To Richard
My long time with Sartonti
and political buddy,
Enjoy!
Ron

Big Orange,
Black Storm Clouds and More

A History of the
University of Tennessee
by
Associate General Counsel
Ron Leadbetter (Retired)

Edited by Martha Rose Woodward

Dedication

I dedicate this history of the University of Tennessee to my wonderful wife, Therese, without whose support I could not have experienced much of what I have narrated in these pages. I also dedicate this literary work to my son, Lee, and daughter, Cara, each of whom blessed me with their presence during UT historical happenings on a number of occasions. Therese received both a Bachelor's and Master's degree from UT and continues to work for the University as a contract employee, conducting seminars for UT employees on a variety of employment issues. Both Lee and Cara likewise received their undergraduate degrees from the University of Tennessee.

First edition published 2015

@copyright 2015

Big Orange, Black Storm Clouds and More by
Ron Leadbetter.

ISBN# Createspace assigned: 13: 978-150286924
10: 15028692X

History-the University of Tennessee's office of general counsel, Ron Leadbetter, UT Knoxville, Tennessee, UT legal cases.

Table of Contents

Prelude ....page 6
Preface ....page 8
Chapter 1-Building a Unique Resume–My Undergraduate Days at UT ....page 9
Chapter 2-Fighting Hippies and Suing the University Leads to Hire ....page 12
Chapter 3-Holding Off the Hippies–The Knoxville 22 ....page 14
Chapter 4-Attacked by Peace Activists–A Resume Enhancement ....page 16
Chapter 5-Leadbetter vs. the University of Tennessee...page 17
Chapter 6-Rally 'round the Flagpole ....page 20
Chapter 7-Political Party Affiliation Not an Obstacle ....page 22
Chapter 8-Hire of Law Clerk as UT's First In-House Trial Attorney ....page 23
Chapter 9-Salary and Job Benefits Received as New Staff Attorney ....page 25
Chapter 10-Bill Bass & Savage Cave–My First Assignment as Staff Attorney ....page 28
Chapter 11-Networking and Building Relationships–a Key To Success.....................page 30
Chapter 12-Team Building in the Office of General Counsel and More ....page 40
Chapter 13-The Board of Trustees is the Client, Not the Enemy ....page 47
Chapter 14-Residency Classification Rules for Admission & Tuition Purposes..........page 53
Chapter 15-The National Association of College & University Attorneys.................page 58
Chapter 16-"BOB," UT's First Basketball Mascot–Almost.................................page 61
Chapter 17-Formal Job Description of University In-House Counsel.........................page 64
Chapter 18-You Won't Find These Listed as Formal Job Duties of Univ. Counsel .....page 66
Chapter 19-Memorable Moments and Special Occasions–Fun & UT Related ....page 71
Chapter 20-My First Trial–Van de Vate vs. UT ....page 76
Chapter 21-The UT Air Force and Near Disaster ....page 78
Chapter 22-Politics Post Hire...page 81
Chapter 23-Gay People's Alliance Petitions for UT Recognition............................page 84
Chapter 24-No Such Thing as a Case That Can't Be Lost-Soni vs. Board.................page 85
Chapter 25-Focus on Integrity by the University Administration............................page 90
Chapter 26-Integrity Without Regard to Position–Patterson vs. Hunt ....page 94
Chapter 27-Do the Right Thing–or Else! ....page 98
Chapter 28-Cheating is a No–No...page 102
Chapter 29-Diplomacy and Friendship Between Adversaries ....page 111
Chapter 30-Three Steps to Success: Train, Advise and Litigate ....page 116
Chapter 31-Bad Settlements: M.Baracuda, P. Manning.....................................page 122
Chapter 32-Author's Resume-A Game Plan Summary ....page 129
Chapter 33-Best Evidence of Success–Wins, Losses and Settlements.....................page 135
Chapter 34-OGC Cost Cutting Proposals ....page 141
Chapter 35-Money Saving Tidbits ....page 143
Chapter 36-A Pot of Money–Birth of the UT Licensing Program ....page 145
Chapter 37-Sports Agent Legislation...page 149
Chapter 38-Tennessee Uniform Administrative Procedures Act ....page 156
Chapter 39-Creation of the UT Police Department ....page 163
Chapter 40-UT Police Officers–Popular Parties to Litigation..............................page 165
Chapter 41-Medical Malpractice–Most Popular Category of Litigation..................page 175
Chapter 42-Honest Plantiff Loses ....page 180
Chapter 43-A "Setup" and Sure Loses Goes Well ....page 183
Chapter 44-The Missing Skull Fragment–Copeland vs. State................................page 190

Chapter 45-Elvis Presley and his UT Legal Defense..page 192
Chapter 46-Tennessee's Charles Manson Alter Ego–Dr. Zed Aydelott......................page 198
Chapter 47-The Flying Nun–Rita Williams..page 201
Chapter 48-Civil Rights–Pinnacle of My University Legal Practice ....page 205
Chapter 49-Civil Rights–Applicable Law and Administrative Agencies....................page 206
Chapter 50-Quantum Shift in Strategy...page 208
Chapter 51-Civil Rights–Plan of Action–the Details ....page 209
Chapter 52-The Concept of Affirmative Action ....page 212
Chapter 53-The Impact of Rita Sanders Geier...page 222
Chapter 54-Best Evidence of Civil Rights Litigation Success ....page 229
Chapter 55-"Race" Leads the Way in Litigation Activity..page 230
Chapter 56-Sex Discrimination Claims Ranked Second in Number..........................page 236
Chapter 57-Title IX and Athletics ....page 253
Chapter 58-Protected Categories with Less Litigation ....page 257
Chapter 59-Veterans and the Body Farm ....page 272
Chapter 60-The First Amendment–Religion and More ....page 275
Chapter 61-Constitutional Right to Due Process ....page 280
Chapter 62-One APA Sexual Harassment Case and One APA Loss ....page 286
Chapter 63-Due Process: Sometimes It Applies and Sometimes It Doesn't...............page 290
Chapter 64-Contracts and Real Estate ....page 296
Chapter 65-Student Right to Know and Campus Security Act of 1990......................page 308
Chapter 66-UT Role in War on Drugs ....page 309
Chapter 67-The Drug War in Memphis: Gilbert vs. UT ....page 317
Chapter 68-The Sam Bozeman Tragedy ....page 323
Chapter 69-Worker's Compensation...page 326
Chapter 70-Whatever Could Go Wrong Did–The Skoutakis Disaster ....page 331
Chapter 71-Boosters Gave Vols Cash ....page 339
Chapter 72-Sport Magazine Expose ....page 347
Chapter 73-Jack Sells and the Blue Chippers ....page 353
Chapter 74-Heath Shuler and UT Associate Dean Roger Jenkins ....page 363
Chapter 75-Phone Fraud Episode ....page 369
Chapter 76-Boston Globe "Expose"..page 376
Chapter 77-The Leslie Ratliff Exception ....page 385
Chapter 78-Jamie Whited NCAA Infraction Tips Prove Baseless..............................page 387
Chapter 79-ESPN Reports Tutoring Scandal...page 389
Chapter 80-Postscript on Tutoring Scandal–Litigation ....page 401
Chapter 81-NCAA Invite to Serve as Southeast Conference Rep. Rejected...............page 404
Chapter 82-The Lola Dodge Purge and the Two-Day Miracle....................................page 406
Chapter 83-Scott Hartman and the Errant Hammer Throw................................./.......page 411
Chapter 84-A Few Cases Qualified as Dumb, Screwy or Just Plain Weird.................page 424
Chapter 85-Joseph Kersavage and the Battle Over Rights to a Bomb Shelter............page 434
Chapter 86-Eric Locke and the Objection Faux Pas...page 439
Chapter 87-Was James Henry Drew Drowned in Tennessee River by UT?.................page 444
Chapter 88-Losing the Case You Expected to Win–Pinson vs. State..........................page 451
Chapter 89-The Malaria Reversal–Elosiebo vs State ....page 454
Chapter 90-Who Won & Who Lost? Adam Manookian & the Threat of Violence......page 458
Chapter 91-Losing Was Cheaper Than Settling–Bobby Moore vs. State ....page 462
Chapter 92-Winning Felt a Bit Like Losing–St. John's United Methodist Church......page 464

Chapter 93-Losing Felt a Lot Like Winning–Henry Grager.......................................page 465

Chapter 94-Even a Loss Can Seem Like a Win–The Mirabella Case ....page 468

Chapter 95-University Health Systems Lease Agreement–30 Year Error ....page 472

Chapter 96-Gilley's Nationwide Search for New UT General Counsel.....................page 476

Chapter 97-The Interview Process Confirmed Suspicion..page 479

Chapter 98-Gilley Sued and the Evidence Grows...page 490

Chapter 99-Pamela Reed Enters the Picture–Gilley's Paramour ....page 497

Chapter 100-Evidence Against Gilley Mushrooms..page 504

Chapter 101-Sworn Testimony Placed Gilley's Truthfulness at Issue ....page 506

Chapter 102-Gilley "Wins"–Did the Courts Get it Right?..page 521

Chapter 103-The Eli Fly Interlude–A Sliver of Orange...page 525

Chapter 104-The Shumaker Presidency–"Go for Two!" ....page 527

Chapter 105-Here We Go Again–First Evidence of Shumaker Corruption................page 529

Chapter 106-Add Lying to the Charges Against Shumaker ....page 535

Chapter 107-Role of the General Counsel in the Shumaker Travesty ....page 539

Chapter 108-Redirection in the Office of General Counsel..page 543

Chapter 109-Networking Focus Removed..page 545

Chapter 110-Life Goes on Quite Well–For Me...page 548

Chapter 111-Joe Johnson, Interim President (2003-2004) ....page 550

Chapter 112-During the Orange Sliver Life Went On..page 553

Chapter 113-Checking Out the Next UT President–John Peterson ....page 555

Chapter 114-The Russia Connection–Easier to Arrange Than Intra-Office Comm. ...page 557

Chapter 115-Russian Connection With UT Blossoms ....page 561

Chapter 116-During the Peterson Presidency All Again Went Well–For Me ....page 565

Chapter 117-Too Many Chiefs ....page 568

Chapter 118-2007 Was a Great Year! ....page 574

Chapter 119-My Litigation Record in 2007–Check the Stats....................................page 575

Chapter 120-The Two 2007 Tort Losses ....page 579

Chapter 121-Two Memorable 2007 Tort Wins..page 580

Chapter 122-The Late Arriving Surgeon and the Missing Skull Fragment ....page 583

Chapter 123-The Sure Loser: An Appeal Not Taken–Chumley vs. State...................page 589

Chapter 124-Political Challenge Leads to Retirement...page 596

Chapter 125-My UT Career's Grand Finale–"The Death of Cupid"...........................page 599

Chapter 126-Post-Retirement UT Activity...page 606

Chapter 127-The Bruce Pearl Tragedy–Who Dropped the Ball? ....page 608

Chapter 128-Conclusion...page 618

Postlude ....page 619

Photos ....page 620

Index...page 632

Big Orange, Black Storm Clouds and More
By Ron Leadbetter

Prelude

My goal in authoring this book is to provide insight into a very important period of history of the University of Tennessee. The story begins during the presidency of UT's 16th president, Dr. Andrew D. Holt, and continues to the present. For more than 35 years during this time period I had a unique opportunity to observe and participate in the making of history from within the inner sanctum of the "Big Orange"–the University's system administration generally and Office of General Counsel, specifically.

Included in my writings are facts well-documented, at least by me, but rarely, if ever, disclosed to the public. My focus is on the events likely to be of interest to you, the reader. Although sufficient detail is included for purposes of historical accuracy, I strive to avoid ho-hum moments. Each chapter of this book aims to produce a "You're kidding!" "Wow!" "I didn't know that," or other evidence of surprise and lack of prior knowledge of the topic covered.

The University of Tennessee has a long history dating back to 1807. Much of that history has been recorded in documents by the University that well describe the its threefold purpose of providing education, research and public service.

University faculty are also a good source of University history, but their writings are generally limited in scope, restricted to the faculty member's discipline and typically of interest only to members of that discipline.

Another obvious source of University history is the news media. While media coverage has been both positive and negative, most coverage germinates from such readily available sources as public events, news releases and review of public documents. Rarely is in depth investigative work involved. Often, the media is unaware there is anything to investigate.

For the purposes of this book, I generally proceed in historical order, from earliest event to latest. But I also address major topics, often on a case by case basis, taking those cases in historical order. Specific dates are used throughout for historical accuracy. Those dates are elicited from my personal diary, telephone logs and correspondence and many other records I have maintained and preserved over the years.

To a large extent I avoid major themes already published purposing to focus on events and incidents you've not previously heard of or read about.

I limit my personal opinions to a great extent, preferring to stick to the facts. If an opinion is offered it is accompanied by careful citation to supporting authority. I'm confident you'll find both the facts and expressed viewpoints helpful in fleshing out a key period of history of the University of Tennessee.

Although it is not always required, I will tyically capitalize the word University when referring to the University of Tennessee-my beloved Alma Mater.

Ron Leadbetter (second from left) and cousin Al Brake (first left) at the entrance to Austin Peay Administration Building (January 16, 1970). The incident that led to Leadbetter's employment by the University of Tennessee.

Preface

Let me say right from the start, I am a Christian. It is my firm belief that God creates each of us with unique characteristics, talents and interests and does so for His purposes. While I do not pretend to fully understand what those purposes for my life might be, this book results, in large part, from the unique characteristics, talents and interests with which I have been endowed by my Creator.

Let's take record-keeping. What is fascinating about keeping records? I don't know, but I have been a record keeper since childhood. Diaries, photographs and copies of every document I considered of interest are filed away in my office and home. Making copies of every check I have ever written has been a lifelong habit. Why? I don't know, however, it is a habit that serves me well.

What about facing a unique challenge where failure can be costly? Or setting out on a path seldom traveled to reach a destination rarely planned? I learned early in life that these questions actually motivated rather than deterred me when a spark of interest arose.

Then, there is the natural human inclination to form cliques. People enjoy joining and bonding with a few close associates at school, in church, and around the workplace. The other side of that coin is to avoid unfamiliar groups in unusual settings at all cost. For whatever reason, I have been endowed with a passion to reach out to others and to develop meaningful relationships with those outside my immediate family and interest groups. For reasons known only to God I am inspired and motivated when thrust into unfamiliar and challenging settings with people I do not know.

Oddly enough these attributes played a vital role in my securing and retaining what I have repeatedly characterized as the greatest job on earth. For more than 35 years I served as legal counsel in the Office of General Counsel at the University of Tennessee. In that role I was privy to and participated in innumerable events of historical significance to the University. Not a typical lawyer's job I can assure you!

I share with you amusing tales, uplifting stories, shocking disclosures and, hopefully, a few useful insights I collected while serving in the inner sanctum of the "Big Orange." As you read this document, you will understand the role played by my unique characteristics, talents and interests in contributing to this history and my reason for sharing this story publicly. It was from this unique position within UT's inner sanctum that, over the years, I watched the Big Orange ripen, then fade, as black storm clouds of corruption moved in, then I saw it transform once again into something yet to be determined.

Chapter 1-Building a Unique Resume–
My Undergraduate Days at the
University of Tennessee

This book is about history of the University of Tennessee viewed from a unique employment setting. Logically, it would seem, such an historical account would begin with my date of employment, not with the accumulation of credentials leading to that employment. In the present case, a review of my history, both as an undergraduate and law student, is absolutely necessary in order to comprehend why I was employed as the University's first in-house trial attorney. Without that review my hire as University legal counsel, a position I held for just shy of 36 years, would appear implausible, if not impossible.

The spring of 1967 marked a significant turning point in my life. For the previous year and a half I had attended Houghton College, a small Liberal Arts college, affiliated with the Wesleyan Methodist Church, in upstate New York. In March of that year, mid-way through my sophomore year, I left Houghton, headed south and enrolled at the University of Tennessee.

I remember well the day I left the freezing cold and snow of my hometown of Wyckoff, New Jersey. The following day I was introduced to the warm and sunny hills of East Tennessee. I instantly fell in love with Knoxville, Tennessee, my new school and my new home.

Almost immediately following my arrival in Knoxville, I became immersed in the politics of the region, both at the University and in the local community. The ongoing war in Vietnam offered a major point of daily conversation and conflict in both settings. Support for American military forces involved in that conflict was hotly debated. Within days after arriving in Knoxville, I became actively involved with both the student body and leaders in the local community in promoting the conservative point of view in this national debate that was tearing deeply at the citizen fabric of our nation.

One of my first friends at the University, who I met only a few days after my arrival in Tennessee, was John ("Jimmy") Duncan, III, the son of U. S. Congressman John J. Duncan, II, a member of the U.S. House of Representatives from Tennessee's Second Congressional District. Years later, in 1988, Jimmy was elected to fill the congressional seat held by his then-deceased father and he continues to serve in that position today.

During our undergraduate years at the University, Jimmy Duncan and I served as conservative columnists for the Daily Beacon, the University's student newspaper. Our political involvement did not end there.

By September 1967, I joined Young Americans for Freedom ("YAF"), a blossoming national organization for college and university conservative activists. The following month I was elected vice president of the UT chapter of YAF. Jimmy Duncan was an avid supporter of YAF, as was his father, and I received their well wishes and encouragement.

In late September I also became actively involved in a community organization organized by prominent members of the Knoxville community for the purpose of promoting patriotic observance activities locally. I was named Sergeant at Arms for the newly organized Patriotic Observance Committee. [The Knoxville Journal, September 28, 1967, page A–11]

Then, in early 1968, I decided to get involved in the UT Student Government Association at the urging of conservatives, both in the UT student body and the Knoxville community. Although a conservative, I elected to run as a candidate for an SGA Senate seat from the College of Liberal Arts on the Student Action Movement (SAM) ticket headed by an unabashedly liberal presidential candidate, Chris Whittle. He later rose to prominence as a highly successful entrepreneur and CEO of Whittle Communications, Inc..

Each SAM candidate was required to contribute $60 to the party for campaign costs. Being a student of meager means, I found it necessary to seek outside funding.

Local conservative activists King and Katsy Benson urged me to contact and seek support from former Knoxville Mayor Cas Walker, the owner of Cas Walker Supermarkets and publisher of a weekly political newspaper, "The Watchdog." I took the advice, met with Walker in his sparsely furnished office in a trailer on Chapman Highway adjacent to one of his stores in South Knoxville and was quite surprised when he directed his secretary to cut me a check for the entire amount needed. This was truly a surprise in light of Walker's reputation for being very tight-fisted with his resources!

Most of the candidates running on the SAM ticket were decidedly liberal and SAM vice-presidential candidate Peter Kami, a native of Brazil and friend with whom I shared frequent coffee time but rarely any agreement on matters political, was generally perceived as being far to the left. While SAM candidates typically campaigned from an "anti-establishment" position, I and a handful of other SAM candidates did not.

Dozens of postcard size campaign cards, stapled to Popsicle sticks and planted throughout the UT campus, announced I was "for RESPONSIBLE student action" and believed that "RESPONSIBLE action initiated by responsible leaders can achieve desirable changes at UT." I openly campaigned for an SGA College of Liberal Arts seat as a conservative Republican who served as vice-president of Young Americans for Freedom. Given the decidedly liberal orientation of the UT student body, particularly among students in the College of Liberal Arts, any expectation of victory might have seemed overly optimistic.

The April 24, 1968 SGA election yielded surprising, at least to me, results. Whittle soundly defeated two more conservative candidates while Kami lost a close race to a "moderate" Program of Progress ("POP") vice presidential candidate, Ford Stuart. I finished third out of 28 candidates for ten liberal arts seats in the SGA senate. Two avowedly liberal candidates each finished less than 20 votes ahead of me. [UT Daily Beacon, April 25, 1968, page 1] I soon discovered that a solid majority of the SGA Senate leaned left and that I was in a distinct minority.

My year of service, 1968-69, as senator with the UT Student Government Association is best described as conservative in orientation and supportive of the University's administration. For example, an editorial appearing in the UT Daily Beacon found fault with my praising an administration the Beacon editor categorized as "arch– conservative," noting that I had introduced and obtained passage of a resolution: "Be it resolved that the administration be heartily commended for its action in granting permission to women 21 and over and senior women with parental consent the right to seek off-campus housing." [UT Daily Beacon, May 15, 1968, page 4].

While Whittle and a solid majority of the SGA Senate pursued liberal, anti-establishment and anti-UT administration positions during my tenure with SGA, ten members of the 35-member Senate, including me, opposed those positions and took a conservative approach.

My undergraduate degree from the University of Tennessee was received on June 9, 1969. Although I took the "Andy Holt pledge" at graduation ceremonies and promised to support my alma mater financially, it was not my intention at the time to remain in Knoxville. I had applied and been accepted to Fordham University Law School and planned to enroll there in the fall. I had not applied to the UT College of Law.

On June 28, 1969, I married the love of my life, Theresa Elizabeth Cecelia O'Brien, from New York City. We rented a home in Palisades Park, New Jersey and I started work nearby as a law clerk at the Patterson law firm of Jeffer, DeCourt, Vogel and Hopkinson.

It was my plan to work for the Patterson firm through law school and following graduation. I had weekend employment as a lifeguard at Paramus Bathing Beach, a privately owned swimming pool where my father served as manager and lifeguard, when not fulfilling his regular duties as a firefighter with the New York City Fire Department. Well settled back home in New Jersey, or so I thought.

One day in late August, only days before the start of law school, life changed. While pacing about my lifeguard station on a slow day at Paramus Bathing Beach, my mind drifted back to Tennessee, the people, the climate, the culture, the University of Tennessee.... Long story short, by evening that day, my new bride and I had made plans to depart New Jersey for the Volunteer State. One problem: only days remained before the UT College of Law's first day of classes and I had not applied, let alone been accepted, to the College of Law.

My problem was quickly resolved in a fashion that would be frowned on today – frowned on and possibly lead to litigation by unsuccessful candidates for admission. Times and circumstances change.

I telephoned the Chancellor of the University of Tennessee's Knoxville campus, Dr. Charles Weaver, "Chancellor Weaver, I don't know if you remember me but this is Ron Leadbetter." "Oh yeah, Ron, I remember you," the Chancellor replied.

Weaver listened patiently as I explained that I had gotten married, lived in New Jersey, was preparing to start law school at Fordham, but wished to return to Tennessee and attend UT's College of Law. Noting that I had neither applied nor been admitted to UT, I asked if there was any way I might "get in at this late date." Chancellor Weaver's unforgettable response: "Ron, you just come on down."

Therese and I departed for Tennessee a couple of days later. At some point, shortly before starting class I filled out standard admissions paperwork. For certain, from the day I walked into the College of Law to register there was never a question raised as to why I had not applied sooner.

Chapter 2–Fighting Hippies and Suing the University Leads to Hire of UT's First Law Clerk

My law school career at the University of Tennessee was anything but typical. Politics on campus supplanted studies for many students. I readily concede the statement applied to me.

Political differences over the Vietnam War created dissension on campus amongst students as well as faculty. This dissension reached out to me and, amazingly, influenced my career path.

Within days after my fall 1969 enrollment in law school I returned to active membership in Young Americans for Freedom. In early October both my wife and I staffed a YAF booth in the University Center during the Activities Carnival. This carnival was an event held to inform students of organized activities available to students on campus and was sponsored by the university. [UT Daily Beacon, October 9, 1969, page 1]

One week later State YAF Chairman, Jim Hager, myself and other YAF members burned a Viet Cong flag at a 2 pm rally in UT's Circle Park while urging a crowd of 500 onlookers to support American troops. In my presentation I "urged the crowd to support President Richard Nixon's current efforts to reach 'peace' ". [UT Daily Beacon, October 16, 1969, page 1]. At the same time, I argued, "Americans must present a united front" so that communists in Vietnam would not think the United States was falling apart. [Id.]

Earlier that same day, during a noon-time Vietnam Moratorium rally at the same location, antiwar advocates, such as UT history professor Dr. Richard Marius, demanded an immediate cessation of American military activities. [Knoxville News Sentinel, October 16, 1969, page 3]

Two days after the Circle Park rally the UT Daily Beacon published my first column as a weekly editorial writer. The title of my column was "No Punches Pulled." From October 17, 1968 through February 4, 1971, I authored a series of editorials unabashedly conservative in their tone.

My editorials were typically complimentary of the University administration. For example, a column titled "Weaver and the 'Daily Beacon Problem'" praised University Chancellor, Dr. Charles Weaver, for appointing a new publications council aimed at avoiding one-sided reporting and editorializing by the Beacon. [UT Daily Beacon, July 14, 1970]

Still, I did not hesitate to criticize the University when I thought it appropriate. In a March 1970 column ("LA Curriculum: An Ailing Sacred Cow"), I opined, "Few ideas have become more accepted in educational circles, in the past few years, than the concept of the Liberal Arts curriculum. To voice criticism of that concept is to invite charges of educational heresy. Liberal Arts has been adopted as the Scared [sic] Cow of the teaching profession but in the view of this writer the beast is ailing and faltering rapidly." [UT Daily Beacon, March 5, 1970].

In a related criticism of the University's education approach during my law school years I may have slightly missed the mark: "Employers don't hire people who know a great deal about campus politics. They don't hire social interactors or well-rounded individuals or socially aware persons or with it students. They hire lawyers, doctors, teachers, businessmen and chemists." [UT Daily Beacon, October 22, 1970]. My own employment history belies the complete accuracy of that statement.

The late '60s and early '70s featured politically motivated campus violence nationwide. The University of Tennessee was not immune from this affliction, although it fared significantly better in that regard than institutions such as Kent State University.

Arguably, the best known incident of campus unrest at the University of Tennessee occurred on January 16, 1970. Incredibly, the events of that day led indirectly, but unmistakably, to my employment by the University.

Chapter 3–Holding off the Hippies–The Knoxville 22

When I first arrived at the University of Tennessee in March 1967, Dr. Andrew D. Holt held the office of president. He was an immensely popular leader even at a time when other University officials were considered part of the despised establishment by a large segment of the student body. Even from my adversaries on the left, I never heard a derogatory comment about President Holt.

As a student I felt President Holt was a personal friend; over the years I encountered countless alumni who felt the same. "Andy" never met a stranger and his unconcealed Christian faith was exemplified by his many acts of kindness in addition to his words.

In 1970 Dr. Holt retired and Dr. Edward J. Boling, UT Vice President for Development and Administration, was chosen by the University's Board of Trustees to replace Holt as president. Left wing campus activists soon made it clear that their apparent respect held for Andy Holt did not carry over to President Boling, UT's 17th President.

The events of January 16, 1970, arguably qualify as the best known incident of campus unrest at the University of Tennessee during the Vietnam era. Amazingly, those events led unmistakably to my initial employment by the University.

On the evening of January 15 Student Government Association president Jimmy Baxter addressed a crowd of around 1,500 at the University Center and called for a campus referendum to ascertain student support for President Boling. The following day a crowd of similar size, gathered on the Hill, adjacent to the Austin Peay administration building. Former SGA vice presidential candidate Peter Kami was the organizer of that demonstration.

Out of curiosity I hiked up the hill to see what my friend Peter might have to say that day. I was not surprised to see a large crowd there nor was I particularly concerned when Kami issued President Boling a challenge to a duel. Kami was speaking symbolically and in no way proposing use of swords or firearms.

I became a bit more concerned when Kami urged the crowd to do more: "We're going to enter the administration building and mill around." My concern grew as I heard vague references to "records" by members of the crowd. That concern escalated when a long-haired student next to me shouted "F – – – the records. Burn the records." Aware of building seizures and record burnings at other educational institutions around the nation, the thought immediately entered my mind: "…those are my records in there. Not going to happen."

Immediately I abandoned my place at the rear of the restless crowd surrounding Kami and trotted briskly to the main door of the administration building. Already standing at the door was a plainclothes UT detective, Ed Yovella. Joining me as I arrived was a student I knew only as Captain Mancuso, who had served in Vietnam as an Army captain, and State YAF chairman Jim Hager, who had also served in the military in Vietnam before entering UT.

Having only moments to act, the four of us instinctively took positions, shoulder to shoulder, blocking the double door entrance to the administration building. A crowd of several hundred surged toward the entrance and reached us only seconds after we took our positions. Fortunately, only one or two blows were struck – fists rather than weapons. The conflict between the four of us and the approaching mob was reduced to pushes and shoves. Although a young lady later claimed her arm was broken in the process, there were no known serious injuries.

A standoff ensued and not a single demonstrator gained access to the administration building. Our foursome held its ground and the records remained secure. Still, the setting was a mob scene that warranted action on the part of the University. Both Chancellor Weaver and the Vice-Chancellor for Student Affairs, Howard Aldmon, came outside the administration building and attempted to persuade those present to leave. Their efforts were ignored and the mob grew louder, refusing to leave the premises.

After an hour or so, I do not know the actual time period, dozens of well-equipped officers from the UT Police Department, the Knoxville City Police Department and the Knox County Sheriff's Department arrived en masse. Entering through the rear basement doors of the administration building and making their way up a stairway to the main floor and out the main entrance, the officers promptly began dispersing the crowd and arresting those that refused to comply. 21 arrests were made immediately, a later arrest increased the number arrested to 22. Peter Kami was one of those arrested.

The entire occurrence was well documented by the news media. [The Knoxville News Sentinel, January 16, 1970, page 1; UT Daily Beacon, January 16, 1970, page 1]. My cousin, Al Brake, was a photographer for the University at the time and assisted in recording the events of the day. Most of the arrestees received minor misdemeanor penalties for their actions. Kami chose to avoid any responsibility by fleeing to Canada. To my knowledge he has never returned to the United States.

Of considerably more importance to me and my future job prospects was the fact that the University of Tennessee's first General Counsel, John Baugh, was standing on the inside of the main entrance with other University officials, observing me as our team of four successfully held off the would-be intruders. I later assisted Baugh's staff and UT law enforcement officials in identifying members of the crowd on the "subject to arrest" list. Unknowingly, at the time, I had a new addition to my job resume.

While the January 16 incident certainly led the way, it was not the only incident of conflict which garnered public attention and received favorable view by my future employer.

Chapter 4–Attacked by Peace Activists–
A Resume Enhancement

Occasionally, acts of campus violence got quite personal. On April 29, 1970, my wife and I ventured from our residence at Laurel Avenue Married Students Apartments to watch student government election returns at the UT Student Center. Shortly after entering the main entrance and approaching the service counter to find out where the election celebrations were being held, I was confronted by four young men and a female.

"What do you think of the United States' invasion of Cambodia?" was the question presented me by one of the young men. Having not yet heard the day's breaking news report of America's military presence in Cambodia, I replied, "I don't know."

My interrogator who was subsequently identified as Bobby Haynes, a Student Government Association council candidate, responded, "Well, we think it sucks and so do you!" With that, a second male who was subsequently identified as Bobby's brother, Kenny Haynes, pulled out and opened a pocket or switchblade type knife. The four males then started toward me, one after another.

In a scene worthy of "America's Funniest Home Videos" I fled my would-be assailants by sprinting toward a nearby study lounge. Quickly realizing the lounge offered no escape, I reversed direction and headed back to where I started, down a long hallway toward an exit, passing my line of attackers in the process.

With me leading the way, my four attackers strung out behind - my wife pursuing them while screaming at the top of her lungs. As we exited the Student Center. I attempted to slam the glass door on my lead pursuer as I exited, but the mechanics of the door foiled my attempt. I leaped over a low wall by the door and headed to the front of the Student Center. There began an assembly of sorts on a small hill in front of the Center. Dozens of students arriving for the election eve festivities looked on in stunned disbelief at the turmoil. At least one joined in the fray.

Two of the male pursuers fled, never to be seen or heard from by me again (and the female member of the group never joined my pursuers after the initial confrontation). Kenny Haynes closed and put up his knife after noting the presence of onlookers. I took his brother down with a blow to his face - sustaining a hairline fracture to my thumb in the process–then landed on top of him. One or two onlookers, evidently unaware of who had initiated the conflict, then piled on top of me in an effort to break up the fight. During the scuffle, I was bitten "on my rear" by Bobby.

Even in the midst of my struggle in the scrum I was quite amazed to overhear

Kenny turn to several students, after disposing of his knife, and ask for help. A large black male with athletic build rebuffed the Kenny's request. "We saw the whole thing and you started the fight," he said. Kenny responded with a racial epithet and the target of the epithet reached to his side, pulled from the ground a campaign sign with wooden stake and headed toward his critic.

UT police Sergeant Jack Thacker and one other UT officer arrived as the melee continued to percolate. With their arrival the scrum on the ground untangled and each of us stood up. The officers approached the Haynes brothers. Thacker was punched in the face by Kenny and responded with a nightstick blow to Kenny's body, bringing him under control. Both brothers were then arrested and transported to the Knox County jail. [UT Daily Beacon, April 30, 1970, page 1]

Less than a month later, as reported in the Knoxville Journal ("SGA voting fight cases bring fines"), the brothers were convicted in Knox County General Sessions Court of assault and public drunkenness and assessed fines totaling $120. [The Knoxville Journal, May 26, 1970, page 8] I testified for the prosecution. I also wrote a scathing editorial for my "No Punches Pulled" column entitled "Hypocrisy Laced Picket Lines" in which I lambasted the Haynes brothers and other campus activists who claimed to support "peace causes" on campus, but used acts and symbols of violence to support their cause. [UT daily Beacon, May 16, 1970]

Several months after the incident, I encountered Bobby Haynes on a campus sidewalk coming from the opposite direction. He approached me and apologized for his conduct on the evening of April 29. I accepted his apology. Following that encounter we met on several occasions for friendly chats over coffee at a nearby cafeteria behind the UT College of Law.

The foregoing incident was not really an extraordinary occurrence given the tense political atmosphere prevailing at the University of Tennessee and nationwide at the time. One positive aspect of the incident, in addition to a memorable opportunity for apology and forgiveness, was its unexpected inclusion in my unofficial employment file. See next chapter: "Leadbetter vs. the University of Tennessee"

Chapter 5–Leadbetter vs. the University of Tennessee

While fisticuffs and other physical conflict with troublemakers might not make anyone's list of recommended resume components for a person seeking hire in a university legal office, a history of bringing lawsuits against that university would surely be considered taboo—a job prospect killer! But, not always.

During my undergraduate years at the University of Tennessee it was always my intent to return to my home in New Jersey following graduation. For that reason it never crossed my mind to object to payment of out-of-state fees charged by the University to students whose permanent residence was outside Tennessee. That changed.

When I returned to Tennessee in August, 1969, my primary purpose was to make Tennessee my home, my permanent residence, not to attend the University. I was now a Tennessee resident entitled to exemption from out-of-state fees, or so I believed. However, under existing University rules and their interpretation, I was denied in-state classification.

My initial application for reclassification was presented to the campus Admissions Committee. Denied! I appealed the committee's adverse ruling to Vice President Joseph E. Johnson and President Holt.

In his October 13, 1969 letter Vice President Johnson explained their adverse ruling as follows: "Under Board of Trustee policy, a person may be classified as an in-state resident if his parents or guardian reside in Tennessee, he marries a Tennessee resident, he owns and lives in a home in this state, he works in Tennessee for a year before becoming a full-time student, or he enters and leaves military service in Tennessee. Unfortunately, you do not meet any of these criteria at this time."

Oddly enough, my wife, Therese, after securing full-time employment in Knoxville, entered UT as an in- state student, excused from payment of out-of-state fees.

I appealed the decision of President Holt and Vice President Johnson to the UT Board of Trustees. On January 9, 1970, I personally appeared before the Board to present my arguments and received a most gracious hearing. Nevertheless, UT General Counsel Baugh advised me by letter of January 14 of the Board's rejection of my appeal.

The services of attorney Charles D. Susano, Jr. (currently serving as a judge on the Tennessee Court of Appeals) were secured by me and, on March 5, 1970, a petition for a writ of certiorari was filed on my behalf with the Chancery Court for Knox County, Tennessee (William P. Newkirk, Chancellor). A transcript of my appeal proceedings before the Board was filed with the Court.

In a September 22, 1970 ruling, following oral argument by counsel for the parties and the Court's review of the case file, the Chancery Court held that the rules applied by President Holt, Vice President Johnson and the Board of Trustees had been improperly applied as exclusive. The Court opined there were other methods of rebutting the presumptions stated in the rules and that the University's action was arbitrary.

While further opining that, "This young man has more than sufficiently, to the reasonable mind, satisfied the fact of his intent, not only to be, but having been, a resident of the state of Tennessee." Chancellor Newkirk held that, under the rules of certiorari, the appropriate action was to remand the case back to the Board for action consistent with the Court's opinion.

The trustees then met, in special session on October 23, 1970 to rehear my appeal. The meeting was chaired by Board Vice Chairman Herbert "Hub" Walters. Among those attending were Trustees Tom Elam, William Miller (Judge on the U.S. Court of Appeals for the Sixth Circuit), Leonard Raulston, Ben Douglas, Clyde York, Marcus Stewart and Wayne Fisher. I made a presentation to the Board and my attorney Charles Susano made arguments on my behalf.

General Counsel Baugh advised, in a November 2, 1970 letter to Susano, that the Board had affirmed my classification as an out-of-state student. According to the Board minutes the vote to affirm was 11 ayes, 4 nays and two not voting. In his letter Baugh added a complimentary note: "The Board of Trustees requested that I also express to you its appreciation and commendation for the outstanding manner in which Mr. Leadbetter has conducted himself while a student at the University." The minutes of the appeal proceeding also contained a number of positive comments by members of the Board.

The Chancery case file was quite voluminous and included a number of my "No Punches Pulled" columns, SGA minutes referencing several bills I had filed while serving as a councilman, and a newspaper article by Jimmy Duncan ("Group to Challenge UT 'hippie establishment'") describing my service as vice president of Young Americans for Freedom. The Board was plainly aware of my activities on campus.

I was quite taken aback when, on November 30, I received a letter, addressed to me personally, from General Counsel Baugh. "Enclosed herewith is Dr. Marcus Stewart's check payable to you in the amount of $200. This check represents a gift of $100 from Dr. Stewart and a gift of $100 from Mr. Clyde M. York. Dr. Stewart and Mr. York are members of our Board of Trustees."

Since my weekly living expenses in 1970 were around $20, the gifts took care of those expenses for 10 weeks and were much appreciated! The checks were in no way conditioned on whether I appealed the Board's decision – simply an act of kindness that further enhanced my positive feelings about the University, its administration and governing board. Moreover, I did, in fact, proceed with an appeal to the Chancery Court contesting the Board's latest action denying my reclassification request.

On March 1, 1971, at its winter meeting, the Board of Trustees adopted new rules for the statewide UT system setting residency requirements for classifying students for tuition purposes. This action was taken in response to a ruling entered by US District Judge Robert L Taylor in a case I filed in federal court challenging the University's residency rules. [The Knoxville Journal, March 2, 1971, page 2]

In a decree entered April 13, 1971 the Knox County Chancery Court affirmed the Board of Trustees' action on my most recent appeal. Under state law I had 30 days to file a notice of appeal. Susano and I discussed the ruling and agreed the Court's reasoning was sound and would likely be upheld by an appellate court.

In a stunning development, just a day or two after the Chancery ruling, I received a telephone call from Assistant UT General Counsel Jim Drinnon. Drinnon related that members of the Board of Trustees and the University administration had very favorable feelings toward me. As a result I was being offered the position of "law clerk" in the office of General Counsel. Drinnon assured me the offer was extended regardless of whether I won or lost any appeal. The sole caveat was that I could not assume the position until litigation was complete.

I responded that I had already decided an appeal would not be filed – that although I certainly preferred the Court had ruled in my favor I agreed with the Court's reasoning. Several days later I became UT's first law clerk and moved into the General Counsel's Office.

As a person of competitive spirit, I don't like losing… unless of course the end result of losing outshines the preconceived benefits of winning. Present case being a prime example of the latter circumstance!

Chapter 6–Rally 'round the Flagpole

Excited as I was about assuming the law clerk position in the UT Office of General Counsel, I had no intention of altering my political involvement on campus or in the community. I continued writing for The Daily Beacon and remained an active member of Young Americans for Freedom.

Do not in any way consider this an endorsement of "how to successfully prepare for a career in the practice of law." I significantly reduced class time so as to accommodate my new law clerk position, a position which offered me a more fascinating way to spend 15 hours each week. My campus and local political activities continued unabated. My grade point average suffered somewhat, but I took it in stride. In this isolated case, the approach taken proved to be a winner, even if unintentionally so. I built my resume in a most bizarre fashion!

One of the tragic incidents of the Vietnam War era was the shooting of several student demonstrators at Kent State University by National Guardsmen sent to deal with the demonstrators. The loss of life at Kent State had repercussions at the University of Tennessee.

On May 4, 1971, I learned that the next day a group of left wing activists known as a Veterans against the War, planned to hold a flag, lowering ceremony on the Hill at UT in front of historic Ayres Hall in honor of the students who had recently lost their lives at Kent State. Other members of YAF and I were opposed to the planned ceremony. Given the great loss of life of men and women serving the nation in the United States military during the Vietnam conflict, we could not stand idly by.

The morning of May 5 a half-dozen fellow YAFers and I beat the opposition to the flagpole and surrounded it. Climbing on the shoulders of fellow YAF member Charlie Thompson, I cut the rope to the flag, wrapped the upper portion of the rope around the flagpole, well out of reach of those below, and used duct tape to fix the rope in place. Soon a couple of dozen members of the antiwar veterans group arrived and discovered the flag had been placed well beyond their reach.

Our small group encircled the flagpole and the protesters in turn encircled us at a distance. There was no physical conflict and the antiwar activists seemed disconcerted by the standoff. Someone representing the group made a call to the Governor.

After an hour or so, the Dean of Students, Dr. Charles Burchett, a military veteran himself and a close political ally and friend with whom I shared frequent conversations in his office, approached us and advised that Tennessee Governor Winfield Dunn had given permission for the antiwar activists to lower the flag. Believing the governor had been misled as to the intentions of the activists, I advised Dean Burchett that we would not abandon our position or permit our opponents to lower the flag. Dean Burchett smiled, turned and walked away. The standoff continued.

Less than an hour later the YAFers developed a plan. I climbed a ladder made available by the University, un-taped the rope and prepared to lower the flag. Before lowering the flag I spoke to those assembled

As the Daily Beacon reported: "Law student Ron Leadbetter, who joined the group surrounding the pole, climbed a ladder supplied by the physical plant and un-taped the ropes. The flag is being lowered to honor people who died fighting for its honor not for the people who died at Kent State,' Leadbetter said." [The Daily Beacon, May 6, 1971, page 1]

The Beacon then reported that "SGA president Charles Huddleston said the lowering honored 'those killed at Kent State, and Jackson State, and in Vietnam.' "[The Daily Beacon, May 6, 1971, page 1]. Notwithstanding Huddleston's comment, the only words spoken at the flag lowering were spoken by me and the flag was lowered by a representative of Young Americans for Freedom, not the opposition, for what we believed to be a right and honorable reason.

Chapter 7–Political Party Affiliation Not an Obstacle

At the time of my hire as UT's first law clerk, the UT administration was completely and unmistakably Democratic in its political affiliation. Tennessee was commonly referred to as a Democratic state.

Both President Boling and Vice President Johnson had worked for State government under the Democratic administration of Governor Buford Ellington. A substantial majority of the members of the Board of Trustees were identified as Democrats. Not a single member of the University administration was known to be a member, let alone an active member, of the Republican Party.

The prevailing political affiliation of the University's higher echelon was best acknowledged by a favorite greeting exchanged with long-time University administrator Betsy Creekmore. Over the first couple of decades of my University employment, whenever we encountered each other, with no one else around, we would smile, thrust a fist in the air and shout, "Rally, rally!" This lighthearted greeting simply reflected the fact that, for many years, the two of us were the only acknowledged Republicans working in the University's administration.

The greeting did not reflect any sense of adverse treatment on that basis. In truth, I discovered during the administrations of Presidents Holt and Boling that conservative orientation weighed more heavily for employment purposes than party affiliation. That was indisputably true in my case.

In April 1971, not long after my hire as law clerk, I announced to the Knoxville news media my intent to run for the office of president of the Knox County Young Republicans. [The Knoxville Journal, April 19, 1971] My April 26 election as president of the organization was also reported by the news media. [The Knoxville News-Sentinel and the Knoxville Journal, April 27, 1971].

During the balance of my clerkship and law school career I served actively and openly in a variety of Republican campaigns and interacted regularly with a number of ranking local, state and national Republican officials.

Never was my political activity as a Republican, or otherwise, criticized or even mentioned by anyone in the University administration. Of course, I never conducted political activities from the office of the General Counsel.

I learned it was possible, even enjoyable, to work with those from different political affiliations on matters of mutual interest with common goals. But, would partisan activity affect future job prospects with the University? In today's political climate the expected answer would likely be "without a doubt". The climate was different in the 1960s and 70s.

Chapter 8–Hire of UT Law Clerk As UT's First In-House Trial Attorney

From April 1971 until my graduation from the UT College of Law in June 1972, I served as the UT General Counsel Office's first law clerk. It was clear to me early on, that neither the General Counsel, nor anyone else in the office, really had any idea what a law clerk's responsibilities should be. It was a new position. For me this was a good thing.

During the period of my law clerk employment almost all University litigation was handled by outside legal counsel—private law firms. The primary purpose of lawyers in the General Counsel's office was to provide legal advice to university officials statewide. Preparation of various and sundry legal documents was another responsibility of the office.

Two attorneys were employed in the office of General Counsel, in addition to the General Counsel, during the time of my clerkship. One, Arthur B. ("Art") Stowers, Jr., reputedly had served as an intelligence officer for the U.S. government before coming to UT. He spoke several languages fluently in addition to English. Art was the epiphany of a true Southern gentleman. He was an avid devotee of wrestling, spent considerable time with the UT wrestling team and was close friends with head wrestling coach, Gray Simons.

Daniel F.B. ("Dan") Rhea was the second office attorney reporting to the General Counsel. Dan was employed as legislative counsel with the Tennessee state legislature in Nashville before his employment with UT. His most widely proclaimed attribute, often proclaimed by Dan himself, was being a "ladies man".

Former Assistant General Counsel Jim Drinnon had moved on to become Vice-President for Administration and, in 1974, became Chancellor of the University of Tennessee at Chattanooga after serving as Interim Chancellor in 1973.

Both Dan and Art presented me with numerous learning opportunities. One challenging request for a legal opinion after another was presented to me for response. I did the research and often wrote the "opinion" for an attorney's signature.

Art would regularly cite my opinion as the basis for his advice ("Ron Leadbetter has advised me that…") with the result that the proffered legal opinions oft were often mine. Art's signature on the letter avoided any charge that I was practicing law without a license.

My frequent encounters with Andy Holt, Ed Boling, Joe Johnson and a host of other University leaders, as well as Trustees and State political leaders paying homage to the State's premier institution of higher education, tweaked my interest in looking for more opportunities to work with leaders I respected so much.

My June 1969 graduation from law school brought to conclusion my career as a UT's first law clerk. A week or so before the end of the quarter, the University being on the "quarter system" at the time, I overheard office chatter that UT would commence handling litigation with in-house counsel. A new attorney would be hired by the Office of General Counsel for that specific purpose. I went to see General Counsel Baugh in his office and expressed my deep interest in the new position.

"Well, Ron, the position requires someone with at least three years litigation experience," replied Baugh. "Mr. Baugh, I know I can do the job if you give me a chance," I responded.

Fortunately, the General Counsel did not ask me the basis for my confidence (given my lack of any litigation experience whatever). Baugh simply repeated, "No, Ron, we need someone with three years of experience." I left his office feeling a bit dejected.

Failing to secure the only job in which I had any specific interest I ventured downtown and inquired at one of the major law firms whether any position might be open there. The answer was "no" and, inexplicably, I was relieved.

I then made a strategic decision which unknowingly avoided my losing an offer of what I later concluded was the best job on earth - I elected not to seek any further job opportunities in the immediate future. Seven years of undergraduate and graduate education had just concluded and I opted to take a short break and clear my mind. My wonderful, understanding wife graciously agreed.

One of my favorite leisure time activities at the University was beach volleyball. The sport was very popular back in the late '60s and early '70s. A beach volleyball court adjacent to the outdoor swimming pool at the UT Aquatic Center was regularly packed with players competing in "jungle ball," played with no rules against touching or even crashing into the net. Others were always sitting or standing in the grass along the court, eagerly awaiting their turn to play. As stated, the rules were lax and teams of as many as 10 or 12 might take to the court. "Quasi- mortal combat" best describes the competition. Many members of the UT football team and a few basketball players, including well-known UT basketball center Len Kosmalski, were jungle ball regulars.

On the afternoon of June 30, 1972, covered with sweat and sand and participating in my favorite leisure time activity, I received word from an Aquatic Center manager that I had a phone call in the office. I raced to the office and took the call. John Baugh was on the line.

"Ron, are you still interested in the new job in this office?" Baugh inquired. "I sure am!" I enthusiastically replied. "Well, the weekend is coming up and we are off for the Fourth of July holiday. So, your first work day will be July 5," Baugh explained.

There was no mention of the obvious caveat that I must take and pass the Tennessee bar exam in order to retain the position. I eventually took the bar in July and, thankfully, on September 10, 1972, received notice I had passed.

Pure, unadulterated joy consumed me following Baugh's unexpected phone call. I returned to an exciting afternoon of beach volleyball, but my real excitement was looking forward with unbridled enthusiasm to sharing the stunning news with my wife Therese at the end of her workday.

An unforgettable professional career as legal counsel for the University of Tennessee was soon to begin. The road that got me there would not be forgotten.

Chapter 9–Salary and Job Benefits Received as New Staff Attorney

Student loans accumulated over my seven years of higher education left me in debt at the time of my graduation from law school. Still, starting salary was never discussed in conjunction with my plea for employment in the UT Office of General Counsel. When I learned I would receive an annual salary of $10,000 as staff attorney, I thought I had struck it rich. In 1972 that was a goodly sum.

Along with my salary I received multiple benefits, both official and unofficial. An excellent state retirement program was attractive to me even as a youthful new employee. More important to me at the time, all exempt employees, such as myself, received two days of annual leave and one day of sick leave each month. In addition, there were paid holidays at Christmas, Good Friday, Easter, Labor Day, Fourth of July and one or two others.

Although in high demand, UT football and basketball tickets were provided at half price to UT faculty and staff. Soon after my employment I remembered the "Andy Holt pledge" I had taken at my graduation ceremony and joined the "President's Club" by purchasing a $25,000 life insurance policy naming UT as beneficiary. I received free parking passes for athletic events in return.

All employees received free access to the swimming and work out facilities at the Student Aquatic Center. Access to dining, library and other campus facilities supplemented the monetary benefits received. These and other benefits of employment at the University of Tennessee completely satisfied me and proved attractive to many others seeking UT employment back then.

In my early years I rarely heard complaints of poor employment conditions at the University. Requests from friends and acquaintances outside the University, including folks already gainfully employed, for help obtaining employment at the University were frequent. Salary was rarely an issue and the University's reputation for having a positive work environment was the driving force.

For me, the best evidence of job satisfaction was my early rejection of two outside job offers, each at a higher salary. The first job offer came from Knox County District Attorney General Ron Webster.

In September 1973, Webster offered me a prosecutor position in his office. Given my student loan indebtedness, the $15,120 salary offer was quite attractive. But, I turned the offer down. I loved the job I had.

Fortuitously, when John Baugh learned of Webster's job offer and my rejection of the offer, he arranged for an increase in my salary. I was elated to learn my salary would increase to $13,000. Baugh told me my salary probably should have been higher when I started. I was happy as could be and thankful for the salary boost.

A second job offer came a year or two after the Office of General Counsel moved to new quarters on the eighth floor of Andy Holt Tower, the new UT administration building, in December 1975. The soon to be departing General Counsel of the governing board of the State University and Community College System (Tennessee's other higher education system established by the legislature in 1972), David Porteous, called and asked me if I would be interested in assuming the position of General Counsel for the Board of Regents.

I expressed appreciation for the offer but, having no interest in moving from Knoxville, politely rejected the offer. The matter would have ended there, but when Therese learned of the job offer and my rejection, she urged me to reconsider, noting the substantial increase in income likely to accompany the position of General Counsel.

I called Porteous back, explained that I had reconsidered and would accept the position, provided I could commute from Knoxville and leave Nashville early on Friday afternoons to return home. The matter was taken under consideration and, to no one's surprise, my counter offer was not accepted. I was quite relieved.

My salary and other "official" employment benefits were highly satisfactory throughout my career. During the nearly 36 years of my employment in the office of General Counsel I never once requested a salary increase and always felt I was compensated fairly. On more than one occasion I joked with friends, "I can't believe I get paid for what I do." I found my job so rewarding I would have done it for free had I been able to afford it. I would not have been the first since former Vice- Chancellor Herman Spivey reportedly worked at the end of his UT career for a dollar a year.

Just as important to me as salary and benefits was the incredible job freedom, flexibility and trust I was afforded. It was this latter category of unwritten, and often unspoken, benefits that bolstered my belief that I had the best job on earth.

I delighted in setting my own work hours. While the typical workday for most non-faculty employees was 8 to 5 or thereabouts, mine was atypical. Throughout most of my career I traveled extensively and for that reason alone the 8 to 5 scenario did not apply. But, even when in town, I operated well outside normal work hours.

With rare exception, I was seated at my desk each morning by 5:15 a.m. (after arising at 4:30 a.m. each day without the assistance of an alarm clock). During most of my career I started each day with prayer and, following a New Year's resolution sometime in the 1980s, readings from the Bible. I spent the remaining quiet hours of the morning, before other staff arrived, reviewing case files, preparing legal briefs and performing other work benefitting from silence in the office.

On Mondays, Wednesdays and Fridays I left my office for a 2½ hour workout, generally between 11 in the morning and 1:30 in the afternoon, a session of weightlifting and paddle ball, a sport introduced to me in the early 1970s by Dr. Andrew J ("Andy") Kozar, a former UT and Chicago Bears football player and executive assistant to President Boling. Only rarely did I accept any request to meet during my allotted workout time; I offered instead to meet any other time during the day, even 10 at night or 3 in the morning. This offer, which I made in all seriousness, gutted any potential claim that I was not accessible. And, to my knowledge, no such claim was ever made during the span of my career.

On Tuesdays I attended meetings of a civic organization, the West Knoxville Sertoma Club, which I joined in December 1972 to further my interest in serving the community as well as working for a salary.

Thursday was the only day of the week retained for lunch meetings. Many, many lunchtime meetings were scheduled on Thursdays over my years of employment with the University.

On the other hand, weekends were family time, particularly Sunday, and I made every effort to avoid bringing work home. I loved the time spent attending our kids' sporting and other activities and weekend activities with friends. A workaholic I was not. Most days I left the office at four in the afternoon.

Responding promptly and effectively to requests for legal assistance was one way I strived to meet my responsibly. This partnership of personal freedom and corresponding responsibility served immeasurably in sculpting the employment position I described as "the best job on earth."

Chapter 10–Bill Bass and Savage Cave– My First Assignment as Staff Attorney

I received word in September 1972 that I had passed the Tennessee Bar Exam. Shortly thereafter I was sworn in to practice law in Tennessee by the Tennessee Supreme Court. No more transactional work such as contract review and legal research. I was ready for my first big case. I was ready to handle litigation.

Eagerly I awaited my first court challenge. Would it be state court or federal? A day or two after being sworn in by the Supreme Court, one of the secretaries let me know I had a caller on the line that needed legal help. My first call from a client had arrived."Excited" would considerably understate my frame of mind.

"Mr. Leadbetter, this is Dr. Bill Bass. I was told to call you and that you would be able to help me." The name given by the caller was not familiar to me but I puffed up with a bit of pride in the fact that someone needed my help on a matter of importance and was told to call me. "How can I help you?"

My pride lasted all of 10 seconds as the caller replied "I need you to explore a cave with me." "What?" I responded. The caller repeated, "I need you to explore a cave with me." During the utterance of my second "What?" and the caller's third "I need you to explore a cave with me," I concluded that one of my friends was pulling a prank on me.

Perhaps detecting my state of mind, the caller explained in more detail that he was a faculty member in the Department of Anthropology and had an interest in human remains as part of his area of research and teaching. He explained that a lady by the name of Pat Savage owned property in Adairsville, Kentucky on which was located Savage Cave. Within the cave was a treasure trove of bones and other human remains of American Indians who had camped there.

The property was for sale. We needed to check it out and see if purchase was feasible.

On September 27, 1972 Dr. William ("Bill") Bass, later to be world renowned for founding and engaging in human cadaver research at the Body Farm on the UT campus, and I drove to Adairsville. We met the owner, Pat Savage, and explored her property. The entrance to Savage Cave reminded me of a long thin orange slice, flat side down. Savage showed us a photograph purporting to show

15 or so members of the Jesse James gang standing side-by-side across the mouth of the cave.

Within walking distance of the cave was a huge, two-story cabin that looked like a fortress. The cabin was only nine or so logs high but each log was thicker than the length of my forearm and the chinks or spaces (now filled with concrete) between the logs were thicker than a large loaf of bread.

Two upstairs bedrooms had balconies overlooking a massive living room. At one end of the cabin was a small exhibit room that had been added on. The exhibit area had display tables with a variety of teeth, bones, arrowheads and other antiquities taken from the cave and put on display for public viewing.

The cabin had been moved by Savage from another location to the present site. Both the cabin and the entrance to Savage Cave appeared well within the boundaries of the property she purportedly owned. According to Savage, National Geographic magazine had an interest in fully exploring the cave. She believed she controlled the entrance to the second-largest cave in the United States, exceeded only in size by Mammoth Caverns in size. Bill and I did a cursory walkabout inside the cave and he was obviously impressed with what he saw.

Returning to Savage's cabin, we learned that her sole interest was in selling the property in its entirety. The purchaser would own the cabin as well as the land controlling the entrance to the cave. The asking price was $1 million.

On the ride home Bill expressed an interest in securing property controlling the cave, but did not believe it was realistic to consider purchase of the entire property. It was his opinion the Alumni Association might be persuaded to provide funding for purchase of the cave property but not $1 million to buy the Savage estate in its entirety. The matter was laid to rest and no further action was taken by Bill to pursue purchase possibilities for all or any portion of the Savage property.

My role as a lawyer in the process was minimal at best. But, my time spent was not wasted. The trip to Adairsville is enshrined in my memory as my first official legal assignment as a licensed attorney for the University of Tennessee. I came away with a far better understanding of one of the of University's academic programs. More important to me was the fact that Bill Bass and I became friends in the process and worked well together for the remainder of my career. An area I deemed of great importance, that of social and professional networking, received an early boost.

Chapter 11–Networking and Building Relationships– a Key To Success

THE ANDY HOLT INFLUENCE

UT President Andrew D. "Andy" Holt became my role model when I was a student at the University of Tennessee. He remains a role model for me today, long after his death.

Dr. Holt's uncanny networking skill influenced my own approach to the practice of law, both consciously and subconsciously. In late 1972, or early 1973, I sat next to Dr. Holt at McGhee-Tyson Airport awaiting a flight. A young lady sat a couple of seats away with her toddler.

"That's a mighty fine looking young man you have with you," said Dr. Holt to the young lady. She beamed and thanked Dr. Holt for his complement. Then Dr. Holt asked the lady where she was from, though he clearly was not acquainted with her. She responded that she was from Des Moines, Iowa. Dr. Holt then asked if she knew an acquaintance of his but she did not. He persisted. Within two or three more questions Dr. Holt had identified someone in Iowa the young lady was acquainted with, a mutual friend.

I was impressed with the entire exchange between Dr. Holt and a complete stranger. With this brief exchange, Dr. Holt had left on me a permanent impression, one that would alter my own focus in dealing with others.

Even before the airport incident I was well aware of Dr. Holt's passion for reaching out a hand of friendship to others in all walks of life. As a student, I heard one story after another of Dr. Holt showing acts of kindness to my fellow students. Whether it was offering a ride downtown or sharing a meal at a local eatery, the recipient of Dr. Holt's kindness came away feeling he or she had made a new friend.

I will not forget the day when Dr. Holt, shortly after becoming President Emeritus, brought a huge wicker basket of candy into the Austin Peay administration building. He went from office to office distributing goodies to all the secretaries, producing one smile after another.

I will also not forget my elevator rides with Dr. Holt. When ladies joined us he would say with great sincerity, "My, my! Aren't we lucky to be here with all these lovely ladies?" Each lady present left with her face all aglow.

With Andy Holt as primary role model, I never doubted the value of networking and relationship building. Both proved invaluable to me in succeeding professionally. They most assuredly enhanced my personal life.

NETWORKING AND RELATIONSHIP BUILDING WITHIN THE UNIVERSITY

Relationships built on trust with UT's first General Counsel, John Baugh, and his successor, Beauchamp E. ("Beach") Brogan, led to more than scheduling freedom for me. With rare exception, I also enjoyed complete freedom in determining HOW to carry out my job responsibilities, and even WHAT those responsibilities should be.

Two secretaries, first Hazel Nicely, then Leticia ("Tish") Griffey, coached and partnered with me for all but one of my 35 years as counsel for the University. I discovered early on that if you really wanted to know what was going on in any office ask a secretary. Absolutely true!

I counted heavily on Hazel and Tish, not only for fast, nearly flawless typing, now known as "word processing," but also skilled diplomacy in scheduling meetings, depositions and a wide variety of other functions as well as "covering for me" when I was away from the office.

Beyond developing relationships in the Office of General Counsel, I made every effort to interact and develop relationships with UT officials and employees statewide. The door to my office was always open (unless a meeting was in progress) and telephone calls came to me directly rather than through my secretary (with the same exception for ongoing meetings). I was told time and again how much this "open" approach was appreciated.

A particularly effective means of networking and building relationships was serving as a presenter at retreats with University faculty and staff and, occasionally, trustees and student leaders. The following is a sampling of these types of events, taken from my personal logs and diary:

- •1976 seminar in Nashville for residency classification officer's. Topic: application of new residency classification rules.
- •1978 retreat at Henry Horton State Park with vice chancellors for student affairs, student government presidents and President Boling's executive assistant, Andrew J ("Andy") Kozar. Topic: current legal issues affecting colleges and universities.
- • 1982 campus retreat at "Hopecote" on the Knoxville campus with vice chancellors for academic affairs. Topic: legal issues of interest to vice chancellors responsible for academic programs.
- •1983 retreat at UT Martin for University employees handling student loan and other debt collections. Topic: collections
- • 1983 retreat at Henry Horton State Park for SGA officers and a number of trustees. Topic: legal issues affecting student housing.
- • 1986 retreat in Nashville for student affairs officers and risk managers. Topic: managing student-related legal risks.
- • 1988 seminar in Knoxville for all UT system administrators. Topic: affirmative action and the law.

- 1988 student leader orientation at Henry Horton State Park for student affairs officers and SGA leaders. Attended by Former Governor and current President Lamar Alexander.
- 1989 retreat at Pickwick Landing State Park for Student Government Association presidents and vice presidents. Attended by UT President Lamar Alexander. Topic: legal issues affecting a university.
- 1991 seminar [location not recorded] for statewide admissions and classification officers.Topic: residency classification regulations of the University of Tennessee and the State Board of Regents.
- 1994 retreat in Gatlinburg for physical plant supervisors. Topic: various legal issues affecting physical plant activities on campus.
- 2000 seminar in Knoxville for UT human resources officers. Topic: legal developments affecting personnel management.
- 2002 retreat in Chattanooga for UTC police officers. Topic: "search and seizure guidelines."
- 2003 seminar at UT medical Center in Knoxville for surgery residents. Topic: "Liability Prevention."

These retreats and seminars served two primary purposes from my perspective. First, I had a chance to develop meaningful relationships with attendees in a relaxed setting. Second, the retreats and seminars afforded me an opportunity to enhance the attendees' awareness of legislation and legal developments in their area of responsibility.

The benefit was mine as well as theirs. Nothing beats a witness well versed in the law taking the witness stand. Immersion in applicable law lessens the chance of ending up in court to begin with.

Over the years I also taught, as "guest lecturer," many undergraduate classes and a host of classes in the UT Colleges of Law, Nursing, Dentistry, Medicine, Pharmacy and Allied Health Sciences.

MY FIRST UNIVERSITY COMMITTEE ASSIGNMENT: RESIDENCY CLASSIFICATION RULES

A couple of years after my employment as staff attorney, General Counsel Baugh requested that I serve on a committee composed of administrative representatives from UT and the Tennessee Board of Regents (State University and Community College System). Our assignment was to rewrite the rules governing residency classification of students for tuition purposes, an area in which I had a bit of experience dating back to my student days. The committee fulfilled its assignment over a period of several months.

On March 15, 1976, following adoption of the newly crafted rules by both governing boards, I flew on a UT plane to Nashville to meet with the residency classification officers from each of the UT campuses. At that meeting I exhaustively reviewed the new rules and provided the officers unlimited opportunity to ask questions. They were urged to contact me if at any time they had a question arise in a particular case they were handling.

SEMINARS AND RETREATS WERE PRODUCTIVE AND FUN

Over the years, I conducted additional seminars for residency classification officers around the state in order to assure that officers were fully aware of any legal developments involving the rules. Numerous appeals were filed over the years, challenging classification rulings. Lawsuits were filed, challenging decisions. But, thanks to dedicated and properly trained residency classification officers, not a single case challenging the University's residency rules or application of those rules succeeded, excluding of course my first Chancery lawsuit against the University which challenged an earlier version of classification rules.

During what I refer to as the "Big Orange" years (from the 1970s until the employment of J. Wade Gilley as president of the University in 1999), I had primary responsibility for legal matters affecting non-faculty employees at UT. Several times each year I met with personnel (now "Human Resources") officers for each UT campus and updated them on legal developments in the employment arena.

From the mid-1970s until 1999 I also had primary responsibility for working with campus "equal employment opportunity/affirmative action" officers. I met with that group also on a regular basis.

My favorites were the chief student affairs officers. We held quarterly meetings throughout the "Orange Years," almost always meeting at one of Tennessee's state parks. A wide variety of issues affecting dealings with students were addressed at those meetings. Legal considerations were intertwined with most issues discussed.

In the evenings we socialized as we dined at the park restaurant. Then we played our traditional game of "nickle ante poker" before bedtime. We followed this tradition for nearly three decades. Results of each game were carefully recorded by Andy Kozar. The overall winner after 30 years had winnings of less than $30 with the overall loser down by a similar amount. My own 30 year winnings were around $15. We were not trying to emulate Las Vegas and did not! We did develop a strong working relationship.

CASUAL, EXTREME AND COMPETITIVE SPORTS NETWORKING

Casual sports competition with University personnel weighed heavily in networking and developing meaningful relationships, many of which I called upon, over the years, in connection with my legal responsibilities.

Shortly after my hire in 1972, I played handball with Jim Drinnon, Dr. Charles Temple, Director of the UT Office of Institutional Research, and S. H "Bo" Roberts, UT Vice-President for Urban and Public Affairs. I learned quickly that I was not adept at playing the game. It seemed that more shots struck my mouth than the walls of the court. Still, it was fun. And a networking opportunity.

My favorite sport was paddleball, a fantastic game similar to racquetball, played almost entirely in Michigan, California, Florida and Tennessee. The one wall version is played outdoors while the "four wall" indoor game is similar to racquetball. A wooden paddle with holes instead of a stringed racquet is used in paddleball and the ball, while almost identical in size, has two-thirds the bounce. Paddleball requires more running than racquetball so the game is a bit more strenuous, but I have enjoyed playing both.

Andy Kozar, author of a 1960s book on the game of paddleball taught me the game when I was a law student. As I mentioned previously, we played together often. Kozar was a running back on UT's 1951 National Championship Football Team who later played pro football for the Chicago Bears. Paddleball is a great game for networking. The game featured a number of prominent members of the University community over the years, in addition to Kozar. **To name a few:**

Ron McCartney (Captain, UT football team and the Atlanta Falcons of the NFL)

James Pippin (Program Director, Engineering Diversity Programs, College of Engineering, UT Knoxville)

Tim Rogers (Vice Chancellor for Student Affairs, UT Knoxville)

Phil Scheurer (Vice Chancellor for Student Affairs, UT Knoxville)

Bill Shmidt (UT track team and Bronze Medal winner, 1972 Olympics, Javelin)

Gray Simons (Head coach, UT wrestling team)

John Trembley (UT Head Coach, Swimming and Diving, and UT swimming Team, "All- American")

Tina Wesson (Winner, "Survivor 2" television series)

Ed Yovella (Chief of Police, UT Knoxville)

I taught the game of paddleball to Charles Temple at his request (at the time I was hired as staff attorney in 1972 Temple served as Director of the UT Office of Institutional Research, became Executive Assistant to the Chancellor at the University of Tennessee at Chattanooga in 1974, then later served as UTC Executive Vice Chancellor, President of Tennessee Tech Community College and then President of Southwest Tennessee Community College).

Temple and I had a unique motivational arrangement: if I held Temple to one point or scoreless in our 21- point games, he paid me three dollars. He paid two dollars when I held him to two or three points and one dollar when I held him to four or five. When Temple scored six or seven points I paid him one dollar. Eight or nine points earned Temple two dollars and ten or more earned him three dollars.

We were both highly motivated to improve our game using this system, and both of us did. For a while the competition was a good moneymaker for me. Then Temple improved to the point we broke even. He relocated to UT Chattanooga before the competition became a moneymaker for him.

One of my favorite racquetball partners in the 1980s was UT Memphis professor William ("Bill") Skoutakis. In later years my favorite was UT Head Football Coach Phillip Fulmer.

Faculty and staff league "flag football" was another favorite of mine. I continued to play for the law school football team after graduation. In 1975 I played for the English Department and we won the intramural championship. I later played for the "Tower of Power"–a team composed of UT Knoxville administrators, including Chancellor Jack Reese, with offices in the Andy Holt Tower administration building. Despite the name we never came close to winning a championship.

I organized rafting trips on major rivers like the Upper and Lower Gauley and New Rivers in West Virginia, the Cheat River in West Virginia and the Upper Youghiogheny River in Maryland. UT Athletic Director Joan Cronan and husband, Tom, UT Lady Vols Volleyball Coach Julie Hermann, UTCHS Vice Chancellor William ("Bill") Robinson, UT Lady Vols Golf Coach Linda Franz, and several attorneys in the Office of General Counsel, were among those who joined me on these rugged adventures.

In the spring of 1985 Central Baptist Church Bearden with $50 donations from 10 members including myself, obtained a used 8-man rubber raft and necessary equipment for a whitewater rafting ministry. I took on the responsibility of organizing and guiding trips on the Ocoee River. The first trip I guided for the ministry was on June 22, 1985.

Two months later, on August 24, 1985, I guided two trips down the Ocoee for a heavily UT flavored group. Participating in the excursion were UT Director of Women's Athletics, Joan Cronan and husband Tom (both members of my Sunday School class), two law clerks from the Office of General Counsel, Susan Fendley and Gwen Fuller, two other UT law students, good friend and private investigator Barry Rice, my son, Lee, and several others.

Joan Cronan later asked if I would take the Lady Vols volleyball team down the Ocoee for head volleyball coach Julie Hermann. I agreed to do so. In August

1993 and, again, in August 1994, I guided several raft loads of volleyball players down the Ocoee. All-American Tamala Brightman was a star paddler on each occasion.

On August 28, 1993 my daughter Cara made her first voyage down the Ocoee. The Cronan's, Jim Pippen, Ron McCartney and UT graduate student Jorge Ureta from Panama, joined us.

My favorite team sport was volleyball and early on I played, first for the UT Knoxville administration, then the English department. I also played for a team at the UT Center for the Health Sciences in Memphis during the 1980s.

From the mid-1980s, until close to the time of my retirement in 2008, I played for a team drawn from various university departments named The Misshits. The team captain, John Rich, was Associate Director of the UT system personnel office.

The Misshits won the faculty staff league championship in 1986, 1987, 1989, 1990, 1991, 1993, 1994 and 1998. By the early 2000s the average age of those on my team was more than double that of its opponents and age took its toll on our championship opportunities.

In 1971 my wife and I started a grasscourt volleyball tradition at our home, first on Friday evenings, then Saturdays then, for the past couple of decades up to the present, every other Sunday afternoon at 2 pm. roughly half of the participants over the decades have been UT affiliated. A great way to burn calories, enjoy fresh air and build friendships at the same time.

NETWORKING–
AS SIMPLE AS SHARING A CUP OF COFFEE

O.D. Larry, a black male, who lied about his age, was hired at age fifteen by the UT Medical Units in Memphis. At the time I commenced work in Memphis for the Office of General Counsel, Larry was manager of food services.

Larry died in February, 1993. On February 24, I sent to his widow, Fanny Larry, a letter by Federal Express. That letter tells the story of a solid networking relationship and friendship:

Dr. Bill Bass with his good friend author Patricia Cornwell in Knoxville, TN.

Dear Mrs. Larry:

For some 20 years I have known O. D., mostly as a dear friend and only secondarily as a colleague at the University of Tennessee. During my numerous visits to Memphis over these past years, it was my custom to begin each day, whenever possible, by arriving at the UT Memphis student center for early morning coffee and breakfast with O.D. the friendship and fellowship we shared on those occasions was truly something special. So special that I consider this friendship that even after O.D.'s retirement I made certain to call each time my travel to Memphis included an opportunity for morning coffee and breakfast. Only a couple of weeks ago I called O.D. for breakfast but, unfortunately, he was unable to come due to problems with his hip.

Why do I consider my friendship with O.D. special? Because O.D. was a very special person, as you well know. Always, O.D. would arrive at the Student Center before me and make sure that a hot pot of coffee was ready for the early arrivals. When I arrived O.D. would greet me, without fail, with a cheery smile and a spirited hello that came straight from the heart. This is not always an easy accomplishment at 6:30 in the morning! For the next hour or so, O.D., his friends, and I would share our faults, experiences, concerns, hopes, and dreams. Never did O.D. have an unkind word for another. His glowing optimism and zest for life were infectious and serve the purpose of getting his own day off to a cheery start. O.D.'s compassion for others is legendary; he received great joy from the opportunity to help folks with drug and alcohol problems, or persons otherwise in need of a kind word of encouragement or a helping hand.O.D. complained a little and gave much praise to others. He gave God the honor He is due and lived his Christian testimony. He not only "talked the talk," he also "walked the walk."

I shall greatly miss my breakfast meetings with O.D., but the great and positive influence he has had in my life, and unquestionably in the lives of many others, shall live on. I am honored to have had an opportunity to share a small part of life of this great man.

Sincerely,

Ronald C Leadbetter
Associate General Counsel

NETWORKING BEYOND UT

My networking and relationship-building efforts extended well beyond the University of Tennessee. I attended a variety of professional retreats and seminars in Tennessee and around the country:

College Law Conference, Georgetown University, Washington, D.C. (7/28/74)

Federal Bar Association, Washington, D.C. (3/21/76)

National Health Lawyers Association, Chicago, Il. (4/28/77)

National Health Lawyers Association, San Francisco, CA. (2/21/78)
Civil Rights conference, Dallas, TX (6/6/78)
Office of Federal Contract Compliance Programs, new procedures review, Atlanta, GA (3/6/80)
Medical Malpractice Risk Management, New Orleans, LA (12/11/81)
Medical/legal seminar, Los Angeles, CA (4/6/83)
Higher education law update, Stetson University, Clearwater, FL (1/29/84)
Intercollegiate licensing seminar, New Orleans, LA (4/23/84)
Affirmative action seminar, New York, NY (11/12/86)
Medical malpractice seminar, Orlando, FL (2/17/87)
Governor's Conference on Human Rights, Nashville, TN (11/12/87)
Drug-free workplace, Washington, DC (3/5/89)
Employment law, Chicago, IL (10/30/89)
Americans with Disabilities Act seminar, Denver, CO (3/6/98)
I also accepted many invitations to speak to higher education and professional organizations, both in-state and nationally:
The Southern Conference of Deans of Faculties and Academic Vice Presidents, "Legal Liability of the Academic Administrator in Personnel Decisions" (Atlanta 1975).
Student College Personnel Association, "The Buckley Act", (Atlanta 1976). UT Conference Center, conference for nurses, "Professional Malpractice" (Knoxville 1976).
Meharry Medical College, administrative retreat (Paris Landing State Park, TN 1976).
Parkwest Hospital, respiratory therapists, "medical malpractice" (Knoxville 1976).
Tennessee College and University Personnel Association (Knoxville 1977). NASPA conference, Tennessee Tech. U. (Cookeville, TN 1977).
TACRAO [Tennessee Association of Collegiate Registrars and Admissions Officers], "Legal Developments in Higher Education" (Henry Horton State Park 1978).
Donelson Police Academy, "Criminal, Civil and Administrative Laws Applying to Colleges and Universities," (Donelson, TN 1979).
Tennessee Association of Financial Aid Officers, "Collections and Bankruptcy", (Paris Landing State Park, TN 1984).
Southeast Regional Group of the National Association of Educational Buyers, "Contracts" (Knoxville 1984)
East Tennessee Chapter of American Association of Internal Auditors (Knoxville 1985).
TACRAO Convention (Nashville 1987)

Medical Educational Services, "Confidentiality of mental health and substance abuse records" (Knoxville 1994)

UTC Police Department, "Search and Seizure," Chattanooga (6/13/02)

UT Medical Center surgery residents, Knoxville (12/10/03)

Student services personnel, legal update, Martin (1/25/06)

Community involvement has been important to me during my entire adult life. Back in December 1972 I joined the West Knoxville Sertoma Club and have maintained my membership to the present. The club raised hundreds of thousands of dollars for charity during the period of my membership (the "Greater Tennessee Sportsman Show" being, until several years ago, a hugely successful fund raising activity for the club). The primary beneficiaries of WKS charitable giving each year have been children with a variety of needs.

Civic involvement has been more than just a means of carrying out the Biblical adage of "help your neighbor." Over the years, a sizable percentage of WKS members have been UT faculty or administrators - another networking and bonding opportunity with employment related benefits.

Weekly Sertoma luncheon meetings also provided many opportunities to invite speakers from the University community. Anthropologist Bill Bass was one of the first to be invited. UT Women's Basketball Coach, Margaret Hudson, a predecessor to world renowned Lady Vols Head Coach Pat Head Summit, spoke to the club at my invitation in January 1974. Coach Summit spoke to the club in November 1994.

Over the years, such notables as UT Football Head Coach Phil Fulmer, UT Memphis Chancellor James C ("Jim") Hunt, UT Athletic Directors Doug Dickey and Joan Cronan, Both the University and the community benefited each time. The networking benefits were priceless. Speaking of which, not a single invited speaker ever received a penny for his or her presentation.

Additional networking benefits resulted from my involvement as a co-founder and long-time volunteer legal counsel and member of the Board of Directors of the non-profit Children's Center of Knoxville (originally named the Knoxville Early Child Development Center). Since the Center's founding in 1975, many of UT faculty and administrators have served on the Board, including the Head of Child and Family Development at UT, Dr. Connie Steele. The founders of the Children's Center looked to the UT Child Development Center as a model.

In 1974, I joined Central Baptist Church Bearden. Since that time I have taught Sunday school, served as Trustee and on church committees and in the Deacon ministry. Many UT faculty, administrators and other employees are members of Central Baptist and have served with me.

I joined Central Baptist strictly for worship purposes, certainly not with any thought that church membership might assist me in performing my job as University legal counsel. Likewise, I did not join the West Knoxville Sertoma Club, co-found and serve the Children's Center, or join and participate in any one of a number of other community organizations for that purpose. Regardless of my intent, my active involvement in community service did in fact assist me greatly in serving effectively as legal counsel for the University.

One of my favorite sayings is "I am not an expert at anything except knowing people who are." I enjoyed success in my professional career as the result of networking with others and developing many invaluable relationships built on trust and friendship. I focused my efforts broadly, not on higher echelons alone. And, not just within the Office of General Counsel or the University administration but throughout the University and well beyond, as is made clear in history recounted in later chapters of this book.

Stated another way, had I not pursued networking opportunities and friendships described herein, it is unlikely I would have enjoyed the a level of success achieved; it is highly probable I would not have reached the 35 year mark of employment in the Office of General Counsel.

Ron, U.S. Senator Howard Baker, Therese and Ann Brake at the Tennessee Young Republican Convention (1971)

Chapter 12–Team Building in the Office of General Counsel–Scandal and Performance Factors

STAFF DEVELOPMENT AND CHANGE

The University of Tennessee's first General Counsel, John Baugh, joined the UT College of Law faculty in 1946. He served as UT staff attorney on a part-time basis beginning in 1947–the year of my birth.

Baugh was named as UT's chief legal counsel in 1965 and served in that position on a fulltime basis until retiring in 1975. As the duties of the Office of General Counsel became more defined, Baugh hired additional counsel to assist in carrying out those duties.

At the time of my employment as staff attorney in 1972, legal services that had formerly been provided by attorneys outside the University were, little by little, redirected in-house. Attorneys Art Stowers and Dan Rhea had nominal litigation responsibilities at the time of my hire, handling primarily transactional and advisory assignments. While my assignments were focused on litigation, there was little of that to be handled early on. Probably a good thing. In all honesty, I learned to handle litigation "by the seat of my pants."

Organization and assignment of responsibilities was minimal at the beginning of my employment in the Office of General Counsel. During the remainder of Baugh's tenure as General Counsel the cornucopia of legal responsibilities directed to the OGC increasingly were directed to one attorney or another as the skills and interests of the attorneys became better known.

Stowers was the attorney who introduced me to the Tennessee Court of Appeals on September 18, 1972. To my knowledge, this was his last appearance in court on behalf of UT.

Rhea was assigned to work with me on UT's first "in-house" case in Federal Court, Nancy Van de Vate vs. The University of Tennessee. Outside counsel, Lou Woolf and I served as co-counsel for the 1974 trial. For reasons unknown to me, Rhea did not participate in or even appear at trial. To my knowledge he never again appeared in court on behalf of the University.

On December 29, 1975 the Office of General Counsel moved to new quarters on the eighth floor of Andy Holt Tower, the University's newly constructed administration building. I had a corner office overlooking the Tennessee River with a nice view of Neyland Stadium and much of the campus. In the summer of '75, John Baugh retired.

I have nothing but praise for John Baugh. After all, he paved the way for my entry into a professional career I consider second to none. He was a man of unquestioned integrity and showed kindness to all. Serving as a role model, he eschewed the spirit of combativeness that so often characterizes the practice of law. He demonstrated a talent for remaining calm in the midst of a storm.

I was only minimally concerned that Baugh's replacement as General Counsel would alter the playing field. My lack of concern was justified.

Beauchamp E. ("Beach") Brogan resigned his position with the office of General Counsel for the Tennessee Valley Authority and assumed the position of Secretary and General Counsel for the University of Tennessee in 1975 – concurrent with Baugh's retirement. Changes were made but the results were quite beneficial from my perspective. For the remainder of Brogan's term as UT General Counsel I regularly bragged to others that the most efficiently run offices at the University of Tennessee, in my view, were Athletics (both men's and women's), Development/Alumni Affairs offices and the Office of

General Counsel.

Shortly after arriving, Brogan terminated the employment of two of the three attorneys on the OGC staff, Stowers and Rhea. The terminations were for entirely unrelated reasons.

Art was a true Southern gentleman. He was well-known for two distinguishing attributes. First, he had a passionate love for the sport of wrestling and was an avid supporter of the UT wrestling team. In any conversation, in almost any setting, Art would bring up the subject of a wrestling if given the chance. "You look like a wrestler. Have you ever wrestled?" His second distinguishing attribute was the one that cost him his job.

When asked to render a legal opinion, which attorneys in the OGC are regularly called upon to provide, Art's trademark conclusion to any opinion offered was, "Now, don't quote me on that." Perhaps more disconcerting, Art's customary caveat issued along with that disclaimer was, in effect, "In response to your question I am of the opinion that… But, it is also possible that a court would find…" leaving the recipient of his advice uncertain as to what course of action to take.

"Beach" (I had always addressed Baugh as "Mr. Baugh" but addressed my new boss as "Beach") made it clear to me that he did not want a staff attorney who would not take responsibility and provide clear direction to those receiving his legal services. Art had to go.

Dan Rhea's involuntary departure, shortly after Stower's, was predicated on personal conduct rather than work quality. Dan was a ladies' man and often said so to his colleagues. He told me more than once he could have any woman he wanted. His speech and behavior vacillated between ultra-diplomatic and stunningly offensive; sometimes a mixing of the two.

In May 1976, Dan and I decided to eat dinner at the popular Wiffle Tree restaurant in Ann Arbor. Michigan. It is located near the University of Michigan where Dan and I were attending an Advocacy Institute. A line of fifty or so waited patiently in line outside the main door of the packed eatery. Except Dan.

Dan walked past the line, disappeared through the front door, then reappeared right outside the entrance minutes later and yelled, "Come on, I've got us a table!" Sheepishly I walked from the rear of the line to join Dan, noting one glare after another as I did.

A pretty little waitress had set a table up for Dan. After taking our seats I commented jokingly, but with purpose, "Dan, someone's going to shoot you. Tell me if I need to duck." No shot was fired on that occasion.

On another occasion Dan climbed onto the second floor balcony of a Sequoyah Hills apartment adjacent to the apartment of his ex-girlfriend. When he attempted to leap, uninvited, to her balcony, he missed, fell to the ground and broke his leg.

A drug arrest a short time later led directly to the termination of Dan's employment. Word of Dan's behavior spread and Beach acted. Dan too was gone. I was the sole survivor of the Baugh legal staff.

Dan moved to Memphis after his dismissal from UT, but periodically returned to Knoxville to visit former colleagues at the University. Dan was an outgoing, friendly sort, but was just tainted by a certain attraction to unacceptable behavior.

Several years after his departure from the University, Dan paid a Friday afternoon visit to UT treasurer Brodie Baynes, one or two others and me. He shared with us that he was going to a family reunion in Maury County over the weekend.

I received word the following week that Dan had made it to the reunion. At some point he announced to his brother that he had to run to the local market to meet someone. He did not return. His automobile was later found in the parking lot at the Maury County Hospital.

Dan's whereabouts were unknown for several years. At some point the TBI received a report from a terminally ill prisoner in the state penitentiary in Nashville that if a search were made in a certain field in Maury County Dan's body would be found. TBI agents, accompanied by Dr. Bill Bass, searched the field and located Dan's body buried 18 inches or so deep, fully dressed with wallet and cash still in his pocket. He had a bullet wound above one eye. Unfortunately my half-joking prediction had come true.

Beach filled the vacancies left by the removal of Stowers and Rhea with attorneys a bit less colorful but more professionally suited to the needs of the office. The "Big Orange" years saw a marked shift to a "team approach" in the Office of General Counsel, an approach that worked with great effectiveness until the black clouds of the Gilley presidency moved in years later.

Brogan's approach to assignment of legal responsibilities was quite simple. Each staff attorney was assigned areas of responsibility based on the attorney's expression of interest in handling that area. I expressed an interest in handling student affairs, personnel and civil rights/affirmative action issues statewide and working with University-wide and campus officials charged with handling those matters. The areas I expressed interest in were assigned to me. Other attorneys were assigned areas such as workers compensation, faculty affairs, and purchasing.

Assignment of responsibilities was also made on a geographic basis. I volunteered to assume responsibility for the UT Center for the Health Sciences in Memphis as well as the UT Martin campus. Responsibility for the UT Chattanooga and UT Nashville campuses, the UT Space Institute and the

UT Institute of Agriculture, was assigned to other attorneys. For each attorney having primary responsibility for a geographic area another was assigned secondary responsibility. The same procedure was followed in assigning responsibility for major topical areas.

An informal "apprenticeship" approach helped identify new attorneys suited for trial work. Most of the new attorneys were assigned to work with me on a case or two. Most acclimated quickly to trial work and went on to handle cases of their own. Several of those assigned to work with me did not pan out as trial attorneys and never tried a case.

Regular staff meetings and occasional weekend retreats were held at Brogan's call. Not too many and not too few. Just enough to assure that all legal matters received adequate attention by attorneys best suited and most interested in handling any particular area. The approach worked well and I never heard a word of dissent. Quite to the contrary, there was a real sense of teamwork at play during the first two and a half decades of my employment in the office of General Counsel.

A FAMILY ATMOSPHERE

Birthday celebrations for OGC staff were a common occurrence during the "Big Orange" years. A 10 minute "coffee break" featuring a few congratulatory words by the General Counsel, a piece of cake and opening of a birthday card signed by everyone else in the office served the purpose.

Office Christmas lunches, sometimes partnering with other offices, were also customary. The lawyers also regularly took the secretaries to lunch on Secretaries Day.

Office picnics, dinners and lunches outside normal business hours were also popular. Almost the entire OGC staff (24 in all) came to our home for late lunch on December 11, 1993.

On October 2, 1994, Therese and I hosted a picnic for the entire office at our home on Creekhead Drive. Sixteen to eighteen OGC attorneys and staff attended. We picnicked outside and the group stayed late.

A luncheon was held at our home for current as well as former OGC staff on February 7, 1999. Office loyalty extended beyond retirement.

Beach was particularly adept at promoting a family atmosphere in the office during the bulk of his career. He actively promoted these and other social activities for the office and was well respected for doing so. Low personnel turnover was one benefit of that approach.

SECRETARIES WERE FAMILY

On December 2, 1989 Therese and I hosted a retirement dinner at our home for my secretary, Hazel Nicely. A second retirement dinner celebrating her nearly 20 years of service to the University was held in the executive dining room of the University Center on December 20. Both events were well attended by OGC staff.

A midwinter lunch was held at our home on February 7, 1999 for both current and former staff. Luncheon guests included both retiree Hazel and current secretary Tish Griffey, the two world-class secretaries with whom I worked for 34 of my 35 plus years in the General Counsel's office.

Hazel taught me the benefits of discussing good fishing locations with courthouse officials in rural East Tennessee when I was a novice lawyer in the Office of General Counsel. Years later it was my honor to sing "Rocky Top" at the foot of her nursing home bed during her last day on earth. At her funeral service several days later rumor had it that she had left to be with the Lord as an escape from my singing. I have assurance that one day I'll be able to ask her if the rumor was true.

The service I gladly rendered to Tish was on a much lighter note: I was pleased to serve as videographer for her November 24, 1996 wedding to Ed Brown.

Even after my March 31, 2008 retirement from the University, Tish (a 2012 retiree and current part time OGC employee) and I continued to share lunch periodically and catch up on University happenings.

Paralegals Bettie Pucket (OGC Memphis office) and Jan Williams Horak (Memphis and Knoxville offices) provided excellent paralegal assistance to me for many years. We maintained our friendship long after our professional relationship ended.

STEVE ROADS AND LITTLE BIG TOWN

One of my dearest workplace friends was Steve Roads. Steve was a member of the Lake Junaluska singers, along with Beauchamp Brogan's son, Jim. Brogan hired Steve as a staff attorney in1989.

Steve traveled with me to Memphis in September of that year for a bit of in-house training under my direction. I was impressed with his legal skills–perhaps more impressed with our commonality of interests and values.

Christian "apologetics" was one interest of Steve's I found appealing. Common interests also included whitewater rafting, skiing and hiking. We worked well together on legal matters as well. Kindred spirits we were in many ways.

Steve was a Republican. At my request, he brought the Lake Junaluska singers to provide entertainment for the West Knoxville Republican club at the December 11, 1989 Christmas dinner.

On December 1, 1990 my daughter Cara and I drove to Georgia for the wedding of Steve and his fiancé, Kimberly. It was a wonderful wedding and Cara and I will never forget hearing Steve and Kimberly sing their vows to each other. Kimberly is a strikingly beautiful, very thin gal with a head full of fuzzy, blonde hair. She became the blonde in Little Big Town. The brunette in the group is Karen Fairchild.

Cara held the mike for the Roads as they sang at the July 1991 West Knoxville Republican Club picnic at the Deane Hill Recreation Center in Knoxville. In May 1992 Steve and I joined UT police officers for a day of marksmanship competition, barbecue and a legal seminar at the Knox County police firing range.

Therese and I joined Steve for dinner and singing by Kim at Amigos Restaurant in August 1993. Around that same time Steve assumed responsibility for legal matters at the UT Medical Center in Knoxville.

A couple of years later both Steve and Kimberly's interest in the music industry, country music in particular, led to their move to Brentwood. Steve became an agent for several country music stars while Kim pursued opportunities as a singer. My work relationship with Steve ended but our friendship continued.

When in Nashville on UT business I occasionally stayed at the Roads' home or more often joined Steve for lunch or dinner. In early December 1998, I spent the evening with Steve and Kim at their home, showing their Bible study group a video based on my 1996 journey to the mountains of Ararat in Eastern Turkey ("Journey to Noah's Ark–the Duripinar Site").

I learned that same evening that Kim had signed a contract with the country music group, Little Big Town. In August, 2001, I spent the evening at the Roads' home following dinner with Steve and an evening at a Nashville studio watching Little Big Town work on their first CD. I was awestruck when I heard their music.

Tragically, Steve died, unexpectedly, at age 41, of a congenital heart defect in April 2005. Amazingly, Kim and Little Big Town appeared for a previously scheduled performance on Market Square in Knoxville, a week or so later, on April 15. My wheelchair-bound dad had the wonderful opportunity to meet Kim and the members of Little Big Town as well as hear their music.

Little Big Town has gone on to win a number of national awards, including the Academy of Country Music's "Top new vocal duo/group of the year" (2006), ACM "Vocal Group of the Year" (2013) and a Grammy award for the song "Pontoon" (2013).

Kim has remarried and has a daughter with current husband Stephen Schlapman. We stay in touch. Therese and I, as well as Cara and husband Dave, visited with Kimberly and Little Big Town backstage prior to a concert with country music star Keith Urban, in February 2014.

The concert was held in Thompson Boling Arena on the UT campus. Kimberly Kneier, a close friend of Kim's and a friend of mine, former secretary in the Office of General Counsel, was also present as Kim's guest.

Little Big Town was awesome in concert in the packed-to-the-gills arena. Had Steve been there he would have been proud. Kim and Little Big Town are quite special to me. I am reminded of my workplace soulmate each time I see or hear them.

TEAM CONFIDENCE

One of my favorite mantras, both in my personal and professional life, is meeting challenges with whatever solution works best—within applicable ethical constraints. I accord Beech Brogan a rating of 9.9 on a scale of 1 to 10 in allowing me to pursue whatever solution to a problem I thought would work best. Innovation was encouraged and "we've never done it that way" was not a bar to improvement.

Employee competence conjoined with supervisory confidence eliminated unnecessary and wasteful levels of supervision. During the Brogan years, as was increasingly true during the preceding Baugh years, each incoming legal issue or lawsuit was automatically directed to the attorney responsible for that area by an office secretary familiar with duty assignments.

For example, a federal civil rights lawsuit filed in Memphis against the UT Center for Health Sciences, would promptly be sent to me without delay, the presumption being that I was capable of determining what action needed to be taken without oversight by one or more levels of supervision. A very cost effective practice that predominated during the "Big Orange" era.

Chapter 13–The Board of Trustees is the Client, Not the Enemy

As a student litigating a claim against the University, one of my early observations was that the General Counsel of the University of Tennessee worked closely with the Board of Trustees. This made perfect sense to me since the University was the General Counsel's client and the trustees were the governing body of the University. High quality legal representation requires good communication between attorney and client.

It was no surprise to me when General Counsel Baugh, from the outset of my employment, invited me to attend and participate in Board committee meetings and meetings of the full Board. After all, as an attorney in the office of General Counsel who would be called upon repeatedly to represent the

University in a wide variety of legal proceedings, it made perfect sense to communicate well with my client's governing board. Of course, with the understanding that such communication would be within any parameters established by my boss.

I was certainly not the first staff attorney to interact with Board members. Assistant General Counsel Jim Drinnon appeared before the Board of Trustees in October 1970, during the board's consideration of my residency classification appeal, representing the University and communicating with trustees as he did.

According to my diary, my first formal presentation to the full Board was on October 15, 1976 when "I made two presentations to the UT Board of Trustees (Salvoni & Grager)." Each presentation reviewed the status of the litigation and provided trustees an opportunity to ask questions.

From the outset of my employment until June 2000, I regularly attended meetings of the trustees regardless of where the meetings were held. For example, the November 14, 1980 Board meeting in Olive Branch, Mississippi was one I attended at the General Counsel's invitation.

I was also generally invited to Board social events. Therese was often invited to join me. I was readily accessible to Board members and was frequently approached by trustees seeking information on a wide range of legal issues affecting higher education in general and the University of Tennessee in particular.

RETREATS FOR TRUSTEES, LEGAL COUNSEL AND OTHERS WERE NOT VACATIONS

A taxpayer might question why university officials, trustees, student leaders and University attorneys would spend of couple of days together at a state park. Good question. From my own perspective such retreats offered an excellent opportunity to network, build bonds of friendship and address issues of common concern free from every day distractions.

A July 5, 1988 memorandum to attendees at the July 17–18, 1988, University of Tennessee Student Leader Orientation Conference at Henry Horton State Park near Lewisburg, Tennessee offers a fine example of a typical retreat. The memorandum, from Executive Vice President and Vice President for Development, Joe Johnson, was addressed to nineteen attendees in the aforementioned categories. Included were trustees Marcia Echols, Jimmy Harrison and Pam Moon, a student trustee. The three trustees were members of the Board's student affairs committee.

The attendees were notified that the "first business session is set for 7:00 p.m. on Sunday in Conference Room A. We will work on Monday morning and close out with lunch." Vice-Pres. Johnson also notified attendees that UT president

Lamar Alexander would join the group for one hour on Monday morning.

An attached agenda listed a variety of topics to be covered during the 7:00 to 9:30 pm meeting Sunday evening:

Organization of higher education in Tennessee–Joe Johnson
University–wide administration–Joe Johnson
Board of Trustees–Beach Brogan
Policies of the University–Ron Leadbetter
Student appointments–Joe Johnson
Travel arrangements and related details–Joe Johnson
Campus administration–Phil Scheurer, Charles Renneisen,
      Bill Robinson, and Phil Watkins

Under each topic was listed a number of subtopics. A similar agenda was published for the following day including "comments by and discussion with President Lamar Alexander" from 9:00 to 10:00 a.m.

Judging from the questions and comments of participants, the retreat went well. It was an excellent opportunity, from my perspective, for networking and bonding with trustees and others present, including President Alexander.

Following a similar retreat years later (June 17–18, 1988), Joe Johnson, then Vice- President of the University, observed in a letter to administrative assistant Katie High, Senior Vice-President Homer Fisher and me: "Board members appreciate the way you do your business." Staff interaction with board members clearly met with the president's approval.

BIZARRE MEETING WITH GOVERNOR AND BOARD CHAIRMAN RAY BLANTON

On February 20, 1975, Therese and I joined John Baugh and Assistant Secretary to the Board of Trustees, Katie Jacobs, for the drive to Nashville to attend the winter Board meeting. Board committees met on the 20th with the full Board scheduled to meet on the 21st.

Gov. Ray Blanton would be attending his first meeting as chairman of the Board of Trustees. Tennessee's governor is officially chairman of the board but often does not attend Board meetings and the Board vice chairman presides. The winter meeting was in downtown Nashville, the State capitol, at the University of Tennessee at Nashville ("UTN").

Gov. Ray Blanton arrived late for the February 21 meeting of the full board. It was later reported that he had turned down an offer to be met by UT hostesses and, as a result, had difficulty locating the meeting site (even though UTN was walking distance from the governor's office).

The meeting room was packed when the governor arrived. As was the custom at the time, the meeting opened with prayer. Matters went somewhat downhill from there.

An announcement was made that the Labor Department had imposed on the University a "back wages" penalty in excess of $100,000 for UTK's failure to pay Safety and Security Officers overtime pay for the 10 minutes they were required to be present before the beginning of each workday in order to be in uniform. Gov. Blanton turned to the General Counsel and asked, "Doesn't the University follow the law like everyone else?" Or something close to that?

Mr. Baugh's memorable response was, "No, Governor, it doesn't." He presumably intended to explain that there was a distinction based on UT's status as a public educational corporation of the state of Tennessee. The Governor did not await nor did he ask for further explanation.

Blanton turned immediately to the Trustees and announced he was appointing a committee to investigate the matter. He announced that trustee William North, a federal judge on the U.S. Court of Appeals for the Sixth Circuit, would serve on the committee.

The Governor did not ask Judge North if he was willing to serve, he simply announced his appointment. Judge North was visibly upset and resigned as trustee that day or the following.

A luncheon followed the conclusion of the Board meeting. Therese and I had the dubious pleasure of being seated directly across from Gov. Blanton and his wife, Betty. I introduced Therese and myself to the Blantons. Gov. Blanton's unforgettable response was, "I see you married beneath yourself, just like me."

The comment was made in jest but the governor got the popular jest inverted. I smiled nervously but did not laugh. My wife was seated next to me. Blanton's wife never cracked a smile; deadpan best described her look. And the Governor himself seemed oblivious to his gaff.

Several years later, on October 20, 1978, Blanton attended his second, and last, Board meeting, in Knoxville. UT employee Dennie Littlejohn had requested an opportunity to address the trustees and the Governor consented.

Littlejohn took the podium and asked the trustees to take action divesting stock ownership in companies doing business in South Africa. After several minutes Blanton advised Littlejohn that his time was up; Littlejohn advised Blanton that he was not through and continued to speak.

Other protesters made their presence known. The governor lost control of the meeting and disruption by the protestors brought the meeting to a close before the agenda had been completed. Police were called and arrests were made.

Of interest is the fact that Littlejohn received no disciplinary action for his conduct at the Board meeting. Of more interest is the fact that Blanton never attended or conducted another board meeting.

In January 1979 Blanton was removed as governor by action of the state legislature which secretly swore in newly elected governor Lamar Alexander early to prevent "Pardon-Me-Ray" Blanton from marketing additional pardons for state prison inmates. Blanton later served prison time for his criminal behavior.

NETWORKING AT BOARD MEETING

The Blanton run Board meetings notwithstanding, most Board and committee meetings were very productive, as were various social events and retreats I attended with trustees.

Sometimes I was included on committee agendas to provide formal presentations on major developments in state or federal law. At other times I was called on extemporaneously to address questions of legal import raised by committee members.

For most of the "Big Orange" years, prior to each Board meeting the trustees would be provided a "litigation status report" summarizing the status of civil cases and administrative proceedings to which the University was a party. These reports provided the trustees an excellent snapshot of the number and nature of proceedings in which the University was involved, as well as the dollar amount of any claims, the identity of the attorney handling each claim and the present status of each case. Case dispositions and dollar amounts and other terms of settlements or losses were made freely available to trustees by the OGC.

An example from the June 1, 1998 status report:

44. SCOTT GRAHAM HARTMAN v. THE UNIVERSITY OF TENNESSEE, Tennessee Court of Appeals No. 01A01-9804- BC-00196 (RCL) (UTK) Complaint filed 4/17/87 alleging UT breached claimant's athletic scholarship agreement by failing to provide for claimant's medical expenses after he was injured at a track meet and failing to exercise due care for claimant's safety at the track meet. Damages sought in the amount of $300,000. UT's answer filed 7/26/88. Plaintiff's Motion for Partial Summary Judgment granted in plaintiff's favor on 9/19/89 on contract issue. Tort claim remains for trial. UT filed second motion for summary judgment on 11–28–95 on tort claim and claimant moved for partial summary judgment in tort claim on 1–17–90 seeking $1,026,000 as liquidated damages for breach of contract. Summary judgment was entered in favor of the University on 3–12–98 and case dismissed. Plaintiffs appealed on 4 –9–98.

PRESENT STATUS: Both parties will file appellate briefs with the Court of Appeals.

Regrettably, the preparation of litigation status reports ceased with the coming of the dark clouds of the Wade Gilley presidency in the summer of 1999. Shortly thereafter, I received word from Catherine Mizell, then UT's General Counsel, that president Gilley was of the opinion there were too many attorneys from the Office of General Counsel at Board meetings and they should not attend.

I found President Gilley's observation rather amusing since I was typically the only attorney in attendance aside from the General Counsel. The Committee and full Board meetings of June 21–22, 2000 were the last I attended while employed by the University.

MEMORABLE BOARD MEETINGS

I found every Board meeting I attended during the "Big Orange" years memorable for the excellent discussions of higher education challenges and plans for the University of Tennessee. Each annual meeting took place in June and always in Knoxville.

Winter meetings were an opportunity for the Board to reach out and meet at other campuses.

Most memorable meetings? A few come to mind and the two involving Gov. Ray Blanton top the list—at least for meetings with a negative connotation. On the positive end was a meeting at which former Governor Lamar Alexander was chosen to be UT's next president.

Alexander shared with the Board that the two jobs he had always wanted were president of the University of Tennessee and president of the United States. The Board voted unanimously to make Alexander the 18th President of the University of Tennessee.

On December 17, 1990, at a news conference in the board room, Alexander announced he had been nominated by President George Bush to the position of U.S. Secretary of Education.

Alexander's successor, Dr. Joe Johnson, was elected president at the June 27, 1991 annual meeting of the UT Board. Seven years later Dr. Johnson announced, at the June 17, 1998 annual meeting, that he would be retiring from the UT presidency.

A year after Johnson's announced retirement J. Wade Gilley was elected as his replacement. I first met Gilley at the Board committee meetings on June 16, 1999, then at the full Board meeting on the 17th. These meetings are not to be forgotten.

The 1999 annual meeting, during which the Board elected Gilley President, ushered in what I will term the BLACK STORM CLOUDS of the Gilley years and beyond. The University's moral focus changed dramatically with the coming of Gilley.

Chapter 14–Residency Classification Rules for Admission and Tuition Purposes– Utilizing My Experience for Victory

The University did not hire me to take advantage of my experience as a litigant in the area of residency classification, at least not intentionally. Yet several of my early high profile cases and projects involved the subject matter of my litigation against the University during my law school days.

HOOBAN vs. BOLING

In May, 1973, UT law student Roger Hooban filed a civil rights action in the US District Court for the Eastern District of Tennessee, against Pres. Boling and Carl Pierce, Assistant Dean of the UT College of Law, asserting that the University had classified him as an "out of state" student for tuition purposes and in doing so had acted arbitrarily and unreasonably and in violation of his equal protection rights under the 14th Amendment to the United States Constitution. Hooban claimed the University's action infringed on his right to travel from state to state.

In less than two months, on July 9, 1973, U.S. District Judge Robert Taylor held trial. Midway through Hooban's testimony on the witness stand Judge Taylor interrupted the testimony and observed, in effect, "Mr. Leadbetter knows all about these residency regulations."

A ruling in the University's favor was issued from the bench immediately after my presentation of the defendants' case. Taylor's official ruling was issued October 2, 1974. Hooban appealed to the U.S. Court of Appeals for the Sixth Circuit.

Oral argument in the appeal was set for June 5, 1974. Each side had 15 minutes to present their case. Hooban attempted to make a speech but was interrupted before he completed the first sentence. First one judge then another interrupted Hooban as he persisted in presenting his speech rather than addressing the questions posed. He truly did not understand how the court operated.

Following the conclusion of the appeal proceeding I joined Hooban back at his hotel room for a bit of socializing. He guessed that he had probably lost the case, saying that he would've fared better had the judges not repeatedly interrupted him. He correctly guessed the outcome.

The three-judge panel affirmed the District Court in a published opinion decided October 2, 1974. [Hooban v. Boling 503 F2d. 648 (1974)]. Hooban appealed to the U.S Supreme Court.

The United States Supreme Court denied Hooban's petition for a writ of certiorari. [421 U.S. 920, 43 L.Ed. 2d. 788 (1975)]

Even while the Hooban case was in progress, measures were taken to improve the University's residency classification procedures. A decision was made to adopt new uniform regulations for both the University of Tennessee and the State University and Community College as the result of a decision issued on June 11, 1973 by the United States Supreme Court in Vlandis v. Kline, 412 U.S. 441 (1973).

Vlandis made clear that public colleges and universities were not permitted to create irrefutable presumptions of non-residence and must permit students to controvert any presumptions of non-residence by producing evidence of bona fide residency in-state.

In a memorandum of July 23, 1973 to all UT chancellors, I summarized the holdings in Vlandis and noted potential problems with residency classification regulations previously adopted by the Board of Trustees - on October 20, 1972.

Over the next two weeks I toured the state with staff attorney Dan Rhea and "met with administrative personnel, from all of our campuses, concerned with the administration of University residency classification regulation.

As I further noted:

"The meetings were most rewarding in that a variety of questions were raised by those present concerning application and interpretation of the reg ulations and Mr. Rhea and I had an opportunity to express our legal opinion as to how that regulations should be interpreted and applied in order to com ply with requirements set down by the recent United States Supreme Court decision of Vlandis v. Kline. It is my impression that the meetings succeeded in resolving a wide variety of questions and apparent or actual conflicts in interpretation of the regulations." (Memorandum of Aug. 3, 1973 to Charles Smith, Executive Assistant to President Edward Boling and all Chancellors).

In the same memorandum I expressed concern over certain aspects of the existing rules, particularly a requirement that those with newly established domicile wait one year before being classified "in-state".

A six or eight member committee, composed of equal numbers of represen- tatives from UT and Regents' institutions, was appointed and asked to hash out a new set of residency classification rules complying with current law. Charles Smith and I were two of the UT appointees.

The committee met several times and reached accord on a number of issues. I prepared the final rule draft for approval by UT Trustees and the Board of Regents. One key provision provided that "every person having his or her domi- cile in this state shall be classified "in-state" for fee and tuition purposes and for admission purposes." A second provision provided that "every person not having his or her domicile in this state shall be classified "out-of-state" for said-purposes." (Rules of the University of Tennessee (All Campuses), Rule 1720–1-1-.03 (1) and (2)).

The term "domicile" was defined as "a person's true, fixed, and permanent home and place of habitation; it is the place where he intends to remain, and to which he or she expects to return when he or she leaves without intending to establish a new domicile elsewhere." (Rule 1720-1-1-.02 (3).

Perhaps the most critical rule in my draft was the one describing the factors to be considered in determining whether a person is domiciled in Tennessee for tuition or admission purposes:

> ...if a person asserts that he or she has established domicile in this state he or she has the burden of proving that he or she has done so. Such a person is entitled to provide to the public higher educational institution by which he seeks to be classified or reclassified in- state, any and all evidence which he or she believes will sustain his or her burden of proof. Said institution will consider any and all evidence provided to add concerning such claim of domi cile but will not treat any particular type or item of such evidence as conclu sive evidence that domicile has or has not been established.
> (Rule 1720–1–1-.06).

The last rule eliminated any specific list of criteria to be considered–such as gave rise to my litigation against the University. Instead, a determination of whether an individual had established domicile in Tennessee was to be made by weighing all evidence supporting or rebutting a claim of domicile. The "rule of reason" was to be applied in determining whether the individual had met his or her burden of establishing domicile.

Some might question why so much effort was spent on revising residency classification rules. Answer: MILLIONS OF DOLLARS ANNUALLY in tuition payments! The taxpayers of the state of Tennessee have a clear interest in bearing the cost of education only for those domiciled in the state with those domiciled elsewhere paying their own way.

Following approval of the committee's proposed rules by both Boards - the UT Board of Trustees approved the rules at its 1975 winter board meeting – a small group of UT officials traveled statewide to educate classification officers on the new rules.

On April 23–24, 1975, Andy Kozar, John Hemmeter, Director of the Office for Institutional Research, Al Berry, Assistant Vice Chancellor for Academics and I, utilizing the University's Aero Commander aircraft, travelled to the Memphis, Martin, Chattanooga and Nashville campuses. At each location I conducted an intense residency classification seminar, with plenty of opportunity for questions and answers.

The revised rules were filed with the office of the Secretary of State, Administrative Procedures Division, on November 23, 1976 in accordance with the rulemaking provisions of the Tennessee Administrative Procedures Act.

Training was a continuing responsibility. On March 9, 1983, as noted in my personal diary, "I went to Nashville to meet with admissions officers of UT and the Board of Regents institutions and discuss student residency classification rules."

The rules filed in 1976 remain in effect today with few revisions. In 1994, nearly twenty years after enactment of the original rules, the Tennessee Higher Education Commission (THEC) suggested a review of the residency classification guidelines to determine whether the changes were warranted.

By letter of January 14, 1994, UT President Joe Johnson thanked Dr. Arliss Roaden, Executive Director of THEC, for "giving us an opportunity to suggest members of a committee to look at residency classification guidelines. I am recommending that Dr. Katie High, Associate Senior Vice President, and Mr. Ron Leadbetter, Associate General Counsel, represent the University of Tennessee. Both Katie and Ron have good communication with admission and records officers throughout the University, and they will stay in touch with these people as they carry out their responsibilities with the committee."

In the ensuing meetings of the new committee little change was made to the rules. The definition of "emancipated person" was shortened and simplified to "mean a person who is no longer in the care, custody and control of his or her parent." No longer was there any reference to the person being someone who had attained the age of 18 years. The only other amendment provided that "unemancipated students of divorced parents shall be classified 'in-state' when one parent, regardless of custodial status, is domiciled in Tennessee."

RARE CONFLICT WITH THE ATTORNEY GENERAL'S OFFICE–WHILE CO-COUNSEL AT TRIAL

Even as work continued on improving the rules, residency classification litigation continued. Roberta Berrien v. The University of Tennessee Medical Units, et.al., a 1973 case in the U.S. District Court for the Western District of Tennessee in Memphis, was unusual in at least one respect.

I arrived in the Memphis office of Dr. Joe Johnson—then Chancellor for the UT Memphis Medical Units - and found Assistant Attorney General Henry Haile, with the State Attorney General's office, waiting there with Dr. Johnson. Taking a seat, I was stunned to hear from Haile that he– not I – would be representing the University defendants in court that day - only the Attorney

General's office had authority to represent the University in a court of law.

I immediately took issue with Haile's assertion and announced that I–not he –would be representing the University. Tempers flared. "Dr. Joe," ever the diplomat, announced that both of us would represent the University.

All three of us went to court. Haile and I sat at opposite ends of the "defendant's table"—as far from each other as we could arrange—much to the consternation of plaintiff's counsel, Irvin Salky, and U.S. District Judge Robert McRae.

Haile and I heatedly disagreed on the facts and pertinent rules addressing Berrien's claim of entitlement to in-state classification by the University. Both Salky and Judge McRae seemed puzzled. They were possibly at a loss as to how to respond to the conflicting arguments of defense counsel. The court took the case under advisement.

Perhaps due to confusion over which defense argument to accept, Judge McRae long delayed any ruling on the defense's motions to dismiss plaintiff's claim. A surprise post-hearing phone call likely saved the University's case. Several months after the Court fiasco – no ruling yet having been issued - Salky contacted the Court and asked to be heard. A hearing was set.

Counsel met in Judge McRae's chambers where the latest development was brought to the judge's attention. Salky reported receiving a telephone call from his client somewhere in the Northeast, where she then resided. Obviously not domiciled in Tennessee. An order of dismissal was entered by McRae on August 20, 1974, bringing the case to a close – The University prevailed.

Other cases have since been brought against the University challenging classifications under the residency rules, but none successfully. Credit goes to classification officers on the campuses for keeping adequately trained in the rules, abreast of applicable law and seeking legal advice when necessary.

Postscript: *The adversarial encounter between Haile and me was an isolated event. During my term of employment, relationships with the Tennessee Attorney General's office were exceptionally benign. The UT Office of General Counsel was even requested by the Attorney General to take on litigation previously handled by that office. Years after the incident with Henry Haile, all workers' compensation cases involving UT employees were specifically reassigned by the Attorney General to the UT Office of General Counsel.*

Chapter 15–The National Association of College and University Attorneys

The National Association of College and University Attorneys is a vast organization that provides one of the best source of legal updates on issues affecting higher education, through annual conferences, sponsored seminars and a variety of publications. Just as important, NACUA provides a nationwide network of hundreds or even thousands of attorneys specializing in higher education. For me, NACUA serve as a reliable source of expert witnesses and professional expertise that greatly benefitted the University of Tennessee.

In 1981, I attended my first annual meeting of NACUA in Salt Lake City. In a short span of time–a week or less–I mentally absorbed countless updates on a wide variety of legal developments affecting higher education. Informal chats with higher education counsel over coffee and meals rendered an even richer source of useful information.

Seminar locations in Vancouver, Honolulu, Toronto, Marco Island, Orlando, Montréal, Seattle, Boston, San Francisco and a host of other popular locations offered the added benefit of visiting some of our nation's premier attractions while networking with colleagues.

My own active participation in NACUA was a necessary component of developing this network. I served as a presenter both at annual meetings and other NACUA sponsored seminars. For example, I spoke at the annual conference in Kansas City, Missouri, in 1988 on the topic of "Broadcast News Comes to Campus: Issues Involved in Dealing with the Media".

In 1991, I served as "Section Reporter" for the NACUA section on Affirmative Action and Nondiscrimination. The same year I was appointed to the Committee on Membership and served as a co-chair (and was reappointed to that committee in 1997). Then, in 1992 I was appointed to co-chair the section on Governance and Accountability, with David R Scott, the University Counsel for Rutgers University.

At the 1993 annual conference in San Francisco, Rutgers University counsel, David Scott, and I co-presented several topics of critical importance including "Who is my Client: the Potential for Conflict of Interest in Representation of College and University Officials, Especially in Lawsuits."

My topic for the 1997 annual meeting in Seattle was "Pre-trial Tactics Including Motion Practice". Of particular interest to defense counsel was my topic at the June 25–28, 2000 annual meeting in Washington DC: "Limiting and Litigating Your Adversary's Attorney Fees".

In 1996 I was appointed to serve on the program committee for the 1997 annual conference in Seattle. I utilized that committee position to promote a future annual conference in Tennessee. That promotion effort was successful and the 1999 NACUA annual meeting was held in Nashville's Opryland Hotel (June 25-31, 1999).

Around 1,000 attorneys–many with families in tow–plunking down cash in Tennessee for the better part of a week. In addition to the networking benefits, I made, UT also gained from my attendance at the NACUA annual meeting in numerous ways for years to come.

I was nominated for a three-year term on the NACUA Board of Directors by Mary Ann Connell, the University of Mississippi's attorney, in a letter on January 20, 1995 to NACUA election committee chair, Lee Liggett, University of Mississippi's chief counsel. Connell's letter states, better than I ever could, much of what I considered important during my years at UT and affirmed my focus on networking and building relationships that mattered:

> "This letter is to nominate Ronald C. Leadbetter for one of the five member–at–large positions on the Board of Directors of NACUA for the three–year term ending 1998. I have known Ron through my 13 years in NACUA and have found him to be throughout this time period one of the most loyal and enthusiastic supporters of the organization. I do not recall very many seminars, workshops or annual meetings when he was not present and actively involved.
>
> Ron has served as Co-Chair of the Governance and Accountability Section for the past two years and as Reporter for the Affirmative Action Section for the year prior to that. He has also served on the NACUA Membership Committee since 1991.
>
> I think Ron's enthusiasm, years of experience in the Office of the General Counsel at the University of Tennessee, and active involvement in the American Society of Hospital Attorneys exhibit the level of professional development and involvement in the profession which are needed on the Board of Directors.
>
> In addition to work within NACUA, Ron has been active in state and community legal and service organizations. He is a member of the Board of Directors and Legal Counsel for the Children's Center of Knoxville and is an active deacon, trustee and Sunday school teacher in his church.
>
> On a more personal note, I learned early on in NACUA that Ron Leadbetter was one of the people who would always stop and give me assistance if I asked him. Because the University of Tennessee is the flagship state university in a neighboring state with problems similar to those of my institution, I have frequently called on him for advice. He has always been willing to help and able to give a level of professional guidance and assistance which I have found invaluable. He demonstrates to me the best we look for in the organization and possesses those qualities of camaraderie, helpfulness, enthusiasm, knowledge and willingness to work which have been outstanding attributes of the leaders of NACUA through the years.
>
> I would appreciate your submitting this letter to the committee on nominations and elections for consideration.
>
> Sincerely,
> Mary Ann Connell
> University Attorney

I was subsequently nominated and approved to serve on the NACUA Board of Directors for a three-year term, 1997–2000. Several of those with whom I served again proved the value of networking and are mentioned elsewhere in this book: Paul J. Ward (Arizona State University, NACUA President, 1997), Mary Ann Connell (University of Mississippi, NACUA President 1998), Sheila Trice Bell (Northern Kentucky University, NACUA Executive Director and CEO) and Pamela J Bernard (University of Florida, NACUA President, 2000).

My director duties were important to me. I took the requirements seriously and rarely skipped a meeting, regardless of location. Best example: On the evening of November 6, 1999 I attended the Tennessee vs. Notre Dame football game at Neyland Stadium. After the game's conclusion - at 11 in the evening –I met my daughter Cara in the parking garage of Andy Holt Tower, next to the stadium. We drove seven and a half hours to Washington, D.C. to attend a NACUA board meeting with Cara sharing the driving while I catnapped.

Immediately following the conclusion of the NACUA meeting we made the return drive to Knoxville. Not the most relaxing way to spend a weekend but for a good cause. And Cara and I had an opportunity to network as father and daughter.

I also had the opportunity to promote the advancement of other high-caliber members of NACUA By letter of January 26, 2000 submitted to NACUA Executive Director, Sheila Trice Bell, I "place[d] in nomination the name of Paul Ward for the Distinguished Service Award." I argued that "Paul has served as General Counsel for at least two major institutions of higher education and rendered exemplary service in many ways to NACUA over the years, including service as President. Paul's high character and winsome personality underscore his suitability for the Distinguished Service Award in my humble opinion."

Ward received the Distinguished Service Award at the June 2000 annual NACUA meeting.

In a separate letter dated January 26, 2000, I advised Executive Director Bell of my recommendation of Kaye Koonce (Trident Technical College) as second vice president and Isis Carbahol-de-Garcia (Florida International University) and William J. Mullowney (Valencia Community College) as Members–at–Large on the NACUA Board of Directors. Each of the nominees was appointed to the recommended positions.

Two of the nominees with solid credentials were women and one was Hispanic. Yet neither gender nor national origin played any factor whatever in my nomination of these highly qualified and committed individuals.

Regrettably, my involvement in NACUA was brought to an untimely conclusion in 2001 by UT's turn from any focus of networking. The benefits of networking also ceased at that time.

Historic Ayres Hall often refered to as "On the hill."

Chapter 16–"BOB"–First Basketball Mascot–Almost

Sports fans and others are well aware that the mascot for the University of Tennessee is Smokey the blue tick hound. Smokey has appeared in form as both an animal and human "cheerleader" dating back to the 1950s. What even the most loyal of fans doesn't know is how close Smokey came to having competition–or even being replaced–at least in the UT Men's Basketball Program.

One of my good friends at the outset of my employment in 1972 was Dr. Grady Adkisson, professor at the Institute of Agriculture. Grady would regularly regale me with tales of his adventures hunting wild Russian boars in Tellico Plains and elsewhere. I was fascinated by his assertion that the Russian boar was the only wild animal that would attack a human without being threatened.

Regardless of the truth of that assertion, I was mesmerized by Grady's tale of a recent incident. On a hunting trip he attempted to shoot a boar, but his rifle jammed. The fierce tusked boar charged. Dropping his rifle, Grady climbed a nearby tree to escape. Then, as Grady told it, the boar pounded the rifle at the base of the tree with his front hooves. I shared this fascinating story with my wife.

At the time Therese was employed as secretary to UT head basketball coach Ray Mears. She shared with Mears my stories of the wild Russian boar.

Evidently, Mears was as mesmerized by the boar tales as I was. Sometime in early fall 1972, I received a telephone call from Coach Mears. "Ron, Therese shared with me the stories you told her about Russian boars." Mears then described to me his vision: For pre-game entertainment cheerleaders would come charging into a darkened Stokely Athletics Center, pulling a wheeled cage housing a huge, ferocious Russian boar banging his tusks against the bars of the cage as the stadium lights flashed about him. This would surely fire the crowd up! Name the mascot BOB-for Big Orange Boar

"Would you be interested in heading up this project," Mears asked. Certainly not your typical legal assignment, but I was excited about the possibility of being involved in such an undertaking. "If you'll check with John Baugh and request his approval I'll be glad to handle the matter," I replied. Mears went one step further. He wrote my boss, asking whether it would be legal to use a wild boar as a mascot. Baugh asked that I prepare a formal response and I did so.

On October 10, 1972, I issued a legal opinion to Coach Mears titled: "Legal technicalities and implications and related information concerning the use of a wild boar, sometimes hereinafter referred to as 'Big Orange Boar' as a mascot for the University of Tennessee Basketball Team."

"Dear Ray:

In answer to your letter of October 5, 1972 to Mr. Baugh, requesting an opinion on the above subject matter, I am happy to inform you that Mr. Baugh and I know of no legal prohibition against the use of a wild boar as a mascot, particularly its use within the confines of Stokely Athletic Center, so long as adequate measures are taken to confine the animal (pen, cage, etc.)

Mr. Bill Roach, Superintendent of Safety Services for the University, informs me that he also knows of no University rule or other safety regulation that would prohibit such use.

According to the Tennessee game and Fish commission's Knoxville office there is a 'pet permit' fee of $1.00 that should be obtained shortly after possession of the boar is obtained.

In checking with Mr. Grady Adkisson and contacting several leads given me by him, I have discovered that Mr. Lawrence Carey, Caronynah Hunting Lodge, Crossville, is interested in trapping a boar for the University for a fee of $150.00. Pursuant to my telephone conversation with you on October 9, I asked Mr. Carey to begin the search for the 'Big Orange Boar.'

As Mr. Carey noted, the transport of domestic or wild hogs or boars is prohibited due to a quarantine imposed by the State. The quarantine is due to end around November 4 or 5 and until that time Mr. Carey will have to retain possession of any captured boar.

I will be most happy to continue to help you in properly obtaining subject boar and helping you to obtain necessary facilities and supplies for its safe maintenance.

Sincerely,
Ronald C Leadbetter
Staff attorney

Upon receiving my letter, Mears called and asked me to proceed. I did so. I contacted the Knoxville Zoo, seeking a home for the new mascot. Zoo director Guy Smith III advised there was no room at the zoo for the boar. This sent me on to "plan B".

In 1972 Therese and I were renting a home on a fourteen acre tract of land in Knoxville's Rocky Hill area. I secured the consent of our landlord, Harold "Hap" Eldridge, to house the boar on the property we rented so long as I secured adequate liability insurance.

Dr. Clark Walker, with the UT Institute of Agriculture, recommended we utilize a mobile cage with dimensions of 6' x 32" x 3.5'. Kyle Crisp, sheet metal shop foreman at the UT physical plant, confirmed his department would construct a cage after receipt of a sketch from a UT graphic artist and a work order or special project request from Coach Mears.

The "Big Orange Boar," or "BOB," our new mascot, would soon be on board. With all major preliminary issues resolved it was time to arrange for a food supply for "BOB." What does a wild boar eat? No better person to ask than Grady Adkisson.

"Why do you want to know what a wild boar eats", queried Grady when I called to ask him. I explained Coach Mears' interest in securing a wild Russian boar as a mascot and described as best I could Mears' vision of how the boar would enter Stokely Athletic Center and help fire up the sellout crowd of 12,500 that typically attended.

"What will you do about the boar's smell?" Grady asked. "I hadn't thought about that. I guess I'll give him a bath beforehand," I replied.

Grady's unforgettable response: "That's not what I mean. What will you do when the boar performs its natural bodily function? When that happens, you will have 12,000 fans heading for the exits."

I then recalled that Therese and I had encountered a wild boar in St. Croix in the Virgin Islands on our honeymoon. The pungent odor accompanying the boar was quite distinct-something so memorable I can still see us scampering with fingers over our noses as we retreated to the safety of our vehicle.Coach Mears and I discussed my findings. It was mutually agreed that plans for a wild Russian boar as a UT basketball mascot were canned.

Smokey had nothing further to fear from Bob.

Chapter 17–Formal Job Description of University In-House Counsel

So what does in-house counsel for a major university like the University of Tennessee do? The answer varies from institution to institution and has always varied within the University of Tennessee itself. The following offers a helpful "hint" though.

During my service in the Office of General Counsel position descriptions for attorneys were rarely prepared. In 1989 an exception was made and a member of the public requesting access under the Tennessee Open Records Act would receive an accurate portrayal of the services I provided the University at that time.

A February 9, 1989 "administrative and professional position data questionnaire," signed off on both by General Counsel Brogan and me, accurately describes my position as it existed throughout most of my 35 years at UT.

My general duties and approximate percentage of time devoted to each duty are as follows:

1. Litigation (including preparation for and trial of lawsuits against the University and its officials) – –80%.
2. Provision of legal advice – –16% (including legal review of documents and correspondence)
3. Conduct seminars and training programs for university officials and employees– –4%.

The rest of the questionnaire detailed other aspects of my position (that of "Associate General Counsel"–a title reflecting salary increases more than any change in duties). Section 2:

"Interpersonal Relationships" emphasized "I have primary work relationships with administrative officials of the system administration and all campuses of the University, including the president vice-president, treasurer and chancellors. At one time or another I have dealt with all, or virtually all, offices and departments of the University statewide. My work relationship with each of these individuals, offices and departments is of an advisory nature (provision of legal advice) or representative nature (representation in courts or before administrative agencies).

The section further noted:

I work extensively with attorneys, judges, governmental officials, company officials, legislators, and a wide variety of other individuals in the course of preparing for and participating in administrative and judicial proceedings, including legal disputes, providing and receiving legal advice and information, and a wide variety of other legal functions.

Section 3 of the questionnaire ("Supervision/Guidance Received") noted:

Occasionally, work assignments are received directly from the General Counsel. However, the vast majority of work assignments result from requests for assistance from university officials and others are self-generated (e.g., preparation and distribution of legal opinions on recent legislation or court decisions).

Major court briefs and pleadings are reviewed and checked by the General Counsel. However, the day-to-day details of the vast bulk of work assignments are not reviewed or checked in any formal fashion. I am responsible for seeing to it that these assignments are carried out appropriately.

The rest of the questionnaire described the importance of avoiding litigation where possible–and prevailing when litigation could not be avoided. Finally, compliance with state and federal law, administrative rules and ethical constraints was emphasized.

With regard to percentage of effort expended in broad areas of responsibility, the litigation factor was less in my first two or three years, due to "lag time," as cases formerly handled by outside counsel commenced to move in-house. Surprisingly, the litigation was greater, as a percentage of total workload, after the coming of the black storm clouds of the Gilley years. But, this was only because my workload in other areas plummeted.

The job description for my position in the Office of General Counsel might appear somewhat bland. However, the actual duties performed were anything but.

Andy Holt Tower-the UT Administration Building

Chapter 18–You Won't Find These Listed as Formal Job Duties of University Counsel

Over my years as university counsel I had innumerable opportunities to interact with my colleagues in the field of higher education law–those within my office at The University of Tennessee as well as those from institutions of higher learning around the nation. Some adhered strictly to the job description under which they were hired. Others performed their formal job duties, but also engaged in networking, bonding and other activities falling outside any normal job description. Yet the latter activities produced job-related benefits.

I unabashedly fell in the latter category and I am of the opinion that the University was better served by my doing so.

VICTOR THE WRESTLING BEAR

My first "off the beaten path" assignment actually occurred during my law clerk days but cannot be overlooked

In 1971 the UT athletics department arranged for a visit by a large black bear, "Victor the Wrestling Bear." Victor participated in a parade in downtown Knoxville before visiting the UT athletics department in Stokely Athletics Center.

My wife, Therese, secretary to UT head basketball coach Ray Mears, received an office visit from Victor. She provided him a soft drink in her office.

The plan was for Victor to wrestle between the first and second games of the Volunteer Classic later that evening. His opponents would be Roger Peltz, a member of the UT men's basketball team known for his unicycle skills, and John Paschal, a well-known local bodybuilder. At the request of Coach Mears, I assumed responsibility for bringing Victor into the arena, on a leash, at the designated time.

All went according to plan. I met Victor and his manager at the home team entrance. Victor seemed to me larger than reported – he certainly exceeded my 210 pounds! The manager handed me the end of Victor's leash, which I grabbed firmly with both hands. We paraded into the arena amidst 12,500 waiting fans.

A large wrestling mat had been placed midcourt. Peltz and Paschal met us in the center of the mat as we arrived.

The wrestling exhibition began immediately. Victor had a muzzle on his mouth but was otherwise free to use his assets against his human opponents. Quite a show! Bodies being tossed about–and Victor's was not one of them.

At the beginning of the match I held the leash tightly with both hands. As the match proceeded it was clear that Victor's attention was on Peltz and Paschal – not me. He made no effort whatever to get away. Thankfully, I felt ignored.

So I relaxed, at one point confidently holding the leash in one hand while wiping away a bead of sweat on my forehead with the other. Not a wise move.

Without any warning whatever Victor suddenly bolted, yanking the leash from my hand. He left his opponents lying on the mat and headed for the exit. Victor was not only big–he was fast! Although momentarily in shock, I recovered my wits and set off in a sprint after him.

As Victor raced toward the entrance through which he had made his debut, two questions popped into my mind as I pursued him. First, where is he going?

Second, what will I do when I catch him? As we exited the arena floor I got my answer to the first question.

Victor sprinted up a flight of stairs, across a concrete hallway, then up a ramp and into an awaiting cage on the bed of a truck positioned at a rear exit from Stokely Athletic Center. The manager, apparently expecting Victor's arrival, shut the gate of Victor's cage after he was safely inside. The truck drove off and I slowly and quietly returned to my courtside seat.

I never learned the answer to my second question.

GUEST COACH FOR THE LADY VOLS

The UT Lady Vols basketball program implemented the idea of "guest coaches" sometime in the 1980s. Therese and I, along with our son, Lee, and daughter, Cara, received and accepted an invitation to attend the Lady Vols' January 4, 1987 contest with the University of North Carolina in Stokely Athletic Center. The game was a good one but Tennessee was trailing at halftime.

As guest coaches Therese and I were invited to join head basketball coach Pat Head Summitt and the Lady Vols in the locker room at half time. Actor David Keith joined us there following a rough first half performance by the Lady Vols.

The three of us entered the locker room and took center seats. Spread around the locker room wall, the team remained standing, as did the coaches.

As I expected, Coach Summitt introduced us to the team and said some nice things about each of us, smiling the whole time. I was at rest and feeling good - really enjoying the experience. In an instant the atmosphere changed.

"SHEILA, IF YOU WANT TO PLAY YOU HAD BETTER …" Summit shouted with venom in her voice as she turned toward Sheila Frost with a glare in her eyes that would pierce steel. I almost had a heart attack!

Sheila had not had a good first half and the Coach let her know in her very unique way that she was displeased. As I recovered from my own shock, I thought, "If I was Sheila, I would be out there leaping over buildings if necessary to avoid any further words or looks from my coach." Sheila evidently felt likewise. She had a far better second half and Tennessee won the game.

Pat wrote Therese and me a nice letter thanking us for attending as guest coaches. My Lady Vols coaching debut under the direction of a world-renowned coach was unforgettable.

On another occasion, UT Women's Athletic Director Joan Cronan kindly invited Therese and I, along with friends Tino LaRosa (a UT graduate) and his sister Carman LaRosa (an Anti-Mafia Judge visiting from Catania, Italy) to join a panel of guest coaches for the January 3, 1998 shellacking the Lady Vols' gave #3 ranked University of Connecticut.

Perhaps Coach Summitt's half-time introduction of Judge LaRosa motivated her team to play well. The Lady Vols won a stunning victory over U. Conn, 84 –69!

Therese, Cara and I presented Judge LaRosa with an official Lady Vols T-shirt when we visited her and the LaRosa family in Sicily that summer.

Our good friends in UT athletics made sure Therese and I had front row seats for the December 9, 1987 basketball contest between the #1 ranked Lady Vols and the #2 ranked University of Texas Lady Longhorns. The game was well advertised.

Customers making a food purchase at a local restaurant chain received a coupon good for a seat at Thompson Boling Arena—first come, first served. What the athletics department administration did not consider was the impact of the vendor coupon arrangement - where a purchase was required in order to get a coupon!

The grand opening of Thompson Boling took place six days earlier with a sellout crowd in excess of 25,000 attending a doubleheader featuring both the UT men's and women's basketball teams.

My wife and I arrived early, as was our custom. We were amazed to see hordes of fans cramming into the arena long before tipoff time. Well before the teams were introduced, radio announcements advised motorists on their way to the game not to bother–the Arena was full. Various reports estimated that approximately 30,000 fans were turned away!

The Lady Longhorns won the game but the events of the evening provided for exciting chatter for the University community for years to come.

ATHLETICS HAD A FEW GRAY MOMENTS FOR ME

Discussed by far fewer members of the University community - a handful - were a couple of incidents that occurred a couple of years later, both involving UT Athletic Director Doug Dickey, other UT athletics department employees and me.

On February 1, 1989 I traveled on the UT plane with Dickey and several others to see the UT vs. Vanderbilt basketball game in Nashville. After arriving in

Music City we stopped for dinner at a local restaurant. The owner entertained us with the story of his lawn mower accident with resulting severe injury to his leg.

I related well to the story since I am an avid lawn tractor operator. Too well! The owner pulled his pants leg up past mid thigh to reveal gruesome scars from his injury. Something clicked in my own mind and I retreated to a seat at a nearby table.

The next thing I knew, Doug Dickey was staring in my face bellowing, "Ron, Ron, are you okay?" I had passed out and was just "coming to".

I felt fine. Despite my protestations, Dickey insisted on taking me to nearby Baptist Hospital. While my Athletics Department cohorts waited outside the emergency room I received a medical checkup before being released.

Our group piled into vehicles waiting outside the emergency room and headed to the Vanderbilt Arena. We made it to our front row seats in the "end zone" a few moments before tipoff.

UT lost the game to Vandy but our hospital detour brightened conversation on the flight back to Knoxville.

A month and a half later (March16) the same outfit flew on the UT plane to Greensboro, North Carolina, for the first round of the NCAA basketball tournament. Coach Don Devoe's Vols got trounced by the University of West Virginia.

Seated next to me in the Arena, Doug Dickey muttered, "He's gone." A few days later Coach Devoe was relieved of his position as UT's head basketball coach and, on April 4, replaced by Wade Houston. The athletics troupe returned from the Greensboro arena to its nearby hotel in a rather somber mood.

The mood lightened after a group of cheerleaders from a college that had just achieved a first-round victory showed up. Our UT contingent joined the cheerleaders in the hotel lounge, which had a large dance floor.

Before approaching the cheerleaders I tipped off my UT colleagues of my strategy for a little fun and a few laughs. I shed my suit jacket, placing it on the back of a barstool–the members of our group were each formally attired and had not had an opportunity to change to casual wear.

Pretending to be rather lacking in gymnastic ability, I asked the young ladies on the cheerleading squad if they might possibly teach me a simple routine. Over the better part of an hour I feigned learning, first one then another simple cheerleading maneuver. I "progressed" –but not too quickly.

I wanted the cheerleaders to think they were training me to do something I had never done (but, which actually had been part of my regular workout routine). My traveling companions enjoyed the charade from the sidelines. I complimented the cheerleaders on their instructional skills.

Finally came time for the grand finale. "Do you think you can teach me how to do a cartwheel?" Evidently concluding they had a teachable student, the cheerleaders demonstrated the basics of a cartwheel.

Pretending to stumble through the process several times, I was ready for the big event–a well-performed cartwheel! I took a couple of steps, leaped high in the air and twisted, with arms and legs properly spread so as to propel my body clockwise. At the apex of my move I heard a loud rrrrrrrrip!

The cheerleaders seemed astonished at my performance. They did not note my embarrassment or recognize the reason for it. I had ripped my suit pants from waste to crotch.

I complimented the cheerleaders on their coaching skills then backed sheepishly off the dance floor toward my fellow Tennesseans and grabbed my jacket. Neither they nor any of the cheerleaders had noticed my predicament. When I revealed my plight laughter permeated the crowd. The glumness of the UT basketball disaster faded temporarily into the background.

WHITEWATER RAFTING GUIDE FOR THE LADY VOLS

Whitewater rafting offers a wonderful bonding experience for participants. As chief guide for the Central Baptist Church Bearden rafting ministry I had ample opportunity to include guests outside the church, including those affiliated with the University of Tennessee.

On August 21, 1993, at the request of Joan Cronan, I guided UT assistant volleyball coach Kim Zenner and ten members of the UT women's volleyball on two runs down the Ocoee River. The following year, on August 20, another Ocoee trip with Coach Zenner and the volleyball team ended prematurely as, halfway down the river, the bottom of the aging raft split from end to end.

The front of the raft caught on a rock, spun the raft crazily around, dumping me from the rear of the raft into the rapids of the Ocoee. As I floated downstream I heard All-American Tamela Brightman yell to her teammates, "Mr. Leadbetter's gone!" No, not really. But the raft was.

All the players eventually made it safely to the bank of the river where I met them. We then headed home–minus one raft that had its last run.

I organized rafting trips on rivers other than the Ocoee. In May 1987 both UT Athletic Director Joan Cronan and husband Tom joined me and others for a weekend trip on West Virginia's Cheat River, followed by a run down the narrow turbulent rapids of Maryland's Upper Youghiogheny River.

On May 30–June 1, 1992 I organized another heavily UT oriented rafting excursion down the same rivers. The rafting crew included Linda Franz, UT Lady Vols' new head golf coach, Julie Hermann, Lady Vols head volleyball coach, and UT Assistant General Counsel Steve Roads.

The following year (August 1993) our daughter Cara attended Hermann's volleyball camp at UT and four weeks later rafted the Ocoee along with Joan Cronan–a little family networking!

SURVIVE THE OCOEE WITH "SURVIVOR II" WINNER TINA WESSON!

Television's 2002 "Survivor II " series winner, Tina Wesson, was an active member of the UT paddleball group birthed in the 1970s by former football UT All-American and Chicago Bears player Andy Kozar. Not only was Tina one of our regulars on the paddle ball court, she was also a whitewater rafter and has guided rafting trips herself.

Even before being declared winner of "Survivor II,"Tina graciously consented to lend her name and presence to a fundraising event aimed at raising sufficient funds to purchase a new top-of-the-line, self-bailing raft for the Central Baptist Church Bearden Rafting Ministry."

The event: "I Survived the Ocoee with Tina Wesson," held on June 8, 2002, featured a kickoff breakfast prepared by Therese at our home, followed by three rafting runs for contributors down the Ocoee with Tina. All but a few dollars of the $4,500 purchase price of the new raft was raised that day, thanks to Tina's generous support.

It may appear there was much focus by me on sports -related events during the course of my professional life. Absolutely! These and many other exciting activities with members of the UT community were "more precious than gold," as the saying goes. Work and play were often intertwined and often hard to tell apart.

Chapter 19–Memorable Moments and Special Occasions–Just for Fun But Still UT Related!

A SIGN OF GREAT THINGS TO COME

On November 30, 1972, I left with UT Knoxville Physical Plant director Bill Roach for my first visit to UT Martin. We spent the night in bug–infested Biltmore Motel in Union City. The following day I met with physical plant officials from all UT campuses. That evening Roach and I left UT Martin, drove to Nashville and attended the Grand Old Opry.

On Saturday, I attended my first UT "away" game ever. I was stunned to see two thirds of the fans in the Vanderbilt stadium in Nashville wearing orange. UT defeated Vanderbilt 30–10. Roach and I arrived back in Knoxville in time for Therese and me to attend UT's victory over South Carolina in basketball.

Not my first work-related trip away from Knoxville, but one that bolstered my belief that I had secured more than just a job. Something more akin to a way of life. And lots of fun!

PICNICS FOR FUN AND NETWORKING

The annual UT faculty-staff picnic was for many years a special event attended by thousands of employees. Lots of entertainment, including a variety of sports contests rounded out the occasion.

On September 1, 1977 I played on three volleyball teams, one softball team and was a member of the UT system tug-of-war team competing against the UT Knoxville team. Susan Cardwell, an employee in the UTK personnel office, and I teamed up to finish second in the three-legged race. I finished first in the sack race.

LOST AT REELFOOT

On April 27, 1981 I flew on the UT plane with Andy Kozar and his executive assistant, Kaddie Barber, to Reelfoot Lake State Park for a UT student affairs officers retreat. In the late afternoon I took the UT pilot, "Spud", and Kaddie out in a special "Reelfoot boat" (with steel plate positioned under the propeller to allow for bouncing over hundreds of tree stumps lingering beneath the surface of the lake.)

We made it to the far end of the huge shallow body of water and began winding our way through a maze of narrow passageways snaking through acres of floating seaweed-like greenery. Then the narrow passageway before me suddenly disappeared. Our engine choked and died and the cause was readily apparent: the propeller was encased in seaweed or something that looked like it.

There was no exit in sight and the park facilities were at the far end of the lake. Darkness was approaching. Worse yet, we would miss dinner.

The watercraft had a reverse oar mechanism by which rowing backwards propelled the craft forwards. But, only so long as the oars did not dip into the water and hang up in the greenery. With lots of practice I managed to get us back to the lodge–just after dark, halfway through dinner–covered with lake debris.

Worth years of ribbing by my passengers and others at the retreat.

RECORD COLD BRINGS WORK TO HALT

1985 marked a record-breaker weather wise. Monday, January 21 was the coldest day on record in Knoxville with the temperature plummeting to 26° below zero at 7 a.m. Seven inches of snow fell Saturday night and Sunday morning.

I had work to do and went to work at 5:15 AM (although UT was closed for Martin Luther King's birthday–not because of snow or cold temps). I sat in my office on the eighth floor of Andy Holt Tower–wearing a winter coat the whole time. At 9:00 a.m. I left, feeling a bit defeated by the frigid temperature in my office. Neil Wormsley, an official in the Treasurer's office, was the only other UT employee in the building. We left together.

HIKES TO MT. LE CONTE AND RUNS TO WORK

The hike to Mount Le Conte in the Smokey Mountains of Tennessee is challenging in nice weather. My favorite hike is 4 and 1/2 miles up the Alum Bluff Cave trail. It typically takes me 2 1/2 hours.

Since the early 1970s it was my practice to organize or join a group for an overnight stay at LeConte Lodge atop Mt. Le Conte, the highest commercial lodging in the eastern United States.

Many of the trips to Le Conte were organized by Tom Cronan and featured a late October overnight stay at the Lodge. One such trip is unforgettable. The following account is taken from my diary of October 31, 1993:

11 crazy folks, with Tom Cronan in the lead, headed for Mount Le Conte this a.m. Snow fell in Knoxville last night – putting us on the alert.
Joan Cronan opted out (giving as excuse that she must travel to Kansas City) (UT business) but was kind enough to prepare a wonderful breakfast as we met at the Cronans' for our 9:30 AM departure.
(Those on the trip included two of Joan's friends from Chattanooga, neither of whom had any real hiking experience).
We arrived at Sugarlands (Visitor Center) around 11:30 – just in time to find Highway 441 closed due to heavy snow. After some debate as to whether we should turn back the group opted to drive to the rainbow Falls trailhead and try that route. By 12:30 we were on the trail in a moderate snowfall and three – 6 inches of snow on trail.
At Rainbow Falls (3:00 pm) we stopped for hot chocolate and made critical decision to proceed to the top.
Despite falling temperatures and increasingly deep snow the first group (Joe and Robb Johnson and I) made it to Le Conte Lodge at 5:30 PM. The last .6 mile was toughest! Pain in the legs! The last group… Did not arrive until 7 pm – more than 1 hour in the dark! Snow depth was 10 inches and temperature in late evening was 9°. Dinner at 7 – nothing special but who cared? Cabin was frigid!!! Water froze inside. All that kept us warm was extra blankets.

One of Joan's friends, Barbara Murray, who had struggled to reach the top in the dark, and was freezing cold when she arrived, announced that she expected to die there, and was quite serious. She made it through the night, was impressed with her accomplishment and joined me for the hike down right after breakfast.

UT WORK–A FAMILY AFFAIR

I was fortunate to be able to involve my wife, son and daughter in a number of my work assignments.

Therese attended numerous Trustee and office events as earlier reported. Not that extraordinary. More so when Therese and the kids joined me on a state-wide work run. Take for example the family "vacation" of August 1991.

[August] 8. Therese, Cara, Lee and I drove to Nashville (my NCAA interview with former UT coach Doug Matthews and NCAA investigator Bill Saum). After the interview the Leadbetters headed for Memphis. We stayed at the condo (UT condo on the Mississippi River).

9. We all had dinner with Charles and Adelle Horton [Charles being an official at the UT Center for the Health Sciences, where I spent the day handling routine office matters while the family toured the city]

10. This morning we drove to UT Martin. Had lunch with former UT basketball coach Ray Mears. Then check Lee into his dorm room at Ellington Hall. Tomorrow is Lee's first official activity as a freshman at UTM. At 2 PM the UT plane picked me up for a trip to Asheville. Dinner at the Hilton with [Pres.] Joe Johnson and our athletic folks to get ready for NCAA hearing tomorrow.

11. NCAA hearing of charges against UT re: former assistant football coach Jack Sells and summer FB campus. The hearing, with 40–50 news people outside lasted 5 1/2 hours. Afterwards the UT plane returned me to UT Martin. Therese, Cara and I left for home around 7:15 PM and got back in Knoxville around 12:30 PM [on the 12th].

Definitely a matter of combining work and pleasure! The same held true when 10-year-old Cara joined me for the 1996 NACUA annual meeting in San Antonio. Two years earlier both she and Therese had joined me for the annual meeting at Marco Island, Florida.

The kids also had a chance to see me in court–and have a bit of fun in the process. On July 16, 1981 staff attorney Karen Brock and I drove to Nashville for a trial scheduled next day. Lee, age 8, joined us for the trip and occupied the courtroom the following morning while we tried our case. At the conclusion of trial, Lee and I headed to Opryland for the balance of the day.

In 1984 Therese and Lee joined to me at Reelfoot Lake state park for a UT student affairs officers retreat. On the second day, April 16, I was scheduled to argue the "Gilbert" case in the Tennessee Court of Appeals in Jackson. The UT plane transported Lee and me to Jackson for the proceedings. We returned to Reelfoot on the plane following the conclusion.

Cara likewise had an opportunity to participate in work–related activities with me. She flew with me to Memphis on November 5, 1987.

After spending the night at the UT condo, I took Cara by the UTCHS security office where the six year old became a "member of the security staff"–complete with security badge. She spent the day in the Security front office while I took a deposition downtown. We returned to Knoxville that evening.

Almost a year later, Cara again joined me in Memphis, midway through a federal jury trial (Itson v. UTCHS) She arrived on October 20,1988 on the evening flight from Knoxville and stayed at the UT condo with me. Cara enjoyed the condo's indoor pool.

The next morning–as on her last visit to Memphis–Cara "reported for duty" to the UT security office. My day was spent downtown at the Federal Courthouse, as the Itson trial continued. That evening Cara and I accepted the invitation of officials from UT's William F. Bowld hospital to join them for a river cruise on the Mississippi River.

On Saturday Cara and I attended a pregame legislative–alumni luncheon at the Liberty Bowl sponsored by the UTCHS Chancellor's office. Following UT's football victory over Memphis State University, Cara and I went to see the ducks swim in the fountain at the Peabody Hotel downtown before dining and returning to the condo for the evening.

We caught an early flight to Knoxville Sunday morning, and I returned to Memphis that evening for completion of the Itson trial. Cara remained at home with Mom.

UT FAMILY SOCIAL EVENTS JUST FOR FUN

An enjoyable aspect of my employment in the office of General Counsel was the many opportunities for me (accompanied by Therese on most occasions) to intermingle–network–with folks from throughout the University in a wide variety of social settings. Here are a few examples taken from my diary:

Christmas party at the home of Dr. Charles Temple, head of Institutional Research (12/17/72).
Dessert at the home of Stu Aberdeen, UT assistant basketball coach (7/18/73)
Christmas party for UTK personnel at the home of Edward Bennett, Dir.
of Personnel (12/10/76).
Volleyball picnic at our home on Creekhead Dr., Office of General Counsel vs.
UT Treasurer's Office (7/19/80).
Dinner in Memphis at the home of UTCHS professor, Dr. Andrew Laszlo and wife, Wilma. Tennessee Supreme Court Justice the William Fones joined us for the meal (11/13/80).
Dinner at home of UT chief pilot Steve Rogers and wife, Kay (5/11/84).

Overnight stay at our Creekhead home for UTCHS Vice Chancellor for Student Affairs, Bill Robinson, and UT Martin Vice Chancellor for Student Affairs, Phil Watkins (the next morning they joined me and a group from Central Baptist Church Bearden for rafting on the Ocoee) (7/5-6/85).

Christmas party for employees in the Treasurer's Office and also of the office of the Vice President for Business and Finance at the home of Butch and Dulcie Peccolo. Sadly, Treasurer's office employee Barbara Musselman, on her way to the party, died in an automobile accident several blocks short of her destination. (12/6/85).

Christmas party at the University Center for more than 200 employees and retirees of the Treasurer's office. I played Santa Claus. (12/17/87)

Dinner for UT administrative staff at Blackberry Farm in the foothills of the Smokies, hosted by newly appointed UT President Lamar Alexander and wife, Honey (7/7/88).

Early-morning drive from Memphis to Martin for breakfast with UT Martin athletic director Ray Mears (6/14/90

Social at athletic director Doug Dickey's house following UT football victory over Mississippi State 26 – 24. (9/21/91).

Andy Kozar, UTC Vice Chancellor for Student Affairs, Rocky Renneison and UT Memphis Vice-Chancellor for Student Affairs Bill Robinson over to Creekhead for evening of "nickel-ante" poker (1/28/97). Same group over again for another round (9/24/98.)

Croquet party at Tom and Joan Cronan's in memory of Tom, who died of pancreatic cancer at 5:45 AM the previous morning, August 18, 2006. A "Celebration of Life" ceremony was held at Central Baptist Church Bearden the following evening, honoring a dear friend I held in high esteem. (8/19 -20/06).

In October 2006 I hiked with a group to Le Conte Lodge for an overnight stay in honor of Tom Cronan. Tom will never be forgotten by me.

Chapter 20–My First Trial–Van de Vate vs. UT

The first day I was to report for work as newly hired staff attorney was July 5, 1972. My level of excitement with my new job was such that I could not wait that long. I paid a visit to the Office of General Counsel on July 3, 1972, although the office was closed for the Fourth of July weekend. I wanted to review the file on the first case assigned to me for trial–although assigned jointly with outside counsel, Knoxville attorney Lou Woolf, and OGC counsel Dan Rhea.

Nancy Van de Vate vs. The University of Tennessee was a civil rights action initially filed with the U.S. Office for Civil Rights and the Equal Employment Opportunity Commission shortly before my hire.

Lou Woolf had been hired as lead counsel for the University and Dan served as co-counsel. I was thrilled just to be added as counsel of record– "chief bottle washer."

Counsel for Van de Vate was John Lockridge (the attorney who represented the Haynes brothers following their arrest for assaulting me during my days as a law student).

Van de Vate's complaint was that the UT Department of Music had refused to hire her as a member of the Music faculty on the basis of her sex; female. I knew Van de Vate's husband, Dr. Dwight Van de Vate, who was my philosophy professor in my undergraduate days. He was one of my favorite instructors.

So, at the outset of my career, I dealt with a factor rarely if ever addressed in law school - handling litigation involving opposing parties and legal counsel with whom I had "connections." Just the tip of the iceberg as I would soon learn.

On July 10, 1972 Dan and I met with Jim Drinnon and Vice-Chancellor for Academics, Luke Ebersole. According to my notes, we met "concerning approach to Van de Vate case–decided to go all the way." Drinnon made clear the wisdom of "gathering all the facts" before doing so.

Meetings with potential and actual witnesses were held virtually every weekday during the remainder of July. Numerous signed statements were collected from prospective witnesses. More meetings were held during the fall and throughout the following year.

Van de Vate filed suit in the U.S. District Court for the Eastern District of Tennessee in December, 1973, following the EEOC's issuance of a "right to sue" letter. In February 1974 U.S. District Judge Robert Taylor set the case for trial. Our case would be heard on Tuesday, May 21, 1974 at 9 a.m.

Lou Woolf and I took depositions of the plaintiff, music department head Al Schmied and Prof. Don Peterson in John Lockridge's office on April 18. Professors David Van Vactor and Mary F. Johnson were deposed on May 9.

On May 13 we took the deposition of UT professor Michael Combs then the deposition of Dr. Robert Harvey – later named as acting, then interim, president of Knoxville College.

The case was tried on May 21, as scheduled, and completed that day. According to my case note, "I did direct exam of Schmied and Sarah Maybry; Lou Woolf crossed plaintiff's witnesses and read Harvey deposition."

Interestingly, Dan Rhea never participated in the trial. I never asked the reason. I was too caught up in the excitement of my own participation.

Judge Taylor announced his ruling from the bench. Judgment for the defense. For certain there was a glow about my head. My first victory–shared, of course, with my mentor, Lou Woolf.

Less than an hour after the close of trial I returned to my office in Andy Holt Tower. I encountered Vice-President Joe Johnson on the front steps and was pleasantly surprised to hear him say, "I hear y'all won the Crocker case."

"How did you know?" I replied.

"Dan told me ya'll won." Interesting. I just smiled and said nothing further.

On June 3, 1974 "Judge Taylor issued his memorandum opinion, dismissing the complaint. The first trial of my career was officially over.

My first trial–and the first civil rights suit against the University–came to a favorable conclusion. I exulted in the result!

Chapter 21–The UT Air Force and Near Disaster

TERROR IN THE SKY

Shortly after my employment by the University, I was pleasantly surprised to learn I would have access to a UT owned and operated Aero Commander airplane, The aircraft was maintained in a hangar adjacent to McGee Tyson Airport.

A two-seater aircraft–a Piper Cub, I believe–was maintained at UT Martin (and I heard stories about a larger UT owned aircraft destroyed in a crash while transporting members of the UT football team, with loss of the aircraft but no serious injury to the players).

I found UT aircraft an efficient means of getting to my destination. For example, the Aero Commander would fly directly from Knoxville to the landing strip adjacent to Reelfoot Lake State Park. Utilizing a commercial flight would require a landing in Memphis, securing a rental vehicle, then a two-hour drive to the park.

In the early years of my employment I often sat in the co-pilot's seat - notwithstanding my complete lack of any pilot training. Future tragedy changed that practice and the presence of a trained co-pilot was required. One other rule generally adhered to–at least during the "Big Orange" years–was that the flight must include at least three passengers. Less than three was not cost-effective.

Since most of my traveling was solo, I typically traveled by commercial airline. Still, in checking with the president's office I often found the plane going my way and would secure a seat. Occasionally, I would be dropped off at my destination then retrieved on the return flight. Commercial airlines don't do that!

Most often, I was part of a small group of UT officials traveling to a retreat. The plane would sometimes hopscotch around the state, picking up passengers at other campuses before heading to the final destination.

Most UT flights were uneventful–but not all. In early December 1973 Charles Smith, Executive Assistant to President Boling, Vice-Chancellor Howard Aldmon and I had scheduled a flight to Birmingham, Alabama to attend a hearing before the Equal Employment Opportunity Commission in a sex discrimination case brought by UT food-service worker Cleo Calage. The flight was canceled due to a forecast of bad weather and the meeting was postponed to the following week.

On December 13, 1973 the three of us arrived at the flight hangar for the rescheduled trip to Birmingham. The weather forecast was as dismal as the previous week's. Pilot George Wallace offered to proceed and we accepted. A big mistake!

A tornado hit a schoolhouse in Meigs County that day. Only minutes after liftoff the Aero Commander flew into the turbulence of the weather pattern from which the tornado evolved. We ended up being tossed around like a toy by giant unseen hands. Then came a horrendous rat–a–tat–tat pounding by hailstones. The aircraft's radar was knocked out.

Both Howard and Charles had looks of total fear on their faces every time the aircraft plummeted or was sucked further up into the sky. Their knuckles turned white as they gripped the arms of their seat.

Our seatbelts anchored us to the seats but did not prevent us from thrashing about. When someone asked our pilot if we would make it, the normally cool and collected George Wallace said, "We should." Not a totally reassuring answer.

I prayed and I am certain my colleagues did too.

After what seemed like hours–probably no more than 15 or 20 minutes but maybe longer–of being tossed about, the plane exited the worst of the storm. We eventually landed in Birmingham, breathing a huge sigh of relief. A cursory inspection of the plane revealed half the paint gone. The orange and white aircraft was now 50% gray. The leading edge of the wings appeared as if sledgehammered. I later learned that repair costs exceeded $10,000. A lot of money back then!

We arrived at our meeting as three of the happiest people to have feet on the solid soil as any you will ever meet. We made it through and were greatly relieved to see sunshine and blue skies. Our weather-beaten, radar-free plane made the return trip to Knoxville with a skilled pilot and grateful passengers on board.

I gained one significant benefit from the flight. Previously I became a bit nervous when a flight I was on would shake, vibrate, or make noise or do anything else to gain my attention. The flight to Birmingham completely cured me and never again did I experience flight-related anxiousness on any of the hundreds of flights taken since. That does not include the flight I missed.

TRAGIC DISASTER AND MIRACULOUS ESCAPE

In early March 1978 UT's director of property management, Henry Morse, and UT development officer, Mike Hitchcox, requested that I accompany them to Morgantown, West Virginia on a project requiring legal assistance. I readily agreed to assist. The trip was set for Friday March 31.

Just three days before the scheduled trip I received a call from the office of U.S. District Judge Robert McRae in Memphis notifying me that Judge McRae had ordered attorneys in a case I was handling to attend a conference in his office on the day I was scheduled to fly to West Virginia. I requested that McRae reschedule the conference but my request was denied.

Henry and Mike said they would go without me. I was angry with the judge.

My anger lasted through the Friday afternoon conference and the flight back to Knoxville. It did not cease until I reached home and received a telephone call from my mom. "I'm so glad to hear your voice," Mom said, exuding clear joy.

I was puzzled by her words and the joyous tone accompanying them. Then Mom added, "Did you hear about the terrible UT plane crash?" My hands started shaking involuntarily as Mom explained that all on board had been killed with the exception of a young woman who lingered in critical condition and died a day or so later. I presumed Henry and Mike had died in the crash but wondered who the other victims were.

Minutes later I learned from another attorney in the office, Alan Parker that Henry and Mike had not died in the crash. I telephoned Henry. In a very shaky voice he explained that after I canceled my plan to accompany them to West Virginia, he and Mike decided not to go. A group of Knox County educators took advantage of the plane's last minute availability and traveled to Maryland.

The crash resulted from the wrong fuel being placed in the Aero Commander's gas tank. Pilot Charlie Lockwood, a friend of mine, reportedly failed to check the color of the fuel as a way of confirming that correct fuel had been added. The plane crashed shortly after takeoff for the return flight to Knoxville (leading to litigation that I had no involvement in handling and regarding which I have no further comment).

My anger with Judge McRae dissipated immediately as I realized how close to death I had come. The tragic incident helped me understand how fragile this life is. I drew closer to the Lord as a result.

Chapter 22–Politics Post–Hire

Partisan politics did not prevent me from being employed by the University of Tennessee. My employment as University counsel likewise did not prevent me from continuing to be involved politically in partisan politics.

Politically motivated preferential treatment in doing my job was anathema to me; politically oriented networking was not. The University benefited from the latter.

I campaigned in Laurel Apartments (UT married student housing) on behalf of "John Mann for State Representative" (October 1972). The Republican candidate was elected and served in the state legislature. In the same month I attended a barbecue at the Knoxville Civic Coliseum sponsored by Congressman John Duncan.

In February 1973 I chaired the Lincoln Day Dinner sponsored by the Knox County Young Republicans. Knoxville Mayor Kyle Testerman and I drove out to McGhee- Tyson Airport, in a limousine provided by the city, to pick up the guest speaker, George Bush. In addition to Bush, then the newly selected Republican Party National Chairman, we picked up U.S. Senator Howard Baker.

At the head table, besides the four of us, were Congressman and Mrs. John (Lois) Duncan, Mrs. Kyle (Janet) Testerman, Congressman Lamar Baker, Gov. Winfield Dunn and Knox County Republican Chairman Warren Webster. More than 1,200 attended the February 12 event at Knoxville's Hyatt Regency Hotel.

In 1974, I served as delegate to the Tennessee Young Republican convention in Memphis. Dave Chesney, the father of country superstar Kenny Chesney, was our Second Congressional District chairman (and also my successor as President of the Knox County Young Republicans). On August 11, 1974, the convention elected Don Sundquist (future Governor of the State of Tennessee) as state chairman of the Tennessee Young Republicans.

On a number of occasions over the years Jimmy Duncan, son of John Duncan and current representative from the Second Congressional District, and his wife Lynn joined us at our home for dinner or invited us to theirs. On one occasion (3/12/83) UT Treasurer David Martin and his wife joined the Duncans at our home for dinner and on another (5/11/96) we were joined by Joan and Tom Cronan and the Duncans, as well as dear longtime friends Doug and Sandra Dutton (Doug and I being UT law schoolmates, political allies in campus politics, as well as having traveled together internationally and attended the same church).

Congressman Duncan and a host of other friends helped me celebrate my 50th birthday with a surprise party at Creekhead organized by Therese. She had invited to the March 16, 1996 event a group fairly evenly divided among political associates, UT co-workers, friends from church and family members. A number, like Joan Cronan and Therese had membership in more than one group. Politics for me was not my sole focus in life – just a significant one.

GOV. DON SUNDQUIST'S BURMA CAMPAIGN

In the fall of 1994 I took leave of absence, for the better part of a month (October 19- November 14), from my UT work to do a bit of free-lance travel around Southeast Asia (Burma- officially "Myanmar"- Vietnam, Cambodia, Thailand, Malaysia and Singapore) with my sister, Gail, and UT videographer David Cann. Regrettably, I was out of the States when the fall elections were held. For the first time in my adult life I did not vote. But, I did campaign.

While in Burma, I posted a campaign poster for Congressman Don Sundquist, candidate for governor of the state of Tennessee, in front of the Strand Hotel in Rangoon, Burma. I took a photo or two and sent those to the Governor-elect when I returned to the United States.

Sundquist responded with a friendly note a short while later (December 22, 1994):

> Dear Ron,
>
> Thank you for your letter of congratulations and best wishes. It only happened because of strong support and hard work by people like yourself.
>
> It was good to hear from you after all these years. I do recall our meeting in Nashville back in 1971. Time surely goes by quickly.
>
> I appreciated the pictures from Burma. If you ever have any questions or concerns, please don't hesitate to call upon me or my staff.
>
> My best to you and your family for the holidays and the coming new year.
>
> Sincerely
> Don Sundquist
> Governor Elect

Sundquist served as Governor of Tennessee for two terms– eight years – and as Chairman of the UT Board of Trustees for the same period. A small planned effort at support–albeit humorous and from a far off land–was the least I could do to stay in touch.

PRESIDENT CLINTON'S STATE OF THE UNION ADDRESS

I avoided, like the plague, letting politics interfere in any way with my University work responsibilities. However, I must confess, I was infected on one occasion.

Returning home from my Memphis office late one evening, I was greeted by Therese, who excitedly announced that I had been invited by Congressman Jimmy Duncan to attend President Bill Clinton's State of the Union address the next evening. I had been offered his wife Lynn's seat as each congressman and senator are allocated one seat at this special event. Without a moment's hesitation I replied that I could not attend–I had a deposition scheduled in Bristol, Virginia the next day.

With Therese's encouragement–and me recognizing the likelihood that this would be my once-in-a-lifetime chance to attend such an event–I opted to let politics trump work. Of course, Clinton being a Democrat and Congress having a new Republican majority, political motivation to attend was non-partisan.

I called my paralegal, Jan Williams, and asked her to call opposing counsel's office first thing the next morning, giving notice of cancellation of the scheduled deposition. She did as requested.

The morning of January 24, 1995, I flew to Washington, D.C. My Congressman and dear friend Jimmy provided me a brief but memorable tour of the capital, including the gallery where I would sit for the special event. He also brought me as his guest to a birthday party for Congressman Bud Schuster (R. Pa.) at Schuster's condominium in Virginia.

Shortly before 9 p.m. that evening I took my front row center seat in the balcony facing the podium. For the first time in 40 years a Democratic president would speak to a Republican congressional majority. Thanks to Jimmy Duncan I felt as if I was personally participating in that historic event. I was quite honored to be present.

There was an unforeseen downside: opposing counsel in the case for which the cancelled deposition had been scheduled did not get word from his office of the cancelation. Attorney Larry Dry drove from Oak Ridge, Tennessee to Bristol, Virginia only to learn the deposition had been cancelled. When we next met Dry expressed his anger and I apologized. My apology seemed to carry little weight. I felt bad about the incident. No more cancelations by me!

Unless of course I receive another invitation to a State of the Union Address.

Chapter 23–Gay People's Alliance Petitions for UT Recognition

During my student days at the University of Tennessee a wide variety of organizations operated on campus with University approval. Each new organization was required to go through a process by which it would seek recognition. The term was commonly understood to reflect the University's approval of the organization's stated purpose for existing.

An organization by the name of "Gay People's Alliance" applied for recognition in 1974. The organization's stated purpose was to "provide a social environment which will enable homosexuals to meet and socialize with other homosexuals, both active and latent, with greater ease and more respectability." (Summer Beacon, June 25, 1974).

The Alliance petitioned the UT Knoxville campus administration for recognition but the petition was denied. The organization's appeal to President Boling was likewise denied.

Under applicable UT Board bylaws the next step for the organization was an appeal to the Board. I was asked by President Boling and General Counsel Baugh to represent the University's position to the Board. Knoxville attorneys Lewis Combs and John Darsie represented the Gay People's Alliance.

A three-member committee composed of trustees Bob McDowell, Paul Kinser and E.S. Bevins was appointed to hear the appeal. The hearing was conducted in the UT Board Room at 800 Andy Holt Tower on February 20, 1974 and lasted from 9:00 in the morning until 4:30 in the afternoon. At the conclusion of the session the Alliance's appeal was denied by the Board's committee.

The various arguments were reported by the news media the following day. Daily Beacon reporter Marcia Edging succinctly stated the trustees' reasoning in denying the appeal.

> Agreeing that such a purpose would "degrade" and prove disruptive to UT as an institution of higher education and would "encourage disrespect for and violation of the state law pertaining to crimes against nature," the trustees unanimously denied the recognition request.

(Summer Beacon, June 25, 1974, p.1)

I received a note dated July 8, 1974, from Executive Assistant to the President, Charles E Smith, (with copies to President Boling, Vice President Joe Johnson and General Counsel Baugh), providing:

"Thank you for your July 2 memos in regard to action relative to the Elsa H. Fine [an unrelated matter] and Gay People's Alliance cases. This is good news and reflects credit on the quality of your work. You have represented the University in some extremely important and sensitive cases in recent months, and we are pleased with the favorable decisions that have resulted."

No court action was taken to challenge the Board's decision. Further application for recognition of a "gay rights" group was not submitted to the University for nearly eight years.

On January 4, 1982 I was called to the UT Chattanooga campus following the campus administration's receipt of a request for recognition of the campus Gay Liberation Front. Several recent court decisions around the country dealing with gay rights groups at other institutions required that the recognition issue be re-examined.

The challenge was met and resolved in short order. Recognition was replaced by registration. The University would no longer be placed in the position of appearing to endorse a statement of purpose provided by the Gay Liberation Front or any other organization. On February 18, 1982, the GLF was approved as a registered organization of the University of Tennessee at Chattanooga.

Since the language change in 1982, to my knowledge, there have been no other purpose focused disputes regarding registration of student organizations on the issue of gay rights or otherwise.

Chapter 24–No Such Thing as a Case That Can't Be Lost–Soni vs. Board of Trustees of The U. of Tennessee

There is a well-known saying among lawyers: "There is no such thing as a case that can't be lost." I gained familiarity with the truth of that saying early in my career.

Dr. Raj P. Soni was born and raised in India. In 1959 he came to the United States to obtain his Ph.D. degree in mathematics from Oregon State University. Soni graduated from Oregon State with his doctorate, in 1963.

In September 1967 Soni was employed by the Mathematics Department of the University of Tennessee, Knoxville, as a Visiting Associate Professor. In October 1968 Department head John Barrett issued a recommendation that "Professor Raj Soni be offered an Associate Professorship with tenure." Later the same month Dr. Donald Dessart became acting head of the Department of Mathematics when Dessart became ill.

Dessart called a special meeting of the Department's tenured faculty for the purpose of considering Barrett's recommendation. At the meeting bizarre point out that Sony was not a citizen of the United States and, therefore, under state law could not be pointed to a permanent position. Therefore, no vote was taken by the faculty to recommend Soni for tenure. However, the faculty recommended Soni be employed as "associate professor" rather than "visiting associate professor." Clearly the faculty had good feelings toward Soni and would have recommended him for tenure had they been able to do so.

Dessart then wrote Soni a letter that read in part: "It was recommended that you be appointed an associate professor without tenure.... The question of recommending tenure will be considered by a similar departmental group at the time you become a citizen of the United States."

On December 15, 1971 Soni became a naturalized U.S. citizen. However, he was not recommended for tenure. Instead, Soni received a letter dated March 8, 1972, from the department chairman notifying him that his appointment would be terminated as of August 31, 1973 because his performance as a teacher and as a research mathematician had not been of the quality expected of tenured staff. Soni was not offered an opportunity for a "due process" hearing of the "poor performance" charge which led to his termination.

Soni filed suit in the U.S. District Court, Eastern District, Tennessee, on September 4, 1973 against the Board of Trustees of the University of Tennessee and UT President, Edward J. Boling. Knoxville attorney Charles Susano (assisted by Caesar Stair) represented the plaintiff and I represented the defendants. The presiding judge was U.S. District Judge Robert L Taylor.

Two main contentions were presented to the court, one by the plaintiff and one by the defendants. Soni claimed he had an understanding that his employment would continue on a permanent basis with the Department of mathematics, even though he was advised in writing that his position was one without tenure. For that reason, Sony's termination without a due process hearing was alleged to deprive him of a property interest in continued employment.

The opposing position of the University defendants was quite simple. Soni could not lawfully have been provided tenure or permanent employment under state law, and there was no claim or evidence the University attempted to circumvent the law. In the absence of tenure or permanent employment Soni lacked a property right entitling him to a due process hearing prior to termination.

Tennessee law on the subject was exceedingly clear:

"It shall be unlawful for the trustees of the University of Tennessee... To employ any... Teacher... To have in any way the custody and care of students of the public educational institutions of this state who is not a citizen of the United States of America; provided that nothing in this section shall be construed to prohibit arrangements whereby professors and teachers who are citizens of other nations may be employed on a temporary basis on the faculties of colleges, universities or public schools in Tennessee...."

Tenn. Code Ann. 49-1303.

The UT Knoxville faculty handbook incorporated state law by providing that "(c)itizens of other countries may be employed in temporary positions only."

When I received the complaint for response I was 100% certain of victory. I was aware of ongoing litigation in other states challenging limitations on employment of aliens legally in the country. But Soni had not raised that issue in his complaint. Even had he done so, his complaint must fail since the University (other than departmental faculty) had never attempted to grant him tenure or permanent employment. Soni's dismissal was based on the University's position that he lacked the skills necessary to qualify him for it tender i.e. permanent employment. As a temporary employee he lacked a property interest entitling him to a due process hearing.

I learned a valuable lesson and contributed to making a bit of notable legal history adverse to the interest of the University that was a long time overcoming.

Judge Taylor denied a motion for summary judgment filed on behalf of the University defendants and set the case for trial. The key witnesses for the University would be Chancellor Jack Reese, Vice-Chancellor Walter Herndon and Lida Barrett, Chairman of the Department of Mathematics–as well as Dr. Dessart. But, the key argument remained focused on applicable state law.

The case was tried by Judge Taylor on February 19, 1994. He rendered no judgment from the bench and I left the court still confident of victory. Judge Taylor's order in favor of the plaintiff, entered February 21, 1974, came as quite a shock–at least to me. Most shocking was Judge Taylor's failure to explain away the defense's reliance on state law, Soni v. Board of Trustees of U. of Tenn., 376 F. Supp. 289 (E.D. Tenn. 1974).

The District Court noted the language of state law prohibiting the employment of non-citizens as professors in public educational institutions of the state except on a temporary basis. The Court likewise noted language of the UT faculty handbook permitting citizens of other countries to be employed in temporary positions only. Id.,p.291.

In the footnote detailing the applicable statutory language, the district court merely opined "[as] the case under examination here is governed by the Roth and Sindermann guidelines, it is inappropriate at this time to make a dispositive ruling on this statute's constitutionality." Id., p.291, fn2.

Although state law and the UT faculty handbook stated plainly that a non-citizen could only be employed on a temporary basis, the District Court used words I characterized as "weasel words" to reach an opposite conclusion.

> Against this factual background [Soni was in many ways treated like
> a tenured faculty member], the court concludes that under Roth and Perry
> there existed sufficient objective evidence to vest in plaintiff a cognizable
> property interest in the form of a reasonable expectation of future and

continued employment. Defendant objectively acted toward plantiff in such a manner as to reasonably lead him to believe that he was a person with a relative degree of permanency in the academic community of this university.

***

If this court is to issue formalistic and technical tests in finding property interest then the mere presence of a formal tenure system, as is the case under examination here, should not be a dispositive distinction between Perry and the case before this court. It is the opinion of the court that under the circumstances here, plantiff had a viable understanding that his employment would continue on a permanent basis with the Department of mathematics notwithstanding the statement contained in the October 29 correspondence that plantiff's was one without tenure. All the evidence and testimony received by the court points toward a mutual understanding of job permanency.

While the issues of the constitutionality of the Tennessee statute restricting tenure to United States citizens is not before the court, plantiff could have reasonably concluded that "but for" the statute's presence he would have been granted tenure in 1968.

Id., pp.292-93.

The District Court concluded that Soni had a property interest in continued employment with the University and was entitled to back pay from August 31, 1973 until the University provided him an appropriate hearing meeting legal requirements of due process. A notice of appeal to the U.S. Court of Appeals for the Sixth Circuit was promptly filed. I was confident the Sixth Circuit would straighten out the District Court's refusal to apply state law and university policy.

Oral argument was held before the Sixth Circuit (Circuit Judges O'Sullivan, Phillips and Edwards) on December 13, 1974 in Cincinnati. The Court's opinion was filed March 12, 1975. Soni v. Board of Trustees of University of Tennessee, 513 F. 2d 347 (6th Cir. 1975).

The Court of Appeals noted the appellant's argument that Soni "could not have acquired a reasonable expectation of continued employment because the University of Tennessee had a well-established tenure system." Id. p. 351. That argument was rejected. In reliance on Supreme Court decisions cited by the District Court, the Court of Appeals noted that the Supreme Court, "Did not say, as it easily could have, that a reasonable expectancy cannot arise in the context of a formal tenure system." Id.

Even though the Court of Appeals acknowledged Tennessee law specifically permitting only temporary employment of aliens, the Court did not address the issue of whether the state law was constitutional. Id., p.350. The law was simply ignored, as was the equally plain provisions of the UT faculty handbook. Also noted–but ignored–was the October 29 letter to Soni from his departmental chairman that it was "recommended" that he be appointed Associate Professor "without tenure" with the question of recommending tenure to be considered at the time he became a citizen. Id. p. 349.

In my opinion the Court of Appeals, like the District Court, opted to disregard plain English and select the result preferred.

The second major issue before the Court was perhaps less clear but likewise attendant with great consequence for the University: was the University of Tennessee an agency of the state of Tennessee and therefore immune from suit pursuant to the Eleventh Amendment to the United States Constitution?

The Court of Appeals was "unable to find any case discussing the University's status under the eleventh amendment" but noted there were "many federal cases from other circuits holding other state colleges and universities to be state instrumentalities that enjoy the protection of the eleventh amendment.[Citations omitted]." Id. p. 352.

The Court of Appeals noted that UT's charter provided it the right to "sue and be sued" in Tennessee or elsewhere. Still, the court acknowledged that "it seems generally agreed that a state's consent to be sued in its own courts does not necessarily imply consent to be sued in federal court." Id. But, because UT was created "only a few years after the ratification of the 11th amendment, with the unrestricted right to sue and be sued 'in any court of law or equity' " the Court saw "no indication that this sweeping consent was intended to be limited to suits brought in the state courts." Id. p. 353. The University of Tennessee lacked eleventh amendment immunity from suit.

Henry Haile, with the Tennessee Attorney General's office, called on March 25 and we agreed to file a petition for rehearing with the Sixth Circuit bearing my name and Attorney General Ray Ashley's. Unfortunately, the petition for rehearing was denied by the appellate court on June 5, 1975.

A petition for a writ of certiorari to the U.S. Supreme Court was filed on behalf of the University. The petition was denied by the Supreme Court on June 7, 1976. The matter did not rest there.

I immediately met with Chancellor Jack Reese and other university officials to discuss scheduling of a "due process" hearing for Soni. The decision was made not to proceed in that direction and Soni was permitted to continue his employment until the date of his retirement.

Soni was cited repeatedly in the years following its issuance–but never again was the University of Tennessee held bound by the principles enunciated therein. The problems created by the District Court and Sixth Circuit rulings got fixed.

And, I learned a major lesson from the Soni litigation: There is no such thing as a case that cannot be lost.

Chapter 25–Focus on Integrity by the University Administration

THE INTEGRITY FACTOR

Sometime in 1975 President Boling called me to his office in the old UT administration building. He explained that UT athletic director Bob Woodruff had brought to his attention a matter involving one of the coaches and a possible violation of NCAA rules.

I don't recall the details of the incident. What I do recall is President Boling's statement before asking that I look into the matter.

"Ron, you can be a coach here at UT and lose some games and we will keep you – for while. But, if you cheat you're gone!" With that statement it was made clear to me that my findings were not to be influenced in any way by the fact the issue arose in athletics. Had Boling suggested otherwise–that integrity depended on who was involved–there is no question my career at the University would have been short-lived.

If I had to name a single factor that created a passionate bonding between the University and me during the "Big Orange" years, it was the unabashed commitment of UT leaders to INTEGRITY! That commitment made me proud to serve "the Big Orange" as legal counsel.

THE IMPACT OF FAITH

It has long been my belief that faith influences integrity. UT President Andy Holt was a man of strong Christian faith. A DVD featuring Andy Holt sharing his faith received accolades from my Sunday school department long after Holt's retirement from UT. "Andy's" integrity was never questioned at any time by anybody during his term of his presidency.

The first president of the University of Tennessee was a Christian pastor as were six of the next nine. Two of the remaining three prepared for the ministry but never held ministerial positions. Other presidents were known to be active in their churches.

The UT Board of Trustees commences each meeting of the full board with prayer. Trustee Ann Baker Furrow and husband Sam were members of my Sunday school department. Over the years, on numerous occasions, I had discussions on matters of faith with Board members.

Such UT notables as football head coach Phil Fulmer and UT quarterback Peyton Manning have spoken at Fellowship of Christian Athletes fundraisers. UT women's athletic director Joan Cronan served on the FCA's national board of directors. I served on the Knox area Board from 1996 to 2013.

Various faculty and administrative staff–and many alumni and friends of the

University – have periodically placed faith-based ads in the Daily Beacon on special occasions. An Easter ad published in the March 16, 1989 edition proclaimed:

I am the resurrection and the life; He who believes in Me shall live

even if he dies, and everyone who lives and believes in Me shall never die… (Jesus).

The names of those sponsoring the ad included many UT department heads, Andy Holt's son, Andy Holt, Jr., the Furrows, future UT trustee Bill Sampson and more than 200 other leaders in the UT community. Therese and I were ad sponsors.

In challenging times and on special occasions it was common practice for a number of the secretaries in the office of General Counsel to approach me with a request that I lead in an office prayer. Not in my job description and not a request I would ever refuse.

During the "Big Orange" years, faith and commitment to integrity within the UT community had far more influence than did power or wealth. Or even friendship. Correspondence regarding a case that ended up in the Tennessee Court of Appeals made this point well.

MICHAEL SANDERSON APPEAL

Nick Dunagan, a Vice-Chancellor–and later, Chancellor–at the UT Martin campus, was appointed to serve as administrative hearing officer in a UT Knoxville case involving a student charged with plagiarism. Dunagan ruled in favor of the student.

I appealed Dunagan's decision to UTK Chancellor William Snyder. Snyder reversed Dunagan's decision and the Tennessee Court of Appeals later affirmed Snyder's decision.

In his memorandum of November 25, 1997, President Joe Johnson made the following inquiry of Beach Brogan and me:

"Thank you for getting to me the favorable Tennessee Court of Appeals ruling in the plagiarism case involving Michael Sanderson. Congratulations!
Why did we appeal a Nick Dunagan decision? Did you discuss this decision with me? Please discuss.
I have reservations about seeking to overrule a good person, like Nick."

Brogan's December 1, 1997 response:

We appealed Dunagan's decision because it was wrong. Dunagan thought Sanderson had to "intend" to plagiarize in order to be found guilty and issued an "initial order" to that effect. Nick did not accept the position of the General Counsel that intent was not required. Likewise, we had no obligation to accept Nick's decision which we thought was wrong. We know Nick is a good person.

However, our job is to represent the University to the best of our ability. Because this was an adversarial proceeding, this is exactly what we did. Accordingly, in accordance with APA procedures, Chancellor Snyder was asked to review the "initial order" by Dunagan. We did not discuss it with you. Snyder's order became the "final order."

In addition to the decision by Snyder disagreeing with Dunagan, four judges also disagreed with him including the Davidson County Chancellor and three members of the Court of Appeals for the middle section. The Court of Appeals held:

After reviewing the entire record, and comparing all three versions of Sanderson's paper to the source material, regardless of whether intent is required, there is clearly substantial and material evidence to support Chancellor Snyder's finding of plagiarism.

Thus, five people above Dunagan agreed Sanderson plagiarized. Accordingly, we believe the action we took was entirely appropriate.

Our job is to protect the integrity of the University regardless of friendship.

If you have any further question about the manner in which this case was handled, please let us know. Thank you.

Not surprisingly, due to his own well-established ethical standards, President Johnson accepted the explanation given. Integrity trumped friendship!

TOILET PAPER CAPER

Friendship ties are easier to ignore when the friends are someone else's. Two of my friends in the early 1970s were UT detective A.D. Earl and Sgt. Jack Thacker. Thacker was the officer who intervened in 1971 when I was attacked in the University Center.

I was quite saddened to learn in fall 1974 that a former UT police officer, Tony Martin, had submitted a 21 page document alleging a variety of wrongdoings by members of the UT Knoxville Safety and Security Department, including Earl and Thacker. It was my responsibility to investigate the allegations.

Among the more serious claims was that Earl had made Friday afternoon stops at Neyland Stadium, where toilet tissue and other supplies were stored, to stock up on personal needs. Thacker was alleged to have entered the UT Knoxville personnel office, without authorization, for the purpose of reviewing employee pay information.

After interviewing dozens of witnesses over a period of three weeks or so, I concluded there was merit to Martin's report. As a result of my findings, the employment of both Earl and Thacker was terminated. [Knoxville News Sentinel, January 27, 1975, p. 2; January 28, 1975, p. 2]. The name of the scandal came from a UT Daily Beacon article titled "Toilet Paper Caper." (The Daily Beacon, January 28, 1975, p. 6)

Did friendship play a role in the way I handled the officers found to have a misappropriated university property for their own personal use? Yes, but only in a way that did not reward their misconduct.

I called A. D. Earl on the telephone and asked him to meet me in my office. When he arrived I told him that I was sorry but I had no choice but to recommend the termination of his employment. I said, "You're a good guy but what you did was wrong"–or words very close to that. I urged him to acknowledge the wrong-doing and move on with his life. A.D. left my office. My advice was rejected.

At a May 9, 1975 hearing before the Unemployment Compensation Hearing Appeals Board, Earl's rebuttal to the University's position that unemployment compensation should be denied because Earl was terminated "for cause," was that others were doing the same thing– stealing supplies from the stadium storage area. My response: "Tell me who they are and we'll take appropriate action against them, too."

On May 22 the review Board announced its decision denying Earl's claim for unemployment compensation.

The proceedings against Sgt. Thacker were a bit more prolonged and somewhat more intriguing. He was initially fired, then reinstated at a lower rank by UTK Chancellor Jack Reese. Nevertheless, Thacker filed suit in U.S. District Court against his superior, Col. Tom Whitehead, Director of Safety and Security. He was represented by attorney Roger Hooban.

Thacker claimed his right of due process had been violated and that he was unjustly penalized. He asked $400,000 in compensatory and punitive damages.

I filed a "motion for summary judgment," asserting there were no facts in the record sufficient to permit the case to go to trial. Judge Robert Taylor granted the motion and entered judgment in favor of Col. Whitehead on January 23, 1976. (Thacker v. Whitehead, 407 F. Supp. 1111 (1976))

An appeal was taken from Judge Taylor's ruling to the U.S. Court of Appeals for the Sixth Circuit. That court likewise found Thacker's case lacking in merit and, on January 20, 1977, affirmed the ruling of the district court (Thacker v. Whitehead, 548 F. 2d 634 (1977).

Over the ensuing years I encountered Thacker on the number of occasions and our meetings were proper. I never again saw Earl. Friendship suffered. Integrity survived.

Honesty and integrity was not just valued during the "Big Orange" years. It was expected! There was a price to pay when students or staff, as well as ad-ministrative personnel, elected to violate ethical standards set by the University. "Do the right thing" was a mandate, not a suggestion.

Chapter 26–Integrity Without Regard to Position
Patterson vs. Hunt

Cheating is a matter of what you did–not who you are. Integrity is important in all aspects of life. That is certainly true in professional programs such as those at the University of Tennessee.

"Honor codes" have been adopted for each of the UT professional schools in accordance with the Tennessee Uniform Administrative Procedures Act. Each honor code focuses on promoting integrity. The code for the UT College of Dentistry in Memphis is no exception.

In spring 1983 first-year dentistry students Richard Patterson, Edward Shaw and Joseph Melton were charged with violating the College of Dentistry Honor Code. As an applicant for admission to the College of Dentistry each had signed the following statement:

> I, the undersigned, signify that I have read the Honor Code and the By-Laws of the Honor Council and hereby pledge my support of them. I understand what is expected of me as a student of the University of Tennessee in the College of Dentistry and realize that a plea of ignorance will not be acceptable by Honor Council. If I have reason to suspect that a breach of the Honor Code has been committed, I will take action in one of the following ways:
> 1. Issue a personal warning to the suspect with the knowledge of a member of the Honor Council.
> 2. Issue a personal warning to the suspect through a member of the Honor Council.

Each of the three dentistry students was charged with cheating in connection with a pathology examination administered on April 22, 1983. Melton asked Shaw to provide him with a copy of the answer key to the examination and Shaw provided the assistance requested.

Patterson, in the top 10% of his class and serving as the class president, did not directly participate in the cheating activity. However, when Melton asked Patterson to determine if the answer key would be posted for the test Patterson agreed to do so. Patterson learned the key would be posted and so informed Melton.

The three were advised they had the option to proceed before the honor council or before an administrative judge in accordance with the administrative procedures act. Each of the three signed a waiver of his right to proceed under the APA and elected to be heard by the Honor Council.

Both Melton and Shaw entered guilty pleas before the Honor Council to the charge of cheating. Patterson pleaded not guilty to cheating but guilty of having knowledge of cheating by Melton and Shaw. After receiving a report from the

Honor Council, the Dean of the College of Dentistry, Dr. William Slagle, advised all three students that they would be dismissed from the College although they could apply for readmission in the future.

All three students appealed the Dean's decision to UTCHS Chancellor Hunt. The Chancellor denied their appeal, affirming their dismissal from the College of dentistry.

On May 19, 1983 all three students filed suit against Chancellor Hunt and the University of in Shelby Chancery Court petitioning for a temporary restraining order preventing their dismissal from the University. Memphis attorney Robert Friedman represented Patterson and Melton while Memphis attorney William Heaton represented Shaw. The presiding judge was Chancellor George Lewis.

Chancellor Lewis issued a "TRO" on the day it was requested. On May 23, I filed a motion to dissolve the order. Instead of ruling on the motion the Chancellor set the matter for trial. The issue for trial was whether the plaintiffs had been denied their constitutional right to due process because they had unknowingly waived their right to a hearing under the administrative procedures act.

The case was tried before Chancellor Lewis on August 1, 2 and 4, 1983. At the conclusion of trial Chancellor Lewis announced his findings in favor of the defendants with respect to plaintiffs Shaw and Melton but in favor of plaintiff Patterson. Judgment incorporating the Chancellor's findings was entered on September 16, 1983.

In October the University appealed to the Court of Appeals of Tennessee from the Chancellor's judgment in favor of Patterson. Shaw and Melton appealed the Chancellor's ruling against them. On May 22, 1984 oral argument was held before a panel composed of appellate judges W. Frank Crawford, Hewitt Tomlin and Alan Highers.

One exchange indicated to me where the court was heading. Patterson's counsel, Robert Friedman observed that his client had continued enrollment while the case proceeded–if the ruling below was reversed his time spent in school would have been wasted. One of the panel responded, as best I recall, "Isn't that a chance he took when he appealed?"

The ruling of the Court of Appeals was rendered on July 13, 1984. The court unanimously affirmed the Chancery ruling against Shaw and Milton. The Chancery ruling in favor of Patterson, on the other hand, was reversed by a unanimous vote of the panel. Patterson v. Hunt, 680 S.W. 2d 508 (Tenn. App. 1984).

The due process claims of plaintiffs Shaw and Melton were quickly disposed of by the Court of Appeals:

Counsel for the plaintiffs have repeatedly asserted throughout this voluminous record that the due process rights of the plaintiffs were violated, because they unknowingly waived their rights to an administrative board hearing. Concerning this issue, we note two points: firstly, as provided by [the Honor Code] the ultimate decision from an administrative board hearing rests with the Chancellor of UT, because he represents the last resort on appeal. Similarly, the Chancellor also possessed the power to make the final decision on the appeal from the honor Council. By either method of appeal, the Chancellor possessed the power for de novo review. [Citation omitted].

Secondly, we note the procedure provided by [the Honor Code].

The respondent is asked how he pleads to the charges; if he pleads guilty, no further hearing may be necessary; if he pleads not guilty, the hearing proceeds.

Once these students plead guilty, the hearing would conclude before the board as the hearing concluded before the honor Council. Again, as to guilty pleas, we can discern no real difference between the two methods of procedure.

Id., p. 515.

Assuming the plaintiffs would continue in their truthful testimony and plead guilty before the administrative board, we cannot conceive of any rights waived. Since the initial procedures would be very similar before the Honor Council and the administrative board and the appeals process to Chancellor Hunt would be identical, we hold no rights were waived and any procedural due process rights violated were cured.

Id. 515-16.

For that reason, the appellate court rejected the plaintiffs' claim that they were denied due process.

The Court of Appeals acknowledged that Patterson entered a not guilty plea to the charge of cheating. It also noted that he admitted guilt of knowing others were cheating:

Q. (By Mr. Leadbetter) my question was this, are you denying that you made the statement I have knowledge of cheating?
A. To be quite honest with you, without some type of recording of everything I said during that hearing, I couldn't tell you what my exact wording was. I'd be lying if I said I was sure.
Q. Did you later on – but you did plead guilty, you did say for whatever words you used–
A. I don't know if you'd say I pleaded guilty. I said I was guilty of having knowledge that someone intended to cheat, but I was not guilty of cheating on the exam.
Q. And then later on I believe you were asked to explain exactly what you did on this particular test date, and I believe at one point in time you are asked, you understand that what you did violated the Honor Code, and you responded yes, didn't you?
A. Yes, sir.

Id., p. 513.

The appeals court noted Patterson's contention that "he did not have notice of the charge against him because he did not cheat as such, but merely knew that cheating was going on and did not report it. We find this difficult to absorb in view of the record in the case which clearly shows that Patterson knew that cheating was taking place and he was in fact asked to aid and abet the cheaters." Id., p. 515. The contrary reasoning of the Chancery Court was rejected. "The trial court apparently felt that Patterson's actions were excusable, and in this regard, we disagree. The Honor Code is clear, and Patterson's actions are a violation of Article III." Id., p.616.

In its concluding remarks the Court of Appeals observed, "[p]rofessional schools should be commended for installing and adhering to the Honor Code. However, if clear violations of honesty under whatever circumstances, are excused, the Honor Code would be transformed into a mockery. This situation should not be allowed in our society." Id.

The Court dissolved the injunction previously issued on behalf of Patterson. He was dismissed from the College of Dentistry retroactive to the date the injunction was issued by the Chancery Court.

Integrity won the day both for the University and the Tennessee judicial system.

At a fundraiser for Congressman Jimmy Duncan preceding the annual Lincoln Day Dinner in Knoxville. Left to right: Senator Bill Frist, Congressman Jimmy Duncan, Therese Leadbetter, Ron Leadbetter, Governor of Tennessee Don Sunquist. (2001)

Chapter 27–Do the Right Thing–or Else!

One of my job responsibilities was to provide legal assistance in enforcing University "Personnel Policies and Procedures" governing employee conduct. When violations qualifying as "gross misconduct" occurred, I served as a "prosecutor" of administrative charges if a hearing of those charges was requested by the accused.

Another responsibility was to provide similar assistance in enforcing the "Code of Student Conduct" for each campus. Stiff penalties were imposed under either system for serious ethical violations, affirming the importance of integrity.

When misconduct, such as theft, resulted in loss of University funds or property it was my responsibility to pursue recovery of the University's assets, and even recovery of punitive damages from the wrongdoer.

In 1977 UT employees misappropriated $223 in university funds. I filed suit in Shelby County Sessions Court seeking recovery of both compensatory and punitive damages. Judgment was entered in the University's favor on April 28 –$223 in compensatory damages and $2,000 in punitive damages! [The University of Tennessee v. Dallas Bradford and Yvonne Lomax, Shelby Sessions Docket No. 375859] The judgment was fully paid. Wrongdoing had a high price.

UNIVERSITY OF TENNESSEE v. OSCAR SEELBINDER

A good case study of how aggressively the University defended principles of integrity and pursued remedies against wrongdoers, in the first decades of my professional career, is found in an early 1980's case involving the past and current directors of purchasing at the Wm. Bowld Hospital (UT Memphis).

University auditors discovered evidence that former hospital purchasing director, William Reed, and current purchasing director, Oscar Seelbinder, were involved in a scheme to purchase hospital scrub suits in quantities far exceeding the amount needed by hospital staff. The excess scrub suits were advertised for sale on local television. One telephone number provided for scrub suit orders was that of the purchasing department.

A third conspirator, William Widgery, a resident of Indianapolis, In., participated in the scheme and shared in the profits.

All three men were arrested in Memphis. Reed and Seelbinder were criminally charged, convicted and sentenced. Widgery was not. Reportedly, while with law enforcement officers, he asked to use the restroom, was given permission, then fled the premises and returned to Indiana. For whatever reason, law enforcement officials elected not to pursue Widgery further.

On June 4, 1980, I filed a civil complaint in the Shelby County Circuit Court against Reed, Seelbinder and Widgery (The University of Tennessee v. Oscar W. Seelbinder, Jr., et.al., Shelby Circuit No. 91591 T.D., Div. 2). The complaint alleged the three defendants had engaged in embezzlement of University property. Both compensatory and punitive damages were sought against each defendant.

Although process was served on Reed and Seelbinder through the Shelby County Sheriff, efforts to serve Widgery by mail failed. I decided to solve the problem by assuming the role of "process server, " and attempt to serve process on Widgery myself.

On October 23, I flew to Indianapolis, rented an automobile and drove out to Widgery's residence. I had confirmed its location in advance, just as I had confirmed as best I could, by means of a "surreptitious" phone call to a lady sounding as if she were his wife, that he would be home that evening.

I arrived at the stately Widgery residence in the early evening hours. His home was located on a cul-de-sac adjacent to an Indianapolis golf course. No one was home.

I pulled my vehicle under overhanging tree branches on the side of the cul-de-sac opposite the residence and parked, hidden from view of anyone approaching Widgery's residence. With windows rolled down, as darkness settled in, I listened to the humming and whining of racecars at the Indianapolis Speedway in the distance.

A little after eight a vehicle entered the cul-de-sac and stopped at the mailbox next to the Widgery's driveway. A gentleman exited the driver's side and retrieved some mail. As he did I exited my own vehicle, approached and addressed him, "Mr. Widgery?" "Yes," the gentleman replied." A look of surprise flashed on his face (and a similar look on the face of the lady in the passenger's seat, who I presumed to be his wife–or at least the lady I spoke with by telephone earlier that day). "I have something for you," I said, in my lawyer's voice.

I handed Widgery the summons. He appeared to know exactly what it was. I turned, reentered my vehicle, drove away and returned to Memphis. Assignment complete.

Widgery never filed a response or appeared in Shelby Circuit Court. Summary judgment was entered in the University's favor in the amount of $100,000 on February 6, 1981. That amount included punitive damages. According to University auditors the actual amount of the university's loss was around $30,000. A very nice "profit" for the University from Widgery's criminal wrongdoing.

Although efforts were made to collect the judgment, they were not successful. Someone beat us to it , namely, the U.S. government. I subsequently located

Widgery, in Joliet prison, serving a conviction for mail fraud in an unrelated case. (United States v. Widgery, 636 F. 2d. 200 (8th Cir. 1980)).

The University did not collect the judgment against Widgery. It did recover the loss from the other defendants along with a good deal more.

On August 11, 1983, Seelbinder agreed to settle UT's suit against him. On September 8, a consent judgment for the University was entered by the Shelby Circuit Court. The University received full payment of its loss and substantially more. A similar result was reached in Reed's case.

Total loss: around $30,000; total recovery: $135,000.

IN RE: BUCK

Enforcing integrity can be difficult when doing so threatens severe damage to a university's academic program. Failing to do so threatens destruction of institutional reputation.

In early 1996 a student in the nursing anesthesia program at the UT Medical Center in Knoxville came forward to report a cheating incident involving six out of seven students in that high profile program (in which, I was told, graduates earned close to $100,000 in annual salary immediately following graduation). The "whistleblower" had actually participated in the activity herself but immediately recognized her mistake and acted to correct the error.

The incident arose when the course instructor administered an examination using the "honor system." After distributing the test to each of the nursing anesthesia students, the instructor left the room. First one, then another of the students in the room began to discuss the test questions and answers.

The student who reported the incident also received assistance from one of her classmates. To her credit, she quickly recognized the conduct permeating the classroom was wrong and reported it to appropriate University officials after the test concluded.

Administrative disciplinary charges of cheating were filed against five of the seven students in the class. No charge was filed against the "whistleblower" because she had promptly acted to correct her mistake and, in doing so, to preserve the integrity of the academic program in which she was enrolled. The seventh student was not involved in the cheating activity but cooperated in the investigative and disciplinary process.

The accused students requested a formal hearing of the disciplinary charges against them in accordance with the Tennessee Uniform Administrative Procedures Act. The hearing was held in Thompson Boling Arena dining room and conducted by Administrative Judge Jennifer Richter, with the UTK office of affirmative action.

The hearing took the better part of two days, May 2-3, 1996, and the proceedings were fully transcribed by a court reporter. Both sides submitted proposed "findings of fact and conclusions of law" following the hearing.

An "initial order" was entered by Richter in July, finding each of the accused guilty as charged. Each was assessed the penalty of indefinite suspension from the University.

A "final order" entered by the UT Memphis Chancellor affirmed the ruling of the administrative judge. The five accused were advised they could apply for readmission "this year." But, for the present, they were suspended from the University and the professional program in which they were enrolled. Integrity prevailed.

ATHLETICS

Athletics and The University of Tennessee's history of compliance with rules of the National Collegiate Athletic Association will be addressed in later chapters. But, a September 27, 1991 letter by UT President Joe Johnson is noteworthy for its reaffirmation of the commitment to integrity enunciated by Boling in 1975.

TO: Malcolm McInnis
    Ron Leadbetter

From: Joe Johnson
Subject: NCAA Investigation

    Thank you for the truly fine work you did on the NCAA investigation. And you got solid applause from the NCAA infractions committee. You are thorough, diligent, and effective. You found our strong points and identified where one of our coaches was at fault.

Cc: Dr. John Quinn
    Mr. Beach Brogan
    Mr. Doug Dickey

The coach referred to was a fine young football coach by the name of Jack Sells. He committed no egregious error except one–he lied!

Despite being urged by me to tell the truth, he lied–first to me then later to an NCAA investigator. His lies cost him his coaching job at the University of Tennessee. [See Chapter 76].

An important aspect of my job as trial attorney was to prepare parties and witnesses for depositions and trial, and NCAA investigations. My standard practice in every preparatory session was to emphasize at the outset, "Tell the truth." For those appearing reticent or possibly needing extra motivation I added words to the effect, "do the right thing–or else!"

To the credit of the University, I was never asked by any University official to alter that advice.

Chapter 28-Cheating is a No-No
The University consistently made clear it would not tolerate academic dishonesty–cheating. A variety of cases demonstrated that commitment.

TIM TURLEY vs. JACK E. WELLS

On August 31, 1979, Tim Turley, a student in the College of Dentistry at the UT Center for the Health Sciences, met twice with the Dean of the College of Dentistry, Dr. Jack Wells. During the meetings, Wells orally confronted Turley with a faculty member's contention that Turley had deliberately failed to carry out an order of a faculty member by not retaking a master impression for a prosthetic appliance, thereby treating the patient improperly.

Second, it was reported that Turley had treated the patient without faculty supervision. Third, it was reported that Turley had falsified records of the clinic by placing the initials of a faculty member on records without the faculty member's knowledge or permission. Turley admitted to the Dean that all three reports were true.

Turley received a disciplinary letter dated September 5, 1979. He was immediately terminated as a student in the College of Dentistry. Although Turley he could have immediately appealed the Dean's action he elected instead to proceed in accordance with the Tennessee Uniform Administrative Procedures Act.

Turley received a formal APA hearing on November 5, 1979–61 days after he was terminated from the College of Dentistry. While Turley admitted the truth of the three allegations presented to the Dean, he argued that his actions were justifiable and not serious. Turley's contention was rejected and he was found guilty of the charges against him. It was ordered that he be permanently terminated from the College of dentistry.

Turley pursued a two-pronged appeal process. First he sought relief from the State courts, by filing a petition for review with the Shelby County Chancery Court. Losing there, he appealed to the Tennessee Court of Appeals for the Western Section. He lost there and filed an application for permission to appeal to the Tennessee Supreme Court. On October 5, 1981, the Tennessee Supreme Court entered an order denying Turley's application.

More critical, from my perspective, was the second prong of Turley's appeal. On September 4, 1980 he filed a complaint with the U.S. District Court in Memphis, contending he had been terminated as a dentistry student in violation of his constitutional right to due process. He alleged that his 61 day suspension between the date he was terminated and the date on which he received an APA hearing, was an unconstitutional deprivation of his right to a hearing before any action was taken.

The case was tried to a jury on February 17, 1981, U.S. District Judge Robert McRae presiding. When the jury failed to agree on a verdict I filed a motion for judgment notwithstanding lack of a verdict.

Judge McRae described the case as presenting "a set of somewhat unusual circumstances from the standpoint of applying controlling authority." While Judge McRae was uncertain as to the reason for a 61 day gap between the termination and the hearing, he rested on the undisputed fact that Turley, by his own admission, engaged in the conduct attributed to him.

The District Court rejected Turley's argument that the conduct was not of a serious nature and entered judgment for the University defendants, Dean Wells and UTCHS Chancellor T. Albert Farmer. Timothy Matthew Turley v. Jack E Wells, et al. Civil Action File No. 80-2495-M (W.D. Tenn. 1981).

In the final analysis, it was a combination of the oral hearing provided by Wells, the formal hearing provided Turley in accordance with the APA and Turley's admission that he engaged in the conduct of which he was accused which allowed the University to dodge liability in this instance.

BARRY SELVIDGE v. THE UNIVERSITY OF TENNESSEE

One case stands out as proof that ethics has no expiration date and cheating may have long-term consequences.

In fall 1983 I investigated and administratively prosecuted a cheating case from the UT College of Law. The facts of the case were quite unique.

In the process of completing paperwork necessary for admission to the practice of law a recent UT College of Law graduate–a female–was impacted by her "conscience." In her last quarter of law school she had observed Barry, Selvidge, a fellow student, cheat, but did not report what she observed.

Eventually the student's conscience got the better of her and she came forward to report her observations to Richard Wirtz, the professor who had administered the test. Wirtz in turn, contacted the UTK Office of Student Conduct. Fortuitously, the professor still had the test submitted by Selvidge. He also had the test Selvidge reportedly copied answers from – an exam submitted by a former UT football player (who was not in any way implicated as an accessory). A comparison of the two tests was quite revealing.

On November 2, 1983 Selvidge was issued a letter charging him with cheating. He was notified that, if found guilty, he faced revocation of his degree and dismissal from the University. Selvidge requested a hearing in accordance with the Tennessee Uniform Administrative Procedures Act.

The requested APA hearing was held on December 19, 1983 in the UT Board of Trustees Room and Andy Holt Tower. The Administrative Judge was Dean of Students, Tim Rogers.

The evidence presented was quite interesting. According to the female law graduate, she was taking a multiple-choice law school examination. While doing so she observed Selvage repeatedly look over in the direction of the examination being completed by his classmate. Selvidge denied he was looking at his classmate's answers.

Both Selvidge's test and that of his classmate were presented for comparison. The multiple-choice examination had 50 questions. The tests presented for comparison were identical.

Selvidge called a professor from the UT Department of statistics as an expert witness. The professor noted that Selvidge and his classmate had studied together. Therefore, statistically it was likely they would give the same answers on examination.

On cross-examination I asked the professor to closely examine Selvidge's test, which had been completed in pencil. He did so and agreed that eight of the questions answered by Selvidge bore erasure marks and evidence of an original answer different from the one submitted as final.

In response to further questioning, the professor agreed he could not testify to the statistical probability that Selvidge would mark eight answers then erase and revise those answers to match his classmate's. Especially when some of the corrected answers were correct but others wrong!

An initial order was entered on January 24, 1984 finding Selvidge guilty of cheating and recommending revocation of his law degree and indefinite suspension from the University. That initial order subsequently became a final order and the recommended penalty was implemented. The UT Board of Trustees voted to revoke Selvidge's degree.

Selvidge subsequently filed a petition for review with the Knox County Chancery Court on April 6, 1984. An order of compromise and dismissal was entered on May 22. Barry Selvidge v. The University of Tennessee No. 81827 (Knox Chancery, 1984). However, Selvidge's degree revocation and indefinite suspension from the University remained in effect.

MICHAEL SANDERSON v. UNIVERSITY OF TENNESSEE

In Chapter 25, I made reference to the case of Michael Sanderson in emphasizing the importance of integrity in the University of Tennessee's disciplinary process. It is more important to reach the right decision then to affirm an incorrect decision of one of the University's administrators. Sanderson also served as an excellent example of what the University construed as plagiarism.

In the spring of 1994 Michael Sanderson was a senior undergraduate student at the University of Tennessee, Knoxville. He was enrolled in a class taught by

Professor Robert Glenn. Coincidentally, one of the course textbooks assigned as reading defined "plagiarism" as "using an author's words or ideas without giving credit."

Sanderson submitted what was defined in the course syllabus as a "first draft" of a term paper due April 20, 1994. He received a grade of 84 from Glenn on the draft–one of the three highest grades in the class. Sanderson also entered his paper in the "McClung Research Paper Contest." A faculty member reviewing contest entries felt that Sanderson's material that was not his own and so advised Glenn.

Glenn concluded that much of Sanderson's "draft paper"–and his contest submission Danish was taken from "Persuasion: Theory and Research," a book authored by Daniel O'Keefe. He confronted Sanderson who, at first, suggested the wrong draft copy had been submitted. However, when a computer disk with another version was submitted it remained clear that much of the work was not Sanderson's. Sanderson was issued an "F" in the course and a plagiarism charge letter by Chancellor Bill Snyder.

During the July 19, 1994 APA hearing by Administrative Judge Nick Dunagan, Sanderson argued that he had not intended to commit plagiarism. Sanderson persuaded Dunagan that he had not intentionally omitted citations from his "draft paper" nor had he intentionally represented the material as being his original creation. For that reason Dunagan concluded that Sanderson had not committed the plagiarism and entered an "initial order" in his favor on September 21.

Appealing Dunagan's decision to Chancellor Snyder, I argued that Sanderson had intentionally submitted the material at issue regardless of whether or not he intended to commit the act of plagiarism. Snyder agreed and, on November 21, issued a final order holding Sanderson guilty of plagiarism and imposing a penalty grade of "F" as well as one year suspension from the University.

Sanderson appealed to the Davidson County Chancery Court. On February 23, 1996, the Chancery Court entered an order dismissing Sanderson's petition for review.

Michael Sanderson v. University of Tennessee No. 94-3806-III (Davidson Chancery 1996). Sanderson appealed to the Tennessee Court of Appeals for the Middle Section. He was represented by Knoxville attorney Marilyn Hudson.

On November 19, 1997 an appeals panel consisting of appellate judges Holly Kirby Lillard, Frank Crawford and David Farmer affirmed the Chancery ruling in favor of the University. Michael Sanderson v. University of Tennessee Appeal No. 01A01-9607-CH-00289 (David Chancery 1997).

The Court of Appeals concluded that Chancellor Snyder was not required to defer to any determination of credibility made by the administrative judge and cited another UT case, Patterson v. Hunt, as supporting authority. The appeals court also cited another UT precedent, Gilbert v. University of Tennessee, in concluding there was no constitutional prohibition on the Chancellor substituting his decision for that of the hearing examiner. Id. p. 5.

Lastly, the Court of Appeals made it clear that plagiarism was not dependent on intent to plagiarize. "Chancellor Snyder appropriately utilized the definition of plagiarism given to the class by Professor Glenn, that is, "using an author's word or ideas without giving credit," instead of the definition of plagiarism utilized by the ALJ which required an intent to pass off the works of another as one's own." Id. p.6.

Ignorance of the "University law" was no excuse.

IGNORING TEST "TIME LIMIT" CONSTITUTED CHEATING–PAPACHRISTOU

In the fall of 1997 Mark Papachristou, a first-year student in the UT College of Law, took his first law school exam. The course instructor, Professor Kennedy, wrote "End 4:30" on the board at the front of the classroom. After the exam began, Kennedy departed, but left a proctor in charge.

During the exam, one student experienced a problem with his glasses, made a repair and was provided an additional 15 minutes to finish his exam. No general announcement was made to the class regarding the additional time provided to that student.

At 4:30 p.m., the proctor called, "It's time to quit," or something to that effect. Most students immediately stopped writing and turned in their exams. A few did not. One student, who had turned in her exam, returned to the room and, in a loud voice, asked the proctor if time had been called. "Yes," the Proctor replied, "but some students have not turned in their papers." The complaining student said, "This was not fair," and went back outside the classroom.

At that point, several other students departed, leaving only the student who had been granted extra time and Papachristou. When the other student later asked how much time was left the Proctor replied he had five minutes. Papachristou replied that if his classmate had time remaining he did too.

Even after the Proctor and classmate explained why the additional time was provided the other student, Papachristou, continued to work on his exam. He finally turned it in at 4:45–roughly 15 minutes after time was called by the proctor.

Several students complained to Law school administration and Papachristou was charged with violating the honor code–cheating, by gaining an unfair advantage over other students taking the exam. The disciplinary charge was heard on May 15, 1998 by Dr. Francis Gross, who was appointed hearing officer by

UT Knoxville Chancellor William Snyder. Papachristou was represented by my friend, Knoxville attorney John Eldridge.

Gross issued an initial order on August 11, 1998 finding Papachristou innocent of charges against him. An appeal was filed to the Chancellor who, on September 29, entered a final order, finding Papachristou guilty of the charges against him and assessing the penalty of indefinite suspension from the University. Papachristou appealed that decision to the Chancery Court for Davidson County.

Irvin Kilcrease, Davidson County Chancellor, reversed Chancellor Snyder's order, contending there was insufficient evidence to support his final order. The University appealed the Chancery ruling to the Court of Appeals for the Middle Section of Tennessee. Appellate judges Ben Cantrell, William Koch and Patricia Cottrell were assigned to the case.

John Eldridge and I drove together to Nashville on January 7, 2000 for oral argument before the appellate court. The proceedings went poorly for Papachristou from the outset. My limited time at the podium–20 minutes, as I recall–went quite favorably. Not so much for the opposition. A minute or so after John took the podium his cell phone rang. The phone was back in the courtroom gallery in John's briefcase where he had left it. Judge Cantrell "invited" John to take care of his phone and it took a couple of minutes for him to do so–valuable time he surely would have preferred to spend arguing his appeal.

The questioning from the panel was notably hostile–to Papachristou. Not that the cell phone had anything to do with it.

On February 29, 2000 the Court of Appeals entered a ruling which reversed the Chancery Court and remanded the case to Chancellor Kilcrease for assessment of costs against Papachristou. Papachristou v. University of Tennessee, 29 S. W. 3d 487 (Tenn. App. 2000). The Court of Appeals thoroughly reviewed the evidence supporting the charge against Papachristou, and determined that the Chancery Court had applied the wrong standard of review and reached the wrong conclusion:

> In light of the applicable law and the facts set out in the record, we agree with the appellant. There was substantial and material evidence from which the University Chancellor could find that the appellee violated the honor code.
>
> The testimony in this record is in conflict. Therefore, what really happened in that classroom and what motivated Mr. Papachristou to do what he did requires the fact-finder to assess the credibility of many witnesses. Mr. Papachristou's credibility may have been seriously affected by his denial of ever hearing anyone say that time had been called. It is clear however, that he knew time was a problem, because he said to Mr. Flores, in effect, "If you have more time, so do I."
>
> ***
>
> With substantial and material proof in the record on which the University Chancellor's findings could be based, the action taken must be affirmed.

Id. pp. 490-91.

The court also rejected Papachristou's argument that the University acted arbitrarily by disciplining him but not of other students who had exceeded the time limit of the exam. Id.

Proceeding "pro se", Papachristou filed an application for permission to appeal to the Tennessee Supreme Court. By order of September 5, 2000, the Supreme Court rejected his application.

On April 16, 2001 the U.S. Supreme Court rejected a petition for writ of certiorari filed by Papachristou proceeding "pro se." (U.S. S Ct. No. 00-8461).

FALSIFYING WORK-STUDY TIME SHEETS–
THEFT OF PATIENT RECORDS
ROXANNE KEELE vs. THE UNIVERSITY OF TENNESSEE

Students enrolled in professional and graduate programs at the University of Tennessee are in a number of ways held to a different and higher standard than undergraduate students. Roxanne Keele, who entered the UT Master's program in the Department of Audiology and Speech Pathology in fall 2000, learned that lesson the hard way.

During orientation, a director of the audiology clinic advised students of a rule prohibiting the removal of client files from the building for any reason. Keele violated the rule by bringing client files home at least four times during the fall 2000 semester.

In February 2002 Keele's removal of a client file from the clinic was discovered when a client came to the clinic and the client's file could not be located by clinic staff. Immediately following this incident, the head of the audiology planet, Jack Ferrell, warned Keele she would receive an "F" in "Clinical Practicum" if she ever removed another client file from the clinic.

On March 28, that same semester, Keel again removed a client record from the audiology clinic. Farrell reported the matter to the head of the Department of Audiology and Speech Pathology, Dr. Ilsa Schwarz. Schwarz advised Keele she would receive an "F" in "Clinical Practicum" for the spring semester and be removed from the clinical program.

Keel continued in the Master's program and enrolled again in the clinical practicum for the summer 2002 semester.

In June of the same semester she was accepted into a university Work-Study Program. This program provides opportunities for students in need of financial aid to be paid for various types of jobs needed in all areas of the university. Keele was assigned to the Department A & SP per her request. In this program she would be given work to do for up to 15 or 20 hours a week assisting Audiology Clinic staff.

Even though Keele notified the department secretary and the head of the clinic that she'd been accepted into the Work-Study program, neither had assigned Keele to a supervisor nor given her any work assignment.

For the months of June and July 2002, Keele submitted timesheets falsely representing that she had worked on days when she had not. Keele also placed the initials of clinic staff on the timesheets, falsely representing staff approval.

On October 24, 2002 Keele was charged with three violations of university regulations:

> Violation of Rule 1720–4–3.03 (1) (b) (Furnishing false information to the
> University with the intent to deceive).
> Violation of Rule 1720-4-3.03(1) (f) (Misuse of University records).
> Violation of Rule 1720-4-3.03(1) (i) (Theft, wrongful appropriation or
> unauthorized possession of property of the University or member of the
> University community, i.e., faculty, staff, student or campus visitor).

The University specified the conduct in which Keele had allegedly engaged: removing client records from the clinic in February and March 2002 and submitting Work-Study timesheets in June and July 2002 "making false representations as to work schedule, hours worked, and persons who supervised Ms. Keele's Work Study work. As a result of Ms. Keele's false representations, Ms. Keele wrongfully obtained university funds for Work Study work never assigned or performed."

Keele requested a hearing in accordance with the Tennessee Uniform Administrative Procedures Act. She was represented by Knoxville attorney Robert Ritchie. Administrative Judge Joanie Sompayrac, a faculty member from UT Chattanooga, was assigned to hear the case.

The hearing was conducted in Knoxville on January 28 1029, 2003. Key witnesses included Craig Holtzclaw, UT Office of Admissions and Records-a long time regular at my home for Sunday afternoon volleyball. Holtzclaw was called to testify regarding the accuracy of the timesheets.

On May 23 Sompayrac issued an initial order finding Keele guilty of two of the three charges against her while finding her innocent of "misuse of university records." She assessed the penalty of "indefinite suspension" from the University. Keele appealed to the Chancery Court for Davidson County, filing a "Petition for Judicial Review" in accordance with the Administrative Procedures Act.

As in all APA cases, the appeal was adjudicated solely on the basis of the record below–the transcript of the proceedings and exhibits introduced into evidence–plus briefs presenting the legal arguments of each party.

Ritchie and I presented "oral argument" to the Chancery Court (Helen Hobbs Lyle, Chancellor) on May 20, 2004. On July 12 Chancellor Lyle issued a Memorandum and Order, affirming the University of Tennessee's decision and dismissing the petition for judicial review. Roxanne D. Keele v. The University of Tennessee, No. 03-2813- III (Chancery Court for the State of Tennessee, 20th Judicial District, Davidson County, Part III, 2004).

Chancellor Lyle addressed several issues in ruling for the University. First, Chancellor Lyle rejected Keele's claim that UT violated its own procedures by dismissing Keele from the Spring 2002 Clinical Practicum without affording her any "fundamental rights of the accused" as outlined in the APA. As the court explained, Schwarz's issuance of a "failing grade for the 2002 Spring semester was an academic decision and, consequently, did not invoke the fundamental rights of the accused contained in the rules of the University of Tennessee." Id., p. 6-7. The court recognized that assessment of a failing grade for Keele's admitted removal of a file from campus was a purely academic matter. Id. p.7.

Also rejected by the Chancery Court was Keele's argument that the disciplinary charge based on removal of clinic files constituted "double jeopardy" since she had already been given an academic penalty. The court rejected the notion that "double jeopardy" attaches to university disciplinary proceedings: "As far as this court can determine from the case law, if the proper hypothetical facts were present, there is nothing to prevent a student from receiving an F, being expelled from school through university disciplinary proceedings, being prosecuted in civil court, and being prosecuted in criminal court–all from the same conduct." Id. p.9.

Keele's argument that she did not intentionally remove files from the clinic was rejected as the court noted that "it is clear from the record that the petitioner discovered her possession of the file over the weekend [March 2002], and continued to possess the file until notified by the clinic." Id. p.10.

Chancellor Lyle also quickly disposed of Keele's argument that she worked the number of hours for which he was paid even if the records were inaccurate, as there was substantial and material evidence of her intent to deceive.

While the Hearing Officer did not make a specific finding on whether the evidence indicated any work study was performed by the Petitioner, it was concluded that "there is no evidence that she actually performed work in the clinic." The Petitioner's claim that she "did her own supervised work in the clinic and submitted time records lackadaisically because she did not feel the times of day were important" does not detract from the substantial evidence in the record.

The petitioner's timesheets were written in great detail recording the specific times of the day, down to the half hour, that she worked in the clinic. The petitioner admitted to many inaccuracies and intentional falsifications recorded in the timesheets. It is undisputed that she was paid university funds for the submitted timesheets. The administrative staff's shortcomings in providing the petitioner with a Work-Study supervisor and particular Work-Study assignments pale in comparison to petitioner's unprofessional behavior of supervising her own hours and assignments, and, in turn, submitting intentionally falsified timesheets with no regard for the accuracy of when the claimed work was accomplished. Id. p. 11-12.

Even under the black clouds of the Gilley era, integrity was aggressively pursued by many within the University. Cheating and other forms of academic dishonesty remained a sure road to disaster.

Chapter 29–Diplomacy and Friendship Between Adversaries

Litigation in the United States is an adversarial process. It is not, however, required that adversaries be enemies.

Judicial and administrative proceedings provide a neutral adjudicator for resolving differences of opinion that cannot otherwise be settled by parties of opposing views. An attorney representing a party is not expected or required to treat the opposing party or counsel as an enemy.

My personal practice aimed in the opposite direction. Several University cases make that point.

WITT BUILDING MATERIAL COMPANY

In November 1977 a complaint was filed in Knox County Chancery Court by Witt Building Material Company, Inc. seeking enforcement of a lien. I filed a motion to dismiss on behalf of the University. The motion was argued in court on January 3, 1978 with attorney Al Witt representing the plaintiff and UT being represented by me. The court ruled in favor of the University.

The plaintiff company was owned by Bob Witt, a member of my Sunday school class and a good friend. His brother, Al, was also a long-time friend dating back to the early 1970s. The litigation did not affect our friendship in the slightest. Bob actively supported me in 2008 and 2012 races for public office, both financially and otherwise.

BILL AND DEBBY FOX

Debby Fox and husband Bill attend church with me and have been friends of mine for many years. Bill is Director of the Center for Business and Economic

Research, UT College of Business Administration, and Debby is an outstanding actress who has performed in many plays on campus, sings in our church choir and fills roles in church skits.

In April 2001 Debby and Bill filed a claim with the Tennessee Claims Commission against the state of Tennessee (the University of Tennessee) in the total amount of $110,000 for a "slip and fall" injury suffered during a play rehearsal at UT's Carousel Theatre. During a period of low or no lighting Debbie fell off the stage and suffered a severe leg injury. The Foxes' son, Knoxville attorney Andy Fox, represented his parents in the proceedings.

Both parties conducted extensive depositions and secured expert witnesses in support of their respective positions. Counsel for the parties thoroughly and vigorously cross-examined opposing witnesses, including the parties, during depositions.

An equally vigorous two-day trial was held before Tennessee Claims Commissioner Vance Cheek on May 5-6, 2004. Immediately following the conclusion of the hearing we all shook hands–and Debby and I hugged!

Judgment was subsequently entered in favor of the State on July 10. The plaintiffs appealed to the Tennessee Court of Appeals and, on October 27, 2004, the appellate court affirmed the judgment of the Claims Commission.

The American judicial system worked. As important, the Foxes and Leadbetters remained friends! A couple of years ago (Dec. 18, 2012) Bill kindly accepted my invitation to speak to the members of the West Knoxville Sertoma Club.

KAY HARTMAN

Maybe the best example of care, concern and friendship trumping an adversarial relationship is found in the Hartman case [see chapter 83]. Despite a coma – inducing head injury to her son, Scott, and 16 years of litigation aimed at determining whether the University of Tennessee was at fault, plaintiff Kay Hartman and I became friends.

The Hartmans' claim against the state for compensatory damages was disposed of in the University's favor by the Tennessee Supreme Court on Monday, March 8, 1999) bring our adversarial relationship to an end.

Kay and I met again on October 18, 2001, in Nashville, for her deposition in a companion case involving her ex-husband's insurance company. Each of us agreed to pray for the other.

When I heard of Scott's death on November 17, 2003, Kay was immediately in my prayers. The Bible says to pray for your enemy but it is certainly easier to pray for a friend. I sent Kay a card sharing my condolences. In November 2004 I received a Thanksgiving card from her. Hardly an adversarial relationship!

OPPOSING COUNSEL TOM MILLER

Unsolicited complements from opposing counsel are highly valued. Without them I could never be certain that my own efforts at diplomacy and friendship – while battling on behalf of my client – were meaningful. In October 2007 I received a copy of a letter written by opposing counsel to the president of the University of Tennessee, Dr. John D. Peterson. The contents were humbling but also strong reaffirmation of my approach to dealing with adversaries, including opposing counsel.

Written only days after the conclusion of a high dollar, intensely litigated proceeding before the Tennessee Claims Commission by a senior partner for the prominent Kentucky law firm of Miller, Griffin and Marks, P. S. C., (See chapter 125, Roseanne Barker, M.D. v. State of Tennessee), attorney Tom Miller's October 30,2007 letter overstates my success but accurately states my intent during my 35 years of practice in the UT Office of General Counsel.

Dr. John D Peterson
Office of the President
University of Tennessee
831 Andy Holt Tower
Knoxville, Tennessee 37996

Re: Ron Leadbetter

Dear Dr. Peterson:

My purpose in writing is to complement Ron Leadbetter, your chief legal counsel at the University of Tennessee.

Because the focus of my practice is litigation, I come across many attorneys with whom I am an adversary all over the United States. In the 34 years I have been licensed to practice, my experience with those attorneys has been widely diverse. Particularly, in more recent years, our profession has become increasingly contentious, in a bad way. Therefore, it is somewhat novel to come across an adversary who is both highly competent while maintaining a professional demeanor and a pleasant personality. Ron fits into that category.

Periodically I deal with the attorneys at the University of Kentucky, and, on occasion, I have represented one of its subdivisions. Therefore, I do have a sense of what is involved in representing a university and its employees.

Ron is an excellent attorney who aggressively defends his clients while playing by the rules and shows every reasonable courtesy toward his opposing counsel, the adversarial parties and witnesses. He is also a very hard worker and, as in a case I have with him, is willing to go to great personal sacrifice to travel to difficult-to-reach locations for depositions.

You are lucky to have Ron in your employ.

Sincerely,

Thomas W. Miller

Regardless of any overstatement of my actual deeds, I could not personally have better stated my intended actions.

WILLIAM L. "BILL" WATERS

Even after retirement, adversaries from my days at UT stepped forward in affirmation of the approach I favor. Knoxville attorney William L. Waters is a "dyed in the wool" Democrat and political opponent dating back to our days in student government at the University. Bill is also a dear long-time friend. He provided financial and other support for my campaigns for the Tennessee State House (2008) and Senate (2010).

BILLY STOKES

Attorney Billy Stokes, a leader in the Republican Party in Knox County and Tennessee, and opposing counsel in the hotly contested Mirabella case, (See Chapter 94) was a major contributor and leader of fundraising efforts on my behalf in the 2010 Senate race.

THE MYSTERY VOTER

Perhaps my favorite story about the benefits of diplomacy is that of a voter in my 2010 Senate race.

One day during early voting several campaign workers and I were conversing in a campaign tent pitched near Knoxville's Downtown West polling station when a the young man on his way to vote stopped by and asked, "You don't re-member me do you?" "No, I'm sorry, but I don't" I replied.

"I'm going inside to vote for you." He proceeded to the polling station and went inside. I was puzzled, as were others standing by.

A few minutes later the young man exited the polling place and again walked past the campaign tent. "I voted for you." "Thanks. I really appreciate it," I replied. "Please tell me where I know you from," I continued. He responded, "You were the University's attorney in an administrative hearing a couple of years ago when I was dismissed from the University. But you were fair in the way you treated me."

It then came back to me. The voter was a former student at the University of Tennessee, Knoxville who had received a formal hearing of disciplinary charges against him which resulted in his dismissal from the University. My case note summarized the matter:

"Ex-boyfriend breaks (cinderblock through glass of fire escape door) and en-ters the victim's apartment while she's gone. When she returns and asks him to leave he refuses; keeps her from leaving, masturbates in her presence; and, when she gets in bed hoping he'll leave, she wakes up to find him in bed, screams and runs to friend's house for help." The student was intoxicated at the time of the event. His ex-girlfriend filed no criminal charges.

The student's conduct warranted his dismissal from the University. Still, when I met him during disciplinary proceedings I sensed he was truly repentant for what he had done. He came across as a truly nice young man who had really messed up due to his abuse of alcohol.

I spoke directly to the young man and explained that his actions warranted his indefinite suspension from the University. However, I shared with him my belief that he could get his life in order and I hoped that he would. If he did so he might apply for readmission to the University in the future. I wished him well.

As the young man left the campaign tent I thanked him for his vote and again wished him well. I never doubted the University acted appropriately in dismissing him from the University. But, our brief conversation also confirmed I had not misread his "hidden character traits" and had not erred in offering encouragement to a young man whose actions warranted firm disciplinary action.

Pursuit of diplomacy and friendship while University counsel was a strategy that proved productive for me in more ways than one. More important, I considered it a moral imperative.

Rafting the Gauley: Tom Cronan (front/raised paddle), Ron Leadbetter (front/2nd on right), Steve Roads (1st on right). (September 1990) Others in photo were guides for the trip.

Chapter 30–Three Steps to Success:
Train, Advise and Litigate (not Capitulate)

TRAIN

Training is a commonly accepted key to success in any workplace setting. Time and effort spent on training is dependent on such factors as needs and benefits. Some needs and benefits are obvious and implemented. Some are not –and overlooked or disregarded.

Training in "the law" at institutions of higher education is sometimes relegated to the second category. Wisely administered colleges and universities assign it to the first.

As noted in other chapter, seminars, retreats and other training activities– those addressing legal issues affecting higher education–were conducted extensively during the "Big Orange" era. Legal training was provided to University personnel ranging from unit supervisors to chancellors and the president. Trustees were included.

Training is a necessity, not a way to justify sending folks out of town for a couple of fun days at a state park. Done properly, training is interesting and even entertaining–but comparable to good health care practices. Greatly decreases the possibility of debilitating injury–monetary and otherwise.

Given the consequences of inadequate training in the law, such activity should be mandatory rather than optional. During the bulk of my career UT's administration concurred.

The following is an example of one UT Chancellor seeing to it that appropriate officials of his campus were satisfactorily trained in key areas of state and federal law:

Office of the Chancellor
February 6, 1989

To: Provost, the Vice Provosts; Vice Chancellors, Associate and Assistant Vice Chancellors and Directors; Deans; Executive, Associate and Assistant Deans; and Department Chairmen

From: James C Hunt, M.D.

Subject: Affirmative Action Workshops–Sexual harassment

Comments:

1. The notice sent to you from Robert E. Taylor, Jr., Ph.D., Affirmative Action Officer and Ronald Leadbetter, J.D., Associate General Counsel, announces that affirmative action workshops dealing with sex discrimination and sexual harassment will be held Wednesday, February 22, 1989, 1:00–3:00 p.m. and Thursday, February 23, 1989, 9:00–11:00 a.m., A137 South Auditorium Coleman.

2. It is important that all University staff members responsible for personnel actions attend one of these sessions. You are requested to assure attendance by appropriate personnel in your area of responsibility.

3. It is the policy of the University of Tennessee, Memphis to comply fully with all federal civil rights statutes and not to discriminate in any manner against employees or applicants for employment. To assure compliance with all provisions of civil rights and non-discriminatory regulations, it is important that all staff are made aware of their responsibility in this area.

Chancellor Hunt made it clear that attendance by his administrative staff at the scheduled civil rights seminar was not optional. Directives such as Hunt's bore fruit.

Being an area of heavy litigation, seminars on the topic of "civil rights" were scheduled frequently and heavily attended. The University's success in defending civil rights claims resulted largely from University supervisory personnel being trained in applicable law (and, of course, putting that training into practice).

READY ACCESS TO LEGAL ADVICE

A solid training program on topics of legal consequence is vitally important. But, training alone is not sufficient. Issues arise which even the best training program cannot address.

And, the law changes. New legislation is enacted and courts issue rulings effecting change. If ready access to legal counsel is not provided it is more likely action will be taken based on gut instinct—what seems reasonable? A potentially costly course of action.

For the first three decades of my UT service I had an "open door" policy with full support of my superiors (the President and the General Counsel). I urged anyone needing legal advice not to hesitate to call me or drop by my office.

Advance appointment was unnecessary (advisable only for convenience of the "client"). An ongoing meeting or my absence from the office were the sole limitations. It was not necessary to go through the General Counsel prior to coming to me.

This simple, one step process assured accessibility for those needing legal assistance. Accessibility increases the likelihood that someone needing assistance will actually seek it.

An inquiry would often begin, "I'm sorry to bother you with a foolish question but …" or words to that effect. My typical response was, "The only foolish question is the one that should have been asked and wasn't."

More than once I had an opportunity to conclude a conversation with "I'm certainly glad you asked your foolish question. We may have avoided a lawsuit as a result." One memorable example stands out.

Back in the 1980s or 90s—I am uncertain of the date but it does not matter for purposes of this example—I learned from a friend in the UT Knoxville bursar's office that a co-worker in the office had been summarily fired for stealing cash from a drawer near her desk. No questions asked. I was told the co-worker's name. She was a friend of mine and I believed her to be a person of integrity.

I called the Bursar, Syl Baldridge, and asked if anyone had actually seen the fired employee take the money. Baldridge replied that no one had but she was the only one with access. I advised that he contact her and ask if she would take a polygraph test. He agreed to do so.

A short time later I received word from Baldridge that the employee had consented to take a polygraph test. I then advised that he ask everyone in the office to do the same.

Five or six young ladies from the Bursars's office arrived in my office the same day, expressing concern with Baldrige's request that they take the test. I explained that the polygraph was a helpful investigative tool and only the person guilty of theft need be concerned. The ladies were satisfied and returned to their office.

The next day I learned that another worker in the office had come forward and confessed to the theft. The innocent "initial suspect" was promptly reinstated and compensated for lost time.

The advisory role of legal counsel served well in this instance and did more than head off a potential lawsuit. The reputation and job of a loyal employee was restored and a thief was removed from the Bursar's office.

UNSOLICITED LEGAL ADVICE

A particularly valuable aspect of my "in-house" position was my ability to offer unsolicited advice based on what I saw or heard in the workplace. Issuing legal updates to the general workforce of a college or university is fine but ability to offer advice regarding developing issues overheard, observed or otherwise brought to the attention of in-house counsel can head off legal problems before they ferment.

Consider the graduate student from Nepal, whose family I had visited in Kathmandu a year or two earlier. The student called me to report that his wife, a UT Institute of Agriculture employee, was pregnant and had so advised her departmental supervisor. The supervisor notified my friend's wife that she would have to resign since he could not have a pregnant employee in his laboratory.

I telephoned the supervisor, discussed the graduate student's claim and confirmed that the employee was asked to resign. The supervisor believed the employee's pregnancy would interfere with his research project,

I summarized the provisions of federal law prohibiting discrimination on the basis of pregnancy. Still the supervisor persisted in insisting that a pregnant employee could not work in his lab.

Then, I advised the supervisor that if he proceeded with his plan I would not be representing him in any legal proceedings. He would be in violation of University policy as well as the law. Any award of damages would come from his pocket. Wisely, the faculty member reconsidered and made no further attempt to compel his lab assistant's resignation.

In this instance a University official had not requested my legal advice but I had offered it to him based on information received from others. The University and the official clearly benefitted from this approach.

CONTESSA and the PYTHON

Some years ago a dancer at a local "strip joint," by the name of "Contessa," was known for using a python in her strip routine. The snake got sick and Contessa brought it to the UT College of Veterinary Medicine for treatment. During treatment the python was kept in a cage at the vet school.

At some point the python escaped from its cage. It could not be located despite diligent search. Contessa was notified and was reportedly quite gracious in her initial response. At least until a couple of weeks later when the vet school sent Contessa a bill for the snake's "room and board." Contessa threatened suit.

I heard about the incident and called the Vet School with a bit of unsolicited advice: "Tear up the bill." The College of Veterinary Medicine wrote off the bill and so notified Contessa.

Days later the python was discovered in the ceiling of the facility where it had been treated, having discovered a way to push its way up through a ceiling tile into the space above. Contessa was contacted and she retrieved her snake. The threat of litigation ended after the python returned to its owner in good health with no bill for services.

CHANGE COURSE WHEN WRONG

The incident with Contessa is but one example of litigation avoidance. Revocation of a flawed hire on the Memphis campus offers another.

I learned that UT Memphis Chancellor Jim Hunt had announced his offer of an administrative position to someone he knew outside the University. The offer was made without going through mandatory University hiring procedures set out in the campus personnel policy and procedures manual.

I contacted the Chancellor, noted the deviation from campus rules and the possibility that someone in a "protected category," such as race or gender, would claim discrimination. The Chancellor immediately understood the problem and suspended the job offer. UT hiring procedures were then followed and even the possibility of litigation was avoided.

The University's legal history is one generally to be proud of, particularly in the "Big Orange" years. In my opinion, that success was tied to legal training provided University personnel, the dedication of UT employees to complying with federal and state laws and regulations, and their willingness to seek and utilize legal advice from the UT Office of General Counsel.

My practice, which received strong support from the University administration–at least prior to the presidency of Wade Gilley–was to do everything ethically and reasonably possible to head off litigation. Compromise, explanation, rule revisions, corrective measures, adherence to legal or administrative guidelines were among categories of measures looked to for the purpose of avoiding litigation.

LITIGATION AS LAST RESORT

There are circumstances under which even reasonable parties to a dispute are unable to compromise their differences. That held true in many cases I handled for the University. When deadlock occurred, my practice–supported strongly by my superiors during the years of the "Big Orange"–was to aggressively defend the University's position (or prosecute those cases in which UT was the plaintiff).

Only rarely did I pursue a monetary settlement once a lawsuit was filed. Once the litigation stage was reached my approach was "litigate, not capitulate!" That approach benefitted the University in many ways as seen in case after case described in the pages of this book.

Still, there were occasions when a lawsuit warranted immediate settlement efforts and I never hesitated to seek settlement when my client was in the wrong. **Case in point:**

In 1999 UT Vice President Eli Fly was involved in an auto accident while operating a UT vehicle on UT business. The accident was admittedly his fault.

Kathleen Wood, the owner and operator of the vehicle struck by Fly's filed with the Tennessee Claims Commission a claim for $65,000.

Liability of the University was quickly conceded. Each party made reasonable concession on the issue of damages. Both parties avoided the cost of unnecessary litigation. The suit was promptly settled for $30,000 and the case dismissed by the plaintiff.

In 1995 a woman attending a baseball game at UT Knoxville's Lindsey Nelson Stadium stepped in a space between a concrete aisle and a bleacher seat and suffered severe leg injuries. Knoxville attorney Jim Owen filed a claim on behalf of the woman and her husband with the Tennessee Claims Commission seeking a half million dollars in damages. [Kay and Lloyd Burnette v. State of Tennessee]

The claim was excessive dollar-wise but the Commission could reasonably have found a dangerous condition on University property with resulting injury to the plaintiff. The $5,000 settlement agreed to by the claimant was more than satisfactory to the University.

Settlement was sometimes preferable even when I felt certain of the merits of the University's position.

Milton Robinson Jr., an employee at the Wm. F. Bowld hospital in Memphis (operated by UT Memphis) filed a civil rights action in the U.S. District Court in Memphis in December 1985. The suit alleged that Robinson had been denied promotion to the position of transportation foreman the basis of his race (black). The relief sought included backpay, front pay, compensatory damages and attorney's fees. I felt strongly the plaintiff had not been subjected to discriminatory treatment and we proceeded to trial.

Robinson prevailed at trial. He secured judgment in the amount $27,645 including $11,390 attorney's fees was awarded on May 29, 1987. I filed a notice of appeal to the U.S. Court of Appeals for the Sixth Circuit on June 16.

On February 18, 1988 the parties received notice setting oral argument before the Sixth Circuit on March 29. I presented Robinson's counsel an offer of settlement provided the offer was accepted before Oral argument.

Four days before the date set for oral argument, the parties settled. The University of Tennessee paid Robinson a total of $13,822.82–one half the amount of the judgment awarded by the court. And, the plaintiff received no promotion!

By virtue of the parties' settlement, the Court of Appeals remanded the case to the District Court, which entered an "Agreed Order Vacating the Judgment and Order of Dismissal."

Settlement in this case cut the monetary loss in half and removed a stain, i.e. a federal court finding of race discrimination, from the University's record. A good result, all things considered.

Cases such as those cited above arguably qualify as good settlements, not capitulation. Litigation should be a last resort—but utilized without hesitation when reasonable alternatives are not available. But mere fear of losing is a poor excuse for settling a claim or lawsuit. Any case can be lost. But, a lot of money and institutional reputation can be saved by rejecting "settlement" as the preferred course of action in addressing lawsuits and claims without regard to the merit of the claim–or lack thereof!

On a number of occasions it was possible to win a case without even going to try by filing and prevailing on a "motion to dismiss". In such cases the court would find the University defendant entitled to judgment as a matter of law based solely on matters alleged in the complaint.

In many other cases "matters outside the pleadings," such as affidavits and depositions, were presented by "motion for summary judgment" and led to judgment without the necessity of the trial based on a court finding that undisputed material facts in the case required judgment as a matter of law.

In those cases where the court concluded that material facts were in dispute –that there was evidence to support the plaintiff's case and also evidence to support the defendant's–the case would proceed to trial (unless, of course, the parties elected to settle).

As General Counsel Beach Brogan stated at a staff meeting on April 17, 1996 (after mildly criticizing one of the OGC attorneys for always settling and never trying a case): "You make better all-around lawyers if you do trial work." I was in complete agreement.

Chapter 31–Bad Settlements–Madame Baracuda, Peyton Manning's "Moon Victim" and a "Would Be" Killer

Legal settlements sometimes waste money needlessly, send the wrong message or create more problems than they solve. I classify these as bad settlements. UT has had a few that qualify as disastrous.

"MADAME BARACUDA"–Diane Crocker

Dr. Diane Crocker and I met in March, 1978. She was Chairman of the Department of Pathology at the University of Tennessee Center for the Health Sciences. One of the department employees under Crocker's supervision, Mr. Ellis, was in the process of having his employment terminated by her.

In my entire history as legal counsel for the University, I rarely felt discomfort with action being taken by one of my advisees. The meeting with Dr. Crocker posed an exception. My assessment was that she was legally correct but morally destitute. Crocker fired Ellis. I had done my job, providing legal advice rather than personal opinion. Still, I felt a high level of discomfort with the treatment afforded a University employee.

Crocker's problems with employees in the department of pathology mounted.

Both faculty and staff complained of the abusive treatment received from her. The complaints increased in frequency and intensity. Crocker was widely referred to by those in her department as "Madame Barracuda."

In response to complaints received UTCHS Chancellor James C Hunt acted in early 1980 to terminate Crocker's employment, both as Chairman of the Department and as a faculty member. Crocker retained the services of Irvin Salky, a prominent Memphis attorney.

Federal civil rights claims were filed by Crocker with the U.S. District Court in Memphis and the Equal Employment Opportunity Commission on March 5, 1980 and March 6, 1980, respectively. A charge of sex discrimination and procedural deficiencies leading to Crocker's termination was argued in federal court. She was afforded preliminary injunctive relief by the court.

According to the Court's order, the University was required to afford Crocker an administrative hearing of the charge of misconduct which led to her dismissal. No problem—the witnesses in support of the charge were legion.

On March 13, 1980, the Chancellor and I spoke to a standing-room-only audience in a campus auditorium. The room was packed with faculty and staff, many of whom voiced their opposition to Crocker's continued employment at the University. I subsequently met with many witnesses willing to testify to Crocker's inappropriate actions toward co-workers of all ranks.

Crocker's counsel made an offer of settlement. If Crocker could retain her faculty position she would not contest the removal of her department chairmanship and would withdraw her federal civil rights claims. The University would only be required to agree, in exchange, and that she would be treated the same as any other faculty member.

I favored rejecting the offered settlement agreement in light of Crocker's well-documented mistreatment of others. To me, her conduct warranted dismissal, not the equivalent of demotion.

In this case Beach and I disagreed. He felt strongly that settlement would resolve the problems tearing at the department of pathology. We would avoid any risk of a courtroom defeat. A consent judgment, implementing the parties' settlement agreement, was entered by the U.S. District Court on May 23, 1980.

Regrettably, the settlement agreement did not resolve the conflict between Crocker and her co-workers. Complaints of abusive behavior continued to flow from secretaries, lab assistants and faculty.

Recognizing the persistence of the problem, a decision was made to offer Crocker a fully paid two-year sabbatical if she would resign. A letter of proposal was drafted by Brogan, signed by Chancellor Hunt and mailed to Crocker.

Crocker declined the offer. Dissension and complaints continued within the department. Efforts were made by the Chancellor to discipline Crocker without success.

In early 1984 Crocker, with new counsel, Don Donati, filed suit in federal court claiming discrimination on the basis of sex under title VII of the Civil Rights Act of 1964, violation of Crocker's First Amendment and other constitutional rights.

A second federal action presented a claim that defendants were guilty of contempt–violation of the Federal Court's 1980 "consent judgment." Numerous depositions, hundreds of pages of motions, briefs and rulings were capped by nine days of trial in the two proceedings.

The litigation lasted from 1984 through entry of judgment on February 28, 1990. On a bright note, Crocker left UTCHS for other employment in 1985, as the proceedings were getting underway.

On February 28, 1990, U.S. District Judge Julia Gibbons entered judgment in favor of Chancellor Hunt and other University defendants on all discrimination, retaliation and constitutional claims. (U.S. Dist. Ct., W.D. Tenn. No. 80-2096). Great result!

Unfortunately, on the same day, Gibbons issued a ruling holding defendants in contempt of court. She found the defendants had treated Crocker "different" from other faculty in violation of the court's 1980 Consent Judgment. A judgment totaling $237,000, including compensatory damages, attorney's fees and costs, was assessed against the defendants. Horrible result!

To add insult to injury, Judge Gibbons opined that Chancellor Hunt had lied at trial by testifying that he had not offered Crocker a two-year paid sabbatical if she would resign. In final argument, I explained that Hunt had simply forgotten the letter offering settlement (for Pete's sake, the UT General Counsel had written the letter for him!) but Gibbons dismissed my explanation.

As a final jab, the State committee charged with determining whether judgments against state employees should be paid by the State, came within one vote (2-1 vote) of deciding that defendants would be personally responsible for paying the judgment obtained by Crocker. Fortunately that did not happen.

Bottom line: the 1980 settlement of Crocker's claims yielded disastrous results. An administrative hearing of the disciplinary charges levied against Crocker would – in my opinion, based on the University's record of success in such proceedings and the wealth of evidence against Crocker– have avoided the monetary loss, the workplace dissension, character assassination and other costs to the University described above. [See: The Commercial Appeal, October 29, 1989, p. 1]

PEYTON MANNING MOONS JAMIE WHITED

Even more disastrous dollar wise than the Crocker settlement was the University settlement of a number of sexual harassment claims asserted by Dr.

Jamie Whited, appointed in 1989 as the first female trainer in the UT men's athletics department.

Underlying the controversy which led to the infamous settlement were a number of claimed incidents of sexual harassment occurring in the athletics department. My own assessment was that each of those claims was either unsubstantiated or of a joking nature– and there was solid evidence that Whited herself participated in jokes and comments of a sexual nature and did little to show disapproval of such conduct.

The event that led directly to mediation–and what I considered an absurd settlement–was an incident not in anyway attributed to a UT employee. The incident involved UT quarterback Peyton Manning.

Whited claimed that in February, 1996, while she was busy about her duties in the UT men's locker room, Manning dropped his pants and "mooned' her. There has been considerable debate over the years as to what actually took place. Manning and Whited tell different versions of what occurred. [See: Knoxville News Sentinel October 26, 2003, p. D6: November 5, 2003, p. 3C]

Beach Brogan and I discussed a proposal to submit the claims for mediation, a proposal initiated, as I recall, by counsel for Whited, Marilyn Hudson and Jim Andrews. I expressed my opinion that Whited's claims were invalid and should be litigated. Beach insisted the matter was a good one for mediation. Attorney Jim London, an excellent mediator, was secured by agreement of the parties.

The first mediation session was held on July 24, 1997. In attendance were attorneys Andrews and Hudson, Brogan and myself, mediator London, Jamie Whited and her husband. The Whiteds were the last to arrive at the meeting and Jamie's entrance emphasized in my own mind some of the frailties of her case.

One of Whited's grievances was that one or more employees in athletics had referred to her as "Bumpers," referring to the size of her breasts. When Whited walked into the mediation conference room, you may be certain that both Brogan and I checked to see what might have led to the nickname.

Brogan said it best, speaking to a female attorney in our office the next day, "Gosh, she's not as big as you" or words to that effect. My co-counsel indicated she was surprised but not offended by Brogan relating his observation. In any event, I likewise saw no basis for the claimed nickname.

A second mediation session was held on July 30 and a third on August 13,1997. Prior to the last session, Brogan stated his belief that a proposed settlement was a good one. I offered my opinion it was not and would prove embarrassing to the University. Beach's response: "There will be an article in Thursday's paper and that will be the end of it." I requested that my signature be omitted from the agreement and my request was granted.

The University paid Whited $300,000 in full settlement of all claims against the University. Contents of the agreement were made confidential (but word got out that Whited resigned her position at the University effective June 30, 1998).

I don't recall what if anything was reported in Thursday's newspaper. I first read about the settlement in the sports section of the Nashville Tennessean on August 16,1997. The very next day, sports commentator Jerry Thompson offered an opinion column titled "Manning 'moon' case just absurd", and called the settlement evidence that "there is no end to the absurd and outrageous." Then another article commenting on the settlement appeared in the Tennessean on the 18th.

On Tuesday, August 19, 1997 the front page of the Knoxville News Sentinel headlined, "33 claims cited by UT trainer". It announced the $300,000 settlement payment as full satisfaction of Whited's grievances, then provided a thorough description of the 33 points of her complaint.

Another front-page headline article, "UT trainer's tapes confidential" appeared in the next day's Knoxville News Sentinel [August 20, 1997, p. 1]. Still another appeared in the Sentinel on August 21, and another front-page Sentinel article on August 24 ("it wasn't for the money").

The University's settlement with Whited may have been the worst ever for several reasons. First, the $300,000 payment far exceeded any judgment ever paid in any civil rights case I ever handled. Second, the vast majority of civil rights cases I handled (almost 95%) resulted in judgment for the University. There was no reason to believe we would have lost this one.

Whited's most ballyhooed claim related to the actions of Peyton Manning. But, Manning was a student, not an employee. Absent evidence the University directed his actions, it would have had no legal responsibility for anything he did.

Oh yes, one more reason: the bad publicity did not appear only in "Thursday's paper" following settlement. It went on and on and on.

FELIPE HERNANDEZ–AN ASSAILANT REAPS REWARD

Felipe Hernandez was a UT Knoxville Physical Plant employee in 1996. He was assigned a UT truck to carry out work assignments with the plumbing department. Work rules prohibited use of University of vehicles for personal business and vehicles were not to be driven outside the immediate work area.

In late February, 1996, Hernandez's supervisors received a report that he had driven his assigned University vehicle out of the work area, attempted to strike his wife with the truck, then threatened to kill her.

On February 28, 1996, Hernandez was issued a letter charging him with gross misconduct and his right to a hearing of the charges against him. He elected to receive a formal hearing in accordance with the Tennessee Uniform Administrative Procedures Act. Malcolm McInnis, a UT administrative judge, was assigned to hear the charges against Hernandez.

The hearing was held on April 22, 1996. Hernandez was represented by attorney Wilfred Nwauwa.

I prosecuted the administrative charges against Fernandez, joined by UT Assistant General Counsel Rhonda Alexander. The basis for the administrative charges were set forth in the testimony of Hernandez's wife, as well as her sister.

(Testimony of Mona Hernandez)

Q. Okay. And did an incident occur on February 27, 1996 at approximately 3:05 p.m. involving your husband, Mr. Hernandez?

A. Yes, it did

Q. Would you tell the court what happened on that occasion?

A. Okay. At 2:00 I went on my break. So, we had to be back at three, so we was running late.

Q. You work at Ramsey's cafeteria?

A. Yes.... So, we started walking down the alley which is – – the apartment building is the fifth apartment building from my work in the short alley at the garage. I started walking down there, and my sister said, wait a minute, I left my time card, and she started walking back. And all of a sudden, I was trying to listen to her and I just heard a roaring sound. I looked over my shoulder and that truck was already – – it just flew up there. And the front wheel came up on the sidewalk and Felipe jumps out of the truck like he's going to hit me, and he said, "I told you, bitch, if I ever catch you out, I'm going to kill you." He said, "You remember what I said."

The sister of Mona Hernandez offered similar testimony.

A. We was going back to work and I had forgot my time card. And I went halfway back up towards the house to holler at my boyfriend to go get my time card for me. We were standing there waiting for him to go get my time card, this gentleman here came up the street pretty fast, and I was like, God, you know. And the next thing I knew, he came up on the sidewalk and I thought he had hit my sister. I stood there in shock for a little bit. I thought, oh, God, but, I mean, I started screaming at him. He got out of the truck and went towards my sister and I went down towards where he was at, and he got back in the truck and left.

Q. Okay. Then after he screamed at your sister, did you hear what he yelled at her?

A. it sounded like to me, I told you if I called you up here I'll kill you. Now, I can't guarantee that's what he said, but I know he said something and he was real hateful to her. And in my opinion he had no business doing what he done.

There was also testimony that Fernandez was operating the UT truck away from his assigned work area at the time of the incident.

Administrative Judge McInnis issued an "initial order" on June 27, 1996 finding Hernandez guilty of three of four charges against him:

1. Disorderly conduct, including using threatening language and attempting bodily harm to another individual on University property and/or while driving a university vehicle.
2. Unauthorized use of a university vehicle.
3. Behavior unacceptable to the University and the community at large.

Hernandez was found "guilty of disorderly conduct by threatening his wife with physical harm with a University of Tennessee motor vehicle and verbal threats to kill her, unauthorized use of [University] motor vehicle... [and] diversion of a university vehicle for personal use in order to engage in threatening conduct to his wife as part of an ongoing domestic dispute...." McInnis then ordered that plaintiff's employment with the University be terminated. Hernandez had a right under state law to appeal the initial order but never exercised that right.

In November, 1994, prior to the incident which led to his dismissal, Hernandez filed with the Tennessee Human Rights Commission a charge that he had been discriminated against and harassed on the basis of his race and national origin (Cuban), and that UT had failed to accommodate his religion. These claims ended up in federal court (U.S. District Ct. No. 3:98-CV-398, E.D.,Tenn) in a claim filed on June 26, 1998–two years after Hernandez was found guilty of the charges of serious misconduct warranting termination of his University employment.

On March 10, 1999 the District Court dismissed all individual defendants from lawsuit. Depositions of prospective witnesses were completed and it was my assessment that there was little evidence to support Hernandez's claims.

In late January 2000, just two weeks before the scheduled trial, a meeting was called by newly appointed UT General Counsel Catherine Mizell. "The case would be settled," she announced.

For what reason? According to my meeting notes Mizell felt "Hernandez should be settled because it might look bad for the University for it to come out in public that the "N" word was used and that the "rectoseal" prank was going on in the workplace."

The decision was made. Final settlement was agreed upon by the parties the afternoon of February 10, 2000. The settlement agreement was executed the following day. An "agreed order of dismissal" was filed with the court on February 16. The University later issued a check in the amount of $100,000 payable jointly to Hernandez and his attorney, Mark Brown.

The price of settlement was steep. In my opinion there was little likelihood of losing the case and, even if we had, the likelihood of a $100,000 judgment - or anything approaching that figure–in favor of a man who tried to hit or kill his wife with a UT truck–was miniscule. As concluded in my final case note:

But… we'll never know! It's "only" money! $100,000 for the benefit of hiding one worker's use of one or more racial epithets in jest and participating in work room antics. A high price for the University!

Absurd! A disastrous settlement in my humble opinion.

Chapter 32–Author's Resume–A Game Plan Summary

In 1999 Beach Brogan announced his intent to retire from the position of General Counsel. It was not a happy occasion for me. I thoroughly enjoyed the two and half decades I served the University under Brogan's superb leadership.

We did not always agree, as evident in several chapters of this book. However, our disagreements were on a professional level. The vast majority of the time I could not have improved on any aspect of Brogan's leadership - certainly not as it applied to me.

The pending vacancy in the position of General Counsel of the University of Tennessee was advertised and I applied for the position in Fall 2000, I submitted my resume and, following a national search, was judged one of two top candidates for the position. Discussion of the search process is left for a later chapter. For now, the focus is on the resume.

My resume was widely available for public inspection, subject to critical review by University trustees and officials and open to question or challenge by them and anyone else. No questions or challenges were posed. Nor were any of concern to me. As noted in the Preface, I am a voracious record keeper and each and every point in my resume is fully documented by records I maintain.

The resume provides a summary of litigation and other activities I handled from 1972-1998. Details appear in other chapters. A review of the resume quickly reveals my overall game plan for handling legal issues affecting the University, the areas of law in which I specialized, and the parameters within which I operated.

Most important, the resume succinctly reflects the extent to which the game plan worked.

RESUME
(2000)
RONALD C. LEADBETTER
719 Andy Holt Tower Knoxville, TN 37996-0170
(423) 974-3247 (Office) (423) 690-0445 (Home) RLEADBET@UTK.EDU

Employment Experience: The University of Tennessee,
Office of General Counsel
•1972-1978, Staff Attorney
•1978-1981, Assistant General Counsel
•1981-Present, Associate General Counsel

Achievements: LITIGATION OF UT CASES
 • Extensive litigation experience in civil rights, Constitutional law, tort, and
medical malpractice. Additional litigation experience in contracts, bank-
ruptcy, unemployment compensation, prosecution of federal embezzlement,
and other areas
 • Litigated cases in every federal district court in Tennessee (Western
District,   Memphis   and   Jackson;   Middle   District, Nashville and
Cookeville; Eastern District, Knoxville, Greeneville, and Chattanooga)
 • Handled litigation in United States Bankruptcy Courts (Western and East-
ern Districts of Tennessee)
 • Argued more than 20 cases before the United States Court of
Appeals for the Sixth Circuit
 • Tried numerous cases in the Sessions, Chancery, and Circuit Courts for
Shelby, Davidson, Knox, Hamilton, and other counties of Tennessee
 • Argued appeals before the Tennessee Court of Appeals
(Western, Middle, and Eastern Sections)
 • Handled petitions for certiorari to the United States Supreme Court and
applications for appeal before the Tennessee Supreme Court
 • Served as University lead counsel in 29 published (reported)
federal- and state cases
 • Handled numerous administrative proceedings before the United
 States Equal Employment Opportunity Commission, Department
 of Education (Office for Civil Rights), United States Department
 of Labor (Wage and Hour Division and Office of Federal Contract
 Compliance Programs)
 • Handled proceedings before the Tennessee Department of Employ
  ment Security and Tennessee Commission for Human Rights
 • Represented UT in compliance proceedings before the National
  Collegiate Athletic Association

- Handled numerous claims before the Tennessee Claims Commission (Western, Middle, and Eastern Sections)
- Handled more than 70 hearings before Administrative Judges under the Tennessee Administrative Procedures Act
- Handled numerous informal UT disciplinary proceedings before student and faculty hearing panels (staff and student hearing panelists)
- Handled more than 500 cases litigated in Tennessee and Federal courts of record and before State and Federal administrative agencies

Overall success rate:

-Judgments, verdicts and other findings completely favorable to UT: 94%
-Settlements: fewer than 3%
-Judgments unfavorable to UT (including cases in which UT prevailed on major issues): fewer than 3% ($1,600,000 paid pursuant to adverse judgments in 15 cases from 1972 to the present)

TRANSACTIONAL EXPERIENCE:
- Directed UT's compliance with all aspects of the Tennessee Uniform Administrative ProceduresAct (1983 to present)
- Conducted or directed all aspects of the promulgation of UT Rules under the rulemaking provisions of the APA (including preparation and presentation of rules to the Board of Trustees and presentation and defense of rules before the Joint Government Operations Committee of the State legislature)
- Authored UT proceduresfor conducting contested cases in accordance with the APA
- Trained UT AdministratiVe Judges handling APA contested cases
- Directed successful negotiations with federal civil rights agencies conductingon-site reviews at UTK, UT Memphis, UTSI, and the Institute of Agriculture

SUPERVISORY EXPERIENCE:
- Supervised UT Memphis branch office of General Counsel's Office, including secretaryand professional staff assigned to the office (1974-1993)
- Supervised main office secretary, paralegals, & attorneys assisting in litigation

INSTRUCTIONAL ACHIEVEMENTS:

- Trained all UT Administrative Law Judges and Hearing Officers for hearings under Tenn. Admin. Procedures Act
- Conducted numerous training seminars for UT officials, staff, and student leaders on subjects such as:
  - *Employment Law
  - *Family Educational Rights and Privacy Act
  - *Federal Copyright Law
  - *Debt Collection
  - *Conduct of University Disciplinary Hearings
  - *Affirmative ActionlEqual Employment Opportunity
  - *Insurance/Claims Commission Coverage for UT Employees
  - *UT Board Policies
  - *Residency Classification
  - *Medical Records Administration
  - *Affirmative Action and Equal Employment Opportunity
  - *Sexual Harassment
- Guest lecturer to numerous classes on Knoxville/Memphis campuses
- Made formal presentations to professional organizations such as: National Association of College and University Attorneys, Southern Association for College Student Affairs, National·Association of Educational Buyers, Health Financial Management Association, Tennessee Association of College Registration and Admissions Officers, Southern College Personnel Association, and Southern Conference of Deans of Faculties and Academic Vice Presidents
- Participated in Annual Orientation for UT Student Leaders

OTHER ACHIEVEMENTS:

- Proposed and directed the establishment of (and initially managed) UT's trademark licensing program (current annual revenue: approx. $4 million)
- Authored UT drug testing program for student athletes
- Drafted Tennessee Sports Agents legislation, Tenn. Code Ann. §§ 49-7-2101, et seq.
- Served on UT/Bd. of Regents Committee which developed the Uniform rules for classifying students for tuition and admission purposes (1973-1974). Successfully defended rules in Court (Hooban v. Boling, 503 F2d 648 (1974) cert. denied 421 U.S. 920 (1975)
- Served as primary legal consultant to statewide Affirmative Action Officers, Student Affairs Officers, Personnel Officers, and Title VI Officers (1970's to the present)

- Served as coordinator of UT compliance with reporting require ments of Federal Drug Free Workplace Act, Drug Free Schools and Com munities Act, Student Right-to-Know and Campus Security Act. and State Crime Reporting Statutes.

EQUAL OPPORTUNITY/AFFIRMATIVE ACTION COMMITMENT ACHIEVEMENTS:

- Drafted UT's Board-adopted Affirmative Action Policy & U'I's first Affir mative Actions Plans. Reviewed succeeding Affirmative Action Plans
- Provided legal counsel to statewide UT personnel, affirmative action, and Title VI officers on Equal Opportunity/Affirmative Action matters (1970s to present)
- Presented numerous training seminars for UT officials and employees on EO/AA and sexual harassment
- Successfully prosecuted administrative charges against faculty, staff, and students for rape, sexual harassment, and other sexual offenses
- Contributed to diversity understanding by extensive independent travel, including numerous home stays in more than 60 countries in Africa, Asia, & Europe, & by providing home stays to visiting African & Asian nation- als & hosting numerous African, Asian, Hispanic, & European visitors
- Maintain numerous personal contacts (pen pal & e-mail contacts) in coun- tries in Africa, Asia, Europe, and Panama

Current Professional Memberships:

- National Association of College & University Attorneys (Board of Directors; Committee on Continuing Legal Education; Committee on Honors & Awards)

Bars of the Following Courts:

*Tennessee Supreme Court

*U.S. District Courts, (Eastern, Middle and Western Districts, Tennessee)

*U.S. Court of Appeals, Sixth Circuit (4-16-74)

*U.S. Supreme Court (9-26-75)

*U.S. Court of Appeals for the Federal Circuit (12-16-76)

Current Community Service:

*West Knoxville Sertoma Club (Board of Directors)

*Children's Center of Knoxville (A United Way Agency) (Board of Directors; Co-Founder and Legal Counsel since 1976)

*Fellowship of Christian Athletes (Board of Advisors) (Member since 1975)

Education: Houghton College, Houghton, N.Y. (1966-67)
        The University of Tennessee (B.S. Degree-1969)
        College of Law of the University of Tennessee (J.D.Degree-'72)
Personal:
• Wife: Theresa (UT B. S. 1988; M.S. 1998)
• Son: Lee (UT B.S. 1995); Westminster Theo. Sem. 1996
• Daughter: Cara (UT freshman; Fall '99)

References:

Joan Cronan
Women's Athletics Director
The University of Tennessee
208 Thompson-Boling Arena
Knoxville, TN 37996-4610
Office No. (423) 974-0001

Douglas A. Dickey
Athletic Director
The University of Tennessee
252 Stokely Athletics Center
Knoxville, TN 37996-3100
Office No. (423) 974-1224

The Honorable R. Leon Jordan
United States District Judge
800 Market Street, Suite 141
Knoxville, TN 37902
Office No. (423) 545-4224

Sammie Lynn Puett
Vice President, Institute for Public Service
The University of Tennessee
109 Student Services Building
Knoxville, TN 37996-0213
Office No. (423) 974-1542

Robert W. Ritchie, Esq.
Ritchie, Fets & Dillard, P.C.
Main Place, Suite 300
606 West Main Street
P.O. Box 1126
Knoxville, TN 37901-1126
Office No. (423) 637-0661

Chapter 33–Best Evidence of Success–
Wins, Losses and Settlements

A detailed explanation of the "Overall success rate" referred to on the second page of my resume in the previous chapter, adds meaningful context to the summary. Of course, "win percentage" alone lacks meaning without knowing what kind of cases were handled. As a general rule, plaintiffs have the option of being selective, avoiding cases with limited likelihood of success. Defendants have no choice and must defend whatever case a plaintiff elects to pursue.

A heavy majority of cases I handled on behalf of the University were cases in which suit was brought against the University or one of its employees. Those cases included cases clearly without merit, cases with a clear weight of evidence in favor of the plaintiff and cases with substantial merit on both sides. Lawsuits and administrative proceedings initiated by me on behalf of the University rarely fell into the loss column. Cases lacking merit were simply not pursued.

Successfully defending complaints clearly without merit sheds little light on defense counsel's commitment or level of skill. Settling cases with a clear weight of evidence in favor of the plaintiff likewise fails to say much about defense counsel's competence or commitment.

The vast majority of cases I handled fit into neither of these categories. Employee training and pre-litigation advice to University personnel and opposing parties served to dramatically eliminate such cases from reaching the litigation stage.

Cases with substantial, credible evidence on both sides of a legal controversy are those which test the confidence, skill and commitment of counsel as well as that of the client.

What about settlement as a means for avoiding the risk of losing? Confidence, skill and commitment play heavily in addressing that question. UT General Counsel Beach Brogan had a favorite saying: "If you've never lost a case you've never tried a case." Valid point!

Any lawyer can settle a case (although the cost may be mind-boggling). I found "stepping up to the plate," with confidence, skill and commitment, far more cost effective in the long run where I found firm evidence supportive of the University's position. Litigation records heavily support that conclusion.

DETAILED SUMMARY OF CASE RESULTS, 1972- 1998

Case totals: 503 (including four instances of joinder of two separate actions for trial) (for the period 1972–1998)

    A. 453 wins

    B. 28 losses

    C. 22 settlements

B. 28 losses
1. 13 losses: No $ paid by UT
2. 15 losses: $1,649,920 paid in total (including attorney fees and costs)

YEAR	OPPONENT	CASE TYPE	$$ (JUDGEMENT)
1. 1976	Soni	CON [constitutional claim]	$50,000
2. 1979	Gurley	CR/ S [Civil Rights/Sex Disc.]	$3,538
	UT won termination claim; lost salary claim		
3. 1980	Croushorn	CR [reverse discrim.]	$42,000
	UT won termination "reverse discrimination" claim; lost salary claim		
4. 1986	Moore	T [Tort]	$62,235
	UT offered $70,000 settlement pre-trial		
5. 1988	Bruwiler	CR/ Sex	$39,290
	Back pay, attorney fees and costs		
6. 1989	Watson	MM [medical malpractice]	$15,000
	Original claim: $200,000		
7. 1990	Ayers	MM	$100,000
	(Judgment entered for $150,000; plaintiff settled, post judgment to avoid UT's appeal)		
8. 1990	Crocker	Contempt of court	$237,000
	UT won sex discrimination claim in separate action		
9. 1991	Skoutakis	CON/ T	$282,500
	$2.5 million claim; jury verdict for UT on discrimination claim; Judgment for plaintiff on libel/slander and the due process claim		
10. 1992	Roberson	CR/ S	$97,820
	Jury verdict; salary, promotion and retaliation		
11. 1994	James	MM	$50,000
	$300,000 claim for damages		
12. 1994	Scarbrough	CR/ Disability	$109,083
	Jury verdict; termination of employee with cerebral palsy		
13. 1995	Pinson	T	$300,000
	Claims commission limit; severe football related head injury		
14. 1997	Davis, Robert	CON	$75,000
	Sixth Circuit reversed jury verdict in the amount of $250		
15. 1997	Hineline	CR/ S, Pregnancy	$186,465
	Jury Verdict		

C. 22 Settlements
    (1). 9 Settlements: No $ paid by UT
    (2). 13 Settlements: $379,030 paid in total

1. 1978	Neese	K [Contract]	$2,797
2. 1987	Summer	T	$1,500
$20,000 claim			
3. 1988	Heathcoat	MM	$5,000
$125,000 claim			
4. 1988	Robinson	CR /R	$13,823
$27,645 judgment vacated; settlement negotiated to avoid appeal			
5. 1988	Sledge	MM	$7,000
$200,000 claim			
6. 1992	Clark	CR/ R	$138,232
$500,000 claim; judgment for a higher amount vacated; settlement for lower amount			
7. 1994	Hatton/Holland	CR/S	$64,227
Judgment for plaintiffs was vacated; case settled			
8. 1994	Snell	MM	$25,000
$300,000 claim			
9. 1996	Ely	MM	$75,000
$300,000 claim			
10. 1997	Burnette	T	$5,000
$500,000 claim			
11. 1997	Walker	T	$5,000
$250,000 claim			
12. 1998	Impact Promotion	K	$6,451
$7,027 claim			
13. 1998	Wood	T	$30,000
$65,000 claim			

Cases listed above are those I handled, either alone or with another OGC attorney assigned to me for training purposes. Not all attorneys in the OGC had litigation experience or the same results.

One objective conclusion may be drawn from the data and history presented for the cases I handled: the University rarely lost. And, rarely did I settle a case.

In those few cases concluding in loss or settlement, the cost to the University was generally a small percentage of the amount originally sought. I submit that my game plan worked and worked well!

As UT Executive Vice President and Vice President for Development, Dr.

Joe Johnson, stated in a memorandum of August 1, 1990 to Beach Brogan and UT Memphis Chancellor Jim Hunt, "We must all recall we win about 98 to 99 % of our lawsuits. We must be doing something right, but it would be useful to have fewer lawsuits because of time, money, publicity, and feelings." The University's willingness to litigate rather than settle helped achieve the results described by Dr. Johnson.

A May 4, 1994 memorandum to me from Dr. Johnson, after he assumed the presidency of UT, again recognizes the positive results of litigating rather than caving:

> To: Mr. Ron Leadbetter
> From: Joe Johnson
>
> Subject: In Re: Sue Hatton v. Jim Hunt and Carolyn Holland v. UT
>
> Thank you for letting me have the good news of the decision of Judge Jerome Turner to dismiss the cases of Hatton v. Hunt and Holland v. UT in relation to an award of $6,000 each to Hatton and Holland and a considerably smaller amount for attorneys' fees than the original request of $85,000. These folks and Donati got a lot less than they sought and the court judgment against the defendants was erased.
> I certainly hope Donati, other attorneys, and some UT staff members earn [sic] a bit from this one.
>
> Thank you for a good piece of work.

(See Hatton and Holland cases)

Not to be ignored is the fact that many litigated cases included in the above statistics were "reported" or formal decisions establishing legal precedent binding, not only on the University and its adversary, but everyone under the issuing court's jurisdiction! Twenty nine such rulings, mostly favorable to the University, were issued between 1972–1998. Most are referred to elsewhere in this book.

Noteworthy is the fact that the TOTAL dollar value of losses and settlements over 26 years of the "Big Orange" era–slightly more than $2 million–was only 50% more than a SINGLE loss (Hartman #2) under new OGC leadership as the black storm clouds of the Gilley era moved in.

LITIGATION STATUS REPORTS

Beach Brogan excelled in keeping the UT Board of Trustees informed. One of his accomplishments was publication of an annual "litigation status report".

A report was presented to the President, members of the Board of Trustees and members of the President's staff prior to each annual Board meeting and the trustees had ample opportunity to ask questions regarding the listed cases. I personally handled many such questions from trustees. The following is a sample memorandum from Brogan accompanying the report:

To: Acting President Joseph E Johnson
   Members of the Board of Trustees
   Members of the Presidents staff

From: Beauchamp E. Brogan
Date: June 17, 1991
Re: Status of Civil Cases and Administrative Proceedings Pending as of June 1, 1991

Attached is the litigation report showing the status as of June 1, 1991 of litigation and investigative complaints involving the University of Tennessee.

Forty-two court cases, 116 Tennessee Claims Commission cases and 43 administrative proceedings are being handled by this office. This is an increase of five court cases, an increase of 39 cases before the Claims Commission and a decrease of one administrative pro ceeding since July 1990.

The 42 cases in various courts and the 116 cases in the Tennessee Claims Commission consist of the following types:

Medical Malpractice	51
Workers' Compensation	17
Other Personal Injury	44
Civil Rights	18
Contract	16
Other	12

The 43 administrative proceedings consist of the following types:

Discrimination Complaints	35
Employee Terminations for Cause	5
Student Disciplinary Actions	3

Following the cover page was a synopsis of every civil case and administrative proceeding pending as of June 1, 1991. For example, the first listing under "General Litigation":

1. ALBERT ALEXANDER v. SAM PATTERSON, ET. AL, U.S. District Court, Western District of Tennessee, Western Division, No. 90–2474–TuB. (JCC/RCL/OH) complaint filed July 8, 1990 requesting damages of $35,000,000. Dr. Alexander alleges civil rights and anti-trust violations.

PRESENT STATUS: Motion to dismiss and/or for summary judgment filed September 21, 1990.

Recipients of the Litigation Status Report could determine the basics of the case and which attorneys were handling it - in this case OGC Memphis attorneys JoAnn Cutting, myself and Odell Horton.

Litigation status reports followed the same format for a number of years. Only the numbers within categories changed:

June 4, 1992 - 61 court cases, 162 Tennessee claims commission cases and 42 administrative proceedings

May 17, 1993 - 54 court cases, 206 Tennessee claims commission cases, and 41 administrative proceedings

June 6, 1994 - 51 court cases, 192 Tennessee claims commission cases and 52 administrative proceedings

June 14, 1995 - 57 court cases, 220 Tennessee claims commission cases and 57 administrative proceedings

June 3, 1996 - 59 court cases, 271 Tennessee claims commission cases and 48 administrative proceedings [1997 -copy unavailable]

June 1, 1998 - 60 court cases, 266 Tennessee claims commission cases and 31 administrative proceedings

It is my understanding that President Wade Gilley directed that litigation status reports be discontinued. From 1999 forward the trustees were no longer provided such reports in any event. Board minutes do not reflect documentation of annual amounts paid for litigation settlements, either in individual cases or yearly totals.

In my opinion litigation status reports helped UT trustees, as well as UT officials, assess whether the Office of General Counsel performed at a satisfactory level. Good accountability practices arguably require a means of comparing current results with those from the past. Without records such as litigation status reports that ability does not exist.

Chapter 34–OGC Cost Cutting Proposals

The 1970s, '80s and '90s were years of budgetary frugality at the University of Tennessee. That doesn't mean there weren't areas for improvement. UT's administration regularly looked for cost-cutting measures. Our office was no exception.

On February 28, 1997, Beauchamp Brogan and Catherine Mizell issued to "All Attorneys" a memorandum titled "Budget Reduction–Taking a Critical Look at What We Do." The document presents an excellent, succinct statement of the University's conservative approach to spending and cost-cutting at that point in time.

> A fundamental tenet of the University administration's philosophy with respect to the current fiscal state of affairs is that there will be no "across–the-board" reductions. In other words, departments cannot simply apply a percentage reduction to their total budgets, cutting all programs and activities equally. Rather, departments must identify lower producing or less essential functions and impose the reduction on those functions rather than on more productive or more essential functions.
>
> In keeping with this tenet, all UWA departments have been charged to conduct a critical review of their functions, seeking to identify and fund those functions that best fulfill the mission of UWA. Specifically, each department must review and identify the following:
>
> 1. Services currently provided that can be eliminated or reduced; and
> 2. Opportunities for generating new sources of revenues.
>
> With respect to the first issue, we are asking all of you to devote some time to thinking critically about the services you perform in this office, seeking to identify any that might be eliminated or reduced. In particular, consider (1) whether any function you are performing is merely perfunctory – more form than substance – and (2) whether the cost of any function you are performing outweighs its benefit to the University. ... In considering this issue, try especially to identify things we do just because we've always done them. Do they really justify the time? Do they serve an essential purpose for the University? Think drastically. Have a "nothing is sacred" attitude.
>
> With respect to opportunities for generating new sources of revenue, we will have to think quite creatively. The most obvious opportunity, of course, would be performing more "plaintiff" work for the University. Unfortunately, unless we are able to eliminate or reduce some non-essential functions, we probably will not be able to devote significant attorney time to litigating plaintiff claims on behalf of the University. Nevertheless, please identify any plaintiff litigation you would recommend pursuing if we had sufficient in–house resources or if we "outsourced" the claim.
>
> Please give this matter your attention over the next few weeks and send us your response before April 1. Our hope is that everyone can identify at least one function that could be eliminated or drastically reduced.

In my opinion, the February 28 memorandum sets the "**gold standard**" for how a public, taxpayer supported university, such as the University of Tennessee, can be operated in an effective, efficient and businesslike manner.

My March 24, 1997 response:

I offer several suggestions for cutting costs and generating new sources of revenue:

1. Limit use of outside counsel to those situations where this office cannot ethically or competently provide legal representation for the University and/or its employees. Consider this an offer to take on any cases identified in this area.

2. Reorganize the office to concentrate litigation with attorneys who actively litigate, freeing up time of attorneys who do not.

Such a move would promote efficiency and inevitably cut costs. It is inefficient for an attorney to expend the time necessary to become thoroughly familiar with the rules of evidence, federal and state rules of civil procedure, and local practices merely to handle occasional litigation. On the other hand, efficiency and proficiency is a byproduct of experience. The old adage of "jack of all trades and master of none" suggests the wisdom of organizing so as to maximize the benefits gained from experience–and the development of expertise–in both litigation and non- litigation aspects of our office's operation. While we surely would not want to specialize too narrowly, it seems impractical to expect every attorney in the office to be a trial attorney given the limited number of cases which go to trial.

Again, consider this an offer to assume responsibility for additional litigation.

3. With respect to revenue, we might consider doing more than merely accepting repayment from individuals caught misappropriating University property or funds. In the past, this office not only sought reimbursement, but also compensation for the expense of recouping the loss. Where litigation was necessary, punitive damages were frequently sought–and in every instance where such damages were sought, they were recovered and almost always collected.

4. We might re-examine our role in collection of debts due the University. For example, in the past this office served as collection agent, whenever practical, for student loan defaults. Any necessary suits sought recovery of principle, interest at the legal rate, plus all collection costs including a reasonable attorney's fee. In a number of instances we collected substantially more than the amount due the University.

Are we presently sending these cases to collection agencies to skim off the "gravy"? In times past we prosecuted in-house those cases which this office could efficiently handle while forwarding the remainder to collection agencies. Perhaps a good practice to resume.

On March 26, 1997 Brogan replied in a manner consistent with past practice–a practice which came to an unfortunate end two years later.

Ron, thank you for your March 24 memorandum regarding ways in which this office could more efficiently operate in order to achieve our goal of reducing our budget. I agree with many of your suggestions. I especially agree that we should attempt to concentrate litigation with attorneys who actively litigate, freeing up time of attorneys who do not. I also appreciate your offer to assume responsibility for additional litigation, which we will gladly accept.

It seems a certainty the Legislature will make changes in the Claims Commission Act to assign backlogged cases to senior judges. ... Once changes are made to the Claims Commission Act and backlog cases assigned to senior judges, we will need your help desperately in helping out wherever needed. I appreciate your cooperativeness.

The game plan described in this chapter is not rocket science. It is one that worked well for the University for nearly three decades.

Chapter 35–Money Saving Tidbits
Benefiting the OGC–and the University

Sometime in the late 1990s Beach Brogan and I traveled together to Memphis. At the airport I rented a midsize automobile. Beach asked why I did not rent a full-size vehicle. I explained that I always rented a midsize since it rented for less and used less gas. "It's just money," was Brogan's reply.

Beach was typically frugal but not on this occasion. I took a different view of spending public funds as reflected in a comment made around the same time by U.S. District Judge Robert McRae to my paralegal, Jan Williams, during a chance encounter outside the courtroom: "Ron's a nice young man but he treats the University's money like it's his own."

Just as I would not waste my own money I would not waste of that of Tennessee taxpayers. I saw it as part of my job to preserve University resources even in circumstances where failing to do so would be unquestioned. Still, one can be frugal and do well.

On one occasion Andy Kozar and I flew to Memphis to attend a UT Board meeting. We stopped at the airport and I rented an automobile, a Lincoln Continental. Vice-President for Business and Finance Eli Fly, who had flown in on the same flight, had just rented a midsize vehicle from another car rental agency. Fly observed that I had rented a Lincoln Continental and asked why I had not rented a less expensive vehicle.

I asked Eli the rental charge for his vehicle then told him the charge for mine. Mine cost less (a "frequent renter special" yielding the lower price). Andy enjoyed a good laugh at Eli's expense. He shared the story at the Board meeting a couple of hours later and received a chorus of laughs in response.

SUBPOENAS RARELY USED

It is common practice for attorneys to have subpoenas issued for attendance of witnesses at depositions and trials. The cost of each subpoena is minimal but costs mount up over time.

Not once during the entire period of my University practice did I have a subpoena issued for a witness, with the exception of those I was required by law to have issued if requested by opposing counsel, in cases brought pursuant to the Administrative Procedures Act.

It was my opinion that networking and "friendly persuasion" served as well, if not better, to secure the presence of witnesses. Multiply avoided subpoena costs by thousands of witnesses and you have significant savings.

FREE OR LOW COST EXPERT WITNESSES

It is often necessary to secure the assistance and testimony of experts. That can be expensive. "Search firms" can be costly and directory listings unreliable. My own preference was utilization of personal contacts.

While I consulted innumerable "expert" resources outside the University over the years, each and every contact was informal and a product of social networking and friendship. UT paid nothing for expert advice offered by friends. Of course on many occasions I returned the favor to colleagues at UT and elsewhere.

Each and every expert witness used by me in court or administrative proceedings resulted from networking. Most experts served without requesting or receiving compensation. Others received compensation but at a low rate resulting from a greater interest in helping the University than raking in a high fee. A benefit of networking.

USE OF IN-HOUSE ADMINISTRATIVE JUDGES

In a later chapter I describe the advantages to the University of Tennessee of appointing University employees as administrative judges or hearing officers to hear cases brought under the "contested case" provisions of the Administrative Procedures Act.

It was standard practice for "extra pay" in the amount of $500 (perhaps more now) to be provided to University employees serving in this capacity. An absolute bargain.

USE OF IN-HOUSE COUNSEL

The use of in-house counsel offers certain networking and other advantages. Assuming a proper staffing level, use of in-house counsel should be more cost-effective than hiring hourly paid attorneys.

During my 35 years of service my work hours were 24/7. I was on call round-the-clock and every day of the week. While effort was made to conduct work during "normal" work hours, exceptions were frequent.

I received the same pay whether I worked 40 hours or 80. There was no extra compensation for Friday nights or Sunday afternoons spent in airports or on planes. My pay did not increase with an upsurge in new cases.

The "hourly fee" clock did not commence to run when I received a 10 p.m. phone call from a UT official needing legal advice. Nor did it start when I received an unscheduled 7 a.m. visit from a "whistleblower."

One case demonstrates well the cost advantage of utilizing in-house counsel. The original contractor on UT's Thompson Boling Arena construction project defaulted in its responsibilities and ended up being sued.

The OGC lacked any attorney on staff knowledgeable in construction law. Given the magnitude of the case, it would've been grossly impractical to expect anyone on staff to develop the needed expertise. Competent outside counsel was employed.

The University prevailed in the litigation and in April 1992 secured settlement in the amount of approximately $6.5 million. However, the University incurred litigation costs of roughly $7 million. A big win with a net loss of around a half million dollars.

Many wins of that nature could lead to severe financial difficulties.

Chapter 36–A Pot of Money–Birth of the UT Licensing Program and Gift of Rights to Rocky Top

Prior to the 1980s anyone desiring to produce and market a hat, shirt or other item bearing a college or university logo was free to do so, and keep all profits. Few, if any, institutions of higher education secured trademark protection of any sort. The University of Tennessee did not have trademark protection for its logos.

Sometime in 1980 or 1981, I met with a small number of attorneys from colleges and universities that had recently established, or were planning to establish, trademark protection for their logos. UCLA, Southern Cal, The University of Michigan, Ohio State University, Notre Dame and two or three other institutions were represented in the meeting.

The attorney for UCLA speculated once UCLA's licensing program was in place it expected to earn as much as $100,000 in royalties each year. I was impressed with the thought that revenue might be earned with little investment, all proceeds being derived from selling the right to use an institution's trademark on items already being sold.

Shortly after returning to Knoxville, I presented to Vice President Joe Johnson a proposal that a licensing program be initiated for the University of Tennessee. Joe's immediate response was, "No, that would anger the alumni." He correctly noted that no one else in the Southeast Conference had such a program.

The following year, after my second meeting with attorneys for higher education institutions having licensing programs, I again proposed establishment of a licensing program. Vice President Johnson again declined approval.

In the winter of 1983, I once again met with Dr. Johnson, repeated my proposal and noted that the University of Alabama was initiating a licensing program. "Okay Ron, go ahead," was Dr. Johnson's immediate reply. Third time's a charm!

Not desiring to reinvent the wheel, it occurred to me that my best course of action would be to consult with someone whose licensing program was already established–or well underway. My first choice: the University of Alabama!

On March 29, 1983, I flew from my Memphis office to Tuscaloosa, Alabama. The following day I met with the licensing program officials at the University of Alabama, including newly appointed licensing director, Finus Gaston. After lunching at the University club, I received from Gaston a thorough review of Alabama's new licensing program. I was impressed and excited about the prospects for a similar program for UT.

Two weeks later I attended a university licensing conference in San Francisco. On April 13,1983, two days after I returned home from the conference, I received a phone call from Bill Battle, UT's former head football coach.

Battle was starting a new business, the Collegiate Licensing Company, which would protect trademark items for colleges and universities and collect and distribute royalty payments from vendors. I thanked Bill for his interest but replied that, at least for the present, I would be setting up and administering UT's licensing program.

In November I was contacted by Barry White, the founder and CEO of Collegiate Concepts, a California operation is similar to Battle's. Same response: I would handle licensing for the University of Tennessee. As UT's licensing director I attended the meeting of "Intercollegiate Licensing" officers in New Orleans in April 1984.

Because I had no expertise in trademark law I secured, on behalf of the University, the services of someone who did. I located a retired judge who formerly sat on the United States Court of Customs and Patent Appeals.

As advised by the judge, I headed to the UT bookstore and sought out all categories of marketable items bearing UT logos. I then prepared a list of all logos to be trademarked, such as "Vols" "UT" and "Big Orange." Others, such as "Tennessee" and "Volunteers" were subject to trademark protection when used along with the color orange or otherwise tied to the University of Tennessee.

I forwarded to the judge the completed the list of categories of items bearing marketed UT logos as well as a list of logos the University wished to protect. The judge applied his expertise and secured trademark registration for the UT logos sometime in 1985.

I assumed responsibility for securing licensing agreements with businesses desiring to market products bearing any UT logo, collecting license fees and taking necessary enforcement action against vendors marketing UT, logo bearing products without executing a licensing agreement.

I discussed with legal counsel for the University of Texas how we would handle the licensing of similar logos ("UT") and colors (orange-although "official"

Tennessee orange is of a brighter shade than "Texas orange"). We reached a "gentleman's agreement" –one never reduced to writing–that the Mississippi River would be the dividing line. Tennessee would not seek royalties from "UT" products sold west of the Mississippi and Texas would not seek royalties from those sold east of the Mississippi, and, no, we didn't discuss bowl games.

Royalty income for the first year or so was less than $200. Enforcement action was limited to writing letters to vendors of unlicensed items stating that I would have no choice but to initiate litigation if a licensing agreement was not signed. One reluctant vendor, a Cumberland Avenue bookstore owner near the University, owned by a good friend of UT women's athletic director, Joan Cronan, looked to be my first enforcement target. Thankfully, he signed the requisite agreement before suit was filed.

As it turned out I never initiated an enforcement action against any vendor. I soon came to the realization that any enforcement measures by me outside the State of Tennessee, especially during Bowl contests or out-of-state games, would be impractical if not nearly impossible. It also became clear that serving as licensing director interfered with my responsibilities as legal counsel.

Sara Phillips, of the UT Office of Business and Finance, and I both attended the annual meeting of Licensing Directors in San Antonio in April 1985. Phillips assumed day–to–day responsibility for the licensing program a short while later.

On September 23, 1985, Vice President for Business and Finance, Emerson H. ("Eli") Fly, Bill Battle, Sara Phillips and I met in Fly's office and set in motion a new plan: Collegiate Licensing Company would manage the University of Tennessee's licensing program. Aside from approving items to be marketed with University logos (no toilet seats) the only remaining responsibility of the University was to bank deposit the 8.5% royalty payments collected by CLC from vendors.

The University of Tennessee currently receives between $2 million and $3 million a year in licensing royalties. After winning the football national championship in 1999 the royalty revenue for UT was $4 million.

As reported by the Knoxville News Sentinel on March 28, 2005, "Since 1998 UT has pocketed more than $18.8 million worth of royalties–$18.5 million coming from UT Knoxville–from the sale of officially licensed items, ranging from apparel to furniture to endless lines of memorabilia." Even in fiscal year 2010–11, with no postseason tournament play for the football team, licensing revenue was $2,800,000.

The best part about the UT licensing program? A heavy revenue stream with only a drop or two of expense! Like the proverbial "buried pot of money."

"ROCKY TOP"

It is sometimes mistakenly assumed that "Rocky Top" is a licensed trademark of the University of Tennessee. It is not.

The song "Rocky Top" was written by songwriters Felice and Boudleaux Bryant in 1967 in Gatlinburg, Tennessee where they lived until their deaths. In the 1970s the song became a popular fight song associated with UT athletics.

Boudleaux Bryant died in 1987. Several years later I learned that Felice Bryant desired to transfer all rights to "Rocky Top" to UT. She, or someone acting on her behalf, I don't recall which, contacted me and requested that I prepare a legal document accomplishing that purpose.

I prepared and mailed the requested document to Felice Bryant for her signature. She signed the document, returned it to me and I, in turn, forwarded the document to the UT Treasurer's office for filing. UT became the owner of rights to "Rocky Top" upon Felice Bryant's execution of the document assigning those rights to UT. The saga continues, however.

During the first week of January 1997, I received a call from Joy Postell, Vols Cheer Coach. UT cheerleading and dance teams were scheduled to appear in a national competition to be televised on ESPN. The team's routines were choreographed to the song "Rocky Top."

The organization sponsoring the national competition, Varsity Spirit Corporation, advised Postell "Rocky Top" could not be used without documented authorization.

Postell sought a copy of Felice Bryant's "assignment of rights" agreement from the UT Treasurer's office, but the agreement could not be located. In its stead I faxed to Varsity Spirit Corporation my assurance the copyright had been transferred to UT:

To: Varsity Spirit Corporation
    Attention: Melanie Berry

From: Ronald C Leadbetter
Date: January 6, 1997

    Felice Bryant, original artist of "Rocky Top," has assigned all rights to the University of Tennessee to use "Rocky Top" in perpetuity. Thus, the University of Tennessee cheerleading squad has the right, per Felice Bryant's assignment of rights to the University of Tennessee, to use "Rocky Top" at the 1997 Universal Cheerleading and Dance Teams National competitions which will be televised on ESPN with Varsity Spirit Corporation.

Ronald C Leadbetter
Associate General Counsel

Varsity Spirit Corporation accepted the substitute. The show went on.

Chapter 37–Sports Agent Legislation–the Role of Suspended Attorney John Mark Hancock

For me, the very best part of practicing law was solving the problems of others. I love a challenge! UT had plenty of legal challenges. Some were addressed by negotiation, others by litigation and a few by legislation.

Winning athletic contests was the responsibility of the athletic directors and coaches. Addressing compliance issues involving rules of the National Collegiate Athletic Association (NCAA) was a responsibility of mine (and UT Athletic Department compliance officers). One major legal challenge involving sports agents and college athletes in Tennessee was addressed by legislation.

NCAA rules prohibit providing "extra benefits" to college athletes. Other rules bar students from competing at the college level if they have entered into a contract with a sports agent. Back in the 1980s the University of Tennessee faced challenges in both areas. One episode had a very sad beginning but a laudable conclusion.

On March 4, 1986 I received a telephone call from attorney John Mark Hancock. He was calling on behalf of a student having an issue with the University. In response to my question as to whether he was the student's attorney, Hancock hedged.

After graduating from UT law school and receiving his license to practice law in 1981, Hancock racked up a record hardly worthy of praise. In 1984 former UT football running back Hubert Simpson and his attorney, Hancock, were convicted on criminal drug charges (sale of cocaine).

Hancock's license to practice law was suspended by the Tennessee Board of professional responsibility in 1984 on the basis of the drug conviction. His license was not reinstated until 1988.

Perhaps I should have reported the 1986 phone call to the BPR but, because Hancock hedged on whether he was the student's attorney. I did not.

On October 24, 1986, I received a telephone call from UT athletic director Doug Dickey. He complained that Hancock had been hanging around Gibbs Hall, UT's athletic dormitory. Dickey was concerned with Hancock's presence with the athletes and asked that I contact Hancock and ask that he stay away from the dorm.

I contacted Hancock the same day and advised that he was not welcome as a guest at Gibbs Hall and should refrain from going on the premises.

Because Hancock was reported as having represented himself as a "sports agent" to several of the UT football players, both Dickey and I were concerned that player eligibility not be compromised. We agreed that current Tennessee law provided little protection against a "sports agent" whose conduct adversely affected a player's eligibility. State Senator James Kyle, D-Memphis, was requested by UT administration to sponsor corrective legislation.

An article in the sports pages of the Knoxville News Sentinel (Feb. 24, 1988) summarized the purposes and potential impact of the legislation sponsored by Sen. Kyle:

Universities and colleges could sue sports agents and others who help students violate the rules governing amateur athletes, under a bill passed by a Senate committee on Tuesday.

***

Sen. James Kyle, D- Memphis, sponsored the bill. He said he wants to protect universities and colleges, which can lose revenues from game attendance when players are deemed ineligible after violating NCAA rules.

***

Kyle said he consulted with the state's attorney general's office and officials at Memphis State University and the University of Tennessee in drafting the bill.

UT officials praised the action. "To put it in a nutshell, I think the whole bill is excellent," said UT General Counsel [sic] Ron Leadbetter. "It's a good thing for college and universities in the state. It will not prevent the honest sports agent from signing student athletes. But it will prevent those who are selfish and take advantage of the athlete to the detriment of the athlete and the college or university."

I'm in favor of anything that would get the agent issue into focus so they do have to pay attention to business regulations in the state," said UT athletic director Doug Dickey. The bill would require both players and agents to notify, in writing, the student's college or university within 72 hours after signing a contract.

"I think that's excellent. It gives the opportunity for the appropriate people in the athletic department to counsel with the student athlete about rendering himself ineligible." Leadbetter said.

The contract must also contain a warning, printed in large type, that the student loses his or her amateur status by entering into a professional contract, under the bill.

***

University officials also praised language which gives student athletes 20 days after signing the contract to change their minds about losing amateur status.

"It accomplishes two purposes. It prevents the student athlete from engaging in a secretive contract in which no one is aware of it until it is too late," Leadbetter said. "And it gives the athlete a pretty good opportunity to think twice about what he is doing. Some of these sports agents give them the hard sale and immediately they think this is very good. But if they thought it through most of them would probably complete their eligibility."

The legislation was eventually signed into law. (Acts 1988, ch. 853; Tenn. Code Ann. 49-7-2101, et. seq.).

In the midst of the legislative process Hancock's license to practice law again became an issue. In early 1988 both co-counsel Karen Holt and I reported to the Board of Professional Responsibility that we had received calls from Hancock on behalf of a female student having legal issues concerning university housing.

A short time later I encountered a Knox County judge in a local supermarket. I was shocked to learn the judge was on his way to Nashville to testify as a character witness for Hancock in a license reinstatement proceeding. Hancock's shortcoming was not persuasiveness. His license was reinstated in 1988.

Controversy concerning Hancock's "sports agent" activity reared its head again in 1995. I received from Gary Wyant, assistant athletic director, football operations, copies of letters sent by Hancock on August 15, 1995 to several current UT athletes with remaining eligibility including football players Peyton Manning and Leonard Little.

Each letter was from "John Mark Hancock, Attorney and Counselor-at-Law." The second paragraph the letter read: "As you may know, I have represented professional athletes in my law practice for over 14 years now, going back to the days of U. T. Quarterback Jimmy Streeter, for whom I started a trust fund, since he had some tough luck in his life since being of all, and as an example of how I care about my clients beyond their careers as football players."

Hancock then advised each recipient that although NCAA regulations prohibited any written or oral agreements until college eligibility ended, he would "...be interested in talking with you regarding your professional potential." Several athletes presented Hancock's letter to athletics department officials.

Wyant wrote Hancock (letter of August 30, 1995), advising him of the UT Athletic Department's adamant opposition to "...any premature contact by any agent or financial advisor with our student athletes prior to the expiration of their NCAA eligibility. Likewise, we will most enthusiastically discourage any of our student athletes from dealing with any agent or financial advisor who prematurely tries to contact and/or negotiate with our student athletes prior to the completion of their NCAA eligibility."

I, along with Coach Fulmer, Athletic Director Dickey, NCAA compliance officer Malcolm McGinnis and UT law school professor Neal Cohen, received a copy of Wyant's letter.

Hancock responded to Wyant with a 6½ page letter, dated September 8, 1995, marked "confidential". The letter expounded on Hancock's qualifications and experience, his contacts with those in positions of power and his commitment to the University of Tennessee. One assertion stood out in Hancock's letter:

"Whatever personal or professional problems I may have had in the past are not only just that, in the past, but they had nothing whatsoever to do with my representation of athletes or my relationships with them."

Hancock concluded with a request for "equal treatment" after earlier stating,

"It is common knowledge, as I have told you that people like Jimmy Sexton and others have been given open access to the locker rooms, practice fields, dormitories, training table, etc., for many years, a clear NCAA violation. It is also apparent from people I know who can give sworn testimony attesting to these facts that some members of the University community have received kickbacks from agents in exchange for their steering of athletes to them. Such under–the–table money is commonplace in various athletic areas at U.T. as well as elsewhere…. I know where a lot of other skeletons are buried, and the media gives me prime attention, due to the credibility I have built with them. I don't think U.T. wants to go that route, and I'd also prefer to "to let sleeping dogs lie". After all, as I said, it's my school, too, I can only be pushed so far."

McInnis, Dickey, Cohen, Fulmer and I received copies of the September 8 letter.

On Monday, September 11, 1995 Hancock called me to express his anger with the letter he received from Wyant. He spent an hour or more on the telephone with me alternately issuing "indirect threats" and suggestions as to how much he could help the University if the University would treat him right.

Contrary to implications in his letter to UT athletes, Hancock stated that his license to practice law was currently suspended, but at an upcoming hearing he would seek reinstatement. He referred to his "good friend" [Knox County District Attorney] Randy Nichols as someone he thought would vouch for him.

Hancock repeatedly referred to all the things he knew about NCAA infractions but added that he would not want to hurt the University by revealing this knowledge. According to my notes of the conversation, "I advised him that a loyal UT fan would disclose wrongdoing if they knew of it in order to head off future problems and I repeatedly advised him that if he were sincere in his loyalty to the university he would assist in that regard and reveal any knowledge of wrongdoing."

By letter September 14, 1995 to Hancock, I confirmed two points made in my conversation with him:

Dear Mark:

First, the University of Tennessee objects to you or any agent contacting an eligible athlete in the manner in which you contacted Peyton Manning and others on August 15, 1995. In my opinion, it is impossible to read your letter as anything but soliciting the establishment of an agency relationship with athletes having remaining eligibility while, at the same time, leading the athlete to believe that you were available to provide legal advice (hence your letterhead "John Mark Hancock, Attorney and Counselor-at-Law").

Second, you stated to me that you were aware of improprieties in the UT athletics program involving agents, players, and athletic staff members. I will repeat here what I stated to you on the telephone: if you are aware of any violation of NCAA rules or unlawful activities affecting the UT athletic program, you are urged to provide me with that information. You can rest assured that appropriate action will be taken to thoroughly investigate any reported illicit activities and that prompt and appropriate remedial steps will be taken where such activity is identified.

Sincerely,
Ronald C Leadbetter
Associate General Counsel
Cc: Mr. Doug Dickey
    Dr. Malcolm McInnis

Less than two weeks later, Hancock advised Tripp Hunt, with the Tennessee Board of Professional Responsibility, that the letter to UT football players "was inadvertently sent on my old law office stationery [listing me as an "Attorney and Counselor-at-law"], I cannot understand how this could have possibly happened."

Interestingly, each letter was individually signed "Mark."

By letter of October 18, 1995, Tennessee Attorney General Charles W. Burson advised Hancock:

The Office of the Attorney General and Reporter for the State of Tennessee is charged with the duty of pursuing civil causes of action against any individual who "causes, aids or abets a student athlete or institution, or both, to violate or be in violation of a rule or rules of its governing national collegiate athletic association...." Tenn. Code Ann. section 49-7- 2103. In this regard, this office has been forwarded letters that were apparently sent by you to Peyton Manning and Leonard Little, who play football for the University of Tennessee.

After investigation, it has been determined that this office will not take action at this time. However, should it become evident in the future that any action by us is warranted, this office will take all appropriate steps to enforce Tenn. Code Ann. Section 49-7-2101, et. seq.

You are reminded that should you attempt to enter into any contract with any student athlete at the University of Tennessee, or any other state institution, that the provisions as outlined in Tenn. Code Ann. section 49-7-2104 must be strictly followed.
Sincerely,
Charles W. Burson
Attorney General & Reporter

cc: Philip Fulmer
    Gary Wyant
    Doug Dickey
    Neal Cohen
    Ron Ledbetter

In late October 1995 Hancock advised the associate athletic director for compliance, Malcolm McGinnis, that he chose not to elaborate on previous general allegations of NCAA violations by UT athletes or personnel. By letter of November 27, 1995, UT President Joe Johnson wrote Hancock regarding his allegations of NCAA violations:

"Thank you for coming by the office a few days ago to discuss your interest in establishing contacts with selected University of Tennessee athletes. You set forth a rationale for such contacts, including allegations of certain illegal NCAA violations by folks in the UT Athletics Department. You allege that certain sports agents have open access to our athletes, members of the University community have taken kickbacks from agents, and other "skeletons."

As I related to you, you have an obligation to set forth formally your allegations to allow them to be investigated and resolved if they are true. If not, you are engaging in the covering up of possible NCAA and legal violations. One challenge and task for all of us with UT is for us to investigate all allegations and questions. So, if you have anything to put on the table, you are urged to do so. Failure to do so tends to smear everyone in the University's community."

By the way, our athletics department leadership assures me that Jimmy Sexton and other sports agents do not have open access to our student athletes. If you know otherwise, let me know.

Finally, Peyton Manning and Leonard Little brought to our staff your correspondence. It was not "intercepted and opened" by anyone other than these young men. They reported the contact by you because of all the current sensitivity about agents and contacts by agents that may lead to in CAA violations.
Sincerely,
Joseph E Johnson
President

In 1997 the Board of Professional Responsibility filed with the Tennessee Supreme Court a petition for an order of contempt against Hancock. On July 6, 1998, the Court issued a ruling sentencing Hancock to 5 days in jail for practicing law on a suspended license. The Court noted Hancock's prior license suspension from 1984–88 on drug charges and his 1994 license suspension for misrepresentation, misuse and misappropriation of client funds. (In re: John Mark Hancock, Tenn. S. Ct. July 6, 1998)

Hancock made another attempt in early 2000 (in a seven page letter to Doug Dickey) to secure Dickey's support and access to UT athletes. Dickey opted not to even respond to the letter. He opposed taking any action to involve Hancock with UT athletes.

(Left to right) UT General Counsel Beach Brogan, Ron's wifeTherese Leadbetter, UT President Ed Boling, and Ron Leadbetter, (December 1982).

Chapter 38–Tennessee Uniform Administrative Procedures Act–How to Enact a Rule or Conduct a Hearing

The Tennessee Uniform Administrative Procedures Act (APA) was enacted into law in 1974, Tenn. Code Ann. 4-5-101 et. seq. Two major components of the Act affect Tennessee state agencies, including the University of Tennessee. I had sole responsible for the University's compliance with both components of the Act for the entire period of my employment in the Office of General Counsel.

RULEMAKING PROVISIONS

The first major component of the APA is its rule-making provisions, Tenn. Code Ann. section 4–5–201, et seq. This section prescribes the manner in which state agencies must proceed in order to enact new or amended rules whenever those rules affect a person's property rights or liberty interest.

As applied to the University of Tennessee, the rulemaking provisions apply to rules such as traffic and parking regulations, student rights and responsibilities, library fines, honor codes and "procedures for conducting hearings in accordance with the contested case provisions of the uniform administrative procedures act".

University rules not required to be implemented in accordance with the APA included those regulating student academic performance and those governing faculty and staff work performance. Neither of those rules affects a "property right" protected by the U.S. Constitution.

Rulemaking involves a multi-step process. My first responsibility was to see to it that new rules and amendments were prepared in proper format, with appropriate designation by number or letter of each paragraph, subparagraph and so forth.

The rule draft was next presented to the full UT Board of Trustees for a roll call vote. The final pages of each rule submission listed the trustees voting and how each trustee voted. My signature appeared on each rule submission as the person responsible for presenting the rules for legislative review.

Next, Board-approved rules were forwarded to Nashville for approval by the State Attorney General. In my years of service only a single rule was rejected at that level.

Over my objection and that of UT Knoxville Vice-Chancellor Tim Rogers, the Knoxville campus adopted a rule prohibiting "hate speech." The rule received Board approval but was rejected by the Attorney General and never pursued further.

All rules approved by the Attorney General are filed with the Secretary of

State, Administrative Procedures Division, the official repository of all rules of agencies of the state of Tennessee. Lastly, the agency rules are placed on the agenda of the Joint Government Operations Committee of the Tennessee state legislature for "rule review".

During the '70s and part of the '80s the State senators and representatives sitting on the committee actually voted to approve or disapprove rules. However, this process was eventually rejected as an infringement on the authority of the administrative branch of government as a violation of "separation of powers." Under new and current procedures, any agency rule not included in "omnibus" legislation at the end of the term becomes null and void. Same result as in early decades, but by a different procedure.

On average I appeared before the government operations committee once each year. More at the beginning and less toward the end of my service to UT. My very first appearance –and the first "rule review" appearance by anyone on behalf of the University–took place on June 8, 1977.

The assembly room in Legislative Plaza in Nashville was packed. More than twenty senators and representatives were seated on stage behind a huge semi-circular dais. I was first on the committee agenda.

It being my first time to testify before the legislature, I was somewhat nervous but felt reasonably well prepared to answer any questions the committee might have concerning various categories of rules listed on the agenda under "The University of Tennessee." The committee chairman called me to the podium.

I was not prepared for the first question. "Mr. Leadbetter, how is the University of Tennessee going to do against Alabama this year?" A five or ten minute discussion of the likelihood of Tennessee defeating Alabama in the upcoming football season was my introduction to the legislative process.

Although I had plenty of opportunities to watch representatives from other agencies go through the meat grinder of a legislative grilling I rarely had a negative experience of that nature.

Between my first appearance before "Government Ops" and my last (March 19, 2007), I made numerous presentations to the committee and addressed hundreds of questions and comments. A single rule was rejected in that 30 year period. And the University continued to use and abide by that rule even though it was rejected by the legislature. There was a good explanation.

In the late 1990s or early 2000s an amendment to the residency classification rules was offered for the purpose of complying with a recently enacted statute permitting residents of a County adjacent to Tennessee to pay in-state fees. The language of the rule merely adopted the language of the law.

When I advised the Government Ops committee that the UT rule simply incorporated existing state law, one committee member blurted, "If I voted for that my constituents should take me out and shoot me [or words to that effect]". The representative then moved the rule be rejected. It was never to be mentioned again.

The University continued to comply with the law–and its "unwritten" rule incorporating the law.

On another occasion, the Government Ops committee considered a rule I had drafted for the purpose of allowing those entitled to a "due process" hearing to waive their right to proceed under the APA's "contested case" provisions. State Sen. Steve Cohen, from Memphis, heatedly opposed the rule

I explained to the committee that the "Contested Case Hearing–Waiver Policy" was completely voluntary and allowed students, employees and others to sign a waiver of APA hearing rights and proceed in accordance with informal University hearing procedures. The latter option typically avoided the expense to the hearing recipient of securing legal counsel and the expense to the University of securing a court reporter. A vast majority of those requesting a hearing elected to sign a waiver and proceed informally. (Note: In my entire career, a single recipient of a traffic citation requested a formal hearing under the APA. The party requesting the hearing failed to show for the hearing and the citation was upheld by the hearing officer).

Senator Cohen did not retreat from his opposition to the waiver policy rule and insisted on a vote. A vote was held and the committee sustained the rule, with Cohen casting the only dissenting vote. The waiver policy remains in effect. (Tennessee Administrative Register, Rule 1720 –01–03).

One minor hiccup in dealing with the Government Ops committee did occur in 1978. Being out of town on another matter I asked my colleague in the OGC, Alan Parker, if he would take my place at a scheduled meeting. He agreed to do so.

When Alan and I next met, his first words were, "Don't ask me to do that again!" A committee member had asked him about a rule change that would permit use of coffeemakers in student housing. The exchange went something like this:

[Legislator] Why were coffeemakers in student housing prohibited in the past?"

[Alan] Possibly, because coffee grounds might clog the sink.

[Legislator] So, coffee makers don't produce coffee grounds any longer? Or they don't clog the sink?

[Alan] I'm really not sure.

The legislator then immediately moved to suspend further consideration of the UT rules until "the University brings someone who can answer our questions." The motion passed.

In the past I had attended Government Ops hearings alone. Vice Presidents Joe Johnson and Homer Fisher and another UT official in the Business office, Ray Jordan, and I flew in the UT plane to Nashville to attend the July 11, 1978 rescheduled hearing for the "coffee maker rule" and other amendments. The rehearing was uneventful and all proposed UT rule amendments passed legislative muster. The price of coffee had gone up.

The revised practice continued for several years, until I sensed I could get by appearing solo without arousing legislative ire.

Although the requirements of the rulemaking process were time-consuming and somewhat of a nuisance, they were not to be ignored. On one occasion an increase in the fee for getting a traffic citation was approved by a UT Knoxville committee charged with oversight of traffic and parking regulations. The increase was then implemented without going through the rulemaking process. Campus traffic and parking brochure listed fines at the higher rate. Additional revenue in excess of $1 million resulted from the increase.

A UT student, while reviewing the University's rules on file with the Administrative Procedures Division in Nashville, discovered the discrepancy between the fines assessed by the University and traffic and parking fines approved in accordance with the rulemaking provisions of the APA. He challenged a fine he had received and those paid by others.

The University eventually mailed refund checks to those paying citations at the illegal rate. The administrative cost of rectifying the $1 million plus in overcharges was also in excess of $1 million. Total loss in excess of $2 million. A very expensive lesson–obey the law.

A majority of rules and amendments submitted for approval under the APA rulemaking provisions fell within the jurisdiction of UT student affairs officers. I met with the officers on a regular basis, typically at "retreats" at one of the State parks. We discussed ways in which the bureaucratic rulemaking process could be reduced.

The "student affairs" team agreed, early on, to utilize uniformity among the campuses, to the extent possible, in the language of major rules. Accordingly, campus rules governing student conduct were relatively uniform, as were rules providing for "maintenance of ethical and professional standards."

The rulemaking process often took a year or longer. The student affairs officers and I reached consensus that only rules and amendments of significant consequence would be pursued. Changes for grammatical improvement alone would no longer be considered.

By limiting utilization of the rulemaking process the number of my appearances before the Government Ops committee was reduced from four times a year in 1977, to one or two times a year in the 1990s and only occasional appearances after 2000. My last three meetings were on March 12, 2001, March 8, 2004 and March 19, 2007. There was no need to meet more often. The cost of promulgating rules had significantly declined as a result of the reduced time spent promulgating rules.

CONTESTED CASE PROVISIONS

The second major component of the APA, Tenn. Code Ann. Section4-5-301 et. seq., specifies the manner in which a state agency must proceed prior to depriving a person of a property right or liberty interest.

Uniform rules for conducting administrative judicial proceedings for such individuals were established by the Secretary of State's office, Tenn. Admin. Reg. 1360-04-01. The University of Tennessee adopted rules closely tracking those of the Secretary of State. Tenn. Admin. Reg. 1720-01-05.

Although I was not the only attorney in the Office of General Counsel having responsibility for trying cases under the contested case provisions of the APA, I handled the majority of them – around eighty in the span of twenty five years.

The first case handled under the contested case provisions of the APA was one I handled in 1981. A UT Martin employee, Vester Newcomb, had a disciplinary charge of gross insubordination heard by a UT administrative judge. The AJ found the charge true and ordered Newcomb's employment terminated.

Newcomb filed a petition for review with the Knox County Chancery Court on February 4, 1981. (Knox Chancery No. 71664). The Knox Chancery Court's final judgment was entered by Chancellor H. David Cate on July 27, 1984, affirming the ruling of the administrative judge.

I had another major responsibility in this area of the law: training administrative judges and hearing officers to conduct hearings under the Act, The University of Tennessee having statutory authority to appoint its own administrative judges and hearing officers.

My approach was to contact the campus Chancellor and request his recommendation of campus officials they considered capable of serving as administrative judge (having a law degree) or hearing officer (not having a law degree). I then contacted the "nominees" and determined if he or she was willing to serve. If so, I conducted a training session for the new prospect.

Each training session included a review of the APA contested case provisions, the UT procedures for conducting hearings in accordance with those provisions and helpful court rulings, particularly those involving UT cases. I offered one additional piece of advice: in weighing argument of counsel on the facts in any case, no greater weight should be given my argument based on my status as University counsel; in weighing argument on applicable law in a given case, great weight should be given my position (or any other OGC attorney) since I must defend that position on any appeal

Ordinarily the training sessions were one-on-one. I conducted training for several administrative judges at the same time in Nashville on August 26–27, 1993. On November 4, 1998 a similar session was held for three administrative judges at UT Chattanooga.

When I received notice of an APA hearing request I immediately contacted the appropriate Chancellor (or President, in a case involving a system employee) and recommended a trained AJ or hearing officer to hear the case.

The first administrative judges included Dr. Malcolm McGinnis, Dr. Timothy Rogers and Jennifer Richter, Associate Director of the Office of Equity and Diversity. Each conducted a substantial number of administrative hearings and did so in excellent fashion. Not one was ever reversed on appeal.

Administrative Judge Karen Weekly earned acclaim in more than one respect. First, she was the only administrative judge or hearing officer to ever have an order reversed on appeal (in cases I handled). (See Chapter 62).

Even in *Wilson*, the administrative judge's ruling was affirmed on appeal by the UTC Chancellor as well as the Chancery Court for Davidson County. Although the Tennessee Court of Appeals reversed the rulings below it did so based on the disciplinary letter's perceived error in relying on language in the UT Chattanooga faculty handbook as a basis for the disciplinary charge against Wilson–essentially, an error of law rather than mishandling of the facts of the case or committing a procedural error.

Judge Weekly can disavow responsibility for any error of law. The APA training program casts that responsibility with the lawyers for the University–in this case, me!

The APA contested case contact with Weekly did yield one superb benefit for the University of Tennessee. A networking bonanza!

Not long after conclusion of the Wilson case I met with Karen Weekly in Chattanooga on another matter. She told me she had heard there was an opening at UT Knoxville for the head coach of the women's softball team and that she was interested.

Karen explained that both she and her husband, Ralph, had a solid background in coaching softball. Ralph had coached softball in the last Olympics. Did I know anyone in Knoxville I could contact on her behalf? I told Karen I knew Women's Athletic Director Joan Cronan and would be glad to contact her and let her know of the Weeklys' interest in the coaching position.

The next day I contacted Joan and told her about the Weeklys. A lunch meeting was promptly scheduled. Joan hired the Weeklys as co-head coaches of the Lady Vols softball team a few days later.

In 2013 the Weeklys led the Lady Vols to the World Series, losing only in the finals to NCAA champion Oklahoma. It is arguable that only a 2 games to 1 loss to defending champ Oklahoma prevented their appearance in the 2014 World Series (UT Lady Vols having defeated World Series champ Florida 3 games to 0 in the regular season). The loss in *Wilson* had a bright aftermath!

WITH UPSIDES THERE ARE DOWNSIDES

While the Tennessee legislature surely intended the provisions of the contested case section of the Administrative Procedures Act to protect property rights and liberty interests, there were certain downsides. Some of these were described by me in a Knoxville News Sentinel article on February 6, 1993: "Releasing players' names mistake, UT's Snyder says." (The Knoxville News Sentinel, February 6, 1993, p. C1).

At the beginning of the article, UT Chancellor Bill Snyder apologized for "releasing the names of 11 current or former [football] players charged with student misconduct for their involvement during a fraternity fight Jan. 17." (Id.) The charges involved a fight between UT football players and members of a black fraternity from Knoxville College.

While the privacy of student records is protected by federal and state law, public hearings of student disciplinary matters mandated by state law are not prohibited.

There were aspects of such disciplinary proceedings, aside from the records privacy that I addressed in the Sentinel article:

The student athletes could have requested a Student Judicial Hearing before a jury of their peers with law students serving as prosecutors and defenders.

Instead, the football players opted for the Administrative Procedures Act, which means their hearings are public. In such cases, UT's Chancellor appoints a hearing examiner or an administrative judge, the difference being the judge has a law de gree and the examiner doesn't.

Ron Leadbetter, UT's associate general counsel, said he will be the prosecutor. He said Friday he had not had a chance to interview any witnesses and could not comment on specifics of the case.

Leadbetter said the APA procedure "take significantly longer" than a student hearing, which is conducted informally.

"Under the APA, both sides have various rights to question witnesses and take discovery," he said. "That takes a bit of time."

"It's not going to be in a week, and for sure won't be in two weeks. I rather suspect it would not be within a month, but don't hold me to that."

Leadbetter said he did not know if the cases would be heard one at a time or en masse.

Leadbetter said most students go the informal route when it comes to a hearing.

"First of all, many feel they'd rather be judged by their peers," he said. "Second, they (student judicial hearings) are very informal and less expensive and rarely do they involve attorneys."

"Whichever way they go, they'll get a fair hearing."

(Id.).

Eleven of twelve players charged with student misconduct hired lawyers to represent them in formal proceedings under the Administrative Procedures Act. After discussing with me the factors noted above and, and the relatively minor nature of the disciplinary offenses charged, each of the attorneys involved advised me that their client or clients would execute the required written waiver of his right to proceed under the APA.

Both the students and the University saved time and money as a result of that decision. My own workload was also favorably impacted.

(Post note: I handled compliance with APA rulemaking procedures, including legislative work, right up until my retirement from the University in March 2008. On March 25, 2008, at the request of the UT General Counsel, I prepared a summary of procedures to be followed by my successor).

Chapter 39–Creation of the UT Police Department

In 1972 UT campus law enforcement officers were referred to as "safety and security" officers. Some officers obtained city or county "commissions" on their own and others did not. Aside from those holding city and county commissions, officers had no more police authority than any other University employee.

Each UT campus established a cooperative relationship with local government. The arrangement worked reasonably well. But, not always.

In 1981 the University of Tennessee Center for the Health Sciences encountered strong opposition to a proposal I initiated to grant UT security officers the same authority as regular Memphis police. As reported in the July 22, 1991 edition of the Memphis Press Scimitar:

> A proposal to grant to security officers at the University of Tennessee Center for Health Sciences the same powers as regular Memphis police has encountered strong objections from police director E. Winslow Chapman.
>
> "We don't need people floating here and floating there that are semi-police," Chapman said.
>
> ***
>
> The idea was advanced by Ronald Leadbetter, associate general counsel to UT, who made the suggestion to the City Council's public safety and judicial affairs committee.

Leadbetter offered a draft of an ordinance granting the 38 UTCHS security officers "full authority to enforce all state statutes and city ordinances and to arrest offenders for violations thereof."

Leadbetter said the UTCHS officers would use their authority, however, only on university property except where "hot pursuit" of a violator was involved.

The attorney said UTCHS would accept all liability involving the security force and the proposal "won't cost the city a cent."

Leadbetter said the thrust of the suggestion is an effort to save the university money and insurance fees. Lawsuits involving the security force, he said, are more likely to result in costly awards against the university if the officers do not have the same status of regular police. "Our guards don't have any more protection than you or I," Leadbetter said.

A corollary benefit, he said, would be a savings to Memphis taxpayers because crimes on the UTCHS campus "would not have to be investigated twice" —once by the security force and again by the Memphis police.

Leadbetter added that if the council approved the ordinance he proposed, UTCHS would pay for advanced training for the security guards.

The ordinance route did not succeed. The state legislative route was then pursued.

I drafted legislation having three basic provisions. First, UT law enforcement officers would have full power to enforce state law.

Second, UT police officers would have law enforcement authority on University property as well as any adjacent public property. Third, UT officers would be required to complete appropriate law enforcement training prior to being commissioned as a university police officer.

Legislative sponsors were secured for the proposed legislation. The legislation was enacted into law in 1987 (Public Acts of Tennessee, ch. 78; Tenn. Code Ann. section 49–7-118). Since that time UT police officers have had full authority to enforce state laws on University property and neighboring areas defined by law.

Chapter 40–UT Police Officers–
Popular Parties to Litigation

For reasons I'll leave to the speculation of others, I spent more time working with UT police officers as parties to litigation, on either the same or opposing side, then any other UT department or budgetary unit. I refer only to cases in which officers were either plaintiffs or defendants - not witnesses (which is, of course, a frequent and expected role for police officers). I hasten to add that some of my very closest friends at UT were Police Department employees, including police chiefs Hugh Griffin and his successor, Ed Yovella.

My earliest cases involving UT police officers date back to 1974 (Detective A.D. Earl and Sgt. Jack Thacker). There were a good number more. Several in particular merit mention in this chapter.

TWYLA LOGAN and DAVID RENO

A particularly odd case involved a female police officer, Twyla Logan. We had an adversarial relationship from the get-go.

Logan filed a charge of sex discrimination (harassment) in December 1980 with the Equal Employment Opportunity Commission. The University rejected Logan's charge as lacking any merit. In March 1982 the EEOC issued a notice declining further action on Logan's charge.

Three months later, in June 1982, Logan filed a new charge with the EEOC alleging acts of reprisal by the UT Police Department based on her earlier discrimination charge. The EEOC entered a "determination" in the University's favor on August 31, 1983.

A little more than a year later I received word from UT Knoxville deputy police chief Ed Yovella that Logan had presented a harassment complaint against a fellow officer, David Reno. Among other actions, Reno had placed an inappropriate photo of Logan on her automobile in the Police Department parking lot, where it was seen by passersby.

I met with Logan at police headquarters and notified her that this time I was on her side – the evidence supported her claim and appropriate disciplinary action would be taken against Reno. Based largely on evidence provided by Logan, Reno was suspended without pay on October 11, 1984 and a disciplinary hearing of "gross misconduct" charges (acts of moral turpitude) against him was set for November 28. Logan would of course be the primary witness against Reno at the hearing.

The November 28 hearing was held before a four-member panel chaired by Associate Dean of Student Conduct and Orientation, Dr.Timothy Rogers. Deputy Chief Yovella and I were present on behalf of the University; Reno was represented by attorney Wayne Houser.

Also present, as expected, was Officer Twyla Logan. She was accompanied by Knoxville attorney Herb Moncier. There was no objection to his presence although it was made clear that he could not participate in the proceedings.

Rogers called the hearing to order, both sides presented opening statements and I called the first witness for the University, Officer Twyla Logan. I was stunned by Moncier's announcement that he had advised his client not to testify at the hearing for fear the University might "use the very same information to fire Officer Logan. For that reason, I feel it's in Officer Logan's best interest not to testify at this hearing. And I'm advising her not to make a statement at this time."

In response I announced that if Logan did not testify I would be advising her superior – seated to my immediate left – to terminate her employment for insubordination. Yovella then advised Logan to testify or risk the consequences.

Despite Yovella's warning Logan refused to testify. She and Moncier left the hearing room. The hearing proceeded without the chief prosecuting witness.

The hearing panel ultimately found the charges against Reno to be true and recommended his employment be terminated. Chancellor Jack Reese accepted the panel's recommendation. The University's action was affirmed both by the Knox County Chancery Court and the Tennessee Court of Appeals.

Logan was also fired. The charge was gross insubordination. Moncier requested a formal hearing of the charge against her in accordance with the Administrative Procedures Act.

On January 3, 1985 UT administrative judge Malcolm McGinnis heard the charge against the Logan. He found Logan guilty of gross insubordination and ruled that termination of employment was the appropriate penalty.

The administrative ruling was subsequently appealed, first to the Knox County Chancery Court then to the Tennessee Court of Appeals, Eastern Section at Knoxville. Both courts rejected Logan's appeal.

The Court of Appeals, in its January 14, 1988 opinion, completely rejected Moncier's argument that Logan had been deprived of her Fifth Amendment right against incrimination. Just as important, in my view, was the Court's rejection of a challenge to the right of the University–in this case, Chancellor Jack Reese – to appoint a University employee–McGinnis–to conduct the hearing of the disciplinary charges against Logan:

"Finally, Appellant questions the constitutionality of the U.A.P.A. hearing before an Administrative Law Judge designated by the Chief Executive Officer of her employer. This issue was not argued, and is discussed only minimally in the Brief; suffice it to say that the U.A.P.A. procedures were scrupulously followed and the fact that the Hearing Officer was an employee of the University [the State] is no more disqualifying of him that it would be of any trial or appellate judge [citation omitted]."

The appellate court essentially affirmed the May 1980 ruling of Knox County Chancellor Frederick McDonald rejecting an argument by UT security officer John Coltharp that the UT Chancellor had no authority to appoint UT law professor John Sobieski to hear "misuse of sick leave" disciplinary charges against him and that the "hearing officer should have been chosen by the Secretary of State with the help of the Attorney General rather than from the UT staff." [Knoxville News Sentinel May 15, 1980]

THE MEMPHIS CHALLENGE-- Cavallo, Nettles and Gregory

During my career Memphis certainly outranked any other UT campus in providing litigation opportunities for attorneys. This was certainly true with respect to cases involving UT Memphis police officers. 1989 was a particularly challenging year in that regard.

On August 4, 1989 UT Memphis police officer Jimmy W. Cavallo, a white male, was fired for theft or dishonesty (collecting wages from the University when he was in fact not at work), immoral behavior affecting ability to perform assigned work and visiting other departments or having visitors during work hours without permission (involving a dalliance with a young lady during work hours).

Since, at the time, no UT Memphis employee had been trained to serve as administrative judge, J. Stovall, with the office of the State Attorney General, was secured to conduct the disciplinary hearing requested by Cavallo. A three-day hearing was held in September 1990 following which Stovall found Cavallo guilty of the charges against him and termination of employment as the appropriate penalty. Stovall's' findings were implemented by the University.

Cavallo appealed the University's action to the Davidson County Chancery Court. On February 4, 1992, the Chancery Court entered a final order in the university's favor, dismissing Cavallo's appeal..

Cavallo appealed the Chancery Court decision to the Court of Appeals for the Middle Section of Tennessee. On October 30, 1992, the Court of Appeals affirmed the Chancery Court ruling.

Cavallo initiated a second legal proceeding in the Tennessee Claims Commission on March 21, 1990, charging the University, UT Memphis Chancellor Jim Hunt, UT Memphis Assistant Vice Chancellor for Security Affairs (i.e. police chief) Warren Shadko and other UT officials with denial of due process, sex discrimination, breach of contract and retaliatory discharge. Compensatory damages in the amount of $500,000 and punitive damages in the amount of $2 million was requested, as well as back pay and reinstatement.

The Claims Commission action was transferred to the Shelby County Chancery Court for trial but subsequently dismissed for lack of prosecution.

The Tennessee Court of Appeals for the Western Section of Tennessee rejected a subsequent effort by Cavallo to reopen case. The appellate court's July 1, 1993 ruling brought to conclusion Cavallo's actions against the State [UT and UT employees].

On November 13, 1989, in the midst of the state proceedings, Cavallo also filed a federal civil rights lawsuit against the same defendants named in the claims commission action and, asserting the same causes of action and abandoning the same monetary damages and other relief.

By "order of dismissal," entered on July 19, 1991, U.S. District Judge Julia Gibbons ordered Cavallo's complaint dismissed for lack of subject matter jurisdiction. Gibbons noted that by filing a claim with the Tennessee Claims Commission, Cavallo waived his right to proceed in federal court against UT–an agency of the state of Tennessee–and any UT employees acting within the scope of their employment. She cautioned that "If the Tennessee claims commission concludes that defendants' acts were outside the scope of their employment, the waiver is void and plaintiff may reinstate his federal cause of action."

No such conclusion was reached by the claims commission. Therefore, Cavallo's federal option never resurrected. And, any chance of success ended with the Tennessee Court of Appeals October 30, 1992 affirmation of Stovall's administrative ruling.

In a bizarre twist, two other UT Memphis police officers filed similar claims commencing in late 1989. The only common factor among the claims of the three officers was the legal representation provided each by Memphis attorney David Sullivan.

Officer Mario Nettles filed a federal civil rights action on November 13, 1989 alleging non-promotion and imposition of a three-day disciplinary suspension based on his race (black) and denial of his due process rights. The same defendants were named as in Cavallo. Nettles sought $500,000 compensatory and $2 million punitive damages.

As in Cavallo a claim was subsequently (March 21, 1990) filed with the Tennessee Claims Commission (and transferred to the Shelby County Chancery Court) replicating the causes of action and requested relief set forth in the federal lawsuit. For the same reasons stated in Cavallo, Nettles' federal action was dismissed pursuant to the U.S. District Court's "Order on Motion to Dismiss or for Summary Judgment" entered November 7, 1991.

In the remaining Chancery Court proceeding I filed "Defendants Motion to Dismiss or for Summary Judgment" accompanied by the affidavit of police chief Shadko and documentary evidence showing that another black officer had been promoted at the same time and that Nettles had a lengthy history of complaints about his job performance. On October 22, 1993 the Shelby County

Chancery Court granted the defense motion and dismissed Nettles' lawsuit.

The same day Nettles filed his the federal civil rights action a white officer, Lieutenant Donald Gregory, filed a nearly identical action, against UT and UT Memphis employees, contending that he too had been denied due process, had had his employment contract breached and that such was done on the basis of his race. The relief sought was the same is that demanded by Cavallo and Nettles: $500,000 compensatory and $2 million punitive damages, back pay and reinstatement.

The most significant difference in outcome between Gregory's litigation and that of Cavallo and Nettles was the fact that neither of the latter was "officially reported". In Gregory, both the U.S. District Court and U. S. Court of Appeals for the Sixth Circuit rendered opinions considered of sufficient legal significance to warrant publication for purposes of citation by members of the legal community.

The headnote of the District Court ruling summarizes the case:

Former state university campus police officer brought action against university and university officials alleging a violation of his civil rights as well as pendant state claims for defamation, breach of contract, procurement of breach of contract, and tortious interference with contract rights, negligent deprivation of statutory rights, and violation of Tennessee Human Rights Act. University officials sought absolute or qualified immunity. The District Court, Turner, J., held that campus police officer failed to establish any violation of his property or liberty interest and, accordingly, university officials were entitled to qualified immunity from liability.

Motion for summary judgment on issue of qualified immunity granted.

Affirmed on appeal, 24 F. 3d 781

Gregory v. Hunt, 872 F. Supp. 476 (W.D. Tenn. 1991)

The District Court concluded that Gregory was an "at will" employee lacking any property right in continued employment and had received all the process he was due. An informal hearing before Chancellor Hunt provided him a legally sufficient opportunity to "clear his name" and rebut any complaints of poor work performance).

The Court of Appeals, in a 3-0 ruling, affirmed the District Court's conclusion. Gregory v. Hunt, 24 F 3d 781 (6th Cir. 1994). The appellate court reemphasized Gregory's lack of a property interest in continued employment and cited one of my earlier cases receiving a favorable ruling from the Sixth Circuit, in doing so.

Even if we were to assume that Gregory did have a protectable property interest in continued employment, we would still have to affirm the District Court's grant of summary judgment with respect to this issue based on this court's ruling in Woolsey v. Hunt, 930 F. 2d 555 (6th Cir.), cert. denied–US–112 S. Ct. 195, 116 L. Ed. 2d 155 (1991). In Woolsey, the plaintiff, a former secretary for the University of Tennessee Center for the Health Sciences, filed a suit in District Court, pursuant to 42 U.S.C. section 1983, claiming that she was wrongfully and illegally discharged without notice of the charges against her and without opportunity for a pre-termination hearing as required by the due process clause of the 14th amendment and by the University's rules and regulations. Just as in the case before us, two of the defendants in Woolsey were Chancellor Hunt and the University of Tennessee.

The Sixth Circuit then cited *Woolsey's* conclusion that "plaintiff does not possess a constitutionally protected property interest in continued employment with the University for the reason that Tennessee has not waived its sovereign immunity with respect to implied contract suits against the state." The same principle of law applied to Gregory's claim of a property right in continued University employment.

Wynn and Bishop Lawsuits against UT Knoxville Police Officers Ivester, Morgan and McReynolds

In the early morning hours of November 20, 1992 Trina Wynn was driving an automobile eastbound along Cumberland Avenue on the campus of the University of Tennessee in the Knoxville. Clifford Bishop was a passenger in her car.

UT police officer Charles Van Morgan observed Wynn's automobile being operated in what he judged to be a reckless manner and suspected the operator of the vehicle of driving under the influence of alcohol or drugs. Morgan activated the emergency lights and siren of his police cruiser and pursued Wynn's vehicle. Following a short pursuit, Wynn pulled her vehicle onto Estabrook Drive near its intersection with Cumberland Avenue on the UT campus. At approximately the same time, UT police officers Dana Reynolds and Jack Ivester arrived at the scene and assisted Morgan in dealing with the incident at hand.

Wynn, a black female, was arrested and charged with DUI. Morgan advised Bishop he was under arrest after exhibiting threatening behavior. Bishop attempted to flee but slipped and fell. He was apprehended by officers Morgan and McReynolds and placed under arrest for "resisting, stop frisk halt and assault on a police officer."

Wynn filed a federal lawsuit in September 1993 against UT and Officer Morgan, both in his "official capacity" and "individual capacity" (although UT and Morgan in his official capacity were quickly dismissed from the lawsuit). She claimed Morgan had falsely arrested her in violation of her constitutional rights and that any unusual behavior on the day of her arrest resulted from side effects of Tegretol, a medication she lawfully used.

With the assistance of co-counsel Robert Walker I completed a thorough investigation of the facts of the case by deposing all known witnesses, then filed a motion for summary judgment. The U.S. District Court granted the defense motion, finding that Morgan was protected by the doctrine of qualified immunity – that Morgan's actions were objectively reasonable when taken and did not violate any clearly established rights.

As beneficial – at least in the long run – as the favorable ruling of the District Court was publication of the District Court decision for future citation. Wynn v. Morgan, 861 F. Supp. 622 (E.D. Tenn.1994).

Bishop likewise filed a federal lawsuit against UT and Morgan, as well as officers Ivester and McReynolds. He claimed that he was deprived of various constitutional rights, including the right to be free from excessive use of force and malicious prosecution, right to be free from cruel and unusual punishment, right to due process and right to be free from harassment because of religion. Specifically, the complaint alleged the University defendants committed an unwarranted stop, arrest and assault on Bishop with resulting severe injury. Compensatory damages in the amount of $10 million were sought from each University defendant as well as $500,000 in punitive damages.

Unlike Wynn, an effort to dispose of Bishop with a motion for summary judgment was unsuccessful–although an attempt was made. Counsel for both plaintiff - Knoxville attorney Gloria Moore represented Bishop and also represented Wynn - and defendants prepared for trial.

U.S. Magistrate Thomas Phillips conducted a three-day jury trial on May 28 –30, 1996. The jury rendered a verdict in favor of each of the defendants.

On May 31, 1996 The Knoxville News Sentinel reported the results in a front-page article, noting that three white UT police officers, charged with falsely arresting and beating a black male, had been found innocent.

Bishop filed a notice of appeal to the U.S. Court of Appeals for the Sixth Circuit. The appellate court dismissed Bishop's appeal by order of August 23, 1996. Another police case win!

Of course not every police case resulted in a win.

RAYMOND A. CLARK--UT MEMPHIS POLICE CHIEF

In late 1989 UT Memphis police officer Raymond A. Clark applied before the open position of Assistant Vice Chancellor for Security Affairs at UT Memphis. Clark, a black male, was initially denied the position. He promptly filed a charge of discrimination on the basis of race with the Equal Employment Opportunity Commission.

Two months later, in March 1990, Clark filed suit in the U.S. District Court for the Western District of Tennessee alleging he had been denied promotion based on race. Another UT Memphis employee, Troy Vaughan, an employee in the campus personnel office, joined Clark as a party plaintiff, claiming that he likewise had been denied promotion on the basis of his race (black).

Named as defendants in the proceeding were Chancellor Hunt, Vice Chancellor Howard Carman and another administrator, Hugh Teaford. Each plaintiff asked $250,000 in compensatory damages and $250,000 punitive damages.

Memphis Attorney Don Donati represented Clark; Vaughn was represented by seperate counsel. Extensive discovery, including numerous depositions, preceded trial. Both plaintiffs continued their University employment during the proceedings.

U.S. District Judge Jon Phipps McCalla held trial (non-jury) on June 24 – 25, 29 and July 10, 1992. On July 13 McCalla announced his judgment from "the bench."

Judgment was entered in favor of the defendants in the case brought by Vaughan. However, McCalla entered judgment against each of the defendants in the case brought by Clark, finding he had been denied promotion based on his race.

A written judgment entered on August 10, 1992 provided Clark the following relief:

1. Injunctive relief
2. Back pay to July 1, 1992
3. Front pay at $50,000 per year
4. Attorneys' fees ($44,507.70) plus costs ($3724.43)
5. Compensatory damages ($60,000)
6. Punitive damages against defendant Teaford ($20,000)
7. Punitive damages against defendant Carman ($30,000)
8. Employment as assistant Vice Chancellor for security affairs, when position becomes available at salary of $50,000 per year.

While the defendants were certainly pleased with the Vaughn victory and the award of monetary damages far less than the half-million dollars sought by Clark, the award of punitive damages against Carmen and Teaford posed a serious problem: in my view the University had questionable authority to pay an award of punitive damages for an employee since such an award is based on a finding of intentional wrongdoing.

This was a case worth settling!

Why would Clark even consider such a proposal? I'll leave that speculation to the reader.

Don Donati and I appeared before the Court on August 24, 1992. The same day an "agreed order vacating the judgment and order of dismissal" was entered by Judge McCalla. Each of the District Court's prior rulings in favor of Clark were vacated (the judgment entered with respect to Vaughan was not affected). The University of Tennessee and Clark entered into a settlement agreement.

Clark was hired as Assistant Vice Chancellor for Security Affairs effective September 14, 1992. While the contents of the settlement agreement are confidential, two results of the settlement stand out. First, the amount paid by the University to Clark and his attorney was more than $6,000 less than the amount awarded by the court.

More significantly, neither Carman nor Teaford paid one penny of punitive damages (nor did anyone else).

My own assessment is that Raymond Clark performed well in the position of Assistant Vice Chancellor for Security Affairs. He served in that position until 1995.

Regrettably, Clark's law enforcement career ended with him on the other side of the law. On June 6, 1998 the Memphis Commercial Appeal headlined: "Ex –law officer sent to prison; shot girlfriend." (Memphis Commercial Appeal, June 6, 1998, p. B1).

The Commercial Appeal reported that Clark was sentenced to "spend the next 6 to 20 years in prison," explaining that Clark said "he gave up a wife and a job for a woman he then nearly killed in a jealous rage in September 1996." (Id.)

The article noted that "Clark won a federal discrimination lawsuit against UT Memphis in 1992 in which a judge ruled he had been unfairly denied the top of security post and ordered his hiring." (Id.p. B2). After Clark "pleaded guilty as charged to aggravated assault for a previous attack on [Athenia] Moore, aggravated burglary for breaking into her house, attempted first-degree murder for shooting more and attempted second-degree murder for trying to shoot her male friend" he was sentenced to "concurrent sentences of three years each for aggravated assault and aggravated burglary, eight years for attempted second-degree murder and 20 years for attempted first-degree murder." (Id.).

A tragic end to the career of a top former UT police official who earned his position the hard way – through litigation. Not the first UT administrator to gain a position in that manner.

MIRABELLA vs. UNIVERSITY OF TENNESSEE

One of my favorite UT police cases commenced shortly after the University of Tennessee's decisive 31 – 14 football victory over the University of Florida on September 19, 1992. A miserable rainy day did little to dampen the spirits of UT fans on that memorable occasion. The same was not necessarily true for several Florida fans departing Neyland Stadium at the game's conclusion.

Florida fans Sam Mirabella and wife Marie had traveled with son Charles Mirabella and wife Joanne to Knoxville to attend the game. As the couples were departing the stadium following the game's conclusion, a dispute developed between UT police officer Keith Lambert and Charles Mirabella. Profanities were shouted at Officer Lambert. Because Lambert detected an odor of alcoholic beverages and heard slurred speech, Lambert believed Charles Mirabella was intoxicated.

Officer Lambert requested Charles Mirabella to immediately leave the stadium but the conflict between the two persisted. Lambert then proceeded to arrest Mirabella.

In the process of arresting Charles Mirabella there was physical contact between Officer Lambert and Sam Mirabella. As a result of the contact, Sam Mirabella fell and broke his ankle

Officer Lambert charged Charles Mirabella with public intoxication, disorderly conduct and resisting arrest. He also charged Sam Mirabella with assaulting an officer and resisting arrest. A Knox County grand jury subsequently returned a "not true bill" as to both and the charges against Charles and Sam Mirabella were dismissed.

On September 17, 1993 all four Mirabellas filed a claim with the Tennessee Claims Commission alleging negligence, assault and improper arrest. Each claimant sought $250,000 in compensatory damages – meeting the million-dollar maximum claim for any single claims commission case.

Seven and a half years of litigation and $1 million in claims were eventually resolved. (See Chapter 94).

There were other winners and losers in cases involving UT law enforcement but the foregoing were those I found most interesting and informative.

Chapter 41–Medical Malpractice–
Most Popular Category of Litigation

During the term of my employment "medical malpractice" became the number one category area of litigation handled by the UT Office of General. Counsel. A March 14, 1997 memorandum from General Counsel Beauchamp Brogan to President Joe Johnson and his administrative staff succinctly describes the University's statewide litigation volume at that time:

> As of March 14, 1997, this office was handling a total of 373 legal proceedings. 285 are Claims Commission cases, 55 are general litigation cases and 33 are administrative claims. Administrative claims include EEOC and the Tennessee Human Rights Act complaints, as well as proceedings under the Administrative Procedures Act and complaints by students.
> Out of 148 medical malpractice cases, the UT Medical Center Knoxville has 60 compared to 88 in Memphis. Also, the UT Hospital in Knoxville has 19 workers comp cases compared to 12 in Memphis.
> As you can see, we have a lot of litigation for a small staff. None of our attorneys does litigation full time. The first Claims Commission cases involving the University started after July 1, 1986, when UT was told to drop its insurance coverage, and has now ballooned to 285.

The 1986 shift from insurance coverage to coverage by the Claims Commission significantly increased my own caseload, particularly in Memphis. My own data from 1999 showed medical malpractice cases as a 40% plurality of all cases handled by the OGC.

Until the employment of Joann Cutting, a former schoolteacher, Memphis resident and recent law school graduate, in 1985, I handled virtually all legal matters for the UT Memphis campus on my own. I did so by commuting to my office in Memphis each week and typically spent 1 to 3 days there depending on the need.

Chancellor Jim Hunt's letter to me of August 25, 1986, described one approach to addressing the need. "... I have mentioned to Beach my belief that we must have a second full-time attorney on the Memphis campus. This should be a senior person, and all we would need to accomplish this is to have you relocate to Memphis."

I opted not to relocate and a second full-time attorney was hired in Memphis. The caseload continued to increase and I continued to commute. Only when a third full time attorney was added in the Memphis OGC office did my routine commuting cease. Even then my work with the UT Memphis campus did not end. I handled several major lawsuits in Memphis during my last year of employment with the University.

I personally found medical malpractice cases to be quite fascinating. But, unlike litigation in other categories, the focus on "applicable standard of professional care," and whether the standard was adhered to, would likely be of interest only to professionals in the field. While many cases were "high dollar" cases of great significance, the facts were of a technical nature and probably not of sufficient interest to warrant their mention in this book. There are a few exceptions.

THE BAD BREASTS STORY

One of my first medical malpractice cases left several participants scratching their head as to what the problem was.

Julie Story filed a medical malpractice claim in Shelby County Circuit Court in June 1986. Her complaint was that she had received "inadequate mammoplasty augmentation" by University plastic surgery faculty and residents. A damage award in the amount of $250,000 with requested. The lawsuit was transferred to the Tennessee Claims Commission by consent of the parties in February 1987.

Story's complaint was that she had breast augmentation (surgical procedure for breast implants) performed by the University's plastic surgery team to correct a significant difference in size between her two breasts. Her contention was that after the procedure "right breast sags, flatter than the left." Story claimed that the surgeons had not completed their work and she was left with one breast that remained smaller than the other.

As the physicians explained in their depositions, the augmentation procedure utilized implants identical in size. They explained that utilizing gel implants differing in size would have resulted in one breast moving and appearing much different than the other. The use of a large implants of identical size substantially reduce the percentage of size difference between Story's breasts even if they were not made equal in size.

Story's deposition was the last to be taken. I'd requested that she bring with her any photographs she intended to use as supporting evidence of her claim. One photograph was produced. I immediately saw victory on the horizon.

The "au natural' photograph had been taken long after healing of the plaintiff's surgery - possibly even after I issued my disclosure request. The photograph depicted a very attractive, bare-breasted, young lady that no man, such as the Commissioner assigned to hear the case, would find deficient or defective in any way. No harm done! Victory in sight!

My confidence eroded when I learned, a short time later, that a new commissioner for the western section had been appointed – a woman. Maybe attention would now focus on such minutiae as "applicable standard of care" and whether an "objective" observer would find the breast size difference sufficient to support Story's claim.

My concerns were unwarranted. By order of March 9, 1990 Claims Commissioner Martha Brasfield dismissed Story's claim.

THE BURNED PENIS

Herman Davis and wife Darnell filed suit against the state of Tennessee and the on July 12, 1993 for injuries arising during a hospital stay earlier that year. The Davis's claim was that on March 15, 1993, Herman Davis underwent a "transurethral incision of the prostate" at the UT Medical Center in Knoxville. The patient experienced discomfort (burning sensation) soon after the procedure. Two days later a Foley catheter was removed from Davis's penis, an examination was conducted and it was discovered that the penis had sustained a burn.

The plaintiff sought a combined judgment of $450,000 for the burn injury. The wife's claim ($150,000) was premised, as might be expected, on interference with the parties' marital relationship. Aside from claimants' allegations, there was never any evidence of lasting permanent injury. The burn itself appeared minor – the sensitive location notwithstanding – and a side effect occasionally associated with the operative procedure Herman Davis underwent.

The shocking aspect of the case was not the pursuit of a claim for a relatively minor injury. Rather, it was the level of effort expended in pursuit of that claim.

Less than one month after filing an answer on behalf of the State, I followed my standard practice of immediately deposing the plaintiff. On March 14, 1994 I took the deposition of both plaintiffs. On the same date plaintiffs took the deposition of Dr. Paul Hatcher, the primary physician in the case.

From that day until February 28, 1995, less than a year later, 32 more depositions were taken by the parties–almost entirely at the instance of the plaintiffs. Anyone whose name appeared anywhere in the medical record was deposed.

UT Knoxville risk manager Murray Edge was deposed as was UT hospital risk management official, John Sherrer. Neither had the slightest clue what caused Davis's injury, let alone whether the procedure used fell beneath the applicable standard of care.

I traveled to Birmingham in January 1995 to depose Dr. Doblar, a witness identified by plaintiffs as their "expert witness." In short order it was clear Doblar had little basis for claiming Davis' injury was either serious or caused by any questionable medical practice.

Several months later I filed a motion for summary judgment asserting and that, notwithstanding the numerous depositions taken in the case, there was a complete lack of any evidence to support a judgment if the case went to trial.

Perhaps due to the massive record in the case the commission denied the State's motion for summary judgment. Still, the case never went to trial. Despite plaintiffs' record-setting effort to identify supporting evidence, none was found.

On March 8, 1999 more than four years after the last deposition was taken and more than a year after the commission denied the State's summary judgment motion, an order of voluntary dismissal was signed by the plaintiffs and entered by the Commission.

If you're wondering what was gained by what can only be described as a "record-setting" litigation effort, don't worry. So did I.

HELEN ASHE AND THE FAIRY PRINCESS

Twin sisters Helen Ashe and Ellen Turner are well known in the Tennessee for their charitable undertaking for feeding Knoxville area poor known as the "Love Kitchen."

A simple "pap smear" conducted in 1995 for Helen Ashe by Dr. Trent Nichols, a UT Medical Center practitioner in internal medicine led to one of my most unusual UT medical malpractice cases.

In June 1995 Helen Ashe filed a medical malpractice claim against the State with the Tennessee Claims Commission seeking recovery of compensatory damages in the amount of $300,000 for the alleged negligence of Dr. Nichols. In August 1998 the case was transferred to the Knox County Circuit Court to be joined for trial in an action connected to the same event filed against another physician, Dr. Thomas McDonald, [Helen L. Ashe v. Thomas W. McDonald, M.D., Knox Circuit No. 1-14-98]. The facts underlying Ashe's complaint are quite simple.

A Pap smear test for cancer was conducted for Ashe under the auspices of Dr. Nichols. Nichols reported test findings showing the presence of cancer cells. On the basis of Nichols report, Dr. McDonald (a private physician not employed by the University) performed surgery to remove the uterus he believed to be cancerous. But testing of the uterus post–surgery confirmed there were no cancer cells present.

The essence of Ashe's claim was that she never had cancer to begin with and Nichols mixed up her test slide with that of another patient. Her claim against McDonald was that he failed to conduct further testing before performing surgery.

The case was assigned to Knox County Circuit Judge Dale Workman – who in 1971 had run against me in my successful race for the presidency of the Knox County Young Republican organization.

One of the more interesting aspects of the case was involvement of North Carolina's "research triangle." Consistent with my custom I issued notice for taking the deposition of plaintiff's expert immediately following the joinder of the Claims Commission case with the Chancery Court action. That deposition

–the deposition of Dr. John Moore–was conducted in Atlanta on September 29, 1996.

Thanks to helpful input from colleagues in the National Association of College and University Attorneys, I was put in contact with Dr. Marcia Eisenberg in Raleigh-Durham, North Carolina. Dr. Eisenberg was an expert in DNA testing. She eagerly offered to assist me and provided me an invaluable education in the hows and whys of DNA testing.

Arrangements were made to test the DNA on the Pap smear slide–which I believed to be that of Helen Ashe–and compare it with a DNA sample taken from Ashe. The samples were tested in Dr. Eisenberg's lab. The results were conclusive.

Plaintiff's counsel took the deposition of Dr. Eisenberg on October 26, 1998. It was Dr. Eisenberg's testimony, based on her testing of both DNA samples, that the cancer cells on the Pap smear slide in controversy contained the DNA of Helen Ashe. The chance of the DNA being someone else's was less than one in several million. I do not recall the exact figure but it was astronomical.

Three weeks later I filed a motion for summary judgment on behalf of the State (Dr. Nichols). The appended deposition testimony of Dr. Eisenberg was my primary evidence in support of my motion. The court set the State's motion for oral argument on January 21, 2000.

My argument on behalf of the motion was that the cervix cancer cells on the pap smear slide were those of Helen Ashe notwithstanding the fact that not a single cancer cell was located in the surgically removed cervix. The DNA on the slide was the same as the DNA test sample taken from Ashe. As to the remote possibility of a mix up of Helen Ashe's slide with that of another patient: "only if a fairy princess alighted on one slide, then flew away and deposited it on the other," was my rebuttal.

At the close of oral argument Judge Workman granted the State's motion. An order to that effect was entered on January 24, 2000. (Interestingly, the case against McDonnell was tried on October 30 of the same year and judgment was entered against him in the amount of $150,000 plus costs.).

So, three extremely remote, perhaps miraculous, likelihoods were featured in this litigation: First, the likelihood that the only cancer cells in Helen Ashe's body were those removed for Pap smear testing. Second, the likelihood that the DNA on the slide was not hers but someone else's. And third, that a fairy princess mixed Ashe's DNA with someone else's cancer cells. I leave the reader to speculate which occurrence was more likely.

My own belief is that God's intervening hand served to prolong the life of a wonderful lady committed to serving others.

Chapter 42–Medical Malpractice–
Honest Plaintiff Loses
Patsy Smith vs. State of Tennessee

It is truly the rare case where a plaintiff eyewitness testifies truthfully, is far more credible than the chief defense witness, completely refutes the key expert witness and loses. The following is one of those rare cases.

PATSY SMITH, AS NEXT OF KIN AND MOTHER OF SHAWN SMITH vs. STATE OF TENNESSEE

Shawn Smith was hospitalized in October 1993 for orthopedic surgery for injuries resulting from the 1992 automobile accident. The surgery was performed on October 6, 1993 at UT medical Center in Knoxville. While recuperating from surgery on the recovery floor, Shawn aspirated vomitus and died sometime during the early morning hours of October 8.

Patsy Smith, the mother of Shawn Smith, filed a $1million claim for damages with the Tennessee Division of Claims Administration on October 5, 1994. The claim asserted that Shawn died as the result of the failure of UT to provide proper medical and nursing care . The two-day trial in January 2004 was a bit gut wrenching - in more ways than one.

The medical record reflected that Shawn Smith, a 26-year-old weighing 300 pounds, with a history of gastric reflux, had orthopedic surgery on October 6 and was moved to the post–surgery recovery room early that evening. He experienced a vomiting episode that same evening and a couple more the next day.

Shawn's physician signed a post–surgery order permitting him to advance to a regular diet even while taking medication for post-surgery pain. The evening of October 7 Shawn requested and ate a cheeseburger around 6 p.m. He went to sleep a couple of hours later.

Around 1 a.m. (October 8) Shawn had another vomiting episode. The registered nurse on duty, Ronald Baer, cleaned up the patient and left the room. Nurse Baer made a 4 a.m. entry in the medical record that his patient was resting quietly and using his morphine pump moderately. Baer reported that between 1 a.m. and 5 a.m. his patient had used 5.1 mg of morphine. He observed no indication of any problem until he entered Shawn Smith's room at 5:45 a.m. and found him unresponsive. Less than an hour later Shawn Smith was pronounced dead. The cause of death was aspiration of vomitus. Patsy Smith filed suit soon thereafter.

Dr. Cleland Blake served as plaintiff's expert witness. A well-known Fulbright Scholar and Morristown pathologist, Blake was nationally recognized for his expertise in the field of forensic pathology. He had conducted thousands of autopsies and was widely sought after as an instructor and expert witness. His expert testimony in this case was scathing.

Blake testified that within a reasonable degree of medical certainty nurse Bayer had acted negligently by failing to use a stethoscope and listen to his patient's lungs after the 1 a.m. vomiting incident. Worse, according to Blake, Smith aspirated vomitus into his lungs after that incident, became unconscious and began slowly dying. In response to my cross examination, Blake described the process as an agonizing struggle during which the patient slowly suffocated.

Claims Commissioner Cheek found "that Dr. Blake was a very credible witness." He found Blake very knowledgeable about his field of specialty, namely pathology.

On the other hand my chief witness performed poorly on the witness stand. Baer recalled little about the patient's condition the morning of October 8. The medical record reflected no evidence Baer had ever used a stethoscope to determine whether Smith was having problems relating to aspiration of vomitus. Without belaboring the point, suffice it to say that my witness did nothing to rebut Blake's testimony.

Commissioner Cheek found fault with nurse Baer's lack of awareness that Smith had eaten a cheeseburger and fries the previous evening. He was also critical of Baer's lack of awareness of Smith's last two vomiting episodes despite each being reported on Smith's medical chart. He was clearly puzzled by Baer's failure to even look at the nursing notes from the previous shift.

> Now as this commission stated earlier, Mr. Baer was a horrible, horrible witness. He may be a good man. The commission makes no judgment or opinion or states no opinion on Mr. Baer as a person, but as a witness, he was horrible. He was evasive. He was elusive. So the image that kept coming to my mind was of trying to nail a piece of Jell-O to the wall.

[Transcript of Commissioner Cheek's opinion of Feb. 4, 2004, p.24]

Another witness for plaintiff, registered nurse Ruby Wiseman, testified that Sean Smith should never been given a cheeseburger and french fries so soon after a vomiting incident. And, lastly, the state was taken to task because the medical record had been reported missing for five and half years. "There is absolutely positively no way this commission can find anything but that such an act, if you will, such an occurrence is unacceptable. There is no proof that the integrity of this chart was maintained."[Transcript, pp. 33 – 34] A gut wrenching disaster in the making for the State. Except for the testimony of one key witness – the plaintiff.

Plaintiff Patsy Smith testified as forthrightly as any adversary I have ever encountered. She told the truth when even a slight deviation would have helped her case. Smith single-handedly destroyed her expert witness's testimony that her son had died an agonizing death. And, she corroborated my own chief witness's shaky testimony that Shawn Smith did nothing to cause alarm between the hours of 1 a.m. and 5:40 a.m. the morning of October 8.

According to my diary note for February 4, 2004: "State Claims Commissioner Vance Cheek issued his findings in favor of the State (Medical Center) in a 45 – 50 minute telephone conference ruling following last week's two-day trial in Johnson City of a case that arose in 1993 – 11 years ago! Great victory!" The Commissioner's oral ruling was transcribed by a court reporter.

Commissioner Cheek's opinion summarized the testimony of plaintiff that mandated judgment for the defense:

At trial the claimant's mother testified that she was with the Claimant the night he died. After the 1 A.M. vomiting episode, Mrs. Smith testified that her son seemed fine. She testified she is a very light sleeper and, of course, chair beds kept in rooms for visiting family in hospitals are not very comfortable. She states she is certain she would have heard any sound that would evidence her son's distress, be it respiratory or otherwise. ...

This Commission must note for the record that Mrs. Smith appears to be a very honest witness, a very credible witness, a very strong woman, a woman who sat literally at my right hand for two days as lawyers and witnesses discussed the gory details of her son's death and acted with poise, dignity and class. She is honest, honest to the point where her testimony became damaging to her claim. The Commission is sincerely impressed with this lady's poise, strength and character, and much of this Commission's decision is based upon her testimony given first as it was offered by the Claimant's counsel.

[Transcript, pp. 18–19]

The basis for rebutting Dr. Blake's testimony is that the Claimant showed absolutely no signs of aspiration at 1:00 A.M. or after. The Claimant did not choke or cough. He did not complain of any burning in his lungs. Additionally, the Claimant conducted conversations with Mr. Baer and his mother after the 1:00 A.M. vomiting episode. Be that as it may, it's interesting that while although he was cleaned up at 1:00 A.M., he spoke clearly to his mother at 1:00 A.M. At the same time he was found unresponsive and the Code was being conducted, the anesthesiologist trying to intubate Mr. Smith found secretions in his throat, in his mouth and in his upper airways while he was trying to be intubated during the Code. This, coupled with the coffee ground emesis found in the Claimant's mouth, evidences that if a final vomiting episode took place an hour prior to the Claimant's death, somewhere around 5:00 o'clock, 5:15 or the like.

[Transcript, pp. 29–30

Commissioner Cheek resolved the "lost file" issue by noting that "the hospital's failure to find the file for five and half years is an abomination, and we would hope that such an event would not be repeated.... And I find that while the integrity of the chart was not proven, that alteration was not proven either. So, in essence, it's a wash."

[Transcript, p. 34]

Judgment for the State, incorporating Commissioner Cheek's oral findings, was entered on March 2, 2004. An appeal was taken to the Tennessee Court of Appeals, Eastern Section. On March 14, 2005 appellate judges Swiney, Franks and Susano affirmed the ruling below, bringing to conclusion a case lasting 10 1/2 years. [Patsy Smith, as next of kin and mother of Shawn Smith v. State of Tennessee, No. E2004-0737-COA-R3-CV].

After a decade of litigation the right result was reached with judgment entered for the defendant-thanks largely to the laudable integrity of the plaintiff, Patsy Smith.

Chapter 43–Med Mal–
A "Set Up" and Sure Loser Goes Well–
Henry Harris and Virginia Harris vs. State of Tennessee

One of the oddest cases I handled for the University was odd not because the case itself was odd but because of the way I became involved in it.

Staffing and assignment of responsibilities in the UT Office of General Counsel became problematic after the University's transition from the "Big Orange" period to the stormy turbulence of the Gilley years. One aspect of that was the addition of a third level of administration in the office, that being the position of Deputy General Counsel. Another related to my own lawsuit against President Gilley.

Peter Foley was hired as UT's first Deputy General Counsel in 2002. He was introduced to the office staff as an experienced attorney with laudable credentials, including trial experience (although no experience in the practice of higher education law). He was immediately assigned a number of cases for handling.

My first surprise came by way of a memorandum to me from General Counsel Catherine Mizell dated April 22, 2003:

> Due to Peter's trial and discovery schedule for the month of August, I need to reassign the medical malpractice claim of Henry Harris v. State of Tennessee to you. The case is set for trial on August 21 – 22. According to my records, you have a TCC claim set for trial on 7/31 and 8/1, but nothing else set in August or September.
>
> Principal discovery in the Harris case has been completed. Peter has taken the depositions of the claimant's wife and claimant's three experts. He has defended the depositions of the res ident and three experts for the state. Peter will be sending you a comprehensive briefing mem orandum on the case.
>
> Thank you,
>
> Catherine

First and foremost, as throughout my career in the OGC, I was excited to have a case assigned to me. At the same time I was greatly surprised by the circumstances.

Surprise No.1. In my entire career I had never had one of my cases reassigned to someone else because of my "trial and discovery schedule." Quite the contrary, I set depositions and trials so as to avoid scheduling conflicts. I even scheduled annual leave, including international travel–occasionally for as long as a month–so as to avoid scheduling conflicts. Not once did I ask someone to take over a case from me because of scheduling conflicts.

Likewise, I have never had another OGC attorney's case reassigned to me except in a few cases where the attorney left OGC employment and a single case where I was requested to assume responsibility for a case due to problems between the attorney and the judge (Mizell and Knox County General Sessions Judge David Creekmore).

The Harris trial was set **four** months from the date of Mizell's memorandum. At the same time Mizell's memorandum noted that principle discovery in the case had been completed. It occurred to me that given those circumstances I would have had abundant opportunity to prepare for trial–or request a court to reset a trial.

Foley had handled the case from the outset (the claim being filed with the Tennessee Division of Claims Administration in March, 2002). For the better part of the year, as noted in Mizell's memorandum, Foley spent a great deal of time on the case, completing "principle discovery" including that of the claimant's wife, claimants three experts, the UT resident and three experts for the State.

It concerned me little that I had only four months to prepare for trial of a case another attorney had spent one year working on–even assuming any additional discovery was needed. But, at a minimum, I knew I would spend countless hours reviewing pleadings, depositions, case law and other matters Foley had spent much time on. A hugely wasteful duplication of Foley's effort! Nevertheless, I personally found the claims set forth by Henry Harris and the wife Virginia Harris quite interesting and was eager to prepare for trial.

Henry Harris had received a kidney transplant in 1993 and was hospitalized at the UT medical Center in 2001 for suspected rejection of the organ. Dr. Jones was a third year UT surgery resident who allegedly removed an "internal jugular Quinton catheter" from Harris without him being placed in the appropriate supine or other recommended position rather than being seated at a 45° angle.

According to the claim, Dr. Jones also failed to hold pressure at the catheter removal site for a sufficient period of time and failed to apply the proper dressing. These claimed omissions allegedly caused Henry Harris to suffer a stroke as well as a heart attack, Harris ending up wheelchair-bound.

Surprise no. 2. Mizell's memorandum contained no hint whatever that I needed do anything more than prepare to try the case.

I soon learned that principal discovery was not complete as Mizell reported. Key depositions remained to be taken prior to the August trial date for both discovery and evidentiary purposes (depositions submitted as evidence in place of a witness testifying in court). Three depositions were hurriedly scheduled and held on separate days during the week preceding trial. One of those was in Stockbridge, Massachusetts.

Surprise no. 3. The memorandum assigning the case to me did not remotely suggested the possibility – let alone the advisability – of settlement. The entire thrust of the document was that the case was all but ready for trial. A lengthy "briefing memorandum" provided me by Foley likewise made no reference whatever to any settlement discussions or recommendations.

By memorandum of May 5, 2003, Deputy General Counsel Foley reiterated information he had provided me the previous week.

> "Ron – just a reminder that, per my lengthy memo to you, rebuttal experts are due to be designated by 5/9. I recommend you fax the supplemental designation I prepared regarding Dr. Goldman to plaintiffs counsel on the 9th."

Less than 15 minutes later I responded to Foley's email:

> Good morning Peter!
> I will fax the supplemental designation on Friday as you suggest.
> I had a chance to review your excellent memorandum and attached materials this past weekend. I get the drift of the case– –although I plan to sequester myself in the next few days and come up to speed on the case.
> Have there been any settlement discussions or offers?

Foley responded less than an hour later:

> "Ron –
> The only 'discussions' were early on when the plaintiffs' counsel suggested that we should simply throw in the towel and pay $600K, saying that we would never find an expert either to defend Jones on the standard of care issue or on the causation issue."

This was the one and only mention of any settlement "discussion."

Surprise no. 4. A couple of days later, in the course of reviewing the rather voluminous case file, I came across the deposition of Dr. Julie Lisa Jones.

I was surprised to read Dr. Jones' discovery testimony essentially **agreeing with** a number of allegations made by the claimant. I was stunned to read Dr. Jones' testimony toward the end of her 128 page deposition.

[Attorney by plaintiffs' attorney Jon Jones]

Q. Okay. And you don't plan to come into the trial of this case and testify that in taking the catheter out you fully complied with the standard of care, do you?

A. No.

Q. Okay. And I don't mean to be too critical because you were put into a situation that night where you'd never had any real teaching or training, is that fair?

A. No. I had pulled catheters before, just not in this particular variant. I'm finished.

Q. Okay. You had never been given any training or teaching about how to prevent air embolism when you pulled jugular catheters, is that fair?

A. Yes.

Q. Okay. And you don't deny because of that lack of training that you did in fact deviate from the standard of care for surgeons or surgical residents in pulling the catheter; is that correct?

A. Can I speak to Mr. Foley?

MR. JONES: Sure. Would you read it back?

THE WITNESS: I mean can I speak to Mr. Foley about that?

MR. FOLEY: You can. You may. You and I can go out in the hall.

MR. JONES: You really can't.

MR. KOKSAL: Not in the course of the deposition session.

MR. JONES: All you can talk about is privilege, and this isn't privilege.

MR. FOLEY: Do you have a question about his question?

THE WITNESS: No

MR. FOLEY: Do you understand his question?

THE WITNESS: Yes.

MR. FOLEY: Okay.

MR. JONES: I need you to answer it.

MR. FOLEY: Then to the extent that you can answer it, please answer it for the record.

THE WITNESS: Would you repeat it, please?(Whereupon, the record was read.)

THE WITNESS: Yes, probably.

MR. JONES: Okay. That's all I have. Thank you very much.

MR. FOLEY: No questions.

[July 16, 2002 Discovery Deposition of Julie Lisa Jones, M.D., pp.126-28]

Dr. Jones admission—with no follow-up questions for clarification by Foley —that she had probably deviated from the standard of care for surgeons or surgical residents in pulling the catheter from Henry Harris, all but destroyed any liability defense. This was definitely a case in which settlement was an option to be pursued.

Surprise no. 5. Coinciding in time with my review of Dr. Jones' deposition, I received a "tip" from a friend who had overheard a conversation between

Mizell and Foley. The essence of the reported conversation was that I was assigned the Harris case with the expectation that I would lose it and be embarrassed–or words to that effect.

Perhaps I should not have been surprised, given the circumstances of the Gilley litigation, but I was.

I ignored the "tip" and focused on the litigation issue at hand. In a telephone call to Foley I offered my opinion that Dr. Jones discovery deposition testimony was devastating and an offer of settlement should be made. Foley agreed without further elaboration.

I called plaintiffs' attorney Ron Koksal and asked if the Harrises would accept a settlement offer of $85,000. The offer was admittedly absurdly low. I simply wanted to initiate settlement discussion.

The response was immediate and clear. "I don't want to waste your time. We will not settle for one cent less than the maximum recovery permitted under state law." I took a huge breath of relief!

Immediately I confirmed by memorandum to Foley the rejection by plaintiffs' counsel of any settlement offer less than the maximum recovery permitted under state law–$600,000.

Gone was the danger that I would proceed to trial, lose a high dollar judgment award against the State (the University of Tennessee), then face accusations of incompetency from my superiors because I had failed to attempt settlement. I proceeded with the remaining depositions and prepared for trial.

As late as August 18, 2003, in a letter to Mizell and me, the General Counsel for University Health Systems, Inc. (private nonprofit operator of UT Medical Center since 1999), Ben Cox, urged "that the state reconsider its settlement offer previously provided to the plaintiffs and make every attempt to settle this case in an amount up to and including the plaintiff's settlement demand of $600,000." The request was declined. Mizell, Foley and I concurred on that response.

Surprise no. 6. Because Dr. Jones' discovery deposition was so devastating I saw no advantage to calling her as a live witness and she refused to attend in any event. I announced to opposing counsel that I would be taking Dr. Jones' deposition–for evidence–in Boston.

I arranged to meet Dr. Jones in Boston on July 28–the day before her deposition was to take place–and spend the entire day reviewing the record with her and preparing her for deposition. There were many "follow-up" questions that should have been, but were not, asked Dr. Jones during her discovery deposition,

When I met Dr. Jones the morning of July 28 I was stunned to learn that Foley had spent little time reviewing Harris's medical record with her prior to her discovery deposition. I was more stunned when she advised that they had met for less than an hour before her deposition commenced. Even a cursory review of Jones' discovery deposition revealed she had not been adequately prepared.

Unfortunately, but not surprisingly, my effort to repair the damage by having Dr. Jones offer further explanation of her earlier testimony did not succeed.

Trial of the Harris's claim was held before the Tennessee Claims Commission, Commissioner Vance Cheek, on August 21–22, 2003. Commissioner Cheek's sixty eight page judgment was entered on July 20, 2004–nearly a year later. [Henry Harris and Virginia Harris v. State of Tennessee, TCC No. 20201438]

Not unexpectedly, Commissioner Cheek keyed in on Dr. Jones discovery deposition: "Finally and quite critically, Dr. Jones was asked if because of her lack of training did she deviate from what she understood to be the standard of care for surgeons or surgical residents when she removed Mr. Harris' IJC. Dr. Jones answered, 'yes, probably.'". [Judgment, p.14.]

Although Dr. Jones was better prepared for her evidentiary deposition, citing published medical authority and offering a far better explanation of her treatment of Harris, the preparatory effort came too late.

After having read and reviewed the extensive testimony in detail, the Commission finds that Dr. Julie Jones was more honest during her discovery deposition than during her evidentiary deposition. The changes in her testimony are too substantial, too self-serving and too critical for this Commission to believe that Dr. Jones simply reconsidered her actions. It is apparent to the Commission that steps were taken by Dr. Jones to explain away intentionally her earlier admission to have violated the standard of care in her treatment of Mr. Harris. Judgment, p. 28

This Commission FINDS that Dr. Jones' change in testimony is too drastic and to dubious to be considered trustworthy, therefore, the Commission elects to give more weight to her discovery deposition over her evidentiary deposition. In fact, it is the Commissioner's view that Dr. Jones evidentiary deposition is to be given little weight, particularly in the areas where she attempts to recant her previous sworn testimony. Judgment, p. 29.

A devastating finding but certainly understandable. Dr. Jones was urged to be–and in my opinion was–truthful in her evidentiary deposition. It was impossible to "correct" testimony given in a discovery deposition by testimony later given in an evidentiary deposition introduced at trial.

The time for restating or correcting testimony given during a discovery deposition was on cross-examination–and there was none in this instance. Better yet, critical issues facing a party should be addressed during preparation by the party's legal counsel in advance of the deposition. That did not happen either.

Dr. Jones was found to have deviated from the standard of acceptable medical care with the result that Harris suffered a stroke leading to brain injury, paralysis and heart damage. Fortunately, the pending disaster ended on a substantially brighter note, if only from a perspective of damages awarded.

While I made every reasonable effort to prevail on the issue of liability the roadblocks to success were clear dating back to my reading of Dr. Jones discovery deposition. My primary focus was on reducing the dollar amount of damages awarded.

I took and introduced the evidentiary depositions of two physicians on the issue of damages. The first was Dr. Denise Rivers, the UT Medical Center physician having primary responsibility for Harris's care. Her key testimony was summarized by Commissioner Cheek: "Dr. Rivers testified that Mr. Harris's diagnosis on admission was that of possible renal transplant rejection. In addition, his pre-admission diagnoses were kidney transplant, Kaposi's sarcoma, hypertension, lung disease, diabetes secondary to steroids in the past, membranous nephropathy ,interstitial nephritis, and congestive heart failure." [Judgment, p. 50]

I also called, as an expert witness for the State, Dr. Darrel Thomas. He was equally clear that Harris' health was very poor before the April 5, 2001 incident with Dr. Jones.

On the basis of the evidence presented on the issue of damages Commissioner Cheek found: "Mitigating Mr. Harris's damages is the clear fact that he is a man who suffered from numerous, grave ailments prior to the events of April 5, 2001." The Commissioner then reviewed the list of ailments testified to by Dr. Rivers and Dr. Thomas. "When assessing damages in this claim, the Commission may not ignore the claimant's delicate health." [Judgment, pp.65-66]

The judgment concluded with what I viewed as a very fair award of damages. Judgment in the amount of $130,000 was entered in favor of Henry Harris and a judgment in the amount of $35,000 was entered in favor of wife for loss of consortium.

While the case goes in the University's "loss" column, plaintiffs' counsel left a lot of money on the table. The University saved $435,000 over the minimum amount plaintiffs would accept as settlement. Stated another way, the judgment against the state was 27½ % of the amount plaintiffs expected to receive.

Of less importance to the taxpayers of the state of Tennessee, my professional reputation survived a while longer. Despite the excellent result, I received no letter of commendation or even an emailed "good result" from the General Counsel or her Deputy. I was not surprised.

Who knows? Perhaps the Harris case reassignment to me was part of a setup. If so, the set up went well–for all UT parties concerned.

Chapter 44–Medical Malpractice–
The Missing Skull Fragment–Copeland vs. State

One of the last cases I handled for the UT Memphis campus concluded in the year prior to my retirement from the University. The case was one of the more unusual cases I tried.

A medical malpractice claim against the State was filed by William B Copeland in the Tennessee Division of Claims Administration (TCC No. 20401644) on April 20, 2004. A virtually identically worded complaint was filed in the Shelby County Circuit Court the same day (Docket No. CT– 002255 –4; Companion Case Docket No. CT–002874-5). The Circuit Court action named Morris Ray, M.D., Mark Smith, M.D. and the Shelby County Healthcare Corporation (The Regional Medical Center at Memphis) as defendants. The Claims Commission claim was later transferred to the Shelby County Circuit Court and joined with the circuit court action for trial.

Smith, a UT-employed third-year medical resident was "non-suited" (dismissed) as a defendant based on his University employment.

The claims set forth in the 49-page complaint were most unusual. The headings appeared on the front page of the complaint.

   I. Bailment
   II. Negligent storage, maintenance, and protection of human body parts
   III. Res Ipsa Loquitur
   IV. Violation of obligations of a warehouseman
   V. Conversion
   VI. Medical malpractice
   VII. Breach of warranty
   VIII. Negligence of physicians
   IX. Replevin
   X. Detinue
   XI. Negligent entrustment
   XII. Negligent entrustment [sic]
   XIII. Special assumpsit

Copeland "prayed for damages" against the defendants "in a sum in excess of Five Million Dollars ($5,000,000.00) and his costs of suit." He was represented by Memphis attorneys Dee Shawn Peoples and R. Linley Richter.

The whittled down version of the facts of the case is that on July 25, 2003 Copeland was admitted to the Regional Medical Center at Memphis ("the Med") following a serious automobile accident during which he was ejected from his vehicle and suffered a serious head injury as well as other injuries.

Dr. Smith and Dr. Ray, a member of the UT surgery faculty performed a craniotomy on Copeland to reduce swelling inside his brain. A small portion of Copeland's skull (a "bone flap") was removed during the procedure and transmitted to another area of the Med for storage. Five days later Copeland was scheduled for surgery to reinsert the bone flap in its original position.

The bone flap could not be located. A "mesh" substitute, identical in size to the missing bone flap, was ordered from a medical supplier. The mesh flap replacement was surgically implanted in Copeland the few days later.

In his complaint Copeland asserted an almost endless list of horrors he experienced as a result of the loss of his original skull fragment and receipt of the mesh substitute.

… As a direct and proximate result of the breach of the duties, obligations, and responsibilities of the defendants, Regional Medical Center at Memphis, Morris W Ray, M.D. and Mark D Smith, M.D., the plaintiff has suffered severe and serious personal injuries that were readily foreseeable, to wit: the plaintiff has been permanently disfigured, and suffers, and will continue to suffer from tinnitus, dizziness, neurological deficits, headaches, blurred vision, loss of balance and vertigo; the plaintiff suffers from anxiety, loss of self-esteem, and nervousness; the plaintiff has lost large sums of money that he otherwise would have earned and will lose large amounts of money in the future that he otherwise would have earned; that said conditions are permanent and progressive;

Complaint, par. 24.

Copeland alleged that the missing "portion of skull is unique and irreplaceable." He then alleged that "the reasonable value of said portion of skull is $1 million a month and the plaintiff has been deprived of the use and enjoyment of said skull since June 30, 2003 when said portion of skull was to have been fixed and united with the remainder of the skull of the plaintiff." Complaint, par.21.

More than a dozen depositions were taken in the case, including that of the plaintiff. The deposition of William Copeland was held in the office of his attorneys on February 17, 2006. A memorable occasion.

I'm not sure what I expected to see when I entered Copeland's attorneys' conference room. Most memorable was what I did not see. I saw nothing remarkable about Copeland's appearance. Photographs were taken to corroborate my conclusion.

Notwithstanding the fact that all but one of the depositions scheduled in the case remained to be taken, I moved forward. On September 20, 2006 I filed a motion for summary judgment together with supporting memorandum of law and a "statement of undisputed material facts." Copeland's deposition testimony and Exhibit No. 1 to the deposition–photographs of the plaintiff–were appended to the filing.

Eleven more depositions were conducted by the parties over the next several months. The State's summary judgment motion was argued before the Shelby County Circuit Court on August 17, 2007. The Court ruled from the bench following the conclusion of oral argument. The State's motion was granted.

The Circuit Court's order granting summary judgment in favor of the State was entered on August 21, 2007. No appeal was filed.

A nice "last hurrah" for my "med mal" practice for UT Memphis!

Chapter 45–Elvis Presley and His UT Legal Defense

World-famous musical entertainer Elvis Presley died in Memphis, Tennessee on August 16, 1977. He arrived by ambulance at Baptist Memorial Hospital at approximately 2:30 PM and was "DOA" (dead on arrival).

Shelby County medical examiner Dr. Jerry T Francisco, an employee of the University of Tennessee Center for Health Sciences, conducted an autopsy on Presley at Baptist Hospital. Francisco eventually prepared a toxicology report detailing his findings.

On August 16, 1979, the same day is Presley's death, a civil action entitled "Complaint for Mandamus," was filed in the Chancery Court of Shelby County, Tennessee (Docket no. 85964 – 3 R.D.]. Plaintiffs in the action were identified as "State of Tennessee, on the relation of James P. Cole and Charles C. Thompson, II." The named defendants were "Jerry T. Francisco, M.D., Shelby County Medical Examiner, and Hugh W Stanton, District Attorney General." I was not immediately made aware of the filing by Francisco or anyone else since the University of Tennessee was not a named party.

On September 11, 1979 plaintiffs filed a "Motion to Compel Answers to Questions Asked on Oral Examination." Two days later I received a telephone call from Francisco. For the first time I learned of his role in performing Presley's autopsy and requests by representatives of ABC TV's 20-20 program for a copy of his findings. I also learned of the pending legal proceedings, and that a hearing on the motion to compel was scheduled for September 28.

My immediate advice to Francisco was to continue denying access to his records until I had an opportunity to conduct a review. On September 17, I flew to Memphis for the day and met with Francisco. I reviewed the report he had prepared following completion of Presley's autopsy (which we consistently referred to as Presley's "toxicology report").

It was my immediate opinion that the Presley toxicology report was a medical record with privacy privileges under state law. My immediate concern was Francisco's potential liability to the Presley family if he released the report to anyone without the consent of the Presley heirs or authorized representative. On the other hand, the University itself had no vested interest in preventing public disclosure of a toxicology report.

I advised Francisco that I would be representing him at the September 28 hearing. The toxicology report was transferred to my possession and I returned to Knoxville later that evening, giving no particular thought to the document in my possession (which I kept in my briefcase).

On September 28, 1979, I took an early morning commercial flight from Knoxville to Memphis, rented a vehicle at the airport and headed downtown for the Chancery Court hearing. I first dropped by my Memphis office, in the UT Memphis administration building, and picked up the volume of Tennessee Code Annotated containing the "medical records" privacy statute (Tenn. Code Ann. 53-1322(C)).

This was a rare–perhaps the only–occasion on which I went to court to argue a motion without first preparing and filing some sort of written response in advance. My reason for not doing so was quite simple: it mattered little if the court granted the plaintiffs' motion; my only concern was that the toxicology report not be released in violation of state law, opening the doors to potential legal liability for Francisco (or anyone else releasing the report).

I headed downtown having little more in my briefcase than the plaintiffs' court filings, my volume of Tennessee Code Annotated and Elvis Presley's toxicology report. The time set for the motion hearing I did not record nor do I recall. But I recall well that I arrived well before the appointed time. I recall a well the packed courtroom greeted me when I walked through the door.

My seat was reserved at the table for defense counsel. There was an extra seat at the table that would remain unfilled. Several attorneys, none of whom I recognized, were seated at the plaintiff's table. Every other seat in the courtroom was taken and a number of observers lined the walls.

Presiding judge, Chancellor D. J. Allisandratos, entered a courtroom abuzz with chatter. The chatter stopped and silence reigned as the bailiff announced, "All rise!" and called the court to order.

Chancellor Allisandratos called the first case on the docket–actually, the only case on the docket that day. Counsel for the parties identified themselves and the party they represented. A Memphis attorney (whose identity I do not recall) identified two attorneys, each from a different state other than Tennessee, who would each be presenting a different aspect of the plaintiffs' position. Plaintiff's table appeared well-stocked with files and reference materials; the defense table

THE COMMERCIAL APPEAL

Death Captures Crown Of Rock And Roll
—Elvis Dies Apparently After Heart Attack

Elvis Went From Rags To Riches

'Are You Sure There's No Mistake?' —The Desired Answer Never Came

'Unclassifiable' Sound Pervaded Elvis' Career

Alabama's Judge Johnson Chosen As New FBI Chief

A Legacy

The Weather

To Test Theory, Sneak Up On A Kurdsman And Yell 'Boo!'

contained only the volume of Tennessee code annotated I had brought with me. I left the toxicology report and several pleadings in my briefcase.

The attorneys representing ABC and seeking disclosure of the toxicology report for the "20-20" television series used the better part of an hour in presenting their arguments. I took no notes, was very relaxed and well prepared when my turn came.

After introducing myself to the court–a formality–I presented my argument. First, I read the one paragraph privacy statute addressing medical records. Second, I observed, "Your Honor, I see nothing in the statute that says 'except for the records of Elvis Presley'." I concluded with a request that the plaintiffs' motion be denied and sat down. I had done my job. It was my expectation that the Chancellor would grant the motion to compel, direct that an order to that effect be prepared and entered. The report could then be released without any fear of legal liability.

Chancellor Allisandratos thoroughly reviewed the plaintiffs' arguments. Only toward the end of his remarks did it become clear that the ruling would not favor the plaintiffs. According to the Chancellor, the report prepared by Dr. Francisco was a medical record, the privacy of which was protected under state law. Plaintiffs' motion to compel was denied!

The ruling was a surprise to me considering my minimal effort to prevail. The Chancellor's final admonishment caused me to break out in a sweat.

"And woe be it to anyone who does anything to cause disclosure of this report to the public" or words like that were said. In a matter of seconds it dawned on me that I was the only person in a position to breach the Chancellor's edict since I had sole possession of the document. It seemed that everyone looked at me as I exited the chamber following adjournment.

Still sweating, I marched directly to the office of the Shelby County Clerk and Master. "I have a document that I wish to file under seal," I explained to one of the office personnel. "Sure, but you'll need an appropriate order signed by all counsel of record in order to do that," was the reply.

Of course. I knew that. I was simply responding to a completely unexpected development.

I headed back to my Memphis office, then on to the airport, making certain that the Presley toxicology report was locked securely in my briefcase. Never, for any reason, did I go anywhere without the briefcase being within arm's reach. Paranoid would be a fair description of my mindset. I imagine that anyone looking at me–from the time Alissandratos announced his ruling until I reached Knoxville and entered my automobile for the drive home–knew I had the report and would take advantage of any opportunity to get it!

I prepared the necessary order and secured the signatures of all counsel of record. The process took more than a month. In the meantime, I kept the report hidden and better protected than gold bullion. My return trip to Memphis, with report and order in hand, was accomplished cautiously and with discreteness an intelligence service would be proud of.

The Elvis Presley toxicology report was filed with the Clerk and Master of the Shelby County Chancery Court on November 9, 1979. My job was complete. Counsel for the Presley family soon entered the fray and pursued defense of the record's privacy all the way to the Tennessee Supreme Court.

The Knoxville News-Sentinel reported the Supreme Court's December 13, 1982 affirmation of Chancellor Alessandratos' ruling with the headline "Elvis Presley Autopsy Results are Private, High Court Rules," The Knoxville News-Sentinel, December 13, 1982, page B-8.

Fourteen years later, a January 6, 1991 front page article in the Knoxville News-Sentinel ("Silence Broken–Pathologist says Elvis Died from Drugs, not Heart Attack") reviews a late-breaking controversy between Dr. Francisco and Dr. Eric Muirhead,who erroneously claimed he was muzzled into silence by Baptist Hospital attorneys when actually the silence was predicated by my advice to him and Dr. Francisco as to whether Presley's death resulted from a heart attack or drugs. No citation to the toxicology report was made by either man.

Whether Presley's report remains under seal, yet to be disclosed to the public, I have no knowledge. I know only that I played no role in its release.

Now, I bet you are wondering, "Did Ron read that toxicology report or not?" Well, of course I did. After all, Elvis was the King and any tidbit of information about him was highly interesting and important. Now, you are wondering, "Will Ron tell us what the report said?" No, or course I won't. I think by this time just about everyone that wants to know has the basic knowledge of what was in that report, but I can always bask in the knowledge that I was one of the few people who knew the truth about the causes of Elvis' death that soon.

I feel the need to also share with you that when I got word of the death of Elvis Presley, my knees nearly buckled. To get that news was something like getting punched in the stomach. For all that he was and became in his life, Elvis was correctly nicknamed "The King," and, since he was from Tennessee, he was even more to us as he was "Our King."

Let me tell you, Memphis after the death of Elvis was a city in mourning. Photos, pictures, flowers, displays of all sorts, signs, messages and anything and everything you could think of could be seen on the streets and Elvis had been dead less than 24 hours. People were milling around, cars were whizzing by and everyone was sad. There would be no smiles in Memphis that year and for a long time to come.

As news spread of Elvis' death every radio station was playing round-the-clock Elvis music and it was blaring from loud speakers on every street. The television stations were providing play-by-play accounts of the death, and showing a live feed from Graceland, Elvis' home. Movie stars and singers like Burt Reynolds and Jerry Reed had already arrived in town and were shown sitting in a chair inside Elvis' house wiping tears from their eyes. Everyone was focused on their own grief, but also reaching out to Mr. Vernon Presley, Elvis' dad, Priscilla, his former wife, and Lisa Marie, his only child. There was nowhere to look or to go to get away from the sadness at that time.

I didn't realize it on that day, but when I walked into that courtroom, several famous people were in the crowd. Members of what was called "the Memphis Mafia" were also there. The Memphis Mafia was the group of men and women who took care of Elvis, some were his relatives, and most were his long-time friends. Others in court were regular citizens who had camped out all night in order to secure a spot inside the courtroom. How would I describe them? Shocked, stunned, numb. Elvis was dead and nobody could believe it.

Whatever you may think of Elvis Presley, his story certainly reads like a novel. Born into poverty, all he had was the love of his parents, a guitar and a talent we can only believe was God given. You may not think of him in this way, but Elvis was a pioneer. He, and some others, invented a new form of music. They blended country, rhythm and blues with some jazz in there, along with a dose of religious or sacred music and called it Rock 'n Roll. The world has not been the same since.

During his short life, Elvis was ridiculed because of the way he dressed and the way he styled his hair. He was once told by Ernest Tubb, a very famous country music star, after his first appearance at the Grand Ole Opry, "Son, you need to go back on home to Memphis, no one is going to want to hear your kind of music." However, staying true to himself and believing in his own talent, helped him to keep pushing forward.

One day while still working as a truck driver, he wanted to record a birthday gift for his Mother. He stopped by Sun Records there in Memphis where he had been meeting with some new friends, Johnny Cash, Jerry Lee Lewis, and Carl Perkins, and recorded, "That's Alright Mama." The disc jockey, Sam Phillips, on duty that day, took the recording and played it on his radio show. His phones began ringing off the hooks and the rest is history.

Elvis' death was a sad chapter in the history of our country. Looking back all these years, it is like I lived in a dream because of the way things played out. I never knew Elvis personally, but I took good care of him after he died when the matter of protecting that report found its way into my hands, and for that I find peace and a little bit of joy in my heart.

Chapter 46–Tennessee's Charles Manson
Alter Ego–Dr. Zed Aydelott

Tennessee's Attorney General from 1988 to 1993 was Charles Burson, Jr. I first met Burson in the early 1970s while he was in private practice. We were on opposing sides in a case involving a UT Memphis College of Medicine student charged with illegal drug use. The case went well and Burson impressed me from the outset as being a "good guy" - a person of integrity.

In May 1995 a Memphis newspaper had a front page story featuring a "father of the year" award given Charles Burson, Sr. by a Memphis civic organization. Burson's wife and daughter received similar awards. A photograph of the Burson family prominently graced the front page.

Charles Burson, Jr. was included in the photograph, standing with his award winning family. So was a gentleman identified as Dr. Zed Aydelott, described as the fiancée of Charles' sister and a member of the faculty at UT Memphis.

On May 18 I received a call from Dr. Bill Webb, the head of the UT Memphis psychiatry department. Webb explained that he had had a troubling encounter with one of his patients, a young male military veteran with psychiatric issues, at the Veterans Administration Hospital in Memphis.

The young man had told Webb of a recent encounter with one of his treating physicians. The psychiatric caregiver reportedly took G__H__ to "Peanuts Bar", a neighborhood bar in Memphis, then on to the doc's residence where G__H__ was offered illicit drugs and aggressively plied with sexual overtures. G__H__ identified Dr. Zed Aydelott, a member of the faculty of the UT Memphis Department of Psychiatry, as the person committing the described acts.

The next morning I caught a flight to Memphis. There I met in Webb's office with him and staff from the VA hospital, Dr. Druff and Mose Hart. I learned that Dr, Aydelott had recently been hired by the University as a resident in the Department of Psychiatry.

According to Webb, the resume submitted by Aydelott with his application for the residency listed several years' employment at the U.S. Naval Academy in Annapolis, Md. No background check was conducted nor were any personal references checked by the University.

I examined the news photo in which Aydelott appeared alongside the Burson family. The four of us agreed that G__H__ could have seen that photo and used it to concoct a sordid story of evildoing, with Aydelott serving as the designated culprit. Perhaps the story was a concoction by a mentally challenged person. But perhaps not.

The claim of professional misconduct was sufficiently credible to mandate further investigation. I left Webb's office, drove to the VA hospital and arranged for G__H__'s release to my custody. We departed the hospital and headed straight for Peanut's Bar, where G__H__ claimed he went with Aydelott.

After arriving at Peanut's around 8 p.m. I asked G__H__ to look around and identify a bartender or anyone else who might have seen him with Dr. Aydelott. He was unable to identify any such person. We took a seat and reviewed, over and over, G__H__'s recollection of his time spent with Aydelott. "Is there anything you recall him telling you that you have not shared with me?" Finally, he did.

"Oh yeah, he said he had his license to practice medicine revoked by the state of California." Bam! What an absurd statement to make if untrue. On the other hand the statement may not have been made. I saw this statement as a potential deal breaker.

I returned G__H__ to his quarters at the VA hospital. Telephone time for me. My first call was to the U.S. Naval Academy in Annapolis. I learned from the Academy that there had never been a Zed Aydelott employed there.

Next call to the State of California. After some intense searching I learned there had been a licensed psychiatrist by the name of Zed Aydelott. His license had been revoked in April 1970, according to the helpful lady with the state office handling matters such as this. Final court action affirming the license suspension was reported as having been taken on April 26, 1973.

I asked if the lady could tell me the nature of the charge which led to Aydelott's license suspension. "The charge was: prescribed drugs on more than one occasion for known narcotic addict. Acts involving moral turpitude and immorality – oral copulation – one case involving a patient." I needed nothing more for the University to proceed. But more was on the way.

The next morning, May 20, I advised Dr. Webb of my findings. Aydelott was immediately called and asked to report to a 10 a.m. meeting. with Webb, Druff, Dr. Aivazian (another psychiatry faculty member) and me. Upon entering the office suite and meeting briefly with Dr. Webb in his personal office, Aydelott left Webb's office and the suite in a visible rage.

A short time later I received a call from Charles Burson. He was calling as the attorney on behalf of Dr. Zed Aydelott. As a friend and colleague I advised Burson to have Aydelott secure other counsel for a meeting to be held in Webb's office the next morning. Burson thanked me for my concern and said he would call back later.

Minutes later I received another phone call. The caller identified himself as a former FBI agent currently employed by the state of Mississippi. He explained that he learned that G__H__ was not the only person seeing the photograph in the Sunday morning paper, that Dr. Zed Aydelott was employed by the University and asked that we "hold" him until he arrived. I explained that Aydelott was currently an employee but would be notified of his dismissal from the University the next day.

"What do you know about Dr. Aydelott?" the agent asked. "I know that he lied on his employment resume about being employed by the military and I also know that his license was rescinded by the state of California."

"That is only the tip of the iceberg," the agent replied.

The agent then explained that Aydelott had also been licensed to practice in Mississippi, and had had his license to practice rescinded. He had committed crimes in Florida, New York and elsewhere and was being sought by a variety of law enforcement agencies.

The agent inquired, "Do you know the young lady in the photograph he is scheduled to marry?" I replied that I knew she was the sister of Charles Burson, Jr. The agent then related that Aydelott was already married, three times, and had wives in Oklahoma, Texas and Mississippi. Each one he had married in either Las Vegas or Reno, Nevada.

I again confirmed that Aydelott would be expected at a meeting the next morning, but would not be employed by the University thereafter. The agent said he was on his way.

Later that afternoon Charles Burson called again. He stated that he understood "what the circumstances were" but would nevertheless be representing Aydelott at the scheduled meeting.

On May 21, I arrived early at Dr. Webb's office. Minutes later Aydelott arrived in the company of Charles Burson and his associate, Knox Walcup. We all took seats. Webb and I explained the evidence supporting the termination of Aydelott's employment. Aydelott's reaction was unforgettable.

Leaping to his feet, Aydelott screamed, "Lies, lies, all lies." I felt the hairs raise on my arms. In an instant I saw before me a lunatic who could have passed, both in appearance and behavior, as the twin brother of crazed California murderer Charles Manson.

Burson and Walcup immediately seized Aydelott, one on each arm, and led him out of the office. Webb and I simply stared at each other in stunned silence.

In a few minutes Burson returned and simply announced "Do what you need to do." Later that afternoon a person called and announced that Aydelott would resign. For certain, he would never be seen again by either me or anyone else at the University of Tennessee.

Some years later I walked into a federal courtroom in Memphis just in time to hear a former UT trustee, Lee Winchester, plead with Judge McRae, "But your honor, I don't know how to respond to Aydelott ..." Later, as Winchester left the courtroom, I asked him if he was referring to Zed Aydelott. He was. Winchester explained that Aydelott was incarcerated in the federal penitentiary and was continuously filing spurious lawsuits which Winchester was responsible for defending.

The Charles Manson alter ego had ample opportunity to pursue a quasi-legal career from his secure residence. The University would be secure in knowing that its failure to conduct a proper background search on a candidate for employment caused no lasting, significant damage to the University or its reputation.

I'm not certain but the agent from Mississippi may have played a role in Aydelott's apprehension and imprisonment. What I do know is that the University's discovery and disclosure of Aydelott's history helped preserve the reputation of the University of Tennessee, and the good name of the Burson family. The wedding plans were reportedly canceled.

Chapter 47–The Flying Nun–Rita Williams vs. Regional Medical Center at Memphis Foundation

One of the oddest cases in my career was a negligence action filed in the U.S. District Court, Western District of Tennessee on April 1, 1988. Rita Williams v. Regional Medical Center at Memphis foundation, et al. No. 88 –2241–HA.

William's lawsuit alleged that she was severely injured in a suicide attempt at the Memphis International Airport resulting from negligence attributed to the Regional Medical Center at Memphis, UT Memphis psychology professor Dr. Keith Wood, UT medical resident Dr. Troy Gene Scroggins, Jr., Memphis airport security, a third-year medical student, a social worker and an airline on which Williams had a scheduled flight. Damages in the amount of $750,000 were requested from the defendants.

Knoxville attorneys Donna Holt and Sid Gilreath represented the plaintiff. I represented defendant Scroggins.

The deposition of plaintiff Rita Williams was taken in Memphis on June 8, 1989 in the office of one of the defense attorneys (possibly that of Memphis attorney Bill Haltom).

At the outset it must be stated emphatically that neither counsel for the plaintiff nor any defense counsel ever questioned William's mental state at the time of her deposition. Nor was any claim ever made that her testimony lacked credibility due to mental issues or due to medication or illegal drug use. In fact the latter issue was disposed of early on in the deposition with William's denial that she had recently used any mind altering drug or was under the influence of any drug.

Williams appeared quite bright and well-spoken. She was a college graduate and had an advanced degree from the University of South Carolina.

My own assessment was that Williams responded to all questions posed in a very forthright manner without any hint of behavior tied to mental illness or drug use. And, therein lies the ultimately stunning evidentiary discovery bringing this case to conclusion.

The bizarre "facts" of the case were laid out by Williams in sworn testimony, responding to questions presented by the various defense counsel present, including myself. Her testimony may be summarized as follows:

At some point prior to the incident giving rise to litigation, Rita Williams became enamored with the "New Age " movement. "Ramtha", a 10,000 year old spirit associated with the movement, "spoke" to Williams and directed her to sell everything she had. And she did as instructed.

Williams was living in Louisiana at the time. After disposing of all her belongings she lacked a means of survival. She left Louisiana and moved in with an uncle in North Carolina.

Not long after moving to North Carolina, Williams again heard Ramtha's voice. This time she was directed to travel to Oregon and meet him there. Because she had sold her automobile and had no means of transportation she borrowed her uncle's car and headed west.

William's route took her through the state of Tennessee. She reached Shelby Meeman State Park near Memphis in the early evening and decided to spend the night there. Williams pitched a tent in proximity to a ranger station.

Once again Williams heard the voice of Ramtha telling her to go to the park ranger's cabin and tell the ranger she loved him. She did as she was directed, went to the cabin and knocked on the door. No one was home.

"Confused" Williams returned to her tent and sat down inside. Yet another voice spoke to her and told her to kill herself. She took out a knife, held it in both hands and, as she demonstrated in her deposition, aimed it at her chest.

Even today I have a vivid memory of asking her, "Did you pierce the skin?" "No," she replied. Williams explained that she became frightened, dropped the knife, burst into tears, ran out of the tent and laid down in the middle of the nearby park road.

Before long an elderly couple approached in their vehicle and observed Williams in the road. She ended up in their automobile and the couple transported her to the Regional Medical Center at Memphis.

Williams' first stop at "the Med" was in the waiting area of the emergency room. I well recall my next questions and could never forget William's response. "Was anyone in the waiting room?" ("Yes.") Do you know who it was?" ("Satan.")

The response was given in a very matter-of-fact" fashion and the questioning continued. Williams explained that she was questioned by various hospital personnel including the psychiatrist, social worker, Dr. Scroggins and others. She said she told them she no longer felt like doing harm to herself. Still, the medical staff and social worker concluded that Williams was not fit to drive home alone.

Williams provided the phone number of her uncle in North Carolina to one of the defendants. The uncle was contacted. He arranged for William's airline transportation from Memphis back to North Carolina.

Williams was released from "the Med" based on the belief that she was no longer an immediate danger to herself and could safely return to her uncle in North Carolina on the next available flight. One of the defendants called a taxi to transport Williams to the airport. More about that later.

To this point, William's counsel at the deposition, Donna Holt, seemed to have full advance knowledge of everything to which her client testified. She may well have believed at this point that the case against one or more of the examining physicians, or even the social worker, was solid. Perhaps she was right.

The facts are that Williams arrived at Memphis international but missed her scheduled flight. Airport security had been made aware of Williams' circumstances and assigned a female security officer to "keep an eye on her" until she could be placed on the next scheduled flight to her original destination.

As the security officer testified in her own deposition, Williams appeared relaxed, laid down and appeared to fall asleep on seating in the waiting area. At some point in time, Williams jumped up and sprinted toward the balcony. The officer testified she knew what Williams was doing and ran after her. Before the officer could apprehend her, Williams dove over the airport balcony, hence the "flying nun," and plummeted to the ground 20 or 30 feet below, sustaining serious bodily injuries in the process.

Had the compilation of facts ended here an effort to settle plaintiff's claim might have been warranted. Certainly the case for any defendant, including Scoggins, who exercised professional judgment and determined that Williams could be released from the Medical Center to return home, with no reason to believe she would make any further effort to harm herself, was debatable at best. A jury might well have taken the defendants "to the cleaners."

There was one tiny blip on the overall timeline that almost escaped the attention of all parties to the litigation. The taxi ride to the airport.

Toward the end of William's testimony I had one more question, one that might seem a bit ridiculous and a waste of time. "Did you recognize the taxi driver?" Or words to that effect. Williams responded, "Satan." I had just another question or two.

When asked to describe what happened after entering the taxi, Williams testified that she was taken to a location and raped, and only after that was she dropped at the airport. Donna Holt had a stunned look on her face as Williams testified regarding this last matter. The taxi incident is what lawyers would call an "intervening cause."

Although I had filed a motion for summary judgment on behalf of Dr. Scroggins shortly after the complaint was filed, I filed a supplemental memorandum in support of that motion following the deposition of Rita Williams. I argued that the plaintiff's own testimony, specifically that she was raped on the way to the airport, served as an intervening cause of her subsequent suicide attempt. There was absolutely no way to prove Williams had any suicidal inclination prior to that incident. I filed a motion requesting entry of summary judgment in Scoggins favor.

On November 15, 1993 the United States District Court entered an Order Granting Defendant Scoggin's Motion for Summary Judgment.

As an interesting postscript, apparently no effort was ever made by plaintiff's counsel to identify the driver of the taxi which transported Williams to the airport. This was not a difficult task to accomplish since there was undoubtedly a record of the call made from hospital. Satan might possibly have been the driver of record.

On a brighter note, look closely in the audience. Ever heard the phrase, "Pat, we've got your back?" Well, Ron, (to left of Pat's head) Therese, (partially hidden) and Lee (to right of Therese) certainly enjoyed watching their friend, Pat Summitt, from the back as she coached the Lady Vols Basketball Team. (1996)

Chapter 48–Civil Rights
The Pinnacle of My University Legal Practice

During the nearly three decade long "Big Orange" period of UT history, civil rights was undoubtedly the number one legal topic addressed by the University. Within the Office of General Counsel I was assigned primary responsibility for assuring University compliance with civil rights law. The vast majority of civil rights litigation arising during that period – more than 200 cases –were mine to resolve.

The civil rights assignment promoted within me deeper passion, caused greater excitement and required more work than any other job responsibility placed on my plate at any time during my UT career. I loved it! For good reason.

From the outset of my University employment I sensed great opportunity to take on exciting and fascinating legal challenges and be a problem solver. I judged the character of those in command as being such as would permit me to "do the right thing" when taking on these challenges.

My civil rights responsibilities constituted the pinnacle of my university legal practice by offering me a unique chance to practice my Christian faith. How so? Quite simple.

One of my favorite songs as a child was "Jesus loves the little children, all the children of the world. Red and yellow, black and white, they are precious in His sight. Jesus loves the children of the world." My favorite Bible verse – a foundation of my own faith – was and is John 3:16: "For God so loved the world that He gave His only begotten Son that whosoever believeth in Him should not perish but have everlasting life." Jesus, a Jew, spoke to a Samaritan woman even though she was scorned as a foreigner by other Jews.

In carrying out my civil rights assignment for the University I admittedly was influenced by a principle of faith - that one person should not be considered of less worth than another based on race, sex, national origin or other characteristic over which he or she has no control. My personal practices hopefully reflected my faith as was my intent.

My wife and I befriended a UT graduate student, Shaojun Wu, from China. She and her daughter, Le Fan, lived with us for almost a year while Shaojun's husband in China processed immigration paperwork to join her and Le Fan in America. "Uncle Ron" was how LeFan referred to me.

For a couple of years I drove to UT each Sunday morning to pick up a graduate student from Panama, Jorge Ureta. Jorge joined my wife and me for church, occasionally lunch and Sunday afternoon volleyball in our backyard during warm weather. Although Jorge graduated and returned to his family in

Panama, we have stayed in touch throughout the years.

I first met Amon Ben ("AB") Chauke, wife Linah and daughters Miyetani, Xaniso and Rulani in Zimbabwe in 1988. We have maintained a close friendship over the years, too. AB and Rulani spent a week with us a couple of years after we first met. On the weekdays Rulani, who is the same age as our daughter Cara, attended Christian Academy of Knoxville (CAK) on a guest basis with Cara.

Miyetani, spent college spring break with Therese and me several years ago. She and I attended two UT Lady Vol softball games after I took her on an extensive campus tour.

In June 2012 the entire Chauke family (except Xaniso) spent the better part of a week at our home to celebrate Miyetani's graduation with a doctorate in neuroscience from the University of California. [See: Bearden Shopper-News, June 18, 2012, p.1] The Chaukes are all refugees from Zimbabwe, black and, most of all, dear friends.

Friends described above fit into three distinct racial and ethnic groups. A variety of fascinating personal attributes led to our long term friendship. Race and ethnicity were not among them.

In carrying out my civil rights responsibilities, I likewise vigorously opposed the use of race or national origin (or any other immutable and legally protected characteristic) for employment, admission or other University purposes. The effort was largely successful. In the process of making the effort I reached what I considered to be the pinnacle of my University legal practice.

Chapter 49–Civil Rights–
Applicable Law and Administrative Agencies

APPLICABLE FEDERAL AND STATE LAW

The 14th Amendment to the United States Constitution provides for "equal protection" under the law and historically applied to prohibit discrimination on the basis of race. In 1971 the U.S. Supreme Court in Reed v. Reed, 404 U.S. 71 (1971), extended the application of equal protection to discrimination on the basis of sex absent a rational basis for such discrimination.

The Equal Pay Act of 1963 protects men and women who performed substantially equal work in the same establishment from sex–based discrimination.

Title VI of the Civil Rights Act of 1964 prohibits discrimination on the basis of race, color and national origin by recipients of federal financial assistance.

Title VII of the Civil Rights Act of 1964 (1972 amendment) prohibits employment discrimination on the basis of race, color, religion, sex and national origin.

Title IX of the Civil Rights Act of 1964 (amendments of 1972) prohibits discrimination on the basis of sex in programs and activities administered by recipients of federal financial assistance.

The Age Discrimination in Employment Act of 1967 bars age–related employment discrimination against persons 40 years old and older. The Age Discrimination Act 1975 prohibits discrimination on the basis of age in programs and activities receiving federal financial assistance.

The Rehabilitation Act of 1973 requires that employers engage in affirmative action to hire, retain and promote qualified persons with disability. Discrimination on the basis of disability is also prohibited by the act. The Americans with Disabilities Act of 1990 prohibits employment discrimination on the basis of disability against persons who are otherwise qualified.

The Vietnam Era Veterans Readjustment Assistance Act of 1974 requires certain federal contractors and   subcontractors to take affirmative action to employ certain categories of veterans and disabled veterans and prohibits discrimination against qualified veterans.

During my tenure the University was also subject to certain presidential executive orders aimed at preventing discrimination. Executive Order 11246, issued by President Lyndon B. Johnson in 1965 (prohibiting discriminatory acts by federal contractors based on race, color, religion and national origin) and Executive Order 11375 (adding "sex" as a protected category) issued by President Johnson in 1967, were those with which the University was most frequently involved.

The University also encountered complaints brought pursuant to the Tennessee Human Rights Act, a State complement to Title VII, prohibiting employment discrimination on the basis of race, creed, color, religion, sex, age and national origin.

FEDERAL AND STATE ENFORCEMENT AGENCIES

The University encountered a variety of federal civil rights enforcement agencies. Federal contract compliance was initially handled by the Department of Health, Education and Welfare ("HEW") and later the Labor Department (Office of Federal Contract Compliance Programs or "OFCCP").

Employment law compliance was handled by the Equal Employment Opportunity Commission ("EEOC"). The Office for Civil Rights ("OCR") handled enforcement involving the programs and activities administered by recipients of federal financial assistance.

The Tennessee Human Rights Commission served as the State agency responsible for enforcing compliance with the Tennessee Human Rights Act. It was part of my job to be familiar with all of the above.

Chapter 50–Quantum Shift in Strategy From Medical Malpractice to Civil Rights Defense.

During most of my career in the Office of General Counsel medical malpractice cases were the number one category of those handled by the OGC with roughly 40% of the total. In second place was civil rights litigation with approximately one third of the total. My approach to handling the two categories of litigation differed sharply.

Over the years I presented many legal seminars to surgery residents, respiratory therapists, nursing students, pharmacy faculty and other healthcare professionals and students. While I focused on ways of avoiding legal liability I rarely commented on specific healthcare practices. I might comment on the need for accurate and timely record-keeping, but not on specific record contents. Never did I attempt to instruct a surgery resident on how best to perform a surgical procedure.

I presented far more seminars concerning civil rights than medical malpractice. The focus was not those within a particular specialty. Instead, the audience was typically composed of any University officials having hiring or employee supervisory responsibilities. Less frequently the audience was composed of University officials having responsibility for student admissions or activities.

Civil rights seminars focused on specifics such as hiring practices to avoid, language to be included in letters of dismissal and how to conduct a legally defensible job candidate search.

In handling a medical malpractice claim my focus was on learning from experts in the profession, such as what constituted the "standard of care" in performing a hysterectomy. Rarely would a search for legal authority on that subject be productive.

With respect to civil rights actions, research into applicable statutory and case law was often of critical importance. Customary practice in an employment setting mattered little if contrary to applicable law.

Stated another way, I rarely defended a medical malpractice action without calling upon a medical expert for assistance in preparation and providing evidentiary testimony. Almost never did I call upon an expert for such assistance in a civil rights case.

Interestingly, I often experienced a very pleasant working relationship with plaintiffs in medical malpractice cases (and most other non-civil rights cases).

Amicable conversation on matters other than the pending litigation was customary.

Animosity reared its head far more often in dealing with plaintiffs in civil rights actions. Friendly exchanges with the opposing party were the exception rather than the rule. Still, I implemented no change in strategy myself. Treat the opponent with the greatest respect possible even where animosity is detected.

Chapter 51–Civil Rights–Plan of Action–the Details

KEEPING ABREAST OF THE LAW

Seminar attendance was quite helpful in staying abreast of legal developments in any area of the law for which I bore responsibility. I found attendance at civil rights seminars particularly helpful. Most helpful was networking with other attorneys, especially higher education attorneys, particularly those having responsibilities in the area of civil rights.

Attendance at an annual continuing legal education ("CLE") seminar was sufficient for keeping apprised of most areas of the law. Not so for keeping abreast of changes in the law pertaining to civil rights. For a period of time the OGC subscribed to the Federal Register, a daily federal publication, roughly half an inch thick, setting forth regulations just issued by various federal agencies. A good number of those affected federal enforcement of civil rights laws and regulations by the OFCCP, OCR and other federal agencies.

During the years immediately prior to the ascendancy of Ronald Reagan to the presidency the volume of newly issued federal pronouncements was so great as to warrant my daily review of the Federal Register. I kept University officials apprised of significant changes in federal regulations affecting the University.

The OGC Federal Register subscription was canceled, soon after Reagan became president, as the number of newly issued federal regulations declined significantly.

Keeping abreast of new case law in the area of civil rights was even more demanding. New cases interpreting and reinterpreting the equal protection provision of the 14th amendment and a plethora of federal civil rights statutes were issued by the U.S. Supreme Court, the U.S. Courts of Appeal and the U.S District Courts almost daily!

Similarly, Tennessee state court decisions affecting civil rights enforcement were issued regularly and required my prompt attention.

Stated another way, months might pass without a new federal or state case of consequence to my medical malpractice practice coming to my attention. On civil rights matters I expected, and typically encountered, significant new cases with each review. I regularly conducted new reviews first thing each morning.

I likewise kept abreast of developments in federal and state statutory developments. On occasion I presented recommendations for new legislation to appropriate University officials.

CIVIL RIGHTS TRAINING FOR UT OFFICIALS

The time I expended keeping up-to-date on civil rights law certainly benefited me in defending civil rights litigation. Utilizing that knowledge to conduct training seminars for University officials having supervisory responsibilities in the areas of personnel (human resources) management and student affairs was just as beneficial to the University.

At seminars, retreats, staff meetings and other gatherings to which I was invited to speak on legal matters, civil rights was addressed far more frequently than any other topic. At meetings with personnel officers and student affairs officers the topic dominated many conversations. With affirmative-action officers civil rights was our number one topic of conversation.

Many areas of civil rights concern were covered during training. One key area covered repeatedly: "Employee selection process." My approach to this particular topic was quite simple but of critical importance.

For example, the following comes from a note card I prepared for a "Civil Rights Seminar" I presented (or co–presented with other legal counsel from the Office of General Counsel), during the spring of 1988, for UT–system officials and university officials of all categories on each campus statewide.

***

    (2) Selection Process
        (a) Set reasonable job criteria (avoid eliminating for reason not critical to job)
        (b) Start w/ adequate pool of candidates (use reasonable recruitment
            methods)
        (c) Select Best Qualified Person for job
        (d) But where underutilized /pref. to female/black (Johnson v. Santa
            Cruz/ Geier) - explain
                * [e.g.] find highly qualified black – hire. (A,G, opinion)
                * otherwise avoid discrimination

As I sometimes explained to seminar attendees, it is **perfectly legal** to set unreasonable job criteria, or pick a best friend for a position to be filled, even one completely unqualified for the position. Foolish but legal as long as discrimination on the basis of race, sex or other legally protected attribute was not a factor. While legal, such cases are often difficult to defend in court.

Adherence to the first three guidelines virtually assured success in defending litigation brought by someone not selected for a contested position, and generally avoided litigation to begin with.

The fourth guideline was one I did not personally favor, but it was lawful until historic underutilization was eliminated.

Well-trained university staff avoided actions and omissions constituting a violation of civil rights law. Or, as happened on occasion, recognized a violation when it occurred and took appropriate remedial action, either directly (such as reversing a decision) or indirectly (such as by reporting a violation to appropriate University officials). In this manner the number of civil rights claims and lawsuits filed against the University was greatly reduced.

Still, there were civil rights actions brought despite involvement of well-trained University personnel acting in accordance with their training. The vast majority of those cases ended favorably for the University.

AVAILABILITY OF LEGAL COUNSEL

It was my customary practice to be readily available for legal inquiries from University personnel and others in the University community. Availability of legal counsel is of a vital importance in the area of civil rights. I had more meetings and telephone conversations with university officials and others on civil rights issues than any other subject.

Availability of legal counsel to University personnel, those voicing a grievance and attorneys representing those having grievances, offers one last chance to resolve differences without litigation. On more than one occasion potential embarrassment or disaster, for one party or another, was avoided simply by having legal counsel readily available and willing to sit down and engage in reasonable conversation.

DEFEND, DON'T CAVE IN

With the exception of those rare cases reassigned to me mid-stream it was my practice to investigate as fully as possible any civil rights action brought against the University or its employees **before** filing a response. If my investigation revealed that a violation had likely occurred I promptly pursued resolution before any litigation was initiated.

In the absence of solid evidence of a civil rights violation it was always my practice, occasionally overruled by a higher up, to aggressively defend those employees who appeared to carry out their responsibilities in a lawful manner and not in violation of anyone's civil rights. It bears mention that one of the frequently asked questions of a defendant in a civil rights action is "Have you ever been sued for violating someone's civil rights?" If the answer is "Yes," the follow-up question is "How was the case resolved?" Any answer to that question which involves payment of money, whether resulting from an adverse judgment or settlement, opens the door to further inquiry, at best!

So, did my civil rights strategy work? You be the judge. I'll provide you the evidence in the next few chapters.

Chapter 52–Civil Rights–The Concept of Affirmative Action During the "Big Orange" Era

A BIT OF HISTORICAL BACKGROUND

Prior to 1961 Tennessee practiced racial segregation in higher education (and elsewhere). "Negroes" were not permitted to attend the University of Tennessee. Employment opportunities at the University for blacks were also severely restricted.

In 1959 Theotis Robinson applied for admission to UT. He was denied admission because of his race, "Negro". He threatened to sue the University for discriminating against him on the basis of his race.

On November 18, 1960 the UT Board of Trustees adopted a policy prohibiting racial discrimination in admission of qualified students. "Negroes" would no longer be denied admission.

On January 3, 1961 Theotis Robinson and two others became the first black students at UT. Robinson did not graduate from the University. Robinson joined the UT staff in 1989. In 2000 he was named Vice President for Equity and Diversity by President J. Wade Gilley.

Admitted to the University in 1967, Lester McClain became the first black to play on the UT football team. That same year, Dr. Robert Kirk became the first black full-time professor at UT. Also, Rita Geier filed suit in federal court in Nashville, seeking to halt construction of UT Nashville and integration of the UT system.

The year I received my undergraduate degree from UT, 1969, was the year Jimmy Baxter was elected as the first black president of the Student Government Association. In 1970 Hardy Liston became the first black UT administrator.

In 1971 Larry Robinson and Wilbert Cherry became the first black players on the UT basketball team under coach Ray Mears. My wife Therese–Mears' secretary–knew and admired both players.

The year I was hired as a staff attorney in the office of General Counsel, 1972, Condredge Holloway was UT's first black quarterback. He was a superb athlete and I enjoyed watching him play and later getting to know him a bit after he was hired as an assistant football coach for the Tennessee Volunteers.

By the time of my employment in the Office of General Counsel in 1972, the

U.S. Supreme Court had extended equal protection under the 14th Amendment to cover sex as well as race. The Equal Pay Act of 1963 and the Civil Rights Act of 1964 had been enacted - and the latter amended - to prohibit employment discrimination on the basis of race and sex as well as other categories.

THE AFFIRMATIVE ACTION DEBATE

The concept of affirmative action developed as a means of "removing the vestiges of discrimination" – the lack of minorities and women in the workforce as a result of discriminatory practices predating enactment of the civil rights statutes. In 1978 federal officials began demanding that "quotas" be established as a means of increasing the number of black and female employees.

For a short while after I assumed responsibility for UT civil rights issues. The concept of affirmative action, in the minds of some, involved replacement of one group of victims of discrimination with another. As the argument went, previous discrimination against blacks as a class was to be corrected by discrimination in favor of blacks as a class–while unavoidably discriminating against those not in the class.

The practice of discrimination was illegal and, in my opinion, morally wrong. It was my further opinion that any remedy penalizing or excluding non-blacks was likewise wrong, both legally and morally. I resolved to do all I could to resolve the problem at the University of Tennessee and perhaps elsewhere.

My goal was to eradicate discrimination, not replace old victims with new. That goal could be achieved by simply eliminating discrimination and substituting lawful employment and admissions procedures. In the period I refer to as "Big Orange,"my effort was largely successful and well documented.

In 1978 I sent to the chief affirmative action officer for each campus a document titled "Required Contents of Affirmative Action Programs," for the purpose of explaining that "The following are required contents of affirmative action programs promulgated pursuant to Executive Order 11246…." Each campus was required by federal regulations to create an affirmative action plan and update that plan annually.

Eleven categories of information were required to be contained in each plan. Paragraph 4 on the document spelled out the requirement for a "Detailed Workforce Analysis" thoroughly analyzing workforce positions and salaries as well as the number of males, females, blacks and other ethnic groups holding positions under each job title.

Paragraph 5, "Identification of problem areas," stated that "The program must analyze all major job groups at the University and explain underutilization of minorities or women." Eight factors were to be considered in determining whether underutilization existed. For example, "(5) the availability of minorities or females having requisite skills in an area in which the University can reasonably recruit."

Paragraph 6,"Goals and Timetables," required that the affirmative action program "establish goals, timetables and affirmative action commitments designed to correct any identifiable deficiencies...." [See Federal Register, Vol. 43, No. 204–Friday, October 20, 1978 for full details of U.S. Department of Labor regulations implementing the Executive Order]

The affirmative action officers and I worked together to develop campus and "University–wide" affirmative action plans which met Labor Department (OFCCP) requirements. Each year I reviewed reports and employment data for the previous year and recommended changes, if necessary.

For example, in a March 3, 1992 memorandum to the UT Space Institute affirmative action director, Patricia Burks – Jelks, I recommended removal of a sentence reading: "However, we will continue to actively pursue the recruitment and hiring of minorities and females," in a job category where underutilization had already been eliminated.

In 1978 the United States Supreme Court made my job a bit easier. On June 28 of that year the court issued Regents of the University of California v. Alan Bakke. By memorandum of July 12, 1978, I provided the President's staff and the University's affirmative action officers a six-page detailed analysis of the split opinion of the Bakke court. I summarized what I perceived to be the impact of the case on race-based decisions with respect to students.

I believe that it can be stated safely that, as a general rule, current policies and practices of the University of Tennessee fall within the Bakke guidelines. UT does not establish quotas in any of its admissions programs or other programs and activities. We must continue to avoid designating job positions, scholarship assistance or other benefits for members of a particular racial group. In accordance with the principles set down in Bakke , individuals must be free to compete for all benefits offered by the University without regard to their race or color. Again, at least with regard to UT's admissions program, race may be considered as one factor of several in determining which of a number of individual applicants should be admitted.

Moving in the right direction! I expressed my great satisfaction with the decision when interviewed later that day by WBIR TV for the evening news.

Yes, moving in the right direction but not everywhere. The Labor Department's Office of Federal Contract Compliance Programs (formerly the "Office of Federal Contract Compliance" in the department of Health, Education and Welfare–"HEW" -but moved to the DOL in 1978) appeared to aggressively search for an institutional example of agency prowess in carrying out its civil rights mandate. Unfortunately, in its early years, OFCCP seemed far more interested in proclaiming victory than determining the true state of a University's employment practices and achievements.

UT BATTLES THE OFCCP

In late spring 1979, I received a word from officials at UT Memphis that OFCCP had scheduled an "on-site review" for the campus. I later learned from UT personnel director Jim Stockdale that such reviews had been scheduled around the same time for Purdue, LSU, Notre Dame and the University of Oklahoma.

On the morning of June 4 Executive Assistant to President Boling, Andy Kozar, and I flew to Memphis for an introductory session. The session was held at the UTCHS University Center.

Attending the meeting for the University, in addition to Kozar and me, were UTCHS Chancellor Al Farmer, Vice Chancellor Earle Bowen, Jim Stockdale and Affirmative Action Director Roland Woodson. Representing the OFCCP was the agency's official in charge of the on-site review program, Clarence Brown. One or two assistants were with Brown.

From the outset of the June 4, 1979 introductory session it was clear to me that our dealings with the federal agency would be adversarial. I sensed an intense desire on the part of Brown to criticize UTCHS civil rights compliance efforts in every way possible. My suspicions proved true.

Following the introductory session, five more meetings were held that day at Brown's request. Included was a meeting with all UTCHS academic department heads and another with all non-academic department heads. During the process Brown requested – and campus officials provided – a vast amount of documents and information from various campus offices.

On June 5 three more meetings were held including an exit interim meeting with the Chancellor's Executive Assistant, Dr. Sam Bozeman. Then, on June 6 an exit interview was held and attended by the same seven officials present at the introductory meeting.

At the June 6 exit interview Brown verbally critiqued UTCHS civil rights compliance ranging from the contents of its affirmative action plan to employment and salary data for blacks and females. He advised that he would get back to us after he and his staff completed review of the materials received.

On October 29, 1979 Clarence Brown called a meeting to announce his preliminary findings. The meeting with Brown was held at UTCHS and attended by Bozeman, Kozar, Mike Brookshire, the UT system's personnel director, and me. Brown's criticism of the UTCHS compliance program was severe.

In a follow-up letter of November 16, 1979, Brown spelled out his extensive criticisms of the contents of the UTCHS affirmative action plan and his conclusion that the campus had engaged in an extensive discriminatory actions against blacks and females. Appended to the report was a list of faculty and staff claimed to have been underpaid based on race or sex. A demand was made that compensation in excess of $1 million was to be paid.

A follow-up meeting with Brown was scheduled at the University's request. On January 23, 1980, UT Vice President for Business and Finance, Eli Fly, Kozar, a number of UTCHS officials and I met with Brown at UTCHS. I and other UT representatives advised Brown of our strong disagreement with his findings. The meeting concluded with my announcement that I would provide a written response to those findings. One last meeting with Brown was held on January 29 and attended by Bozeman, Brookshire and me. No progress made.

The University's encounter with the OFCCP led to a two-day University-wide retreat at Henry Horton State Park. The event was attended by all UT affirmative-action officers and personnel directors, Kozar and me. Also in attendance were Betsey Creekmore and Vice Chancellor Luke Ebersole from UT Knoxville, Steve Sprouse from the Office of General Counsel, Director John Hemmeter of the Office of Institutional Research and Kaddie Barber from the President's office.

The entire focus of the March 4-5, 1980 retreat was on the OFCCP findings and the University's pending response. A seven page summary of discussion at the retreat was prepared by Kozar and sent to all participants. A few excerpts from the March 14 document well describes the combative relationship between UT and the OFCCP at that time:

Kozar welcomed the group and explained that the meeting was being held so that what had been learned from the on-site visit of Clarence Brown of the OFCCP Memphis office could be conveyed to the participants of this meeting. Kozar said the switch from enforcement of affirmative action regulations from HEW to DOL had created some confusion concerning what we need to do to comply with federal regulations. He concluded that we still have some confusion because of Brown's hesitancy in telling us what was right even though he frequently told us what was wrong. We plan to proceed with good faith efforts in providing equal employment opportunities through affirmative action.

Leadbetter commented on the alleged deficiencies included in a letter dated November 16 from Clarence Brown of the Memphis OFCCP to Chancellor Farmer. Because of the in-house, confidential nature of the information, only highlights of the discussion will be included here.

***

Many of Brown's criticisms were directly related to the operation of the UTCHS personnel office. Although alleged discrimination was indicated against a group of applicants, Brown and his staff did not pursue any follow-up on these individuals. When follow-up was accomplished by UTCHS staff, no discrimination could be found. ...

Brown was opposed to performance appraisal and said it was discriminatory to minorities and females. We held that job performance is a legitimate, nondiscriminatory basis for salary increase determination. Several hundred persons were listed as having been discriminated against.

***

During the discussion of the alleged deficiencies at UTCHS, it was pointed out that according to the Tennessee Supreme Court, the plaintiff in cases of discrimination has the burden of proof.

***

Leadbetter reviewed with the group the October 1979 version of the UTCHS affirmative action plan, indicating that it is the surest thing we have. [He then reviewed the contents required by federal regulations].

In summary, the University was committed to and practiced equal employment opportunity. The Labor Department findings to the contrary were rejected.

Not long after the Henry Horton retreat I provided the OFCCP a detailed written response to Clarence Brown's findings. All findings of discriminatory action were denied.

The OFCCP claim that hundreds of blacks and women listed in Brown's findings were victims of discrimination was rejected. In like manner, the request for compensatory payment to those individuals in excess of $1 million was rejected.

Eventually the conflict was resolved. Agreement was reached to redraft portions of the UTCHS affirmative action plan. No finding of discrimination on the basis of race or sex was further pursued. Not one cent in compensation was paid by the University to anyone on the OFCCP list. The war was over.

There were other skirmishes over the next decade with the Office for Civil Rights, the U.S. Department of Agriculture and EEOC, as well as OFCCP. Those encounters ended more quickly and with less hostility. Still, a combative atmosphere prevailed at times.

DEMAND FOR DIVESTMENT OF STOCK IN COMPANIES DOING BUSINESS IN SOUTH AFRICA

During Lamar Alexander's term as UT president demands were made by certain activist groups that UT divest itself of ownership of stock in any company doing business in South Africa because of that nation's apartheid (segregated by law) system of government. My boss, Beach Brogan, got personally caught up in the controversy on one occasion.

Beach and I were standing outside the UT Board room, next to our offices in Andy Holt Tower one morning. Several campus ministers were in the lobby and complained about South Africa's apartheid system of government. Beach responded that if it concerned them they should go to South Africa to work on the problem. His comment was construed as "go back to Africa" although, as I recall, most of the ministers were white.

A demand was soon made that Beach meet with representatives of various campus groups promoting stock divestiture. President Alexander requested that Beach attend. Beach, in turn, asked that I accompany him to the meeting.

The meeting was held in the UT Board room. When Beach and I walked in the room was full and all seats around the circular conference table were taken except two reserved for us.

Beach responded very well, in my opinion, to questions posed by those present. The focus of the questions was on whether Beach had a racist inclination of some sort. He made clear that he did not. The comment which led to the meeting was simply an offhand remark by Beach offering his opinion that the problem at hand–apartheid–would best be handled by efforts in South Africa.

I thought the meeting went quite well until the very end. One of the black faculty members berated Beach, "… and another thing, I'm sick and tired of you constantly referring to us as "y'all!" Beach, noticeably flustered, hesitated a moment before replying, "Why, I've been saying that since I was little." He explained that no insult was intended.

The meeting adjourned. Beach and I retired to his office. He was visibly upset and voiced his anger with the faculty member asking the last question. I told Beach I knew he intended no disrespect–that "ya'll" was a term we all used. The faculty member was completely off-base.

There was no follow-up to the session in the Board room and the brouhaha which led to the meeting subsided. Still, the session was indicative of how easily a remark could be taken out of context, during that period in history, on civil rights related issues.

The divestiture debate continued. In 1989 President Alexander requested that Executive Vice President Joe Johnson organize a panel to address the issue in an open forum on the UT Knoxville campus.

On February 16, 1989 a panel composed of Vice President Johnson, Treasurer David Martin, Vice President for Business, Planning and Finance Eli Fly and I participated in a forum sponsored by the Student Government Association. The forum was held in the University Center and well attended.

There was seemingly complete agreement between the panelists and attendees that apartheid was wrong; there was cordial disagreement over the issue of stock divestiture. [The Daily Beacon, February 20, 1989, p.1]

The demand for divestiture never gained traction with the Board of Trustees and the issue died when South Africa abandoned apartheid in 1991. Other struggles over civil rights issues continued.

By letter of June 14, 1991 Larry Stanley, District Director (Nashville district office) of the OFCCP, notified Chancellor that a review of UTCHS compliance with federal law administered by his office had been completed. "The results of this review indicate that your establishment is not in compliance with the requirements of executive order 11246, as amended, section 503 of the rehabilitation act of 1973, as amended, and the Vietnam Era veterans readjustment assistance act of 1974, as amended.... Consequently, we are issuing the enclosed notice of violations which set forth the violations and necessary remedies."

Stanley further advised, "In order to come into compliance you must enter into a conciliation agreement (CA) which encompasses all remedies prescribed herein." A 10 page conciliation agreement was attached.

By letter of June 26, 1991, I advised Stanley that I had reviewed the "notice of violations" and that it was "my opinion that the University has not violated the executive order or the implementing regulations." As in the earlier OFCCP encounter, I spelled out a number of changes in the UTCHS affirmative action plan the University was willing to make. Just not as part of any conciliation agreement.

"Since it is the University's position that it has not violated the executive order or the regulations, I cannot recommend that the University execute a conciliation agreement. However, I am quite willing to recommend to Chancellor Hunt that he execute a letter of commitment, committing UT Memphis to proceeding in accordance with such plan and related items as are found to be mutually acceptable by the University and your office." I wrote a similar letter the same day to Frederick Norton, the assistant district director of the OFCCP Memphis office.

In a follow-up letter (August 2, 1991) to Stanley, President Joe Johnson advised Stanley, "I concur with the thoughts expressed by Mr. Leadbetter, in his letter to Mr. Norton, that the University should not be compelled to execute a conciliation agreement in view the University's good faith efforts to comply with the law, serious doubts as to whether specific provisions of the regulations have been violated and the University's reliance on past assistance provided by your office in developing an affirmative action plan which your office now finds to be defective."

The University did not cave, satisfactory changes in the affirmative action plan were made, no conciliation agreement was executed and the skirmish ended peaceably.

Since 1991 I had no further skirmishes with any federal civil rights agency. The University simply continued to meet its civil rights obligations and comply with the law.

ELIMINATING THE SOLE LEGAL BASIS
FOR PREFERENTIAL TREATMENT

In an April 23, 1987 memorandum to all UT chief personnel officers I commented on the recently issued U.S. Supreme Court case of Johnson v. Transportation Agency, Santa Clara County, California. I noted that the Court permitted, but did not require, preferential treatment of "minorities or women" in employment categories where a "conspicuous imbalance" existed. The Court cautioned that "...while preferential employment practices may, under the restrictions described above [sex or ethnicity may be considered as a factor in hiring, but a specific numbers of positions may not be set aside for minorities or women], be utilized as a permissible means of attaining racial or sexual balance in a job category, such preferential practices are not a permissible means of retaining a racially or sexually balanced workforce."

I further reported that "[w]hile the court permits preferential treatment within the above specified guidelines, it does not mandate that such preferential treatment be afforded to anyone. It remain settled law that a court will order preferential treatment only upon a finding that an employer has discriminated on the basis of race, sex or other impermissible basis.

I explained the reason for my recommendation. "As you know, the law requires affirmative action to eliminate vestiges of discrimination. However, where vestiges of discrimination no longer exist, the law prohibits making employment decisions on the basis of race or sex." The recommendation was accepted and implemented.

In a memorandum of March 30, 1994 I advised the UT system director personnel services, Sarah Phillips, as follows:

I have reviewed the affirmative action plans for UT Martin and UT Knoxville and have nothing to add to what John Rich has said. However, I have a recommendation that might go a long way toward putting our affirmative action efforts in proper perspective.

Each year one or more of our plans makes reference to job categories in which underutilization of minorities or females is eliminated. For example, the 1993–1994 affirmative action plan for UT Knoxville refers to elimination of underutilization in six categories. Such elimination of underutilization stands as evidence of the University's commitment to affirmative action. Yet the overall affect of this achievement is lost as the same section of the UTK plan makes reference to eight instances of underutilization appearing "for the first time." From this one might infer that we are sliding downhill in our efforts.

My recommendation is that each affirmative action plan contain a one page chart listing all job categories and, under appropriately headed columns, indicating the date on which historic underutilization was eliminated for each category where such has occurred. Such a chart would reflect the true progress of each campus in eliminating under representation in the workforce resulting or appearing to result from historic discrimination against minorities and females as opposed to disproportionate representation occurring, by mere chance, as the result of normal ebb and flow of persons in the workforce. It is well recognized, legally and otherwise, that our workforce–let alone individual job groups in that workforce–will not always the mirror the percentage of qualified and available females, blacks, or total minorities in the workforce in which the vestiges of historic discrimination have been completely eliminated, and there is no current discrimination.

While it is legally imperative that we be vigilant against discrimination which results in new underutilization, the law requires and endorses affirmative action only where underutilization results from historic discrimination.

My advice was accepted and by memorandum of July28, 1994, from the office of personnel services, all University affirmative action officers were so advised.

While reviewing our affirmative action plans, Ron Leadbetter suggested adding a chart that would provide an indication of the historical elimination of underutilization at our campuses and units. Such a chart would show that we have made progress in our affirmative action efforts whereas our current plans provide a "snapshot" at a given point in time and do not normally provide a history.

It is recommended that such a chart be added to the plans for the affirmative-action year 1994–95.

From that point on each campus affirmative action plan identified each job category in which historic underutilization had been eliminated. That approach made clear that historic underutilization had been eliminated throughout the University. For example, John Rich advised Sarah Phillips the very next year (memorandum of July 11, 1994) that underutilization had been eliminated in every University wide administration job group.

Enclosed is a chart depicting elimination of underutilization by job group and protected class in the University administration affirmative action plan. The changes based on Ron Leadbetter's suggestion that the plans should indicate when the historical vestiges of any unintentional discrimination were eliminated.

The chart itself indicates the earliest year in which underutilization was eliminated based upon a review of University Administration AA plans from 1974 through 1994.

The appended chart showed that 1991 was the last year in which under utilization existed for female ("professional" and "secretarial/clerical" categories). For blacks the last year in which underutilization existed ("UWA paraprofessional" and "technical/paraprofessional" categories) was 1993.

By memorandum of March 18, 1999 Sarah Phillips confirmed to all University Vice Presidents, Directors and Department Heads of the University-wide Administration and the Institute for Public Service that "...in prior years the University administration has eliminated underutilization in all applicable job groups."

Elimination of underutilization was likewise reported on each campus throughout the University. The legal basis for preferential treatment, i.e. discrimination, on the basis of race or sex, no longer existed.

Chapter 53–The Impact of Rita Sanders Geier

The University of Tennessee's record in defending Civil Rights litigation during the "Big Orange Era" was certainly one to take pride in, as evidenced by the results reported in the next chapter. Its record in rebuffing over-the-top accusations and demands by federal civil rights agencies during that same period was spotless.

There was a single major blemish on an otherwise stellar civil rights record. One that cost the University an entire campus and one that diverted focus from eliminating racial discrimination to determining what discrimination was permissible.

RITA SANDERS vs. ELLINGTON

The biggest Civil Rights lawsuit in Tennessee history was filed before my arrival in the Office of General Counsel. While never assigned responsibility for defending the case, although I requested that assignment more than once, the litigation had monumental impact on higher education in the State of Tennessee. My responsibility for handling Civil Rights matters was noticeably impacted.

Rita Sanders (later Rita Geier) was one of several plaintiffs who filed suit in 1968 against Governor Buford Ellington, as governor of the State of Tennessee and chairman of the Board of Trustees of the University of Tennessee, various officials of the Tennessee State Board of Education, the University of Tennessee and its president, Andy Holt, Tennessee A and I State University and a number of officials of that university. The thrust of plaintiffs' claim was that the previously segregated system of higher education established by law in Tennessee had not been dismantled and historically white institutions still had overwhelmingly white enrollment while Tennessee A and I State University still had overwhelmingly black enrollment.

It was requested that the University of Tennessee be prevented from constructing a new facility in downtown Nashville aimed at expanding its program at that location. Plaintiffs claimed the new facility would further segregation by attracting white students who would otherwise attend Tennessee A & I State University.

The litigation lasted from 1968 until 2006. Names of the defendant, the Governor of Tennessee in office at the time of any court proceeding, changed as did circumstances. A brief synopsis of the litigation follows.

On August 23, 1968, U.S. District Judge Frank Gray issued the first ruling on the matter presented by Geier. Sanders v. Ellington, 286 F. Supp. 937 (M.D. Tenn. 1968). Judge Gray made a number of critical findings.

First, Judge Gray found that "now all institutions of higher learning are at this time pursuing an open–door policy." He found that neither UT nor the State Board of Education (which at the time was operating the other Tennessee public institutions of higher education) "are now or have been in the recent past, and I emphasize recent, guilty of any constitutionally impermissible acts in the administration of the institutions. Rather, it appears to the court clearly evident that the present situation is the result of mistakes and inequities in the past." Geier, p.940.

Judge Gray observed that UT had established a national center 20 years earlier "to provide evening courses for employed persons who could not attend regularly scheduled classes at ordinary day institutions." He further concluded that "the record clearly indicates and the court finds that, in its expansion program for the Nashville Center, the University of Tennessee seeks only to provide a quality continuing education and public service center for Nashville and middle Tennessee with overwhelming emphasis being placed upon the provision of educational opportunity for employed persons of all races who must seek their education at night." Geier, p. 942.

Finally, Judge Gray concluded that with respect to historically white institutions in the state, "It appears that genuine progress is being made [in increasing the number of black students]." However, Judge Gray found that "nothing has been done to dismantle effectively the dual system so graphically illustrated by the enrollment [of blacks] at Tennessee A & I State University." Geier, p.942.

The Court concluded by announcing it would enter an order "requiring the defendants to submit to the court a plan designed to affect such desegregation of the higher educational institutions of Tennessee, with particular attention to Tennessee A & I State University, as to indicate the dismantling of the dual system now existing." Id.

Judge Gray did not address the fact that the University of Tennessee was a public educational corporation of the state of Tennessee. [See: Public Acts of Tennessee 1807, chapter 64] with all other public higher education institutions in the state of Tennessee separately governed under the administration of the Tennessee State Board of Education. UT's Board of Trustees had no jurisdiction over the Board of education and vice versa. Tellingly, UT was represented by General Counsel John Baugh and Assistant General Counsel Jim Drinnon of the UT office of General Counsel, while all non-UT defendants were represented by attorneys from the State Attorney General's office.

GEIER vs. DUNN

The defendants submitted to the District Court, on April 1, 1970, the plan requested by Judge Gray. In 1972 the parties were back in court with the addition of the United States as a plaintiff–intervener. Geier v. Dunn, 337 F. Supp. 573

(M.D. Tenn. 1972).

The court recognized that significant progress had been made in integrating the traditionally white institutions. For example, black enrollment at all institutions except Tennessee State University - formerly Tennessee State A & I - had increased from 2,720 to 3,869. Contrasted to this 42% increase TSU had no gain in white students. Geier, p. 575.

It was the court's "opinion that, with the exception of TSU, defendants are proceeding to dismantle their dual system of higher education, taken as a statewide hole, at a constitutionally permissible rate of speed." Geier, p. 580. TSU's racial composition was deemed "of a severe and egregious nature." The defendants were told they "must carry out their affirmative duty, and, if an open-door policy will not work, then more radical remedies are required." Geier, p. 581.

The defendants were ordered to present to the court, by August 1, 1972, a report including the feasibility of some form of merger or consolidation of TSU with UT Nashville. Judge Gray suggested possible relocation of Nursing and School of Social Work programs from UTN to the TSU campus.

GEIER V. BLANTON

Of the parties appeared before Judge Gray once again in 1977. This time the court took note of a "division" between the parties, something that should have weighed in the University's favor.

> "Both the division between the boards governing UT-N and TSU and the power the University of Tennessee system was demonstrated at the outset by counsel for the defendants. From the beginning, the University of Tennessee and its Board of Trustees have retained their own counsel. In the initial stages of the action, UT was represented by in-house counsel; in the later stages, private counsel was retained by the system. The remaining defendants, including the Board of Regents as the governing board of TSU... Have been represented by the Attorney General for the state of Tennessee...."

The court recognized, once again, that UT Nashville operated in a nondiscriminatory fashion. The problem remained TSU. The fact that UT's approach was nondiscriminatory and effective was disregarded. "There is no reason why one university in the Nashville area could not effectively utilize both the home campus of TSU and the downtown campus now occupied by UT-N." Geier, p. 661. It was then ordered that UTN and TSU "be merged as a single institution under the governance of the state Board of Regents, such merger to be completed by July 1, 1980." Id.

The District Court ruling was appealed by the University to the U.S. Court of Appeals for the Sixth Circuit. Nashville attorney Tom Steele represented the University in Cincinnati. I attended oral argument but did not otherwise participate in the case. It seemed to me that we did not sufficiently emphasize the independent corporate status of the University of Tennessee. Regardless, the appeal did not succeed. See Geier v. Blanton, 597 F2d 1056 (6th Cir. 1978).

GEIER v. ALEXANDER

Although it should come as no surprise, Judge Gray's effort to address racial composition on the TSU campus by removing the successfully desegregated UTN campus from UT did not work. Judge Thomas Wiseman (replacing Judge Gray) so knowledged: "Since the merger, re-segregation has taken place at PSU, and inadequate progress has been made at the remaining colleges and universities. The deterioration at TSU has been particularly disheartening." Geier v. Alexander, 593 F. Supp.1263 M.D. Tenn. 1984)

The percentage of black, first-time freshmen at TSU rose from 69.7% in 1979 to 90.2%. During the same time the percentage of black administrators at UT and TSU combined went from 58% to 72.6%. There were 195 black faculty members at TSU and only 44 at all other State Board of Regents institutions, UT not included.

Unfortunately, Judge Wiseman implemented a remedy which I did not personally agree with, nor did the United States Department of Justice. The court approved a "Stipulation of Settlement" approved by all parties except the US Department of Justice because of the inclusion of numerical goals and objectives. In my view, the establishment of numerical goals was nothing more than a code word for racial preferences i.e. race discrimination.

The August 31, 1984 Stipulation of Settlement set several goals: First, the Board of Regents and UT would collaborate on implementing goals and objectives established by the stipulation of settlement. Second, for the five-year period beginning in 1985 75 black college sophomores would be selected each year for pre-enrollment in five professional programs (law, dentistry, pharmacy, veterinary medicine and medicine). Those selected would be admitted to the professional program so long as they completed their undergraduate work and met "minimum admissions standards" for the program. Third, a staff development program would be instituted to "enable black staff members to obtain advanced degrees and become eligible for positions of higher salary and higher rank within all institutions of higher education and state of Tennessee."

In February 1988 Tennessee Attorney General Michael Cody called a meeting in his office of several of his top assistants, as well as Beach Brogan, Catherine Mizell and me from the UT Office of General Counsel. He requested our assistance in meeting the goals set forth in the Geier consent decree.

By memorandum of February 26, 1988, to those attending the meeting, Cody thanked us for advising him of progress being made by the institutions we represented. He also noted "...since the end of the period covered by the stipulation of settlement is rapidly approaching, I feel it would be useful for us to continue to meet on a periodic basis." Immediately following the meeting with Cody, civil rights seminars, with Geier updates, were scheduled throughout the State.

On April 4, 1988 I traveled to Memphis and met with UTCHS Chancellor Jim Hunt and his top staff along with President Boling and Vice Presidents Fly, Johnson and Prados. I announced my plan to conduct seminars for middle management personnel having employment responsibilities, reminding those officials of their EEO/affirmative action obligations under federal law and specific requirements of the Geier stipulation of settlement. The following day Assistant General Counsel Alice Woody and I conducted such a seminar at UT Martin for Chancellor Margaret Perry and 65 top and middle management personnel.

On April 29 Catherine Mizell and I presented a three-hour seminar on civil rights for Vice President for Agriculture Pete Gossett and more than 80 supervisory staff from the Institute of Agriculture and the College of Veterinary Medicine. The Institute's Affirmative Action Coordinator, Clinton Shelby, and affirmative-action officers were also present. At Vice President Gossett's request I had earlier presented the seminar to Institute of Agriculture deans, department heads and supervisory staff at the Experiment Station in Jackson (April 18) and the Experiment Station in Nashville (April 19).

On May 3 Assistant General Counsel Karen Holt joined me to present a seminar to Chancellor Fred Obear and around 45 management staff at the University of Tennessee at Chattanooga. Then on May 11 Mizell and I conducted an affirmative action seminar for 38 directors and managers of the UT system-wide administration with introductory comments by Eli Fly and Sarah Phillips.

On May 12, I presented the Geier/Civil Rights seminar to Vice Chancellor for Clinical Affairs Bill Rice and several dozen administrative staff at the UT Medical Center in Knoxville. I traveled to UT Memphis on May 31, 1988 and presented the same seminar to Chancellor Jim Hunt and more than 150 administrators, including deans, department chairmen and vice chancellors.

The last seminar on Civil Rights in this state-wide effort was one presented by Catherine Mizell and me on September 22 to UT Knoxville Chancellor Jack Reese and his administrative staff.

Contents of each of the above mentioned seminars were essentially the same although discussion varied from session to session depending on unique challenges faced locally. Topics covered and points made at each session follow (taken from my two-sided 4 x 6 index card titled "Civil Rights Seminars/1988").

Side 1
I. Purpose of Being Here/ two- fold
   (1) Fed. Civ. Rights Statutes [review]
                                    ***
      (c) HISTORICALLY – excellent record due to (1) well intentioned
      (2) Well-trained e.g. seminars-best evidence: time and again go into court
w/necessary records demonstrating …[non- discrimination]
      (2) Geier v. McWherter ; 1960s Statewide deseg./elim dual syst of higher
ed 5 Yr. Stip of Settlement/UT to seek out Black students, fac & admin.
      (a) Stip of Settlement expires August 31, 1989
      (b) A.G. Mike Cody wishes term. Of lawsuit/ Cts supervisory function
at that time
      (c) …to accomplish must:
   1. Demonstrate compliance w/ Stip of Settlement
      a. Progress in attracting blacks (stud, fac & admin)
      b. B/F [i.e. bona fide] Recruitment Effort Where Goals Not Reached
                  (Goals NOT Quotas)
         Side 2
II. Method of Assuring Greatest Likelihood of Success
   (1) Recruitment - key to attracting Black, female in "problem areas"
      (areas of underutilization – job groups/ key: availability of qualified
applicants)
         (a) Methods – 1. Appropriate means (media, telephone, personal)
                  2. Appropriate length
                  3. Avoid unnec job restrictions   (e.g. UT grad)
   (2) Selection Process
         (a) Set reasonable job criteria (avoid eliminating for reasons not critical
to job)
         (b) Start w/ adequate job pool of candidates/ and special effort to in-
clude blacks in interview pool
         (c) Select Best Qualified Person for job
         (d) But where underutilized / Pref. to fem/Black (Johnson v. Santa
Clara County/ Geier - explain Acad/Admin/Fac -ok , highly qualified black –
hire (AG opinion) * otherwise avoid discrim
         (3) Documentation [importance of documenting recruitment efforts, race
and sex of all applicants, availability and reasons for exclusion, selection or
non-selection of each candidate]   ***
   IV. Conclusion
   - Over yrs you've come through
   - Special effort between now and '89 Geier

My focus was on promoting sound, well-documented, nondiscriminatory employment and admission practices by the University. I advised compliance with the racial preference aspects of Geier, as well as setting goals for blacks and women in underutilized job categories, as required by federal law, but always promoted a conservative approach to engaging in what I considered to be just another type of discrimination.

Two major developments allowed me to eliminate the "permissible discrimination" instructions from my seminars. First, elimination of underutilization of blacks and women in all or virtually all job categories throughout the University by the mid-1990s erased any obligation under federal law to grant employment preferences based on race or sex–and removed any legal basis for doing so.

Second, although the affirmative action mandates of Geier ended up being extended, in one form or another, until 2006, the sole remaining legal basis for race discrimination ended that year. In 2006 all parties to the Geier litigation joined in a "Joint Motion for the Entry of a Final Order of dismissal."

Judge Thomas Wiseman granted the motion on September 21, 2006. [Geier v. Bredesen, 453 F. Supp. 2d 1017 (M.D. Tenn. 2006)]. In his final order of dismissal Judge Wiseman concluded that the defendants had fully complied with the most recent consent decree (2001). He further ruled that any remaining vestiges of discrimination had been removed from the Tennessee system of public higher education to the extent practicable and as required by law.

Rita Geier was hired by the University of Tennessee, Knoxville in 2006. Chancellor Loren Crabtree hired Geier in the position of "Associate to the Chancellor" and made her an integral part of his "Ready for the World" initiative. Her role in promoting desegregation of Tennessee's higher education system had been fulfilled and she moved forward.

Chapter 54–Best Evidence of Civil Rights Litigation Success–Wins, Losses and Settlements

The University enjoyed great success in dealing with federal Civil Rights agencies during the "Big Orange" decades. While making numerous alterations in affirmative action plans and a few record-keeping and administrative changes the University paid **zero dollars ($0)** in compensation in any form to anyone as a result of action by any of those agencies.

Geier has been discussed in some detail in the last chapter and stands as the primary example of Civil Rights litigation mandating huge expenditures by the University of Tennessee.

I had a major role in advising others of implications and rulings associated with Geier. Also, I had considerable responsibility to assure University compliance with judicial mandates and stipulations of settlement. However, I was not assigned responsibility for litigating the case. As a result, I cannot cite Geier as evidence for or against my strategy for handling civil rights litigation. I was responsible for more than 200 other civil rights cases. Those cases shed light on the extent to which my overall strategy worked.

Total number of Civil Rights actions (cases alleging discrimination in violation of federal or state civil rights statutes) against the University and/or its employees concluded between July 1, 1972 and December 31, 1998:

Cases Won –   204 (95.8%

Cases Lost –   6 (2.8%)

Cases Settled –   3 (1.4%) = 213

CASES LOST

Year	Plaintiff	Campus	Claim Category	Total $ Judg.
1979	Gurley, Laverne	UT Knoxville	Sex	$3,538
1980	Croushorn, James	UT Knoxville	Race (Reverse D)	$42,000
1988	Bruwiler, Sallee	UT Memphis	Sex	$39,290
1992	Roberson, Deborah	UT Knoxville	Sex, Retaliation	$97,820
1994	Scarbrough, Gerry	UT Knoxville	Disability	$109,083
1997	Hineline, Ginger	UT Knoxville	Sex (Pregnancy)	$186,465
			Total	**$478,196**

CASES SETTLED

1988	Robinson, Milton	UT Memphis	Race	$13,823
1992	Clark, Raymond	UT Memphis	Race	$138,232
1994	Hatton/Holland	UT Memphis	Sex	$64,227
			Total	**$216,282**

Each of the cases lost or settled is mentioned again in another chapter. It is my firm belief that more is often learned from a loss, or even a settlement, than even a long series of wins. For that reason I describe a number of the cases that ended in a loss or settlement.

The University's civil rights litigation record during the "Big Orange" era is one the university can be proud of. And I take pride in the integrity, commitment to non—discrimination and competence of hundreds or even thousands of University personnel whose contribution to building that record was nothing short of phenomenal–total judgments and settlements less than $700,000 over a period of more than 26 years! Only nine payouts statewide–roughly one every three years for the entire UT system.

Go Big Orange! And my hat is off to all my friends and former colleagues in the University administration, faculty and staff who contributed so much to the establishment of an awesome record!

Chapter 55–Civil Rights–
"Race" Leads the Way in Litigation Activity

MELVIN WOODS EEOC WIN–THEN LOSS

My first race discrimination case of any kind was filed by C. W. Mathis with the U.S. Department of Health, Education and Welfare in July 1974. The targeted department was the Department of Vocational and Technical Education, UT Knoxville.

The claim of employment termination on the basis of race was investigated by HEW and found to be invalid. Two months after the charge was filed resolution was reached. No appeal was filed to any court and the case ended

Seventeen race discrimination cases later the University had suffered no finding of race discrimination and paid no adverse judgment. The 18th case was filed with the Equal Employment Opportunity Commission in August 1976.

The claimant, Melvin Woods, a UT Memphis police officer, claimed he was denied promotion and subsequently terminated on the basis of his race (black). The EEOC ruled in Woods favor but filed no suit to enforce the ruling. Instead, the Commission issued Woods a "right to sue letter."

Woods filed suit in U.S. District Court alleging that his University employment was terminated based on his race. An EEOC representative testified on Wood's behalf. Two black police officers, brothers Lonnie and Perry Batts, both friends of mine, offered testimony helpful to the University. Personnel director James Stockdale and several UT Memphis Safety and Security officials and employees did likewise. The trial lasted three days.

The District Court entered judgment in the University's favor on May 22, 1978 and came close to granting the University's request for an attorney's fee. [U.S. Dist. Ct., W.D. Tenn., Civ. Action No. 77-2582}. General Counsel Brogan so advised the members of the UT Board of Trustees by memorandum of May 25, 1978.

To: Members of the Board of Trustees

From: Beauchamp E. Brogan, General Counsel and Secretary

Subject: Melvin Woods v. University of Tennessee Center for the Health Sciences

(US District Court, Western District of Tennessee)

Attached is a copy of the Court's judgment dismissing this action against the University and a copy of the Court's decision on which the judgment is based.

This was an action by a former black employee at UTCHS seeking reinstatement and back pay, claiming that he was unlawfully discharged because of his race, that he was not promoted during his employment because of his race and that the University maintained a racially discriminatory promotion system within its security department in Memphis. In holding that the University had not discriminated against Woods, the Court held that Wood's improper performance on the job was the reason for his discharge and that "any officer, black or white, would have been discharged for similar behavior." Also, the Court held that promotions in the security department were, and are, made on the basis of ability, not race.

We sought attorney's fees in this action in the amount of $3,860 – – for time spent trying the case – – because we felt that Woods' case had no merit and that he made allegations knowing them to be untrue. You will note that the Court came close to allowing us attorneys' fees but stopped just short of doing so.

Ron Leadbetter of this office tried the case for the University and did his usual good job.

Those truly earning credit for the victory were the University staff members who performed their jobs in a lawful manner and offered the court convincing testimony that no discrimination had taken place.

The winning spree continued. Not until the 29th case of alleged discrimination on the basis of race was a loss suffered by UT. A most unusual case it was.

A WHITE MALE PREVAILS
CROUSHORN v. THE UNIVERSITY OF TENNESSEE

James Croushorn was a white male faculty member employed by the UT Knoxville School of Social Work, Nashville branch. The program operated on the campus of Tennessee State University.

In Fall1976 Croushorn filed suit with the U.S. District Court in Nashville contending that he was paid a lower salary than black faculty based on his race. He also claimed he had been retaliated against by his superiors for complaining.

In February 1977 this lawsuit, naming the Dean of the School of Social Work, Ben Granger, and the Vice Chancellor for Academics, Hilton Smith was joined with a separate action against the Tennessee Commissioner for Human Services, Horace Bass, for trial. The case was tried by U.S. District Judge L Clure

Morton on June 11 and 12, 1979, in Nashville, then concluded on June 15 in Cookeville. Judgment was not entered until June of the following year.

On June 19, 1980, Judge Morton entered judgment, partially in favor of the UT defendants and partially in plaintiff's favor. On the subject which incited litigation to begin with –salary discrepancy based on race– the University prevailed. However, the District Court found that School of Social Work officials denied Croushorn summer employment in retaliation for filing a salary discrimination complaint with the EEOC. The court awarded Croushorn compensatory damages in the amount of $42,000 on the retaliation claim. [James Croushorn vs.The University of Tennessee, U.S. District Court, M.D. Tenn. No. 77-3051]

Federal law bars any act of retaliation against an employee pursuing a claim of discrimination with the EEOC or other civil rights enforcement authority. There was without doubt evidence in the record that Croushorn was denied summer employment because he had filed a complaint with the EEOC. Although I introduced into evidence ample opposing evidence I lacked any sound basis for arguing that the court's evaluation of the evidence was arbitrary, capricious or otherwise lacking in merit. No appeal was filed and the judgment was paid.

In the late 1970s it was well understood by UT administration, faculty and staff that employment discrimination on the basis of race was unlawful. The University won yet another race discrimination claims as a result.

Less well understood was the fact that employment retaliation of any sort against an employee claiming to be victimized by discriminatory treatment– even if there was no discriminatory treatment – is likewise unlawful and leads to risk of litigation and resulting monetary loss. Lesson learned! When faced with a civil rights complaint "get out of the way" – let the legal system adjudicate the claim - don't retaliate!

Although Croushorn was a civil rights case resulting in a judgment against the University for retaliation, that judgment did not blemish the University's reputation for being free of any finding that it discriminated on the basis on race. Not until 1988, after seventy five (75) civil rights actions alleging race discrimination by UT in one form or another, was there a judgment against the University with a finding of race discrimination.

MILTON ROBINSON vs. WILLIAM F. BOWLD HOSPITAL

Milton Robinson was employed in 1981 as a nursing assistant at the University's William F. Bowld Hospital in Memphis. In September 1983 the position of transportation service foreman was created by the University. Robinson was one of four candidates for the position, two white and two black. One of the white applicants was selected for the position. In December 1983 Robinson filed with the EEOC a charge that he had been denied promotion on the basis of his race (black).

The EEOC investigated Robinson's charge. A "fact-finding conference" was held by the EEOC at the Hospital in February 1984 and a full day of interviews of hospital officials took place in May 1985. The administrator of Bowld Hospital, Leslie Herring, explained that although Robinson was a good worker, he was frequently absent or late without providing adequate advance notice. On the other hand the successful candidate was rated "very reliable" and "good with the public".

On July 19, 1985 the EEOC issued a "Determination" finding the University innocent of discriminating against Robinson. Robinson requested and received a "right to sue" letter and proceeded to federal court.

In December 1985 Robinson filed a "Title VII" action in the U.S. District Court in Memphis alleging he had been denied promotion on the basis of race. He requested an award of front pay, back pay, compensatory damages and attorney's fees.

The case was tried on January 5, 1987 before U.S.District Judge Robert McRae. The witnesses appearing before Judge McCrea were essentially the same as those who testified in the EEOC proceeding. The testimony of both plaintiff and defense witnesses remained unchanged. Hospital officials testified that it was Robinson's work performance that prevented his promotion not his race.

Judge McCrae opted to accept Robinson's explanation over that of Hospital officials and ruled in his favor "from the bench" at the conclusion of trial. By order of March 12, 1987 the District Court ordered that plaintiff be awarded his attorney's fees in the amount of $11,390. The court's "findings of fact and conclusions of law, entered on May 29, awarded plaintiff judgment in the amount of $27,645.64. [Milton Robinson vs. William F. Bowld Hospital, U.S. District Court, W. D. Tenn. No.85-3073-MA].

The University promptly appealed to the U.S. Court of Appeals for the Sixth Circuit. In its appellate brief the University argued that the District Court's findings were "clearly erroneous".

On February 18, 1988 the Clerk of the Court of Appeals issued a notice setting oral argument on the appeal for March 29, 1988. One week later, on February 25, Robinson accepted an offer of settlement I had previously extended on behalf of the University. A confidential settlement agreement was executed by the parties on March 14, 1988.

The University paid Robinson the sum of $13,822.82. Judge McRae's judgment was vacated by order of March 14, 1988 on the same day the settlement agreement was executed. His finding of race discrimination by the University was thereby eradicated from the record. The monetary cost to the University was cut in half and its reputation restored.

ITSON AND WATSON

One of the more unusual race discrimination cases involved UT Memphis employees James Earl Itson and Michael Jerome Watson, both of whom were black males employed as "senior storage clerks" at William F. Bowld Hospital. In 1987 each was charged with gross misconduct (specifics not recorded) and notified that his employment at the hospital would be terminated. Each requested a formal hearing under the Tennessee Administrative Procedures Act.

An administrative judge from UT Knoxville, Tim Rogers, was assigned to hear the cases. Both cases were heard in Memphis on April 22, 1986. In his "initial order" of July 22, 1986, administrative judge Rogers concluded that Watson should be dismissed but that Itson should be reinstated.

UT Memphis Chancellor Jim Hunt later issued a "final order" directing that both men be dismissed.

Concurrent with the APA proceedings, both Itson and Watson pursued charges of race and sex discrimination, as well as retaliation, with the Tennessee Human Rights Commission and the Equal Employment Opportunity Commission. In October 1986 Watson was issued a "notice of right to sue" letter in each of his agency proceedings and in April 1987 Itson received letters in each of his.

Watson filed suit in U.S. District Court in Memphis on January 16, 1987 under various civil rights statutes alleging discrimination on the basis of race and sex and retaliation. Back pay in the amount of $20,000 and punitive damages in the amount of $100,000, plus attorney fees, was requested. Named as defendants were UT employees Rudolf McDaniel, Pauline Mashburn and Robert Nolley.

Itson filed suit in the same court on May 28, 1987 making essentially the same claims and requesting the same relief–although he requested $10,000 more in compensatory damages. He named the same defendants.

In early 1988 Itson filed a motion to consolidate his lawsuit with that of Watson. Although I fully expected the District Court to grant the motion, I filed a statement in opposition on behalf of the defendants. To my surprise, by order of July 14, 1988, the Court (Turner, District Judge) denied Itson's motion to consolidate. On August 16, a like order was entered in Watson's case.

Both Itson and Watson were then set for trial. Itson was tried by a jury on October 17–21 and 24, 1988. A verdict was entered in favor of all defendants on the issue of race discrimination although the district judge entered separate findings on sex discrimination claims brought pursuant to Title VII of the Civil Rights Act of 1964. Judgment was entered in favor of all defendants in November 1988. [Itson v. McDaniel, U.S. Dist Ct., W.D. Tenn. No. 87-2376-TU/B]

Watson was set for trial on October 11, 1988. The notice of setting was issued August 15, 1988–one day before entry of the Court's order denying Watson's motion to consolidate. Perhaps Watson was clairvoyant and foresaw the result in Itson. Or just didn't want to be first. There was no trial. An order of dismissal was entered in favor of all individual defendants on March 15, 1989 and judgment in favor the University was entered on March 28, 1989. [Watson v. McDaniel, U.S. District Court, W.D. Tenn. No. 87-2038-MG].

The last case threatening UT's blemish-free record in race discrimination cases during the "Big Orange" period was the Clark case out of Memphis. (See Chapter 42) As in Robinson, described above, the adverse judgment initially entered by the trial court was subsequently vacated, leaving the university with a clear record.

BLACK STORM CLOUDS BRING CHANGE

With the hiring of J. Wade Gilley, in 1999, as president of the University of Tennessee came black storm clouds of change–change that adversely affected the reputation of the University from a legal perspective and otherwise. I will focus on the legal perspective.

As in earlier years, the University's record with respect to race discrimination claims remained without blemish of a loss. Two such cases were settled with a loss being removed from the record in each case.

The first settlement was very ill-advised to say the least. The second was a good example of the settlement option used wisely in a rare case where a reputation damaging and more expensive loss would otherwise be sustained.

My responsibility for civil rights litigation ended in 2001 in conjunction with my civil rights litigation against President Gilley. All of my pending civil rights cases were reassigned to other attorneys in the office of General Counsel.

I closed out my last three years of dwindling civil rights work with 14 wins, zero losses and two settlements totaling $202,011.09. A record I can live with.

Chapter 56–Civil Rights–Sex Discrimination Claims Ranked Second in Number

When I enrolled in the UT College of Law in 1969 there was one female student. Currently, around 40% of the enrollees are female.

Both judicial interpretation of the "equal protection" clause of the 14th Amendment to the U.S. Constitution and the Civil Rights Act of 1964 changed the playing field for women, as well as blacks, in higher education, with respect to education programs and activities as well as employment.

By the date of my employment in the UT Office of General Counsel the law was well established that, with rare exception, employment opportunities could not be determined on the basis of sex. The same was true for educational opportunities.

Vigorous debate continued regarding the role of "preferential treatment" as a permissible ingredient in affirmative action as a means of addressing under representation of females attributed to discriminatory policy and practice predating the change in law. That debate was, in my judgment, less intense and ended sooner than the similar debate concerning underrepresentation of blacks in higher education.

While court-ordered numerical goals and recruitment practices were established for blacks at the University of Tennessee (see chapter 55) such was never done for females. Implementation of nondiscriminatory employment and admission practices sufficed ("Title IX" and the gender factor in athletics being addressed separately in Chapter 57).

As was true for "race," "sex" as an employment factor was addressed in each of the numerous seminars I conducted for University personnel from 1972 until my responsibilities in that area ended in 2001. The only legal basis for different treatment of the categories, where sex is a legitimate factor for consideration (a bona fide occupation qualification or "BFOQ"), such as assignment of responsibility for monitoring toilet facilities or conducting police "pat downs." A BFOQ never arose as a factor in any of the numerous sex discrimination claims I handled.

LITIGATION RECORD

The overall litigation record for sex discrimination cases I handled was comparable to that for race discrimination cases. 61 cases ended favorably for the University. Four cases ended with judgments against the University totaling $327,113. One case was settled for $64,227.

Of the 65 sex discrimination claims I handled 44 were disposed of between 1974 and 1984, roughly 2/3 of the total. Sex discrimination claims declined dramatically after 1984. Slightly more than one per year, on average, were filed statewide in this latter period.

Three of the four losses sustained by the University occurred during the latter period. Grievants and their attorneys became more selective in prosecuting sex discrimination claims–avoiding prosecution of those lacking significant evidentiary support.

The first sex discrimination litigation I handled, and successfully, was Van de Vate. As noted earlier, I actually picked up the case file during my first week of employment in the OGC. The case concluded favorably on June 3, 1974. Not until 1979 would the University be saddled with a monetary judgment in a sex discrimination case. However, there were interesting challenges along the way.

CLEO CALAGE vs. UNIVERSITY OF TENNESSEE

In 1967 Cleo Calage was hired by the Food Services Department of the University (Knoxville) as catering supervisor. In February 1973 Calage filed a sex discrimination charge with the EEOC contending she was paid less than several male food service managers on the basis of her sex. The EEOC conducted an on-site review in June.

Key UT officials were interviewed by EEOC investigator Alan Gosa including President Boling's administrative assistant, Charles Smith, Vice Chancellor Luke Ebersole, Vice Chancellor Howard Aldmon and Personnel Director Ed Bennett. Director of food services, Norm Hill, and his second-in-command, Bob Norris, were also interviewed.

An EEOC "determination" of August 21, 1973 went "almost entirely against us" according to my file note. Things went downhill from there, in one sense.

A November 13 meeting was called in Vice Chancellor Aldmon's office to discuss Calage's refusal to comply with Norris' order to submit "timesheets" indicating her hours worked. Further attempts were made by Norris to secure Calage's compliance, but without success. Norm Hill issued a letter of termination to Calage dated November 19.

Attorney Charles Susano, who had represented me in my litigation against the University, provided notice of his representation of Calage and her request for a grievance hearing (although he did not appear with her at the requested hearing). Following an adverse grievance finding Calage filed a second charge with the EEOC, this time alleging "reprisal" (retaliatory discharge). But this time the EEOC issued a determination favorable to the University.

Susano represented Calage in an unemployment compensation appeal hearing on June 11, 1974 but that appeal was denied.

Calage filed suit in U.S. District Court in Knoxville on January 6, 1975. She alleged wage disparity and denial of promotion, based on her sex, in violation of Title VII of the Civil Rights Act of 1964 and the Equal Pay Act. The judge handling the case was U.S. District Judge Robert L Taylor. Attorneys for the plaintiff were Charles Susano and L. Caesar Stair, III, of the law firm Bernstein, Dougherty and Susano.

Judge Taylor had a reputation for being abrupt with attorneys but also had a reputation for having the second most current docket in the entire nation. He was one of my favorite judges in the state of Tennessee.

Both sides engaged in extensive discovery and several motions were filed and disposed of by the court. The trial was set for March 12, 1975–a little more than two months after the complaint was filed!

The trial began in a most unusual way. My friend Caesar Stair rose from his seat at the plaintiff's table to present opening argument on behalf of his client, Susano was present as was the plaintiff. No sooner had Stair introduced himself than Judge Taylor interrupted, "My, my, you're awfully young to be handling a case like this."

With his client seated a few feet away I'm sure Caesar was a bit stunned. Perhaps not as much as me. I was roughly the same age and had no one of Charles Susano's reputation, or anyone else, seated with me. Fortunately, when my turn for opening argument came, Judge Taylor made no mention of my age, I was 27. The Judge was in his 80s, possibly explaining his assessment of youthfulness.

An even stranger occurrence took place shortly before lunch. Judge Taylor commented it was nearly lunchtime (and I recall turning and seeing the clock at 11:45) and asked how many witnesses I had left. "Two," I replied. "Just tell me what they're going to say," Judge Taylor continued. I quickly summarized the expected testimony of the two witnesses I had planned to call. There was no objection from the plaintiff's table. The first, and only, time I ever had a judge ask me to "testify" in place of the witness.

At the close of the March 12 trial Judge Taylor ordered the parties to submit briefs by the 19th, setting out the applicable law and pertinent facts as we saw them. Both parties met the one-week deadline.

Yet another strange occurrence took place. Judge Taylor ordered that a second evidentiary hearing, a resumption of the trial, be held on April 7. Prior to that day the deposition of Norm Hill was taken in the office of Caesar Stair.

Hill, as well as Calage and one other witness for the plaintiff, testified on April 7. Judge Taylor's memorandum and order dismissing the complaint were entered two weeks later–on April 21, 1975. Even looking back I remain incredulous that so much could be done in such a short time. The results were good; I had no complaint

The District Court thoroughly analyzed the evidence of record. It noted that "[i}t is significant in this regard that plaintiff at no time charged the University with sex discrimination in hiring." Calage v. The University of Tennessee, et. al., 400 F. Supp. 32, 38 (E.D. Tenn. 1975).

The court took note of evidence presented by the University that the pay of male food service directors Calage sought to compare herself with was "based upon job complexity, responsibility, educational and managerial credentials, seniority and job performance and not on a person's sex." Id, pp.38-39. "The court cannot say that the reasons set forth in exhibit B for salary differentials constitute an artifice for sex discrimination." Id.

Judge Taylor concluded by finding "on the basis of exhibits 1–16 [and] 26, the evaluations of plaintiff and other females, and the affidavit of Mr. Hill, the contents of which were verified by the oral testimony of Mr. Hill at the April 7 hearing, the court is of the opinion that plaintiff was not the object of unlawful discrimination under title VII of the Civil Rights Act." Id. p. 39. Calage appealed to the U.S. Court of Appeals for the Sixth Circuit.

In its opinion of November 3, 1976 the Court of Appeals, in a unanimous opinion of the three-judge panel, rejected the plaintiff's contention that the trial court erred in reopening the case. It also concurred with the District Court's rejection of "the theory that equal title demands equal pay" - that it is job content, not title, that is determinative. Calage v. University of Tennessee, 544 F.2d 297 (6th Cir. 1976).

SUE HATTON

In 1977 Sue Hatton (UT Memphis) filed a sex discrimination charge with the equal employment opportunity commission. The EEOC rejected her claim and no appeal was taken. But we would hear from her again 12 years later. Hatton's voice would then have impact–in more ways than one.

The following year, 1978, the Equal Employment Opportunity Commission issued findings of discrimination in favor of three separate claimants bringing sex discrimination claims. I viewed the evidence cited by the EEOC in its findings as exceedingly weak - so weak that two of the three cases were pursued no further by the claimants. I misjudged the third.

LAVERNE GURLEY vs. THE UNIVERSITY OF TENNESSEE

Claimant Laverne Gurley, a UT Memphis employee, filed a charge of sex discrimination (salary) with the EEOC on October 13, 1974. Following issuance of a determination sustaining Gurley's charge against the University, the commission issued Gurley a "right to sue letter."

Gurley filed suit in federal court on May 1, 1978. U.S. District Judge Robert McRae, by far my least favorite judge in the state of Tennessee because of his extremely liberal judicial perspective, was assigned to hear the case.

Judge McRae announced his findings following the trial held on July 19-20, 1979, partially in favor of the University and partially in favor of Gurley. He rejected Gurley's claim that she was twice denied promotion to the position of Chairman of the Department of Radiologic Technology on the basis of her sex. However he ruled that she was discriminated against on the basis of sex with respect to her salary.

Judgment was entered on November 1, 1979 awarding plaintiff the very modest amount of $1,769. But attorney's fees were also awarded in an equal amount, thereby doubling the award. While a bit disturbed by McRae's finding that a small salary differential was attributed to sex discrimination I was more disturbed by the fee award.

My unbroken string of 19 sex discrimination cases without an adverse monetary judgment was broken. And my attention was drawn to the issue of attorney's fees.

PROPOSED LEGISLATION ADDRESSING ATTORNEY'S FEE DISPARITY

On December 4, 1981 I drafted and sent an eight page letter to Congressman John J. Duncan criticizing the application of civil rights law provision for discretionary award of attorney's fees to the prevailing party in a civil rights action. The problem, as I described it:

Despite the seemingly even-handed and clear meaning of the language of Title VII and [section] 1983 the courts have seen fit to interpret these attorney's fees provisions to mean that, as a general rule, only a prevailing plaintiff may recover his attorney's fees. Moreover, the courts have also interpreted [section] 1988 as requiring that an award of an attorney's fee to a prevailing plaintiff extend to all legal services rendered, including services aimed at establishing major claims on which the defendant prevails. The result of this two-fold manipulation of the language of Title VII and [section] 1988 has been to inequitably burden civil rights defendants, including public institutions and universities such as The University of Tennessee. These defendants have been denied recovery of attorney's fees, even when they prevail in lawsuits having little merit, and are compelled to pay attorney's fees even in cases in which they prevail on most or even all of the major issues in dispute.

I suggested corrective language that might be introduced as an amendment to the misapplied federal statutes. ("A party shall not be awarded fees with respect to those substantial issues on which it does not prevail" and "[i]n determining whether and the extent to which an attorney's fee should be awarded to the prevailing party , the Court shall make such determination without regard to whether a party is a plaintiff or a defendant"). Attached to my letter were copies of the *Woods, Gurley and Croushorn* judgments against UT awarding attorney's fees to the plaintiff under circumstances described.

On December 10 Executive Vice President and Vice President for Development Joe Johnson sent an identical letter to Senator Howard Baker. Corrective legislation was not passed but the problem was identified and eventually resolved, in future litigation.

MARIE JOSBERGER vs. THE UNIVERSITY OF TENNESSEE

In 1982 Marie Josberger, former Dean of the UTCHS College of Nursing, was removed from her faculty position in the College based on a charge of failure to carry out work assignments. Josberger filed a complaint with the EEOC claiming she was terminated because she was female. A determination in favor of UT was issued by the EEOC on February 25, 1983.

Two months later Josberger filed suit in Shelby County Chancery Court challenging the process by which she was dismissed. She was represented by Memphis attorney Don Donati.

Josberger lacked sufficient supporting evidence to even get to trial. Shelby County Chancellor Neal Small entered summary judgment in favor of defendants UT and Chancellor Jim Hunt on June 11, 1984. [Marie Josberger v. The University of Tennessee, et. al., Shelby Chancery No. 90145-1] The Chancery ruling was appealed to the Tennessee Court of Appeals.

In a published opinion of Feb. 5, 1985, the Court of Appeals confirmed the Chancery Court's conclusion that there was "clear and convincing proof that the plaintiff was guilty as charged, and there is material and substantial evidence to warrant her discharge. We further hold that the actions of the university officials were not arbitrary or capricious, or characterized by abuse of discretion." Josberger v. University of Tennessee, 706 S.W.2d. 300, 303 (Tenn. App. 1985).

Don Donati recovered no fees from the University in this case because he did not prevail in any respect on any claim. He would later be a key player in improving the law governing award of attorney's fees.

SALLEE BRUHWILER vs. UNIVERSITY OF TENNESSEE, ET. AL

In 1973 Sallee Bruhwiler was hired as a research toxicologist in the toxicology laboratory at UT Center for the Health Sciences. In 1977 the director of the laboratory, Dr. D. T. Stafford, asked Bruhwiler to assume responsibility for running the laboratory, but did not officially promote her or offer a salary increase. A male with less seniority was subsequently promoted.

Stafford, having had an opportunity to observe Bruhwiler's interaction with others, did not promote her because he felt she did not get along well with other people in the laboratory.

Bruwiler filed a charge of discrimination with the EEOC in August 1982, contending she was denied promotion on the basis of sex. The EEOC issued a determination in favor of the University and issued a "right to sue" letter to the claimant.

Both the University of Tennessee and Dr. Stafford were named as defendants in a federal civil rights action filed by Bruhwiler on October 28, 1982 in the U.S. District Court in Memphis. The case was assigned for trial to judge Robert McRae.

The case was tried before McRae on April 2–3, 1986. At the conclusion of trial McRae entered judgment in favor of the plaintiff. He found that Bruhwiler was denied promotion on account of her sex and was also "constructively discharged." Damages were awarded in the total amount of $39,290 ($29,000 in back pay, $9,480 in attorney's fees and $810 in court costs). Bruhwiler v. University of Tennessee, et al., U.S. District Court, W.D. Tenn. No.82–2819M (1987).

I filed an appeal from the District Court judgment with the U.S. Court of Appeals for the Sixth Circuit. In a split, 2-1, decision the Court of Appeals upheld McRae, but just barely. The majority (Circuit Judges Boyce Martin and George Clifton Edwards) concluded that the District Court's findings were not clearly erroneous and that "[i]f the District Court's account of the evidence is plausible in light of the record viewed in its entirety, the Court of Appeals may not reverse it even though convinced that had it been sitting as the trier of fact, it would have weighed the evidence differently...."Bruhwiler v. University of Tennessee, 859 F.2d 419, 421 (6th Cir. 1988).

Circuit Judge David Nelson issued a strong dissenting opinion. He agreed with the majority that the Court of Appeals could not reverse the District Court if the District Court's "account is plausible in light of the record viewed in its entirety." However, Judge Nelson went on to explain that he had read the record in its entirety and "having done so, I am bound to say that the District Court's stated reasons for finding Mrs. Bruhwiler a victim of sex discrimination, as opposed to being on the wrong end of a personality clash and a victim of insensitivity or managerial incompetence, do not strike me as 'plausible.' " Id., p.426.

In arriving at his dissent Judge Nelson made a number of references to Judge McRae's own statements of record. One reference Nelson made I remember quite well:

> If the district judge (a male) had found himself working in a small group
> with Dr. Stafford, one senses that there would have been an "obvious personal
> tension" between the two of them also. As the judge commented to defense
> counsel from the bench,
> "Mister Ledbetter, you have got a bunch of dodos to protect in this. Really, I
> don't understand. You know, you get some tough ones. The University of Tennes-
> see, they have, that outfit, academia out there, they are the worst personnel

managers I have ever seen in my life.

They really are. They are a bunch of silly children. They don't – they all are 'poppycock,' you know, proud and gossip and all that stuff. I have had several of these cases and every one gets worse than the other."

If a male who considered Dr. Stafford a "dodo" had been passed over for promotion, and for all we know plaintiff's witness Edward Vaughn was passed over for precisely that reason – it would hardly have constituted sex discrimination.

Id., p.426.

A Petition for Rehearing and Suggestion for Rehearing En Banc was filed to no avail. The Sixth Circuit denied the petition. This was just one of those cases destined for the loss column. It did give meaning to a phrase often used in the legal profession, "bad facts make bad law."

Bruhwiler also provided some new material for my seminars and "consultations." When someone sought my advice on a course of action that was completely legal but grossly insensitive I would opine, "Yes, what you propose is legal." Then, I would share the Bruhwiler saga and lesson learned.

DEBORAH ROBERSON–A LOSING BATTLE
(BUT MORE LESSONS LEARNED)

Deborah Roberson was employed by the UT Agricultural Extension Service in 1980 as an assistant agent. A male, Richard Skillington, hired the previous year as an assistant agent, was promoted in 1986 but Roberson was not.

In April 1987 Roberson filed a complaint with the Knox County Chancery Court contending that she was denied promotion on the basis of sex in violation of the Equal Pay Act and the Tennessee Human Rights Act. She also alleged that the University had retaliated against her earlier filing a discrimination charge with the Equal Employment Opportunity Commission.

The first issue addressed was whether Roberson could pursue her claims in Chancery Court rather than the Tennessee Claims Commission. Knox County Chancellor Frederick McDonald agreed she could not and, on August 17, 1987, ordered her suit dismissed for lack of jurisdiction. Roberson appealed.

On July 19, 1988 the Tennessee Court of Appeals reversed the Chancery decision. Although noting that the Tennessee Claims Commission Act granted the Claims Commission "exclusive jurisdiction to determine all monetary claims against the state [including] negligent deprivation of statutory or constitutional rights....", the appellate court also held that the Human Rights Act took precedence since "the more specific comprehensive legislation addressing the special subject matter of human rights and discrimination was intended to survive the more general language of the Claims Act. Deborah Roberson v. University of Tennessee, C.A. No. 754 (Tenn. App. 1988). See also Roberson v. University of Tennessee 912 S.W. 2d 746 (Tenn. App. 1995) (specifically holding that the State was a "person" within the meaning of the Human Rights Act and, thereby extending jurisdiction to the University of Tennessee).

Roberson's claims proceeded to trial by jury. A four-day trial (January 14-17, 1991) ended with a jury verdict in the plaintiff's favor. The jury awarded Roberson $13,600 in back wages based on her sex discrimination claim and $50,000 on the retaliation claim.

The Chancery Court also granted plaintiff's request for attorney's fees in the amount of $26,000. Total judgment: $97,820, including court costs. The University appealed. Knoxville attorney Gerald Becker represented Roberson, being the third attorney to represent her, with the first being Harry Wiersema, Jr. and the second being Greg Grisham.

On January 15, 1992 the Tennessee Court of Appeals affirmed the Chancery Court's judgment. The court found material evidence supporting the jury's verdict that the University had discriminated against Roberson because she was female and in retaliation for her filing an EEOC charge. Also the appellate court found that the amounts awarded for damages and attorneys fees were proper. Roberson v. University of Tennessee, 829 S.W.2d 149 (Tenn. App. 1992).

As in other cases with rulings adverse to the University, I found useful tips in the Court of Appeals' ruling.

It is not seriously contended that plaintiff did not make out a prima facie case, because Skillington, the male employee who did comparable work, earned more money and received promotion in the year he was eligible. The focal point is whether defendant's failure to promote plaintiff was based on a lack of merit or on the basis of her sex.

***

At the time plaintiff inquired why her peer earned more money than she, defendant's management provided contradictory answers. First, her manager denied that Skillington made more money, then plaintiff was told that Skillington made more money because he was a man with a family to support. Finally the Dean sent plaintiff a letter advising the relatively low MBO scores and her failure to take extra coursework had kept her from receiving a raise and promotion. Merit was but one of the defendant's three explanations for the distinction made between the agents, and the jury was the judge of this fact issue.

Id., p. 151.

Lessons learned: be truthful and forthright, don't fabricate reasons for employment action. And of course, don't discriminate on the basis of sex or any other legally protected category. From my perspective, these lessons were nothing new but I had another good case study to share in future seminars and advisory sessions.

HATTON & HOLLAND–
A LOSING BATTLE PROVES BENEFICIAL

Rarely does a litigation loss result in more celebration by the loser then the winner. One particularly unusual case from Memphis fell in that category.

Sue Hatton was employed by UT Memphis in 1959. From 1977 she served as assistant to the chairman of the Department of Pharmacology in the College of Medicine. Prior to that she had served as a research technician in the Department of Physiology.

As noted earlier in the chapter, in 1976 Hatton filed a sex discrimination charge (wages, terms and conditions of employment and reprisal) with the EEOC. That case was administratively closed in January 1977.

Twelve years later, in 1989, Hatton filed a new charge with the EEOC alleging discriminatory treatment on the basis of sex with respect to salary. Her claim was brought pursuant to Title VII as well as the Equal Pay Act. The EEOC ruled in Hatton's favor on the former and the University's on the latter.

Hatton requested and received from the EEOC a right to sue letter and proceeded to federal court. On May 1, 1990 she filed a complaint with the U.S. District Court in Memphis. Hatton named UT Memphis Chancellor Jim Hunt and Dr. Robert Summitt, Dean of the College of Medicine, as defendants.

A second plaintiff, Carolyn Holland, was employed by UT Memphis in 1974 as a secretary in the University's Cancer Center. In 1978 Holland was promoted to Office Services Supervisor and served as assistant to the Chairman of the Department of Physiology and Biophysics in the College of Medicine.

In May 1989 Holland filed with the EEOC a charge of sex discrimination (salary) and retaliation, She filed a second charge of retaliation with the EEOC in May 1991 but subsequently withdrew that charge. Like Hatton, Holland received a "right to sue" letter and proceeded to federal court.

On December 31, 1990 Holland filed a sex discrimination complaint against the University of Tennessee with the U.S. District Court alleging she was paid less then a male counterpart performing work requiring substantially equal skill, effort and responsibility, and performed under similar working conditions.

The lawsuits filed by Hatton and Holland were joined for trial pursuant to the District Court's order of January 24, 1991. A four-day trial was held on August 22 and 26 through 28, 1991. U.S. District Judge Jerome Turner presided.

Following the conclusion of trial, on August 29, I contacted Hatton's attorney, Don Donati, and Holland's attorney, Hite McLean Jr., and proposed a settlement.

According to my litigation note card:

I offered to settle for $25,000 for both plaintiffs [each plaintiff].
Plaintiffs countered with offer to settle for approximate $1,300 pay increase
for three fiscal years ($3900) each; plus $6,000 back pay plus $6,000 damages,
plus retirement benefits, plus $45,000 attorneys' fees
– Hunt said NO to counter
No settlement was reached – at the time.

Judge Turner's "Findings of Fact and Conclusions of Law" were entered September 17, 1991 (followed by entry of judgment on June 19, 1992 after incorporation of an award of attorney's fees.)

The University defendants prevailed on the title VII claim. Hatton and Holland prevailed on their Equal Pay Act claim. In other words, the plaintiffs failed to meet their burden of proving, by a preponderance of evidence, that they were paid less then males doing the same work based on sex. On the other hand, the University failed to prove that the pay differential between plaintiffs and their male counterparts was justified by "(i) a seniority system; (ii) a merit system; (iii) a system which measures earnings by quantity or quality of production; or (iv) a differential based on any other factor other than sex). Hatton v. Hunt 780 F. Supp 1157, 1165 (W. D. Tenn. 1991).

Although I argued that the pay differential was premised on a "factor other than sex" Judge Turner rejected that argument. "The court concludes that defendants have not met their burden of proving by a preponderance of the evidence that the salary disparities at issue were based on a factor other than sex." Id. p. 1166.

In awarding relief, Judge Turner rejected each plaintiff's claim that a $3,000 merit raise each received in 1988 should not be considered in awarding back pay.

The Act requires equal pay, not that the reasons for equal pay be based on an intent to comply with the Act. For whatever reasons, as of July 1988 plaintiffs received substantial raises in excess of the raises Banton received and much of the disparity between their salaries was dissipated with those raises. The court does not have authority under this act to compel merit raises, only to insist that the congressional edict of equal pay be met."
Id. pp. 1167-68.

Accordingly, Hatton was awarded $2,884 in back pay and Holland was awarded $2,869. Id.

In his Judgment entered June 19, 1992, Turner awarded attorney's fees totaling $14,046 -less than one third of the amount Donati alone demanded for settlement at the conclusion of trial.

Both plaintiffs and the University filed appeals with the U.S. Court of Appeals for the Sixth Circuit. The parties' appellate briefs were filed and oral argument before the Court of Appeals in Cincinnati was set for December 7, 1993.

Donati and I appeared at the designated hour (McLean opting not appear and leaving to his colleague the argument on behalf of the plaintiffs). As customary, our case was listed on the day's docket and each side was allocated a specified time – either 15 or 20 minutes – for oral argument. Quite contrary to customary procedure were the opening remarks of the presiding judge after Court was called to order and the three judge panel (Appellate Judges Boggs and Norris and District Judge Bell) was seated.

Following the reading of the name of each party to the proceeding and inquiry being made by the presiding judge as to who represented the parties, first Donati then I stood and introduced ourselves. A stunning "directive" by the presiding judge followed: "Gentlemen, we suggest you go out and try to settle this case." No explanation for the "suggestion" was given. My best guess was that the panel found merit with both parties' positions–or neither. Had the court felt strongly in favor of either position - or was uncertain as to which position was more meritorious – the panel surely would have entertained argument (and later issued a ruling on the appeal).

Donati and I exited the courtroom and made our way to the adjacent conference room. Don was plainly troubled. Recalling the previous offer of settlement in the amount of $25,000 for each plaintiff, I reiterated that offer. This time the offer was accepted.

A settlement agreement was subsequently executed by the parties. On April 22, 1994 an "order of dismissal" was entered by the U.S. District Court, vacating the judgment previously entered. The University's "pay-out" to the plaintiffs and their counsel was in the amount of $38,083.48 for Hatton and $26,144.21 for Holland, the total amount being slightly more than what Donati had demanded just for his fee!

Several years after conclusion of the Hatton/Holland cases Donati shared with me, during a chance encounter in the Memphis airport, that he was rarely taking cases against the University because we rarely settled. I had earlier been present in Judge Turner's chamber when Donati complained that inability to secure reasonable attorney's fees discouraged him from handling civil rights actions.

While I greatly admired Donati for his prowess in civil rights litigation I likewise felt that prosecution of civil rights cases should not be the "Las Vegas" of the legal profession.

A May 4, 1994 memorandum to me from President Joe Johnson accurately portrayed our "celebratory" mood following the final results of Hatton and Holland cases.

Thank you for letting me have the good news of the decision of Judge Jerome Turner to dismiss the cases of Hatton v. Hunt and Holland v. Hunt in relation to an award of $6,000 each to Hatton and Holland and a considerably smaller amount of attorney's fees than the original request of $85,000. These folks and Donati got less than they sought and the court judgment against the defendants was erased.

I certainly hope Donati, other attorneys, and some UT staff members [l]earn a bit from this one.

Thank you for a good piece of work.

cc: Beach Brogan

    Eli Fly

    Bill Rice

There were lessons learned in these two cases. The most valuable was that civil rights actions with minimal risk of sizable award of damages should not be settled for fear that a "jackpot" award of attorney's fees will follow.

Post script: Holland pursued one last claim of sex discrimination and retaliation with EEOC in 1995 with litigation in federal court the following year. That litigation went nowhere, being devoid of any evidentiary support as confirmed by U.S. District Judge Jon McCalla's March 28, 1997 "Order Granting Defendant's Motion to Dismiss and/or for Partial Summary Judgment." [Carolyn A. Holland v. University of Tennessee, Memphis Campus, No. 94-3009 Ml/ V (W.D. Tenn. 1997)].

BIGGEST SHOCK--GINGER HINELINE vs. THE UNIVERSITY OF TENNESSEE

Not counting Hatton and Holland, which were settled, the only "sex-discrimination" litigation loss I handled from 1992 through 2001, my final year of handling civil rights litigation for the University, was one I least expected. In actuality it did not qualify as a "sex discrimination" case since all the actors were female and no male received preferential treatment. Discrimination on the basis of pregnancy more accurately describes the claim. The facts of the case are quite intriguing.

In June 1991 Julie Hermann was hired as head coach of the UT women's volleyball team. Hermann in turn hired Ginger Hineline as assistant coach despite the concern of women's athletic director Joan Cronan that Hineline lacked collegiate coaching experience. Hineline had coached high school volleyball for a brief period of time but never at the collegiate level.

During the first four years of Hermann's tenure as head coach, the women's volleyball program failed to achieve the level of success expected by Cronan and Hermann. The fall 1994 season was particularly disastrous as the volleyball team ended the season with an overall record of 10 wins and 21 losses. The team won only two Southeast Conference matches while losing 12 to conference opponents.

Hineline was perceived by Cronan as being a contributing factor to the losing record for a number of reasons. First, Hineline had failed to recruit any highly talented prospects and was judged unsuccessful in establishing a relationship with players she recruited. Her lack of recruiting ability was evident from the fact that none of her home visits ever produced a recruit for the women's volleyball program.

Hineline had engaged in angry disputes with players as well as University personnel. She received a reprimand from Cronan, on one occasion, for speaking rudely on the telephone to the UT chief of police and hanging up on him. Hermann was of the opinion that the players did not feel comfortable coming to Hineline for help.

On October 25, 1994 Cronan called a meeting with Hermann and told her she felt a staffing change was needed and directed that Hineline be terminated as assistant coach. Hermann agreed but a decision was made not to inform Hineline of the decision until after the season was over, so as not to disrupt the season. Neither Cronan nor Hermann knew it at the time the termination decision was made, but Hineline was pregnant.

On October 31, 1994, Hineline informed coach Hermann of her pregnancy. Hermann relayed this news to Cronan on November 1. Herman did not advise Hineline of the termination of her employment until January 25, 1995. She was told she would be permitted to remain employed with the University in an administrative capacity until August 1, 1995. Hineline requested maternity leave, which was approved by Cronan.

In April 1995 Hineline filed a charge with the EEOC contending the University terminated her employment based on her pregnancy. The following March the EEOC case was administratively closed.

Hineline filed suit against the University in the U.S. District Court in Knoxville on January 25, 1996. She alleged that she had been discriminated against on the basis of sex (pregnancy). U.S. District Judge Jimmy Jarvis was assigned to the case. Plaintiff's attorneys were Gary Ferraris and Scarlett May.

Seven depositions were taken by the parties between August and December 1996, including those of the plaintiff, Julie Hermann and volleyball assistant coach Kim Zenner. The focus of discovery was challenging Hineline to explain a lengthy list of interpersonal conflicts attributed to her. She did not deny the conflicts existed. Also, she offered no evidence of discriminatory animus on the part of her head coach or the Lady Vols athletic director.

On January 8, 1997 I filed a motion for summary judgment with the U.S. District Court, appending Hineline's deposition and affidavits of Cronan and Hermann in support. My argument for summary judgment was simple:

Where a plaintiff "has failed sufficiently to demonstrate that defendant's legitimate nondiscriminatory reasons for [an adverse employment action] are pretext," summary judgment should be granted. [Citation of legal authority omitted]. In the instant case, the University's non-discriminatory reasons for terminating the plaintiff's employment are clearly articulated and–in the absence of any legally sufficient proffer of evidence of pretext–requires entry of summary judgment in the University's favor.

Memorandum in Support of Defendant's Motion for Summary Judgment, U.S. District No. 3:96-CV-31 (E.D. Tenn.).

Although I often prevailed on motions for summary judgment I was not particularly concerned when Judge Jarvis denied the motion. If there is any evidence of substance in the record supporting the opposing party, the law requires the motion be denied. Judge Jarvis clearly preferred that Hineline receive her "day in court". On March 20, 1997 he entered a memorandum and order denying UT's summary judgment motion.

The trial by jury commenced June 2 1997. Attorney Scarlet May joined Hineline at the plaintiff's table while Joan Cronan joined me, as the University's representative, at the defense table.

Trial proceeded as well or better than any I'd ever tried. On every disputed motion or objection during trial, the University prevailed - to the point it was a topic of discussion even before a jury verdict was rendered. The evidence summarized above (from discovery) was presented to the jury in considerable detail. Plaintiff offered into evidence only a single morsel of evidence in support of her claim that she was fired because she was pregnant.

Hineline testified that Hermann and Zenner were bridesmaids in her June 4, 1984 wedding. During wedding festivities Hermann joked loudly to the gathered celebrants " I hope this doesn't mean you're going to go out and get pregnant" or words to that effect.

That Herman's remarks were a lighthearted effort at humor during a festive moment seemed clear. And well-documented – by a wedding video clip introduced into evidence by the plaintiff.

The nationally publicized pregnancy of UT women's basketball head coach Pat Head Summit was described to the jury by Cronan as was the pregnancy of a coach of the UT women's rowing team. Neither coach was fired or subjected to any other adverse treatment.

At the close of trial, following final arguments, the jury was released to deliberate. Following the jury's exit from the courtroom, and Judge Jarvis's departure for his chamber, a sizable audience remained, including Cronan and myself. The Court bailiff, friends and onlookers, and even Scarlett May, offered the opinion, in one way or another, that the University had surely won. I had little doubt that was true.

The jury returned to the courtroom late in the afternoon of June 4. Judge Jarvis asked the jury if they'd reached a verdict. The jury foreman said it had. My memory beyond that point is a bit foggy. Only the word "plaintiff" stands out. Verdict for the plaintiff.

The jury awarded Hineline $50,000 in backpay, $50,000 in front pay and $50,000 in compensatory damages. Attorney's fees in the amount of $36,465 were later awarded by the District Court.

Virtually everyone in the courtroom appeared in a state of shock, except the jury and those seated at the plaintiff's table, the latter understandably beaming with joy.

My dear friend Joan Cronan was stunned, as was I. Almost immediately Joan asked if we could appeal. My response was one never previously given following a loss. I explained that because we had prevailed on all objections and motions during trial, including objections to introduction of evidence, we lacked any procedural errors to assert on appeal. Any claim there was no material evidence to support the jury verdict would likewise have failed. Although minimal, there was evidence of record to support the jury's verdict. The wedding video.

The jury elected to believe the Hineline's interpretation of events over that of Cronan and Hermann. It necessarily dismissed their testimony that they were unaware of Hineline's pregnancy at the time a decision was made to terminate her employment. I knew the jury was dead wrong. I knew Joan Cronan would not testify falsely. And I felt the same way about Julie Hermann. But I was only counsel for the defendant, I didn't get to testify to what I knew to be the truth.

The next day's Knoxville News-Sentinel (June 5, 1997) headlined "Ex– UT volleyball coach awarded $150,000 over firing" and noted that "Ginger Hineline celebrated her third wedding anniversary with an unlikely feeling – vindication." The article also reported my state of mind. "I'm in a state of shock, Leadbetter said. 'I can't possibly believe a jury could believe that (women's athletic director) Joan Cronan would discriminate against a woman because she was pregnant.' "

A sports page story the next day headlined "Cronan is baffled by decision of court in discrimination case" and reported that the outcome "still has Leadbetter and Lady Vols athletic director Joan Cronan baffled and frustrated." Knoxville News-Sentinel, June 6, 1997, p. C1.

What lessons were learned from this $186,465 loss? Write more frequent and caustic reprimands to an employee failing to perform as expected? Fire a poor performer immediately rather than wait for a more convenient time?

My own thought: this was simply a great example of "You can't win 'em all!"

Postscript: Julie Hermann was named Athletic Director for Rutgers University in 2013. I was pleased to hear good news for an old friend.

STEFANOVIC v. UNIVERSITY OF TENNESSEE–
COVERING THE WATERFRONT

One last sex discrimination case deserves mention. The case could have been covered in a number of other chapters since the plaintiff's claims were brought pursuant to various federal and state statutes, alleged various categories of discrimination and named a variety of defendants.

On July 2, 1993 Dragan Stefanovic applied for the position of Coordinator of International Programming for the UT Center for International Education. He later learned that he had not been selected as a finalist to be interviewed for the position. Still later, he learned that a female had been hired.

In December 1993 Stefanovic filed with the EEOC a charge alleging discrimination on the basis of sex, age, national origin and veteran status. He received a "right to sue letter" from the EEOC on February 2, 1995.

Stefanovic filed suit in U.S. District Court in Knoxville on May 1, 1995. Named as defendants were the University of Tennessee, UT Board of Trustees, UT Center for International Education, UT Affirmative Action Office, William T. Snyder, Philip A. Scheurer, James A. Gehlar, Joseph W. Flory, Lola R. Dodge and Camille Hazeur. The individually named defendants were sued in their "official" as well as "individual" capacities.

The plaintiff alleged violations of Title VII of the Civil Rights Act of 1964, the Vietnam Era Veterans Readjustment Assistance Act, Executive Order 11246, the 14th Amendment to the United States Constitution, and the Tennessee Human Rights Act.

The defendants' failure to employ Stefanovic as Coordinator of International Programming was allegedly based on his sex (male), national origin (Eastern European) and status as a military veteran. Blount County attorney David Duggan represented Stefanovic. U.S. District Judge James Jarvis was assigned the case.

A variety of motions, and the court's April 8, 1996 ruling on those motions, also "covered the waterfront." Various defense motions to dismiss resulted in eliminating all claims except Stefanovic's Title VII action and his Fourteenth Amendment claim against the defendants in their individual capacities. Stefanovic v. University of Tennessee, 935 F. Supp. 944 (E.D. Tenn. 1996). On April 25, I filed a supplemental motion to dismiss the individual defendants and, by order of July 8, 1996, the District Court granted that motion. Stefanovic v. University of Tennessee, 935 F. Supp. 950 (E.D. Tenn. 1996). "Thus, the only remaining cause of action is a title VII action, and the only remaining defendant is UT." Id. p. 954.

The parties deposed 12 witnesses including Chancellor Snyder, Vice Chancellor Phil Scheurer, Affirmative Action Director Lola Dodge and members of the search committee which declined to recommend Stefanovic for the coordinator position. In September 1996, I filed a motion for summary judgment, much as I did in the Hineline case, appending sworn testimony of witnesses to the motion. As in Hineline I argued there was no substantial evidence of record entitling the plaintiff to a trial.

This time Judge Jarvis agreed. By Order and Memorandum Opinion of December 18, 1996, Jarvis granted the University's motion for summary judgment. The U.S. Court of Appeals later denied Stefanovic's appeal from the District Court judgment. Stefanovic v. University of Tennessee, No.97-5125 (6th Cir. 1997).

This time my expectations were met. UT's excellent civil rights record was renewed!

Chapter 57–Civil Rights–Title IX and Athletics

Title IX of the Education Amendments of 1972 prohibits discrimination on the basis of sex in any program or activity conducted by a recipient of federal financial assistance. The law has many applications but one in particular warranted my active involvement: Title IX's application to the University of Tennessee's program of intercollegiate athletics.

Shortly after enactment of Title IX the Department of Health, Education and Welfare (HEW) requested input as to how proposed Title IX guidelines might affect an institution of higher education. Based on input received from chancellors on each campus in the fall of 1974, I drafted a 25-page response. The document was mailed to Peter Holmes, director of the Office of Civil Rights (HEW) on October 2, 1974. Several key points were made in the UT response.

In section 3 of the UT response ("Affecting Intramural Athletics") I explained that "the University of Tennessee offers an intramural sports program on four of its five campuses (the fifth, an evening institution, having none)." It was then explained then explained: "Based on the expressed desires and interests of students, the university has organized some intramural teams and leagues for men only, others for women only, and still others for both men and women. We emphasize that this procedure has been followed because it permits equality in opportunities offered for both sexes to participate in intramurals."

Objection was made to the requirement in the proposed title IX guidelines that "every intramural activity be conducted on a coeducational basis." There are documented cases of lawsuits resulting from serious injuries caused by larger members of teams to smaller participants engaged in intramurals and all-male sports, and the chance of such incidents will be greater if both men and women are mixed on a compulsory basis."

The HEW guidelines were eventually amended to eliminate the requirement that an intramural sports league be conducted on a coeducational basis.

The University's greatest concern was set forth in section 4 of its response ("Affecting Intercollegiate Athletics"):

> The University of Tennessee conducts an intercollegiate athletics program on three of the five campuses in the institution's statewide system. On these three campuses the University is fully committed to provide its students with the greatest possible opportunity to engage in competitive athletics with other institutions, and this commitment is made equally to students of both sexes. However, the financial support that can be offered a given intercollegiate team on a given campus is heavily dependent upon factors other than the sex of the participants, and it is dangerously impractical to measure equality on the basis of the dollar distribution between the sexes.

The University's response then explained that that some teams justified larger expenditures on the basis of income produced, such as men's football. The argument was made that "[g]iven adequate time for growth and development, as was the case for men's athletics, these women's programs should eventually produce a substantial income that can be returned to the support of their teams. Otherwise, in the face of drastic and immediate demands for increased expenditures to finance women's athletics, the University may not be able to afford continued participation in intercollegiate sports in any form. This, we believe, would be detrimental to the entire student body, both men and women, as well as to the institution itself, its alumni, and its other friends and supporters."

It was suggested that the Title IX regulations be amended to provide "nothing in this section shall be interpreted to require that athletic opportunities, necessary equipment, supplies and other benefits be provided equally where factors other than sex, such as ability to produce revenue, level of student interest, level of public support, quality of student participation, and other non–sex related factors justify an unequal provision of such opportunities and benefits." The Title IX guidelines were subsequently amended, meeting some but not all of the university's concerns in this area. As a result certain changes were made by the University in administering intercollegiate athletics.

In a memorandum of May 8, 1978 Andy Kozar provided information to UT trustees Tom Elam, Ann Furrow and Bill Johnson. "Notes from meeting of special board committee to consider future funding of women's athletics on Saturday, April 29." Present at the meeting were: President Boling, Vice Presidents Fly and Johnson, Board Secretary Brogan, Staff Attorney Leadbetter, Executive Assistant Kozar, Vice Chancellor Howard Aldmon, Athletic Director Gloria Ray, and Bob Gilbert of the UT Public Relations Office.

The Kozar memorandum described a variety of efforts that might be undertaken to raise funds for women's athletics. "Mr. Brogan and Mr. Leadbetter were asked if UT is in compliance with title IX regulations, and it was stated that, as far as we know, UT is in compliance. It was explained that Title IX does not specify equal expenditures, but it does require equal opportunity and good faith efforts to provide comparable financial and other support for women's athletics." Still, it was uncertain as to how the final Title IX regulations would deal with expenditures which varied from one sport to another. The question was answered by an interpretation published in the December 11, 1979 issue of the Federal Register.

By memorandum of December 14, 1979 to President Boling and his senior staff ("Subject: Title IX Intercollegiate Athletics Policy Interpretation") I provided a "copy of the latest policy interpretation by the Office for Civil Rights regarding application of the Title IX regulations to intercollegiate athletics." I offered my opinion that the new policy interpretation was:

> ...far superior to the interpretation issued by OCR at the beginning of this year. For example, there is no more vague talk about "average per capita expenditure" and "presumed" compliance. There is now a more explicit recognition that basketball, football, and sports in general have peculiarities that may justify different levels of support for male and female athletes. I do not believe that the new interpretation poses any significant problem for us.

I noted other highlights of the new policy interpretation. For example, "separate men's and women's teams in intercollegiate athletics are permissible" and that there was no requirement to sponsor a separate team for the excluded sex if there is not "sufficient interest and ability among the members of the excluded sex to sustain a viable team...."

"The mere interest alone is no longer sufficient to warrant a requirement that a separate team be established." However, "intercollegiate athletic programs and benefits provided for females must be equivalent to those provided to males unless the lack of equivalency is based on legitimate, nondiscriminatory factors." In my opinion UT was compliant with Title IX.

I addressed the issue of pay equity for athletic coaches in a July 26, 1990 memorandum to Executive Vice President Joe Johnson.

I have looked over the NACUA College Law Digest article (EEOC notice) regarding application of the Equal Employment Opportunity Act and the Equal Pay Act to coaches' salaries. It is clear, as the notice points out, that salaries paid to male and female coaches cannot be set at different levels on the basis of sex.

On the other hand, salaries paid to the coaches of male and female teams, whether those coaches are male or female, may be paid different salaries based on differences in the coaching positions unrelated to sex. For example, the men's basketball team at a major college or university may be under substantially greater pressure to produce a "winning" program in order to sustain substantially higher ticket sales and monetary income than the coach of the women's basketball team at the same institution. As the EEOC notice suggests, the question of whether or not two coaching positions are equal is one of fact. With respect to both the EEO Act and the Equal Pay Act it is clear that an employer must be prepared to defend any pay differences between male and female coaches by reference to legitimate non-discriminatory business factors other than sex.

The same considerations apply under Title IX.

By memorandum of January 24, 1996 President Joe Johnson provided all UT chancellors and athletic directors a copy of a document issued by the Office for Civil Rights titled "Clarification of Intercollegiate Athletics Policy Guidance: The Three-part Test." I was asked to assist in reviewing the document. In a January 30 memorandum I reiterated "The opinion I expressed in October that we are in full compliance with both Title IX and the implementing regulations."

The concept of "proportionality" (spending on intercollegiate athletics in proportion to the percentage of males and females in the student body) remained a heated litigation topic in the late 1990s. Cohen v. Brown University, 101 F.3d 155 (1st Cir. 1996)) led the way with the First Circuit ruling against Brown University's contention that Title IX did not require proportionality. Unfortunately, the U.S. Supreme Court refused to hear Brown's appeal.

By memorandum of May 13, 1997 ("NCAA Gender Equity") I listed a number of problems facing the University of Tennessee if "proportionality" were imposed on UT today.

***

2. The UT intercollegiate athletic program is operated in a nondiscriminatory manner which provides women as much opportunity to participate in intercollegiate athletics as men. Evidence of UT's nondiscriminatory approach is found in the comparable level of funding provided to all nonrevenue sports in which teams are fielded for both men and women. Further evidence of UT's nondiscriminatory approach is found in the recent addition by UTK of women's teams in golf, crew, soccer and softball – and the most recent change in men's program being the dropping of wrestling in 1984.

3. While UT clearly provides "equal opportunity" for women to participate in intercollegiate athletics, that opportunity does not yield "equal results." In the UTK program numerical parity does not exist between the percentage of women participating in intercol-

legiate athletics (34%) and the percentage of women in the student body (49%).

4. To achieve numerical parity UTK, given the dominant influence of football (165 athletes), it would be necessary to double the number of female participants in intercollegiate athletics or slash in half the number of male participants (or undertake a combination of cuts and additions). Fairness and common sense aside, such a move would have a significant fiscal impact on the University.

5. Eliminating all "non-profitable" men's sports, retaining only football and basketball, would still not achieve parity (male athletes would still significantly outnumber female athletes) and such an approach would eliminate nationally ranked teams with strong public support.

6. The expense of women's athletics currently exceeds revenue by more than $2 million. Doubling the number of female athletes would predictably move in the direction of doubling that deficit.

7. At UTK, men's football and basketball foots a good portion of the bill for all other sports, both men's and women's. In a recession (God forbid!) or a decrease in football or basketball revenue, any effort to achieve or maintain numerical parity would require reallocating funds from academics and other non-athletic sources to athletics or gutting the athletics program....

***

By letter of June 17, 1998, I provided the U.S. Department of Justice, Civil Rights Division, in Washington D.C., the 1997 annual report prepared by the University of Tennessee, Knoxville in compliance with the Equity in Athletics Disclosure Act. (enacted in1994). Annual reports for UT Chattanooga and UT Martin were provided separately. The reports reflect that proportionality was not achieved on any of the three campuses.

My involvement in Title IX enforcement concluded with the hire of President Gilley in 1999. To that point UT never achieved proportionality. All the same, UT was Title IX compliant. At least in my opinion.

Chapter 58–Protected Categories with Less Litigation

The vast majority of Civil Rights actions brought against the University of Tennessee alleged race or sex discrimination as the primary complaint. However, I handled a good number of cases alleging discrimination on other bases: age (28), disability (22) national origin (14), religion (4) and veteran status (2).

Approximately 88% of the Civil Rights actions I handled involved plaintiffs asserting a single basis for discrimination. However, 12% of claimants alleged multiple categories of discrimination. The record in that regard likely goes to Chandan Vora, an applicant for a faculty position in the UT Martin Math Department in 1985. Vora claimed denial of employment on the basis of race, color, sex, religion and national origin. The University prevailed in that case.

Twenty-one of these miscellaneous claims came from the Knoxville campus.

19 cases came from the Memphis campus, eight from the Martin campus and a single case from Nashville. The latter was an age discrimination claim filed with the EEOC in 1985 and again in 1990 by Robert Rowan, a member of the faculty of the UT School of Social Work (affiliated with UT Knoxville but located in Nashville on the Tennessee State University campus). The University prevailed on both occasions.

Oddly, over 80% of age discrimination complaints were concluded between 1982 and 1991. On the other hand two thirds of actions claiming discrimination on the basis of disability were fully litigated between 1993 and 2001.

Only a single Civil Rights action in the above listed categories, a federal Civil Rights action alleging discrimination on the basis of disability, resulted in a judgment against UT. Not a single discrimination claim based on national origin, age, veteran status or religion was adjudicated against the University.

The Hernandez case was settled-foolishly (see chapter 31). Not one other suit alleging discrimination outside the categories of race or sex was settled.

THE SCARBROUGH ANNOMOLY

Jerry Scarborough was an employee in the University housing department at UT Knoxville. He was hired without regard for his being afflicted with cerebral palsy.

Scarbrough's superiors soon perceived his work as unsatisfactory. In 1990 Scarbrough was transferred to another position housing officials thought more suitable for his capabilities. In the new position as well Scarborough's work was judged to be unsatisfactory. His employment was terminated in 1992.

Scarbrough filed suit against the University of Tennessee on January 12, 1993 in U.S. District Court, Knoxville. He claimed he was discriminated against on the basis of his cerebral palsy from the date of his employment being some time prior to 1990.

Also, Scarbrough claimed he was dismissed in retaliation for having earlier filed a charge of discrimination on the basis of his handicap with the U.S. Office for Civil Rights (May 1990). Plaintiff's counsel was Knoxville attorney Todd Moody

In its answer, the University denied the plaintiff's allegations of discrimination and retaliation. The University contended that Scarbrough was simply an unsatisfactory employee from the start. I secured a friend, Dr. Jerry Lemler, as expert witness for the University.

U.S. District Judge Thomas Hull presided over the litigation. In October 1993 he granted a defense motion to dismiss much of the plaintiff's claim except as to alleged acts of discrimination and retaliation occurring after January 12, 1992. Scarborough had failed to pursue claims of earlier discrimination in a timely fashion.

A three-day jury trial was held in Greeneville on June 11, 14 and 15, 1994. The adversarial proceeding featured sworn testimony of UT management personnel, including UTK Personnel Director Ed Bennett and Housing Director Mike West that, despite warnings to Scarbrough that his work performance was unsatisfactory, improvement was not forthcoming and termination was warranted. They denied Scarborough's disability played any role in his dismissal.

Scarbrough presented contradictory evidence that his work performance was satisfactory, leading to the conclusion that he was terminated because of his disability and in retaliation for earlier complaints of discrimination.

The jury resolved the swearing contest with a verdict in plaintiff's favor. Scarborough was awarded damages in the amount of $75,000. Judge Hll tacked on an award of attorney's fees in the amount of $34,082.84. Total judgment: $109,083. Scarbrough v. The University of Tennessee, No. 3-93-0018 (E.D. Tenn. 1994)

I filed a motion for a new trial with Judge Hull on March 25. His order denying the motion was entered April 6, 1994. Given the presence of material evidence supporting the jury verdict no appeal was filed.

Another "you can't win 'em all" case. One that concluded with my congratulating opposing counsel, Todd Moody, for a job very well done. The first and last disability discrimination lawsuit defeat for the University.

Now for a look at a few of the unusual cases that were winners.

MAHENDRA KUMAR JAIN–
A BASELESS CAREER OF LITIGATION

In my career I encountered a number of bad cases, meaning those lacking evidentiary support that went nowhere. They are not mentioned in the pages of this book. There were a number of completely meritless cases that merit no attention. There is the exception.

Mahendra Kumar Jain was a member of the faculty of the Department of Math and Computer Science at the University of Tennessee at Martin. He was a native of India.

On May 29, 1974 Jain filed with the EEOC a charge that he had been discriminated against by UT Martin on the basis of his national origin (Indian) both with respect to salary and denial of promotion. By "determination" issued November 18, 1976, the EEOC concluded that Jain's charge could not be sustained. Jain proceeded to federal court.

In a complaint filed February 8, 1977 Jain alleged discrimination on the basis of national origin and that the University had retaliated against him for filing a complaint with the EEOC. He was represented by Paris (Tennessee) attorney

Bill Neese, a classmate of mine in law school.

The case was tried in Memphis on November 17 and 18, 1977 before U.S. District Judge Robert McRae. At the close of the two day trial Judge McRae announced his findings from the bench. In doing so he expressed understanding and sympathy for the plaintiff while voicing a few criticisms of UT administrators. Unfortunately, Jain construed the Judge's remarks as a ruling in his favor. Judge McRae ruled in favor of the University.

Judgment for the University was entered on December 6, 1977. (Jain v. The University of Tennessee, U.S. District Court, W. D. Tenn., Docket No. 77 – 1011). Then the foolishness began.

First, Jain terminated his attorney–client relationship with Bill Neese. All future litigation was handled by Jain "pro se."

On April 24, 1980 Jain filed with the District Court an "Answer to Ruling of the Court." The plaintiff just didn't like the Court's ruling. By order of August 8, 1980 the District Court dismissed plaintiff's answer.

On August 18 Jain filed an "Answer to Order of Court." He did not like the Court's order denying his April 24 motion. Judge McRae didn't like Jain's answer and, on October 24, entered an order rejecting that pleading.

Jain filed an appeal to the U.S. Court of Appeals for the Sixth Circuit. The University moved to dismiss the appeal and the appellate court agreed. Jain's appeal was dismissed, by order of the court entered April 9, 1991. (Mahendra Kumar Jain v. The University of Tennessee at Martin, United States Court of Appeals for the Sixth Circuit, No. 80 – 5412).

Six days later Jain filed a letter with the Court of Appeals requesting additional time to file a motion for rehearing. On June 15, 1981 the Sixth circuit entered an order denying plaintiff's petition for rehearing.

Jain then filed a new complaint with the U.S. District Court in Memphis (Docket No. 81–1122). In Complaint II, Jain essentially repeated the claims set forth in Complaint I. The second lawsuit was initially assigned to U.S. District Judge Harry Welford. Once Judge Welford learned of Judge McRae's prior involvement with Jain he transferred the new case to him. (Order of July 21, 1993).

On July 25, 1984, Judge McRae wrote Jain a letter advising him that he had lost his case and should file nothing further or risk sanctions by the court. A futile request.

In February 1985 Jain filed "Further Arguments and a Response to Judge McRae's Letter of July 25, 1984." Additional motions and responses were filed by Jain and the University over the next few months.

On August 6, 1986, the District Court entered an order denying plaintiff's "prayer" for reconsideration and granting a defense motion to dismiss. As might be expected by now, Jain appealed that ruling to the Sixth Circuit. (Docket No. 86–5966).

A variety of motions and responses were again filed both by Jain and the University with the Court of Appeals, including another University motion to dismiss. By order of March 16, 1987 the Court of Appeals dismissed Jain's appeal.

In May 1987 Jain again filed pleadings with the District Court. The University's motion for summary judgment was granted by U.S. District Judge James Todd's officially reported order of August 17, 1987. Jain v. University of Tennessee at Martin 670 F. Supp. 1388 (W. D. Tenn. 1987).

Judge Todd's opinion was one cited in future cases questioning whether the University of Tennessee was an agency of the state of Tennessee entitled to the same "11th Amendment" immunity from suit as any other state agency.

> UTM is an entity created by legislative charter. [Citations omitted]. Case decisions have consistently held, with one exception, that UT and its various campuses were arms of the state for 11th Amendment purposes. [Citations omitted]. One case did hold that the legislature might have waived sovereign immunity with respect to the University of Tennessee as a result of ambiguity perceived by that court in a Tennessee statute allowing the university to sue or be sued. Soni v. Board of Trustees of the University of Tennessee, 513 F. 2d 347 (6th Cir. 1975), cert. denied, 426 U.S. 919, 96 S. Ct. 2623, 49 L. Ed. 2d. 372 (1976). However, Soni now has questionable validity. Following the Soni decision, the Tennessee legislature amended the state's sovereign immunity statute to provide:[n]o statutory or other provision authorizing the University of Tennessee and its board of trustees to sue and be sued shall constitute a waiver of sovereign immunity.
> Tenn. Code Ann. [Sec.] 20-13-102(b).

Jain appealed to the Sixth Circuit. Docket No. 87–6068. The Sixth Circuit's order affirming the District Court ruling for UT Martin was entered April 6, 1988.

Jain's "Request for Extension of Time to File a Petition for Rehearing En Banc" was denied by order of the Sixth Circuit entered May 17, 1988. Two days later Jain filed an age discrimination complaint with the EEOC. Then, in June Jain filed a petition for writ of certiorari to the United States Supreme Court from the Sixth Circuit. On October 3, 1988 the Supreme Court entered an order denying his petition.

By this time I had concluded that the various courts would not act effectively on their own to discourage further filings by Jain. Judge McRae's letter to Jain had encouraged rather than discouraged such activity. Time for a new strategy.

In November 1988, I filed with the U.S. District Court a motion for award of attorney's fees. Being a salaried employee of the University, such a motion was quite unusual; the first one I ever filed. The motion was granted.

On February 1, 1989 Judge Todd entered an order granting defendant's motion for attorney's fees and costs:

> The court finds that the documents filed and signed by the plaintiff in which he argues "fraud" on the court were neither well grounded in fact nor warranted by existing law nor good faith argument for the extension, modification, or reversal thereof. The allegations were "frivolous, unreasonable, [and] without foundation."
>
> ***
>
> The court concludes that an appropriate sanction for the Rule 11 violation is an award of attorney's fees. Defendant will be awarded a reasonable fee for the time spent by counsel from September 9, 1982, the date plaintiff first sought to amend the complaint to allege "fraud," through September 8, 1986, when the plaintiff filed his notice of appeal from the May 28, 1986 order, plus the time spent preparing the motion for attorney's fees. Defendant's counsel, Ronald C. Leadbetter, has documented 25.35 hours of work during this period.
>
> ***
>
> Accordingly, plaintiff is hereby ordered to pay to the defendant the sum of $2,535 in attorney's fees, and the cost incurred in this action since September 9, 1982. Defendant is directed to file a bill of costs incurred since September 9, 1982 soon as practicable.

Mahendra Kumar Jain vs. University of Tennessee, Civil Action No. 81-1122. Court costs in the amount of $62.75 were later added to the amount due from Jain. And, quite predictably, Jain appealed to the U.S. Court of Appeals for the Sixth Circuit.

A PER CURIAM decision was issued April 25, 1990 by Circuit Judges Guy, Norris and Conti. Mahendra Kumar Jain v. The University of Tennessee at Martin, No. 89-5621. (6th Cir. 1990). In its fifteen page ruling the Court of Appeals succinctly reviewed Jain's history dating back to his 1977 initial filing with the District Court. The Court noted Jain's attempt to re-litigate matters previously litigated and his failure to proceed in timely or proper fashion.

The Sixth Circuit also concurred with the District Court's rejection that Jain's claim that UT General Counsel Beach Brogan, Judge McRae, and even his own attorney, Bill Neese, had engaged in fraudulent conduct, was "frivolous, unreasonable, [and] and without foundation." For example:

> Plaintiff has filed numerous complaints, motions and memoranda attacking the honesty and impartiality of Judge McRae during the time period specified by the District Court for the award of attorney's fees. These allege that Judge McRae's annoyance and hostility toward plaintiff were the real reasons for his inability to prevail, that Judge McRae signed fraudulent instruments, that he made secret deals with the attorneys behind plaintiff's back, that the oral rulings he gave from the bench were part of a sellout, and that he fraudulently

narrowed Jain I to Title VII. Plaintiff does not offer any evidence to support his outrageous charges. A review of the record discloses no indication of bias on the part of the district judge.

Id. P. 11.

The Court of Appeals affirmed both the District Court's dismissal of plaintiff's claims and the lower court's award of attorney's fees for services I rendered defending Mahendra Kumar Jain's frivolous litigation.

Jain paid the attorney's fee and cost award. I presumed he had now learned his lesson and would never be heard from again. Wrong. Just not in federal courts or agencies.

In June 1999 Jain filed a claim with the Tennessee Claims Commission alleging breach of contract and entitlement to worker's compensation. In January 2001 a motion to dismiss for lack of jurisdiction was filed by the University. On May 10, 2001, the motion was granted.

Jain filed a rambling three-page "Petition for Reconsideration of Order to Dismiss" on May 23, 2001. The document began: "references of past injustices toward me, claimant, are made in order to show prevailing reality that people like me cannot get any justice in this country where prejudices are deeply rooted and where power of the government seems to control." He then proceeded to narrate a litany of perceived wrongs ("Mr. Leadbetter violating ABA codes of professional responsibility and remained silent and Judge Todd stuck to his concocted erroneous holding by not correcting his error when I had filed my petition for reconsideration pointing out his error. Judge Todd also did not award me judgment by default when Mr. Leadbetter did not file the University responses within required 20 days given in summons").

On June 18, 2001 the Commission entered an order denying Jain's motion to reconsider. Already retired from the University of Tennessee Martin, Jain also retired from his primary calling and filed no further litigation against the University. His last filing concluded with the following paragraph:

I have lived in USA for 34 years and know the realities because of which I do not expect any justice. I am putting my frustration on record for inclusion when I am able to find a publisher for my book which will also include this trauma. I am 72 and a God knows when will go away before such publication takes place. M K J

Perhaps my inclusion of Jain's 27-year litigation history in this book will serve the purpose.

RALPH GLAZIER v. UNIVERSITY OF TENNESSEE HEALTH SCIENCE CENTER–
AN AGELESS TALE OF VICTORY

While the University suffered no litigation losses to claimants alleging discrimination on the basis of age, at least one case in that category deserves mention.

In the early 1980s Ralph M. Glazier was employed by the University of Tennessee Center for the Health Sciences in the position of Director of Medical Photography and Illustration.

Sometime in 1983 Glazier's superiors became dissatisfied with his work conduct and terminated his employment. Glazier filed suit in U.S. District Court in Memphis alleging that his constitutional right to due process had been violated in that he had not been provided a hearing of charges against him. He was represented by Memphis attorney Don Donati.

Donati secured a preliminary injunction from the Court of U.S. District Judge Robert M. McRae. Case: Ralph M. Glazier v. James C. Hunt, MD, et. al., No. 83-2907M-B (W.D. Tenn. 1983). By order of November 23, 1983, Judge McRae enjoined the University from terminating Glazier's employment without affording him an opportunity for a hearing of the charges against him. The University proceeded immediately to comply with the Court's order.

Chancellor Jim Hunt personally held a hearing for Glazier on December 5. A week later he issued a decision finding Glazier guilty of conduct warranting his dismissal. Still, the federal lawsuit remained active. I took Glazier's deposition on April 10, 1984.

For reasons I no longer recall a decision was made by University officials to offer Glazier a second chance. A settlement agreement was reached whereby Glazier was reinstated and his suit against the University was dismissed. There was no monetary settlement. A pending age discrimination claim filed with the EEOC was dismissed at the same time, around April 30, 1984.

The second chance effort did not work and Glazier was fired again in late 1985. Glazier again filed a suit in federal court, this time alleging that he was terminated on the basis of his age. He requested a jury trial and sought $350,000 in damages, reinstatement and attorney's fees. Don Donati was again Glazier's counsel of record.

A jury trial was held from September 14-17, 1987 with U.S. District Judge Julia Gibbons presiding. The jury's verdict in favor of the UT Center for the Health Sciences was rendered the afternoon of September 17. Judge Gibbons entered judgment in favor of the University on September 21, 1987. A noteworthy victory in view of Donati's status as one of the top rated and most respected civil rights attorneys in Tennessee.

FOOTBALL COACH ROBERT MADDOX–
DRUNK DRIVING IS NOT ADA PROTECTED

On February 17, 1992, UT Knoxville athletic director Doug Dickey, at the recommendation of head football coach Johnny Majors, hired Robert Maddox as an assistant football coach. Maddox was expected to coach the defensive line.

In late May 1992, I received a phone call from Doug Dickey while I was in Memphis. He advised me that Coach Maddox had been arrested for DUI. More specifically, it was reported that Maddox had recklessly backed his car, going in the wrong direction, across Kingston Pike in Knoxville, into a parking area where he was confronted by a Knoxville police officer.

Maddox was found with his pants unzipped. He was apparently intoxicated. When asked if he would take a breathalyzer test Maddox refused.

Dickey asked what action I recommended. Given the circumstances surrounding Maddox's police stop and the importance of having good role models on the coaching staff. I recommended the termination of Maddox's employment. Dickey agreed. Maddox was issued a letter of dismissal by Dickey and Majors on June 22, 1994.

On May 10, 1993 Maddox filed suit against the University of Tennessee in the U.S. District Court in the Knoxville. He claimed his employment with the University was terminated on the basis of his disability, he defined as being alcoholism, in violation of the Americans with Disabilities Act and section 504 of the Rehabilitation Act of 1973. He requested back pay, $300,000 in compensatory damages and his attorney's fees. Maddox was represented by Knoxville attorneys John Lockridge and Scarlet Beaty.

I filed an answer to the Maddox complaint on May 26, 1993. On the same day I issued notice for the taking of Maddox's deposition. I completed his deposition on October 5. On November 17, 1993 I filed a motion for summary judgment on behalf of the University, appending the deposition testimony of Maddox as well as affidavits of Coach Majors and athletic director Dickey.

On May 31, 1994, U.S. District Judge Leon Jordan granted summary judgment in favor of the University. The judgment was premised on Judge Jordan's conclusion that there was no evidence in the record which could lead a "rational trier of fact" to find in favor of Maddox. The decision of Dickey and Majors to terminate Maddox's employment was based on his misconduct (his arrest for driving under the influence of alcohol and the resulting bad publicity) not on the basis of any alcoholism disability. Maddox v. University of Tennessee, 907 F. Supp. 1144 (E.D. Tenn. 1994).

Maddox appealed to the U.S. Court of Appeals for the Sixth Circuit on June 21, 1994. He secured the services of attorney Michael A. Valente, with a

Louisville, Kentucky law firm, to handle his appeal.

Appellate argument was held on July 25, 1995 before U.S. Circuit Judges Bailey Brown, Herbert Milburn and Alan Norris. The District Court judgment was affirmed by unanimous ruling of the appeals panel on August 21, 1995. Maddox v. University of Tennessee, 62 F.3d 843 (6th Cir. 1995).

In affirming the District Court ruling in favor of the University the appellate court noted that Dickey and Majors denied even having knowledge that Maddox was an alcoholic. In any event, according to the court, Maddox was terminated for misconduct because he was not "otherwise qualified."

> It is obvious that as a member of the football coaching staff, Maddox would be representing not only the team but also the University. As in the instant case, UT received full media coverage because of this embarrassing incident. The school falls out of favor with the public, and the reputation of the football program suffers. Likewise, to argue that football coaches today, with all the emphasis on the misuse of drugs and alcohol by athletes, are not role models and mentors simply ignores reality.

Id., pp. 848-9. Case closed!

General Counsel Brogan issued a memorandum of August 21, 1995 notifying President Joe Johnson, UT Trustees and members of the President's staff of the Sixth Circuit's ruling. He added "[w]e are glad the court recognized the University's right to terminate an alcoholic because of his conduct." Finally, Brogan advised the recipients of the memorandum that I had handled the case for the University.

HARRISON LANCE v. UNIVERSITY OF TENNESSEE

A later case alleging discrimination on the basis of disability got one step closer to the finish line but still failed.

Harrison Lance was employed in May 1985 as a carpenter in the physical plant at UT Knoxville. In July 1995 Lance suffered a temporary, non-work related, hand injury which prevented him from carrying out his carpentry duties.

Lance's physician advised John Parker, Executive Director of the physical plant, that Lance "possibly" could return to work the following October but "probably be more likely early November before his hand is mobile and strong enough to be a helping hand for carpenter." Id. p. 742. Because Lance had exhausted all accrued annual leave his employment was terminated on August 31, 1995.

Lance filed a complaint against UT with the U.S. District Court, Knoxville, on January 20, 1998. He alleged that his hand injury constituted a disability and that the termination of his employment was discriminatory and constituted a violation of the Americans with Disabilities Act. He further alleged that the University failed to make "reasonable accommodation" for his disability by assigning him to another position not requiring the use of his injured hand.

Lance requested $1 million in punitive, compensatory and general damages. He was represented by Knoxville attorney Stephen Heyder.

As in the Maddox case, I filed a motion for summary judgment. By order of January 29, 1999 U.S. District Judge Jimmy Jarvis denied that motion. Lance v. University of Tennessee 46 F. Supp. 2d 740 (E.D. Tenn. 1999).

In denying the university's motion for summary judgment Judge Jarvis opined that "[q]uestions of material fact remain to be determined with regard to whether the plaintiff has a physical impairment that substantially limits one or more of his major life activities." Even if the injury did not fall in that category, according to Jarvis, "a question of fact remains with regard to whether plaintiff has a record of such an impairment or was regarded by UT of having such an impairment." Id. p. 744.

Therefore the case proceeded to trial.

The trial by jury commenced on April 27, 1999 and concluded the following afternoon. At the close of plaintiff's proof I presented to the District Court a motion for a directed verdict, roughly equivalent to a motion for summary judgment, arguing once again that there was no evidence of record upon which a reasonable fact finder could rule in Lance's favor. This time the University's argument prevailed.

The District Court granted the motion for directed verdict. A memorandum opinion and order to that effect was entered on May 5, 1999. Lance v. University of Tennessee, U.S. District, 60 F. Supp. 2d 773 (E.D. Tenn. 1999). Judge Jarvis's reasoning is described in the following excerpt from his opinion:

> Initially, the court notes that there is a substantial question with regard to whether plaintiff was actually "disabled" within the meaning of the Act. However, even assuming that plaintiff's proof satisfies this threshold element, plaintiff cannot meet the second element for a claim under the ADA. The court finds that, based on the uncontroverted facts, the only conclusion that a reasonable jury could reach is at the time of the plaintiff's termination plaintiff had not suggested an objectively reasonable accommodation which would qualify him to perform the essential functions of his job.

Id. p. 776.

Judge Jarvis concluded that although Lance suggested an accommodation to the University [unpaid leave of absence], "a jury could not reasonably find that he suggested a reasonable accommodation." Lance's suggestion that the University provide him an unpaid leave of absence of indefinite duration was not reasonable. "Accordingly, it was reasonable for the defendant to hire someone to replace the plaintiff, particularly in light of the shortage of carpentry workers in the physical plant. Plaintiff has therefore failed to produce sufficient evidence on an essential element of his claim; that is, that he was a qualified individual who could perform the essential functions of his job with or without accommodations at the time of his termination." Id. p.777.

FRED HARRIS v. THE UNIVERSITY OF TENNESSEE

One other disability discrimination claim got closer yet to a ruling against the University.

Fred H. Harris was employed by the University of Tennessee, Knoxville, on March 18, 1991, as Vice Chancellor of Computing and Telecommunications. At the time Harris was hired, John Quinn was Chancellor. In late spring 1992 Quinn resigned.

William L Snyder replaced Quinn, first as acting Chancellor then, on July 22, 1992, as Chancellor.

Chancellor Snyder was aware of problems with Harris's performance as Vice Chancellor early on. For example, in fall 1993 Harris received criticism for his "lack of communication skills" and "failure to articulate a vision for his unit" during the administrative review process for University officials reporting to the Chancellor, from faculty, students, staff and outside constituents providing input.

Unfortunately, none of the performance criticisms were conveyed to Harris until a short time after Harris advised the Chancellor that he might have (and later confirmed as having) Parkinson's disease. Worse, Chancellor Snyder notified Harris that his employment was being terminated effective October 31, 1994, one week after Snyder learned of Harris's Parkinson's disease.

In fall 1994Harris filed suit against the University, both with the EEOC and the Tennessee Human Rights Commission. He alleged that he was terminated on the basis of disability in violation of the Americans With Disabilities Act and the Tennessee Human Rights Act. Both agencies issued Harris a "right to sue" letter and he proceeded to Federal Court.

Harris filed suit on May 31, 1995 in the U.S. District Court in Knoxville, alleging that his dismissal from the University was based on his disability–Parkinson's disease. The case was assigned to U.S. district Judge Jimmy Jarvis.

As was my custom, I promptly scheduled and took the deposition of Fred Harris.

University officials, including Chancellor William Snyder, Vice Chancellor John Peters, the Chancellor's Administrative Assistant, Marianne Woodside, and others, were deposed by Harris's attorneys. Even before the depositions scheduled by Harris were completed I filed a motion for summary judgment, seeking dismissal of Harris's lawsuit.

Judge Jarvis denied the motion:

Although the University contends that the timing of plaintiff's termination is mere coincidence, the court is of the opinion that there is a material factual dispute as to when the decision to terminate plaintiff's employment was actually made—i.e., before or after plaintiff informed Mr. Snyder of his diagnosis of Parkinson's disease. Thus, while there is some evidence that Mr. Snyder had already formed the intent to terminate plaintiff's employment before he knew of the diagnosis, the record is clear that plaintiff was not informed of the termination decision until one week after he had spoken with Mr. Snyder about his condition. Clearly, then, there are issues of fact present in this case rendering summary judgment inappropriate at this time.

The case proceeded to trial on April 8, 1996. Trial concluded on April 11 with a jury deadlocked, 7-4, unable to reach a verdict. Counsel were not told who had the 7 and who had the 4.

I later filed a "motion for judgment notwithstanding lack of a verdict." The motion was denied. A retrial would be necessary.

On May 6, 1996 the second jury trial began. Trial complete, the jury was released to deliberate at 3:30 p.m. on May 8. Not until the afternoon of May 9 did the jury reach a verdict. It was with great relief I heard the words "for the defendant" at the end of the juries announced verdict. The court's judgment was entered in favor of the University the same day. Fred H. Harris v. The University of Tennessee, No. 3:95-cv-307 (E.D. Tenn. 1996)

Minutes after departing the courtroom with Chancellor Snyder the jury foreman approached us on the street. He asked if he could share his thoughts with us. Both Snyder and I agreed.

According to the foreman, at the outset of deliberations the jury was split 50-50 with half the jurors favoring a verdict for Harris. Two factors were seized upon. First, the university's failure to notify Harris of complaints against him so that he could take remedial action. Second, action the jurors viewed as insensitive–providing Harris with notice of termination one week after he advised Chancellor Snyder of his serious health condition.

The foreman then explained that he argued to the jurors that the jury's role was to apply the law, even if in doing so inconsiderate behavior was rewarded. He then shared with Snyder and me his personal feeling that Harris was handled poorly–even if legally. Both Snyder and I expressed our appreciation to the jury foreman for sharing his thoughts with us. Another lesson–this one not nearly as costly as it could have been–to be shared with others!

SARAH LEDBETTER v. UNIVERSITY OF TENNESSEE MEDICAL CENTER

One of my last major civil rights cases, one alleging discrimination on the basis of disability in violation of the ADA, merits attention for several reasons. The first–how the case reached my desk–gains more meaning as the black clouds of the Gilley years swept over the University in general and the Office of General Counsel in particular. (Yes, our names are similar, but different spelling and no relation).

Sarah Ledbetter was employed by the University of Tennessee Medical Center and claimed in a filing with the EEOC that she was forced to retire because of her disability–a hearing impairment. The case was assigned to OGC attorney Ben Cox, who had primary responsibility for handling legal matters for the Medical Center. Cox obviously did a fine job since the EEOC entered a determination in favor of the University. Ledbetter then filed suit with the U.S. District Court for the Eastern District of Tennessee, naming the University of Tennessee Medical Center and Andrea Clapp as defendants (Clapp being the Ledbetter's Medical Center supervisor). I was a bit surprised to find the case reassigned to me by the General Counsel, but quite happy to get it. The reason for the unusual reassignment was spelled out by Brogan in a memorandum of November 17, 1998 to President Joe Johnson, Vice President and Medical Center senior administrators and Bill Rice and Mickey Bilbrey.

Re: Sarah Ledbetter v. University of Tennessee Medical Center and Andrea Clapp, U.S. District Court, Eastern District of Tenn., CA No. 3:98-cv-694

Attached is a copy of a complaint by Sarah Ledbetter against the University of Tennessee Medical Center and Andrea Clapp claiming she was discriminated against under the Americans with Disabilities Act of 1990 because of a hearing impairment. She claims a constructive discharge, alleging she was forced to retire from her job under a disability retirement.

In my opinion this action is without any merit. In fact, the EEOC found in favor of the University on Ledbetter's complaint. However, she has a right under the federal law to file the lawsuit notwithstanding the finding of the EEOC.

Although this is an action involving the Medical Center, I have assigned it to Ron Leadbetter since he is our resident expert under the ADA and our most experienced trial lawyer in federal court. To the extent necessary, Ben Cox will assist him since he is familiar with the facts of this case.

A jury trial is demanded. Plaintiff asks for punitive damages of not less than $1 million and compensatory damages of not less than $1 million.

As indicated, I was pleased to have the case reassigned to me for handling. I was also pleased to learn that opposing counsel was David Duggan from Blount County, a gentleman I respected and had enjoyed getting to know while litigating the Stefanovic lawsuit (See Chapter 56; more about Duggan in Chapter

97).

In accordance with my standard operating procedure, within three weeks following the filing of the complaint I filed a motion to dismiss aimed at cleaning up the case as much as possible. By order of May 5, 1999, United States Magistrate Judge Thomas W. Phillips dismissed Andrea Clapp as a party defendant and dismissed Ledbetter's "section 1983" claim. Only Ledbetter's disability discrimination claim brought against the University pursuant to the Americans with Disabilities Act remained.

In July, I deposed Ledbetter in preparation for filing a motion for summary judgment. Around the same time I became aware of developing case law questioning whether a state or a state institution such as UT had 11th Amendment immunity from suit even though the ADA specifically held: "A State shall not be immune under the Eleventh Amendment to the Constitution of the United States from an action in Federal or State court of competent jurisdiction for a willful violation of this chapter (the ADA)." 42 U.S.C. section 12202.

On September 13, 1999, I filed a "Motion to Dismiss or for Summary Judgment," arguing that the University had 11th Amendment immunity from suit under the ADA. In support of my argument I cited an unreported decision by U.S. District Judge Leon Jordan (Satterfield v. Tennessee, No. 3:97–cv–478 (E.D. Tenn., Mar. 31, 1998).

In the alternative, I argued, summary judgment should enter due to lack of any material evidence in the record supporting Ledbetter's claim. The court never had to address that alternative.

In a "Memorandum and Opinion" filed February 7, 2000 Judge Phillips granted the University's motion to dismiss based on his finding that the University had 11th Amendment immunity from suit under the ADA. Sarah Ledbetter v. University of Tennessee Medical Center, No. 3:98-cv-694 (E.D. Tenn. 2000). The court's order dismissing Ledbetter's claim under the ADA was entered the same day.

Judge Phillips acknowledged that the ADA expressly provided that states were not immune under the Eleventh Amendment from actions alleging violation of the ADA. He also found "[t]he Supreme Court has not expressly addressed application of the Eleventh Amendment to actions brought against the states pursuant to the ADA. The U.S. Court of Appeals for the Sixth Circuit has likewise not ruled on the issue [citations omitted], but has noted a split of authority on the issue. [Citation omitted]."

Id., p. 4.

Citing Judge Jordan's ruling in Satterfield, Judge Phillips found "[i]t does appear that the ADA impermissibly attempts to subject state action to higher level of judicial scrutiny than the Supreme Court has found appropriate under the Fourteenth Amendment. [Citation omitted]. Thus, it seems that Congress exceeded its power under section 5 of the Fourteenth Amendment by enacting the ADA. "

Id. pp. 7-8.

Judge Phillips concluded, "[t]he undersigned agrees with Judge Jordan that the ADA's purported abrogation of the States' sovereign immunity is invalid [citation omitted]. Accordingly, the court finds plaintiff is precluded from arguing her claims against UTMC in this court. This suit is dismissed for lack of subject matter jurisdiction."

Id., p.10.

Ledbetter filed a notice of appeal with the U.S. Court of Appeals for the Sixth Circuit on March 2, 2000. On April 25 Chief Circuit Mediator for the Sixth Circuit, Robert Rack, arranged a conference call with David Dugan and me. During that call we agreed that a case pending before the U.S. Supreme Court (Board of Trustees v. Garrett), would control the disposition of Ledbetter.

The U.S. Supreme Court rendered its decision in Board of Trustees of the University of Alabama v. Garrett on February 21, 2001. The Court held the University of Alabama immune from suit under the Americans with Disabilities Act based on UAB's status as an agency of the state of Alabama. Duggan forwarded a copy of that decision to Rack.

By letter of April 17, 2001 Rack thanked Duggan for sending him a copy of the Supreme Court's decision and forwarded to Duggan a "form Motion for Voluntary Dismissal" to be executed and returned to his office. Duggan promptly complied. An order was entered by the Sixth Circuit on April 27, 2001 dismissing the appeal and bringing to a favorable conclusion the last civil rights action I would handle in federal or state court.

David Duggan and I would meet again in the federal civil rights with Judge Phillips, but under incredibly different circumstances.

Chapter 59–Veterans and The Body Farm

Only twice in my career was I confronted with litigation claims of discrimination on the basis of veteran status. In Stefanovic veteran status was clearly treated as secondary to sex as the basis for the plaintiff's claim of discrimination. The only other claim of discrimination related to military service dates back to 1976.

My records show that in April 1976, UT Knoxville transportation services worker, Rodney Q. Nelson, filed a claim with the Office of Federal Contract Compliance Programs that he had been discriminated against in some fashion on the basis of his status as a U.S. military veteran. Employment Opportunity

Specialist Katherine Tuve, with the OFCCP, conducted a daylong investigation of Nelson's charge. She interviewed UTK personnel officials Ed Bennett, Joe Robustelli, Toni Debusk and Helen McWaters, as well as Transportation Center official John Beason.

On November 26, 1976, the OFCCP issued a determination in the University's favor (although finding the University's affirmative action program deficient in several respects and directing that corrective action be taken, the specifics of which I did not record and do not recall.)

In sum, the University's litigation experience involving the legally protected category of "veteran status" was negligible. I was, however, involved in several matters of an administrative nature which ended on a high note.

BODY FARM CONFLICT WITH VETERANS' AFFAIRS RESOLVED

Some conflicts defy reason. One that immediately comes to mind was initiated by telephone calls I received on March 20, 1995 from Hardy Mays of Memphis, representing a Veterans' Association, and Fred Tucker, Commissioner for Veterans' Affairs for the State of Tennessee. Mays informed me that he had received reports that the bodies of three armed forces veterans were buried at the University of Tennessee Anthropological Research Facility often referred to as "The Body Farm."

The Anthropological Research Facility is located a few miles from downtown on Alcoa Highway behind the University's Medical Center. It was first started in late 1981 by anthropologist Dr. William M. Bass as a facility for the study of the decomposition of human remains. Bodies that are not claimed by relatives may, and often do, wind up as a source for experimentation at the Body Farm.

Dr. Bass, his colleagues and students worked in relative obscurity for numerous years until writer, Patricia Cornwell, heard about him and his work. Cornwell actually traveled to Knoxville on several occasions sitting in on lectures Bass was giving his students and touring the site. The publication of Cornwell's novel, "The Body Farm," based on Bass and his work, sent the reputation of the professor and his facility into world-wide orbit. Cornwell has written other books including investigative techniques she learned from Dr. Bass and the two became close friends. Dr. Bass has been the focus of numerous television programs, too.

According to Mays, having veterans buried in such a place could not be tolerated. A call from Tucker followed who demanded that the University immediately release the bodies for what he called "proper burial."

I suppose it is ironic that, nowadays, burial at the Body Farm is seen as a kind of status symbol so much so that the University has a waiting list for donors who request that their final resting place be on a hill full of beautiful trees along the shores of the Tennessee River. Many people like the idea of donating their bodies to science thinking that students may learn something that will help mankind.

Although my conversation with Tucker began on a rather tense note I advised him I would work to address the issue. Tucker expressed satisfaction with my commitment.

First, I contacted State Medical Examiner, Dr. Charles Harlan, who had arranged for the veterans' bodies to reach the Body Farm to begin with. Would he be willing to retake possession of the bodies? Harlan declined. He also offered the opinion that under state law neither he nor the University could lawfully release the bodies to anyone other than a relative of the deceased (citing Tenn. Code Annotated 68–4–104 and 105). Section 104 seemingly barred an institution receiving a body from the medical examiner for medical, dental, surgical or anatomical study from disposing of the body except pursuant to a claim for burial by relatives. The institution, and even the chief medical examiner, was barred from "giving, selling or delivering a 'body' to any other person, firm, society, association or corporation."

My next step was to draft an amendment to state law that would permit a research institution, such as UT, to summon an undertaker to take possession of a body if the institution elected to discontinue use of the body for research purposes. UT President Joe Johnson asked that I convey the proposed amendment to Tucker with a request that he contact appropriate legislators and solicit their help in obtaining passage. Tucker expressed approval of the proposed amendment.

On March 29, 1995, Beach Brogan and I received a letter from Fredia Wadley, Commissioner of the Tennessee Department of Health, and Richard Knight, General Counsel for the Department of Health, advising that the University might lawfully release the bodies to the Department of Veterans Affairs, for burial with military honors, without violating Tennessee law. It was their opinion that "[o]nce the transfer from the state medical examiner is accomplished the body becomes the property of the institution. " Further, what we believe the law implies is that a receiving institution under T.C.A. section 68–4–104 can, without legal liability, release the remains of bodies for the internment that they would have received but for their transfer to the institution."

Wadley and Knight then requested, on behalf of the Department of Veterans Affairs, the release of the bodies of three veterans identified by name and Social Security number, to Mortuary Associates of Nashville.

The bodies were released, the law was amended to resolve any doubt and the controversy between the Anthropological Research Facility, aka, The Body Farm and the Department of Veterans Affairs was resolved to everyone's satisfaction.

In December 1996, Commissioner Tucker once again contacted Bill Bass, requesting that skeletal remains of six veterans located at the Body Farm be released for transfer to the Department of Veterans Affairs. Bass responded with a request for a short delay. He explained that one of the skeletons was buried to be used in training law enforcement officers how difficult it is to locate a buried body in Tennessee after leaves fall from the trees in the fall. Bass explained that his graduate assistants would not be back in town until the start of the second semester on January 15 and, as soon as the weather permitted, the skeletal remains would be excavated and cleaned up for return to the Department of Veterans Affairs.

Commissioner Tucker wrote back, several days later, that he appreciated Dr. Bass for his "cooperation in arranging for the surrender of six sets of skeletal remains of honorably discharged veterans to this Department for interment," and agreed it would be more logical to pick up all sets of remains on one trip. He requested that Bass contact Mortuary Associates "when the remains of Thomas Arlington are available, hopefully this month, weather permitting."

In March, 1997, Commissioner Tucker again wrote Dr. Bass and thanked him for his cooperation in surrendering skeletal remains of 15 honorably discharged veterans for interment with military honors at the Middle Tennessee State Veterans Cemetery in Nashville. I was copied on the letter and very pleased to see that any hint of controversy between the University and the Department of Veterans Affairs was fully resolved.

Indeed, it was always my commitment to work in support of the U.S. military and the men and women who have served our nation so well.

Chapter 60–The First Amendment–Religion and More

During the period of my responsibility for Civil Rights matters I handled a total of four cases with a primary allegation of discrimination on the basis of religion. All four cases were resolved with rulings favorable to the University.

Marginally more problematic for the University was dealing with religious expression, something addressed by the First Amendment to the United States Constitution. Occasional attempts by University officials to regulate campus visitors preaching on campus approached the margin. Readily accessible legal advice from the UT Office of General Counsel—and willingness to heed the advice—headed off major legal problems.

With strict exceptions speech may be limited only as to time, place and manner. In my experience, public colleges and universities in the U.S. historically have avoided problems in this area. I mean, if you can't express different thoughts on a college campus where can you?

One exception to the rule has been occasional efforts to limit outsiders preaching or evangelizing on campus. For example, back in 1981, an evangelistic religious group announced it would protest a policy of the State Board of Regents and Memphis State University, "prohibiting religious groups from recruiting converts on University property." (Memphis Press-Scimitar, January 22, 1981, p. 8). The University of Tennessee had no such policy at any time during my employment and I so advised the Press-Scimitar.

> But Ron Ledbetter, legal counsel at the University of Tennessee Center for the Health Sciences, said UT has "no rules prohibiting students or recognized campus organizations from going around trying to convert people."
>
> "We don't try to monitor that kind of behavior. I would be the last person to stop it, as long as it doesn't disrupt business on campus," he said.
>
> Ledbetter said he thought the applicable case law centered on a person's right to freedom of speech in a public place and not on whether a university was appearing to advance, promote or inhibit institutional religion.

> Id.

But the scope of my opinion was not limited to speec by students or recognized campus organization. "'Universities are public places much like airports, and like airports, should allow anyone to solicit converts or distribute literature.' he said." (Id).

I repeatedly taught in numerous UT seminars, and issued many legal opinions that when the public was provided open access to the University as invitees or guests, speech could be regulated only as to time, place and manner, not content. For example, speaking, at least loud speaking, might be restricted during late evening hours in campus housing accessible to the public. Speakers might be banned from doorways or otherwise blocking building access. Bullhorns might be banned everywhere.

Religion may not be singled out for special restriction any more than political speech favoring one party over another. If a campus visitor is free to yell "Go Vols!" on a campus plaza he or she is free to follow that with "Call upon the name of Jesus. He will set you free!"

Nationally known campus preacher Jim Gilles often telephoned me or came by to see me in person when appearing on the Knoxville campus. Our first visit was in April 1992.

Gilles had a propensity for going to court whenever a university administration attempted to block his activity. He was well versed in the law governing "free speech" at public institutions of higher education. Being a "free-speech" proponent myself I did everything necessary to assure that UT did not needlessly end up in court with Gilles. He and I got along just fine.

On a couple of occasions UT police officers called me after asking Gilles to leave a particular site on campus, explaining that Gilles had suggested contacting me. On each occasion, after determining that Gilles was preaching in locations where other members of the public were permitted to speak openly on other matters, I advised that he be allowed to continue preaching. My advice was followed and litigation was avoided.

Not until after my retirement in 2008 did UT sustain a litigation loss for attempting to restrict a traveling evangelist from preaching on campus. (See Knoxville News- Sentinel, August 3, 2013, p. A4). The plaintiff in that case, John McGlone, actually called me sometime after my retirement to ask my opinion on his right to preach on campus. I provided him my standard "bare-bones" seminar, explaining that the law protected his right to preach on campus in those areas where members of the public were free to speak on other issues, subject to reasonable restrictions on "time, place and manner."

Several years ago I received a call from Matthew Scoggins, a fine young attorney in the UT Office of General Counsel who asked my thoughts on McGlone's campus preaching. I confirmed that McGlone had contacted me and the advice I had provided him. The same advice I provided Matthew.

Evidently U.S. District Judge Thomas Phillips had reason to believe the University could lawfully bar McGone from preaching on campus without sponsorship from a student group or invitation from faculty, staff or a student and entered a ruling to that effect. McGone appealed to the U.S. Court of Appeals for the Sixth Circuit seeking reversal of the District Court's decision and preliminary injunctive relief, enjoining the University from barring him from campus

By order entered August 2, 2013 the Sixth Circuit, by unanimous opinion of the three-member panel (U.S. Circuit Judges Boyce Martin, Jr. and John M. Rogers and U.S. District Judge Arthur J. Tarnow), held that UT had two "sponsorship" policies which were contradictory on their face and that it was unclear to a person of ordinary intelligence as to who had authority to grant sponsorship to a visiting speaker such as McGone. The Court of Appeals reversed the District Court and instructed that court to grant McGone preliminary injunctive relief. John McGone v. Jimmy Cheek, et. al., No. 12-5306 (6th Cir. 2013).

I never lost, or even handled, a lawsuit involving alleged deprivation of the First Amendment right to espouse religious beliefs on campus. However, I did lose a First Amendment case which emphasized the fact that freedom of speech is not dependent on the message being conveyed.

THE BANNER ON VICTOR ASHE BRIDGE– ROBERT DAVIS v. UNIVERITY OF TENNESSEE, ET. AL

On the evening of September 13.1991, Robert Davis, a UT Knoxville student, and other demonstrators hung banners from and displayed signs on the Victor Ashe pedestrian bridge spanning Cumberland Avenue. The demonstration was in response to an incident in which a Knoxville police officer shot and killed a lady by the name of Darlene Grant in the presence of UT police officers. The signs and banners were critical of the police.

UT police officers Anthony Bowman and Robert Wyrick ordered Davis to remove the banners from the bridge. They and officer Burl Harris arrested Davis when he failed to comply and became combative.

On September 10, 1992, Harris filed suit in U.S. District Court alleging that the banner was unlawfully seized in violation of his First Amendment rights. He also sued for unlawful arrest and use of excessive force in the process. The University and three arresting police officers were named as defendants as were UT Chancellor William Snyder and UT Police chief Edward Yovella. Davis sought $250,000 in compensatory damages and $250,000 in punitive damages. UT was dismissed as a party defendant before the case was tried.

The case was tried by jury before U.S. District Judge Leon Jordan on September 13–16, 1994. Evidence was introduced by plaintiff that other individuals and groups often hung banners from the pedestrian bridge prior to football games. There was evidence the banners in controversy were permitted to hang from the bridge for as long as five weeks or so before Davis' arrest.

Police Chief Yovella and other officers denied having knowledge of those banners and permitting them to be hung (and in my pretrial investigative work I concluded they did not). Regardless, the jury reached a conclusion to the contrary.

The jury found that Officer Bowman had violated Davis's "Civil Rights" but failed to specify whether that referred to Davis's First Amendment right of free speech or his Fourth amendment right not to be subjected to use of excessive force in connection with his arrest. Davis was awarded $250 in "compensatory or nominal" damages for the civil rights violation by Bowman. Wyrick and Harris were exonerated and the jury awarded no punitive damages against anyone.

The jury specifically found that Chief Yovella and Chancellor Snyder had violated Davis's First Amendment rights. But no damages were awarded.

Judge Jordan did award attorneys' fees and costs totaling $17,915.16 by Order of July 6, 1995. Robert Davis v. The University of Tennessee, et. al., No. 3-92-634 (E.D. Tenn. 1995) Both Davis and the remaining defendants appealed to the U.S. Court of Appeals for the Sixth Circuit.

On April 2, 1997 the Sixth Circuit, in a 2-1 decision (Circuit Judges Gil Merritt and Guy Cole in the majority and U.S. District Judge Patrick Dugan in the minority), entered an order denying defendants' appeal but granting Davis a new trial on the issue of damages assessed against Officer Bowman. The Appeals Court was of the opinion that the damages awarded by the District Court were insufficient regardless of whether the jury was referring to a First Amendment or Fourth amendment violation. Robert Davis v. Ed Yovella, et. al., Nos. 95-5415/95-5450/95-6036 (6th Cir. 1997).

Better to settle than go through another trial when the issue of liability had already been adjudicated in favor of Davis. A settlement was duly negotiated with Davis's attorney, Peter Alliman of Madisonville.

An order of compromise and dismissal was entered by the Court of Appeals on August 28, 1997. The University issued a check in the amount of $40,000 for the plaintiff and $35,000 for attorney's fees and court costs.

Lesson confirmed: the First Amendment protects speech without regard to subject matter. A banner lambasting "police brutality" has no less First Amendment protection then one urging the Vols to victory!

Personally, I did not need a reminder. It was my position throughout my career that the First Amendment protected popular speech as well as unpopular.

"HATE SPEECH"

In Chapter 38, I referred to a single rule rejected by the State Attorney General during the rulemaking process of the Administrative Procedures Act. The proposed rule, adopted by the UT Board of Trustees in May 1989, provided that UT, Knoxville "standards of conduct" would include prohibition of conduct often referred to as "hate speech." The rule, amended the definition of prohibited disorderly conduct: "Specifically prohibited are both actions and language which tend to incite an immediate breach of the peace by making reference to another's race or ethnic origin." Rule 1720-4-3-.03 (n).

State Attorney General Charles W. Burson solved my concern, and that of UTK student affairs administrator Tim Rogers, by returning the rule to me unsigned. In his letter to me of June 16, 1989, General Burson explained:

Although the proposed rule is directed at statements "which tend to incite an immediate breach of peace" it appears that standards set out by the United States Supreme Court require more than a tendency to justify suppression of First Amendment rights. For example, in [Tinker v. Des Moines Independent Community School District] the Court stated that undifferentiated fear or apprehension of disturbance is not enough to overcome the right to freedom of expression. In [Brandenburg v. Ohio] the Court held that the critical line for determining the permissibility of regulation is the line between mere advocacy and advocacy directed to inciting or producing imminent lawless action. Under these standards, it is doubtful that the language "which tend" would survive a constitutional challenge.

The rule died and was not further pursued, at least not during the period of my employment with the OGC.

Overall, the University of Tennessee's record in adhering to the free speech provisions of the First Amendment to the United States Constitution is, in my opinion, solid although not perfect.

Chapter 61–Constitutional Right to Due Process– When it did Not Apply

During the decades of my legal service to the University I handled, in one way or another, hundreds of hearings mandated by the constitutional principle of due process. However, in a public educational institution such as the University of Tennessee, there are several circumstances under which the institution may act without affording due process.

ACADEMIC DECISIONS AND DUE PROCESS– STEVENS v. HUNT

One issue resolved early in my career was whether a UT student had any property right warranting a due process hearing in which to challenge an academic decision.

Several students enrolled in the UTCHS College of Medicine in 1977. Rules adopted by the College after the date of entry required that all medical students pass Part I of the National Board of Medical Examiners examination at the end of their second academic year. The rules further provided that any student failing the exam may be sponsored by the Progress and Promotions Committee to retake the examination a second or third time.

James Stevens and a couple of his classmates completed two years of medical school then failed the NBME twice. The Progress and Promotions Committee voted to allow them a third chance to pass the test. Dr. Robert Summit, Dean of the College of medicine, disagreed, based on the students' academic records, class standing and two failures of the NBME examination. The students' appeal to UTCHS Chancellor Jim Hunt was denied.

On January 4, 1980 the students filed suit in U.S. District Court in Memphis, claiming they had been deprived of a property right to take the NBME examination a third time and had been subjected to "arbitrary and capricious" action by University officials. Preliminary injunctive relief was sought, preventing the University from dismissing the students until the case was fully tried.

On February 21 the U.S. District Court entered an order denying the plaintiffs' motion for preliminary injunction. James R. Stevens, et. al., v. James C. Hunt, M.D., et. al., No. C-80-2004 (W.D. Tenn. 1980). Plaintiffs appealed that ruling to the U.S. Court of Appeals for the Sixth Circuit.

In a unanimous, 3–0 decision rendered April 20, 1981, the Sixth Circuit ruled that the plaintiffs were not "vested with a property right to take the NBME examination a third time when the Committee voted to sponsor each of them for a third attempt." Further, the court found that the plaintiffs had not offered evidence that the Dean acted arbitrarily or capriciously by rejecting the Committee's recommendation. James R. Stevens, et. al., v. James C. Hunt, M.D., et.al. No. 80–1238 (6th Cir. 1981).

Although the University prevailed in Stevens, the case served as reminder of the need to include non-binding language in academic materials whenever matters were to be left to academic judgment. As a general rule, the courts of the United States have been extremely reluctant to interfere in matters involving academic judgment, unless, of course, an academic institution makes a binding commitment to act or refrain from acting without any reference to exercise of academic judgment as would have been the case had the UT College of Medicine rule stated "a student failing the examination will be permitted to take the examination a second or third time."

IN ABSENCE OF CONTRACT THERE IS NO PROPERTY RIGHT IN EMPLOYMENT–STOKES v. UNIVERSITY OF TENNESSEE AT MARTIN

Raymond Stokes was employed by UT Martin on September 1, 1967 as Associate Director of Financial Aid. Randall Hall, Director of Financial Aid, issued Stokes a letter of November 29, 1983 notifying him of the termination of his employment, effective December 31, 1983, for "inadequate work performance." Stokes filed suit in Chancery Court, Weakly County, contending he was deprived of his property right to continued employment without due process, in violation of the U.S. Constitution. 42 U.S.C. s1983.

Weakly County Chancellor Homer Bradberry denied the University's motion to dismiss in an opinion filed February 20, 1986. The University filed a motion for summary judgment on March 26 and, Chancellor Bradberry granted that motion on October 20, 1986. Stokes, represented by Dresden attorney Harry Max Speight, appealed that decision to the Tennessee Court of Appeals.

On June 19, 1987, the Tennessee Court of Appeals for the Western section, at Jackson, affirmed the ruling of the Chancery Court. The court ruled "It is well-established that the University of Tennessee is not a 'person' amenable to suit under 42 USC 1983 (citing an earlier case I had participated in litigating, Gross v. University of Tennessee, 448 F.Supp. 245 (W.D. Tenn. 1978) aff'd 620 F 2d. 109 (6th Cir. 1980)).

Stokes v. University of Tennessee at Martin, 737 S.W. 2d 545 (Tenn. App. 1987) Permission to Appeal Denied Sept. 8, 1987.

The court of appeals specifically rejected the plaintiff's argument that his suit was not barred by the doctrine of sovereign immunity because he sought injunctive relief rather than monetary damages. Id.

In the absence of a written contract of employment UT employees serve on an "at will" basis, subject to termination for "good cause, bad cause or no cause whatever–just not an illegal cause." This was a brief statement of settled constitutional law I shared repeatedly at employment law seminars. Next, I explained that terminations for "bad cause or no cause whatever" might well be perceived by a judge or jury as termination for an illegal cause such as discrimination on the basis of race, sex, etc. As lawyers say, "bad facts make bad law."

ONLY EXPRESS CONTRACTS CONVEY PROPERTY RIGHT– WOOLSEY v. HUNT

As is by now surely evident from reading other chapters in this book, the amount of effort consumed in litigation, the importance of issues resolved and the level of any monetary award may be largely unrelated. In the following case, both sides expended great effort and issues critical to the University were resolved. The litigation would have been very costly to the University had the final results been different. In more ways than one.

Telena Woolsey was employed at UTCHS on February 9, 1977 as a senior secretary in the Division of Connective Tissue Diseases, College of Medicine. In 1981 Woolsey was promoted to the position of office supervisor. In the new position she not only performed secretarial tasks but also administrative duties as well as training and supervising office personnel.

In a 1983–84 evaluation Woolsey's supervisor, Dr. Robert Pinals, rated Woolsey's job performance as excellent. A few months later Pinals departed UTCHS to accept the position of Chairman of the College of Medicine at Princeton University.

The incoming director, Dr. Arnold Postlethwaite, made it clear he did not want Woolsey as his office supervisor and would do whatever necessary to get rid of her. As soon as he assumed the directorship he announced a plan to reorganize his office.

On July 17, 1984 Woolsey filed a grievance under the University's grievance procedures with the chairman of the department of medicine, Doctor Albert Kang. At the same time Howard Carman, Vice Chancellor for Facilities and Human Resources, and Paula Harris, Director of Personnel Services, to continue Woolsey's employment for an unspecified time beyond July 31, 1984 in order to afford her additional time to seek other employment within the University.

Postlethwaite confirmed the extension of employment and advised Woolsey that her employment would be extended. But she would no longer serve as Office Supervisor and would function in a "temporary role as secretary". On July 26 Woolsey began moving personal belongings from her office and in the process injured her wrists, aggravating a pre-existing job-related injury. She was placed on leave of absence with pay by the University following her physician's recommendation that she not return to work pending resolution of her wrist injuries. Because of those injuries Woolsey never assumed the temporary secretary position agreed to by Postlethwaite.

Kang declined to grant Woolsey the relief she had suggested in her grievance and Woolsey appealed to the Dean of the College of Medicine, Robert L Summitt, M.D. Summit, appointed Associate Dean of the College, Ray Colson, to handle Woolsey's appeal. In a memorandum of September 4, 1984 Colson wrote: "I recommend that Mrs. Wolsey be retained as a regular full-time employee within the Rheumatology Division for up to six months at her current rate of pay while she looks for a suitable transfer."

In the same month Postlethwaite twice offered Woolsey secretarial positions in his division. She declined both offers. By a letter of October 8, 1984, Postlethwaite notified Woolsey that because she had declined his offers of continued employment and had failed to report to work in the "temporary secretary" position her employment was terminated. Woolsey was not offered an opportunity for a hearing to contest her termination.

Woolsey filed suit in U.S. District Court on November 9, 1984 claiming she was discharged in violation of her due process rights under the 14th Amendment to the United States Constitution. Named defendants were Chancellor Hunt, Postlethwaite and the University of Tennessee. Representing Woolsey were Memphis attorneys Donald Donati and his wife, Wanda. The case was assigned to U.S. District Judge Julia Gibbons.

I filed motions on behalf of the defendants, contesting the District Court's jurisdiction under section 1983 and invoking qualified immunity on behalf of the individual defendants. All motions were denied by Judge Gibbons.

JoAnn Cutting, from the Memphis office of the Office of General Counsel, provided wonderful assistance to me in representing the University defendants in what would prove to be an intensely fought and labor–intensive lawsuit.

Trial before Judge Gibbons commenced on September 17, 1987, continued on September 23–24 and October 29 and concluded the morning of November 2. Both sides were requested to submit proposed "findings of fact and conclusions of law" for Gibbons' consideration. Those were filed in January 1988.

Nearly a year later, on December 14, 1988, Judge Gibbons entered her findings of fact and conclusions of law. She held that "[p]laintiff's written and oral communication with Colson, combined with the actions of university officials, letters from Ballwin, Harris and Postlewaite, and the employment status policy, created a mutual understanding, both implicit and explicit, of continued employment of at least six months from September 4, 1984." Judge Gibbons further found that Woolsey was terminated without a pre or post–termination hearing and, therefore, had been deprived of her constitutional rights.

A consent order of dismissal as to the University and to Hunt and Postlethwaite in their "official" capacities was entered on April 5,1989. Hunt and Postlethwaite remained defendants in their "individual capacities."

On June 21, 1989, the District Court entered judgment for Woolsey holding Postlethwaite alone liable for lost wages in the amount of $52,183.68 and compensatory damages for emotional distress in the amount of $5,000. The court further ordered that Woolsey be reinstated "to her previous position as senior secretary in the division of connective tissue diseases" and enjoined defendants "from terminating plaintiff until she is given notice of the charges against her and provided a pre–termination hearing in accord with the procedure set forth." Telena Woolsey v. James C. Hunt, et.al. No. 84-2949-GB (W.D. Tenn. 1988).

Defendants were ordered to provide Wolsey with appropriate raises, establish her salary at $17,725 per year and pay contributions into her pension fund and Social Security fund. Woolsey was also awarded attorneys fees in the amount of $45,240.63 and expenses in the amount of $2,016.20.

I filed a motion for a new trial or to reconsider the judgment on June 29. The motion was denied by Judge Gibbons by order entered on August 4, 1989. Notice of appeal to the U.S. Court of Appeals for the Sixth Circuit was filed on behalf of the defendants on August 15, 1989.

Don Donati and I argued our respective positions on oral argument before the Court of Appeals on November 5, 1990. The appeals panel consisted of Circuit judges Damon Keith, Cornelia Kennedy and Richard Suhrheinrich. Much was at stake from the University's perspective.

On May 9, 1991, by a unanimous decision, the Court of Appeals reversed the District Court's June 21, 1989 judgment and vacated the District Court order granting Woolsey reinstatement, restitution, attorney's fees and costs. Woolsey v. Hunt, 932 F. 2d 555 (6th Cir. 1991).

The Sixth Circuit took note of the District Court's reliance on the Soni case which I had managed to lose for the University in both the District Court and the Sixth Circuit back in the 1970s (See Chapter 24). However, the appellate court made short shrift of the district court's reliance on Soni:

> In *Soni*, this Court held that the 11th Amendment did not bar a monetary judgment against the University of Tennessee. This conclusion was based on the court's finding that the Tennessee legislature might have waived sovereign immunity with respect to the University pursuant to a statute allowing the University to sue and be sued. [Citation omitted].
>
> However, following the decision in *Soni*, in 1977, the Tennessee legislature amended the state's sovereign immunity statute to provide: "[n]o statutory or other provision authorizing the University of Tennessee and its Board of Trustees to sue and be sued shall constitute a waiver of sovereign immunity. "Tenn. Code Ann. 20-13-102(b).

Id., p.565.

The appellate court noted that at the time Woolsey filed suit Tennessee had "waived its sovereign immunity only with respect to suits against the state based on an express contract or breach thereof." Id., p. 565.

However, as the court noted, Woolsey conceded that her suit was based on claimed breach of an implied contract-not an express contract. Id. p. 566-67.

Then the Sixth Circuit cited the Tennessee appeals court decision in Stokes:

> The Stokes court stated that even if the suit were based on an express contract, [Tenn. Code Ann.] 29–10–101(a)(1) mandated dismissal of the suit because the statute related only to express contracts and specifically provided for suits thereon in the courts of Davidson County. Implied contract claims against the state of Tennessee are not recognized and are not enforceable in any court in the state. [Citation omitted].

Id., p. 567.

The District Court erred in holding that plaintiff possessed a constitutionally protected property interest in continued employment for a period of six months or more. The District Court failed to conduct the requisite analysis of state law in this case. [Citations omitted] Had it done so, no property interest would have been found to have stemmed from Tennessee law based on an implied contract.

***

This conclusion, that plaintiff does not possess a constitutionally protected property interest in continued employment with the University for the reason that Tennessee has not waived its sovereign immunity with respect to implied contract suits against the state, compels a finding also that the District Court erred in holding Dr. Postlethwaite liable for damages in his individual capacity because Dr. Postlethwaite did not deprive plaintiff of a recognized property interest under state law.

Id., p. 568.

The devastating effect of the District Court decision was completely erased. Good news for the University. General Counsel Brogan so notified the members of the UT Board of Trustees by memorandum of May 20, 1991. He advised the Trustees that that more than $170,000 in savings resulted from reversal of Judge Gibbons' judgment, that the Court of Appeals had relied on several earlier UT cases in reversing the District Court and that "Ron Leadbetter of this office handled the trial of this action." I would have added that JoAnn Cutting provided valuable assistance.

Woolsey stands as a good example of a case with positive results derived from "staying the course," defending a position believed to be correct and refusing to cave in for fear of losing to a competent adversary.

Postnote: The Sixth Circuit's reversal of Judge Gibbons' District Court ruling came shortly after Gibbons was appointed to a position on the Court of Appeals.

Chapter 62–One APA Sexual Harassment Case and One APA Loss–Richard Wilson vs. UTC

Sexual harassment is a topic I regularly included in my civil rights seminars presented to UT affirmative-action officers, personnel/human resources officers and others. It was included within the general topic of sex discrimination.

The University's firm opposition to sexual harassment was stated clearly and repeatedly. That is made clear in documents such as a February 6, 1989 memorandum from UTCHS Chancellor Jim Hunt to every campus official having any authority whatever over students or employees.

SUBJECT: affirmative action workshops–Sexual harassment
COMMENTS:
1. The notice sent to you from Robert E Taylor, Junior, Ph. D. Affirmative Action Officer, and Ronald Leadbetter, J. D., Associate General Counsel, announces that affirmative action workshops dealing with sex discrimination and sexual harassment will be held Wednesday, February 22, 1989,1:00-3:00 p.m. and Thursday, February 23, 1989, 9:00- 11:00 a.m., A137 South Auditorium Coleman.
2. It is important that all University staff members responsible for personnel actions attend one of these sessions. You are requested to assure attendance by appropriate per-

sonnel in your area of responsibility.

   3. It is the policy of the University of Tennessee, Memphis to comply fully with all federal civil rights statutes and not to discriminate in any manner against employees or applicants for employment. To assure compliance with all provisions of civil rights and non-discriminatory regulations, it is important that all staff are made aware of their responsibility in this area.

During the period I handled civil rights matters, the University had a praise-worthy record of avoiding sexual harassment claims. Most complaints, whether against students, faculty or other UT employees were resolved by informal means, such as counseling and letters of warning. In only a single instance over nearly three decades did I handle litigation involving sexual harassment. It had several unusual aspects.

RICHARD WILSON vs. THE UNIVERSITY OF TENNESSEE AT CHATTANOOGA

In 1995 Dr. Richard Wilson, a professor of political science at UT Chattanooga, was the subject of a sexual harassment complaint filed by one of his female students. Following issuance of an administrative order finding Wilson guilty of sexually harassing the student, Acting Provost and Vice Chancellor for Academic Affairs Charles Summerlin wrote Wilson and cautioned him to stop telephoning students unless specifically requested by them to do so. He also instructed Wilson to stop inviting students to his home. Wilson was also cautioned, "students have the right to expect a non–threatening environment for their classes and for their interactions with faculty."

On April 9, 1998, Wilson requested a female student, Diana Oo, to do typing for him. Oo agreed. Wilson asked her to come to his home to perform the requested secretarial services.

When Oo arrived at Wilson's home, she was led to a basement room in which a laptop computer and dictaphone was located–a guest bedroom. Although Wilson left for a period, he subsequently returned to the room, commented on the work Oo had done and proceeded to massage her shoulders and back. She became uncomfortable and informed Wilson that she had to meet a friend for lunch. Oo began to put a shoe back on that she had removed while typing. Wilson reached to assist her and placed one hand on Oo's ankle in the process. Wilson's actions were not invited by Oo and upset her.

Wilson requested that Oo return after meeting her friend for lunch. She returned, as requested, but brought the friend with her. Upon seeing Oo in the company of her friend, Wilson advised that he no longer needed her services.

Oo subsequently filed a complaint about Wilson's conduct with the acting head of the Department of Political Science. After submitting this complaint Oo encountered Wilson in a campus parking lot and was angrily interrogated by him regarding her report to the department head. The encounter greatly distressed Oo, particularly since she was a student in Wilson's class.

I received a call from the UTC academic affairs office requesting that I handle the matter for the Chancellor, Another attorney in the Office of General Counsel, Karen Holt, had handled the previous matter involving Wilson.

By letter of November 22, 1998 Chancellor Bill Stacy notified Wilson that he was charged with (1) "Persistent refusal to comply with University policies," and (2) "Serious violation of the university's standard of professional responsibility in personal relations of students." He was provided a summary of Oo's allegations against him.

Wilson requested a hearing in accordance with the Tennessee Administrative Procedures Act. Chancellor Stacy named Karen Weekly, a member of the UTC faculty (and later co–head coach of the UTK women's softball team), as administrative judge for the hearing.

The hearing was held on May 16, 1999. Weekly entered an initial order on September 16, 1999, finding Wilson guilty of both administrative charges placed against him. One key finding of the administrative judge addressed the credibility of the witnesses: "[c]onsidering the record as a whole, Oo's testimony is far more credible and plausible than that of Wilson."

With respect to the first charge, Weekly declined to determine whether Wilson's activities were sufficiently severe to constitute hostile environment sexual harassment. Instead, she found that UTC had "the right to take prompt, effective remedial action to see that liability for the creation of a hostile environment is avoided." The University should not be required to "tolerate the misconduct of an employee until sufficient acts of wrongdoing are committed to subject the employer to liability." The University certainly had no interest in tolerating Wilson's conduct until it resulted in Oo filing suit against the University!

Weekly also found that Wilson's actions constituted "a serious violation of the University's standard of professional responsibility in personal relations with students. As a matter of professional responsibility, a professor should not engage in behavior which included uninvited, inappropriate touching of students."

Wilson appealed Weekly's findings and conclusions to Chancellor Stacy. Stacy entered a final order, dismissing Wilson's appeal, on December 15, 1999.

Wilson then appealed Stacy's ruling to the Chancery Court for Davidson County. On September 13, 2000, Davidson County Chancellor Irvin H. Kilcrease, Jr. entered judgment affirming the University's final order. Wilson then appealed the chancery court's ruling to the Tennessee Court of Appeals for the Middle Section of Tennessee in Nashville.

The panel assigned to hear Wilson's was composed of appeals judges Houston

Goddard, Charles Susano and Herschel Franks. Franks did not participate in the opinion issued by the court. Representing Wilson were Hamilton Lake County attorneys Rebecca Wells Demaree and Andy Berke.

The ruling of the appellate court was entered on December 28, 2001. Judges Goddard and Susano both ruled in favor of Wilson, reversing each of the three preceding adjudicative bodies. Richard Wilson v. The University of Tennessee at Chattanooga, No. M2000-02573-COA-R3-CV (Tenn. App. 2001). The Court of Appeals found Wilson innocent of the two charges against him.

In reviewing the facts of the case, the appellate court concluded "we do not find that Dr. Wilson's actions toward Ms. Oo were of such severity [as required for a single incident to be actionable as sexual harassment]". Id.p.7.

Significantly, the Court of Appeals did not suggest that UTC could not have designated Wilson's conduct as grounds for a charge of misconduct, only that it had not done so. "It is our conclusion that the sexual harassment policy of UTC as set forth in its faculty handbook did not sufficiently apprise Dr. Wilson that UTC might consider the conduct attributed to him in this matter to be sexual harassment." Id. p.10.

"We find that nothing in the letter which would have placed Dr. Wilson on notice that UTC would consider his behavior toward Ms. Oo in the present case to be sexual harassment." Id. p.9.

An application for permission to appeal was filed with the Tennessee Supreme Court on February 26, 2002. The Supreme Court denied the application by order of September 9, 2002.

Wilson subsequently filed a motion for discretionary costs as well as pre-and post trial interest. The Davidson County Chancery Court awarded Wilson court costs but refused to award him the interest.

While this case registered as a "litigation loss" I lost little sleep over it. It was the only one of more than 135 APA cases I handled which resulted in a final court ruling against the University.

The University did all it could to support Ms. Oo. At the same time it made clear to Wilson that his behavior was unacceptable, even if the Court of Appeals found he was not previously given notice that such conduct was unacceptable.

The process was a costly one for Wilson (even if his attorneys worked for free). In addition, the case demonstrated clearly the University's commitment to opposing sexual harassment, notwithstanding the Court of Appeals' finding that sexual harassment had not occurred. No further complaints of inappropriate conduct by Wilson were received by UTC. Presumably he learned his lesson.

Chapter 63–Due Process–Sometimes it Applies and Sometimes it Doesn't

Early in my career I took on responsibility for assuring that the University followed Constitutional principles of due process whenever acting to impact the rights and privileges of students, employees and others. My first effort of University-wide application started with a memorandum of February 7, 1975 sent to President Boling, General Counsel Baugh, Vice President Joe Johnson, Administrative Assistant to the President, Charles Smith, and Chancellors Jim Drinnon (UTC), Al Farmer (UTCHS), Larry McGehee (UTM), Roy Nicks (UTN) and Jack Reese (UTK).

I have had the opportunity in recent weeks to review several of the current and proposed appeals procedures utilized or proposed to be utilized by the University in handling complaints, grievances, and appeals from disciplinary actions. In doing so I have come to the realization that some of these procedures may require strengthening in order to comply with the due process requirements of recent court decisions and avoid possible future litigation.

I then proceeded to outline a number of key areas in which improvement was necessary such as provision of hearings prior to imposing disciplinary action except where immediate action "is necessary to avoid substantial threat of harm to property or the health or safety of fellow employees, students or other individuals." Also recommended was specifying specific time limits for filing grievances, hearing requests and appeals.

Also addressed were the necessary steps in a legally sufficient hearing, from required contents of a charge letter to matters to be covered in a final order. There were other suggested rule improvements, not least of which was clarity, simplicity and, where beneficial, uniformity of language among the campuses.

Much input was invited and received. By September the project was ready for presentation to the UT Board of Trustees.

By memorandum of September 17, 1975 Andy Kozar, Executive Assistant to the President, confirmed with Board Chairman Harry Laughlin and Members of the Student Affairs Committee that a meeting of the Student Affairs Committee would be held at 4:00 p.m. on October 9 in the Board Room at Andy Holt Tower to "discuss the enclosed 'Hearing Rights and Procedures' statement, which has been developed to assure due process for all persons connected with the University of Tennessee, that is, its students, faculty, administrators, and all employees." Kozar added that a meeting of the Academic Affairs Committee of the Board would be held on October 10 for the same purpose.

The Kozar memorandum was copied to President Boling, Vice Presidents, Chancellors, Student Affairs Officers and me.

I presented my own one–page memorandum to Harry Laughlin the day of the meeting for the purpose of providing him "some of the background information which provided the impetus for the development of the proposed Hearing Rights and Procedures Statement."

Both Board committees met, discussed and approved the proposed regulations "outlining minimum legal requirements below which the campuses and system must not go in handling matters requiring due process hearings." The full Board subsequently approved the regulations at its winter meeting in 1976.

All University hearing procedures subject to new regulations were promptly brought into compliance. There would continue to be questions to be addressed on a case –by-case basis but the framework was set.

A good example of the approach taken by the University in addressing the concept of due process is found in a memorandum I addressed to UT System Personnel Director Mike Brookshire on February 16, 1978.

> Jim Stockdale has indicated to me that you would like a response to several questions raised in the recent meeting of personnel directors in Nashville.
>
> **Question 1.**: Does an individual entitled to a hearing have a legal right to be assisted by counsel?
>
> **Response:** The preponderance of available legal authority suggests that an individual having a legal right to a hearing does not have a legal right to counsel. However, there is some authority that would suggest the contrary. This office has recommended that individuals whom we are required by law to provide a hearing opportunity be permitted to have assistance of counsel. Permitting such legal assistance certainly avoids any possible necessity of defending a policy whereby we prohibit the presence and assistance of legal counsel in our hearings. Also, from a public relations viewpoint, we avoid any appearance of attempting to "railroad" individuals entitled to hearings. Naturally, counsel from this office should be present at any hearing at which counsel is present for the individual receiving the hearing.
>
> It is recommended that counsel not be permitted to participate in hearings which the University elects to provide to its employees but which are not required to [be] provid[ed] by law. For instance, it is not recommended that counsel be permitted to participate in grievance hearings or hearings held to discuss an employee's termination for inadequate work performance.

Formal procedures for conducting hearings in accordance with the Contested Case provisions of the Tennessee Uniform Administrative Procedures Act, applicable to All Campuses, were approved by the Board of Trustees in 1991 and became effective October 29 that same year.

No successful legal challenge to the University's procedures for implementing the Constitutional right to due process was ever successfully pursued during the nearly three decades I handled that subject matter for the University. There were challenges, however.

THE FIRST RAPE CASE TRIED UNDER THE
APA–FRAKER / FLEMING

A rape case from the mid-1980s provides a good example of how a charge of egregious misconduct was handled at the University of Tennessee when the accused requested a formal hearing in accordance with the Administrative Procedures Act.

During Fall Quarter 1985 a UT Knoxville student, Jennifer Standifer, was reported to have been raped by one or two other UT students, Scott Fleming or Stephen Fraker. After interviewing Standifer, I concluded there was ample evidence to proceed with administrative charges against both. Standifer elected not to pursue criminal charges against either of her assailants.

I drafted a charge letter for Chancellor Jack Reese addressed to each of the accused. Fleming and Fraker were jointly charged with raping Standifer on October 12, 1985 in violation of UTK standard of conduct #27 ("Commission of an act or an attempt to commit an act on University property or involving members of the University community... That would be in violation of the Criminal Code of the State of Tennessee" [in this case, "rape" as described in T. C. A. 39 –2–604]) (rule 1720–4–10 –.03 (aa) Tennessee Administrative Register).

At my recommendation Malcolm McInnis, Jr. was named by Chancellor Reese to serve as administrative judge. The hearing was conducted on January 24, 1986 in the conference room of the UT Office of Student Conduct. Both of the accused were present, represented by Knoxville attorney Lawrence Ault. After introductory remarks by McInnis, both Ault and I were afforded the opportunity to make opening remarks, present witnesses, cross examine opposing witnesses and offer closing argument.

On April 18, 1986 McInnis entered an "Initial Order", containing his findings of fact and conclusions of law. The basic facts, found from the evidence introduced into evidence, were as follows:

On the evening of October 12 Standifer visited several bars on Cumberland Avenue adjacent to the campus, accompanied by a female friend, Terri Sutherland. Around 2 a.m. Standifer left the "University Club" with Terry, who had secured transportation home with her friends, Fleming and Fraker.

After a stop at the Kappa Alpha house and another stop to pick up beer, the group went to a parking lot across from Standifer's apartment. Fleming escorted Sutherland to her apartment and Fraker escorted Standifer to hers.

Fraker and Standifer watched television for a while. Then Standifer, quite tired and drunk, went into her bedroom, closed the door, got in bed and went to sleep.

As noted in the Initial Order:

> Sometime later she [Standifer] awoke to find a nude male in bed with her. Another male was also present in the room and was undressed, at least from the waist up. Ms. Standifer screamed at the two individuals to get out and the one standing at the foot of the bed left immediately. The other individual took his time walking over and starting to get dressed. When Standifer yelled at him again to get out he said, "just a minute Jennifer, I'm trying." Ms. Standifer

was quite upset and called a friend, Lisa Dates, and told her she thought she had been raped.

Shortly after calling a friend, Dates, Standifer called the UT police.

When Dates arrived, Standifer was dressed but crying and unable to talk. Dates took her to UT hospital where she was examined by "Dr. Montgomery" who confirmed the presence of semen. He found no evidence of trauma but noted Standifer's complaint of pain in the vaginal area.

As noted by McInnis there was ample evidence that Fraker and Fleming were the two males in Standifer's bedroom. A checkbook with Fleming's name on it was found in the apartment and he returned shortly after the incident looking for it. A dry-cleaning receipt with Fleming's name on it was also found in Standifer's bed.

The next issue for resolution was whether Standifer was raped or had consensual sex. McIinnis found the former by noting that Standiford was drunk and that the accused knew or had reason to know that she was physically helpless. State law (T.C.A. 39–2–604) defined rape to include unlawful sexual penetration of another when the actor knows or has reason to know that the victim is physically helpless. Moreover, McInnis found that Standifer's actions after discovering the men in her room completely refuted any notion of consent.

McGinnis also resolved the issue of whether it was Fleming or Fraker who raped Standifer, noting that "[u]nder of the law of Tennessee, one who is present and aids or abets, or is ready and consenting to aid and abet in the commission of an offense shall be deemed a principal offender." In other words, it mattered not who was the principal and who was the accessory.

McInnis concluded that both Fleming and Fraker were guilty of the charge of rape. He assessed the penalty of "indefinite suspension" (from the University) on both. McInnis advised that his "initial order" would become a "final order" unless a petition for reconsideration was filed within 10 days. "Either party" might seek administrative review by filing a petition with Chancellor Reese. McInnis also advised that either party could seek judicial review by filing a petition for review with the appropriate Chancery Court within 60 days of entry of the final order.

On May 29, 1986, Fraker and Fleming filed a petition for judicial review with the Knox County Chancery Court. The case was assigned to Chancellor H. David Cate. Chancellor Cate issued his Findings of Fact and Conclusions of Law and entered Final Judgment on October 27, 1986. Scott Fleming and Stephen Fraker v. Jack E Reese, Chancellor of the University of Tennessee, ex rel Jennifer Lynn Standifer, No. 88916 (Knox County Chancery Court 1986)

The Chancery Court considered three issues on appeal: (1) whether the University's administrative judge was without jurisdiction to hear or conduct any type of proceedings, (2) whether the hearing was premature and placed the appellants in jeopardy of waving immunity if the matter ever came before a grand jury, and (3) whether the decision affirmed in the final order of Chancellor Reese was supported by the evidence. Chancellor Cate concluded "all three issues should be answered in favor of the respondent's." Id. pp.1-2.

Cate included McInnis's entire nine page "initial order" in his own the ruling, then issued two of his own findings of critical and lasting importance to the University. First, Cate noted that "[w]hile it is true that prosecution of a criminal charge and resulting punishment, if found guilty, is to be accomplished in the courts which have proper subject matter jurisdiction, this does not preclude the determination of a violation of an administrative rule through the contested case procedures prescribed in the Uniform Administrative Procedures Act." Id. p.12. The University was free to reach an administrative decision as to whether a rape had been committed; it was not required to await action by a criminal court.

Second, Cate rejected the notion that requiring the accused to testify, although neither testified at the hearing and neither was asked to do so, would have placed them in jeopardy, that they had voluntarily waived immunity if the matter came before a grand jury. "If credence is given to this position, an administrative agency would have to wait until the statute of limitations had run or a criminal prosecution concluded.... Thus, the administrative agency would be powerless to act, even in the case where the health and safety of the agency was in jeopardy." Id. p.13.

Cate noted that it was "not unusual for civil litigation to occur concerning the subject matter of potential criminal prosecutions prior to such criminal prosecutions, particularly in tort cases and bank failure cases." Id. In other words, the University was free to prosecute administrative charges without regard to any claim that an accused party or witness might be forced to either refuse to testify or offer testimony of a potentially incriminating nature in criminal proceedings. Id.

Lastly, Chancellor Cate concluded that Chancellor Reese's final order was supported by substantial and material evidence in the record. The court ordered the petition for judicial review dismissed. Id. pp. 14-15.

In November 1986 the petitioners appealed to the Tennessee Court of Appeals. On August 7, 1987 the Court of Appeals enter judgment in the University's favor–upholding the findings of Chancellor Cate.

DUE PROCESS NOT ALWAYS REQUIRED–
WILLIAM DAN JOHNSON v. W. TIMOTHY ROGERS

In August 1994 I received a visit from UT Knoxville Associate Vice Chancellor for Student Affairs Tim Rogers. Rogers and I had worked together very effectively on many legal matters over the years and this time was no different. Well, not exactly. On this occasion Rogers was the target of litigation. He shared with me a copy of a complaint recently filed against him and other University defendants in the U.S. District Court. The facts were set out in the complaint.

On August 30, 1993 William Dan Johnson, applied for admission to the University of Tennessee, Knoxville. Johnson, a 35-year-old white male, provided the University with considerable information regarding his previous imprisonment for various criminal offenses. The application was denied by the UT Office of Admissions.

Johnson paid a visit to Rogers' office requesting a hearing. Rogers declined to provide one.

On August 17, 1994 Johnson filed suit in federal court alleging he had been denied admission to the University, without a hearing, and in violation of his Constitutional right to procedural due process. He also claimed that he had been denied equal protection and was subjected to arbitrary and unreasonable discrimination in violation of the 5th and 14th Amendments to the United States Constitution. $350,000 in compensatory and punitive damages was sought, as well as attorney's fees and costs.

Several weeks later, on September 16, I filed a motion with the district court seeking dismissal of the complaint. On December 20, 1994 U.S. District Judge James H. Jarvis issued a memorandum opinion granting that motion. William Dan Johnson v. W. Timothy Rogers, et al., No. 3:94-cv-500. (E.D. Tenn. 1994).

Most important, Judge Jarvis ruled that Johnson was not entitled to a hearing– "procedural due process" –in connection with the University's decision to deny him admission. He reached that conclusion since "plaintiff has failed to allege any facts sufficient to support the existence of a property right or liberty interest." Id. In so ruling Jarvis made clear that an applicant for admission to UT has no right to a hearing if the application is denied.

Judge Jarvis also opined that Johnson received no treatment different from other applicants with criminal records and rejected Johnson's contention that he was in a "suspect class" denied equal protection. Id. pp.5-6. The University remained free to deny admission to applicants with criminal records if it wished to do so. And it was free to do so without affording a rejected applicant a hearing to contest the decision.

Chapter 64–Contracts and Real Estate

From 1972 until the early 1990s I was responsible for reviewing contracts between the University of Tennessee and other parties. Over this period I reviewed thousands of contracts. On a number of occasions I was responsible for crafting contract documents and on others seeing to it that documents were properly executed. And, on still others it was my job to enforce contract terms through litigation. The following are a smattering of contract–related transactional services I was called upon to provide, as noted in my diary.

In December 1972, I drove to Nashville to meet with agents of the Internal Revenue Service. An issue had arisen concerning UT anesthesiology contracts. I do not recall the details but all ended well. No tax penalties.

In September 1974, I traveled to New York to negotiate a contract with Lort Theatres for the UT Theatre department. Then, in 1976 I drafted the deed conveying the West Tennessee Chest Disease Hospital to the University of Tennessee.

By letter of May 7, 1982 General Counsel Brogan advised UT Center for the Health Sciences Chancellor Jim Hunt that he had "redrafted the memorandum of agreement concerning services to be provided by the University and FMPC to the City of Memphis Hospital for the period July 1, 1982 to June 30, 1983." Brogan concluded the two-page letter by advising Hunt, "Ron Leadbetter will be in Memphis on Thursday and Friday of next week, and he will be available to work with you and Bill Rice. I've instructed him to get with Bill and representatives of FMPC [Faculty Medical Practice Corporation] and SCHCC [Shelby County Health Care Corporation] and work out a satisfactory agreement which you are willing to recommend."

My work on another UT Medical Center contract was referenced in Hunt's May 8, 1989 letter to UT Vice President for Business and Finance Eli Fly:

> Thanks for your letter of April 24, 1989, concerning the proposed contract with the University Physicians Foundation for management services for the University of Tennessee Medical Center. I have reviewed your questions and have discussed the issues again with Ron Leadbetter. It is my understanding that Ron has discussed the contract with Beech Brogan.

From the mid-1970s until at least 1989 I routinely handled contract matters for the UT Memphis Center for Health Sciences. As attorneys were hired for the Memphis campus, contract and other transactional responsibilities for shifted to those attorneys.

I also had responsibility for handling real estate transactions. On January 2, 1979, for example, my diary entry records that "I left for Columbus, Mississippi to close the sale of the Reagan property to Sloan Implement Company for $2.7

million. [UT officials] Henry Morris and Henry Gigou went with me."

In addition to contract transactional matters I handled contract litigation. Several contract cases were rather unique.

PUNITIVE DAMAGES AWARDED IN A CONTRACT CASE– SLY AND THE FAMILY STONE

One of the more interesting contract cases I handled involved the rock, funk and soul band Sly and the Family Stone. The band had a contract to perform at the University of Tennessee but failed to appear for the scheduled performance. I contacted Ken Roberts, manager for the band and sought a settlement but to no avail.

On August 9, 1973, I filed suit for the University against Sly and the Family Stone in Knox County Circuit Court. Included in the University's "prayer for relief" was a request for compensatory and punitive damages.

An attempt to serve process on the out-of-state defendant, utilizing the Secretary of State's office, failed. Knox County Circuit Judges Edward Cole and James Haynes, both of whom I knew. Each suggested I serve process myself (since I was not a party to the litigation). Good idea!

On September 20, 1973, I flew to New York City and located and served process on Ken Roberts, Sly's agent, in his office at 25 Central Park West in Manhattan. Roberts was quite surprised to see me.

An answer to the complaint was not timely filed by Sly and, on October 24, 1973, I filed a motion for judgment by default. The motion was heard before Knox County Circuit Judge Chester Mahood on December 14, 1973.

Judge Mahood asked if I had heard from the defendant. I replied that I had contacted Sly's attorney, Sanford Goldman, in New York and notified him of the motion setting. I was also asked by Mahood if he could award punitive damages in a contract action. To the surprise of many attorneys in Mahood's court that day I replied that he could. I read language from a contract case which suggested that might be possible, probably a strained interpretation.

Judgme Mahood ruled from the bench, entering judgment for the University. He awarded requested compensatory damages in the amount of $11,356. Amazingly, Mahood also awarded punitive damages in the amount of $7,500. I had requested $10,000. A total award of $18,856! University of Tennessee v. Sylvester Stewart, et. al. No. 1-442-73 (Knox Circuit 1973). As pleasing to me as the positive outcome for the University were the numerous stunned looks on the faces of fellow attorneys as I exited the courtroom.

The case was later turned over to a collection agency in San Francisco for collection. I am not certain whether the full amount was ever collected. Regardless, the case was a vital cog in my professional development. No such thing as a case or argument that cannot be won.

NO PUNITIVE DAMAGE AWARD IN CONTRACT CASE–
BLACK vs. UT

The issue of whether punitive damages can be awarded for breach of contract arose once again less than a year later (Black et.al. v. University of Tennessee and Christina M. McKinney). Same court (Knox Circuit), same judge (Circuit Judge Chester Mahood) and same issues (may punitive damages be awarded for breach of contract?) as in *Stewart*. Knoxville attorney Geoffrey Kressin–a classmate of mine from law school–served as counsel for the plaintiff.

The plaintiffs sued UT and McKinney, head resident of Morrill Hall dormitory for $10,000 compensatory and punitive damages. They alleged that defendants wrongfully assessed all residents of the floor on which the plaintiffs lived for property damage on the floor caused by a number of unidentified residents.

I filed motions to dismiss for failure to exhaust administrative remedies and also to strike the request for punitive damages. I argued that punitive damages were not recoverable in a contract action. Judge Mahood gave me a quizzical look during oral argument–apparently recalling the opposite position I had taken on the contract breach by Sly and the Family Stone. He agreed with my current argument and sustained the Univerity's motion on both grounds.

THE ORCHID CASE–UT v. BURNSIDE

In late1974 or early 1975 I received a phone call from E.J. Chapman, an official with the UT Institute of Agriculture. According to Chapman, 100 dozen or so orchid plants had been gifted to the University by Mr. and Mrs. Walter Messick of Chattanooga, owners of Messick Nursery.

Having no "in-house" need for orchid plants, the University advertised the plants for sale. Burnside Nursery in Florida purchased $15,000 worth of orchid plants - around 30 dozen as I recall. A contract was entered into between UT and the Burnsides providing for a monthly payment for the plants purchased.

The Burnsides drove a truck from Florida to the Messick Nursery in Chattanooga a year earlier , picked out 30 dozen plants, loaded the truck and returned to Florida. For several months the Burnsides made the agreed-upon monthly payment. Then, the payments stopped. The Burnsides claimed the orchid plants purchased would not produce orchids.

As was my practice, I interviewed available witnesses before initiating litigation, Mrs. Messick being the most critical. Messick assured me each and every orchid plant donated to UT would produce orchids. Based largely on her assurance, I filed suit against the Burnsides in the U.S. District Court in Chattanooga. The case was initially assigned to U.S. District Judge Frank Wilson. University of Tennessee v. Burnside No. 1-75-37 (E.D. Tenn. 1975).

Burnside requested a trial by jury and was represented by Nashville attorney Larrimore Burton. After preliminary matters were disposed of trial was set for August 4, 1975. I went on family vacation the preceding week.

My wife, son, niece Deirdre and I drove from Knoxville to Laurel Lake, near Binghamton, New York for the annual Leadbetter family reunion on July 28. In those days before cell phone service, I had little contact with the outside world during our stay at "Uncle Bert's" cabin on the lake.

On the last Friday afternoon of July I made the mistake of finding a phone booth and calling my office. A new judge–U.S. District Judge W.A. Bootle of Alabama had been assigned to replace Judge Wilson in the Burnside case and wanted me to call him. I had no choice.

At the beginning of our telephone conversation Judge Bootle requested that I provide him with a memorandum outlining the details of the Burnside case so he could review it before trial. I explained I was in a remote location in New York State and had not planned to return to Tennessee until Sunday–the day before trial. Bootle's response caught me by surprise.

"That's fine, just come by my hotel room when you arrive in Chattanooga Sunday evening. I'm staying at the Sheraton. You can tell me then what the case is about."

After a delightful family reunion on Saturday afternoon at Reid and Louise Barton's (my cousins) my family foursome departed for Tennessee. We spent the night in Virginia and arrived back in Knoxville late Sunday afternoon. By 6 p.m. I had packed my suitcase, grabbed my briefcase and hit the road to Chattanooga.

By 8 p.m. I had checked into the Sheraton Hotel. I found Judge Bootle's room. He greeted me at the door, invited me in and offered me a drink and a comfortable seat. We engaged in what I would describe as "banter" about the case to be tried the following day. After an hour or so Judge Bootle thanked me for updating him on the case and I departed. A most unusual proceding–even for a jury trial.

The trial commenced on Monday August 4. Judge Bootle presided and a six person jury–three men and three women was seated. The University's proof was rather mundane, consisting of itemization of amounts paid and those remaining due. Then, there was the testimony of Mrs. Messick who testified at length to the high quality of the orchid plants in her nursery – all of which had produced and were capable of producing orchids!

The Burnside's proof included introduction of six orchid plants into evidence. The potted plants were placed on a table, roughly equidistant between the judge's bench, the jury box and tables for the plaintiff and the defense.

The six plants were the focus of everyone's attention– "stars of the show."

They were from the truckload of plants taken from the Messick Nursery by the Burnsides. Amazingly, Mrs. Messick not only recognized the plants but knew each by name. One was "Princess Blue Bells." Each plant had a similarly attractive name. I asked Mrs. Messick–seated next to me at counsel's table - if she observed any defect in the plants. She did not. This was good. My game plan to this point was to insist there were no defects in the plants and that the Burnside's had simply failed to pay the amount due.

The defense called as its last witness Mr. F. L. Stephenson. Stephenson was the president of the American Orchid Growers Association.

Stephenson was asked by counsel for the Burnsides to leave the witness stand, approach the table on which the orchids had been placed and examine the plants. He did so, then returned to the witness stand after inspecting the plants for several minutes.

"Have you ever seen those plants before today?" asked the Burnside's attorney. "No," Stephenson replied. "Will those plants produce blooms?" "No." Stephenson was certain that none of the six plants would produce blooms.

There was no point in having my key witness, Mrs. Messick, return to the witness stand. If she agreed with Stephenson we would lose; if she disagreed with him it was unlikely the jury would accept her testimony over that of the president of the American Orchid Growers Association. Time for a change in game plan.

"Mr Stevenson, I noticed that it only took you a couple of minutes to inspect the plants and determine that the plants would not produce orchids," I observed on cross examination. "That is correct," he replied.

"Now, you're the president of the American Orchid Growers Association. I know nothing about orchid plants. How long would it take you to teach me how to determine these plants will not produce orchids?" "About ten minutes," Stephenson responded. "Thank you, sir." I had no further questions.

In final argument to the jury I pointed out that the Burnsides were experienced nursery operators. They had driven their truck from Florida to Tennessee. Each orchid plant placed in the truck was selected by the Burnsides. If the plants were defective at the time of selection they would certainly have noticed the defect.

The truck used by the Burnsides was unheated and the weather in Chattanooga was cold when the plants were picked up from Messick Nursery. The cold likely damaged the plants on the long trip to Florida. There was nothing wrong with the plants when the Burnsides made their selection from the stock at the nursery in Chattanooga.

The jury rendered its unanimous verdict at 4p.m. on August 6. The University was awarded $12,041.89 principal balance on the contract and $746.61 in interest. The District Court's judgment, incorporating the jury's verdict, was entered the same day.

Lesson of the day: set a carefully researched course of action but do not hesitate to deviate when necessary. Second lesson: the "other side" may have something of value to say.

MORE CONTRACTUAL AND RELATED MISCELLANY

On January 2, 1979, I traveled to Columbus, Mississippi with Henry Morse, director of UT properties and Henry Guigou, with UT development. We attended the closing on the "Reagan property" -a gift to the University of Tennessee–yielding $2.7 million for the University.

In July 1979, I proposed a number of amendments to a draft contract between UT and FMPC (Faculty Medical Professional Corporation). One recommendation was that the contract "be simplified by eliminating the page and a half of whereases (pages 1-2)."

UT v. DR. CHARLES GROSS

While the University recognized the value of having medical faculty receive compensation for treating "paying patients" at UT medical facilities, the University imposed income limits so as to assure that medical faculty not ignore their teaching and research responsibilities. A 1978 case involving a member of the UTCHS medical faculty, Dr. Charles Gross, made that point.

Suit was filed in Shelby County Circuit Court on October 25, 1978, seeking recovery from Dr. Gross of money he received for "private practice" in excess of limits imposed by the University. Gross was represented by Memphis attorney Irvin Salky.

A motion for summary judgment, filed on behalf of the University, was denied by the Circuit Court in 1979. The matter was set for trial by jury on February 13, 1981(and later reset to October 6). On July 29 Salky called to offer settlement of the case in the full amount of UT's claim, $16,140.

On September 21, 1981-one week before the scheduled trial–I met Salky in his office and received a check in the full amount of UT's claim. I signed an order of dismissal which Salky filed with the Court. University of Tennessee v. Dr. Charles Gross , No. 84677 (Shelby Circuit 1981).

Years later–I don't recall the exact year–Dr. Gross presented to the UT Board of Trustees an appeal challenging the limit placed on his "private practice" earnings. I attended the board meeting at which his appeal was presented. I will not soon forget the commentary provided by UT Trustee Bill Johnson. While not a quote the following is close: "Dr Gross, I agree with you. You should be able to earn as much money as you want - you just can't do that and still work for the University of Tennessee."

In my personal opinion, Trustee Johnson's statement should have been enshrined and placed throughout the University for all to see. A University employee's need for reasonable income commensurate with experience and position is understood. However, the University's primary focus should be on education, research and public service. Any employee or recruit whose primary focus is on amassing income best serves the University by going elsewhere.

GO THE EXTRA MILE TO GET THE JOB DONE–
UT v. RON TALIAFERRO

Ron Taliaferro had a research related contract with the UT Research Corporation back in the late 1970s. Under the contract a particular research development was to be marketed by Taliaferro with royalties paid to the University. In 1981 Taliaferro stopped making agreed upon royalty payments. In addition, he moved to Texas–or moved locations in Texas–so that he could not be located.

The UT Research Corporation not only was deprived of the royalties due from Taliaferro, it was also unable to market the product through anyone else since Taliaferro held contract rights.

On December 9, 1981 I filed a complaint on behalf of the UT Research Corporation with the U.S. District Court in Knoxville. The lawsuit against Taliaferro requested a finding that the contract had been breached – was therefore null and void – and an award of damages in the amount of $12,252.69 plus interest for unpaid royalties.

One major hurdle prevented the litigation from proceeding. Repeated attempts to serve process on Taliaferro through the U.S. Marshals Office failed. I applied to U.S. District Judge Robert Taylor for appointment as a process server – a U.S. Marshal – for the purpose of serving process on Taliaferro. By order of April 15, 1982 Judge Taylor granted my request.

Repeated attempts to contact Taliaferro by telephone and mail failed. I obtained several residential addresses for him but it appeared he was constantly relocating to avoid service of process by creditors, including the UT Research Corporation. In early May I made a final decision to personally track him down in Texas–concurrent with the opening of the 1982 Worlds Fair in Knoxville.

I flew to Houston, Texas, arriving at 4:45 a.m. the morning of May 3. After renting a vehicle I commenced my tour of Houston and investigated several locations where Taliaferro had lived in the past–confirming only that he no longer resided at any of those locations. Then, fortuitously, I located a neighborhood where a "Taliaferro" was reported to reside.

I encountered a young lady walking her dog near the address given and told her I'd come to visit "Ron" but perhaps he had moved. The young lady kindly advised me that it was his sister who resided nearby but she had moved. However, the young lady had the sister's new address and provided it to me. A very unexpected gift.

By midafternoon I located the new address, knocked on the door and found no one home. Mail in the mailbox confirmed the residence to be that of Taliaferro's sister. I departed and met a friend at her office - former UT Memphis auditor Maureen Witt who had relocated to Houston to take an auditing job there.

During an early dinner I explained why I was in Houston and asked if she would like to accompany me as I attempted to locate my target and serve process on him. She readily agreed–she had a truly adventurous spirit as an auditor and loved a challenge.

After dinner Witt and I drove out to Taliaferro's sister's. Still no one home. We parked across from the residence–a second-floor apartment – turned off the car lights and reviewed "old times" at UT. Around 8:30 or 9 pm a middle-aged lady arrived, walked up the stairs to the apartment and entered. Presumably the sister.

Leaving Witt in the automobile as a lookout, with process papers and Marshall identification in hand, I approached the apartment and knocked on the door. A lady opened the door and I stated I was looking for her brother. "I'm the housekeeper," the lady replied. "Mr. Taliaferro should be here in a little while." No mention of the sister's whereabouts but that was not a particular concern of mine.

At this point I identified myself is a federal marshal and stated that I would take a seat by the door and await Taliaferro's arrival. The lady seemed genuinely disinterested in my presence and went about her business, cleaning the apartment.

I spent the next hour or so in a straight back chair a foot or so from the door I had entered. Basically "twiddling my thumbs."

At exactly 10:05 PM I heard a key being inserted in the door lock. The door opened and a middle-aged white gentlemen walked in–rather shocked to see me standing at the doorway. "Mr Taliaferro," I announced–not questioned. "Yes, " he replied. "I'm a U.S. Marshall and I have something for you.." I then handed him court papers I had been duly authorized to serve on him.

I departed the apartment, returned to my rental vehicle where Witt was waiting and drove her back to her own vehicle. After thanking Witt for her company and assistance I proceeded directly to the airport. I caught a late night flight, first to Atlanta then to Knoxville, arriving home at 7:30 in the morning of May 4. Later that day I returned to the court certification that process had been served.

I had a good laugh when, several days later, I received a phone call from Taliaferro. "I don't know if you're aware but a federal marshal served process on me several days ago." Then, for the first time, Taliaferro expressed an interest in discussing settlement. In this case, "too little, too late." I declined his offer. He filed a "motion to dismiss" the lawsuit against him with the District Court in Knoxville.

Judge Taylor conducted a hearing on the parties' motions on July 2, 1982. Taliaferro did not appear for the hearing. Taylor denied Taliaferro's motion and entered judgment in favor of the UT Research Corporation, awarding the $12,552.69 requested and 8% interest from December 9, 1981.

The excellent result reached in this contract action was well worth the atypical effort expended. To my knowledge, Taliaferro never learned the identity of the U.S. marshall who visited his sister's residence the evening of May 3.

J B DICKS AND THE UT SPACE INSTITUTE PROBE

Use of University property for personal gain was a definite no-no. As reported in the December 9, 1981 edition of the Tullahoma News & Guardian, p. 16-A.

> A University of Tennessee investigation of possible misuse of UT Space Institute equipment and personnel concentrated on one Tullahoma firm and other "spinoff" industries at the Institute, a UT official said this week.
> The investigation, conducted by Ron Leadbetter, UT Associate General Counsel, resulted in a report recently by the state comptroller's office critical of John B. Dicks and Associates for its use of the Institute's equipment and personnel in carrying out energy research projects.
> ***
> "The good thing is I found out there was that there was not a hornets nest with all sorts of things going on," Leadbetter said.

The investigation had been initiated at the instance of UTSI Dean Charles Weaver. My investigation of "rumors" of inappropriate use of University equipment and personnel proved largely unfounded. Minor misunderstandings of University policy regarding use of University equipment and personnel were immediately corrected.

UT v. PROFESSIONAL FOOD SERVICES MANAGEMENT

In October 1981 I filed suit on behalf of the University to collect profits due from Professional Food Service Management, Inc. ("PFM") under an agreement with the University for operation of food services in the University Center at UT Center for Health Sciences. At issue was whether PFM had improperly excluded UT – paid staff in determining operating costs and whether PFM was entitled to income from all University Center vending machines.

It also requested that the court award interest at the legal rate (8%) on unpaid revenue due the University from the date UT terminated its contract with PFM.

PFM filed a counter claim against the University, claiming it was due additional income from the contract. Memphis attorney Ron Krelstein represented PFM.

Shelby County Chancery James Tharpe held trial on July 17 – 18, 1984. Judge Tharpe's findings in favor of the University, awarding damages in the amount of $25,712.69, were issued on October 1. Judgment for the University was entered on October 29, 1984. University of Tennessee v. Professional Food Service Management, Inc. No. 95859 TD (Shelby Circuit, Div. III, 1984). PFM appealed the Chancery judgment to the Tennessee Court of Appeals, Western Section.

On January 6, 1986 the appellate court (appellate judges Hewitt Tomlin, Frank Crawford and Alan Highers) entered judgment for the University, affirming the court judgment below. University of Tennessee v. Professional Food Service Management, Inc., Shelby Equity No. 70 (Tenn. App. 1986).

The appellate court made clear the importance of a well-written contract:

> We begin with the invitation to bid or request for proposals and move from
> that document to the contract itself. Both documents are clear. They state that
> it is the intent of UT to secure "a professional management service program
> to manage the food service operations of its Center for the Health Sciences...."
> Both documents clearly describe the food service operations – that is, the
> cafeteria, the faculty dining room, the snack bar, and two sandwich machines.

Id. p.5.

The appellate court concurred with the trial court's rejection of PFM's claim that it was entitled to revenue from video games, cigarette machines, laundry machines and even soda machines not directly related to serving food. As the Court of Appeals added, "it would make almost as much sense for PFM to claim fees from the operation of a park–for–pay parking lot as it would for commissions derived from the operation of video amusement machines."

Id. p.6.

Rejected by the Court of Appeals was PFM's claim that UT utilized "reckless accounting practices." Also rejected was PFM's claim that management costs attributed to UT employees should not have been included as operating expenses. Id. p.8.

The appeals court also rejected PFM's claim that there were certain oral agreements supporting its position. "The contract as negotiated between UT and PFM clearly stated that the books and records of UT were open and available to PFM at any time. PFM never chose to avail itself of the opportunity to determine from those records what was and what was not included as income from food sales. Id. p. 11.

PFM's claims of fraud and misrepresentation on the part of UT were likewise rejected. "Again, we heartily concur with the trial court as to fraud and misrepresentation PFM has failed to carry the burden of proof, and the trial court's findings pertaining to these oral representations are clearly supported by the evidence." Id.

Finally, the appeals court affirmed the trial court's award of prejudgment interest dating back to the date of termination of the agreement – November 30, 1979–rather than the date suit was filed. "Awarding prejudgment interest is left to the discretion of the trial court". Id. p.12.

A hard-fought contract action with a good result! This was a rare instance in which a University contractor refused to meet its contractual commitments.

UNIVERSITY PHYSICIANS FOUNDATION

In 1983 I prepared an "Affiliation Agreement between the University of Tennessee and University Physicians Foundation, Inc." and in 1987 I prepared a similar document for a UT agreement with the Tennessee Pharmacists Foundation, Inc. the purpose of both documents was to facilitate income for UT faculty from private practice but with certain limitations to assure that such practice had monetary limits and did not interfere with faculty education and research responsibilities.

In 1988 UTCHS Chancellor Jim Hunt and the UT system administration reached accord that an agreement should be developed for UPF management of the UT Medical Center–William F Bowld Hospital–in Memphis. In a memorandum of November 14, 1988, Hunt advised Executive Vice President Joe Johnson:

> We will proceed with the development of the "contractual" relationship between the University Physicians Foundation and the UTMC at Memphis, involving Ron Leadbetter to assist Steve Burkett and Ray Colson in developing the document. We will hold any announcement concerning Steve Burkett's appointment as Vice Provost until we have a mutually agreed upon document.
>
> We will ask Ron Leadbetter to assist us in finalizing the renewal of the contract among the Shelby County Healthcare Corporation (SCHCC), the University Physicians Foundation (UPF) and the University of Tennessee.

UPF had its own attorney involved in the contract development process. Although UPF and the University had many mutual goals (patient care, education and research), they were separate legal entities. As a matter of integrity, it was my responsibility to assure the University's legal interests were well protected. In that regard, I related a "conflict of interest" concern involving the appointment of Burkett as both director of the Bowld hospital (and employee of UPF) and as Vice Provost of UT Memphis having primary responsibility for representing the University in matters relating to the Hospital.

My concern was expressed to Vice President Johnson in a January 1989 memorandum, "Both Steve and I agreed that this dual role would constitute an apparent, if not actual, conflict of interest; there is no way that Steve could represent the University and see to it that UPF fulfills its role as manager of the Hospital while, at the same time, serving as UPF's top administrator at the Bowld Hospital." The problem was resolved and Burkett was not placed in a compromising position.

The requested document was drafted and final agreement reached by the parties. Under the agreement, UPF assumed responsibility for managing the Medical Center. The University retained ownership of all assets of the Center. It was further agreed that the net revenues from the Center would be retained by the Medical Center and "expended under the auspices of the University to enhance the mission and goals of Medical Center at Memphis". UPF would be compensated for its management services.

A final agreement between UT and UPS (as well as Shelby County Healthcare Corporation) was executed in June 1989. The agreement was implemented and, to my knowledge, administered without any complications of a legal nature.

FLEETWOOD FLOP

My last contract case was one which remained active at the time I retired to run for State office. In my absence the University took the easy way out.

Fleetwood One Hour Photo, Inc. filed a claim with the Tennessee Claims Commission against UT in August 2006 claiming UT had breached a UT Knoxville purchasing agreement to purchase a "market basket" of items from Fleetwood at greatly reduced prices. Damages in the amount of $575,000 was sought.

According to Fleetwood's complaint every single purchase of photographic services was contractually required to be made from Fleetwood. A UT faculty member was not free to secure photographic services on his own, at any time for any reason in Fleetwood's view.

After reviewing "bid" documents, UT's purchasing agreement with Fleetwood and meeting with UT purchasing and business officials it was clear to me Fleetwood's claim lacked merit. Plaintiff's depositions of Purchasing Director Jerry Wade and UT finance officer Cindy Stockdale, confirmed my belief.

While there is no such thing as a case that cannot be lost, I was of the opinion there was little chance of an adverse ruling in this case. The fact that a motion to dismiss filed in August 2007 and a motion for summary judgment filed in

March 2008 were denied, did nothing to change that opinion. Denial of the summary judgment motion simply meant there existed "some" material evidence which "could" lead a rational fact finder to rule in favor of Fleetwood. I felt the odds were heavily against that possibility.

The University took no chances. After my retirement I learned the case was settled, following arbitration, for around $99,000 plus payment of arbitration fees. Perhaps I missed some critical piece of evidence. Or perhaps it was just easier to "cave" and avoid even the possibility of a blemish on the University's litigation record. Of course, that assumes a needless settlement is not a blemish.

Chapter 65–Student Right-to-Know and Campus Security Act of 1990

Roughly concurrent with my responsibility for University compliance with federal legislation concerning illicit drugs and alcohol was my responsibility for compliance with the Tennessee College and University Security Information Act of 1989 and the federal Student Right to Know and Campus Security Act of 1990.

Vice President Joe Johnson issued a memorandum on May 26, 1989 to all University chancellors, the Dean of the University of Tennessee Space Institute, Dick Roberts, all chief student affairs officers and me, providing a copy of the state law and advising that "Ron Leadbetter is to work with campus and institute officials to be sure we follow the law." By memorandum of February 15, 1991 I provided Vice Presidents Joe Johnson, Homer Fisher and Pete Gossett, all chancellors, and all Vice chancellors for student affairs a copy of the federal legislation and a five-page outline of crime data required to be maintained by each campus and contents to be included in annual reports provided to each student and employee, as well as the Department of Education on request.

It was my responsibility to review all annual crime reports. On rare occasion I called for correction of data that had been fudged.

The federal campus security act was amended in 1997 to require that campus crime reports report crime statistics on a calendar year rather than academic year basis. Crime occurrences rather than arrests were to be reported. Arson was to be added to the list of reportable occurrences. Finally, crime occurrences in non–campus buildings and property and "reasonably contiguous" public property, as well as the campus itself, were required to be reported.

While compliance with federal and state crime reporting legislation was admittedly a bit of a nuisance, I viewed it as being of considerable value to the public. A friend and neighbor, S.Daniel Carter, was hugely responsible for enactment of the state legislation and was active in monitoring compliance with the federal legislation. He served as a leader of the national organization, Clery Center of Security on Campus. We worked together well on a number of minor issues that arose from time to time concerning UT annual crime reports.

Possibly my last involvement in monitoring University compliance with campus crime reporting related to compliance with the "Victims of Trafficking and Violence Protection Act of 2000." The Act required that college and university crime reports be revised to include information concerning state–registered sex offenders. I notified appropriate University officials of the need to revise UT crime reports by October 28, 2002, the effective date of the new law.

Chapter 66–UT Role in War on Drugs

LSD was the drug of choice of a good number of my classmates during the late 1960s and early '70s. One of my colleagues in student government, while under the influence of LSD, attempted to leap from an upper floor window in Laurel Avenue married students apartments where my wife and I resided during law school. Someone had "spiked something he had eaten at a party" with LSD.

While transporting a young lady friend from McGhee-Tyson Airport to campus I received a thorough education in the benefits and harmless, non-addictive qualities of cocaine. In less than a year the young lady was dead; a cocaine overdose being the culprit.

Martha, one of my far left political adversaries, nevertheless a friend, was another student. She was an unabashed fan of marijuana and other mind altering drugs. In May 1980, I learned that her body had been discovered in an apartment off campus. She had apparently been dead for three or four days from a self–inflicted gunshot wound. I was quite shocked. (Knoxville News-Sentinel, May 13, 1980, p. 14). I was not surprised to hear the suicide was drug-related.

My position within the Office of General Counsel offered me a very welcome opportunity to actively combat something I perceived as a scourge on society –a cancerous tumor to be removed before infecting and corrupting the University community. On the list of "legal categories" for which I was responsible throughout the "Big Orange" years was assuring compliance with federal and state law governing possession and sale of illicit drugs, and administrative prosecution of violators. I received strong support for my efforts from the University administration.

University regulations published within campus personnel policy and procedures manuals and student handbooks made clear that possession or sale of illicit drugs on campus was prohibited. During the course of my career I administratively prosecuted many violations of that prohibition. I did not maintain a listing of such administrative proceedings prior to 1982, and did not include such cases in my case card catalog unless the matter proceeded to state or federal court. Several summary observations are still possible.

While alcohol abuse was a common problem throughout the years of my employment rarely did a student charged with an alcohol offense request a formal hearing. Only on one or two occasions did I participate in informal hearings available to those who waved their right to proceed under the administrative procedures act. On average I handled less than one alcohol related administrative proceeding each year. None made the headlines.

With respect to possession or sale of illicit drugs, there were far fewer cases than those involving alcohol related charges but a far higher percentage of those charged with a drug related violation requested a formal hearing. There were, roughly, five drug cases for every four alcohol-related cases presented for formal hearing. And a number of drug cases made the headlines.

DRUG INVOLVEMENT NOT TAKEN LIGHTLY–
JAMES ALLEN BREWER

My earliest record of active involvement in a drug investigation was a diary entry dated June 10, 1975 with explanatory file card entries.

On June 10, I traveled to Memphis to confer with Dr. Pat Wall, regarding an applicant to the College of Medicine and the applicant's suspected involvement with illegal drugs. The next day I met with several faculty members at Lambuth College in Jackson, Tennessee who were familiar with the applicant, James Allen Brewer. My visit to Lambuth concluded with a meeting with the Dean of Men and Lieutenant Jackie Moore a former narcotics officer with the Jackson Police Department. Based on the information received, I scheduled a meeting with the applicant himself.

On June 24, 1975, I met with Brewer but learned nothing favorable. I drafted a letter from the Dean of College of medicine advising Brewer he was denied admission but had the right to a hearing to contest his rejection. The letter was issued by the Dean on July 1.

On July 18 Brewer received a hearing before a five-member committee of faculty from the College of Medicine. Brewer testified at the hearing, as did Jackson Police Chief Marcon, "Lieutenant Moore" and "Sergeant Holt." The intriguing testimony is summarized on my case card.

- 3 –4 years ago Brewer dropped out of school

- 4 years ago or more–LSD trip; (Lt. Moore can confirm), ran naked in public.

Mother and Dr. Baker Hubbard (Jackson–Madison Co. Hosp.) picked him up (he was naked again).

***

4:30 PM, June 1, 1974 – on basis of informants tips, Lt. Jackie Moore & Sgt. Bobby Holt staked out house on Northside (runs parallel to Muse St.) car had been to Memphis to pick 1 pound of marijuana.

When car came down St., Jim got out on forest. Police followed car; Mike threw grass out; police arrested him (bag had his initials). Mike insisted that the marijuana was his –would not implicate Jim. Mike admitted that Jim had gone to Memphis with him. House used by Jim and Danny Ward (arrested later for growing marijuana); Mike said he was bringing the grass to the house (frequented by known drug users)

The committee unanimously voted to affirm denial of Brewer's application for admission to the College of Medicine. And so concluded my first drug case.

FOOTBALL PLAYERS TONY ROBINSON AND B.B. COOPER

In 1985 UT quarterback Tony Robinson was considered by many a candidate for the Heisman Trophy. An injury to his right leg during the 1985 season took Robinson out of the running for the trophy. His poor choice of ways to spend his time away from class and football did far more damage.

On February 10, 1986, I met in my office with Knoxville Metro narcotics officers, Captain Stan Bullen, Captain Jerry Day and Mike Duncan. They provided me details of the January 8 arrest of Robinson and teammate Kenneth B. B. Cooper on a total of eight charges of sale and distribution of narcotics (cocaine). The sales were reportedly made to an undercover police agent at the Paper Mill Square Apartments off-campus on November 8,1985 and January 7 and 8, 1986.

The following day, February 11, I met with athletic director Doug Dickey, Vice Chancellor for Student Affairs Phil Scheurer and General Counsel Beach Brogan. I brought them up to date on the evidence supporting the charges against Robinson and Cooper. There was unanimous concurrence that administrative disciplinary charges should be issued against both.

UT Knoxville Chancellor Jack Reese issued letters charging Robinson and Cooper with violating the campus code of student conduct. Each was charged with conduct violating the rule published in the student rights and responsibilities section of "Hill Topics" prohibiting "the sale, distribution, manufacture and possession for sale or distribution, owned any drug in violation of federal law, or the Tennessee Drug Control Act of 1971." The accused were warned that possible penalties ranged from a warning to indefinite suspension or dismissal from the University.

Both Robinson and Cooper were advised of their right to a hearing of the charge against them. Each opted to be heard and each elected to proceed in accordance with the Tennessee Administrative Procedures Act rather than the informal procedures set forth in the student handbook, "Hill Topics."

Robinson was represented by Knoxville attorneys Robert Ritchie and Tim Priest, Priest being a former UT football player and his is the voice often heard on the radio giving play-by-play accounts during UT football games. Cooper was represented by Knoxville attorney Don Coffey. "Not guilty" pleas were entered by both of the accused.

Chancellor Jack Reese appointed Dr. Francis Gross, UT Associate Vice Provost and Director of Management Services (also referred to as "Chief Auditor") as hearing examiner. The hearing was scheduled for May 23 and, in accordance with the APA, was open to the public.

The hearing for Robinson was held on May 13, 1986. Metro narcotics officer Mike Duncan testified that he was tipped off to Cooper's and Robinson's drug activities by a paid informant and holder of a past criminal history, Donnie Dockery. It was Dockery who arranged the drug transactions between the accused and Duncan. Dockery had been subpoenaed to appear at the hearing but did not show.

Duncan testified during the five-hour hearing that Cooper took a more active role in promoting the drug transactions than Robinson, but that Robinson was still present during some of the transactions and was personally involved. On one occasion, January 7, Robinson took a bag with nearly two grams of cocaine from the hem of his sweatpants and handed it to Duncan, is saying it was "good"- clearly evidencing his awareness that it was cocaine. Duncan also testified that Robinson referred to Cooper as his partner "T–Rob" and that Robinson had put up $220 to purchase cocaine when Duncan was short of cash.

Richie argued that Robinson was "entrapped." Robinson elected not to testify at the hearing. I addressed both Richie's argument and Robinson's failure to testify, as noted in the next day's edition of the Knoxville Journal Newspaper.

Richie's allegation of police entrapment of Robinson was disputed by UT's Associate General Counsel Ron Leadbetter.

"My own personal view is that entrapment is a non-issue. More than that, the evidence is clear that Mr. Robinson was not entrapped," Leadbetter said. Only Duncan testified during the hearing, which was attended by Robinson and his mother. "Robinson's lack of testimony," Leadbetter said, "could be a factor in what punishments for Robinson the University requests from Gross."

(The Knoxville Journal, May 14, 1986, p.1. "Police 'induced' Robinson to sell drugs–attorney").

I explained to the press, "Common sense tells you violation of the law takes place at the time of the act. Entrapment is a defense for a criminal charge. It is not a defense at an administrative hearing. You don't sell cocaine lawfully because you're entrapped. You won't be convicted, but you're still breaking the law." (The Daily Beacon, May 14, 1986,p.1. "Robinson hearing delayed for witness").

Gross afforded Robinson an opportunity to secure the testimony of the informant, Dockery. I objected to a continuance of the hearing in order for Dockery to be subpoenaed. I made what some might consider a bold pronouncement in order to avoid unnecessary delay.

UT counsel Ronald Leadbetter, however, convinced Gross that the absence of Dockery did not require a postponement of the hearing for Dockery to be subpoenaed again.

"I'm willing to stipulate he would say everything he (Richie) says he will say. But I don't see any reason for a postponement." Leadbetter said.

Id.

Around May 23 a document containing the stipulated testimony of Dockery, signed by Richie and me, was filed with the hearing officer. The document noted that Dockery had been charged with criminal offenses in 1982 (burglary), 1985 (shoplifting) and 1986 (drunk driving). It also contained a statement that Dockery was "totally surprised and shocked" that Robinson was charged with possession of cocaine for resale in the University disciplinary letter. In my opinion, nothing Dockery said mattered.

UT's attorney said that although he signed the document, it does not mean that he agrees with the statement or its wording.

"In a stipulation you're saying it's not worth arguing about," said Leadbetter. "As a practical matter, we're not going to have a hearing whether every word is accurate. We're basically saying it doesn't matter if everything in there is true."

"You will not see a statement by Dockery that he got Cooper and Robinson to sell drugs and they didn't want to do." He said, "Our whole position is they willingly made these sales to make money."

(The Knoxville News-Sentinel, May 22, 1986, p. 1,"Informant 'surprised' by Robinson arrest").

The hearing for Cooper to place on May 23. The University's proof was essentially the same. Cooper did not testify. In final argument, I submitted that Cooper should be indefinitely suspended from the university.

Coffey argued that the University lacked jurisdiction over Cooper and Robinson because the accused acts occurred off-campus. I responded that the UT student code of conduct applied to drug sales off-campus. He also argued that the University should take no action because criminal charges were pending. I replied that the University had no obligation to await disposition of criminal charges before enforcing its disciplinary rules.

Hearing officer Francis Gross issued his initial order on August 8, 1986 finding both Cooper and Robinson guilty of the disciplinary charges against them. As reported by the media the penalties differed. Cooper was indefinitely suspended while Robinson was suspended for the fall quarter.

"Although Cooper was given the maximum penalty allowed under Hill topics, UT's student code of conduct, Robinson's penalty was less severe because he was the 'lesser partner' in alleged drug sales," said Ron Leadbetter, UT associate General Counsel.

"I think it has probably been apparent to everybody… That he (Cooper) was the senior partner and that Tony was the junior partner," Leadbetter said.

(The Knoxville News-Sentinel, August 9, 1986, p. 1,"UT suspends Cooper, bars Robinson for term").

Both Robinson and Cooper were subsequently convicted of criminal charges and sentenced respectively to 90 days and 150 days in the Knox County Penal Farm, with the remainder of their six and eight year sentences, respectively, to be served on probation.

One final point, contrary to an argument Coffey made during the Cooper hearing: neither the administrative prosecution nor the penalties requested by me were influenced in any way by Robinson and Cooper's status as athletes. Although I am and have always been a UT athletics fan I refused to ever let that influence my handling of legal matters involving athletes or athletics

Post note: Another APA hearing of drug charges against a UT Knoxville student was heard on April 18, 1986, a little more than one month before the Cooper hearing. The hearing officer issued an "initial order" on June 5, finding the student guilty of the charge against him and assessing my recommended penalty of "indefinite suspension." From this anecdotal evidence one should conclude that the University neither penalized nor rewarded "athlete status" when handling violations of UT regulations concerning illegal drugs. Integrity would not permit such distinction.

TACTICS FOR COMBATING THE DRUG CHALLENGE

I found good relations with law enforcement most helpful in addressing drug issues on campus. I became acquainted with FBI agent Clyde Merryman during workouts at the UT Aquatic Center. He was a good source of information in identifying drug violators in the University community.

A front-page article published in the Knoxville Journal on August 26, 1986 ("UT athletic probe queried FBI narc"), made no reference to the recently concluded Robinson and Cooper hearings, but noted my contact with Merriman in relation to a recently concluded investigation of possible infractions of rules of the National Collegiate Athletic Association.

Clyde Merryman was on a list of witnesses that UT released Friday with its final report on the six–month athletics probe of alleged gifts and ticket sales among UT athletes and boosters.

***

Philip A. Scheurer, chairman of the four–member investigating committee and vice chancellor of student affairs, declined to say what the rumors concerned or who suggested Merryman be interviewed.

***

Ronald C. Leadbetter, UT Associate General Counsel and a member of the [investigative] committee, said, "The rumors had nothing to do with athletic boosters or national collegiate athletic Association violations."
Leadbetter described his contact with Merryman as "very brief."
"The information we discussed was information I was trying to confirm and I could not do so," said Leadbetter. "He shared with me information he had which was not of a nature that we could do anything with it."

***

Merryman is one of two agents who lived in Knoxville more than 18 months under assumed names while working undercover on the drug related cases of two East Tennessee Sheriffs.

Networking and relationship building with law enforcement offered one means of combating drugs on campus; networking and relationship building with those on the other side offered another.

DRUG TESTING OF ATHLETES

During 1985, as the result of discussions with other higher education attorneys involved with intercollegiate athletics, I became acutely aware of developing interest in having athletes tested for illegal drug use. A few higher ed institutions may have already instituted drug testing for their athletes.

I drafted a proposed drug testing program for UT athletes and presented it to Tim Kerin, Head Trainer for UT men's athletics, for his review and input. A few days later I mentioned my proposal for drug testing to Vice President Joe Johnson. He vetoed the idea, for the time being, because no other institution in the Southeast conference had such a program, not even Alabama.

Months later, in January 1986 I attended the mid-winter NACUA–Stetson (higher education law) conference in Clearwater, Florida. One of the presenters was a good friend, Paul Dee, University of Miami General Counsel (who later served as U. Miami Athletic Director from 1993 to 2008).

Dee's presentation to an auditorium packed with University attorneys concerned drug testing of athletes. He reviewed a program that had recently been adopted at Miami. After he completed his presentation I approached Dee and congratulated him on a fascinating presentation. I asked if he would be willing to provide me a copy of the Miami testing program. He laughed.

"Do you know where I got my program?" "No," I replied. "From Tim Kerin. He said you developed it." In the not-too-distant future UT Incorporated a drug testing program using the guidelines I developed. Miami beat UT to the punch with our help.

FEDERAL LEGISLATION

UT leadership during the "Big Orange" years was quite serious in combating illegal drugs on campus. Enactment of two pieces of federal legislation helped encourage that commitment and served to document UT's efforts.

In 1988 Congress enacted the Drug-Free Workplace Act requiring that federal contractors act to control use and possession of illicit drugs on campus. As noted at the outset of this chapter, the University already had such regulations in place in both its employee manuals and student handbooks.

The Drug-free Schools and Communities Act of 1989 was enacted by Congress the following year. UT personnel policy and procedures manuals and student handbooks required only minimal revision, to include "unlawful possession, use or distribution of alcohol."

In addition, it was required that the the University develop a method of annually notifying employees and students of the University's rules prohibiting unlawful possession, use or distribution of drugs and alcohol, applicable penalties under local, state or federal law for violations, health risks associated with the use of illicit drugs and abuse of alcohol, available counseling and treatment programs available to university employees and students and a clear statement that the University will impose penalties on students and employees violating standards of conduct governing drugs and alcohol.

A biennial review of the University's compliance with the law was also required.

As noted in a March 19, 1990 memorandum from Executive Vice President Joe Johnson to UT Memphis Vice Chancellor for Student Affairs Bill Robinson:

> Bill, I appreciate very much your thoughtfulness in writing to ask Ron Leadbetter and me for guidance on ways to respond to the... letter from the U.S. Department of Education on requirements of the 1989 Drug Free Schools and [Communities] Act. ... .
>
> We do not want to go off in several different directions on framing language and policies to get in line with this act. Accordingly, Ron has been asked to work with our personnel, student affairs, and faculty officials to reach accord, direction, and the wording at the statewide level and at campuses and institutes.

I served as coordinator of compliance efforts with respect to both federal acts. Working with campus student affairs officers, it was my responsibility to assure that the required biennial review reports were correctly prepared for each campus and submitted to the federal government in a timely fashion. The job got done and the University received no complaints of noncompliance from the federal government.

Chapter 67–The Drug War in Memphis–Gilbert vs. UT

In the latter part of 1980 I learned from Bill Derrington, Chief of Police for the UT Center for the Health Sciences, illegal drugs were being sold on campus. Suspicion focused on a number of university employees including a University police officer and one or more employees in the UTCHS business office, where students went to pay fees and conduct other financial transactions.

On January 15, 1981, a strategy session was held in my office in the UTCHs administration building at the corner of Union and Dunlap Avenues in Memphis. Attending the meeting were Vice Chancellor for Business Robert Blackwell, University internal auditor Maureen Witt, two drug agents with the Shelby County Sheriff's Department, Warren Young and Jim Zachary, and me. We agreed that we would meet on a regular basis and keep our meetings secret while drug reports were investigated. The "secret" aspect sometimes came close to failing

For example, on February 27, 1981, a meeting of the initial group, along with Chief Derrington and police Inspector John Butler, was held in my office. It was Blackwell's birthday. As we were seated around my conference table, discussing investigation strategy, we heard a knock on the door to my office. Blackwell got up, went to the door and cracked it open.

To our surprise a noisy group in the hallway pushed its way in with a young lady who turned out to be a striptease dancer. The business office had decided to surprise Blackwell with an unscheduled bit of entertainment. We opted to let the entertainment proceed. There was not actually a complete striptease. After the celebration concluded and Blackwell's co-workers left my office, along with the unexpected guest, we resumed our meeting. The secret mission of the group had not been compromised.

At the end of February we included in our group a young lady by the name of Leslie. The plan was for her to be employed as an undercover agent in the cashier's office. She did an excellent job. The investigative group met on several more occasions between late February and early May. Then we met with Leslie one last time. We all had a good laugh as Leslie shared that the chief cashier and his top assistant had advised her to be careful in handling any illegal drugs because it was rumored that law enforcement agents were making inquiries about the presence of drugs on campus.

Arrest warrants were served on a number of UTCHS employees in mid-May 1981. One of those arrested was Denise Bobbitt, a cashier in the business office. She was charged with possession and sale of illegal drugs (UT drug transactions took place by a a customer approaching a cashier's window and exchanging cash for a paper sack containing illegal narcotics). Bobbitt entered a plea of innocent and was released on bond pending trial.

Although it was rumored that head cashier Gilbert was involved in the illegal drug operation, he remained free for lack of evidence. When arrested, Bobbitt had declined to speak to the arresting officers. There was no evidence of any other person having personal knowledge of Gilbert's involvement in drug trafficking.

I was well acquainted with Denise Bobbitt, as I was with many other UTCHS officials and employees. On May 19, 1981, the morning I learned of Bobbitt's arrest from another friend, Inspector Butler, I advised Butler I would contact Bobbitt and seek her cooperation. Butler chuckled and said, "She won't talk to you". "We'll see," I replied.

I telephoned Bobbitt at home. She did not answer. I hopped in my rental vehicle and drove to her residence. She was not there. I left a hand written note suggesting she contact me, stating my belief that it would be to her benefit.

Later that afternoon, Bobbitt appeared at my office, saying she wanted to talk. I offered my opinion it would be a shame if she suffered a criminal conviction while her boss got off scot-free. She agreed.

I asked Bobbitt for a written statement of her involvement in the illegal drug possession and sales and she provided one. She specifically included transactions between herself and Gilbert. She also agreed to testify against Gilbert at a University administrative hearing. I thanked her for her cooperation but made no commitment in return.

Vice Chancellor Blackwell issued a termination letter to Gilbert the following day-May 20, 1981. The termination was based on Gilbert's alleged purchase and possession of drugs on University premises. Gilbert requested a formal hearing in accordance with the Tennessee Administrative Procedures Act.

UTCHS Chancellor Jim Hunt appointed, Dr. Samuel Bozeman, Executive Assistant to the Chancellor, to conduct the hearing. Bozeman (brother of Knox County Judge Howard Bozeman) was a friend of mine who frequently joined me for coffee or meals. I had trained him as an APA hearing officer.

In preparation for the hearing I met with Butler, Blackwell and investigators Young and Zachary on June 30. Knoxville OGC attorney Karen Brock (daughter of Tennessee Supreme Court Justice Ray Brock and newly hired by the OGC) joined us as part of her training as a new attorney in the OGC. Later the same day Brock and I met with Denise Bobbitt and her attorney, Charles Holt.

The following day, July 1, 1981, Bozeman called the hearing to order in the Chancellor's conference room. After an introductory explanation of procedures to be followed and a reading of the charge letter, each side made a brief opening statement. I was then asked to present the prosecution's case.

My first and primary witness was Denise Bobbitt. She was accompanied by her legal counsel. After being sworn in by the court reporter and responding to a few introductory questions I asked Bobbitt a few brief questions.

Had she been involved with her boss, James Gilbert, in the sale of illegal drugs in the cashier's office? She replied that she had.

I asked her to describe the specific illegal drug she had handled with Gilbert and she did (marijuana). Bobbitt was then asked to state the first time and last time she had engaged in a drug transaction with Gilbert. She gave the dates. I asked nothing further.

Gilbert's attorney, Mark Baretz of West Memphis, Arkansas, commenced his cross-examination by asking Bobbitt what other dates she had been involved in drug sales. She responded, "On the advice of my attorney I refuse to answer that question on the ground it may tend to incriminate me," or words close to that. Additional questions by Baretz were responded to in the same fashion.

I called one or two other very brief witnesses and rested the State's case after 15 minutes or so. Baretz then called Gilbert to testify. He denied any wrongdoing. Both sides presented final arguments and Bozeman adjourned the hearing after announcing he would issue his decision.

On August 3, 1981 Bozeman issued his "findings and conclusions," holding that Gilbert was not guilty of the charge against him and should be reinstated. Bozeman based his holding on his conclusion that Gilbert had been denied the right to cross examine the chief prosecution witness, Bobbitt, since she had refused to answer questions posed by Gilbert's counsel. I appealed Bozeman's finding to Chancellor Hunt.

On September 4, 1981 Hunt wrote Gilbert a letter stating that he had carefully reviewed the record in the matter, as well as Bozeman's findings and recommendations, and that he could not agree with those findings. Hunt found the charges to be fully documented and ruled that Gilbert's employment would be terminated.

Gilbert filed suit in the Chancery Court for Shelby County on October 23, 1981. Both sides filed motions for summary judgment and the motions were argued before Shelby County Chancellor Wil Doran on July 15, 1982.

Chancellor Doran entered judgment in favor of Gilbert on August 13, 1982. He held that "while there may be substantial evidence to support either Dr. Bozeman's and/or Dr. Hunt's decisions, this Court only finds that there is substantial evidence to support Dr. Bozeman's findings."

Chancellor Doran held that Hunt had no right to substitute his judgment for that of Bozeman–and that doing so violated Gilbert's substantive and procedural due process rights. The Chancery Court ordered that Hunt's final order be set aside and that Gilbert be reinstated to his position of cashier in the

UTCH's business office, with compensation for all lost income dating back to his termination on May 20, 1981. James P. Gilbert v. University of Tennessee, et. al. No. 88739-2 (Shelby Chancery, Tennessee 1982).

I filed an appeal on behalf of the University defendants (University of Tennessee, James C Hunt, M.D. individually and as Chancellor of UTCHS) with the Tennessee Court of Appeals, Western section, Tennessee on September 13. Attorney General William Leech, Jr. and Assistant Attorney General Stephen Doughty agreed to be added "of counsel" on the brief filed by the University.

Oral argument before the Court of Appeals was held on January 18, 1983 before appellate judges Charles Nearn, Paul Summers and Frank Crawford.

By unanimous vote, the Court of Appeals entered judgment on January 31, 1983 reversing the Chancery ruling. The panel noted that, under provisions of University regulations promulgated in accordance with the Administrative Procedures Act, "the Chancellor (or President), after reviewing the entire record, shall enter a final decision. " James P. Gilbert v. University of Tennessee, et. al., From the Chancery Court, Shelby County No. 3 (Tenn. App. 1983).

> Contrary to the decision of the trial judge below, the law on this topic is crystal clear that administrative agencies are not bound to accept the findings and recommendations of hearing examiners.

***

> The trial court below stated that "while there may be substantial evidence to support Dr. Bozeman's and/or Dr. Hunt's decisions, this court only finds that there is substantial evidence to support Dr. Bozeman's findings." This holding was improper because Chancellor Hunt's decision was the final agency decision. It was his decision, not Dr. Bozeman's findings, that was subject to review according to the standards of T.C.A. 4–5–117 (now T.C.A. 4–5–322).

Id.p. 5, 6.

The Chancery Court decision was reversed and the entire matter remanded to the Chancery court for review of Hunt's decision in accordance with the proper standard. Id. p. 7. Gilbert applied for permission to appeal to the Tennessee Supreme Court and the Supreme Court denied that application by order entered April 4, 1983.

The parties re-argued the merits of their respective cases before the Shelby County Chancery Court on August 11, 1983. This time Chancellor Doran ruled from the bench- and in favor of the University. The court's judgment in favor of the University was formally entered on September 9, 1983. Gilbert again filed an appeal to the state Court of Appeals.

On the second go-round the appeal was assigned to appellate judges Hewitt Tomlin, Charles Nearn and Alan Highers. The panel heard oral argument on April 16, 1984. One particular exchange tipped me off where the case was heading.

Baretz argued that Gilbert had been unlawfully denied the right to cross-examine Bobbitt, the chief witness for the state since she refused to answer any questions he, meaning Baretz, asked. Because Bobbitt refused to answer his questions her testimony lacked credibility, Baretz contended. I never had a chance to respond as one of the panel members beat me to it (I believe it was Judge Highers, but I am not certain).

"You were not denied the right to cross examine he witness, she just wouldn't answer your questions," was the essence of the judge's comment. "The witness pleaded innocent to a criminal charge of possessing and dealing illegal drugs, then testified at the hearing that she had possessed illegal drugs and provided them to Gilbert. I find her testimony very credible in light of this statement against interest." I felt confident of victory following this exchange.

My expectation was confirmed by the Court of Appeal's opinion and judgment entered September 26, 1984. Judge Tomlin, writing for the Court, rejected Gilbert's argument that Bozeman's ruling was "res judicata" and that Hunt erred in disregarding it. That matter had been finally disposed of by the appellate court previously according to Tomlin.

Only the issue of whether there was substantial evidence in the record to support Hunt's decision (as the Chancery Court found in its latest ruling) remained. The Court of Appeals found there was:

> As we are obliged to do, we have reviewed that record in its entirety.
> The only actual witnesses to the transactions bringing about the plaintiff's dismissal were the plaintiff himself and that of Mrs. Denise Bobbitt. Obviously, the plaintiff denied any wrongdoing. On the other hand, Mrs. Bobbitt testified that on several occasions the plaintiff came to her requesting that she furnish him with drugs. She stated that she in fact sold him marijuana and, on occasion, qualudes. These transactions took place on the campus of the University.

***

> Although at the time of plaintiff's hearing Mrs. Bobbitt was under indictment for illegal activity in drugs, none of the events for which she had been indicted involved the possession and/or sale of drugs on the University campus, or her activities with the plaintiff. Furthermore, Mrs. Bobbitt testified, as did an official of the HSC, that no deal of any type had been struck with the district attorney general in order to obtain favorable testimony from Mrs. Bobbitt, who testified voluntarily as a witness against the plaintiff.

***

> Several of Mrs. Bobbitt's co-workers testified to the effect that she frequently told lies, but that they were types of lies to make her "look better." Chancellor Hunt, in his find-

ings, disregarded this testimony, noting that the testimony of Mrs. Bobbitt was against her legal interest, and rather than being designed to make her look good, it only made her look worse, but could likely subject her to further criminal prosecution.

James P. Gilbert v. University of Tennessee, et. al. Shelby Equity (Tenn. App. 1984).

The appeals court also noted that "the Chancellor below concurred in the finding of the agency head that in so far as the drug transactions between plaintiff and herself, Mrs. Bobbitt testified truthfully at the hearing. Thus, this finding is binding on the court and again, reinforces our conclusion that the finding below was supported by substantial and material evidence." Id.

Gilbert appealed the Court of Appeals judgment to the U.S. Supreme Court, applying for a writ of certiorari. The appeal was dismissed by the Supreme Court on April 22, 1985. Gilbert v. University of Tennessee, No. 84-1429 (471 U. S. 1050, 85 L. Ed. 2d 474). Hard fought litigation reached a just conclusion. The UT Center for the Health Sciences business office was eliminated as a center for criminal activity.

On October 28, 1981, while the Gilbert litigation proceeded, I testified in Shelby County Criminal Court at the request of Denise Bobbitt. I had made no commitment to do so but was pleased to accept her request and advise the Court of her cooperation in pursuing administrative charges against Gilbert. It was my hope that Bobbitt had learned a lesson and would turn her life in a more positive direction.

In the final analysis the Gilbert litigation ended on a high note and restored integrity to a key component of the University's operation. One aspect of the Gilbert litigation did end on a heartrending note–the destruction of a valued friendship.

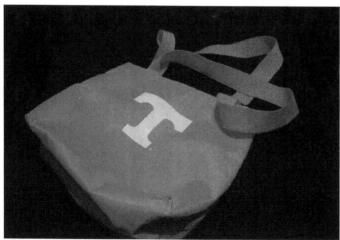

Sample item purchased through UT licensing agreement.

Chapter 68–The Sam Bozeman Tragedy

When Sam Bozeman, Executive Assistant to UTCHS Chancellor Hunt, learned that I had appealed his initial order in the Gilbert case, and that Hunt had rejected his findings and entered a final order terminating Gilbert's employment, his attitude toward me changed dramatically. All social contact ceased. Worse, Bozeman allowed his hurt feelings to impact his responsibility to the University.

On April 4, 1983 the Tennessee Supreme Court rejected James Gilbert's application for permission to appeal the Tennessee appellate court's holding that Chancellor Hunt was not bound by the Bozeman's findings in his favor.

Hunt called me to a meeting in his office on April 25 and showed me a memorandum Bozeman had written to him. He asked what I thought. I initially opined that I saw no problem with the opinions expressed. Only when Hunt noted that a copy had been sent to legal counsel for a party (Jonathan Lipman) in another case involving the University did I express shock.

I opined that such conduct by an Executive Assistant to the Chancellor warranted termination of employment. That was my advice. Hunt took the advice and issued Bozeman a termination letter. Since he was not charged with misconduct and was a non-contract "employee at will" Bozeman was not entitled to a hearing of any sort.

Initially, on June 20, 1983, Bozeman filed an age discrimination complaint against the University with the equal employment opportunity commission (which was administratively closed in November of that same year). Bozeman moved quickly to a higher battleground.

On August 29, 1983 Bozeman filed a complaint with the U.S. District Court in Memphis. He alleged his employment had been terminated in violation of his free-speech rights under the First Amendment to the U.S. Constitution. A trial by jury was requested.

Named as defendants were the University of Tennessee, UT President Ed Boling, Chancellor Hunt and me. UT and Boling were dismissed as defendants by the Court's order of January 3, 1984 for lack of jurisdiction. Bozeman was represented by Memphis attorneys Don Donati and Deborah Ford. Alan Parker, a colleague of mine in the UT Office of General Counsel, served as legal counsel for Hunt and me. The case was assigned to U.S. District Judge Julia Gibbons.

Depositions of Bozeman and Hunt were taken on March 20, 1984. Hunt's was actually completed on May 4. The same day a motion for summary judgment was filed on behalf of Hunt and me. Judge Gibbons denied the motion by order entered June 12, 1984. The deposition process accelerated. Fifteen more depositions were taken in Tampa, Florida (from retired UTCHS Vice Chancellor, Dr. John Shively), Memphis and Knoxville before trial. I was deposed as were Vice Presidents Joe Johnson and Eli Fly.

The jury trial commenced April 29, 1985 and continued over a five-day period ending May 7, excluding a long weekend. On May 7 the jury rendered a verdict in favor of the defendants. Judgment entered in favor of Hunt and Leadbetter!

What should have been over had a good ways to go. After the jury verdict was rendered Parker asked the Court's permission to speak with the jurors. Judge Gibbons granted permission for all attorneys to do so and imposed no limitation on what interrogation was permissible. Turmoil resulted.

Bozeman filed a motion for a new trial after his counsel interrogated the jurors. The complexity of the matter is best evidenced by the fact that Judge Gibbons did not rule on the motion for a year. It was not until July 3, 1986 that Judge Gibbons entered a 14 page Order Denying Motion For New Trial. Samuel R Bozeman v. James C Hunt, M.D. and Ronald C Leadbetter, No. 83-2714 G (W.D. Tenn. 1986).

A summary and a few quotes from Judge Gibbons helps explain the extraordinary delay:

Although plaintiff makes several arguments in favor of a new trial, the one requiring most detailed discussion involves an assertion that the jurors considered extraneous prejudicial information in reaching their verdict. Id. p.1.

Although Local Rule 19 states that the court will determine the scope of the interrogation and other limitations upon it, the court made no specific ruling as to what interrogation [of jurors] was permissible.

The affidavit of plaintiff's counsel Deborah Ford states that Ms. Forde called the jury foreman Harold James on the telephone the night of May 7 and that she spoke with six of the eight jurors between the end of trial and May 15. Ms. Forde states that the foreman told her that the statute of limitations question [there was a factual question as to the date plaintiff knew or should have known of his cause of action, and this issue was submitted to the jury for decision] was decided in plaintiff's favor. "Virtually all" the jurors with whom plaintiff's attorney spoke told her that defendants "prevailed because of these considerations: (a) the plaintiff's financial status was such that he need not win the case; (b) the plaintiff's age was such that he should be retired because he was 'too old;' (c) the plaintiff sent a copy of the memo to Dr. Hunt to the lawyer representing Jonathan Lipman. [A footnote pointed out that the memo to Hunt was not protected speech and it could not provide a basis for recovery by Bozeman]. The affidavit also indicates that juror Ruth Blackwell told plaintiffs attorney she saw plaintiff in the parking lot during trial, noted in that he had a relatively new car, and thus knew that he "had money."

Id. pp. 2-3.

Judge Gibbons noted that both Alan Parker and I filed affidavits, which the plaintiff moved to strike as inadmissible evidence. The court refused to strike our affidavits because "the information they contain is no different from that included in plaintiff's affidavits."

Id. p.3.

According to Parker's affidavit:

> Over a week after the conclusion of trial he received a call from the jury foreman Mr. James. Mr. James told Mr. Parker that Ms. Blackwell had called him and was concerned about some of the interrogation she had received from plaintiff's counsel, including questions about whether she was related to a UTCHS official who had been a witness at trial [presumably the Vice Chancellor for Business and Finance Robert Blackwell]. Mr. Parker states that Mr. James told him the case was decided in defendants' favor on the statute of limitations issue.

> Mr. Leadbetter's affidavit states that he talked with one juror, Lucille Stephens, who told him the verdict was based on the statute of limitations. He also says that he spoke with plaintiff's counsel Don Donati after trial.

Id. pp. 3-4

Judge Gibbons then related that the plaintiff's attorneys requested permission to obtain and file affidavits from the jurors but she denied the request. She likewise rejected their alternative suggestion for an evidentiary hearing to determine the influence of "extraneous information" on the verdict.

The Court clearly concurred with the defense argument that "any parking lot observations of plaintiff's car by Ms. Blackwell and any observation of plaintiff's age are not extraneous prejudicial influences and are not a basis for new trial."

Id. pp. 4-5.

Judge Gibbons held that a new trial was not warranted for two reasons. First, the plaintiff had failed to provide any allegations which, if proven, would entitle plaintiff to a new trial.

Id. p.5.

Seven pages later in her ruling, Judge Gibbons offered the second reason.

> A second reason compels the conclusion that no new trial or further inquiry is warranted in this case. Although this court permitted the juror interrogation conducted by counsel, it should not have done so.

Id. p. 12.

She did not blame our attorney, Parker, for the snafu.

> Although the court did not anticipate that plaintiff's counsel would conduct the type of questioning pursued here, particularly since the request to interrogate came from defense counsel, obviously this court's failure to refuse the request

or define the scope of questioning permitted an intrusive and undesirable inquiry into the bases for the jury's verdict. The court will not compound its earlier error by permitting a resumption of the questioning, as plaintiff urges, or by holding an evidentiary hearing. Moreover, because the court should not have allowed the initial questioning, it will not grant a new trial based on its results.

Id. p. 13.

The District Court then concluded that the verdict was not against the clear weight of evidence and denied plaintiff's motion for a new trial.

Happily the case was concluded; no appeal was filed. Sadly, Sam Bozeman's overall laudable history at the University was likewise concluded and a valued friendship disengaged.

Chapter 69–Worker's Compensation

One area of the law I avoided most of my career at UT was workers' compensation. While I eagerly volunteered to handle almost any other area of the law involving the University, I let it be known that I preferred not to handle workers' comp cases. Such cases were perceived by me as more akin to handling insurance claims where the only real issue was how much to pay.

At the outset of my employment all UT workers' comp claims were handled by the State Attorney General's office. At some point the Attorney General asked General Counsel Brogan if the Office of General Counsel would be willing to handle workers' comp cases. Brogan's agreement to do so was announced at a staff meeting and Assistant General Counsel Steve Sprouse took on primary responsibility for handling those cases. He developed real expertise in handling workers' comp cases for the OGC.

In 2001, without any explanation, Sprouse's workers' comp cases were reassigned to me. To some extent, my original distaste for handling such cases was confirmed. The Tennessee Claims Commissioners assigned to hear workers' comp claims appeared heavily predisposed in favor of an employee seeking compensation for any injury or illness occurring at work whether or not the injury was work related.

My workers' comp litigation experience was rather limited: between 2001 and 2008 I tried 16 cases to completion with eight wins, six losses (state payments totaling $117,500) and two settlements (state payments totaling $56,000). All but five of those cases were concluded in 2006 and 2007. Seven additional cases remained active at the time of my March 2008 retirement.

The 50% win rate for workers' comp cases would have caused me to be far more settlement oriented had it been my success rate in other litigation. Still, much to my surprise, I found this area of litigation enjoyable and challenging.

The proceedings before the Tennessee Claims Commission were not perfunctory as evidenced by the eight claims litigated to favorable conclusion. Still, there were a couple of litigation losses which demonstrated, at least from my perspective, the high hurdle faced when challenging a questionable workers' comp claim.

FALSE TESTIMONY PREVAILS–MORRIS v. STATE OF TENNESSEE

Ken Morris was employed at the UT Martin experiment station. He suffered a muscle spasm injury in 2002 while employed by the University. Morris applied for and received workers' compensation payment from the State. At some point the State office handling workers' comp payments declined to make further payments. Morris filed a complaint with the Tennessee Claims Commission on January 13, 2004. The State's (University's) answer was filed March 1, 2004 and responses to claimant's discovery requests were served the following day. Nothing further was heard from the claimant or his attorney, Kyle Crowe, for more than one year.

State law provides: "Absent prior written consent of the Commission, it is mandatory that in any claim filed with the Claims Commission upon which no action is taken by the claimant to advance the case to disposition within any one year period of time be dismissed with prejudice." Tenn. Code Ann. 9-8-402(b). [Emphasis supplied]

Commissioner Nancy C. Miller–Herron wrote Crowe on September 20, 2004, observing that the file "reveals no activity since defendant's answer filed March 1, 2004." On February 25, 2005 the Commissioner again wrote counsel advising "the referenced file reveals no activity since your replies to the status letter dated September 20, 2004, indicating that answers to the defendant's first set of interrogatories were being prepared and that scheduling a trial was in the near future." Despite the two letters from the Commissioner nothing whatever was filed with the Commission or provided to me prior to the expiration of the one-year statutory period.

On March 7, 2005, after numerous unsuccessful attempts to secure answers to requests for discovery of documents and information from claimant, I filed a motion to dismiss. I received the claimant's response to the state's interrogatories two days later–several weeks beyond the expiration of the one-year period.

Commissioner Miller–Herron refused to dismiss the case based on Crowe's contention that he made an attempt to schedule an independent medical exam prior to expiration of the one year period. Kenneth Morris v. State of Tennessee,

Tennessee Claims Commission No. 20101860 (Order Denying Defendant's Motion to Dismiss, entered April 8, 2005). Nothing was ever filed to substantiate Crowe's claim and the independent exam was not conducted until March 21, 2005, two weeks after the filing of the State's motion to dismiss. In my view, the Commissioner disregarded the clear mandate of state law. Her handling of the facts of the case I viewed as worse.

In interrogatories to the claimant, the State requested identification of all healthcare providers who "examined or treated [claimant] within the 10 years prior to the incident until the present date, stating the inclusive dates of each such examination or treatment, the nature of the examination or treatment and, if applicable, their status as either outpatient or inpatient."

Morris's answer, sworn to under oath, was "Dresden Medical Associates for minor colds and injuries, outpatient; Dr. David West, back, outpatient; Dyersburg." At trial, Morris first denied he had any injuries prior to the work related lower back muscle strain in 2002, for which he received workers' compensation payments. When confronted with medical records I had received from "other sources" he proceeded to admit that he'd suffered a shoulder injury in 1996, a chest injury involving two rib fractures and a fracture of the nasal bone in 2000, a finger injury requiring medical attention (and documentation of degenerative bone disease) in 2001, and medical treatment for trauma to the left upper chest (and identification of borderline hypertension) in 2001.

Although, at trial, claimant claimed excellent memory of all aspects of his lower back injury, he denied memory of each of the incidents noted in the medical record, but quickly recalled most of them when confronted with the record.

Morris was asked if he had filed any previous workers' comp. claims, he testified the only claim he recalled was one file 30 years earlier. In fact, he filed two workers comp claims: one for the 2000 chest injury and another for the 2001 finger injury. His testimony at trial coincided with the answers given in response to the State's interrogatories.

One of the more interesting entries from the record of Dr. David West regarding a December 3, 2003 lower back injury:

> Patient is a 61year-old white male who presents to the clinic today with a chief complaint of back pain. Patient has an annular bulging disc at the L4 area. He was working on his tractor today and basically the tractor broke down in the back 40. He is having some pain and would like a refill of his medication. The last time I refilled his medication was approximately one year ago which was Ultraset. We will refill that for him. I have refilled his Viagra.

At trial Morris testified that after the 2002 word–related injury he could no longer operate a tractor. Only when confronted with Dr. West's medical record did he admit he'd been out on a tractor.

In a sworn affidavit, Dr. Joseph Boals made reference to the medical record he prepared at the time he examined Morris on March 21, 2005. He concluded that the condition of Morris's back was related to the 2002 muscle strain. As I argued to the Commissioner, Boals' lack of records or other information concerning Morris's 2003 tractor related injury and other documented injuries rendered Boals expert opinion as to causation of Morris's Medical condition in 2005 incompetent–after Morris admitted at trial that he did not tell Boals of any injuries preceding the lower back muscle pull in 2002, I asked him why he didn't. Morris replied, "Because he didn't ask."

Despite blatant falsification of testimony and discovery responses, on February 15, 2006, Commissioner Miller–Herron granted judgment for Morris. He was awarded a lump sum payment of $13,149.50 plus $2,629.90 in attorney's fees, and future medicals. I felt strongly that an appeal to the Tennessee Court of Appeals was warranted. My recommendation to that effect was declined by Mizell.

FALSIFICATION WORKS WELL–
CLEMENTS v. STATE OF TENNESSEE

The second case in the falsification duo has a tie-in to the first. Critical issues in both cases bore an uncanny resemblance.

Cecil Clements was employed by UT Martin as a campus police officer in July 1990. Previously he had been employed as a police officer with the city of Martin.

Clements reported to work at 7a.m. on May 9, 1992. It was graduation day at the University. Clements began his regular duties, which included setting up barricades and directing traffic. During the morning Clements began feeling bad. His symptoms progressed and around 11:30 a.m., while directing traffic, he left his post and went to the hospital.

Clements filed a workers' compensation claim on July 16, 2003. His attorney of record was R. David Strickland. Also involved in Clements' case was a second attorney–Kyle Crowe. At one time the two operated out of the same office and appeared to be partners.

Cardiologist Thomas Stern, M.D., conducted an independent medical examination of Clements on January 29, 2004. An EKG and a stress echocardiogram were performed that day on Clements. Stern concluded that Clements had suffered a heart attack as the result of work-related stress the morning of May 9. Just one problem, Stern did not review a single medical record in reaching that conclusion.

As Stern testified at his deposition, "[his] medical opinion was based entirely on what Clements told him during the January 29 examination in his office". Clements related to Stern information regarding lab evidence of a definite heart attack, elevated enzymes, and "a history of myocardial infarction documented by appropriate laboratory results."

How did Stern know this medical information was accurate? "I have to assume he was giving me accurate information," was Stern's explanation during deposition. For this reason alone Stern was, arguably, completely incompetent to testify as to Clements' heart condition any time prior to the January 29, 2004 office visit.

Why didn't Stern review Clements' medical records from 1992? Once again, Stern relied on Clements' representation that both Martin and Jackson hospital records of the 1992 event had been lost. Commissioner Miller–Herron noted claimant's testimony that "he thought these records had been lost when his family physician closed his practice. In fact, it is undisputed that claimant's prior counsel produced these records during discovery." Cecil Clements v. State of Tennessee, Claim No. 94–001–464 Workers' Compensation, (Tennessee Claims Commission, Western division 2006)).

Notwithstanding this devastating testimony of the claimant's sole medical expert, Commissioner Miller–Herron enter judgment for the claimant, in the amount of $34,135.20, attorneys' fees in the amount of of $8533.80 for a 45% permanent partial disability to the body as a whole. Id.pp.18-19. A number of undisputed facts were totally disregarded by the Commissioner.

On May 3, 2004 Clements' attorney mailed the hospital records to me in response to interrogatories on behalf of the State. On November 1, 2005, after those hospital records were mailed to me - claimant's counsel obtained from Dr. Stern an affidavit falsely representing, once again, that the hospital records were not available. Even during his deposition (January 19, 2006) Stern testified he had not been provided the records or told of their existence.

Without having ever reviewed the missing records Stern testified that it was "probable that the events [of May 9, 1992] triggered the heart event." Id. pp. 7,15. Hospital records from 1992 completely refuted the story Clements told Stern.

The Volunteer General Hospital record from Martin noted that Clements' chief complaint was "substernal chest pain since 6 p.m. last night." The Jackson –Madison County Hospital medical record likewise documented that claim. Tellingly, the Jackson–Madison County Hospital record stated that Clements "spent an extremely restless night," and "that he had not experienced any sensation like this in his lifetime." The Jackson–Madison County Hospital discharge summary succinctly stated Clements' medical circumstances:

"This is a 45-year-old white male, who began having chest discomfort on Saturday, May 8, 1992, at about 6 PM. He described this as indigestion or pressure in his chest radiating to his arms and his neck he was restless most of the night and woke up intermittently with this discomfort. The pain became fairly constant at about 8 a.m. on5/9/92 and it endured for 3–4 hours."

While Stern testified to the possibility that Clements had discomfort the night before, the hospital records document the fact that he had pain!

In his deposition, Stern testified it would've been better to have had the hospital records to look at: "The medical records would have given me what he said at the time, obviously fresher than his recollection of ten years previously." Stern admitted he failed to call the hospitals to see if they had the records.

Six weeks after I recommended that Morris be appealed to the Tennessee Court of Appeals, I recommended the same for Clements. This recommendation was likewise declined by General Counsel Mizell.

In May, 2006, I presented a request to the Tennessee Board of Professional Responsibility, asking that it determine whether attorneys Crowe and Strickland had violated the "rules of professional conduct" for attorneys, with respect to their handling of the Morris and Clements cases. Due to limitations of rules of the Tennessee Supreme Court I will decline further comment on those proceedings.

The lessons learned from this case are best forgotten.

Chapter 70–Whatever Could Go Wrong Did– The Skoutakis Disaster

Vasilios ("Bill") Skoutakis, a tenured professor in the UTCHS College of pharmacy, was one of my good friends in Memphis back in the 1980s. We worked out together and frequently competed on the racquetball court. Our friendship had a serious setback in the late 1980s.

In 1986 Skoutakis founded the Memphis Pharmacotherapy and Clinical Research Center, Inc. ("the Center"), a for-profit corporation. Later the same year he requested approval for a change in employment status from full-time to 80% part-time in order to promote his private business. Initially, the department chairman for Skoutakis, Dr. Richard Evans, and the Dean of the College of Pharmacy, Dr. Michael Ryan, approved.

Matters went downhill when Ryan's wife brought home a copy of a proposed contract with the Center which was mailed to hospitals in a is six state area, including the Regional Medical Center at Memphis ("The Med") where Ryan's wife was employed as a pharmacist.

Although Ryan had at least cursorily examined the contract when Skoutakis presented his proposal to go part-time, Ryan was angered by the contents of the proposed contract. He advised Skoutakis that the proposed contract created a conflict of interest between the Center and the College of Pharmacy because the College planned to offer the same services. Ryan called Skoutakis to his office and demanded that he retract the proposal or be fired.

A day or so later Skoutakis contacted Ryan and advised him that the Center's board of directors had approved providing all profits from the Center's contracts to the College of Pharmacy so long as Skoutakis remained employed in the College of Pharmacy. Ryan rejected the offer, advising Skoutakis he believed it was inappropriate for a faculty member to compete with the College.

Ryan proceeded to remove Skoutakis from membership on College committees as well as other positions he held as a result of his faculty position. He contacted Evans, who was on sabbatical in Switzerland, and UTCHS Chancellor Jim Hunt, to let them know what was going on. At Hunt's urging, or at least with his concurrence, Ryan changed Scoutakis' status back to full time for the 1988–89 academic year.

On August 19, 1988, Skoutakis filed suit in U.S. District Court against Evans, Ryan and Hunt, both as officials of the University of Tennessee and individually. Skoutakis' claims were manifold. He claimed the defendants had entered into a conspiracy to violate his constitutional rights. Specifically, it was alleged that the defendants deprived him of due process by changing his employment status and also violated his First Amendment rights to free speech. It was further alleged that the defendants discriminated against him on the basis of his national origin (Greek) in violation of federal law. Skoutakis alleged that Evans and Ryan had defamed him in their trans–Atlantic communications, that Hunt and Ryan had breached his contract, and that Evans had "tortiously" interfered with his contract of employment.

Skoutakis demanded permanent injunctive relief, a declaratory judgment in his favor, $1 million in compensatory damages, $1 million in punitive damages, $500,000 compensation for the alleged libel/slander by Evans and Ryan, and his attorney's fees.

Hunt and Ryan were represented by me, and I in turn was assisted by JoAnn Cutting, an attorney in the OGC Memphis office. Evans, although Chairman of the College of Pharmacy, was employed by St. Jude's Hospital and secured separate legal counsel. Skoutakis was represented by Memphis attorney Donald Donati. The case was assigned to U.S. District Judge Robert McRae.

The "'Answer" of the University defendants was filed on September 2, 1988. "Plaintiff's First Request for Production of Documents" was filed on September 22. From that day through mid-December 1989 the parties engaged in discovery, demand for production of documents and deposition of potential witnesses, which could well be characterized as excruciating.

Thousands of pages of documents were requested by the plaintiff from various University offices. These were located and produced. More than 25 depositions were taken by the parties, one of the highest number of depositions taken in any employment lawsuit I handled.

A number of the depositions were exceedingly long. For example, Ryan's deposition extended over a number of days: November 3 and 4, November 17 and 18 and January 18, 1989. My deposition of Skoutakis also covered several days: October 9, 10 and 12, November 3, 8, 14 and 15 (although on the last two dates other depositions were also scheduled).

In accordance with my standard procedure, on January 16, 1990 I filed a motion to dismiss or for summary judgment, with appended affidavit and deposition testimony of witnesses, including affidavits of Ryan and Hunt, requesting that judgment be entered in favor each of the defendants as to each claim filed against him. At that point in time, aside from the extraordinary complexity of the discovery process, the litigation appeared to be going well. And, as was typically the case, Donati, his assistant–name not recalled–JoAnn Cutting and I got along quite well and enjoyed our time together.

On July 20, 1990 Judge McRae entered his "Order on Pending Motions", disposing of the defendants' summary judgment motion, as well as several motions filed by Skoutakis. The District Court granted summary judgment in favor of the defendants as to Skoutakis' procedural due process and First Amendment claims. Summary judgment in favor of Evans as to plaintiff's state law claims was also granted. In addition Hunt and Ryan were granted summary judgment on Skoutakis' breach of contract claim. Motions seeking summary judgment on Skoutakis' conspiracy, substantive due process, discrimination, equal protection and defamation claims were denied.

Plaintiff's motion for summary judgment, motion to strike (certain materials filed by plaintiff) and a motion for "sanctions" were also denied. Vasilios Skoutakis v. William Evans, et.al. No. 88-2627-4B (W.D. Tenn. 1990).

Since the denial of summary judgment means only that the opposing party has introduced "some" evidence sufficient to support a verdict or judgment in his favor I was not concerned. After all, Judge McRae found that a number of plaintiffs' claims were not supported by any evidence sufficient to sustain a judgment or were contrary to the law. A jury would have to decide.

SCREW-UP ON MY PART–AND UT PRESIDENT LAMAR ALEXANDER'S RESPONSE

As the Skoutakis litigation was ongoing there were other important occurrences at the University–one being the UT Board's election of a new president to replace Edward Boling following his announced retirement.

Lamar Alexander served as governor of the state of Tennessee from 1979 to 1987. At the fall 1987 meeting of the UT Board of Trustees Alexander was elected president of the University of Tennessee to replace the retiring Ed Boling. I was present at that meeting and felt the Board had made a good decision despite Alexander making clear that he would not be in the position long-term –he desired to run for the Presidency of the United States.

The President's Office was on the eighth floor of Andy Holt Tower–as was the Office of General Counsel when Alexander assumed the UT presidency. Alexander's first day on the job was July 1, 1988 and he visited my office on the eighth floor the morning of his first day. The two of us had a nice chat as Alexander nibbled popcorn from a bag he had brought with him. I admired his "down to earth" approach. My diary entry for that day read:

Lamar Alexander's first day on the job. I met him as he arrived (7:45 A.M.)
and was honored with a visit to my office by him 45 minutes later as he
started a tour of the campus. He will be a great president (UT and the U. S.)

For the bulk of Alexander's UT presidency we worked together extremely well. We attended seminars together at State parks and I kept Alexander up-to-date on litigation matters. With a single exception–an admitted screw-up that proved embarrassing to me.

At some point during his deposition in the Skoutakis case Pharmacy Dean Ryan was asked by opposing counsel if he had ever used drugs with students while serving as Associate Dean of the College, prior to his promotion to the Deanship. He admitted that he had. The deposition questioning continued, but in a different direction.

Although surprised by Ryan's admission, it did not relate to Skoutakis' claims against Ryan and the other defendants and I refocused on other matters. I had knowledge of Ryan's admission of past serious misconduct but did not inform Ryan's superiors, including Alexander, of the information I had received.

Embarrassment followed, for me, but prompt corrective action was taken by UT administration after learning of my oversight. The Memphis Commercial Appeal carried the news on the front page of the February 24, 1989 edition: "Pharmacy Dean at UT admits use of drugs." (The Commercial Appeal, February 24, 1989,p.1).

The Dean of the College of Pharmacy at the University of Tennessee,
Memphis, has admitted in a sworn deposition to using marijuana and co-

caine with university students and falsifying expense accounts.

Michael R Ryan, 44, said he used the drugs with students while he was an associate dean and before he became Dean in 1983. The expense report practice involves reimbursements made in recent years.

UT lawyer Ronald C. Leadbetter said he could not comment on the matter. Ryan and his boss, UT–Memphis Chancellor Dr. James C. Hunt, directed questions to Leadbetter.

The deposition, taken in Leadbetter's presence, was given in November in connection with a federal lawsuit by a tenured professor against Ryan, Hunt and Dr. William D. Evans, who is chairman of clinical pharmacy. (Id.)

The article noted that "at least two members of the search committee that recommended hiring [Ryan] as Dean of the College of pharmacy at the University of Tennessee, Memphis, knew of his drug use with university students…." And, that the depositions implicating Ryan "are contained in a $7.5 million lawsuit filed by a tenured professor against university officials." (Id. p. A12).

The Comptroller of the State treasury, William R. Snodgrass, wrote President Alexander on April 21, 1989:

> Dear President Alexander:
> Subject: Failure to Report Irregularities as Required by Law
>
> On Friday, February 24, 1989, this office was advised of the apparent falsification of officialstate records by Dr. Michael R. Ryan, Dean of the College of Pharmacy at the University of Tennessee, Memphis. This office became aware of this matter through newspaper articles and inquiries by the media concerning the investigation of these problems and other matters by the University of Tennessee, which apparently began in November 1988. We immediately contacted top officials of the University to learn more about the matter.
>
> At that time we were advised that although Mr. Ronald C Leadbetter, an attorney for the University of Tennessee, became aware of this information during depositions in November 1988, he had failed to advise appropriate university officials or this office as required by law.
>
> I call this to your attention so that appropriate actions may be taken to see that the law relative to reporting such matters is complied with.
>
> Very truly yours,
> W.R. Snodgrass

President Alexander responded to Snodgrass by letter of May 4, 1989:

Dear Bill:

I appreciate your writing about the delay in properly notifying your office, as required by state law and policy, of some irregularities with some travel expenses and other matters in the University of Tennessee College of pharmacy. Information on this subject came to the attention of Mr. Ron Leadbetter, one of our staff attorneys, during the deposition phase of a lawsuit involving a college of pharmacy faculty members. Eli Fly, Joe Johnson, and others of us were not informed because of the status of the preliminary work on the lawsuit. Mr. Leadbetter did not intend to conceal what he knew to violate any laws or regulations. He simply made an error in judgment under unique circumstances.

However, Mr. Leadbetter should have passed along information about irregularities, and your office should have been made aware of them. We have discussed the situation with Mr. Leadbetter and our General Counsel, Beach Brogan, to ensure no recurrence. We are well aware of the legal and policy requirements for prompt reporting of fiscal misconduct and are committed to compliance.

Sincerely,

Lamar Alexander, President

Alexander was correct in stating my error was unintentional and occasioned by unique circumstances. The pressure of focusing on the defense of a multi-million dollar lawsuit was the unique factor that led to my screw-up. But that is an explanation–not a justification. I should not have made the error and it was a one-time occurrence. Lesson learned!

The error was not held against me by the President or anyone else. My relationship with Alexander remained solid during the remainder of his brief presidency. His letter to me of January 31, 1991 confirms that.

Dear Ron,

Honey and I want to thank you for being so helpful to us while we've been at UT. We hope that you and Theresa will join us for a reception at our home at 3801 Topside Road on Friday, February 8 between 5:30 and 7:00 p.m.

Parking will be available at the Clayton Homes corporate offices on Alcoa Highway, and vans will run to and from the house. Please call Judy Flanagan at 974–2225 to let her know your plans.

Sincerely,

Lamar Alexander

Any damage from my mistake had no lasting effect. Just a lesson learned, at least by me.

ON TO TRIAL

The *Skoutakis* jury trial commenced on October 22, 1991. It continued on October 23, 24, 25, 28 and 29 and November 4 and 5. The trial concluded on November 8. During the course of the trial the plaintiff, without any explantion, dismissed all charges against Evans.

The case was actually presented to the jury for its deliberation on November 6. Deliberations continued over a three-day period and a verdict was reached on November 8.

The jury's verdict was entered in favor of Ryan and Hunt on the issue of discrimination on the basis of national origin. Unfortunately, from that point on the verdict was in the plaintiff's favor.

On the substantive due process claim the jury awarded plaintiff $40,000 in compensatory damages and $40,000 in punitive damages against Ryan and $30,000 in compensatory damages and $30,000 in punitive damages against

Hunt.

The jury also awarded $30,000 in compensatory damages and $30,000 in punitive damages against both Ryan and Hunt on the conspiracy charge. Ryan suffered a further award of $50,000 in compensatory damages and $50,000 in punitive damages on the defamation claim. The total damages award: $360,000! The news was reported the next day, November 9, in the Memphis Commercial Appeal.

Attorney's fees were later added on top of the verdict. Donati requested $244,956.57 (although the University took the position that $163,304.38 was the correct amount since more than one third of his documented hours were expended on pursuing the national origin discrimination claim). Worse was yet to come- before the expected award of attorney's fees.

MOTION FOR SANCTIONS AGAINST UT COUNSEL

On or shortly after December 9, 1991, I received word that Don Donati had filed with the District Court a motion requesting sanctions against Hunt and Ryan as well as Brogan, Cutting and me as counsel of record. The basis for the motion was two-fold.

First, Donati claimed that false affidavits had been filed with the summary judgment motion I had filed on behalf of the defendants in January 1990. He claimed Hunt stated in his affidavit that he had "directed" Skoutakis' return to a full-time position, but testified at trial that he had "strongly urged" such action. It was Donati's contention that all three attorneys had collaborated with the defendants to file a false affidavit with the Court.

Second, and more critically, Donati asserted that defendants and counsel had, during discovery, "carefully purged from the [University's] files" three documents which were important to plaintiff's case.

Judge McRae ordered all attorneys to attend an oral discussion of the sanctions motion in his office in the federal courthouse in Memphis on January 3, 1992. Accompanying me to the meeting were Cutting and Memphis OGC attorney Odell Horton, Jr. The proceedings were in, in my opinion, most inappropriate.

Judge McRae, having clearly reviewed the motion for sanctions, initiated the session by vigorously criticizing the defendants and me for the conduct described in the sanctions motion. After several minutes of being excoriated by the judge I asked if I would have an opportunity to respond. Only then did Judge McRae cease his diatribe and say, "I've probably already said too much," and announce that a hearing on the motion would be held after both sides had an opportunity to conduct discovery on the matter.

Brogan, Cutting and I could no longer represent Hunt and Ryan since we were now essentially defendants. We retained former State Attorney General Michael Cody (1984-88) as our defense counsel. Memphis attorney Leo Bearman became counsel for Hunt while Memphis attorney Lee Cagle assumed Ryan's defense. Horton became the legal representative for the UT Office of General Counsel.

A host of depositions were scheduled starting less than two weeks after the meeting in Judge McRae's office. The depositions of Donati and Skoutakis were taken on January 14. Depositions of Brogan, Ryan and Cutting were taken on February 4.

The following day depositions of my paralegal, Jan Williams, and me were taken in the offices of the attorney representing former defendant Bill Evans. It seemed there were more attorneys in the office than clients.

Evan's attorney had earlier informed Donati that one of the alleged "purged" documents (a memorandum having Hunt's initials in the upper right-hand corner evidencing his receipt and awareness of the document), had not been provided to them either. It being understood that counsel for co-defendant would receive a copy of all University documents produced in discovery at plaintiff's request.

At the beginning of my deposition I suggested to Evan's attorney that he look in a particular file in his office since I was certain he had received a copy of the memorandum initialed by Hunt. We took a break from the deposition and Evan's attorney went back to an office file room. A short time later the attorney returned with the subject memorandum in hand. The document had not been purged as Donati claimed. Counsel for co-defendant had a copy of the document in his copy of the pile of documents provided to Donati.

My deposition continued that day and was completed the following, on February 6. Seven more depositions were taken in February. At the conclusion of these proceedings it was clear to all parties that the motion for sanctions lacked any basis.

On April 27, 1993 Judge McRae entered an "Agreed Order of Dismissal with Prejudice" making that point absolutely clear. McRae said:

Plaintiff's counsel represents that during the course of discovery following his filing on December 9, 1991, of a motion for sanctions against defendants James C. Hunt and Michael R. Ryan and their counsel, Beauchamp E. Brogan, Ronald C. Leadbetter and JoAnn C. Cutting, facts were discovered leading him to believe that said motion for sanctions is not well-founded and said motion should be withdrawn and considered stricken from the record. Accordingly, plaintiff withdraws and disavows the claims of misconduct and other claims asserted in said motion for sanctions.

Vasilios A. Skoutakis vs. William Evans, et. al. No. 88-2627-4 BRO (W.D.

Tenn. 1993).

One major problem resolved but the devastating results of the judgment against Ryan and Hunt remained, and the amount of the award of attorney fees had yet to be set. Worse, by law, the state was not responsible for an award of punitive damages against a state employee such as Ryan and Hunt. Payment would have to come out of their own pocket. An appeal to the Court of Appeals for the Sixth Circuit was possible but the likelihood of winning questionable.

On the other hand, three University attorneys had a potential cause of action against the plaintiff and his attorney for a baseless motion for sanctions. An excellent time to consider the possibility of settlement!

By letter of September 22, 1992 Brogan contacted Tennessee Attorney General Charles Burson and requested his approval of a settlement agreement, explaining the tortuous route taken by the Skoutakis litigation. Burson agreed to the proposal. A settlement was reached in April 1993 as referenced by the District Court in its April 27 order dismissing Skoutakis' lawuit "with prejudice".

The settlement results were quite good considering the alternatives. By agreement all parties released the opposition from any liability claims. Skoutakis was paid the sum of $150,000. A second check in the amount of $150,000 was issued to Donati in payment of attorney's fees and costs.

Most important, in my personal estimation, was sworn affirmation by Skoutakis and Donati that the sanction motion alleging misconduct on my part and that of Brogan and Cutting was "not well founded" and that any asserted claims of misconduct were disavowed. As a Christian, I accepted the retraction and held no grudge against my former racquetball partner or his attorney. I had at least one very cordial conversation with Donati after *Skoutakis* concluded. *Skoutakis* certainly does not qualify as my best litigation foray. Then again, it is fair to say that the "disaster in the making" could have ended on a far more drastic note.

Chapters 71–Boosters Gave Vols Cash

From the outset of my employment at the University of Tennessee I was assigned responsibility for handling legal matters for the UT athletics departments. One of my first assignments was a venture to Kentucky sometime in the early 1970s, at the request of UT head basketball coach Ray Mears, to investigate a report that a player had received an automobile in return for signing to play for Kentucky. I traveled to Lexington to investigate but found no evidence to support the claim.

Between 1972 and 1986 my interaction with both men's and women's athletics–the departments being separately administered–was largely advisory. For example, on March 18, 1980, my birthday, I met with UT women's athletic director Gloria Ray, all Lady Vol coaches and Ray's entire supervisory staff. The meeting was an opportunity to keep athletics supervisory personnel up-to-date on legal developments affecting higher education in general and UT and athletics specifically.

Prior to 1986 my athletics responsibilities were almost entirely educational and advisory. Little occurred that garnered news media attention. Dramatic change took place in 1986.

"BOOSTERS GAVE VOLS CASH"

On February 11, 1986 the Knoxville News–Sentinel headlined a front-page article by Al Browning, "UT players given free rooms for 2 decades, innkeeper says." The article quoted area motel operator Trent Richey as claiming he had provided free hotel rooms valued in excess of $100,000 to "UT players, the families of UT players and UT coaches" from the early 1960s until he sold his motel (Old English Inn) in 1964.

In the same article the News-Sentinel made reference to an earlier report that Knoxville physician, Dr. Robert Overholt, had loaned an automobile and credit card to UT quarterback Tony Robinson so he could attend the Sugar Bowl in New Orleans, because Robinson was injured and did not travel with the team to the game.

The Knoxville Journal contained a far more shocking front-page headline the following day: "Boosters gave Vols cash, gifts." The Knoxville Journal, February 12, 1986, p.1. Co-authors Tim Smith and Cindy McConkey reported that 15 ex-players, including such notables as football stars Bill Bates, Fuad Reveiz, Carlton Peoples, Steve Kluge and Mike Cofer, and former basketball player Willie Burton, had either received gifts or knew of teammates who had.

For the next several months the news media regularly covered the scandal involving UT athletics. The following headlines told the story, at least as seen by the news media.

"Vols profited from tickets" and "UT starts probe of booster activities," The Knoxville Journal, February 13, 1986, p.1.

"Panel named to probe UT's alleged NCAA violations," "Vol violation reports stir ire, disbelief," The Knoxville News–Sentinel, February 13, 1986, p.1.

"UT staff knew of motel stays, ex–coach says," The Knoxville News-Sentinel, February 14, 1986, p.1.

"UT denies knowledge of wrongdoings," The Daily Beacon, February 14, 1986, p.1.

"UT silence may spur NCAA", Knoxville Journal, February 16, 1986, p.1.

"Betrayed," announced The Knoxville News-Sentinel, "Boling picks outside review panel," February 17, 1986, p.1.

"Motel owner tells of housing '66 recruit for the Vols," The Knoxville News –Sentinel, February 17, 1986, p. C1.

"Sports' scandal' ", "Ex-Vols deny gifts charges," The February 22, 1986 February 18, 1986, p.1.

"Faculty concerned over exclusion from probe," The Daily Beacon, February 19, 1986, p.1.

"UT probes ticket letter– 'you owe me for basketball tickets,' player was told," The Knoxville Journal, February 22, 1986, p.1.

"'We shouldn't have rules if they can't be obeyed,' "The Atlanta Journal and Constitution, March 2, 1986, p.18D.

"Faculty Senate questions UT probe procedure," "Probe of UT Athletics not documented, faculty says", The Knoxville News–Sentinel, March 4, 1986, p. C!.

"UT athletics probe turns to current players", The Knoxville News–Sentinel, April 22, 1986, p. B1.

"It's up to NCAA–2 athletes suspended after UT's investigation", The Knoxville News–Sentinel, June 4, 1986, p.1.

"UT suspends Ziegler and Reveiz, asks NCAA to OK reinstatement," The Knoxville Journal, June 4, 1986, p.1.

"Questions surround probe of UT Athletics," The Knoxville News–Sentinel, June 17, 1986, p.1.

"NCAA may give UT credit for internal probe," The Knoxville News–Sentinel, June 18, 1986, p.1.

"UT athletic probe queried FBI narc", The Knoxville Journal, August 26, 1986, p.1.

"NCAA pass violations affect 28 Vols", The Knoxville Journal, September 5, 1986, p.1.

These and other articles in the news media may well have led readers to conclude the UT athletic program was in deep trouble. One important lesson from this chapter: don't unquestioningly believe everything you read.

Before the ink was dry on either the Journal's or Sentinel's February 11, 1986 articles an investigation was underway to determine whether any rules of the National Collegiate Athletic Association had been broken. General Counsel Brogan, Athletic Director Doug Dickey, Faculty Chairman of the Athletics Board, Dr. Malcolm McInnis, Vice Chancellor for Student Affairs, Phil Scheurer, and I attended a called meeting on February 11.

Two days later, at a specially called news conference, President Ed Boling stated that the University had no knowledge of any NCAA rule violations but that a committee of four had been appointed to investigate the matter. "Panel named to probe UT's alleged NCAA violations", The Knoxville News–Sentinel, February 13, 1986, p.1.

"Boling asked that anyone with 'verifiable information' concerning rule violations call Associate General Counsel Ron Leadbetter." The Daily Beacon, February 14, 1986, p.1. The Knoxville News – Sentinel concluded a February 14 front-page article ("UT staff knew of motel stays, ex–coach says" / "Probe won't hide facts Boling vows") with an invitation: "Anyone with information for the committee is asked to call Leadbetter at 974 –3245."

Even a UT publication, "Context" (February 26, 1986 edition), urged "students, faculty, and staff who have questions or information pertinent to the investigation" to come forward. "I [Scheurer] encourage anyone with information that might be helpful to us to write or call Mr. (Ron) Leadbetter." Id. Scheurer chaired the investigative panel.

The investigation commenced immediately. As I noted in my personal diary entry for February 13:

> I appeared at a specially called news conference called by Pres. Ed Boling
> to announce the formation of a four member committee (Athletic Director
> Doug Dickey, Vice Chancellor for Student Affairs Phil Scheurer, Faculty
> Athletic Committee Chairman Malcolm McGinnis and I) to investigate allegations that athletes had violated NCAA rules by receiving cash, free car use,
> credit card use, etc. from alumni and other athletic supporters. My intention
> is to run a fast, thorough, accurate and probing inquiry to reveal the truth.

On February 12 the investigative team met with Trent Ritchey. That meeting took place two days after I met with law enforcement officers investigating drug sales by UT quarterback Tony Robinson (See Chapter 66). Although I attended President Boling's February 13 news conference I left Knoxville shortly thereafter–I had work to do at the other end of the state. Early the next morning I flew to Memphis.

I met for two hours on February 14 in my Memphis office with former All-American UT defensive tackle Reggie White, then playing pro football with the Philadelphia Eagles, and former UT defensive back Carlton Peoples. White stated he had never accepted, or even been offered, cash or gifts from boosters while at UT. Moreover, he had no knowledge of any other player receiving such benefits. Peoples offered virtually identical denials. Both White and Peoples signed affidavits affirming the essence of their statements to me.

Later that evening I returned to Knoxville and arrived in the midst of a blinding snowstorm. During the two-hour drive home, arriving to find the rest of the family had been stranded in other locations, I had much to contemplate. I found the athletes statements to me very credible; credible but in complete contradiction to the tone of reports published in local news media.

During the days that followed I contacted, or attempted to contact, every former player mentioned in the news media as having been involved in any way with receipt of cash or benefits in violation of NCAA rules. Not an easy task. In my diary for February 21, I referred to "the busiest couple of weeks since I've been at UT (I've been putting in 14-18 hours a day work on investigation of alleged improprieties in the UT athletic program)."

A February 24, 1986 interview with Fuad Reveiz closely replicated the denials set forth in the statements of White and Peoples. February 18 interviews with ex-UT and current Dallas Cowboy safety Bill Bates and former UT lineman Bill Marron offered special insight.

I telephoned Bates in Dallas and questioned him about news reports that he had admitted knowledge of players receiving benefits. Bates' responded with a denial. He explained that he had recently received a phone call from a gentleman who represented that he was conducting a survey. According to Bates the presentation began with, "you hear that athletes receive cash or benefits when they score a touchdown or catch a pass" or something to that effect. Bates' response to the caller was, "Yeah, you hear those kinds of things." However, Bates denied he told caller he had personal involvement in or knowledge of such activity.

A nearly identical phone conversation took place less than an hour later with Marron, then residing in New Jersey. There was little likelihood that they collaborated on the information they provided me. A pattern was beginning to develop.

While I handled the bulk of witness interviews on my own, members of the investigative committee sometimes joined in. On February 17 all four members of the panel met with and questioned various coaches throughout the afternoon. The following day the panel interviewed a number of current athletes. All day February 19 was spent interviewing a variety of witnesses as was a good part of the following day, February 20.

Early the morning of February 20 I had a one and a half hour meeting with Cindy McConkey. [She had recently left her position at the Knoxville Journal and was now reporting for the Knoxville News–Sentinel]. "Ron, I need your help. I keep getting "scooped" on stories about athletes receiving cash or benefits." My reply–in so many words, "Cindy, the reason you are getting scooped on those stories is they didn't happen." I offered an unofficial explanation for my conclusion and left it at that. The investigation was not yet complete.

THE ROBERT JONES DISCLOSURE

On March 5 I had a telephone conversation with Robert Jones, a former UT third string running back then residing in South Carolina. Jones advised me that he had knowledge of players receiving cash and benefits and was willing to disclose what he knew. I invited Jones to meet with the committee in the Knoxville. He accepted the invitation.

Two days later, on March 7, the investigative panel met with Jones in a conference room in Gibbs Hall (athletics dormitory). After introductions of those present by the panel chair I led the questioning. "Mr. Jones, you indicated to me on the telephone that you can identify players who received cash or benefits from boosters. Would you tell us who received such cash or benefits?" Jones replied, "I would prefer that they give you that information."

Several times, several ways, I asked Jones "who is 'they'?" "Who is it we need to talk to?" Despite my repeated efforts, and those of one or two other panel members, to entice Jones to either identify the alleged recipients of booster benefits or at least provide the names of potential witnesses to be interviewed. Jones refused to provide the requested information and the meeting was adjourned. I removed Jones from my list of prospected witnesses.

BOB OVERHOLT AND TONY ROBINSON

Dr. Bob Overholt was a huge UT basketball fan. His corner front row low balcony seats in Stokely Athletic Center were directly adjacent to my front row floor seats. We were close neighbors and I had ample opportunity to see how enthusiastically Overholt supported the Vols, cheering on his team to victory at every opportunity. I understood that he purchased eight season tickets each year dating back well before my arrival in the Office of General Counsel.

I also knew Overholt to be a kind and generous man, strongly supportive of the community as well as the University. It was with much chagrin that I shared with him, at a February 19 meeting in Stokely Athletic Center, my information that he had provided Tony Robinson free use of his automobile for travel to the Sugar Bowl and had paid the cost of Robinson's fuel for the trip. Overholt confirmed the accuracy of my information.

It was clear to me that Overholt's gifts were not intended for any illicit gain on his part or for any recruiting advantage, but simply an act of benevolence. Unfortunately, because Overholt qualified as a booster under NCAA guidelines, the University had no choice but to address the violation.

Overholt left the meeting noticeably upset. I was not much happier. Had much of my career involved actions such as this I would likely have looked for a different career path.

The University subsequently removed all but two of Overholt's season tickets for basketball. Of more consequence to the University, Head Football Coach Johnny Majors and the UT football program were penalized because Majors had learned of the extra benefits Overholt provided Robinson, had confronted

Overholt and had instructed him to refrain from such conduct in the future. Unfortunately, Majors had failed to report the infraction to the NCAA.

On April 4, 1986, p. B-1, the Knoxville News-Sentinel headlined "UT investigators to begin writing report." The article reviewed the status of the investigation:

A University of Tennessee committee investigating alleged NCAA violations by athletes or athletic department officials hopes to begin writing a report on its findings within two weeks.

However, it may be "6 to 8 weeks" before the investigation is complete and the report prepared, said UT Athletic Director Doug Dickey.

***

"Like all investigations, you start fast and furious, but we have slowed up," said Ron Leadbetter, UT associate general counsel and a member of the committee. "We have become bogged down."

Committee members have had to attend to other business and UT's spring break slowed the investigation, Leadbetter said. Also, committee chairman Phil Scheurer, vice chancellor for student affairs, has been out of town this week, UT officials said.

Leadbetter said the committee has "some isolated points to cover" before the investigation is concluded.

The committee has not decided whether to grant immunity to athletes who come forward and testify, Leadbetter said. If granted immunity, athletes who may have violated NCAA rules would not be subject to disciplinary action on the basis of the information they provide.

"UT athletics probe turns to current players," announced the Knoxville News-Sentinel, April 22, 1986, p.1. Sure enough on April 23, 1986 the investigative committee met with all UT scholarship athletes at 9:30 in the evening. It was made clear that any added benefits needed to be immediately reported and restitution made. Little new information was elicited as a result of this meeting.

A few loose ends were tied up but little new information was received over the next few weeks. I prepared a "draft" report of the committee's findings. I felt comfortable with the contents and confident the investigation had been thorough.

On May 22, 1986 President Boling, Vice President Joe Johnson, and the investigative committee met with a 13 member panel chaired by UT Vice President for Administration Charles Smith. The panel was appointed by President Boling for the purpose of determining whether the committee had done a good job. Members of the panel included UT women's athletic director Joan Cronan, former UT football player Kelsey Finch, and former two-term president of the NCAA, Earl Ramer, among others.

The committee review took 3 1/2 hours and I worked on matters related to the investigation until 2:15 the next morning. While the language of the report would be tweaked the investigative committee stood by its conclusions, first and foremost of which was that there had been a no recruiting violations or cash payments made to players.

On May 27, President Boling, Phil Scheurer, Charles Smith and I flew on the UT plane to Destin, Florida to meet with Southeastern Conference Commissioner, Boyd McWherter. We reviewed the report with him and he expressed no concern with the contents.

One final four and a half hour meeting with the 13-member review panel was held on in June 2. A press conference was held the following day and the committee's preliminary report was released at that time. For the first time, it was announced that two current players, placekicker Carlos Reveiz and linebacker Kelly Ziegler, had been suspended for several violations of an NCAA rule limiting reservation of game passes two family members or students. See: "UT suspends Ziegler and Reveiz, asks NCAA to OK reinstatement," The Knoxville Journal, June 4, 1986, p.1. "It's up to NCAA," The Knoxville News-Sentinel, June 4, 1986, p.1.

Several additional self-imposed penalties were included in the report and reported by the media:

Public reprimand of coach Johnny Majors for failing to report NCAA violations.
Bob Overholt and Trent Ritchie barred from involvement with UT athletics
Refund of $8,000 to Overholt for priority seating in the new, but unfinished basketball arena.

Id.

UT also requested that the eligibility of Ziegler and Reveiz be reinstated. (Id).

As evident from the above listing, not a single penalty of substance was self-imposed by the University. The final decision rested in the hands of the NCAA.

The first step in that process actually took place on May 30, 1986. Charles Smith and the investigative committee flew in the UT plane to NCAA headquarters in Kansas City to meet with NCAA investigators. The UT committee report was presented at that time for discussion. The discussion went well. Our report was released to the press several days later–on June 3.

Perhaps the press got the good word. On June 18, 1986 the Knoxville News-Sentinel headlined "NCAA may give UT credit for internal probe."

On September 25 the investigative committee, President Boling, Vice President Smith and Coach Johnny Majors loaded into UT's King Air and headed for Portland, Oregon to meet with the NCAA infractions committee. We appeared before that committee the following day, September 26. The hearing went well and no challenges to the committee's findings were posed. There was nary a hint the NCAA would conduct its own investigation.

The Knoxville News-Sentinel's front page story of October 18, 1986 ("NCAA puts UT on probation") well documented the final paragraph in this tumultuous chapter of UT history:

The National Collegiate Athletic Association Thursday placed the University of Tennessee on one–year probation–without penalties or loss of scholarships–because of violations in the school's football program.

The ruling, which concludes the NCAA's investigation of the UT athletic department and follows an NCAA hearing on UT's case two weeks ago, will not be appealed, said UT President Edward Boling.

"The athletics program has been placed on one–year probation for the purpose of assessing the effectiveness of our corrective actions, but it is important to note that no sanctions or penalties were assessed against the university," Boling said. "We have conveyed our acceptance of the ruling."

In less than nine months the wagonload of media claims that numerous UT athletes had received cash or other impermissible benefits was laid to rest. The eligibility of two athletes who innocently, in my opinion, committed a "secondary infraction," was restored. Chapter closed.

But, the Chapter would be reopened.

Chapter 72–Sport Magazine Expose

One year after the UT investigative committee, and NCAA, concluded that boosters did not give Vols cash and the UT coaching staff, with one minor exception, had violated no NCAA rules, SPORT magazine dropped a bombshell:

"On October 9, the University of Tennessee will finish serving a one-year term of NCAA probation, the result of its six-month, in-house investigation into charges of widespread rules violations by players and officials of the athletic department. The conclusion of the investigative committee members was that, except for a few isolated incidents (mostly involving quarterback Tony Robinson and a basketball player, Willie Burton), the charges were groundless. Their report was forwarded to the NCAA, whose enforcement department accepted its findings after a cursory review. Last fall, the NCAA committee on infractions, meeting in South Portland, Maine, placed Tennessee on one-year probation without sanctions–essentially a warning against further abuses.

But conversations with dozens of players, coaches, boosters and officials have turned up evidence that the UT investigation was itself improper and many of its conclusions false. Participants in the football program say the university failed to investigate itself thoroughly and instead misled the NCAA through conclusions based on false affidavits and suppressed testimony. Witnesses who testified before the committee say they lied. Another says he was represented to the NCAA in an erroneous, unsigned affidavit. And still others, who testified to abuses say their statements were ignored."

SPORT, "Trouble in Tennessee", November 1987, pp. 68-79.

Many of the allegations in the article dealt with matters beyond the "limitations period" for which the University was responsible or were attributed to unidentified persons. A few claims were directly contradicted by affidavits included in the committee's report or would be contradicted by affidavits I obtained after reading the Sport article.

My first "heads up" on the Sport magazine article came on June 29, 1987 when I received a call from co-author David Whitford. I recall only his inquiries regarding the investigation and my response that the investigative report was completely reliable. Questions were asked and answered. I sensed a reporter looking for a story. I was correct.

"In most cases the conclusions of the official UT investigation have been found to be false or misleading;

Payments to players. "The committee has been unable to identify a single, credible report or otherwise confirm a single instance of a player receiving a cash payment from a booster." In fact, at least six former volunteers, among them Philadelphia Eagles lineman Reggie White and Cincinnati Bengals wide-out Tim McGee, say they received cash payments ranging from postgame "hundred dollar handshakes" to outright gifts.

Clothing, meals and other benefits. "The committee... was unable to identify a single UT athlete [apart from Robinson and Burton] received any clothing, meals or other material benefits from UT boosters." A half-dozen players, including White and former San Diego Chargers lineman Tony Simmons, say otherwise. They describe free airline tickets and trips to clothing stores for new wardrobes...."Id. p. 68.

SPORT also reported that "Leadbetter's notes on the committee's proceedings have never been made available to the NCAA. When SPORT asked to see the rest of these notes, Leadbetter said that the excerpts had been released without his authorization, and that he would not release the rest until ordered to do so by a judge." Id. p. 78.

As the Knoxville News-Sentinel reported on October 6, 1987, p.C1, ("NCAA continues evaluation of UT cover-up report") "UT officials have denied any wrongdoing and said the school's investigation was properly conducted." The article also reported:

"In a related matter, UT General Counsel, Beauchamp Brogan said the university has sent the NCAA the personal notes one in-house investigator made during the course of the probe last year.

Sport magazine said the notes, which belong to UT attorney Ron Leadbetter, indicate that UT overlooked the testimony of at least one former football player when investigators compiled their final report.

The university sent Leadbetter's original notes to the NCAA so the association could determine whether the school covered up any wrongdoing,Brogan said."

As occurred in 1986, the news media jumped on board even before the SPORT article appeared on the newsstand.

"Magazine story charges Vols coverup to NCAA," The Commercial Appeal, September 29, 1987, p. D1.

"UT denies NCAA violations cover–up," The Knoxville Journal, September 29, 1987, p.1.

"Cover-up charged-UT hid football violations, magazine says," The Knoxville News-Sentinel, September 29, 1987, p.1.

"Ex-Vols claim rules violations," "Gault admits shoe deal in college," USA Today, September 29, 1987 p. 1C.

"NCAA uncertain if it will investigate UT," The Knoxville News-Sentinel, September 30, 1987, p.1.

"Another in–house investigation isn't enough," The Knoxville News-Sentinel, September 30, 1987, p.1C.

"Tennessee officials stand by their '86 investigation," USA Today, September 30, 1987p. 3C.

"NCAA to study magazine report on UT," the Knoxville News-Sentinel, October 1, 1987, p. C1.

"Ex-Vols Differed on coaches' involvement," The Knoxville News-Sentinel, October 5, 1987, p. C1

"NCAA continues evaluation of UT cover–up report," The Knoxville News -Sentinel, October 6, 1987, p. C1.

"Magazine: UT probe incomplete," the Nashville Tennessean, October__, 1987, p. C1.

"NCAA extends UT's probation," The Daily Beacon, October 23, 1987, p.1.

"NCAA puts Vols back on probation," The Knoxville News-Sentinel, October 23, 1987, p.1.

"Shy '60 Minutes' here to probe UT," The Knoxville Journal, November 19, 1987, p. 1.

Members of the investigative committee, Scheurer, Dickey, McInnis and I, immediately went back to work investigating new charges and charges previously denied. This time the committee worked more informally, but just as diligently. The results were the same. Here are a few key examples of evidence refuting infraction claims contained in the Sport article. If an infraction was not described the committee ignored the claim.

REGGIE WHITE

During the 1986 investigation I had obtained a sworn affidavit from Reggie White. In that affidavit White attested he had never received any cash or other benefits from a booster and had no knowledge of anyone else having done so.

Sport magazine reported that White admitted having received such benefits and that his affidavit to the contrary was false. The October 1, 1987 issue of the Memphis Commercial Appeal (Sports Section, p. D1) reported that "Reggie White yesterday denied several points about a Sport magazine article that implied Tennessee football coach Johnny Majors tried to coerce or intimidate White into a cover-up of possible NCAA violations."

Still, the article related that "White admitted receiving money–'in cash amounts of $10-$20 but never more,' he said–and clothes while at Tennessee from a friend in Chattanooga, a man he refused to identify. He denied that the man had any connection with the UT football program." Id.

White appeared at a press conference in Memphis on September 30 for the purpose of explaining a number of "inaccuracies" in the Sport article. Two days later I spoke with Reggie White and asked that he explain the discrepancy between his affidavit and his statement to the news media that he had in fact received benefits.

The following is a very close approximation of our conversation:

(**My statement**) "Reggie, you told me you never received any cash or benefits from anyone."

(**Reggie**) "I know I did. But when I left your office I kept searching and searching my mind. I later remembered that Uncle_____ [Reggie stated his name but I do not at this time recall what it was] provided me two suits back when I was in high school."

(**My question**) "What is Uncle _____'s connection with the University of Tennessee?"

(**Reggie**) "None. He's never even been to a UT football game. He's not really a relative but just like a member of the family.

When I was still in high school in Chattanooga I would often preach on Sundays and Uncle ____ would be present to hear me preach. On one occasion he came up to me after the service and said "Reggie, if you're going to preach you have to get something better to wear." He then went out and bought me two new suits to wear when I preached."

The described activity did not remotely constitute an NCAA infraction. White added one more helpful observation during our conversation. "Mr. Leadbetter, it's amazing to me that a third string running back [Robert Jones] claims to have knowledge of players receiving cash payments and I, an All-American, never had anyone offer me cash and never saw anyone else being offered cash." Confident of Reggie White's high moral values and integrity, I weighed his statements firmly against the Sport article's credibility.

TIM McGEE

Tim McGee played football at the University of Tennessee from 1982 to 1986 and, like Reggie White, was cited by Sport as an example of a player who had received cash and benefits from boosters. I elected to take McGee's deposition before a court reporter.

On September 30, 1987, I deposed McGee (Ginger Truesdale, court reporter) in the fourth floor Andy Holt Tower office of Vice Chancellor Phil Scheurer. Malcolm McGinnis was also present. Under questioning McGee made a number of critical points.

> **A.** No, I've never received a cash payment.
> **Q.** Okay. Have you ever received any cash from any coach?
> **A.** No.
> **Q.** Okay. How about any alumnus of the University?
> **A.** No.
> **Q.** And do you recall anyone connected with the University or let's say, a fan; someone who might just be a fan of the university, ever come up to you and say, "here's some money for a good game"?
> **A.** No.
> **Q.** Okay. Now, you're sure about that?
> **A.** Yeah, I'm sure. I've heard of them, but I've never directly received money.
> **Q.** And, no one has ever come up after a game and tried to slip you money where you said, "I don't want it."
> **A.** No, they missed me.

Through 41 pages of interrogation McGee repeatedly stated he had never received any cash or other benefits from any booster, coach or anyone else associated with the University. Aside from seeing Tony Robinson using a booster's automobile–Overholt's–he had no knowledge of any other player receiving cash, credit card or other benefit from any booster.

Aside from a face value sale of his own tickets to Willie Gault, McGee never sold his tickets to anyone else. He also testified he had no knowledge of others selling tickets beyond face value. The pieces of the puzzle were beginning to fit together.

On October 2, 1987, General Counsel Brogan provided a "public statement" explaining why all of my investigative notes had not been released to the NCAA:

"Because the SPORT article suggested that the University had suppressed information given to the investigative committee, Dr. McInnis told a member of the NCAA enforcement staff that he would send to them all remaining materials related to UT's investigation. The sole remaining unpublished document consisted of the personal notes of Ronald Leadbetter, associate general counsel of the University and a member of the UT Investigating Committee.

The notes contained unsubstantiated statements about individuals which unjustly attack their character. They also contained other statements not substantiated by the committee and statements concerning matters not under the jurisdiction of the NCAA. I want to emphasize that the final report submitted to the NCAA and released to the public included all written statements and every allegation of rules violations the committee could substantiate.

Because of the contents of these personal notes, they were not released with the final report. Because the University's athletic program is answerable to the NCAA and so as not to lend any credence to suggestions of cover-up of information given to the investigating committee, the only copy of the notes was sent to the NCAA on Thursday, October 1, in order that the Association could examine them."

ROBERT JONES–
THE THIRD STRING RUNNING BACK BACKTRACKS

An article in the October 7, 1987 Nashville Banner (page D7) featured a disclaimer by Robert Jones, who in 1996 claimed knowledge of NCAA rule infractions. "Ex–Vol claims no cover-up," headlined the article, serving as confirmation of what I had reported to the NCAA in 1986.

Jones had been invited to Knoxville, was encouraged by UT investigators to share any information he had regarding "wrongdoing in its athletic program" and agreed that he did not provide any names, faces or places requested by the committee. "But I would not do that. Those people have to come in on their own. I won't finger anyone." Jones opined that "under the present rules of recruiting Tennessee is a clean program." Id. Not the opinion reported by SPORT.

An October 9 conversation with Willie Gault confirmed that he likewise had no involvement in or knowledge of prohibited booster gifts to himself or other UT athletes. In sum, while alleged NCAA infractions were described in the SPORT article, those allegations lacked any credible supporting evidence.

The investigative committee flew to Atlanta, on the UT plane, on October 20, 1987, to meet with representatives of the NCAA infractions committee. Investigative materials collected since publication of the SPORT magazine "exposé" were thoroughly discussed with the NCAA representatives.

Two days later, on October 22, the NCAA issued a news release, announcing "[t]hat the probationary period imposed last year upon the University of Tennessee, Knoxville, which was due to end on October 9, has not expired. The probationary period will not end until the NCAA enforcement staff reviews information relating to recent published reports of alleged violations of NCAA regulations and a cover-up in the University's 1986 investigation of its football program."

The news release noted that "[m]embers of the NCAA enforcement staff have met with Tennessee officials, and at the university's request the NCAA will conduct its own independent inquiries." No timetable was set for completion of the NCAA review. During the waiting period others apparently reached the same conclusion I reached – there was no merit to the claims posited by SPORT.

"60 minutes" correspondent Ed Bradley spent time in Knoxville, reportedly working on a "60 minutes" segment on UT and the matters reported by SPORT magazine. "Shy '60 Minutes' here to probe UT", the Knoxville Journal, November 19, 1987, p.1. Bradley left Knoxville after short stay without a story worth sharing.

The NCAA agreed. The SPORT story was just that–a story. In May 1988 the NCAA completed its probe of the UT investigation and concluded there was no cover-up. No new infractions were identified. No additional penalties were set. Instead, as headlined on the front page by the Knoxville News-Sentinel on May 27, 1988, "NCAA takes UT off probation". For a second time, extensive allegations and "suggestions" that UT was guilty of NCAA infractions were rejected as baseless.

This chapter of UT history was closed again! It would not be reopened.

Chapter 73–Jack Sells and the Blue Chippers

In early 1990 the NCAA enforcement office received an anonymous letter indicating possible violations of NCAA legislation involving the University of Tennessee's football camps.

Interviews were conducted by NCAA enforcement staff regarding the summer camps. Additional interviews were conducted regarding possible violations involving UT assistant football coach Jack Sells and his recruitment of prospective student–athletes.

I first learned of the NCAA's interest in the summer football camps when UT athletic director Doug Dickey telephoned me and asked that I attend a Friday, December 14, 1990, meeting in his office with NCAA investigator Bill Saum to discuss camp recruiting practices. Sells was a soon asked to join the meeting since he had considerable responsibility for operating the camps.

At the outset of the meeting Sells was asked to describe the extent to which summer football camps were open to the public. Sells' responses to questions on this topic raised no red flags, in my estimation.

Saum then shifted his focus. He questioned Sells about his contacts with several "blue-chip" campers he attempted to recruit to play football at UT. Sells' responses to those questions were a bit shaky. Still, nothing major. NCAA regulations strictly limit coaching contacts with recruits and family members. Often, conversation beyond a brief greeting ("courtesy of the day") constitutes an infraction. But, a "secondary infraction," is not a major violation for which a significant penalty is imposed.

Unfortunately, matters went downhill when Saum asked Sells if he had been involved in securing airline tickets for Brian Thurman, a prospective camper and "blue-chip" athlete. Saum asked Sells if he had been involved in Thurman's purchase of an airline ticket for travel to the camp. Sells denied involvement.

When asked whether he had contacted Mary Fran Lawson with Plaza Travel Agency, Sells denied he had. Sells denied requesting that she make reservations for Thurman's travel from Chicago to Knoxville.

With Sells' denial of involvement with Thurman's acquisition of airline tickets the meeting concluded. As Sells prepared to leave I warned him, "Do not speak with anyone about what we have discussed." Sells replied that he would not and was going to his office–not far from our meeting site. I had a hunch.

Fifteen or twenty minutes later–with Dickey and Saum listening in–I placed a telephone call to Mary Fran Lawson. "Ms. Lawson this is Ron Leadbetter. I understand that you just spoke to Jack Sells about the purchase of an airline ticket for Brian Thurman." Lawson hesitated for several seconds before replying, "Yes." In further discussion she made it clear that the full price of the airline ticket had been paid–as Sells assured her it would be–and it was clear from furthering investigation that the money paid came from Thurman rather than Sells.

Sells involvement with the acquisition of Thurmond's airline ticket was a violation of NCAA rules–a secondary infraction. But providing false information to the NCAA constitutes a primary infraction leading to serious penalty. Saum was well aware that Dickey and I made every effort to discourage such conduct.

Two additional meetings were held that day, one with head football coach Johnny Majors and another with assistant athletic director Bill Higdon. Saum left Knoxville and returned to Kansas City. On Monday morning Dickey advised Sells that he was suspended indefinitely (with pay). See: "Vols suspend Sells after NCAA talk," The Tennessean, December 18, 1990, p. 1C.

Additional on-campus interviews were conducted by Saum on January 18, 1991 and February 15, 1991. The first meeting was attended by Dickey, Malcolm McInnis, Saum and Sells, as well as Knoxville attorney Tom Jones – representing Sells–and me. At this meeting, Sells admitted misleading Saum in the December meeting.

The same group attended the February meeting. On that occasion, Sells clarified that he had "intentionally" misled Saum during the December meeting –

he had been untruthful because of the stress of the unexpected inquiry presented him at that time. From that time forward both Sells and his attorney, Jones, co-operated fully with both the NCAA and me in the investigation to come. Sells was reinstated to his university position on March 26 – coaching responsibilities only – pending completion of the University's investigation into possible rules infractions.

As a result of the January and February interviews, NCAA assistant executive director for enforcement, David Berst, issued an official letter of inquiry to the University. His April 8, 1991 letter was addressed to Acting President Joe Johnson. The three-page letter requested that 10 copies of President Johnson's response be forwarded to the NCAA national office and one copy sent to each member of the committee on infractions.

I was pleased to see that one of the five members of the committee was Beverly Ledbetter, Vice-President and General Counsel at Brown University–a friend with whom I had actively served as a member of the National Association of College and University Attorneys. Occasionally NACUA conference attendees would "mix us up" –I would get her mail or she would get my phone call. We enjoyed a good laugh over it.

Attached to Berst's letter of inquiry was a nine page "Official Inquiry to the Chief Executive Officer of the University of Tennessee, Knoxville." The official inquiry set forth a lengthy list of alleged violations of NCAA bylaws. According to Berst, "based upon a review of the alleged violations set forth in this inquiry, this case appears to be "major" in nature. Accordingly, please note that if the committee on infractions concurs with this conclusion following the hearing in this case, the institution and the involved members of the football coaching staff could be subject to penalties as set forth in Bylaw 19.4.2.1 of the 1991–92 NCAA manual."

The official inquiry was released to the news media. A detailed front page story appeared in the Knoxville News-Sentinel on April 18, 1991 ("UT to respond to NCAA allegations"). The article noted that the University had until June 10 to respond to the allegations and that it would be up to the NCAA infractions committee "to decide if UT is to be placed on probation, with or without sanctions. Possible sanctions would be reduction of scholarships and a ban on television appearances and/or postseason play."

"Intense" best describes the investigation undertaken following receipt of the NCAA official inquiry. Between April 29 and August 8 I spent all or part of at least 37 days meeting with or otherwise contacting witnesses. A few examples:

4/29 Met with football players Bill Shoenle, Mark Needham, Dave Thomas, Tom Myslinski, Tom Fuhler, Armandos Fisher separately and in that order.

5/1 Call to Carole Kaesebier (219/ 239-6411) Notre Dame. Set up meeting with two players. [Kaesebier, a friend of mine from NACUA, and glad to help].

5/3 Call to Larry Templeton (A.D. [Athletic director], Miss. State), set up
    meeting with three players.
5/6 Deposition of Jack Sells - [154 pages in length. During deposition Sells
    admitted that he was not completely truthful during his first meeting with
    the NCAA. "I was wrong in telling them what they wanted to hear." At the
    end of his deposition Sells admitted that he had called Mary Fran Lawson–
    despite being told not to – and asked her to deny that he had called].
5/7 Met with football players Tony Harris, Keo Coleman and Nate Williams
    (after introductory meeting with Miss. State AD Larry Templeton) separ-
    ately and in that order.
5/14 Met with the following separately, in order: Mark Fletcher, DarylHardy,
    Jeremy Lincoln, Shawn Truss, Bill Schoenle (re–interview)
    Evening telephone call to Mr. and Mrs. Schoenle
5/20 Met in Chicago (Law firm of Mayer, Brown and Platt) with Phil Facenda
    (Notre Dame's attorney [another friend of mine from NACUA]) and, first,
    Oliver Gibson, then Pete Bercich.
    Telephone call to Mrs. Bercich (approximately one hour, 20 minutes)
5/27 Met with Bill Higdon
    Met with all football coaches except Jack Sells
5/31 Meeting with Johnny Majors

Approximately 40 football players, recruits and others were interviewd by
telephone or in person. I interviewed athletic directors Bob Devaney (University of Nebraska) and Bob Frederich (University of Kansas) as well as athletic
directors previously identified. Then there were a host of calls to parents and
siblings of football players who had attended the UT football camps.

On June 5, 1991 a meeting was held in Doug Dickey's office, attended by
Majors, Johnson, Brogan, McInnis and me. Special guest was SEC Commissioner Roy Kramer. After the meeting a decision was made to terminate Sells'
employment. A UT press release issued June 7, 1991 explained:

    Dickey said he approved Sells' dismissal with the concurrence of head
    football coach Johnny Majors, UT Knoxville Chancellor John Quinn, and act-
    ing UT President Dr. Joseph E Johnson. Dickey said that following an investi-
    gation by UT legal counsel Sells' actions as an assistant football coach and
    recruiter were judged inappropriate and unacceptable.

On June 8, 1991 Acting President Johnson provided a 28 page letter to David
Berst, detailing the University's response to the NCAA's official inquiry. In
short, it was denied that the UT summer football camps violated NCAA rules.
However, it was readily admitted that Sells made impermissible recruiting contacts with athletes and family members and did so intentionally–notwithstanding Sells claim to the contrary.

It was further conceded that Sells violated NCAA rules of ethical conduct by
providing false and misleading information during the December 14,1990 meet-

ing with NCAA enforcement representative Saum. Johnson also noted that Sells was initially suspended on December 17, 1990 but permitted to return to his coaching duties on March 25–although barred from any recruiting activities – pending UT's completion of the investigation and "determination of the magnitude of any offenses committed by Sells." Johnson then explained that, having completed the investigation, "the University has judged Sells' actions inappropriate and unacceptable. Accordingly, Sells' University employment was terminated on June 7, 1991."

Sells likewise provided to the NCAA a detailed response to the official inquiry. He "admitted to providing false and misleading information, and within a few days after the December 14 interview he (through his counsel) contacted the NCAA in an effort to arrange further interviews to rectify the situation. Subsequently, Sells was interviewed on January 18 and February 15, during which he provided truthful information and during which he cooperated fully with the NCAA."

Sells explained his previous untruthfulness as follows:

While this is not intended to be an excuse of Sells conduct, this is evidence of the situation which was at hand – Sells not fully recalling all of the details, being pressured for answers by the NCAA and by athletic director Doug Dickey, being scared and fearful of the situation, and being without counsel. In a situation such as that, Sells committed an unfortunate yet human mistake–he said something that wasn't true.

Sells response, p. 19. [Sells response was provided to me by Saum at my request].

On June 10, 1991 I spent the day in Kansas City at NCAA headquarters. The University's response was the topic of discussion with Saum. It was a friendly meeting but one thing became clear to me: NCAA staff believed UT's summer football camps recruited "blue-chip" athletes in violation of NCAA rules.

I departed Kansas City, returned to Knoxville and went back to work. I contacted 33 high school football coaches–mostly from Tennessee but one from Columbia, South Carolina, another from Morrow, Georgia and a third from Snellville, Georgia. Each was asked to write a brief letter commenting on whether any UT coach calling to advertise UT summer football camps placed any limitation on those who could attend. An excellent sample response was a August 2, 1991 letter written by Bennie Hammonds, head football coach for Gatlinburg–Pitman High School in Gatlinburg, Tennessee.

Mr. Ron Leadbetter
719 Andy Holt Tower
Knoxville, TN 37996 – 0170

To whom it may concern:

As head football coach at Gatlinburg–Pitman high school for the last 19 years I have had a long-standing working relationship with the University of Tennessee's football staff.

For the last several years, Coach Phillip Fulmer has "recruited" our school. We have had several boys who have attended the "Johnny Majors Football Camp" and the "Senior Football Camp."

Coach Fulmer has never stated to me that either camp was closed to any of our football players. We have had players who have attended both camps. I have never felt that the "Seniors Camp" was closed to any of our athletes or that it was only available to certain athletes. Our staff and players have always felt free to participate in any one of the two camps.

Please feel free to contact me if necessary.

Sincerely,
Benny P. Hammonds
Head Football Coach

The remaining 32 letters stated the same conclusion even though different coaches interacted with different recruiters at UT. Not a single high school coach I contacted suggested that any limitation was ever was placed on camp attendees.

On July 2 NCAA investigative staffers Bill Saum and Richard Hilliard hosted Malcolm McInnis and me in Kansas City for a "NCAA pre-hearing." The meeting was most helpful in explaining how the hearing would proceed.

There would be introductions, opening statements by UT (Joe Johnson), Sells and NCAA staff. Allegations would be presented one–by–one with a presentation addressing each point followed up by questions from the committee. Each party would have the opportunity to make a closing statement.

The estimated time for the hearing it would be four hours (8:30 or 9:00 to 1:00). Any appeal of penalties or findings were required to be filed within 15 days.

On July 14, 1991 The Knoxville News-Sentinel headlined, "UT understated camp report" (p.C-1). The Sentinel accurately reported that UT had erred in reporting the percentage of campers considered division 1-A football prospects for the years 1986–1990. For example, in 1986 UT reported a 14% attendance rate while the Sentinel reported a 27.7% attendance rate. For the most recent year–1990–UT reported 6% while the Sentinel reported 15.6%. Id.

Sports editor John Adams headlined "Sheer numbers blurring UT's description of camp" Id. Adams opined , "UT must convince the NCAA that the second of its two summer football camps from 1986–1990 was not in violation of NCAA rules. So far, its defense has been less than overwhelming." Perhaps – perhaps not.

Adams later noted that "Ronald C Leadbetter, UT's associate general counsel who prepared the official response to the NCAA, said the figures were provided by Bill Higdon, an athletic department administrative aide who is director of the camp…. Leadbetter said the figures came from 'Bill Higdon's recollections' of where prospects signed scholarships." While Adams thought the discrepancy in the figures had relevance I did not. The vast majority of those attending the "Senior Camps" did not sign division 1-A football scholarships.

One last claim made by Sells–that UT coach Tim Mingey had been involved in providing prohibited transportation to Bereich, was disposed of by a trip to West Point. Saum and I met with Mingey–then a football coach at West Point –on July 1, 1991. Mingey denied the infraction activities attributed to him by Sells. In my opinion–and apparently Saum's–his denial was credible.

By letter of August 9, 1991 President Johnson–elected President by the UT Board of Trustees on June 27, 1991–provided an update to the five members of the infractions committee and David Berst. First, Johnson explained the University's reason for suspending, then reinstating and finally dismissing Sells from his UT position. He confirmed that Sells' unethical actions were the basis for his June 7, 1991 termination.

On a second front, although "no evidence has been discovered that head football coach John Majors or any other individual associated with the university's athletic program was aware of coach Sells' recruiting violations", Johnson announced that the full-time coaching position vacated by Sells would not be filled , "re-emphasizing the need for the head coach to exercise control over recruiting and other administrative activities." As Johnson noted, "this self-imposed penalty will accelerate by one year the NCAA–mandated reduction in the number of full-time assistant football coaches from 9 to 8."

"For the same reasons, the University will limit, for the next two years, the number of overall scholarships and football to 85. This penalty will accelerate by two years the NCAA–mandated reduction."

Lastly, Johnson asserted that it was the university's position that the UT football program had been operated in compliance with NCAA regulations–although the "senior camp" had been suspended pending the NCAA's resolution of the issue.

By letter of July 18, 1991 President Johnson was informed by Berst that "[a]n appearance by the institution's representatives before the committee has been scheduled for 8:30 AM on Sunday, August 11, 1991, at the Grove Park Inn in Asheville, North Carolina."

Arrangements were made for the UT plane to pick me up on Saturday afternoon at UT Martin–where I was meeting with UT Martin athletic director Ray Mears. My wife and I were also helping our son, Lee, check into dormitory housing on campus as he prepared for the start of his freshman year at UTM.

After picking me up the UT plane proceeded to Knoxville where the rest of the team boarded. Included were Johnson, Majors, McInnis, Higdon, Brogan, Quinn and Assistant Director of Athletics for Compliance and Operations, Gene Moeller. We spent the night in an Asheville hotel–not the Grove Park Inn. I estimated between 40 and 50 news reporters were congregated in front of the Grove Park Inn when we arrived the following morning.

The hearing proceeded as expected. Introductions were followed by opening statements. Johnson's opening statement brought a smile to my face: "President Edward Boling, my former boss, had a favorite saying, coined sometime in the 1970s, which was repeated to each of the University's athletic directors and members of the coaching staff: 'you can lose games and keep your job–at least for a while. But if you cheat, you're gone.' " The same statement Boling made to me before my first NCAA assignment.

Johnson emphasized the University's commitment to integrity in operating its athletic program. He concluded his opening remarks "by expressing my appreciation to the committee for the assistance provided to Mr. Leadbetter and other university officials in carrying out the investigation at hand." "You have my assurance that, as president, I have insisted and will continue to insist that our athletics program be conducted with integrity and in strict compliance with NCAA rules."

In concluding his introductory remarks Johnson announced, "Ron Leadbetter will be the University's representative for the purpose of responding to the specifics of the official inquiry." Johnson also reminded the committee that I had "handled the bulk of the investigative effort relating to the 1986 NCAA official inquiry. " Now it was my time to enter the firing range. A tough but exciting challenge.

The questioning proceeded as expected. Infractions Committee members–Beverly Ledbetter was no longer on the committee that reviewed our case–asked questions that were challenging, direct and fair. At the conclusion of the proceedings the members of the UT team expressed consensus that all had gone well. We would not know if our assessment was accurate until the committee's report was released.

On September 17, 1991 we received the answer. Alan Williams, Chair, NCAA Committee on Infractions, conveyed "Infractions Report No. 64 (Case No. M

43)" to President Johnson.

The nine page, single spaced, report detailed the committee's findings. Most findings were expected. Some were suprising. Several merited particular attention:

> The violations alleged in category (c) above related to the University's operation of a summer "senior" football. The committee concluded that the information presented did not establish a violation of NCAA legislation.

***

> …the enforcement staff did not sustain its burden of proving that the university failed to give the public adequate notice through information disseminated orally and personally by the coaching staff to high school programs throughout the area of the general availability of the senior camp. In view of the information from the University indicating there was widespread knowledge among area high school football programs of the general availaiblity of the senior camp. In view of the information from the University indicating there was widespread knowledge among area high school football programs of the availability of the senior camp to all entrants the committee concluded that no violation occurred.

Report, p.3. The first surprising -and favorable–finding of the committee was its acceptance of UT's position on summer football camps over that of NCAA investigators:

Although the committee did not find a violation relating to the football camp, the committee concluded that this was a major case under Bylaw 19.02.2. There were a series of recruiting violations, including arranging an airline ticket on a credit basis for a prospect to attend the university's football camp, that were knowingly committed by a member of the University's football coaching staff for whose conduct the University is responsible. Moreover, the University's compliance and rules – education program did not require newly employed coaching staff members to participate in any rules – compliance orientation or demonstrate familiarity with NCAA recruiting rules before recruiting for the university.

Id. p.4.

A completely expected finding. But, the report on this aspect of the investigation then continued in an unexpected direction: Although this is a major case, it is unique. The university fully cooperated in the processing and investigation of this case. It acknowledged violations when the evidence supported such conclusions and admitted that a member of its coaching staff violated the principles of ethical conduct in Bylaw 10.01.1. The university took timely corrective and disciplinary actions that included dismissing its assistant football coach, suspending its senior football [canp], and self – imposing substantial recruiting and athletics grant – in – aid penalties. For these reasons, as explained in Part III of this report, the committee did not apply the full schedule of minimum penalties that bylaw 19.4.2.1 otherwise requires in the case of a major violation.

Id. p.4.

Because of the institutional corrective and disciplinary actions described previously, the committee did not impose additional penalties involving restrictions on postseason competition, television appearances, expense–paid visits by prospect of student–athletes and off-campus recruiting. Had the university not taken the actions it did to correct the violations, discipline the assistant coach who was primarily involved and self-impose penalties on its football program, the committee would haves considered imposing the penalties in these categories required by bylaw 19.4.2.2.

Id. p. 9.

The integrity of the investigation paid off–although integrity is not, in my opinion, in any way dependent on "payoff."

One more committee finding was a major surprise–a finding which *rejected* a NCAA staff finding of infraction after UT admitted the infraction occurred:

The committee did not find the former assistant coach violated the ethical–conduct standards pertaining to the provision of false and misleading information during the course of an NCAA investigation. All parties agreed that during the assistant coach's initial interview with an NCAA enforcement representative, which occurred in the presence of representatives of the university, the former assistant coach gave false and misleading information in response to some of the questions seeking information relevant to possible NCAA violations in which he was involved. Further, at the beginning of this interview, the NCAA investigator specifically called the former assistant coach's attention to the provision of the NCAA bylaws applicable to giving false and misleading information during an investigation of possible NCAA violations and indicated to the assistant coach the seriousness of the consequences that would result from a violation of this bylaw. A separate NCAA bylaw (Bylaw 32.3.6) also places an additional duty on the NCAA enforcement staff, however, to inform an individual prior to the interview that the purpose of the interview is to obtain information about the individual's personal involvement in NCAA violations when that, in fact, is the purpose of the interview. The record before the committee did not establish that the NCAA investigator had given the assistant coach the notification required by this bylaw.

Because the notice called for in Bylaw 32.3.6 was not given, the committee believed it was not appropriate under the circumstances of this case to find that the assistant coach violated the rules of ethical conduct in Bylaw 10.1–(d) by giving false and misleading information during this initial interview. Among the circumstances that led the committee to this conclusion were: (1) the assistant coach was not represented by personal legal counsel during this interview; ... (4) after the initial interview, the former assistant coach promptly consulted personal legal counsel and was prepared to correct the false and misleading statements.

Id. pp. 2-3.

There was no further editorial comment on the quality of the UT investigation by columnist John Adams.

Chapter 74–Heath Shuler and UT Associate Dean Roger Jenkins–Did Jenkins Wine and Dine Quarterback Shuler and Other UT Recruits?

Heath Shuler had a successful career as quarterback for the University of Tennessee's football team starting in 1990 and went on to play pro football in 1994. For a while Shuler operated a real estate business in Knoxville. For several years of my service on the Knox Area Board of Directors of the Fellowship of Christian Athletes, Shuler hosted the Board's monthly meetings at his business headquarters on Kingston Pike.

Shuler was elected to the United States House of Representatives, serving the people of North Carolina's 11th Congressional District from 2007 to 2013).

Heath Shuler's younger brother, Benjie, also had a successful career as punter for the UT football team from 1994 to 1997. The Shuler brothers, along with their parents, were also saddled with claims they received "extra benefits" in violation of NCAA regulations in connection with their UT careers.

By letter of October 25, 1994, Mark Jones, NCAA director of enforcement, it notified Atheletic Director Doug Dickey that his office had received reports of "possible violations of NCAA legislation in the operation of the institution's football program."

The reports were as follows:

The information indicates that during the recruitment and then enrollment of former football student–athlete Heath Shuler that Roger Jenkins, a then associate Dean in the College of business at the institution and now president of Goodys clothing store in Knoxville, Tennessee, and who originally was from North Carolina, may have violated NCAA legislation. Specifically, it was reported that Mr. Jenkins offered to assist the athletics department in its recruitment of Mr. Shuler when the young man was a prospective student--athlete from North Carolina and then took it upon himself to become involved in his recruitment. According to the information, Mr. Jenkins "wined and dined" the Shuler family on no less than five occasions during the institution's recruitment of the young man. Subsequent to Mr. Shuler's enrollment at the institution, Mr. Jenkins frequently provided Mr. Shuler: dinner at no charge to the young man, sometimes at the Club Le Conte and occasionally in the company of other student–athletes; the use of his beige and red four-by-four pickup truck; and took him to the movies and on hunting and fishing expeditions at no cost to the young man. The information also indicated that Mr. Jenkins is a friend of the Shuler family and was quoted in feature stories about Mr. Shuler that appeared in *Sports*

Illustrated and the *Sporting News*. The information indicates that Mr. Jenkins continues to provide meals at his home to football student–athletes at no cost to the young men and may be involved in recruiting current prospective student–athletes. Carman Tagano [Tegano], an academic advisor with the athletics department, also was reported to be knowledgeable about the violations regarding Mr. Jenkins.

Jones noted that any recruiting violations involving Heath Shuler "would have occurred during the 1988–89 academic year and fall outside the NCAA's statute of limitations." However, the University was asked to investigate whether Jenkins had provided "extra benefits" to Shuler after his arrival on campus.

The University was also requested to address Jenkins' role in recruiting student athletes and whether he had ever provided meals to any student athlete. Specifically requested was information regarding Jenkins involvement with the Shuler family. A response was requested by December 15, 1994. UT president Joe Johnson and UT Knoxville Chancellor Bill Snyder requested that I handle that responsibility.

The investigation process in this case was quite straightforward in the absence of an identified informant. Each of those mentioned in the letter from the NCAA would be interviewed. As was my custom, I recorded each of those interviews. The first was with Roger Jenkins on November 25. Jenkins was very forthcoming.

Roger Jenkins held the position of Associate Dean for Academic Affairs for the UT business school until his departure in March 1993 to assume the position of president of Goody's clothing store. He had no responsibilities for recruitment of athletes.

Contrary to reports referenced by the NCAA, Jenkins insisted he "never met the Shuler family until Heath's sophomore year here at the University." In fact, he "never knew the University was recruiting Mr. Shuler until after he was recruited."

During Shuler's sophomore year and continuing while he was at the University, [Jenkins] served as his academic advisor. Jenkins worked closely with Shuler and they would occasionally have lunch together. According to Jenkins,"[o]n those occasions, who would buy the meal? We pay for our own lunches because I was very aware of not providing benefits to the student athlete." Jenkins denied ever paying for the meal of any athlete – specifically including Heath or Benjie Shuler. He denied ever taking any member of the Shuler family to Club LeConte.

Jenkins denied providing any extra benefits to any athletes. He and Heath Shuler went to the movies on four or five occasions but each paid his own admission. Jenkins never went fishing or hunting with Heath or Benjie.

On the other hand, Jenkins unapologetically admitting having both Heath and Benjie to his home for dinner on occasion. "… after I had met Heath during his sophomore year and met Joe and Marge [Heath's parents], his family members, our family and the Shuler family became very close." Jenkins noted that, to his recollection, he never invited any other athletes to his home for a meal. On the other hand, he shared that "when it is a holiday such as Thanksgiving or Christmas or whatever, I will have 20–30 students at my house.… I never acted any differently with Heath Shuler than I did with any other students that I have become close to over the years."

As indicated, Jenkins had "fairly extensive social interaction with the Shuler family after he became a student" ("Absolutely"). Jenkins candidly admitted that "as I indicated earlier, after I had met Heath during his sophomore year and met Joe and Marge, his family members, our family and the Shuler family became very close. There would have been occasions where Joe would be in town and would ask to borrow my four-wheel-drive, so I let him have it. I never owned a four-wheel-drive vehicle, to my knowledge, that Heath has ever used." Jenkins offered an "estimate" that Joe used his Ford Bronco on 2–3 occasions.

During a December 1, 1994 interview, Benjie Shuler confirmed to me at the outset that he understood he was obligated to be truthful under NCAA rules. He confirmed he had eaten at Jenkins' home with his family but that Jenkins never paid for any meal at a restaurant or provided him any other extra benefit. On one occasion, Benji had forgotten his wallet and Jenkins paid the bill "at Grady's restaurant off Cedar Bluff. … He paid for my meal. He reminded me that I needed to pay him back, so it was out in my vehicle, so when we got outside, I reimbursed him with the money." Although it was Jenkins recollection that he was repaid a day or two later, Shuler was absolutely certain that reimbursement was made a short time after the meal. The difference in recollection mattered not for NCAA purposes but demonstrated to me the integrity of the witnesses. Nothing worse than "canned" responses.

On December 5, I had a lengthy telephone conversation with Joe Shuler. He corroborated almost everything in Jenkins "testimony". One exception. He insisted that he borrowed Jenkins' vehicle only once–when he drove to Knoxville and his own vehicle "broke down". He handed Jenkins a $20 bill after he returned the vehicle. Joe Shuler could not say whether Heath had driven the vehicle and suggested that I "ask him that".

A recorded call from me to Heath Shuler was conducted from 9:50 PM to 10:22 PM on December 7, 1994. We reviewed the allegations, one by one. Shuler confirmed that they did not meet Jenkins until his sophomore year. His family and the Jenkins family became close friends thereafter. A number of meals were had at the Jenkins' residence.

He had never been to Club Le Conte nor had he gone fishing or hunting with Jenkins. Movies and restaurants, yes – but each had paid their own way. Shuler had never driven Jenkins' vehicle. His testimony was clear and highly credible:

Leadbetter: Has Roger ever provided you any benefit other than meals? You've already indicated that he didn't provide any meals other than at his own home. But has he provided you anything of value other than the food he provided at his own home?

Shuler: Wisdom only.

Leadbetter: On any occasion, to your knowledge, did Roger ever pay for Benjie's meal?

Shuler: No, my father always picked up whenever Benjie ate with them or something. I'm sure Benjie picked up everything. That was always the understanding when I went.

Leadbetter: Okay. On any occasions did Roger ever provide transportation for you to get to or from the restaurant?

Shuler: No.

Leadbetter: Well, Heath, I believe that responds to all the questions contained in the letter.

Shuler: Okay.

Leadbetter: And I appreciate your help in responding to this.

Shuler: You are welcome. I couldn't believe that when Benjie told me. I was, like, I couldn't believe that. I mean, I guess it's just someone out for either me or Dr. Jenkins or Benjie or someone.

Leadbetter: Well, as you know, frequently these reports are provided to the NCAA and the person providing the report is not identified. Occasionally they will be. In this case we have not had the person making the complaint identified. We don't know what their motivation is.

Shuler: What is the ruling through the NCAA as far as eating at someone's house? I always understood…

Leadbetter: My understanding is that it's permitted. Malcolm McInnis, I don't know if you know about him, but he is our rules expert–he's the faculty representative and I'll be meeting with him and discussing the fine details of what extent you can provide meals. Now, one of the issues here is what happens when you have two families that have had a close friendship, and I don't know where that goes. Based on whatever I know, I don't have any reason to believe that anyone did anything wrong and that it if there were a violation it was certainly not intentional. I guess you know enough about the NCAA rules to know that they are – some of the interpretations are very narrow.

Leadbetter: As I am sure you know, we try our best to comply with the rules and if we find a violation, even a technical one, we are bound to report it.

Shuler: How often do you have allegations like that?

Leadbetter: Fortunately, not very often.

Shuler: Really?

Leadbetter: No, we really don't. I don't know if you remember, I'm trying to think when you were in school–do you remember Jack Sells?

Shuler: Yes, uh-huh.

Leadbetter: Well, that was the last one.

Leadbetter: He was a very aggressive recruiter. He was a good recruiter, but he was very aggressive and he stepped over the bounds of bit. I think the average person, even knowing the rules, would say he didn't step far over the bounds. For example, you know, during certain periods of the year that coaches are not allowed to even…

Shuler: … make contact with players.

Leadbetter: Right. Or parents. What he would do is that he would go out of his way–did wear a Tennessee jacket. He'd go up to watch a baseball game up in Chicago and he just accidentally ran into the parents of this player in the parking lot and said "hi. I'm Jack Sells good to see you around." That was a technical violation. It wasn't a big deal – he didn't give them money or anything like that. What happened was that when the NCAA conducted its investigation and he was asked if he had done something like that, he denied it. He said he had never done it. The NCAA considers that a far worse violation than actually the contact. The contact was a secondary violation. They would have written it up and issued some kind of little reprimand and said don't do that again. Those kinds of little things happen actually with some frequency, no action is taken if it is unintentional and wasn't a major violation. When he lied he committed a major violation and it cost him his job as a coach."

My investigation was rapidly drawing to a close. Carmen Tegano (December 8 telephone interview) denied knowledge of any dealings between Jenkins and the Shulers, just as Jenkins and the Shulers denied any involvement with Tegano. In other words, UT athletics was not involved in any interaction between the Shulers and the Associate Dean of the College of Business. A December 12 follow-up phone conversation with Jenkins revisited the issue of whether a violation had occurred when Jenkins loaned Joe Shuler his four-wheel-drive vehicle.

It was finally agreed that the duration of the loaned vehicle was likely a weekend when Joe Shuler's vehicle was being repaired. From Jenkins testimony it was clear to me he had not intentionally done wrong: "I guess I didn't realize that loaning a vehicle to Joe would have been a violation." I replied "I don't see it as being any kind of significant matter long as we report it. So, we'll do that if that's what's appropriate, and it probably is. If in doubt, we would report it and then have the NCAA say they were not concerned about that."

I prepared my investigative report and had it reviewed by Dr. Malcolm McInnis, Associate Athletic Director in Charge of Compliance, and by Dr. Carl Asp, Faculty Representative. Athletic Director Dickey replied to Jones by December 14. Two minor "potential infractions" were addressed concurrently.

First, I requested and received from Joe Shuler a check which I forwarded to Jenkins with my letter December 23, 1994: "Enclosed is Joe Shuler's check in the amount of $14.99 in payment of the balance due on the fair market rental value of your vehicle which you loaned to him a couple of years ago. Hopefully, this payment, together with the $20 cash payment Joe previously made to you, will be satisfactory to the NCAA."

Second, the University temporarily ruled Benjie Shuler ineligible to play football (since Jenkins had paid for Benjie's meal even though he had been promptly repaid) but requested that the NCAA restore his eligibility. The University's approach worked. By letter of January 19, 1995 Louis Onofrio , NCAA Eligibility Representative, so notified McIinnis.

Dear Malcolm:

This is written confirmation of action taken on behalf of the NCAA eligibility committee and/or the NCAA committee on infractions.... Based upon the information submitted and a review of previous similar eligibility and/or secondary infractions cases, the following action has been taken.

***

Institutional/Conference Action: The institution will require Mr. Shuler to reimburse Mr. Jenkins for the actual cost of use of his car.

NCAA Eligibility Action: Eligibility restored.

NCAA Enforcement Action: The information you have submitted will be reviewed by S. David Berst, NCAA assistant executive director for enforcement and eligibility appeals, as a secondary case and will be forwarded to a member of the NCAA Committee on Infractions for review. Once this process is completed, you will be advised of the result.

The NCAA subsequently accepted Joe Shuler's $14.99 payment to Jenkins as reimbursement for the remaining actual cost of the use of his car. No further enforcement action was taken by the NCAA. The University's investigation and rejection of the claims originally presented–was accepted in full by the NCAA.

Aggressive investigation, commitment to integrity and networking worked to the University's benefit once more.

Chapter 75–Phone Fraud Episode

The years 1995 and 1996 saw an incredible spike in NCAA related incidents at the University of Tennessee. My own calendar during this two-year period was dominated by investigative work on NCAA rule infractions – both real and alleged.

One major episode during this period involved unauthorized use of a telephone access code by UT student athletes. The matter was briefly summarized in my July 31, 1995 interim report to Charles Smrt with the NCAA:

In October 1993 the UT Department of Telephone Services assigned several telephone access codes to the UT athletic department for use by its Office of Student Life. This action was taken at the Athletic Department's request to prevent unauthorized persons from making long distance telephone calls from Student Life phones.

At the beginning of April, 1995, University telephone services officials confirmed a breach in security of its telephone system, over a period of some 15 months, allowing approximately 17,000 telephone calls from over a hundred student dormitory rooms to be the charged to an access code assigned to Kirsten Benson, an academic counselor in the Athletic Department's Office of Student Life. The number of calls attributed to individual students ranged from 1 to 1793, while the value of the calls ranged from $.13 to $2,231.89 (and totaled nearly $26,000). Of course, these numbers are subject to change as the investigation continues.

Because most of the unauthorized phone calls were made from the rooms of student athletes in the Gibbs Residence Hall, [and a small number of unauthorized calls (102) made directly from Benson's phone] and because the compromised access code was Benson's, the University considered the possibility that Benson or another university employee having access to the code knowingly provided the code as an "extra benefit" to one or more student athletes in violation of NCAA Bylaws, Article 16.

Almost immediately after discovery of the breach–no more than a day or two –an intensive investigation was undertaken to determine the source of the breach and whether NCAA infractions had occurred. Several highlights in the investigative process follow.

On April 5, 1995 the task of identifying the source of the leaked telephone code and matching callers with numbers called began. The initial base of investigative operations was located in a conference room in Stokely Athletic Center (Athletics Department).

With two or three roommates to a suite it was necessary to determine which of them made calls using the code. Occasionally, more than one did. 16 athletes –and several others–were interviewed on April 5. Tim Rogers, Dean of Students, and Richard Boring, Director of Audit and Management Services, were present with me during the witness interviews.

Identifying those utilizing the code was somewhat time-consuming but not particularly difficult, as shown by a summary of notes from the first day's interviews (with results given in the order in which witnesses were called, names omitted):

1. Did not use code. His roommate (no.4) did.
2. Did not use code.
3. Used code. R. D. wrote it on a piece of paper and gave it to him so he could call his girlfriend.
4. Used code. Got it from "girlfriend who have a lot of money and wouldn't mind paying for it." who said it was "some girl's code" and okay to use it. No.4 gave code to no.7 and said okay to use it.
5. Never used the code. All calls home made "collect".
6. Used code. Received code from no.18. No. 6 says his roommate also used code.
7. Got code from E. G. who said he "got it from girlfriend who had a lot of money and wouldn't mind paying for it." No.7 gave code to no.12.
8. Got code from N.J. Thought it was his.
9. Denies making calls.
10. Got code from no.7. Used it.
11. Did not have or use code.
12. Obtained code from E.G. Said he got it from a girl he talked to and "she was taking care of it."
13. Has his own calling card but E.G. dialed the code for him several times but would not give him the code. His girlfriend, A. H. Is from Clarkesville, Tennessee. Many calls made to her home–perhaps by her.
14. Basketball player always calls collect. Roommate is no.18.
15. One of three from Memphis. All had code–got his from former roommate JW who is now in Memphis.
16. [An academic counselor who confirmed that each academic counselor had his own code]
17. [Another academic counselor–never heard of the code getting out-even recently. Heard rumors concerning Kirsten Benson–possible relationship with athletes. Nothing specific.]
18. At first denied hearing E.G. mention code. Then changes story. E. G. punched in the code for him 10–12 times. Also claim that A. R. punched in the code, at five dollars a call, for calls to California. **My conclusion**: "LYING."

You get the picture. Identifying the parties making calls with the university code was not particularly difficult. Somewhat more challenging was determining whether the released code–the code provided to Kirsten Benson–was intentionally released by her to one or more athletes. If so, the NCAA was involved; If not, the matter was one for student disciplinary action and recovery University funds expended for personal phone calls my athletes and other students (with the caveat that student athletes would be subject to the same disciplinary treatment as other students).

The following day seven more interviews were conducted. "A.R." admitted using the code and providing it to no. 18, but denied that no.18 paid him to use the code. Instead, A.R. wrote the code on a piece of paper for no.18 after he punched in the code on one occasion for no.18 and the call did not go through.

That same day a lengthy meeting was held with Kirsten Benson. She stated that Ron Davis told her in one occasion "I know the first digits of your code and I'm going to get the rest." On another occasion, "Give me your code–I'm going to get your code." Benson stated she had seen Davis using her phone on many occasions, but thought he was using his own calling card. I had doubts as to Benson's credibility. She agreed to take a polygraph test.

On April 15, 1995 Benson was administered a polygraph test by Advanced Polygraph Services of Knoxville. When asked, "Did you ever knowingly give your long distance telephone access code to any unauthorized person?" Benson replied, "No".

When asked,"In reference to your long distance telephone access code did you ever deliberately allow an unauthorized person to get it?" Benson again replied, "No".

"Deception Indicated" was the "Final Call" by the examiner–and I was not surprised by the conclusion. But there was an unexpected development. When informed of the test results Benson said, "The only thing that I could think of as to why I was reacting so strongly to the questions was 'There were two or three occasions that this particular student came to her and got her to place long-distance calls for him.'" She stated that he told her it was some type of emergency, so she dialed the numbers and gave him the phone. She said that she knew that this was a violation but she felt that it was an acceptable thing to do at the time.

An interview with Ron Davis on April 19 largely resolved the issue of whether Benson had knowingly provided the code to student athletes. That day, Dickey and Vice Chancellor for Student Affairs Phil Scheurer and I flew to Memphis on the UT plane to meet with Ron Davis in the office of his attorney, Don Bourland, and in the company of his agent, Kyle Rote.

During the meeting Davis admitted using the code and stated he would pay for any calls made using the code. At first he denied knowing who gave him the code, saying, "It just was floating around." When pressed, he "guessed he got it from [Reggie Ingram]." Davis admitted making calls from Reggie Ingram's room. He also admitted making calls from Benson's desk using the code. Significantly, he stated that Benson "probably" did not know he was using the code. He never told any UT employee he was using the UT code. Further, he denied getting the code from anyone in athletics (but also denied ever saying to Benson "I'll get the code," or "I have the first three digits and I'll get the rest," or anything to that effect).

An interview with graduate student, N. S. on May 9–with Rogers and Boring present–confirmed that he had it used the code, provided by Benson, on a single occasion. Three long distance calls were made to universities, on an emergency basis, in connection with an academic project N.S. was working on. N.S. did not retain the code and never used it again.

In a single-spaced, carefully detailed letter of May 11, 1995, Benson wrote me that she had: "Asked one of our office graduate assistants, [N.S.], to make some calls to other SEC schools to find out information on their study hall policies." She had written the code on a piece of paper and said, "He took it and made the calls from another phone in our office. He made all the calls in one afternoon."

Later in her letter, Benson confirmed that she provided her code to another student, T. M., "Who was doing a practicum with me that semester, to make calls to a variety of schools to inquire about their academic facilities." She later learned from T. M. that he had made some of the calls from his room in Andy Holt Residence Hall, where he was assistant hall director. "As was true for N. S.," T.M. said, "I did not use the code for any other purpose, nor did I give it to anyone else."

Benson then detailed a request from Ron Davis to tell him her code number. His car was stolen and wrecked and she "allowed Ron to make two or three calls to his home, regarding problems he was having".

She claimed Davis later asked again for her code but that she refused the request. According to Benson, "[Davis said] He knew the first three numbers of my code, and that he could get the rest of the numbers and use it. I told him it was impossible, and besides, he couldn't use the number anyway, because the calls would show up on the bills, and my boss, Carmen Tegano, would see them."

Benson concluded her letter by stating, "[I have] never given my code to any unauthorized person to use, for any reason, and I did not deliberately allowed anyone to get it."

During an earlier meeting with Carmen Tegano (May 1), Tegano had little to offer by way of explaining how student athletes and others obtained Benson's code. With one exception. He described one rumor that Benson had a relationship with football player Reggie Ingram and another that she had a relationship with Rodney Riddick.

I flew to Milwaukee, Wisconsin on May 22 and met with Reggie Ingram for more than an hour. Ingram played football for UT from 1989–1994. At the time of our interview he was playing for the Milwaukee Mustangs.

During his entire time as a student at UT Ingram resided in Gibbs Hall dormitory. Part of that time Ron Davis was Ingram's roommate. Even after Davis moved out of the dorm he continued to visit. And he made a lot of phone calls. "I mean, that's one thing I noticed about Ronnie, he stayed on the phone."

Then there was a helpful disclosure concerning a December 21, 1993 call to 901/345-3967–Ingram's mother's home telephone number in Memphis.

Ron [Leadbetter]: …Did you make that call?
Reg: No.
Ron: Do you know who did?
Reg: Yeah, Kirsten used to call my house in Memphis a lot. I be for sure that this was probably the call- she probably tried to call my house. I see the number 480. I probably wasn't there.
Ron: When you say she called your house a lot, this is the only number we have that's to your house…. This is the only one that we know of billed to the University.

Ingram explained that Benson usually called him from her home. He further explained that all calls made to his mother were made collect. The same was true for all calls he made to his girlfriend in Atlanta.

All calls billed to the University, except the December 21 call, Ingram attributed–accurately it turned out–to Davis, teammate Cory Stone or someone else. Ingram denied Davis' claim that he–Ingram–was the original source of the code. As I later shared with Ingram, "Well, the best proof of that is you don't have any numbers on here." The telephone records fully supported Ingram's version of events.

As a final note, Ingram described his relationship with Benson. He specifically addressed rumors of their "sex scandal."

A lot of people says I guess, you know, I don't know how to identify them or I don't know why, but I guess when they see two people that's real close and cool with each other, plus me and Kirsten used to do things outside of the University of Tennessee, you know, go to a movie or whatever, I mean it's boring around there. I mean, there's nothing to do. I mean, once you're an athlete people really don't understand it, but it's boring. We used to do a lot of things outside. I'd help her in her yard work, just help her around her house, help her play with her little kids and everything, but never nothing sexual.

Although my job was not to determine the nature of Ingram's relationship with Benson, I found his version credible.

By mid June 1995 the telephone fraud investigation was in the wrap-up stage. Internal auditors continued to work with Telephone Services to identify telephone numbers and associated charges to be included in the collection pool. Emphasis on my part shifted from investigating culpability for release of the code to making a good-faith effort to collect money due from suspected code users no longer attending the University. At the same Student Conduct pursued collection of money due from currently enrolled students.

On June 28, I sent collection letters to 16 former students seeking payment ranging from $1.43 to $2,231.89. A number paid their debt, partially or in full. For example, checks for $100 or more from Ed Gray, Ron Davis and Courtney Epps were mailed to me, then forwarded to the UT Treasurer's Office.

It was the consensus of the University administration that litigation to collect any unpaid balance would be unproductive. Instead, holds were placed on records of those failing pay. Collection from 60 "matriculating" students–including 44 student athletes–went more smoothly. Out of $16,000.72 owed the University $14,865.10 was collected by February 28, 1996.

Far more significant than the miniscule amount collected from unauthorized users of the University's Athletic Department code was resolution of NCAA compliance issues.

The UT Athletics Department levied penalties on 31 current student athletes (29 football players and two basketball players). The level of penalty depended on the extent to which the player utilized the code. Two football players, Leland Taylor and Jason Parker, were suspended by Coach Phil Fulmer from athletic competition for the 1995 season. Each lost his scholarship.

Four football players and one basketball player suffered the loss of $850 in scholarship assistance, two season game tickets and suspension from the opening game by Coach Fulmer and basketball Coach Kevin O'Neill. Eight football players suffered loss of $850 in scholarship support and two season game tickets. Each member of the last group of 15 football players and one basketball player was assessed 100 hours of community service as well as loss of two season game tickets.

In addition to the penalties imposed by the Athletics Department, student athletes and other students were assessed disciplinary penalties by the UT Office of Student Conduct. Parker and Taylor were each assessed a two-term suspension based on the number of calls made (more than 400) and a prior disciplinary record. Three players making more than 400 calls and having no prior disciplinary record received one-term suspensions.

Eleven athletes and two non-athletes making 201-400 code calls were assessed probation for two terms. 16 athletes and two non-athletes making 51-200 calls were assessed a one term probationary penalty. The remaining offenders - those making 50 calls or less–were issued written warnings. In total, 16 non-athletes and 45 athletes received disciplinary action by the Office of Student Conduct.

As mentioned earlier, I presented an interim report to the NCAA on July 31, 1995. The Knoxville News-Sentinel reviewed the report and results of the University's internal investigation in its sports section on August 2, 1995. "UT declares two more ineligible," The Knoxville News-Sentinel, p. D1.

My final report was presented to Charles Smrt, NCAA, by letter of October 12, 1995. Critical findings reported were as follows: First, the telephone code disclosure has been treated by the University as a student disciplinary matter rather than an NCAA bylaw infraction. Student athletes and student non–athletes were treated according to the same standard.

Second, the University billed all students and former students for improper calls and made a diligent effort to collect money owed–whether by student athletes or student non-athletes.

Third, notwithstanding lack of evidence that the athletic department code was intentionally disclosed, two occurrences were reported as infractions or possible infractions of NCAA bylaws, article 16. Included was Benson's temporary provision of the code to former student athlete Brian May for "the purpose of seeking an academic internship in sports management" and "a couple of emergency long-distance calls to former student athletes home regarding the reported theft of his automobile. I emphasized that although Benson believed these calls to be appropriate and were not intentional violations of NCAA regulations, each call might be construed as an extra benefit.

The University's focus on integrity and "playing by the rules" worked once again. Smrt's letter to me of November 16, 1995 made that clear.

Dear Ron:
This is in reference to your October 12, 1995, letter that supplemented the institution's previous submissions concerning student athletes' use of a university athletics department telephone access code.

I understand that the University determined that from December 9, 1993, to February 9, 1995, 17,472 unauthorized telephone calls totaling $25,971 were made using the access code of Kirsten Benson, an academic counselor in the institution's Office of Student Life. Of the 61 students who were identified with making these calls, approximately 48 were student–athletes. I understand that the university's auditors were not able to determine how the access code became available to the students. Based upon the information provided by the institution, it appears that no further action in this matter by this office at this time is warranted.

Smrt concluded his letter by advising that the two instances of potential violation of NCAA bylaws would be forwarded to the appropriate NCAA official for "review under the provisions of a secondary violation." On January 26, 1996 I received from Cynthia Gabel, NCAA enforcement representative a letter announcing the NCAA ruling on that final issue.

Gable confirmed that Benson's permitting two student athletes to make long-distance telephone calls from her office at no cost to them was "contrary to the provisions of bylaw 16.12.2.2.2." Notwithstanding, the NCAA's ruling was highly acceptable. Benson continued, "in that regard, it was determined that the case should be classified as secondary and that, inasmuch is the institution's actions in this case were substantial and meaningful, no further action should be taken by the NCAA in this matter."

A conclusion the University relished. Once again, the University dodged serious consequences by acting with diligence and integrity.

Chapter 76–Boston Globe "Expose"

On September 12, 1995 The Knoxville News-Sentinel republished an "expose" first published in the Boston Globe (written by investigative reporter Daniel Golden). The Sports section headlined "Did ex–Vols buck the system?" Goldman's article was headlined "Receivers reportedly were money players before NFL." The Knoxville News-Sentinel, September 12, 1995, p. D1.

A photo insert of former UT players Carl Pickens, JJ McCleskey, Corey Fleming and Alvin Harper, contained the introductory caption "These four former Tennessee wide receivers are among those accused in a widespread scandal involving agents and college athletes." Id.

Golden wrote that Pickens "reportedly received a cellular phone from California agent Bruce Feldman, and a Nissan 300ZX and shoebox full of cash from rival agents". McCleskey and Fleming "reportedly were given hundreds of dollars in cash by an employee at Royal Oaks Country Club in Maryville, for which Chicago financial planner Michael Weisberg has been a managing partner." Harper "reportedly received thousands of dollars from agents for whom 'runner' Jesse Martinez worked." Id.

The Sentinel also reported UT athletic director Doug Dickey's announcement that the University would conduct an internal investigation into the allegations reported by the Globe. "UT will investigate charges, Dickey says." Id.

There were a number of key actors to be investigated. One was sports recruiter or "runner" Jesse Martinez. One excerpt from the Boston Globe report referencing Martinez put me on notice that the upcoming investigation was not one to be taken lightly:

By Martinez' account, told publicly here for the first time, he worked 1989–90 for five agents and a financial planner who paid or gave other inducements to at least 20 prospects at 10 football powerhouses: Ohio State, Tennessee, Southern California, Miami, Florida, Nebraska, Texas A&M, Baylor, Houston and Arizona State.

***

So many agents were pursuing the same players that Martinez often lost out. Last year, disenchanted with the secret bidding war for college talent and feuding with his employers over money, he stopped working for agents–and began exposing them.

His information led the NCAA to suspend two All–Americans, University of Arizona point guard Damon Stoudamire and Ohio State receiver Joey Galloway, and to investigate gifts from agents to college stars Lawrence Phillips of Nebraska and Keyshawn Johnson of Southern California.

"Jesse obviously has been very involved in the world of agents and recruiting athletes for agents," says NCAA enforcement representative Bill Saum. "He's tuned in. The information he's provided us in the past has given us reason to regard him as credible."

Id. p. D5.

Martinez worked as a "runner" for California sports agent Bruce Feldman, then–according to Martinez–left Feldman to work for Weisberg. Id. According to Martinez, Feldman and Weisberg plied the named UT players with piles of cash and other benefits and he assisted in the process. Id.

Virtually all the allegations in the Globe article were provided by Martinez. Several "denials" by players and other "witnesses" were included but the bulk of the report consisted of statements provided by Martinez.

Writer Golden did take brief note of one key sliver of contrary evidence: "Martinez acknowledges that he had shaky ethics in a shady business. He helped players break NCAA rules by putting them in contact with agents who paid them. He had no scruples about deceiving his employers. For example, he pretended to have a fatal illness to wrangle a better financial settlement from Weisberg." Id. Credibility would definitely be a factor in this investigation.

My own role in the investigation commenced immediately. McInnis and I met the day following the publication of the Boston Globe exposé to discuss investigative strategy. But in fact, I first learned of the matters reported by the Boston Globe upon my receipt of a copy of a August 9, 1995 letter to Dickey from Saum who discussed rumors of cash-filled envelopes allegedly provided to UT players by Weisberg.

Mr. Douglas A. Dickey
Director of Athletics
University of Tennessee
1720 Volunteer Boulevard
Knoxville, Tennessee 37996 – 3100

Dear Mr. Dickey:

This office has received information regarding the University of Tennessee Athletics Department. The information involves Mike Weisberg, a financial advisor to professional athletes from the Chicago, Illinois, area; the Royal Oaks Country Club in Maryville, Tennessee, and University of Tennessee football student – athletes.

The information indicates that Mr. Weisberg is involved in some capacity (possibly ownership) with the Royal Oaks Country Club. It has been reported that Mr. Weisberg has instructed Angela Brown, an employee at Royal Oaks, to provide envelopes with cash to certain student – athletes enrolled at Tennessee. Allegedly, the student athletes receive their envelopes of cash from Ms. Brown at the golf course.

In light of the above – mentioned information, please indicate Mr. Weisberg's relationship with the Royal Oaks Country Club, Ms. Brown and the University. Please provide any documentation relative to these relationships. Also, indicate whether any university personnel or coaching staff members are familiar with Mr. Weisberg. Please review this information and indicate to this office your findings by September 22, 1995. Please feel free to contact this office if any further assistance is needed.

Sincerely,
William S. Saum
Enforcement Representative   C: McInnis

On September 14, I spoke by telephone with JJ McCleskey's agent in New Orleans and a meeting was set for September 18. I learned from the agent that McCleskey was highly concerned with his image in Knoxville and was very willing to cooperate.

One week after the publication of the Globe article I was sitting in the Airport Hilton Hotel in New Orleans with McCleskey and his agent, Benjamin Geller, with Sports Management of Texas. The room was provided courtesy of the New Orleans Saints. Our meeting commenced around 4:25 in the afternoon.

McCleskey explained that he graduated from UT in 1992 after completing five years of football–including one "red shirt' year. At present he resided in New Orleans and was playing for the New Orleans Saints.

Cory Fleming was a suitemate of McCleskey's at UT and Carl Pickens was a roommate for three months in "off-campus housing." Alvin Harper was simply a teammate.

McCleskey had met both Feldman and Martinez and believe both to be sports agents–although Martinez later stated he was a "recruiter".

When asked, "did you ever get from any agent any money or free meals, airline tickets, or anything else of value?" McCleskey responded firmly, "No." When asked "did you ever see or hear about any other player getting any money or anything else of value from sports agent or anyone you understood was asking on their behalf?" McCleskey again responded with a firm "No."

It was McCleskey's assessment that Pickens and Martinez were close friends. But, when asked whether he had reason to believe that Martinez made any arrangement to get Pickens money, McCleskey's response was "No, not at all."

I read McCleskey a number of excerpts from the Boston Globe article including one that alleged that he and Cory Fleming had been "given hundreds of dollars in cash by an employee at Royal Oaks Country Club in miracle which had been operated by Weissberg." When asked if the statement was true McCleskey's response was, "That's very false."

McCleskey added that he never even been to Royal Oaks while he was playing for UT. Post-graduation was an entirely different matter. He was there "all the time". He was good friends with Weisberg who served as his accountant–financial advisor. Weisberg had never provided McCleskey cash before he finished his eligibility ("Not at all").

Even after McCleskey's collegiate eligibility was over, Weisberg did not provide him cash. Instead, as McCleskey explained, "Well, he doesn't like give you money or whatever. He gets you a loan." Moreover, as McCleskey clarified, "I know for a fact I didn't meet Weisberg until after the season. I might have talked to him couple times on the phone, but… After my last season."

When questioned as to whether he had an opinion as to whether Martinez was "truthful or a reliable individual" McCleskey had a clear response.

> **J.** One word to sum up Jesse Martinez would be deceitful.
>
> **R.** Okay. Any particular reason you feel that way?
>
> **J.** I mean basically because he told us he had cancer–he told Brooke he had cancer–he told Mike he had cancer. And to my understanding, he was getting a lot of money from Mike about the cancer. He tried to borrow money from me and I told him no.

At the conclusion of our interview, McCleskey expressed his "hope [that] this doesn't hurt my reputation in Tennessee because, I mean, I received a lot of phone calls about it." My reply: "Well, I believe the truth shall be known."

The meeting concluded with McCleskey providing me the telephone numbers of his former girlfriend, Brooke Bowie, Mike Weisberg, and several other potentially helpful witnesses.

I was able to reach Mike Weisberg, by telephone, in Chicago. We agreed to meet during the first week of October.

While on the telephone Weisberg readily admitted that he provided a pair of shoes worth $200 to an Ohio State player (Galloway) at the end of his in junior year but only after Galloway announced he was turning pro. Galloway later changed his mind about turning pro and the gift was reported to the NCAA.

According to Weisberg, he had never been to a UT game, practice or any other activity connected with UT football. He met Pickens through McGee and had never met Harper. He revealed that Martinez had work for Royal Oaks for approximately 2-3 weeks before being fired by the club pro.

September 20 was a busy day. I made a call to the front office of the Cincinnati Bengals seeking Carl Pickens. Another call was made to the front office for the Dallas Cowboys. I left a message for Corey Fleming. Another call was made to the Tampa Bay Buccaneers and I left a request that Alvin Harper give me a call.

My call to Jesse Martinez was answered by a young man who claimed not to know his whereabouts. I left my phone number with him nevertheless. Lastly, I made a call to the NCAA office of Bill Saum. His assistance would be crucial. He was not in at the time but would return my call.

Early the following day I received a call from Brooke Bowie- McClessky's former girlfriend - from Nashville. She had been quoted in the Sentinel as stating that McCleskey told her that Weisberg had paid him a "couple of thousand" dollars during his college career. Id. Although preparing to leave for work – Bowie was an engineering consultant–she was more than willing to discuss the call she received from Boston Globe reporter Daniel Golden.

Bowie said she understood that Golden had recorded her remarks to him. She also was made aware that I was recording her conversation with me. When asked whether she had ever heard of players receiving money Bowie replied that she "had heard that through Jesse. Jesse said he was–I mean, I assumed the money was coming from Jesse." However, when I asked whether it was Jesse who told her he was giving money to players Bowie replied, "No, he never said that."

Bowie likewise denied that any player ever told her he was receiving money from an agent or Jesse. Commenting on Golden's report in the Globe, Bowie stated "I don't know how he put that together 'cause I knew about Maryville about the country club being down there in Maryville, but JJ definitely never said anything about that 'cause when I dated him it was after he had finished playing football anyway. I was not even in school his senior year of eligibility. I was a co-op in New Jersey."

Although Bowie could not say for certain that she had not told Goldman that McCleskey had received money from Weissberg ("I'm not sure on that"), she was absolutely certain no such comment was made which related to the time he was a student athlete. She likewise had not heard of any Tennessee players, such as Fleming or Pickens, receiving payments from agents.

Bowie insisted that quotes attributed to her by Golden were in error: "I read the Boston article 'cause my sister lives in Boston, coincidentally, and she told me about it, so I got the paper down here and it–just one minute he has me saying it and then the next, in another article, he said Martinez says the same thing. I'm thinking he got a quote screwed up somewhere 'cause I didn't say that." Our telephone conversation concluded at 8:55 a.m. and Bowie left for work.

Later that day–September 21–Saum and I finalized plans to question Martinez in person at the NCAA offices in Kansas City (Overland Park).

On September 29 I received a phone call from Jimmy Sexton, sports agent for Alvin Harper. Sexton was most cooperative and agreed he would contact Harper and arrange a meeting.

During our conversation Sexton revealed that some time ago Martinez had asked him for a job. During conversation, Martinez refer to Tennessee as "jerks" and complained that UT football assistant coach Steve Pederson had run him off from a UT practice where he was hanging around "by the fence." Sexton turned down Martinez's job request.

In discussions with Sexton and other agents it became increasingly clear to me that Martinez was well known and had a poor reputation among sports agents. It also became increasingly clear to me that the poor reputation was based on Martinez's shady conduct–not his revelation of misconduct on the part of the agents.

A key meeting in that regard was held on October 27, 1995 with Mike Weisberg at the Royal Oaks Country Club in Maryville. We spent approximately one and a half hours discussing the "Boston Globe" article and the allegations that he provided money and other benefits to football players around the country, specifically including Tennessee players. Weisberg shared with me the following:

Martinez reportedly stole files from Steve Feldman containing some of the information included in the Globe article (Feldman represented Martinez in a personal injury claim and apparently gave Martinez access to his office).

Martinez also purchased and financed an automobile from a dealer in Blount County and misrepresented that he was employed by Weisberg. On another occasion Martinez admitted lying about having cancer. According to Weisberg, Martinez approached Reggie White (former UT and pro football player and partner in Royal Oaks) and many others for money for treatment of his nonexistent cancer.

With respect to his own conduct, Weisberg asserted he had never given money to any of the four UT athletes mentioned in the Boston Globe article. He had had no contact whatever with Alvin Harper.

Weisberg explained that he had arranged for a loan for Corey Fleming from his bank but only after Fleming was done playing at UT. Likewise, he had provided no financial assistance to JJ McCleskey until his collegiate eligibility was complete.

Weisberg was introduced by Tim McGee to Carl Pickens after the 1991 NFL season. He estimated that he had obtained half of his clients through McGee. But he asserted that he never gave or loaned money to Pickens or anyone else. He denied that he ever purchased an airline ticket for any player at the collegiate level. On one occasion, Weisberg did contact "his bank" (where he has an account but no directorship or other control) and asked the bank to extend a loan to Pickens. But he did not make a loan to Pickens.

Also addressed by Weisberg was a claim by Globe reporter Golden that he had received corroborating information from Royal Oaks Country Club employee, Angela Brown. According to Weisberg, Brown called him immediately after the Globe article came out and stated she had adamantly denied to the Globe reporter that she gave money to McCleskey or Fleming–and in mid-December I reached Brown in Joliet, Illinois and she confirmed Weisberg's account).

According to Weisberg, he fired Martinez in June 1993 after paying him for a brief stint as a "freelance recruiter."

In sum, I found Weisberg was helpful, forthright and cooperative. I judged his words to be credible.

After numerous phone calls and many meetings the pieces of the puzzle were beginning to fit together. With the help and cooperation of Bill Saum the project was brought to a fitting conclusion.

At 7:50 a.m. December 11, 1995 Malcolm McIinnis and I met with Bill Saum in his office at NCAA headquarters in Overland Park, Kansas City. Shortly we were joined by the focus of our gathering, Jesse Martinez. Although McInnis and Saum participated, by consensus I led the questioning of Martinez. A 54 page transcript resulted.

Martinez testified extensively that UT athletes received cash, loans and free meals from sports agents. For example, he described an event that purportedly occurred in November 1991.

>   **JM:** ...I had just met with Mike Weisberg through Feldman. He said he wanted to manage his money. So in their off–week Carl flew into Chicago.
>   He flew Carl into Chicago to go to the Bears–Packers game. And we stayed at the downtown Marriott in Chicago. And that's when Weisberg had already met Carl because he had been to Royal Oaks, etc., but at that time that's when Weisberg started getting Carl a lot of money–what I consider a lot of money. In other words, he knew he was going to be a high draft prospect, so, you know, I think right off the bat he put $5,000 into Carl's account. After that we...
>
>   **RL:** Okay, when you say he started giving him a lot of money, he put $5,000 into his account. How do you know he put $5,000 into his account?
>
>   **JM:** Because he told me he did–Mike did.

Martinez stated that he also knew that Weisberg purchased Picken's airline ticket to Chicago ("I'm just going by what Mike told me."). He stated that he also saw a ledger (" the only reason I had the copy of Carl's ledger is that Steve wanted to get reimbursed from Carl the money that he loaned him other than money that he had recruited him with...."

It was also Martinez's contention that during his junior year at UT, JJ McCleskey asked him and Weisberg for money.

JM: ... And so that's when Weisberg started giving him money. And the way Weisberg would do that is at that time they had already opened, I guess, the front–yeah the front nine–at Royal Oaks, the new front nine. So they had a lot of greens fees coming in. So he would send JJ out to the country club and she would just hand him cash – Angie would. Angie Brown. And at that time when I had come to Knoxville I saw a lot of those transactions.

...But I used to see all these transactions cause J.J. like to play golf and we did go out there. And of course, he wouldn't pay for anything–as a matter fact J.J. played a lot of golf out there on Weisberg's dime, so to speak. Um, that started then and so did Cory Fleming. Okay?

And I'm sure Jimmy Sexton will talk to you because he's an alumni and he confirmed this with Bill–that Cory Fleming signed with Sexton and what an agent usually does is ask the player do you owe anyone any money and the agent sends money and says we'll pay them back now and get them out of our hair. And you talk to Jimmy and Jimmy told you how he had paid Weisberg back some money from Fleming and that was–that was like around January 7th–after Cory's eligibility. In other words, after the bowl game.

When I asked Martinez if personally observed McCleskey getting money at the country club he insisted that he did.

JM: Usually it wasn't–she'd just hand him cash. It wasn't like it was in an envelope or a check or anything. She'd just give him cash cause she'd walk over to the bin where they–the register, you know, where greens fees were rung up. She'd open the register and take it out and sign Mike Weisberg–$200 to J.J. McCleskey or $300 or whatever it was.

RL: This was during JJ McCleskey's junior year?

JM: Yeah, his spring of his junior year and then all of his senior year this went on–constantly.

Martinez stated that he paid for meals for McCleskey and other athletes. When I asked if he "paid for one meal, for McCleskey" Martinez replied, "No, millions of meals." (But clarified that he paid for only one meal on the occasion being discussed). He stated, "Sometimes I used Mike's charge card, sometimes I paid cash just depending if I had cash on me or what."

Martinez also contended that "those guys all got free cars there [Nissan dealership on Kingston Pike]. I saw what's his name there getting a free card–Ron Davis. I've seen Cory Fleming get cars there. I've seen Ratliff, I seen–I could go on and on." I then asked, "So you were actually there when the transaction took place?" Martinez's response: "Yeah, cause Carl's real good friends with Ronnie Lay."

While Martinez extensively described sports agent involvement with UT athletes he offered little evidence of UT athletic department involvement in the process. He cited hearsay evidence–purported statements of Harper, Pickens, McCleskey and Fleming–that former coach Kippy Brown would loan or give them money "but to give and to loan is two totally different things." Martinez conceded that he could not think of a specific instance where one of the four athletes said that Brown gave him money.

A number of documents were identified as providing evidence in support of Martinez's claims that cash and benefits were provided to the UT players. Martinez repeatedly offered to provide those documents. He offered assurance that he would but never produced a single document.

Martinez conceded his own lack of integrity, admitting that he falsely represented to Weisberg he had cancer. He denied telling anyone else he had cancer and claimed he made the false representation to Weisberg for the purpose of collecting money owed him. "It was a way of me being sneaky, in other words, quite honestly, with Weisberg and trying to get what [I was owed]."

Martinez conceded he had no information that football coach Phil Fulmer had any knowledge of players receiving cash or other benefits. He offered little by way of specifics to support his contention that former coach Johny Majors and academic counselor Derrick Carter had knowledge of an airline ticket or meal being provided to any athlete.

In his "testimony" Martinez claimed that McCleskey, Feldman, Weisberg, Pickens and the others had all failed to pay him money they owed him. In a key concession Martinez agreed that Brooke Bowie was a truthful person, "Just like Alison [Sexton]."

Following the conclusion of our meeting with Martinez, consensus was reached that no further action need be taken–and none was. The basis for this conclusion was several-fold.

First, Martinez's credibility was lacking–to say the least. There was little if any evidence supporting any of his contentions reported by the Boston Globe (and Knoxville-News Sentinel).

Second, McCleskey, Bowie, Weisberg and Brown appeared highly credible. Each un-categorically and vehemently denied involvement in or knowledge of cash or other benefits being provided to UT athletes-contrary to the claims of Martinez.

Third, there was no evidence that Weisberg or Martinez had any relationship with the University of Tennessee or its athletics department.

Lastly, there was no tangible evidence that current or former UT athletics staff had any knowledge of or participation in provision of "envelopes with cash" or any other benefits to UT athletes.

This case was moved to inactive status. The NCAA agreed and pursued the matter no further. The Boston Globe "expose" was exposed for what it was–completely lacking in credibility or substance.

Chapter 77–The Leslie Ratliff Exception

As investigation of the Boston Globe "expose" led, little by little, to the conclusion that news media reports of UT athletics infractions were contrary to the facts, there were a few exceptions. The case of UT offensive tackle Leslie Ratliff constitutes the most notable exception.

On September 13, 1995 the news media reported Ratliff's arrest for assaulting his girlfriend, Antoinette Huntley. At the same time allegations were reported that Ratliff had received gifts from UT boosters. My investigation of the claim concerning Ratliff's receipt of gifts was short-lived.

On October 4, 1995 I met with Ratliff in UT Athletic Director Doug Dickey's office in Stokely Athletic Center. The meeting lasted 45 minutes. During the course of the meeting valuable information and a number of critical admissions were elicited from Ratliff.

A gentleman by the name of Mose Phillips had introduced Ratliff to Nashville resident Charles Walling and Lebanon resident Charles Hicks. Twice Ratliff had visited McCabe's Pub in Nashville with Walling and Hicks. On one occasion Nashvillian Chuck Holmes joined in.

In the summer of 1994 Ratliff had a meal at McCabe's, together with teammates Cory Stone, Mose Phillips and Ron Davis. Antoinette Huntley was also present–as was Walling. Walling paid for the meal with a $100 bill. Ratliff kept $45 in change.

While traveling through Nashville on another occasion Ratliff had car trouble. He stopped and called Walling. Walling arranged for repair at a local auto repair shop–a "little plastic tube" needed replacement–at no charge to Ratliff.

A third incident took place in the summer of 1995. Walling invited Ratliff to a barbeque at the Budget Inn in Lebanon. The barbeque was attended by teammates Chester Ford, Greg Gaines and Mark Kovaine as well as a number of non-athletes. Walling paid for a motel room and allowed Ratliff and his girlfriend to stay there for the evening.

There was no question in my mind that an NCAA rules infraction had occurred and I so reported. (Interestingly, Ratliff stated he could identify only one other player – Ron Davis – as having received anything of value from boosters and the only way he knew that was "Ron was always flaunting his clothing and jewelry").

Athletic Director Doug Dickey immediately suspended Ratliff from completion and ruled him ineligible to practice and participate for the rest of the season –thus ending Ratliff's collegiate eligibility. No petition for restitution of eligibility was filed with the NCAA.

Three "boosters" were penalized by UT (for involvement in providing benefits to players) as was one assistant coach, Steve Marshall (for "failure to manage information received about possible NCAA violations in a timely and appropriate manner"). The NCAA was asked to consider the reported conduct "secondary infractions".

By letter of July 17, 1996 NCAA Enforcement Representative Cynthia Gabel notified Dickey "that the NCAA enforcement staff and a designated member of the NCAA Committee on Infractions have reviewed this matter …and determined that the following violations occurred:" Gabel then outlined, almost verbatim, the findings of the University as being those of the NCAA.

Gabel reviewed the "corrective and punitive actions" taken by the University*:*

1. The institution immediately ruled then football student–athlete Leslie Ratliff- ineligible for participation in competition on September 14, 1995. After completing the preliminary investigation, he was ruled ineligible for practice and competition for the remainder of the season, thus ending his collegiate eligibility. The institution did not petition the NCAA for restitution of eligibility.

2. As a result of his failure to manage information received about NCAA violations in a timely and appropriate manner, then assistant football coach Steve Marshall was issued a letter of reprimand by the institution. Mr. Marshall was prohibited from receiving any bonus payment for postseason competition during the 1995– 96 academic year. This stipend normally is awarded based on university policy and was approximately one–twelfth of his annual salary. It further is understood that such loss of compensation will not be included as part of any future salary adjustments.

In addition, the Southeastern conference informed Mr. Marshall that he would not be permitted to recruit off campus for seven days during the contact period between January 1, 1996, and the National Letter of Intent signing day. The sanction was accepted, and Mr. Marshall did not recruit off campus during a seven–day period beginning January 7, 1996. On January 15, 1996, Mr. Marshall left the University and was employed as an assistant coach at the University of California, Los Angeles.

3. While Charlie Watling is not a donor or a season–ticketholder, the university has determined that since he provided benefits to a student–athlete, he became an institutional representative based on NCAA Bylaw 13.0 2.11. Therefore, Mr. Walling will be disassociated from the athletics program of the University for a period of five years. After that date, Mr. Walling will be allowed to associate with the program only after a thorough review of his activities during that period of time and after receiving a thorough review of NCAA regulations regarding booster involvement in the athletics program.

4. While the institution has determined that Charlie Hicks is not an institutional representative under NCAA regulations, he has been prohibited from associating with the

athletics program for a period of five years.

5. Chuck Holmes is a donor to the athletics department and has been purchasing 24 season tickets, including two through the University's priority ticket plan. The investigation of the allegation in this case did not find that he was involved directly in providing extra benefits. It was believed that he provided tickets to Charlie Walling from time to time. During the next three years, Mr. Holmes will be prohibited from purchasing more than four non-priority season tickets, and also will be informed in writing of NCAA booster regulations and receive a strong admonishment to avoid any involvement with either Messrs. Walling or Hicks that would place student–athletes' eligibility at risk.

6. The University will look for opportunities to enhance its rules–education program by emphasizing the risk of ineligibility from involvement with alumni and boosters.

While accepting the University's assessment of the facts–and largely endorsing the penalties implemented by the University–the NCAA expressed concern with "(a) the failure of an institutional staff member to report a possible violation at the time he became aware of the matter, particularly in as much as the University is subject to the provision of the repeat–violator legislation and should be engaged in a period of heightened awareness and monitoring, and (b) the involvement of an athletics representative in violations of NCAA legislation."

The NCAA agreed the case should be considered "secondary." However, to UT's self-imposed penalties, the NCAA added the requirement that initial grants-in-aid be reduced by one for the following (1997-98) academic year.

This infractions case was a reminder of the importance of educating student-athletes, university staff and others associated in any way with the University about "extra benefit" limitations imposed by NCAA rules.

Chapter 78
Jamie Whited NCAA Infraction Tips Prove Baseless

It was my undeviating practice to urge University employees, students and others to come forth with any reliable information that others in the University community had engaged or were engaging in illicit activity. UT Athletics' Department trainer, Jamie Whited, seemingly followed that advice–from myself or someone else – possibly ignoring the "reliable" aspect.

In 1996 Whited reported a number of alleged NCAA infraction activities by Head Athletic Trainer Mike Rollo and one or two other Athletics Department employees. In accordance with standard practice, the allegations were promptly investigated.

On September 10, 1996 Athletic Director Doug Dickey, NCAA Compliance

Director Malcolm McInnis and I met with and interviewed Rollo regarding the allegations.

As was my practice in major interviews, a verbatim transcript was prepared. Contrary to my standard practice, advice typically given by me prior to the beginning of the questioning was included in this transcript. It is repeated here as a good example of the emphasis placed on truthfulness.

RL: "Mike, we're here in Doug Dickey's office this afternoon, September 10th, and we're meeting here to discuss some allegations made concerning possible NCAA infractions. You've been around here a long time so you know that the most important or the most serious infraction is not telling the truth and it's important that you do so and answer honestly any questions that are asked. I might say, and this is the best I understand it, the alleged infractions if they occurred would be minor. I haven't been able to identify any allegation which even if true would involve a serious infraction of NCAA rules. So, please keep that in mind. But let me just go through the allegations and get you to respond as thoroughly as you think appropriate and just see where we go."

Emphasis on truthfulness was something I stressed each and every time I prepared a witness for a deposition or trial - or an NCAA inquiry. In NCAA cases I cautioned that lying to the NCAA was a serious infraction even if the matter lied about was not.

In this particular case I summarize the allegations and Rollo's responses as follows:

1. ALLEGATION: In Fall, 1995 Rollo co–signed, as surety, for George Kidd in order to enable Kidd to obtain KUB service.

RESPONSE: Rollo admitted doing this. He stated that he co-signed for many individuals and agreed to provide me a copy of KUB records noting that he had done so. After Rollo received notices from KUB that Kidd had not paid his bills, Rollo notified Kidd and advised him to pay his bills and notified KUB requesting that he be removed as surety. Rollo also reviewed information from Malcolm's office and determined that he should not participate in any co-signings in the future. He is not a co-signer for any current student athlete.

2. ALLEGATION: Rollo provided free Tiva sandals to track athlete Malcolm Saxson.

RESPONSE: Rollo admits providing a free pair of sandals to Malcolm. He explains that Malcolm is a friend and that he has ordered several dozens of Tiva sandals and given those samples out to friends. Rollo views this as an act of friendship not as an attempt to give an extra benefit to an athlete since he treated Malcolm the same as other friends.

3. ALLEGATION: In the summer of 1995 Rollo-paid for dinner for Tory Edge and other football players at Sam & Andy's.

RESPONSE: Rollo admitted doing this. He was supervising a group of athletes who were "sentenced" by Coach Fulmer to work in a community service project at the World's Fair Site. The athletes worked late, missed dinner at Gibbs and Rollo felt that it was only fair that the players be fed. Some, but not all, of the players on the work crew went with Rollo to Sam & Andy's. Rollo paid the bill out of his pocket. He did not request and did not receive reimbursement from the University.

4. ALLEGATION: Rollo told Jamie that C[ ] was permitted to play in the January 1994 citrus bowl after receiving his third positive drug test and that he had met with Dr. Val Gene Ivens to make sure that the doctor would "support our story."

RESPONSE: C[ ] received two positive drug test but the third was not within protocol since it was conducted within 28 days of the second test. The test was, therefore not considered valid under the policy and was not treated as a third positive. While both consulted with Dr. Val Gene Ivens as far as how the matter should be handled, [Doug Dickey confirms that it would be the decision of Dr. Ivens and himself as to what action should be taken on a third positive–not the decision of the trainer].

None of the conduct attributed to Rollo was ultimately determined to constitute an NCAA infraction. Allegations that several other Athletics Department personnel–and the manager of O'Charley's restaurant on Cumberland–provided "added benefits" to players, were denied and credible explanations were given in each instance.

In my own mind the tips provided by Whited were driven by workplace conflict between her, Rollo and others. The motivation really did not matter–our investigative focus was on determining the truth. In this instance it appeared true that no NCAA infractions had been committed. Our investigation concluded and the allegations presented by Whited were not pursued further, either by the University or the NCAA.

Chapter 79–ESPN Reports Tutoring Scandal

"ESPN alleges UT academic fraud, cover-up" read the September 27, 1999, front page headline of the Knoxville News-Sentinel. The allegations were serious:

While the University of Tennessee Volunteers were en route to winning the national championship last season, high-level administrators in the athletics department were alerted to situations in which four tutors may have written papers and done schoolwork for at least five football players, in possible violation of the honor code and NCAA rules, ESPN.com reported Sunday night in a copyrighted story.

Robin Wright, the coordinator for academic programs in the UT Athletics Department, messaged her boss, Jerry Dickey, last December about what she considered a case of plagiarism involving a football player, ESPN.com reported. The note was carbon-copied to his boss, Carmen Tegano ESPN.com reported the alleged case of academic fraud was not isolated, according to internal documents the network obtaine ESPN.com reported that none of that information was passed on to the proper campus authorities charged with investigating possible rules infractions, said Malcolm McGinnis, NCAA compliance officer for Tennessee, and Carl Asp, NCAA faculty athletic representative....

The possible cover-up could present problems for Tennessee, even if none of the allegations are proven. NCAA rules require member schools to follow school procedure in investigating and report any rules violations:

***

Billy Stair, executive assistant to UT President J. Wade Gilley, confirmed Sunday night the university had been investigating the rumors for the past "two to three weeks."

He said Assistant General Counsel Ronald Leadbetter had been assigned to investigate the rumors and was working with the athletic department.

According to the Sentinel, ESPN.com cited the existence of documentary evidence supporting the allegations of academic fraud going back to 1995. "The most serious concerns were raised by Linda Bensel-Meyers, director of composition in the English Department, who said she threatened at the time to bring up charges of 'institutional plagiarism' against the athletic department unless the English Department was given greater oversight over tutors." Id. p.A6.

Several UT football players (Leonard Scott, Reggie Ridley, Keyon Whiteside and Ryan Rowe) were suspended by athletic director Doug Dickey from further play pending completion of the investigation into the report.

One of the first persons I met with was Linda Bensel-Meyers. The two of us met in my office on September 14–nearly 2 weeks before the ESPN story broke. As usual, a transcript–25 pages in length–was prepared from the tape recording of the meeting.

At the outset Bensel-Meyers revealed she had been contacted by Tom Ferry with ESPN. Ferry shared with her information he had reportedly received from a UT track athlete who "had emailed ESPN.com a message about how this track athlete cared about his studies and works really hard and so he just couldn't keep quiet any more and he was at that moment watching a coach write a paper for a football player."

Bensel-Meyers proceeded to describe a number of "rumors" of inappropriate assistance to student athletes documented by Robin Wright. But when asked whether any of those Wright had written about had done anything inappropriate Bensel- Meyers responded:

"There was a real problem is they hire a lot of people who aren't trained in tutoring and so they don't know where the line is so it's excessive collaboration.

Whether or not they were intentionally writing papers for the students is, I think, hard to prove. But at times they would be actually re–writing a paper on the computer while the student talked or something which is transgressing."

The direction in which this investigation was heading becomes clear from the following exchange:

L [Leadbetter]: Is there anyone that's currently employed by the University that would've done anything inappropriate in that regard [writing papers for students].

M [Linda Bensel-Meyers]: The only–I don't have proof of anyone but the Ron Payne person – that's the rumor that is going around–he's the one.

L: Well, I mean aside from rumor where someone has said "I saw him do it" or an athlete saying this tutor wrote my paper?

M: No.

L: the problem I've had in a few of these other cases is the rumors get rampant.

M: Yeah.

L: And–do you have any reason to believe–now not even for what you've seen yourself, but do you have any–let's take Ron Payne or anyone else that you suspect did provide inappropriate help to a student or an athlete?

M: No, I haven't–the person who is employed over there right now is since the interim director in place of Robin Wright–she says she sees no problem going on over there and that she does see Carmen giving the right information as the original orientation. The one thing we had set up is that all writing for all courses–not just English courses–go up to the English department tutoring staff and I was a little worried with some of the changes when Robin left and Jerry Dickey went with David Cutcliff that that would sort of get lost. And they would go back to some of the other tutors and some of the other tutors would start doing that. But I don't have any evidence that's happened. It's just that I knew that things needed to be monitored really carefully.

L: Let me ask a couple of specific questions. Have you talked to any athlete that has reported receiving…

M: No.

L: … excessive help?

M: No.

When asked whether she had received anything in writing identifying someone who had allegedly received inappropriate help, Bensel-Meyers identified a report of "a Ph.D. student from education working in special needs and disabilities [who was asked] to work with an incoming freshmen who had a documented learning disability."

According to Bensel-Meyers, in 1995 an athletics staff member–not a tutor –by the name of Melissa Privlovsky reportedly construed the Americans with

Disabilities Act as permitting her to "write the papers for [the student athlete] because it said that he could not type and he could not read. Which made me question why he was even admitted at that point. We worked that through and got him with a tutor in the English department and after taking the course a couple of times, he did really well and now he's a good student, I think."

Bensel–Meyers conceded that she had not had any reports since 1995 that Privlovsky had done anything wrong. "No, I think once we got it straightened out what the line is, I think she understands it …" Simply put, Bensel-Meyers conceded – aside from the single instance described in the preceding paragraph – she could not identify a single tutor (or other University employee) who wrote a single paper for a single student athlete.

On September 30 Dickey and I flew on a private corporate jet (provided by one of Dickey's friends) to Birmingham, Alabama to meet with Southeast Conference Commissioner Roy Kramer at Conference headquarters. We discussed the status of the investigation and no concern was expressed by Kramer. It was his opinion we were proceeding in the right direction.

On October 4, I flew to Shreveport, Louisiana to interview "tutoring" witness Victoria Gray. The following morning I flew from Shreveport to Nagadoches, Texas to interview the second most frequently cited source of ESPN material –Robin Wright.

Wright served as director of the "Writing Center" in the UT English Department, but was assigned full-time to work with the Athletics Department. She reported to Bensel-Meyers (and Kirsten Benson) in the English Department, Wright was responsible for providing tutoring assistance to UT athletes.

The meeting in Nagadoches was attended by Wright's husband, Gary. We met from 9 a.m. until 12:15 p.m. A 49 page transcript resulted. Much of our conversation centered on allegations supposedly documented by letters and other materials Wright provided to ESPN.

First addressed was whether she claimed to have any knowledge of student athlete Spencer Riley receiving improper assistance in 1995 by having a tutor type a paper for him. Wright stated she had no information on that matter ("that was before my time") although she tutored Riley after the incident and opined that he improved greatly as a student and was "a fine young man"). Wright made no claim that Riley had committed plagiarism or cheated.

Repeatedly, Wright stated that she had "caught" tutors or other athletics department personnel typing papers for or tutoring athletes. For example:

L: [Leadbetter] All right. Reggie Ridley, third player. Now I understand there were some questions about Victoria Gray and whatever she did or didn't do as a tutor in assisting Reggie Ridley.

W: [Robin Wright] That's not quite right.

L: OK. That's what I was going to ask–if you can shed some light on what knowledge you have of the tutorial relationship between Victoria Gray and Reggie Ridley and whether you observed any impropriety in whatever that relationship was?

W: That memo–I mean I put it in her file because it was an ongoing thing. I think there were like 10 e-mails going back and forth that day over this situation. I was upset with Victoria because I kept catching her at the keyboard, all right, and I had caught her with Jason Adams for the same.

Wright was questioned about each of the athletes mentioned in the ESPN.com report. My focus was on whether she had observed any activity that might constitute a violation of NCAA rules.

Wright explained that she had on many occasions observed athletic department tutors typing papers for student athletes and had on the number of occasions taken the papers from the athletes–including players specifically mentioned by ESPN–and ordered those athletes to redo their work.

A critical distinction soon developed between evidence of a potential UT rule violation and the possibility of NCAA infractions.

L: If you learned that a player, if there was a instance where you learned that a player had gotten, had submitted a paper and got credit for it, that they shouldn't have, well, first of all, do you know of a situation like that?

W: I don't know of a situation.

L: And the reason is, the instances where you discovered that a player had prepared a paper that was not his own, you confiscated it or in some way made them re–do the paper?

W: Right.

With reference to her description of an athletics department employee "spoon –feeding answers to players (often the wrong answers)" I asked Wright, "When you refer to spoon–feeding answers, are you referring to cheating, are you claiming that he gave answers?" Wright responded, "No, I'm referring to bad tutoring methods. He should be eliciting those answers from the players by saying, 'well, what do you have in your notes?' That's what tutoring is."

Wright's focus became crystal clear. She was concerned that the UT athletics department had assumed responsibility for an educational activity she believed to be properly under the auspices of the English department.

W: When I was director of the Writing Center every spring I sent out a memo saying what they [athletic department personnel] could and could not do. And I put on my memo to all tutors not to type papers for players. However, I was made aware–you know I just took over the rest of the tutoring job in August–July and August–I was made aware that it had been athletic department policy–they even had a form–that they could type up paper for players if they were paid, you know, because and this is the reason given to me, because any student on campus could hire someone to type his papers.

The problem, as Wright saw it, was not that tutors were typing papers for student athletes but that the wrong tutors were doing so-those not employed in the English department.

H: [Gary Wright] are you saying because of problems they had before. It had been established that it would only be the English Department tutors that would work on papers?

W: Right.

Wright reprimanded Leonard Scott–one of the players prominently identified by ESPN is having received inappropriate assistance–with "that is absolutely inappropriate and you cannot let Jenae help you with papers. Because she's not a qualified English tutor."

It was clear to me that Wright was upset by learning that student athletes preferred help from athletics department tutors to assistance from English Department tutors:

W: She [Jenai] told me that she was helping them with their papers–not just typing. She was tutoring English basically because they didn't like the help they got from the English Department tutors. Roderick has told me the same thing. So basically she admitted she was tutoring English.

***

And I'm trying to find out why I had such a poor attendance rates suddenly last fall. And that's what they would tell me and it would be either Roderick or Jenai.
***

I know that the reason there are memos and so forth about Roderick is because he was helping the students. They weren't coming to their appointments and so when I would talk to the students I would say, "Why aren't you showing up for your Writing Center appointments?" They would say "Roderick helped me with the paper."

When I talked to Roderick about it he said he didn't think they were getting the right kind of help with the Writing Center tutors.

Wright blamed the athletics department for not enforcing the requirement–as she saw it–that athletes seek tutoring assistance only from the English Department:

L: You don't recall an incident where you were I guess upset with Victoria's assistance to Dominique [Stephenson] over her working with Dominique in some fashion?

W: No. Once again there were rules that both Tegano and Gerry backed up on that–no one but English Department tutors were supposed to be working on English assignments, especially writing assignments. There were several instances with Victoria on and off where I said, you know, this is past–this is all you're supposed to be doing. So just send them to us, we're sitting over here not doing anything.

L: So even if what the non--English tutor or mentor was doing was simply sitting with the athlete and saying, well, this paragraph is not clear, how about taking another shot at it? That alone would have been inappropriate…

W: Right.

L: … since they are not an English tutor?

W: Right, and this wasn't just my little rules, this was the athletic department rules that were officially put out in their handbook, and I went over it at every tutor meeting.

L: Spending a lot of time with a player, working on a paper, by itself would not be inappropriate, would it?

W: Well, it would be for Chris [Bumpus] , because he wasn't an English tutor.

Because it was Wright's opinion that "tutoring writing is the hardest subject to tutor because it's so easy to cross that line between collaborative learning and excessive collaboration... . It needs to be in the hands of English Department tutors..."

What Wright made clear during her lengthy interview was a complete absence of any knowledge of plagiarism or cheating being facilitated by any UT Athletics Department employee. This was evidenced by her description of what she knew of the activities of athletic department employee Ron Payne.

L: Was there anything you observed, or at least had personal knowledge of, that he [Ron Payne] did, that would have been inappropriate, in other words, giving inappropriate assistance to a student or a player?

W: I objected, and I sent you the memo that I sent Jerry. I objected to his tutoring methods because he didn't know how to tutor. Tutoring, academic assistance is a complete discipline, as you can see by my operation here. He'd never had any training, he didn't want training, he had been in for a long time, and, maybe 15 years ago, just lecturing to students and having them write down what you say, was okay. I don't know. But it's not a good tutoring method, and that's what I saw, and I objected very strongly to it... .

L: Was there anything that he did that you know about, that you have personal knowledge of, that would have fallen in the category of plagiarism or cheating, in other words, not just a general sense that he was not competent to tutor, but something specific he did with a specific player?

W: No.

It was also stated clearly by Wright that she did not recall ever reporting to Linda Bensel–Meyers any incident of cheating or plagiarism. This is because "I tried to handle them in-house, and to the best of my knowledge, everyone I caught at the keyboard, Carmen let go, or Lois let go..."

I explicitly asked Wright, "If you learned that a player, if there was an instance where you learned that a player had gotten, had submitted a paper and got credit for it, that they shouldn't have, well, first of all, do you know the situation like that?" Wright replied, "I don't know the situation."

Wright admitted that she had written a memorandum, dated October 28, 1998, which read: "Victoria is getting out of hand, she is essentially doing all the work on the papers for these guys." and "She has just gotten bolder and bolder until she is essentially taking their classes for them."

By way of explanation, Wright explained, "I was mad," and her statement was "probably hyperbole." More precisely, she conceded, "It was definitely a hyperbole, but you had to take it within the context of months and months of my discussing this with Victoria... ."

I made clear in a statement to Wright's husband that if a tutor composed a paper for a player that would constitute an NCAA violation ("Absolutely."). I further explained that possible infractions were reported to the NCAA but that "not every problem gets reported to the NCAA. Academic disputes would not be reported to the NCAA."

My polite but intensive interrogation of Wright boiled down to whether she had knowledge of athletic department personnel–tutors and others–facilitating cheating or plagiarism by UT student athletes. Wright made clear she did not have such knowledge.

L: I want to make sure to ask you if when you say, "the program should eliminate excessive collaboration or cheating" that you are really talking about eliminating the possibility of that happening, not addressing actual cheating that you had identified. Am I accurate in saying that?

W: Right. Who are doing too much, like Gary said when you tutor math and your tendency is that, "Well, this is how you work it," and it might actually be a homework problem, you shouldn't do that. If they are well trained, that won't happen, they will know.

L: One reason I'm asking this is I've had a call from the Dean of Students, and the Dean of Students handles cheating cases, so, if there is a case where we catch a person cheating, that is a student copying answers off of someone else's paper, intentionally, then we prosecute them through the Dean of Students' office. They don't have any reports, so I would also ask you to make sure I've covered that, did you ever report any instances of cheating, and that could of course include plagiarism, did you ever report any cases to the Dean of Students?

W: No. To my knowledge, there were no cases of blatant cheating.

L: How 'bout non–blatant cheating?!

W: No cases of cheating that I observed.

In the final analysis, it was now clear to me there were no NCAA infractions associated with tutoring activities for UT athletes.

So how did ESPN arrive at such a diametrically opposite conclusion in alleging academic fraud and cover-up by the University of Tennessee? Wright provided some insight needed to answer that question:

L: Okay, let me make this easy. You have given me a copy of the memorandum that starts off, "Who am I? I am a teacher, I taught English", and so forth. And this is a one-page memo that you provided to Tom Farrey [ESPN] on September 23. Is that all the information you gave to Mr. Farrey?

W: Well, we talked some we talked the night before. That's all I would agree to say on camera.

Wright then went through a process of explaining a number of implicating "disclosures" made by ESPN. For example:

W: Yeah, the ESPN guy, he was reading from the memos, and putting words... in Robin's mouth...

***

That's the Keyon thing [Unnamed instructor who is accusing a player plagiarism] But that's not the, see, that's taken out of context. The Keyon issue was an instructor was not about a paper, or anything….

***

I don't know what that means. Believe me, I was surprised by this.

***

[Responding to a question as to whether a paper Wright believed was at least co-written by Victoria Gray: "Would that have been Spencer Riley?"] Unless he's mixing up all his facts again. He's got everything screwed up.

***

L: One sentence here says Wright confirms she wrote the memos obtained by ESPN.com and insists she wasn't exaggerating in them. And I assume you weren't exaggerating.

W: No, well, there was a bit of hyperbole there.

L: Right, right.

W: But I didn't know everything he [ESPN reporter] had, you know.

Our conversation concluded on a relatively high note–at least from the University's perspective. Wright's comments were directed at academic practices at colleges and universities in general and not a focused attack on practices at UT.

H: But you know when they [ESPN] show Tennessee run out on the field and they talk about academic misconduct and then they show all this orange and then they show a 15 second clip of her [Robin Wright] saying something it makes it look like she's talking about Tennessee.

L: Yeah, that all the players are cheating.

W: But I do – I wasn't – I told him I didn't want to talk about Tennessee and that was actually in the context of when I was saying that Tennessee did a better job than most colleges from my talking with other student coordinators. There is you said who knows what is excessive collaboration. We do in the profession know that but that's why I have 5 people here working 40 hours a week with 80 tutors. It is a very difficult thing to train tutors and oversee them and make sure nobody oversteps the bounds. That's the kind of stuff I was talking about.

L: See, and that's an important comment too, because the NCAA–again we're talking about for purposes of this investigation–not the best way to run a program but whether there is a violation of NCAA rules, namely giving an extra benefit to the player which you would be doing if you allowed them to plagiarize and get away with it.

L: There's two issues–there's academic issues which are being dealt with by the way.

W: Right. John Peters–or Peter's office?

L: Exactly. And that's an ongoing process, of course. And then there's the NCAA compliance issue. That's different.

My last interviews in the tutoring investigation were completed on October 19. I received a phone call from Victoria Gray on the 20th. From her comments litigation against ESPN and Robin Wright appeared imminent. Around the same time I received calls from Tom Farrey with ESPN, Jimmy Hyam with the Knoxville News-Sentinel and other members of the press. I revealed only that a report of my findings would soon be complete.

I met with Dickey, McInnis and Asp on October 21 and shared the results of my investigation. An earlier meeting with Vice Chancellor Peters and Chancellor Snyder was held for the same purpose.

My final report was released on October 28, 1999, As noted in my personal diary, "Today I released my report on the ESPN.com 'tutor scandal' to Doug Dickey, President Gilley and the rest of the world."

In a bit of an odd twist, when I met briefly with newly appointed UT President Wade Gilley in his office to share my report-I found no evidence of NCAA violations-his only response was, "I'm not worried." Unlike the approach of past UT presidents, there was no questioning whatever as to how I reached that conclusion. Not when I was in his office or on any other occasion. Odd.

The October 28, 1999 issue of the New York Times, p. C29, ("Tennessee Report Says Rules Weren't Violated") headlined the good news:

The president of the University of Tennessee, J. Wade Gillery, said yesterday that the school's general counsel's office had not found any "kind of systemic, unwarranted or tutorial help" in the school's athletic department and said that none of its student athletes violated National Collegiate Athletic Association rules.

Gilley said he had received an oral report from the Associate General Counsel, Ron Ledbetter, who conducted the month-long review into allegations reported by ESPN.com on September 26 that some Tennessee football players, including at least one member of the 1998 national title team, were suspected of turning in plagiarized papers or papers co-written by tutors. He said the report clearing the program will be forwarded to the Southeastern Conference and to the NCAA.

***

Ledbetter said he will deliver the three-page report to Gilley today. And it will be made public perhaps as early as tomorrow. He would not comment on the specifics of the report, but said in a telephone intervview that the review was "very thorough."

"The University does not find itself in difficulty," he said.

Ledbetter said he spoke with every person cited in the ESPN.com report which alleged that at least four tutors may have done schoolwork for as many as five players–dating to 1995–and that high level administrators in the athletic department were made award of instructors' and staffers' suspicions but did not pass them on to the school's compliance officials.

"We spoke with everyone who had useful information, some people multiple times," Ledbetter said, declining to say how many. "We talked to anyone who remotely might have had first-hand knowledge of the allegations."

***

Ledbetter said, however, that though the focus of the report was to determine whether NCAA violations occurred that he was bound to report any other violations that broke university rules. He indicated he discovered none. "The report is very positive," he said. Id

The final report to the NCAA was, as previously indicated, released on October 28, 1999. the Nashville Tennessean reported the investigation results the following day, October 29, ("UAT says it didn't find a violation").On October30 David Climer, columnist for the Tennessean, offered a commentary: "Vols'investigative plate full of home cookin'." Climer offered the following assessment of the investigation:

> UT dropped the ball on this one. Rather than follow the trend of hiring an outside law firm to rifle through the laundry–dirty or otherwise–Tennessee adopted its standard operating procedure and speed–dialed an on-campus number.
>
> Be it mountains or molehill, UT likes to keep it all in the family. The prevailing wisdom: why put some $300-an-hour attorney from Atlanta on retainer when you have a good law school right across Cumberland Avenue?
>
> Timeout, I should note right here that nobody is questioning the integrity of Ron Leadbetter, UT's associate general counsel and the point man on the investigation.
>
> Around the UT campus, Leadbetter is regarded as a good man and a good lawyer, thorough and fair, an I–dotter and T–crosser.
>
> But he is a University of Tennessee employee, which compromises the investigative process and orange–flags its findings, at least in the court of public perception.

Id.

Of course I appreciated Climer's assessment of my character but disagreed with his conclusion as to whether a University employee could properly represent the University. After all, Tennessee Supreme Court justices are employed by the State and entertain suits by and against the State regularly.

Of course, my primary concern was whether the NCAA–not the Tennessean –would concur with my investigative report one. I believed the NCAA would.

On the morning of November 12 NCAA investigator Ron Barker met with me to discuss the investigation and review supporting evidence. The meeting was held at my home–away from the probing press. We carefully reviewed the case from start to finish. It was an entirely cooperative meeting. Barker later conducted a follow-up investigation for the NCAA. I expected he would reach the same conclusion I reached.

The Knoxville News-Sentinel reported several weeks later, in a front-page article, "NCAA checking into UT probe." The Knoxville News–Sentinel, January 7, 2000, p.A1. The Sentinel noted my assessment. "Our position is that we have done nothing wrong, and we are confident the NCAA will find likewise," Leadbetter said. "But I can't speak for the NCAA." My assessment proved correct.

By letter of March 13, 2000, Thomas Hosty, NCAA Director of Enforcement advised me as follows:

Dear Mr. Leadbetter:

   This letter serves as a follow-up to prior correspondence regarding the inquiry into the football program at the University of Tennessee, Knoxville by the institution and the NCAA enforcement staff.

   Based upon the available information, the enforcement staff has determined that there appears to be no need to conduct any further inquiry at this time into alleged violations including academic issues and the Tennessee football program.

   Should you have any questions please contact me. Thank you for your cooperation in reviewing these issues.

The Knoxville News-Sentinel reported the NCAA action on March 21, 2000 in another front-page announcement: "NCAA ends probe into UT tutoring—'No need' for more inquiry." UT President Wade Gilley was reported as saying he wasn't surprised by Monday's news. "I think that it reinforces our beliefs that we have the proper structure, the proper processes and we have people of integrity in positions of authority," Gilley said.

   Id.

I was quite pleased with Gilley's expressed appreciation for integrity. It was a characteristic I likewise believed to be inseparable from the University's success as an institution let alone its history of success in dealings with the NCAA.

On April 18 the Knoxville News-Sentinel announced the findings of a 5-member UT Faculty Senate panel chaired by Dr. Burton English: "UT Faculty panel finds no fault with athletic tutoring" (Knoxville News Sentinel, April 18, 2000, p. A4.).

Then on May 2, I received a phone call from Ron Barker asking me to advise him if there were any changes in UT's position on recruiting violations. I replied there were not.

The next day Barker called again. Complaints had been received by the NCAA that evidence of violations had been overlooked. He would need to conduct additional investigation. I offered my full cooperation and assistance.

Sunday, May 7, 2000 headlines read: "NCAA reviewing UT complaint." The [Nashville]Tennessean, May 7, 2000, p.1. The Tennessean reported:

   The NCAA, which cleared the University of Tennessee of academic wrongdoing in March, will return to campus May 23 and meet privately with English professor Linda Bensel–Myers.

   Bensel–Myers said the NCAA wants to review her records, which she says reveal questionable academic practices at UT to keep athletes eligible.

   Ron Barker, a member of the NCAA's enforcement staff, also has notified UT General Counsel Ron Leadbetter of his plans to return to campus and meet with Bensel–Myers. Leadbetter conducted the university's internal investigation, which concluded there were no NCAA violations last fall.

The same article reported "Leadbetter said yesterday Bensel-Myers continues to misinterpret the difference between academic concerns and NCAA violations. He said she's been asked repeatedly to provide any specific information that might constitute an NCAA violation and has repeatedly come up empty." Id. p.17A.

The Tennessean reported Bensel-Meyers' response:

Bensel-Meyers said during her initial interview with Barker, she was prevented by Leadbetter from bringing her records. She also said Leadbetter sat in on the interview.

Said Leadbetter: "We never told her she couldn't bring her records. She can bring a truckload if she wants. But that doesn't mean we're going to look at them."

Id.

Some in the news media misinterpreted this remark. The point was, I was looking for evidence of NCAA infractions - not a mountain of paper documenting an academic dispute between the English department and Athletics.

I invited Barker to meet with Bensel- Meyers in my office and he agreed. Although he certainly did not need my assistance I suggested that he asked her directly: "Can you name one athlete who had his paper written by tutor?" And, "Can you name one tutor who provided such assistance?"

The three of us met in my office on May 23 and Barker asked the suggested questions. Bensel-Meyers' answers remained the same. She could not identify a single player who had received assistance constituting a violation of NCAA rules. Neither could she identify a single tutor who had collaborated with an athlete to submit plagiarized work.

The meeting was short. Barker left. The outcome was as expected–and final. UT heard nothing more from the NCAA on the tutoring scandal. Case closed!

The ESPN-initiated tutoring probe was the last NCAA matter I handled for the University. With a new president and other administrative changes at the University, my job changed dramatically.

Chapter 80–Postscript on Tutoring Scandal–Litigation

My official role in investigating the tutoring scandal reported by ESPN.com ended with the NCAA's affirmation of the University's finding that no NCAA infractions had occurred. But the controversy surrounding the ESPN report was just beginning to percolate.

In early spring 2000, even before the NCAA determined no further investigation was required, I heard rumblings that litigation was in the pipeline. The rumblings were confirmed when I received a copy of a letter from David

Buuck, a Knoxville attorney representing Robin Wright, addressed to UT Deputy General Counsel Catherine Mizell.

The April 28, 2000 letter began, "I am in receipt of your letter of March 27, 2000, in which you decline representation of Ms. Robin Wright for actions taken in the course and scope of her employment at the University of Tennessee." Buuck then argued that the University should be responsible for defending legal actions brought against Wright:

> It is our position Mr. Ron Leadbetter, in his capacity as Associate General Counsel, traveled to Ms. Wright's home to visit with her. Mr. Leadbetter at that time, in his capacity as an attorney, assured Ms. Wright anything she said to him would be held in the strictest of confidence. To that extent, Mr. Leadbetter was holding himself out as counsel to whom Ms. Wright had a reasonable reliance to believe was she could confide in him as an attorney representing her. She therefore made confidential statements to him.
>
> Ms. Wright was sued, inter alia, for statements made to Mr. Leadbetter. To that end, it is our position that Mr. Leadbetter is already representing her and that the University of Tennessee has a duty to come in and defend Ms. Wright in this instance. Mr. Leadbetter can certainly not divulge to any party whatsoever under any circumstances anything said to him in confidence. If he has done so, the university, not Ms. Wright, is liable for the statements if they are slanderous.

Buuck then concluded by suggesting that it was to the University's public-relations advantage to support a faculty member who had aimed to promote the highest degree of academic integrity.

Strangely, I received no inquiry from Mizell regarding the facts of the case before she responded. I would have quickly documented the fact that I made no representation of confidentiality to Wright and that she was well aware that my entire purpose of visiting her was to investigate the validity of allegations attributed to her, then report my findings to the NCAA. Additionally, it was certainly not within her job description to provide to ESPN.com the package of letters and documents which led to the tutoring scandal story.

On February 26, 2000, Reginald [Reggie] Ridley brought suit in the federal court for the Eastern District of Tennessee against Robin Wright, ESPN, Inc., Starwave Corporation, and ESPN Internet Ventures. No. 3:00–CV–119 (Jarvis/Phillips).

Ridley's primary complaint was that the defendants had publicly and maliciously disseminated false and defamatory statements about him publicly. Included in the complaint were Wright's conversations with "counsel for the University of Tennessee and with NCAA investigators." Id. p.3. Compensatory damages in the amount of $1 million and punitive damages in the amount of $500,000 were demanded as well as a trial by jury.

Victoria Gray brought suit the same day in the same court with a very similar claim that she had been publicly and maliciously defamed by the defendants. *Victoria Gray v. Robin Wright, ESPN, Inc., Starwave Corporation, and ESPN Internet Ventures*, No. 3:00–CV–118 (Jarvis/Phillips). Gray demanded $1,500,000 in compensatory damages and $1 million in punitive damages. She requested trial by jury.

Both Ridley and Gray were represented by Knoxville attorney Sidney Gilreath.

Spencer Riley ("individually and as a member of a class of all others similarly situated") filed suit against the University of Tennessee, Linda Bensel–Myers and the NCAA on May 15, 2000 in the same court. No. 3:00–CV–268 (Jordan/Phillips). Riley was represented by Knoxville attorneys Tim Irwin, Robert Watson, Jr. and Richard Hollow

The primary thrust of Riley's complaint was that his student records–particularly those referring to learning disability–had been publicly disclosed in violation of Riley's confidentiality rights under federal law (the Buckley Act) and state law. Riley sought injunctive relief, preventing further dissemination of his and other students' records, and ordering return of all student records to the University with protective measures being taken to assure future confidentiality.

To me the most puzzling aspect of each of the above cases was the failure of Mizell–who became UT General Counsel in December 1999–or the OGC attorney (Memphis office) assigned to represent the University in these matters, Tom McAlexander, to seek from me any information I had regarding any of the cases. There were no meetings or any other form of communication with me aimed at determining the facts of these cases. Very, very puzzling!

In fact, my only involvement in the tutoring litigation was to appear for deposition on August 22, 2001, in the federal actions brought by Gray and Ridley. I was called to testify on behalf of the defendants. McAlexander spent no more than a few minutes discussing the case with me beforehand–a very unacceptable method of "witness and case preparation" from my perspective. My deposition took the better part of a day. The deposition transcript was 248 pages in length.

Questioning by defense counsel Russ Hedrick (for ESPN) and David Buuck (for Wright), as well as plaintiff's counsel, Bryan Capps, covered every conceivable aspect of my investigation of tutoring fraud claims reported by ESPN.

Following my deposition I heard nothing further concerning the tutoring litigation until reading a Knoxville News-Sentinel front page story published on December 15, 2001 ("ESPN claims UT blocked questioning of faculty member").

The article reported ESPN's contention, in court–filed papers, that Tom

McAlexander, halted the deposition of Dr. Carl Asp just as he was "on the verge of obtaining testimony indicating that the direction of, and the fallout from, the investigation went all the way to the top–to UT's then president, J. Wade Gilley, and his then assistant, Eli Fly." Id.

The article later reported, "ESPN contends UT attorney Ron Leadbetter was charged with conducting the investigation in 1999." ESPN then criticized the manner in which I conducted the investigation.

"… despite having in his possession all the information needed to conduct a proper investigation, (Leadbetter) failed to take any action to further that investigation for weeks," the motion [filed by ESPN with the federal court] states.

McAlexander defended Leadbetter's actions, saying he moved forward with his investigation as soon as the University directed him to do so.

Id. p.A7.

Earlier in the article McAlexander was quoted as saying, "Our position is that neither Dr. Gilley nor Eli Fly had any impact on this investigation at all… They didn't prevent it from going forward. Dr. Gilley initiated this investigation." Id.

McAlexander was absolutely correct in stating that neither Gilley nor Fly had any impact on the investigation–neither played any role whatever in direct thing the course of the investigation. At the same time, McAlexander was completely wrong in stating that "Dr. Gilley initiated this investigation." I initiated the investigation before Gilley became president. We never had even a passing reference to the investigation until I presented Gilley a copy of my findings.

Although employed in the office of General Counsel until March 31, 2008 I heard nothing–and read nothing–further about the tutoring litigation. Whether the litigation was non-suited as baseless or settled for a sizable amount I do not know. I am quite certain the matter was not brought to trial.

One thing I do know: my investigative report, rejecting ESPN's claims of tutoring fraud, was never revisited by or overturned by the NCAA.

Chapter 81–NCAA Invite to Serve as Southeast Conference Representative Rejected

Elsa Cole served as the General Counsel for the National Collegiate Athletic Association from 1997 to 2011. Cole was also actively involved with the National Association of College and University attorneys.

Cole and I developed a solid friendship in the course of our NACUA activities. She was also well aware of my extensive experience handling UT athletics cases involving the NCAA.

On May 30, 2000 I received a phone call from Cole. She explained that the

NCAA was formulating a committee of higher education attorneys for the express purpose of developing and improving NCAA rules and procedures–with recommended changes being presented to NCAA membership for approval.

Cole asked if I would be willing to serve as the Southeast Conference representative on the committee. I replied that I was honored by her request and would be pleased to serve. I would need to obtain the approval of my boss, Catherine Mizell, and would seek that approval immediately.

That same afternoon I sent an explanatory memorandum to Mizell:

> Elsa Cole called this afternoon to see if I would be interested in serving on a committee of higher education attorneys Elsa is putting together to provide input to, and receive output from, the NCAA on legal matters of mutual interest to the NCAA and the institutions represented.
>
> The committee will be composed of 10 attorneys including 6 from Division I institutions. I would be the SEC representative (others have already been appointed to represent the Pac 10, Big 10 and most other major conferences).
>
> Since meetings would coincide with NACUA and NCAA annual meetings there would be a minimum of additional expense involved.
>
> This is an excellent opportunity for UT to have a notable influence on and opportunity to stay abreast of NCAA legal matters. Do you agree?
>
> Elsa asked that I let her know as soon as possible if I had approval to serve on the committee.
>
> Thanks.

Cole called again the morning of June 1 to see if I had heard anything from Mizell. I replied that I had not but would send her another email. Minutes later I e-mailed Catherine:

> Elsa Cole called again this morning to see if the decision had been made to participate in the NCAA advisory committee because she wanted to finalize the committee membership before Fed Xing materials to the members. I asked if we could have until tomorrow to respond, since you are out of town, and she agreed.

The following morning Mizell responded that she had "a call in to Elsa to get additional information about the advisory committee." That afternoon I received from Mizell what I considered a bizarre response.

> I told Elsa that I think a General Counsel of one of the SEC schools should serve on the advisory committee. She had asked a couple of GCs, but they were unable to serve. She will probably ask Pam Bernard.

For certain Pam Bernard would have been an excellent representative to the NCAA. She and I worked well together in carrying out leadership responsibilities with NACUA and we had a long-standing friendship. Signifying that solid relationship was a personal letter Bernard later wrote me on June 27, 2001 thanking me for my service.

As a friend, I would certainly have supported Bernard as the SEC representative had Elsa Cole offered her that opportunity. But it was clear to me that friendship played no role in Mizell's decision to suggest Cole recruit a general counsel as SEC representative.

What I found stunning was Mizell's rejection of an opportunity for the University of Tennessee to have an influential role in the NCAA and encouraging redirection of that golden opportunity to the General Counsel of the University of Florida.

I sensed the UT General Counsel permitted personal jealousy or other questionable motive to take precedence over the best interests of the University of Tennessee.

The black clouds of the Gilley years stretched beyond the office of the President.

Chapter 82
The Lola Dodge Purge and the Two-Day Miracle

Prior to 1994 Dr. Lola Dodge served the UT Knoxville campus as director of the office of affirmative action. She and I cooperated in handling many civil rights cases and affirmative action matters. We worked well together.

In 1994 Dodge was promoted to the position of Director of Human Resources Management. My wife, Therese, held the position of Assistant Director in the department and had been employed in the department for more than 20 years. She reported to Dodge.

Within a matter of months following Dodge's assumption of the directorship my wife and other administrators in Human Resources became concerned about Dodge's management style. Their efforts to resolve those concerns by conversation with Dodge proved unproductive.

In October 1995 Therese and two other assistant directors, Linda Francisco and Mike Herbstritt, arranged for a meeting with Chancellor Bill Snyder for the purpose of sharing with him–on a confidential basis–their concerns with Dodge's management style. According to a reliable source the assistant directors shared with Snyder very specific examples of problems they perceived as resulting from Dodge's approach to managing the department.

The morning of November 1, 1995, Therese, Francisco and Herbstritt were called to Dodge's office. Each was handed a letter announcing: "This letter is to inform you that your position as an assistant director in the office of human resources management will be eliminated as of November 30, 1995, due to a reorganization and, therefore, your employment will terminate at that time." I was shocked to hear the news later that day and made the following entry in my diary:

Therese was notified at 10 AM that she was laid off effective immediately–along with Linda Francisco and Mike Hertzberg. To clear their belongings out of their offices by 5 PM !!! Therese called me at 11 to share the news. Her pay runs through Nov. 30. Although I will request prayer for Lola and those above her – as well as Therese and the others THIS CANNOT STAND!! The battle is on for the "soul" of the University and "RIGHT" will prevail!

All three assistant directors appealed their termination to Vice Chancellor for Business and Finance, Ray Hamilton, the following day. The same day I met with President Joe Johnson and voiced my extreme displeasure with what had occurred. Johnson was supportive, but in his diplomatic style urged patience, "Let's see what happens." He made no commitment to take any action and as it turned out he did not need to.

As noted in my diary for November 2, "I met with Joe Johnson today–and unofficially talked to many others. Support for Therese is very strong. The Commission for Women has voted to condemn the layoffs and many folks are writing letters, sending email or visiting Chancellor Snyder in person."

Hamilton denied the appeal filed with him by Therese, Francisco and Herbstritt. The three immediately appealed to Snyder that same day, November 2.

The news media quickly picked up the story. "Layoff of 3 at UT sparks protest," read the front page headline of the Knoxville News–Sentinel on November 3, 1995.

The sudden layoffs Wednesday of three longtime University of Tennessee personnel administrators has set off a wave of campus and community protest.

UT's Commission for Women presented Chancellor Bill Snyder with a resolution Thursday asking for the reinstatement of the three workers while their layoffs are reconsidered. Dhyana Ziegler, president of UT's Faculty Senate, was working on a similar resolution.

"You have these people who are well respected, who had given years of service to this institution being treated like criminals, being treated like dogs," said Ziegler, adding the situation was even worse because it occurred within the Human Resources Department.

Dr. Lola Dodge, UT's executive director of human resources, said the three assistant directors were laid off as part of departmental reorganization aimed at reducing administrative costs. Dodge's supervisor–Vice Chancellor Ray Hamilton–said layoffs in other departments are not expected.

Hamilton confirmed the laid- off employees had met with them in the past to express their concerns about Dodge's leadership of the department.

He and Dodge stress those complaints had nothing to do with their layoffs. Linda Francisco, one of those who was terminated, disagreed.

"This is definitely recrimination," she said Thursday.

***

John Parker, executive director of the physical plant and a 34-year employee of UT, said the campus was "consumed" by outrage as news of the layoffs spread Thursday.

"In the years I've seen people come and go, I don't believe I've ever seen the entire campus as upset," he said.

"I was astounded and shocked. I've never really seen a reorganization where there was a wholesale termination of exempt (administrative) employees."

Parker added the three employees laid off were widely known and liked throughout the University.

Id, pp.A1, A6.

Both Therese and I received numerous phone calls, emails and personal visits from members of the University community expressing support.

Miracles do happen! My diary entry for November 3 acknowledges that fact.

Around 4 this afternoon the message was officially released: Therese, Linda & Mike are back to work Monday. Lola Dodge is out–will have a "special assignment." Praise the Lord for his fast & effective work through hundreds of people. Never in the history of UT has such a thing happened.

Sertoma dinner at the faculty club tonight. The "comeback kid" (Therese) was introduced by new president Harvey Carruth (biggest comebacks since?). It has been a wonderful week. We know that God is with us and that MANY friends are with us.

The front page headline of the next day's Sentinel shared the good news with the entire community: "Dismissals of 3 UT personnel officials rescinded/department head is reassigned." The Knoxville News-Sentinel, November 4, 1995, p.1. Following the headline came details:

The sudden termination of three longtime personnel administrators at the University of Tennessee were rescinded Friday by UT Vice Chancellor Ray Hamilton.

***

Effective Monday, Nov. 6, Joe Fornes, executive director of business serv ices, will assume the role of interim executive director of human resources management while a review of the office is completed. He will serve until a search to identify candidates for a permanent appointment also is completed, Hamilton stated.

"I believe this decision is in the best interest of the individuals and of the university," Hamilton's statement said.

Theresa Leadbetter, one of those dismissed Wednesday and reinstated Fri day, expressed "overwhelming gratitude" for the outpouring of support she received from her colleagues at UT.

"I'm very, very delighted and encouraged that the University has made the right decision. I'm very grateful to have my job back. I love the University and what I do," said Leadbetter, a 25–year employee of UT.

(The Knoxville News-Sentinel, November 4, 1995,p. A1, A3).

A magnificent affirmation of the University of Tennessee's commitment to integrity and loyalty to valued members of the University community-at least during the "Big Orange" years–is found in a November 6, 1995 memorandum from President Joe Johnson to Chancellor Snyder:

TO: Chancellor Bill Snyder
FROM: Joe Johnson
SUBJECT: UT Knoxville Human Resources

You and your crew made a wise decision to reverse the decision to lay–off three Associate Directors of the UT Knoxville Human Resources Office for the following reasons:

1. The method for handling the lay–off was a massacre without a bit of humanity, concern, or care. It can never be defended. UT does not treat dogs like these long – term employees were treated. We only use such methods for thieves and abusers of people.

2. Your administration stresses diversity, conflict resolution, and kindness. The episode in human resources violates each of these notions to which you are firmly committed.

3. A person in a UTK leadership role made a horrible mistake that cannot be defended.

4. It is hard to defend an unwise person who does not treat people fairly and does not foresee adverse reaction.

Your major remaining chore is to decide what to do with Lola. I would return her to a more protected environment.

I will be glad to discuss. You and I need to chat about Lola and Ray.

Thank you.

Dodge was later fired. She filed suit against the University of Tennessee in the Chancery Court for Knox County seeking injunctive relief, preventing the termination of her employment.

Needless to say I did not handle that litigation. I was, however, called upon to provide an affidavit describing my role in terminating Dodge's employment. My affidavit, filed with the Chancery Court for Knox County, made clear I had no such role:

[Case caption omitted]

Affidavit of Ronald C Leadbetter
Ronald C. Leadbetter, having been first duly sworn, deposes and says as follows:

***

4. I had no knowledge of the proposed terminations [of my wife, of Dr. Linda Francisco and of Mr. Mike Herbstritt].

5. After I learned of the terminations, I initiated a conversation with only one University of Tennessee administrator, Joseph E. Johnson, President, to discuss my wife's termination. I did not talk with Chancellor William T. Snyder or Vice Chancellor Ray Hamilton about my wife, the other OHRM employees who were terminated by Dr. Dodge, or Dr. Dodge's removal as director of OHRM and eventual termination.

6. Even though I talked with Joseph E. Johnson about my wife, the termination of Dr. Dodge was never discussed with him or anyone else until after the fact.

7. I had no knowledge of the termination of Dr. Dodge until after it occurred.

8. I never solicited anyone to write letters or electronic messages to Chancellor Snyder on my wife's behalf. If anyone asked me whom they should contact, I told them Chancellor Snyder.

Further, this affiant saith not.
Ronald C. Leadbetter

(Lola R. Dodge v. University of Tennessee, Chancery Court for Knox County, Tennessee, No. 132087–2). The affidavit was executed and filed in January 1998. Dodge's case was eventually dismissed by the Chancery Court.

What started as a terrible personal tragedy–having grievous effect on me due to its impact on Therese–came to an incredibly rapid and positive conclusion. A stunning reversal of events–and what an unforgettable answer to prayer!

Go Big Orange !

Chapter 83–Scott Hartman and the Errant Hammer Throw–Horrific Injury, Longest Case, Huge Win and Stunning Loss

THE OPENING TRAGEDY

Scott Hartman was born on October 12, 1967. In fall 1986 Hartman enrolled at the University of Tennessee, Knoxville as a freshman. He received an athletic grant- in -aid from the University for his participation on the UT track and field team. Conditioned on his receipt of a scholarship, Hartman earlier received from the University a "letter of intent," whereby the University agreed to be responsible for his "medical attention due to athletic participation."

On April 17, 1987 the UT track team participated in a track meet at the University of Kentucky in Lexington (Fayette County), Kentucky. Accompanying the team to the meet was George Watts, UT assistant track coach.

Hartman's event was the hammer throw, an event using a 16 pound steel ball at the end of a cable. A number of hammer throwers from various colleges and universities were warming up for their event while other scheduled events were in progress. Coach Watts was away from the hammer throw warm-up area, attending events already underway.

After completing one of his warm-up throws, Hartman walked down one of the sidelines to retrieve his hammer. Another thrower, from Berea College, entered the throwers circle and commenced his own warm-up throw. Although Hartman initially kept his eyes on the thrower, at some point he apparently concluded the Berea thrower had decided to abort his throw and looked away. A serious mistake. The Berea thrower released his hammer and the device flew down the sideline on which Hartman was walking. Cries of "heads" rang out from other athletes present. It was too late. The hammer struck Hartman in the head just as he was turning back toward the thrower.

Hartman suffered a horrific brain injury and was rendered "level 2" comatose – one level above completely comatose. His condition was so severe that it was generally expected by medical personnel that Hartman would live only a short time following his injury. That expectation proved to be quite wrong.

FLURRY OF LAWSUITS FOLLOWS

By the following spring litigation had been filed by Hartman's mother, Kay Hartman, on his behalf, and by both her and Hartman's father, Cleon Hartman, on their own behalf. Lawsuits were filed in four separate jurisdictions for the injuries Hartman sustained at the track meet.

Suit was filed in the United States District Court for the Eastern District of Kentucky, the United States District Court for the Middle District of Tennessee at Nashville, the Board of Claims of Commonwealth of Kentucky (against the University of Kentucky, University of Kentucky Athletic Association, University of Kentucky track coach Donald Weber, Berea College and Berea track coach, Mike Johnson). The Hartmans also filed suit against UT, the state of Tennessee, UT head track coach Douglas Brown and George Watts in the Fayette Circuit Court, Kentucky. Finally, the Hartmans brought suit in the Tennessee Claims Commission against the University of Tennessee and the State of Tennessee.

Although listed as counsel of record in the Kentucky state litigation, I served only as an assistant to Kentucky attorneys hired by UT to handle the Kentucky litigation–the Lexington, Kentucky firm of Stites and Harbison. The firm's work was quick and efficient.

The Fayette Circuit Court dismissed the Hartmans' suit against the University defendants on January 24, 1989. An appeal was filed as to the individually named defendants. By order of January 26, 1990 The Court of Appeals of the Commonwealth of Kentucky affirmed the lower court ruling dismissing the plaintiffs' action against UT coaches Brown and Watts. The appellate court's reasoning was as follows:

The trial court granted the defendant's motion to dismiss for two (2) reasons: (1) to acknowledge Tennessee's policy of a limited waiver of sovereign immunity and deferring to that policy under the principle of comity; and (2) pursuant to a specific clause contained in the Tennessee statute relating to actions before the claims commission, all causes of action against the state employees individually were waived. This appeal was filed only in regards to the two (2) individual defendants....

Tennessee Code Annotated 9–8–307 (b) specifically states: claims against the state filed pursuant to subsection (1)... Shall operate as a waiver of any cause of action, based on the same act or omission, which the claimant has against any state officer or employee. The waiver shall be void if the commission determines that the act or omission was not within the scope of the officer's or employee's office or employment.

***

We agree with that holding [a case from the U.S. Court of Appeals for the Sixth Circuit holding that "by initiating proceedings with the Tennessee Claims Commission a party had waived his option of submitting his cause of action against the state employees before any other tribunal."] and the Fayette Circuit Court's ruling in that regard.

Scott Graham Hartman by and through his court–appointed guardian and next friend, Kay Hartman; Kay Hartman, individually; and Cleon Hartman v. University of Tennessee; State of Tennessee; Douglas Brown; and George Watts, Commonwealth of Kentucky Court of Appeals, No. 89–CA–000381–MR.

Thereby the Kentucky actions against the UT defendants were concluded. The actions against the University of Kentucky defendants were reportedly settled for $1 million and the actions against Berea College defendants were likewise reportedly settled for $1 million.

The plaintiffs' federal lawsuit in Tennessee was withdrawn–presumably in recognition of the waiver provision of Tennessee law. With that withdrawal and final action by the Kentucky Court of Appeals the only litigation remaining was the Hartmans' Tennessee Claims Commission claim.

The Hartmans' case was filed with the Tennessee Division of Claims Administration on April 15, 1988 and transferred to the Tennessee Claims Commission, Middle Division, on July 18. The case was assigned to Claims Commissioner Richard Rucker.

Both negligence and contract claims were asserted by the Hartmans. Maximum recovery–$300,000–was requested by each of the three claimants on the negligence claim. On the contract claim, the Hartman sought "an amount not yet ascertained to cover Scott Hartman's medical expenses arising out of his participation in the sporting events mentioned herein pursuant to contract."

As a matter of fact, athletic director Doug Dickey traveled to Nashville to meet with Kay Hartman soon after the accident to see what Scott's needs were. He expressed a strong interest in assisting in every way possible.

THE CONTRACT CLAIM

The Hartmans did not contend the University breached its agreement with Scott. Rather, the Hartmans sought a "declaratory judgment"–a declaration of precisely what the University's obligations were under the "letter of intent."

At the time of Scott's injury, the University had an insurance policy providing coverage–with a $1 million limit, and that coverage kicked in immediately. The Hartman's made no claim during the litigation that the insurance carrier refused coverage or that the University in any way failed to meet a contractual obligation.

The problem rested with the meaning of language in the "letter of intent". While the athletics department had issued a letter committing the University to providing "medical attention due to athletic participation" no definitions were provided and no dollar limits specified.

Because the athletics department did not consider the letter a "contract" the document was never sent to the office of General Counsel for contract review –during most of my early career all contracts are required to be reviewed by an OGC attorney. Had I reviewed the agreement, the failure to specify a dollar limit on coverage would have resulted in approval being denied. "Water under the bridge," as the saying goes.

Both sides filed motions for partial summary judgment seeking a judicial determination of the nature of UT's contractual obligation to provide Scott with medical attention. By order of September 27, 1989 Commissioner Rucker denied the University's motion and granted the claimants'. Quite frankly, I had little difficulty accepting the reasoning of the Commissioner:

6. The expression "medical attention due to athletic participation" is phenomenally broad. It does not require that an injury have occurred. "Attention" could cover advice, examination, nutritional evaluation, and preventative treatment in addition to treatment after injury. The term "medical" could cover anyone trained in medicine or medically related fields. The only limitation appears to be that the medical attention must be "due to athletic participation" and would exclude such things as injuries occurring from automobile accidents during school vacation. The commission concludes that the options of the university are very broad so long as the medical attention is provided. Thus, the University could either pay a third party to provide this medical attention, or the University could, through university personnel, hospitals, and/or medical schools provide the attention "in kind".

Scott Graham Hartman, et al. v. The University of Tennessee et al. Claim No. 85209, p. 2-3.

The Commission concluded:

In short, the commission concludes (1) that the reasonable interpretation of the expression "medical attention due to athletic participation" obligates the State to provide reasonable medical treatment appropriate to Scott Hartman's condition without limitation as to time or dollar limit. … (4) the State, through the University of Tennessee or otherwise, may provide the medical attention either (a) in-kind by taking over the care of Scott Hartman using State medical employees, or (b) the State may pay third parties to do this.

University officials were quite satisfied with the ruling for two reasons: first, Doug Dickey was adamant about seeing to it that Hartman received proper care. Second, the University had many options for providing that care by utilizing its own internal resources. Considerable time–many years–would pass before the contract issue again raised its head.

In 1989 the Tennessee law permitting contract actions against the state was amended to permit only a contract action for "breach of a written contract between the claimant and the state which was executed by one (1) or more state officers or employees with authority to execute the contract." Public acts of 1989, Ch. 491, Sec.2. That legislation was aimed at eliminating situations such as occurred in the Hartman "letter of intent."

On June 19, 1992, Dr. Fred Killifer, UT athletics trainer Tim Kerin and I flew on the UT plane to Nashville to visit with Kay Hartman and see how Scott Hartman was getting along. Soon after arriving at the Hartman residence it became painfully evident that his condition had not improved and likely never would. At some point a decision would be required as to whether the University could provide better care in its own facilities. As of the time of our visit UT's insurance carrier was making those decisions. Prior to that (between April 17, 1987 and February 1990) Cleon Hartman's employment-based insurance, "the Bell-South plan," had paid for Scott's care until the plan's dollar limit was exhausted.

THE NEGLIGENCE CLAIM

The Hartmans' negligence claim was based on the contention that Coach Watts acted negligently in failing to be personally present and supervise Scott Hartman during warm-ups in what was indisputably an activity with potentially dangerous consequences. In order to address that issue it was necessary to not only identify acceptable practice in track and field events at the University of Tennessee but also the national standard for track and field. For that purpose depositions were taken from UT athletics staff: George Watt, Doug Brown, Bill Webb, Doug Dickey, Mike DePalmer

The process then went national, involving noted track and field coaches and athletes outside Tennessee:Charles Ruter (Louisville); Dr. Phil Henson (Atlanta); Bill Skinner (Lexington); Ray Sabatini and Tony Dehner (Lexington); Stan Huntsman (Austin, Texas); Mel Rosen (Auburn, Alabama); and Judd Logan (North Canton, Ohio)

Both Huntsman (former UT track and field head coach) and Skinner (Javelin thrower for UT track and field during my student days) were friends of mine from the past and accepted my request for help. Both agreed to serve as expert witnesses without pay.

Skinner, a one-time national champ in the javelin throw, was actually present at the track meet when Hartman was injured. He was one of those that yelled "heads!" when it appeared the Berea thrower's hammer was heading Hartman's way.

For me, the most memorable aspect of my flight to Lexington on August 21 –for Skinner's August 22 deposition–was the fact that I was severely impacted by a case of phlebitis in my left foot and ankle. I had contracted the infection the previous day while guiding the Lady Vols volleyball team on a rafting trip down the Ocoee River. From an emergency room physician examining me that evening I learned that folks regularly died from phlebitis before penicillin was discovered.

The general consensus of the coaches and athletes interviewed was that there was no national standard and, as such, but it was not customary practice for a coach to be present whenever an athlete in the throwing events was warming up. The matter never made it to trial. The Hartmans failed to unearth sufficient

Big Orange, Black Storm Clouds and More   415

evidence to get there.

RESOLUTION OF THE CLAIMS

In November 1995 the University moved for summary judgment on the liability issue (as well as the contract issue). Then, in January 1996 the claimants cross–filed for summary judgment on the same issues

On March 12, 1998–nearly 10 years after the action commenced–Commissioner W.R. Baker (succeeding Commissioner Rucker) granted the University's motion for summary judgment on the negligence issue while denying the Hartmans' cross-motion.

On the contract issue: the Commissioner noted that neither party had appealed any aspect of the 1989 order entered by Commissioner Rucker. Therefore, all aspects of the 1989 interpretation of the contract language was considered res judicata–not subject to further debate.

Baker then addressed claimants' argument that BellSouth had paid a net amount of $1,026,666 for Scott Hartman's care between April 17, 1987 and February 1990 and that judgment should enter against the University in that amount. Claimant's argument was rejected for three reasons, according to the Commissioner: First, although the University is required to provide for Scott's medical care, and although the University failed to do so with reference to the period before February 1, 1990, the claimants have suffered no loss as a result of that failure. The BellSouth plan has paid for Scott's medical care, and there is no indication that the claimants have paid any medical expenses for which the university is responsible. Further, it appears that the plan made such payments because it was contractually obligated to the claimants to do so. Certainly there is no indication that the plan has any claim against any of the claimants for the medical expenses in question. Thus the claimants seek an award for expenses which have already been paid by a third party…. In short, if the University had fulfilled its contractual obligations which are in question herein, Scott's medical care expenses would have been paid and the claimants would have had no responsibility for any of these said expenses. As it is, all of Scott's medical care expenses have been paid and the claimants have had no responsibility for any of these said expenses. The claimants have suffered no loss.

Id. pp. 3-4.

Secondly, the commission conceded that the BellSouth plan might have a claim against the University or the state based on the theory of subrogation but that "neither in the original pleadings instituting this claim, nor in the subsequent pleadings and filings, have the parties claimed, asserted, discuss, or raise the issue of subrogation, except for a mention of the plans potential subrogation rights in the form of an order the claimant submitted in connection with the motion now under consideration." The commission ruled that any claim for subrogation belonged to Bell South and not the claimants–and Bell South was not a party to the claim. Id. p.4.

Third, the Commission found that "the terms and conditions of the coverage provided by the BellSouth plan have not been submitted to this commission. Thus this Commission has no way to ascertain whether the terms of the coverage provided under the Bell-South plan anticipated that it would be primary to any other coverage available, whether it would be secondary to any other available coverage, whether some pro rated division of responsibility was contemplated, or whether some other provision is provided."

Id. p. 5.

For the reasons given Commissioner Baker found in the University's favor on the contract issue: "For each of these reasons, the claimants' motion on their contractual claim is denied, and the university's motion for partial summary judgment as to this claim is granted." Id. p.5.

With respect to the negligence issue Baker observed that to overcome UT's motion for summary judgment, the claimants needed to show that Scott Hartman's injury resulted from negligence of the University. "Stated simply, claimants must establish duty, breach of duty, proximate causation of injury, and loss."

Id. p.6.

The Commission noted claimants' contention that space for warm-up activities at the track was too small and there were an insufficient number of officials present to supervise warm-up activities. "These allegations appear sufficient to establish a claim against the Kentucky authorities which sponsored the event in question, but do not provide an adequate basis on which the University's liability can be based." Id.p.7. Baker concluded that the testimony of Ruter and Henson "placed the responsibility for event safety with the host institution." Id.

In addition the Commission noted an absence of any evidence the University knew of unsafe conditions in the warm-up area, Id. p.7. Another major finding by Baker dismissed the idea that there was a "standard of care" requiring coaching presence during warm-ups:

> The depositions and affidavits, when viewed most favorably towards the claimants, indicate that it was not the normal practice for coaches to be present at warm-ups, except at a national–championship event, and that there is an insufficient number of coaches to supervise athletes in warm–up areas as well is to perform other coaching functions because of factors beyond the university's control (national athletic–conference restrictions on the number of coaches allowed). Such evidence of industry practice, while not conclusive, is evidence about a proper standard of care."

Id. p.8.

Finally, no evidence was presented that the presence of coaching staff would have made any difference. Skinner and Logan "were present at the warm-ups [and] said they did not notice any particular danger." Id. Claimants failed to indicate "what danger a coach could have noticed that Scott and these two witnesses did not perceive. Nor is it at all clear what a coach could have done to avoid the accident." Id.

The commission then concluded, "After almost 10 years from the initiation of this action, during which the parties have had ample time to complete discovery, the claimants have not shown this Commission evidence or testimony from which it could infer that Scott's injury was a proximate result of any negligent conduct or omission by the University." Id. Accordingly the Commission dismissed the Hartmans' claim. The Hartmans appealed the Commissioner's ruling.

On September 14, 1998 the Tennessee Court of Appeals (Judges Cantrell, Todd and Cain) affirmed the Claims Commissions ruling. Then, on March 8, 1999 an application for permission to appeal to the Tennessee Supreme Court filed by the Hartmans was denied. Case concluded–after nearly 11 years of litigation!

Wrong!

BELL SOUTH CORPORATION WAITS 11 YEARS TO JOIN THE FRAY

On March 10, 1999–two days after the Tennessee Supreme Court rejected the Hartman's application for permission to appeal–the Hartmans filed with the Claims Commission a "Notice of Joinder of BellSouth Corporation" and "BellSouth Corporation's Ratification of Claims." I filed a "Motion to Strike," on behalf of the University of Tennessee, contending the filing was untimely–to say the least.

The Claims Commission agreed with the University's motion and, by order of May 10, 1999, Commissioner Baker dismissed BellSouth's claim. His reasons for doing so made sense to me.

First, Commissioner Baker rejected BellSouth's argument that the Tennessee Court of Appeals had earlier ruled that the Commission could join BellSouth as a claimant and re-litigate the claim. According to Baker, "It is abundantly clear that the Court of Appeals did not envision BellSouth's joining this claim but rather its filing a separate claim of its own: '… the way is open for the third-party subrogee to assert its rights, if any, in a separate claim.' "

Id. p. 2.

Second, the Commission rejected BellSouth's argument that it had not been provided reasonable time for filing a "ratification." The Commission noted that the University had denied that BellSouth was the real party in interest in its February 1996 filing. The Commission had concurred with the University's position in its March 1998 Judgment and BellSouth had not filed its ratification until March 1999. "Even under the most liberal reading of this [procedural] rule, this much time is not reasonable." Id. p.2.

Third, BellSouth had argued: "Complete relief cannot be accorded among those already parties without joinder of the additional party." This was rejected. The Commission noted that neither the University nor the Hartmans–the only parties in the case–faced "any substantial risk of inconsistent obligation" since the Commission had already denied BellSouth's claim against the University and "this Commission cannot conclude that any 'substantial risk' exists to the Hartmans as required by this Rule." Id. p. 3.

Commissioner Baker concluded his ruling with a "common sense" observation with which most readers –with or without legal training–will likely agree:

> Finally, BellSouth's position must be rejected on sound judicial–policy grounds. To let BellSouth enter this claim after the action taken by the Court of Appeals and the Supreme Court would mock finality of judicial decisions, and would invite a waste of appellate courts' time and resources.
>
> BellSouth has just waited too long.

Scott Graham Hartman et al v. State of Tennessee, No. 85,209, Tennessee Claims Commission, Middle Division, May 11, 1999.

Case surely over now. Not hardly. An appeal on behalf of the Hartmans was filed with the Tennessee Court of Appeals for the Middle Section, at Nashville. I expected the appellate court would review the record and quickly reject the appeal as lacking in merit. Not so!

In a published decision, the three-judge appellate panel (appellate judges Caine, Cantrell and Koch) reversed the Claims Commission judgment and "remanded for trial on the merits of the issues drawn between the claimants and the defendants as ratified by BellSouth Corporation." Hartman v. University of Tennessee, 38 S.W. 3d 570 (Tenn. Ct. App. 2000). How did the appellate court reached this stunning decision roughly 12 years after the Hartmans filed suit? Cause the "rules" say so.

> In spite of the difference in wording between [federal and state rules of procedure], the need to bind the subrogee under res judicata principles is the same, and no reason is apparent why the ratification procedure in [cited cases of authority] cannot be used for that purpose. The subrogee insurance company under such a ratification mechanism does not have to be made a party plaintiff but does have to bind itself to the outcome of the litigation in res judicata effect.
>
> Id. p.574.

What about the Claims Commission's reasoning? The Court of Appeals addressed that as well:

> Having observed that the failure of the Hartman claimants to disclose in their pleadings prior to March 10, 1999 that they were representing a subrogee and the failure of BellSouth Corporation to affirmatively bind itself to accept res judicata effect of final judgment in the case caused their problems in the first place, it is necessary now to look to the other side of the coin.
>
> Id.

In ruling that BellSouth's claim should be permitted to proceed the appeals court found:

> There has been no adjudication on the merits in this case as to whether or not or to what extent BellSouth Corporation may be entitled to recover from the defendants on their subrogation claim. There is little or no prejudice to the defendants by allowing trial on the merits on a claim of which they have been aware since February 1996. On the other hand, to sustain the position of the defendants would produce a harsh result for BellSouth Corporation.

Id. p.576.

My personal interpretation of the appellate court's reasoning was "no harm, no foul." The University and State of Tennessee filed an application for permission to appeal to the Tennessee Supreme Court. That application was denied on February 12, 2001.

The Court of Appeals' ruling seemingly defined the issue now to be tried as which insurance provider had primary responsibility for paying the bills already paid by BellSouth. However, I took the position that the University and the State were not insurance carriers; the courts had already entered judgment that the University's contractual obligation was to "provide reasonable medical treatment appropriate to Scott Hartman's condition without limitation as to time or dollar amount" and that the University could carry out that contractual responsibility either by paying others to provide the service or by utilizing its own medical resources.

The factual issue remaining was whether the University had acted reasonably and in good faith to meet that obligation. In order to address that question I felt the best place to start was with the only witnesses in a position to testify that the University had not met its obligation–Kay and Cleon Hartman.

I arranged to meet with and take the deposition of Kay Hartman in her home in Nashville on October 19, 200. Our meeting went very well on a personal level.

Later the same day, I took the deposition of Cleon Hartman in the State penitentiary (South Central Correctional Facility) in Clifton, Tennessee where he was incarcerated for a criminal offense. His deposition likewise went well–not nearly as well on a personal level as with his ex-wife.

One of the problems resulting from the appellate courts' disregard for the passage of time as a factor in determining whether a party to any litigation had been disadvantaged was found in Kay Hartman's response to my question as to when UT athletic staff met with her at the UT hospital:

A. ... I remember Tim Kerin, but I don't remember– –I don't
   remember at what time, but he was there. I can't remember.
Q. Did he get they are either that day or the following day?
A. One of the days. I don't remember which. It's been almost 15 years.

Q. Oh, yes. And at some point in time, did coach Dickey, the athletic director, appear at the hospital?

A. Sometime, but I don't remember at what time.

At some point in time the decision was made to move Scott Hartman closer to home. Kay Hartman testified she didn't have anything to do with the arrangements and that it was her ex-husband, Cleon, who made the arrangements to move Scott to Vanderbilt so he would be closer to home.

Q. During this entire period [June 25, 1987, until April, 1989]–that's roughly 3 years or 2 1/2 years–were these arrangements, as far as where Scott was hospitalized, where he was moved to, the treatment he received, was that all satisfactory to you?

A. It was the only choice we had.

Q. Okay. Did you ever ask any officials at the University of Tennessee to intervene and make some different arrangements?

A. No, I didn't.

Both Kay and Cleon Hartman agreed the University never rejected any medical care request they presented. In addition, UT Risk Manager, Murray Edge, testified by affidavit that Bell South had "never requested the University to assume responsibility for any medical care needs of Scott Hartman."

In sum, both Kay and Cleon Hartman confirmed in their depositions that the University had met its contractual obligation to their son. That deposition evidence was presented to the Claims Commission in "Defendants' Motion for Summary Judgment as to BellSouth's Subrogation Claim" filed in January 2002

The University's last argument, in its memorandum in support of defendant's motion for summary judgment, was one never addressed by the Claims Commission-or the Court of Appeals:

> Presumably, the Hartmans proceeded as they did out of a desire that BellSouth assume responsibility for payment of bills for Nashville area medical treatment opted for by Kay Hartman rather than relinquish to the University the option of determining in what reasonable manner it would provide Scott's medical treatment, risking the possibility the University might provide medical care in a manner less acceptable to Kay Hartman. Because the University is responsible for Scott Hartman's athletic–related medical expenses "without limitation as to time or dollar," had Kay Hartman at any time following the April 17, 1987 accident called upon the University to assume full responsibility for Scott Hartman's medical care, there's no question the University would have been obligated to do so. Had such request made, the University might well have opted to transfer Scott from the hospital facilities in Lexington to the University's Medical Center in Knoxville, to its hospital in Memphis, or to other state facilities. Alternatively, the University might have opted to provide medical care through a public or private caregiver of its choosing within or even out-

side the Nashville area. Of course, the University never had the opportunity to exercise these options with respect to those services for which BellSouth paid since it was never called upon by Kay Hartman to do so.

The University's failure or refusal to reimburse BellSouth its cost for medical attention Kay Hartman never requested or afforded the University an opportunity to provide cannot possibly constitute a breach of the University's contract with Scott.

On May 13, 2002 the Claims Commission filed its order on the contract issue, granting the Hartmans' cross–motion for summary judgment and awarding a recovery–payment to BellSouth–in the amount of $1,026,666.71. On the positive side, the Commission refused to award prejudgment interest on the amount expended by BellSouth–an amount that would have approximated the amount of the award, more than $1 million.

The Commission seemingly disregarded the University's argument that it had never refused to assume responsibility for Scott's care ("The University argues that it never refused to provide medical care for Scott because it was never asked to do so, and that it has never breached its contractual commitment to Scott. From this it concludes that Scott has no right to which BellSouth can be subrogated."). Id. p.8.

Further, the Commission concluded, "Medical care was provided to Scott which the University was contractually required to provide. The University is required to pay for this care. It appears that the University seeks to have a requirement that Scott demand treatment implied as a condition precedent to its duty to provide such treatment." Id. p.9.

The Commission's conclusion disregarded the fact that a final judgment had already been entered, ruling that the University had the option of determining how to provide Scott Hartman's medical care. At the same time, the Commission seemingly implied that the University was in a position to direct the Hartman's how Scott should be cared for; should the University have demanded that the Hartmans surrender control over Scott's care?

These and a number of other legal issues deserved full explorations on appeal. A notice of appeal to the Court of Appeals was filed on June 7, 2002.

Of course, there is never a guarantee of success in any litigation–as should be clear from a number of other cases described in this book. Still, to this point in the Hartman case, the University had yet to involuntarily pay one cent in judgment.

I felt confident in pursuing an appeal. But a stunning and unexpected event intervened.

In 2002 UT General Counsel Mizell hired attorney Peter Foley in the position of Deputy General Counsel. A short time later I was advised by Mizell that Foley would be in charge of handling the Hartman appeal.

Foley solicited my input in preparing an appellate brief. Some suggestions were accepted. Most were not. A couple of arguments I deemed critical were rejected.

Foley signed my name to the appellate brief without asking my approval–something that never happened in the past, but a sign of what was to come. I was never presented a copy of the Bell South reply brief. Nor was I advised of the setting of oral argument before the Court of Appeals or invited to attend – let alone asked to argue the appeal before the appellate court. With a million-dollar judgment now facing the University I was quite shocked no effort was made to solicit my input I before oral argument took place.

The decision of the Court of Appeals (Appelate Judges Crawford, Highers and Lillard) was filed on April 14, 2003. I was quite amazed to learn that, in affirming the Commission's decision, the Court focused almost entirely on Bell South's contract obligations as the insurance carrier for Cleon Hartman's employer. That likely was due to the fact, according to the Court, that the University contended the Claims Commission erred in only three ways:

> The University presents for review the issue of whether the Commission erred
> in granting summary judgment in favor of BellSouth. Specifically, the University
> contends that the Commission erred in the following judgments:
> A. By concluding that BellSouth had a contractual obligation to make
>   payments for which it now seeks recovery in this action;
> B. By concluding that BellSouth's subrogation rights are contractual by nature, and
> C. By concluding that BellSouth's subrogation rights were superior to those
>   of the University.

The issue of whether and how the University breached its contract obligation to provide "medical care" if the Hartmans opted to pursue a different care route was not addressed–and presumably never raised in argument before the court. The same was true for the issues of "timeliness" of BellSouth's intervention and the State's sovereign immunity from suit brought to recover subrogation costs.

The approach and arguments I preferred might well have failed. That will remain unknown. The approach taken by new counsel, intervening in the final stages of a 16-year lawsuit, unquestionably failed. There might be a lesson there.

I was afforded one last opportunity to participate in the Hartman proceedings. After the Court of Appeals denied the University's appeal Mizell directed that I have a check prepared in payment of the judgment against the University and State and personally deliver the check to claimant's counsel in Nashville. Of course I did as directed.

On May 13, 2003, I drove to Nashville and hand–delivered a check in the amount of $1,129,333.38 to Paul Davidson, counsel for claimants–a gentleman

I grew to highly respect during the course of the litigation.

And so concluded the longest case I handled in my career. One with notable successes and high points–but with less than a satisfactory conclusion. Lots of unforgettable lessons over the 16-year duration of the case. Particularly toward the end.

Postscript: Scott Hartman departed this life on November 17, 2003, 16 years and 7 months after the horrific accident which devastated his life and severely impacted that of his family. There was one last occurrence I will never forget.

A day or so before Thanksgiving 2004 I received a Thanksgiving card. "Thank you Ron for your prayers throughout the years–God always has a better plan–someday I'll understand."

The card was signed, "Kay Hartman."

More valuable than silver or gold!

Chapter 84–A Few Cases Qualified as Dumb, Screwy or Just Plain Weird

While the legal work I performed for the University generally fell into a variety of well–recognized categories, such as "civil rights", "medical malpractice" and "constitutional law", there were other assignments more extraordinary in nature. "Dumb, screwy or just plain weird" describes a number of those assignments.

THE EUGENE HALLWORTH CASE– HOW EMBARRASSING!

One of my acquaintances from law school was Eugene Hallworth. "Gene" was a year or two ahead of me and most of our contact was while playing "hearts" –a card game–along with fellow law students, at Evan's cafeteria behind the UT law school. I knew Gene to be a nice guy, but knew little else about him.

Just a couple of years after graduating law school and starting work for the University, the UT Knoxville Bursar's office sent me a request for help in collecting a past due student loan account of Hallworth's. Because of our past law school kinship I made a telephone call to him, rather than sending the "standard collection letter."

During our conversation I pleaded with Gene to bring his account up to date because I certainly did not want to initiate legal proceedings against a former law school colleague. He said he would comply with my request and appreciated the call.

Months went by and again the Bursar's Office advised me that Hallworth had not made payments. In December 1975 I filed a civil complaint against Hallworth in the Circuit Court for Maury County (Columbia), Tennessee. Judgment was requested in the full amount of the balance due on the loan plus interest and court costs.

The UT Knoxville Bursar, O.S."Syl" Baldridge, accompanied me to Columbia for the January 26 trial. We arrived a good bit earlier than the scheduled 10 AM docket call. That was my standard practice and likely proved beneficial in this case and certainly did no harm.

My first secretary, Hazel Nicely, offered a good deal of invaluable advice. One such piece of advice was that when handling legal matters in rural communities, and Maury County met that standard, engage the locals in conversation about fishing opportunities in the area. Although I was not a fisherman, I heeded Hazel's advice.

When Baldridge and I arrived at the Murray County Courthouse the courtroom was not yet open. A gentleman in the courthouse lobby greeted us and I immediately commented, "It sure looks like you have some great fishin' places around here." A lively discussion ensued describing a number of local fishing holes and discussing the types of fish that might be caught there. No mention of whether it mattered that this was January 26–the middle of winter.

After thoroughly reviewing the available local fishing opportunities our new friend excused himself, "Gotta go, nice to meet you." About the same time the court bailiff opened the door and invited Baldridge and me in. Hallworth arrived about the same time.

A couple of minutes past 10 the judge entered through a courtroom door behind the bench and the bailiff called the court to order. I immediately recognized my new "fishin' buddy." For what it was worth I was treated more like a long time acquaintance rather than an out of town stranger for the duration of the morning's proceedings.

The bailiff called the docket and there was only one case called–ours. I introduced myself–again–and announced that I would be representing the University of Tennessee. Baldridge would be my sole witness. Hallworth announced that he would be representing himself.

Calling Baldridge to the witness stand, I led him through the plaintiff's case, first introducing Hallworth's student loan promissory note into evidence, then explaining the defendant's default in making the agreed-upon monthly payments. After the University "rested" its case Hallworth took the witness stand. He acted as his own attorney, examining of his only witness–himself. He answered the questions he posed to himself. He noted that he operated a law office in Columbia–as sole practitioner–a fact the court seemed well aware of.

Hallworth explained that he had failed to make the agreed-upon loan repayments because UT had improperly classified him as an "out-of-state" student and charged him much more than he should have had to pay to attend the University. I asked on cross examination if he had ever filed an application for reclassification with the University. He admitted he had not.

At the conclusion of trial, Hallworth requested time to prepare and file a supporting brief. The judge gave him until February 5 to do so. That brief was received a week late. I mailed the court my responsive brief on March 17.

Judgment for the University was entered on February 20–a mere three days after I mailed the University's brief. The University was awarded all that it requested–the grand sum of $827 including $15.75 court costs plus interest at the rate of 12% per annum. Despite numerous stories of home cookin' in the rural courthouses of Tennessee I heard in the early part of my career, that was not my experience in this case–and never was. Perhaps, much to Hallworth's surprise.

Two weeks later Hallworth and I spoke by phone. He confirmed he would not appeal the court's decision and asked if the judgment could be paid off in $40 monthly installments. I agreed, conditioned on his providing me with a signed agreement to that effect. The agreement was duly executed and the first installment was paid. Several more installments were paid. Then the payments ceased. Phone calls to my law school colleague were not returned.

Reluctantly, I proceeded to execute the balance of the judgment on Hallworth's property. The only property belonging to him, I could locate, were his law office assets. I filed appropriate paperwork with the Circuit Court Clerk in Maury County and requested the University's judgment be executed on those assets.

Several days later I received a call from Hallworth. The essence of his plea was as follows: "Ron, I am so embarrassed in the community–everyone knows that Sheriff's deputies have sealed off my office and that a lien has been placed on the contents."

I extended my sympathy but noted his failure to comply with our original agreement. In order for the judgment lien to be released the entire balance would have to be paid immediately

Hallworth promptly paid the judgment balance. I had the lien released.

At the very least, my secretary's "fishing advice" did no harm–and possibly helped me. Classify this case as a bit weird. Yet, to this day it reminds me of the value of identifying a topic of interest to those with whom you wish to network.

CIA DIRECTOR'S HARRASSMENT OF UT AGRICULTURE EMPLOYEE

A particularly bizarre meeting occurred in my office on the eighth floor of Andy Holt Tower during the early or mid–1980s.

I arrived one morning for work around 7 a.m., considerably later than I normally did. After parking on the lowest level of the Tower parking garage, I entered the building and caught the elevator. A number of other workers entered with me and more joined us as the elevator stopped on the second and third parking levels. The elevator was soon packed.

There was a good deal of friendly banter with co-workers on the elevator. Some reference was made to my being a university attorney–or at least being an attorney. The comment was of no consequence to me at the time it was made.

As the elevator stopped at each succeeding office level more and more of those packed into the elevator departed. By the time the elevator reached the eighth floor only two passengers remained–a middle-aged woman and me.

I was not acquainted with the lady and was a bit surprised when she addressed me, "I understand you are a lawyer. I need to talk to you." Although the circumstances were a bit unusual it was my common practice to meet with anyone that requested a meeting so long as I had no conflict on my schedule. I invited the lady, who was professionally dressed but otherwise unassuming in appearance, into my office.

After opening the doors and turning on all the lights I led the way back to my office in the corner farthest from the entrance. I showed the lady to a seat in front of my desk, then proceeded to my own chair on the opposite side. "How can I help you?" I asked.

"I'm being harassed by the director of the CIA," the lady replied. I asked for a bit more detail–and received it. The lady stated that the director of the CIA–whose name she mentioned but I've since forgotten–appeared several times at the Krystal Restaurant on Cumberland Avenue where she was eating. "What did he do to harass you?" I asked.

"He stared at my bosom," was her response. As she spoke I was looking at her eyes. I made certain my gaze stayed focused in that location. Next question.

"Why would the director of the CIA be harassing you?" The lady then explained that she was employed by the UT Institute of Agriculture. Her boss was a department head or faculty member–I forget which–who worked on a contract with the CIA. According to her, the harassment had something to do with her presence in the department and the CIA contract.

Fortunately, at this point someone else entered the office. It was clear to me that the lady had a problem but I was not the one to solve it. I advised her that, unfortunately, there was not much I could do to help her. With that she departed my office.

Later that morning I made a phone call to the Institute of Agriculture and asked to speak with the faculty member she claimed she worked for. The gentleman got on the phone and confirmed she worked under his supervision. Further, the professor confirmed that my early morning visitor was experiencing some mental health issues. No surprise to me.

Now confident that I had a good picture of what the problem was–a lady experiencing psychological problems–I added, with a bit of humor in my voice, "Yeah, she says you are working under contract with the CIA." There was a long pause- silence on the phone–before the professor replied, "I am."

Momentarily dumbstruck, I regained my composure and asked one or two additional questions before concluding that there was nothing for me to do as University Counsel. I had little choice but to let this one go.

(Postscript: Names are not mentioned for the sake of privacy–and because I could not locate them in my records.)

CHAPLAIN REVEREND DOCTOR
JOHN CLARENCE DAVIS, JR.

Back in the late 1960s–during my student days– "left-wing" students on campus organized what was referred to as the "free University." A wide variety of "offbeat" subjects were taught by anyone desiring to teach. No credentials required. One of many volunteer instructors was a gentleman who always signed his letters with the longest title imaginable. One used frequently was: Chaplain Reverend Doctor John Clarence Davis, Jr. On occasion he added the title "Colonel," although I saw no evidence he ever earned that title from the military despite my repeated requests that he produce such evidence.

I had dealings with Davis from the beginning of my employment in 1972 until 1990. During that entire period I was sporadically involved in repeated attempts by Davis to secure employment at the University. At least in his view, he was qualified for virtually any position the University had available–including administrative positions and a variety of faculty openings.

On one occasion Davis ran for public office in Knox County and the local news media quoted him as saying he had held employment at the University "in high places." I called to advise the news media Davis had never been employed by UT. Following that call I telephoned Davis and confronted him with his reported misrepresentation.

Davis responded that when he presented a seminar for the "free university" back in the '60s he was employed by the SGA and the seminar was held in one of the upper floors of a UT building. "SGA does not hire employees for UT," I responded. I did not waste time commenting on the misleading nature of the "high places" reference.

Davis' "letters of application" –and letters of complaint when he was not selected for a position–were always fascinating to say the least. From the recipient(s)' address to the body of the document to the signature space, nothing could be considered ordinary.

One thing for certain–Davis was unrelenting. He came close to securing UT employment on a couple of occasions but "intervention of legal counsel" headed off the potential for disaster.

Davis was born on June 14, 1921–a white male. His home address was Fair Drive in Knoxville. From that point on, Davis' job applications were unlike any I had ever seen. The following examples are taken from a job application he submitted in 1985.

Educationally, Davis reported receiving a BS degree from "Metropolitan University" in "Education Business" in 1958. A Masters in "Bible interpretation" was reportedly received from "Kingdom Bible Institute" in 1959. Then, in 1960 Davis reported receiving a doctorate in philosophy and industrial management from Metropolitan University.

Davis's employment history included the position of "career personal counselor" from July 1966 to June 1972. The identity of the employer is not given but the reason given for leaving is "Knoxville office closed. Didn't want to relocate."

The next position held was "marketing specialist" at J.C. Penney at West town Mall, Knoxville. Date of employment was given as "July 72" and the date of separation was also given as "July 72." Reason for leaving was "laid off."

For the period December 1970 through August 1972 Davis listed his position as "rental agent, property supervisor" with a "family owned business." The address given for the business was Davis' home address. Davis identified his supervisor as "self." "Too much travel involved" was given as the reason for leaving the "rental agent, property supervisor" position.

Davis's last listed employment position was "teacher" in the Knoxville City School System. Dates of employment 1971 to "present." The "reason for leaving" was given as "presently part-time."

Later it in his application Davis more accurately described his position with the Knoxville City School System as "substitute schoolteacher" and noted that he "started substitute teaching 1971 still doing it when needed." A "progress report" was attached with a hand written listing of more than 50 classes where Davis served as substitute e.g. "Gresham Middle–Mrs. Pettit–Academic."

On the same page a typewritten note was added, "It should seriously be noted that where teaching has been done for several days or weeks if applicable for the same teacher this not given." Other entries included "Waiting to serve you (1) makes classroom layouts as much as possible. (2) Tries to address each child by name.... (6) As your substitute responds on first call each time. (7) If required, will renew certification by taking classes at the University if time and opportunity does permit.

The terms "gobbledygook" and "overstated credentials" repeatedly came up when Davis applied for employment with the University. Or when he appealed the University's refusal to hire him.

In February 1987 I forwarded one such appeal to my friend and UT Vice President for University Relations, Sammie Lynn Puett, along with a handwritten note, "You don't have any openings on your staff do you? Rev. Chaplain Dr. Davis is still looking for a job. Thought you might find the enclosed material interesting."

Puett responded with a handwritten note of her own: "Aren't you glad to see the new "credential" of party leadership? And–aren't you glad to see which party it is. That explains a lot of things! I do hope the transition committee can find a position for him. 'twould be mutual justice." (And I hasten to add that our note exchange was entirely of a humorous nature).

The package producing our "good laugh" was addressed to "Honorable Tracy Cloyd, Administrative Assistant to Representative James Naifeh, State of Tennessee Democrat" and "Honorable Michael R. McWherter, Administrative Assistant, McWherter Inaugural Committee, Also on Transitional Committee." It had been mailed to their offices in Nashville.

Introductory paragraphs of the three page single-spaced epistle explains the humor of the situation.

> Dear Fellow Colleagues and Democrats and all on the transitional committees and others connected with the Honorable Governor David McWherter's Administration,

> Greetings:

> Your Dr. Davis is most grateful to both of you as addressed for specifically looking into the matter of obtaining the solid, up to date, right now, in the present time, the deep concerns that the University of Tennessee has against our family, now we seriously emphasize family in the present, because on all the occasions of contact, realizing how important this matter is, wife self and son were all present or in proximity when we are as a family were assured that all records of the past were purged or were of no consequence because of Statute of Limitations or any of the other many reasons from the various past disclosures point of view. However, when one of the top trusted Administrators explained to us out of the blue as a family, and unsolicited, that he knew positively that nothing had been done to change the status quo of the concerns, and that any

and all past and present concerns were in the files to possibly rise up behind our backs and devastate our family, we as a family became very seriously concerned, and this too, because we did not have anything in writing to indicate what terrible things were on file without our knowledge against us in the now present syndrome.

I must confess, I was in all probability the "Administrator" Davis referred to. And, no, the University had no intention of cleaning out Davis' record of endless applications and appeals

Davis concluded his lengthy letter by detailing his wife's extensive service to the Democratic Party–and her recent stay "in the hospital with total services to hospital bill amounts to over $10,000 and there are a host of other expenses that are added to this. In order to be solvent and to pay his bills, he Dr. Davis needs desperately to have a State position, but over and above these bills for his wife, he wants to serve our State of Tennessee as a challenge and an opportunity with an appointed position if this is in order."

The letter was signed "Chaplain Rev. Dr. John Clarence Davis,Jr.,[handwritten, and followed by] In and For The Family, Chaplain Reverend Doctor John Clarence Davis, Jr. Also on the Executive Advisory."

Sometime later Davis received a response, hand-written and signed by Michael McWherter. "Thank you for sending me the correspondence regarding your matter with the University of Tennessee. I have forwarded these letters to Mr. Tracy Cloyd of my father's office for him to look into the matter. He will be back in touch with you shortly. His phone number is 741–3937 or 741–1230. Thank you, Michael R McWherter."

More than a year went by with no action taken and Davis wrote again, this time to Governor Ned McWherter, UT General Counsel Beach Brogan and the entire UT Board of Trustees. At the very top of the three-page letter was typed, "Due to wife not feeling well, we have delayed our trip to Nashville." The letter itself opened with "Dear Governor McWherter, Secretary Beauchamp, the Board of Trustees, Members of the Democratic Party, and to whom it may concern."

Among the suggestions in the letter was that "Governor and others… Issue an executive order to initiate through your office, a most complete and comprehensive investigation to determine what the status is of in the now, that is the present time, from this time forward, in connection with all concerns as they, the University of Tennessee see existing in the now, taking into consideration all laws pertaining to the Statute of Limitations and all other guidelines as would be uncovered."

Among many suggestions was one that the Governor "if you cannot see a thread of continuity of what we are trying to accomplish as a family, and you cannot figure what the letters are inquiring about, that you feel free, or your

Executive Secretary to feel free to underline in yellow marker, the portion that does not make sense to you, and then we can take that turn around correspondence and carefully rewrite or correct or spell out in words and pictures what we seriously mean in this connection."

According to my records and recollection, this was the last of numerous items of correspondence authored by Davis regarding his failed attempt to secure employment at UT. As one might suspect, neither Governor McWherter nor anyone else accepted any of the challenges issued by Davis.

The Davis saga ended in a more traditional fashion–with litigation. In November 1988 Davis filed a discrimination charge against the University with the Tennessee Human Rights Commission and the Equal Employment Opportunity Commission. (THRC No. KE–0134–89; EEOC No. 25A–89–0293)

Davis claimed employment discrimination–refusal to hire–on the basis of age and handicap (hearing loss). Both claims failed. The May 9, 1990 "notice of file closure" received from the EEOC constituted my last entry in the file of the Chaplain, Reverend, Doctor John Clarence Davis, Jr. A lengthy and bizarre segment of UT hisytory ended.

SAVED BY AN ELK–TIMOTHY LAIRD v. STATE

Knoxville's campus has always had a sizable motor pool of various types of vehicles. Periodically the University disposes of used vehicles in the motor pool by public auction. One such auction was held in late 2003 or early 2004.

Chairs for the public auction were rented by the University from Party Rentals, a Knoxville business. The chairs were set up by Party Rentals in a campus building to be used for the motor vehicle auction.

Timothy Laird, a used car dealer from Williamsport, Pennsylvania attended the auction. During the auction, the chair on which he sat collapsed, sending Laird to the floor. Onlookers rushed to assist and but Laird appeared not to be seriously injured–if at all.

On April 6, 2004 both Laird and wife, Rebecca Laird, filed suit against the State with the Tennessee Claims Commission (TCC No.20401586). A second action, against Party Rentals, was filed with the Knox County Circuit Court.

The Claims Commission action alleged that Timothy Laird suffered severe injury as a result of negligence on the part of the State and, as a result of these injuries, his wife suffered a "loss of consortium.' Claimants requested damages in the amount of $600,000. The Circuit Court action featured similar allegations and claim for damages.

A number of depositions were taken on November 11 for the purpose of identifying the party responsible for the chair's collapse–it being a foregone conclusion that the culprit was not Timothy Laird. Deposition testimony was taken from my friend Nate Rothchild, owner of Party Rentals. The Lairds and several UT employees had the responsibility for the auction.

By day's end, the Lairds had testified at length to the severity of the injury–and its devastating impact on the life of both Timothy Laird and his wife, Timothy Laird being largely immobilized. Four other depositions that day left open the issue of what caused the chair to collapse–and who would be responsible for what he called the "severe" resulting injury.

In order to avoid the possibility of inconsistent results–and in accordance with applicable state law–an "order of transfer," moving the Claims Commission action to the Knox County Circuit Court, was entered on June 30, 2005. Defense counsel for both parties then made arrangements with the Lairds' attorney for deposing Timothy Laird's primary physician, Dr. Tuffala. The deposition was scheduled for the morning of June 23, 2006 in Dr. Tuffala's office in Williamsport.

As was my custom, I showed up early at the doctor's office and was shown to a waiting area. I was soon joined by a Pennsylvania attorney–"Joe"–who had been hired to represent Party Rentals at the deposition. During our time together "Joe" entertained me with a fascinating account of an encounter he had the previous afternoon.

Having a bit of spare time, Joe visited the Williamsport Used Car Lot, looking for a vehicle he might be interested in purchasing. In the process he struck up a conversation with one of the sales representatives. The conversation turned to hunting and the salesman regaled Joe with a tale of a recent hunting trip during which he bagged a large buck and transported the buck home in his pickup. Before departing the used-car lot Joe learned the identity of the salesman/elk hunter: Timothy Laird.

Shortly after Joe completed his tale of the elk hunt, an office secretary opened the door to a conference room and invited us in. A court reporter joined us. Dr Tuffalo did not. Instead an attorney representing the Lairds entered the room and announced the deposition of Dr. Tuffalo was canceled. No reason was given and no further comment made. I asked the court reporter to record my response: "Counsel for the defendants are here and prepared for Dr. Tuffalo's deposition. The deposition has been canceled without any advance notice to us," or words close to that.

I suspected that Dr. Tuffalo made clear to the Lairds' attorney during their pre- deposition meeting–that he would not be testifying that Timothy Laird had been seriously injured during the incident at the University auction. At the same time, I was a bit disappointed not to have the opportunity to ask the Doc how much he knew about elk hunting and how physically fit one had to be to participate in such activity.

The Lairds made no further effort to pursue their case. Eventually the case was dismissed for lack of prosecution. A dead elk gets some credit for the positive outcome for the University.

Chapter 85–Joseph Kersavage and the Battle Over Rights to a Bomb Shelter

I was admitted to practice before the United States Court of Customs and Patent Appeals on November 24, 1976. My purpose in seeking admission was to handle a patent matter that never went to court. It was not until 1988 that I handled my first– and only–patent litigation. An extraordinary case with several side issues of import.

Perhaps the first issue was whether–and under what circumstances–an attorney with no experience in an area of practice takes on a case in that area. With respect to patents, there was no attorney in the UT Office of General Counsel having experience. Given the fact that UT had only a smidgen of involvement in patent cases over the years, it would not have been unreasonable for the University to secure outside counsel to handle the rare case in that area.

On the other hand, given sufficient time to prepare, and in the absence of excessive complexity, there are advantages to handling any case internally. Cost savings to the University was one – I received the same salary whether I assumed responsibility for a patent lawsuit or stood by as outside counsel assumed responsibility for the case. Outside counsel would receive an hourly fee for services and–in this case–the total fee for services would have been quite hefty.

It is a sensitive judgment call for in-house counsel since losing such a case runs the risk of criticism that the case would have been won had competent outside counsel with expertise in the area been hired. Making such judgment calls–and being correct most of the time–is part of what I consider a component of leadership.

Professor Joseph Kersavage, a professor in the UT Knoxville College of Art and Architecture, filed suit on December 21, 1988 in the United States District Court, Eastern District of Tennessee. No. 3-88-1002. Named as defendants were the University of Tennessee and two members of the UT faculty, Thomas Moriarty, a research professor in mechanical engineering, and Peter Von Buelow, a faculty member in the College of Art and Architecture.

Kersavage sued for patent infringement, claiming defendants infringed his patent rights to a structure known as a "hyperbolic paraboloid (hypar)" – a structure believed to have an incredible ability to deflect the force of a bomb blast – in the process of working on a research contract between the University and the United States Air Force. Relief in the form of $200,000 in compensatory damages, $200,000 for "willful infringement," $250 per violation, "accounting for profits," injunctive relief and attorneys' fees were demanded by the plaintiff.

Legal counsel for Kersavage was Stan Emert with the Knoxville law firm of Lockridge & Becker. U.S. District Judge Leon Jordan presided over the litigation.

My first order of business was to seek dismissal of the lawsuit on the ground that such action was barred by the State's sovereign immunity. That effort was partially successful.

In a somewhat unusual published opinion, Judge Jordan granted summary judgment as to the University and dismissed UT as a party defendant in an October 2, 1989 memorandum opinion. In so ruling, Judge Jordan cited an earlier case I had handled for the University, in determining that immunity applied in patent cases:

"No question is raised by the parties that the University of Tennessee is an arm of the State of Tennessee; this is now well settled law. See Jain v. University of Tennessee [citations omitted]".

Kersavage v. University of Tennessee, 731 F. Supp. 1327, 1329 (E.D. Tenn. 1989).

"The Court is, therefore, convinced that the University is itself absolutely immune from suit for damages for patent infringement under the Eleventh Amendment." Id. p. 1330.

However, the District Court determined that the individual defendants did not possess "qualified immunity" and remained defendants in the lawsuit. In its October 2 ruling the District Court deferred ruling on the plaintiff's request for injunctive relief and requested that both parties brief that specific issue.

Two months later, in a December 5, 1989 "Memorandum Opinion on Injunctive Relief," the District Court held that the Eleventh Amendment barred suit seeking injunctive relief against the University but, "Nevertheless, the prospect of injunctive relief against a state official sued in his official capacity is not necessarily barred by this amendment." Id. With respect to Moriarty and Von Buelow the motion for reconsideration of their claims of qualified immunity was thereby denied, "leaving them as the remaining party defendants in this case." Id.p. 1332.

With the University itself no longer party to the litigation the question might be raised, "Who will serve as legal counsel for the individually named defendants?" In reality that question was never raised during my years of service in the office of General Counsel–just as long as the employee was acting within the scope of his duties and not engaging in criminal actions, willful misconduct or for personal financial gain.

So I continued to represent Moriarty and Von Buelow since there was no evidence either had engaged in conduct precluding my representing him. My focus turned–at least for the moment–from jurisdictional issues to discovery of the facts on which plaintiff based his patent infringement claim. The discovery process was most interesting.

I scheduled the deposition of Kersavage for June 12, 1990. Without any notice both Kersavage and Emert failed to appear at the designated time and place for the deposition. Kersavage's deposition was reset for August 23. Both counsel and client appeared for the rescheduled event.

I had requested counsel to provide me with all documents supporting Kersavage's patent claim and received a several inch thick pile of documents in response. When I questioned Kersavage about those documents his reply, in effect, was a question, "What does this have to do with the case?" "I don't know, it was provided me by your attorney," I replied. I presented Kersavage the stack of documents I had received from counsel and asked him to identify which documents did relate to his claim.

It soon became apparent a different approach was required. By agreement the deposition was adjourned–to again be reset to a later date. Following the deposition I served detailed interrogatories on the plaintiff, requiring explicit identification of documents supporting his claim.

I did a retake of Kersavage's deposition on January 4, 1991. This time we got right to the point:

> Q. Now, as I recall, from our first deposition, you indicated that your main complaint was that the process which you had patented was violated by Dr. Moriarty and Mr. Von Buelow. In other words – –
> A. These are violations of patents which were issued in 1987 and 1975, yes, which cover structural configurations.
> Q. As I understand from your first deposition, your complaint is limited to the third contract. In other words, you gave permission for the use of your patents in the first and second contract between the University and

the Air Force?

A. Again, this involves bookkeeping to which I have not been privileged.

***

Q. You're aware that there were three contracts between the University of Tennessee and the United States Air Force?

A. There may be more than three.

***

Q. Do you have a basic understanding that there was three separate contracts, as far as you know?

A. There are at least three, there are, at least, probably four, if not more.

Deposition, pp. 6-7.

Kersavage testified that the first contract dealt with "comparative geometries" and constructing a "one-fifth scale model." With regard to the second, Kersavage testified the contract was to construct to full scale models–"two modulars interconnected, yes. ... Yes, full-scale and testing with the full-scale semi–armor–piercing thousand pound bombs, yes." Id.p.18.

When asked if he had worked on the contract between UT and the Air Force, Kersavage replied, "Yes, and I gave the University the right to use my patents. Id. Kersavage explained that the third contract "involved the same configurations [as the second contract] except prefabrication of the modulars."

Kersavage complained, "I did not work on that, and that is a violation of both my patents, 1975 and 1987." He conceded that he had worked on the first and second contracts as a full time, paid employee of the University of Tennessee.

When shown a number of photographs of modulars utilized under the third contract, and asked, "Do you see anything in those pictures that would indicate a violation of your patent?" Kersavage replied "No, sir." Id.p.76.

I concluded the deposition by asking, "Dr. Kersavage, do you have any knowledge of any use of your patent by Dr. Moriarty or Mr. Von Buelow outside of the Air Force contract?" His initial response was "I have heard it rumored that Professor von Bulow utilized the–or suggested the use of the patent by a student for private, outside construction, but I have no specific information on that."

When asked to clarify what he knew, Kersavage did so. "To the best of my knowledge, they used it, generally, under the Air Force contract. But I have–I can't say that they did not use it because I have no other specific information." In so saying, Kersavage made clear that his entire claim–and any claimed admissible evidence–against the individual defendants was premised on their work on the Air Force contract. This was all the information I needed.

On January 10, 1991, I filed an amended answer on behalf of Moriarty and Von Buelow adding, as an affirmative defense: "Defendants are not subject to this action in this court. Plaintiff's sole remedy, if any, is against the United States Claims Court. 28 U.S.C. section 1498 (a)." Three weeks later, on January 30, 1991, I filed a new "motion to dismiss or for summary judgment" with the U.S. District Court. Relevant portions of Kersavage's deposition testimony were appended.

By memorandum opinion and order of March 18, 1991, the U.S. District Court gave Kersavage until April 1 to seek transfer of his case to the Federal Claims Court or, in the alternative, have the case dismissed. Kersavage complied and, on April 8, 1991, the District Court ordered the case transferred to the U.S. Court of Federal Claims (formerly the U.S. Court of Customs and Patent Appeals to which I was admitted in 1976).

Given Kersavage's admissions under oath I suspected the case against Moriarty and Von Buelow would reach favorable disposition. But, never in the way it did.

On July 10, while in my Memphis office, I received a call from Wendy Thomas with the Claims Court in Washington, D.C. She stated that Chief Judge Loren Smith wished to have a conference call with counsel in the Kersavage case. Within minutes the conference call was in progress with Chief Judge Smith, Stan Emert and me online.

Virtually the entire call–the only part I specifically recall–was consumed by Judge Smith blistering Emert with accusations of incompetency and actions warranting disciplinary action by the appropriate professional board. The conduct by Emert which led to this stunning call–and the court action taken–is partially described in the final ruling issued by the Claims Court on July 25, 1996, (Joseph A. Kersavage v. The United States, No. 91-1233 C).

After noting the April 8, 1991 transfer of the Kersavage case from the U.S. District Court in Tennessee to the Claims Court, Chief Judge Smith described plaintiff's counsel's major faux pas:

> The government alleged that it never was served with plaintiff's "amendment to complaint," nor with the original complaint. On August 9, 1991, the U.S. Court of Federal Claims dismissed the action, after plaintiff's then attorney of record, Stanley G. Emert, Jr, failed to respond to three consecutive orders to file plaintiff's complaint and comply with other provisions of the Court's rules. On March 19, 1992, plaintiff, through different counsel [John Lockridge] filed a motion for relief from judgment, which this court granted. The court dismissed the remaining defendants in this action, Thomas F. Moriarty and Peter von Bulow. The government filed a motion for summary judgment and the Court held oral argument.

An order dismissing Moriarty and Von Buelow as defendants in the Claims

Court action was entered on September 14, 1992. I continued to assist counsel for the remaining defendant–the United States–for the duration of the litigation. By letter of July 29, 1996 from Edward H. Rice, Attorney, Commercial Litigation Branch, Civil Division, U.S. Department of Justice, I received the good news:

Dear Mr. Leadbetter:

I am pleased to inform you of the favorable resolution of the Kersavage patent infringement suit. Last week, Judge Smith granted all aspects of the Government's summary judgment motion and entered final judgment for the United States. I am enclosing a copy of the decision and judgment. Mr. Kersavage has 60 days in which to file a notice of appeal.

Thank you again for your assistance in this case. Also, please extend my thanks to professors Thomas Moriarty and Peter Von Buelow, both of whom were extremely cooperative and helpful. Their efforts were instrumental in the success of this case.

So ended a particularly fascinating chapter in UT legal history–at least from my perspective as new patent attorney. And my record for handling patent infringement actions was unblemished. One win–no losses.

Chapter 86–Eric Locke and the Objection Faux Pas

The world does not and should not revolve around lawyers. Nevertheless, it is sometimes advisable to secure and retain the services of competent counsel.

Football running back Eric Locke graduated from Murfreesboro Riverdale High School (Tennessee) in 1998 and enrolled at the University of Alabama on a football scholarship. On June 22, 1999 Locke transferred to the University of Tennessee.

Locke resided in Gibbs Hall dormitory while at UT. His suitemate was Jason Witten, another member of the UT football team (currently playing pro-football for the Dallas Cowboys).

On February 8. 2001 Locke entered Witten's room, found his automatic teller machine personal ID number in a desk drawer and removed Witten's ATM (automatic teller machine) card from Witten's wallet.

Locke proceeded to a nearby bank and, using the acquired number and card, withdrew $600 from Witten's bank account. He did the same thing on February 12, 13 and 14, withdrawing $600 on each occasion. Locke attempted to withdraw cash again on February 21 but was denied service (Witten having discovered, following the February 14 incident, the unauthorized withdrawals from his account and reporting the matter to proper authorities).

Locke learned from head football coach Phil Fulmer on March 2 that some of the events had been captured on film at the ATM. He then returned to Witten all the money he had stolen. On March 5 Locke provided UT police with a written statement that he had taken money from Witten's account on four occasions. Witten elected not to pursue criminal charges and none were filed.

On March 6 Coach Fulmer announced Locke's dismissal from the football team. Knoxville News–Sentinel, June 27, 2001, p.D1. Regardless of the absence of criminal charges, Locke's conduct constituted a violation of UT Knoxville rules governing student conduct. The UT Office of Student Judicial Affairs (Bryan Coker, Director) issued a letter charging Locke with theft of property of a member of the University community–a violation of rule 1720–4-3-.0211 (Tennessee Rules of Administrative Procedure).

Rejected were the efforts of Coker, Vice Provost for Student Affairs Tim Rogers and Dean of Students Vinnie Carilli to secure a "plea agreement" whereby Locke would plead guilty in exchange for a possible one-year suspension from the University.

Locke secured the services of Knoxville attorney David Buuck who requested that the case proceed in accordance with the contested case procedures of the Administrative Procedures Act. This was an arguably wise decision give the severity of the charge. The case was transmitted to me for handling.

I prepared a formal charge letter for issuance by Provost Clifton Woods, naming Jennifer Richter, with the UTK Office of Diversity and Equity, as Administrative Judge. An administrative hearing of charges against Locke was scheduled for June 28.

Locke had secured the services of Buuck even before issuance of the charge letter. Prior to the scheduled hearing we discussed the prospect of Locke withdrawing his request for a hearing, given the solid evidence against him, and accepting a disciplinary penalty of indefinite suspension.

I recommended that Locke submit a letter acknowledging and apologizing for his wrongdoing, to be included in his UT record, The record would be confidential under state and federal law, there would not be a public hearing and the prospect of a formal adverse administrative ruling in his record would be avoided. Buuck was very receptive to my proposal and a reasonable resolution of Locke's disciplinary charge appeared at hand. Until I received word prior to the hearing that Buuck was no longer representing Locke.

I was advised that Locke would be represented instead by his father, Richard "Juicy" Locke, a former Nashville police officer. I made several attempts to contact Richard Locke and reach a resolution reflecting the University's commitment to enforcing its standards of student conduct while at the same time providing Eric an opportunity to admit wrongdoing and demonstrate commitment to acceptable conduct in the future. My effort failed.

The Locke hearing was held in a large conference room of the UT Student Services Building on June 28, 2001. Notice of the hearing had been published in the local news media and a number of reporters, as well as other members of the public appeared for the hearing. Both Richard Locke and Eric Locke's mother were present.

The hearing commenced with Administrative Judge Richter reading the charge against Eric Locke. "You are charged with violating rule 1720–4-3-.0211, which is; theft.... A little more specifically, it is alleged that you engaged in the following conduct in violation of the above rules; that during February 2001 you made fraudulent use of a credit card belonging to UT student Jason Witten to withdraw from various ATM machines approximately $2,400 from Mr. Witten's First Tennessee Bank account." (Transcript of June 28, 2001 administrative hearing, "In re: Eric Locke" Before the University of Tennessee, Knoxville, Tennessee).

Richter then asked Locke, "How do you plead to the charges that I've just read?" "Guilty," Locke replied. Id. pp. 7-8. With this somewhat surprising admission of guilt the only matter left to be resolved was a penalty. I announced I would present a single witness on that issue, the Director of Student Judicial Affairs, Bryan Coker. Id.p 14.

Coker described unsuccessful efforts to negotiate a "plea agreement" with Eric Locke with the possibility of a one-year suspension from the University. Id. pp.18-19. He testified that the "plea agreement was out there for some time and Mr. Locke did not accept that, was not willing to do that, which is fully within his right." Id. p.25.

Coker described Locke's misconduct as " theft, looking at a monetary amount of $2,400 ... very serious," Id.p24, and read from a "witness statement" to police in which Locke stated that he stole the money to pay expenses for his car and cell phone. Id. pp. 30-31. The disciplinary action recommended by Coker was "indefinite suspension."

Coker then explained that "indefinite suspension" was the penalty routinely applied in the case where a "plea agreement" could not be reached. Id. p. 25. Under cross examination from Richard Locke, Coker also explained that, in the absence of a plea agreement, any grades received after the issuance of the disciplinary letter would be nullified in accordance with standard procedure. Id. pp.44-45. Finally, Coker explained that while he worked with the athletic department he received no pressure from Fulmer or anyone else in the athletic department to treat Locke different than any other student. Id. pp. 45-46.

Richard Locke then called his son to testify. With respect to the punishment recommended by the University, Eric Locke was asked by his father:

Q. Do you feel that the punishment that has been imposed upon you is severe or – – what would you like to see happen to you?

A. Yes, the punishment put on me is very severe. You know, knowing that not only myself but others have done worse, this, I don't believe this could be viewed as serious. No one was harmed, I returned every cent back to Jason, and, you know, I wasn't charged with any felonies or anything like that, so...

Id. p.62.

Eric Locke completed his testimony by testifying:

A. Like I said, I think the penalty is just too severe. I'm on course to graduate. I've been a good student, you know, I had just this one incident and it'll never happen again. Jason and I are best of friends, I returned every cent of his money back to him. No charges were filed against me, I was not arrested or anything like that. So, you know, I just feel the punishment is too severe.

Id. p.66.

Cross examination of the accused produced a very unexpected windfall:

CROSS EXAMINATION By MR. LEADBETTER:

Q: Mr. Locke, let's start with the statement you've made that you'd never do this again. Do you feel you've learned your lesson now?

A. Yes, sir.

Q. Is this the first time you've ever taken anything that didn't belong to you?

Id. p.66.

And, I digress for a moment to explain that I had no idea whatever if Eric Locke had stolen anything in the past. This was nothing more than a "shot in the dark."

Continuing:

RICHARD LOCKE: I object, Your Honor.

THE COURT: What is the objection?

RICHARD LOCKE: The objection is the fact he is a leading to the fact that Eric had a incident, a shoplifting incident in high school. But Eric had that shoplifting in high school where he stole a jacket. Philip Fulmer still came to the house and wanted to sign him.

(Laughter)
***

MR. LEADBETTER: Maybe I should call Mr. Locke as my witness.

RICHARD LOCKE: I guess.

MR. LEADBETTER: Appreciate the help, but I'd like to ask Mr. Locke, the accused, to respond to that question.

THE COURT: I'm going to allow the question, because it relates directly to Mr. Eric Locke's statement that he's learned his lesson. So I'm going to allow the question. Id. p.67.

Eric Locke then testified that he had been apprehended shoplifting in high school and explained that it was "you know, a incident where, you know, being young, being out of control, you know, just made a mistake." Id.p.68. When asked if he was still young and out of control, Locke replied, "No, I'm not." Id. p.68. His own testimony suggested otherwise.

Locke testified that he used his roommate's credit card because he needed money to pay a high cell phone bill and for auto repairs. Id. p. 69. He admitted knowing he was doing wrong on each of the four occasions he used his suite-mate's card to withdraw cash from his account. Id..pp. 70-71. And, he admitted returning the stolen cash only after being confronted by Coach Fulmer, advised that he had been caught on bank film at the ATM machine, and ordered by Fulmer to returned to Whitten what he had taken. Id. pp. 73-74.

Wise counsel might have urged silence following the administrative hearing. Eric Locke apparently received none. The Knoxville News–Sentinel (June 29, 2001, p.C1) reported Locke's post–hearing comments: "Afterward, Eric repeated what he said in testimony; namely that he thought this case would be a football matter: 'I was under the impression it was a team issue,' he said."

"I wasn't charged; I wasn't arrested," he said. "It's not like I'm on double murder charges, Timothy McVeigh or anything like that." Id.

Locke's father was reported as claiming there was a conspiracy at work to "use his son in an effort to aid the NCAA in its investigation of the University of Alabama" and that Fulmer was somehow involved. " 'This isn't over,' he said. 'This is just beginning.' " Id.

By initial order entered by Judge Richter on August 6, 2001 Locke was found guilty as charged. In determining appropriate disciplinary action Richter observed:

> Disciplinary probation would be inappropriate in view of the serious and repeated nature of Mr. Locke's behavior.
>
> It is unnecessary to delve into any past actions on the part of Mr. Locke as his present activities, conducted while Mr. Locke was a University of Tennessee student, are of a serious enough nature to support the penalty issued below.

Eric Locke was assessed the penalty of "indefinite disciplinary suspension effective the end of the University's spring semester 2001. Mr. Locke will remain under indefinite disciplinary suspension until such time that the University shall determined that readmission would be appropriate." Initial Order, In Re: Eric Locke, p.5.

The initial order became a final order and was not challenged in court. Still,

Richard Locke hardly remained silent. "Most recently Locke said UT committed NCAA rules violations when it recruited his son. He also indicated that Vols' boosters offered his son money to attend UT, though he has yet to release their names." The Knoxville News Sentinel, September 20, 2001,p. D1-D5.

My response to the latest bluster was suggested in the story's headline: "UT unfazed by Locke's latest salvo." Id, p. D1. The first paragraph accurately stated my position:

> University of Tennessee officials have grown weary of Richard "Juicy" Locke's accusations and threats.
>
> "To be honest, I've lost interest in him," UT Associate General Counsel Ron Leadbetter said. "He's barked an awful lot, and he's been given ample opportunity to come forward with evidence."
>
> "At some point in time, you want a witness or a document to work with. I'm not good at working with abstract accusations."

Later in the article Locke was quoted as claiming that Head Coach Fulmer and former offensive coordinator David Cutcliff had committed NCAA infractions in recruiting Eric. Id.p. D6. Both denied wrongdoing and I found their denials credible, contrary to my assessment of Locke's claims. Id.

As the Sentinel correctly noted, "At this point, UT's administration doesn't plan on following up on the latest of Locke's allegations.' If someone wants me to look into this, I'll do it,' Leadbetter said,' but I haven't heard from the president or athletic director yet.'" Id.

Three years later Richard Locke presented State authorities with a claim that I had dealt with him and his son in an unethical fashion. As with various other claims he articulated in various forums, this claim too was unsupported by any evidence.

The ethics claim did nothing more than add one final bizarre note to a chapter which could have concluded almost before it began with a father's admonition: "Son, you have messed up big time but been provided an opportunity to set things straight. Take your lawyer's advice, admit your wrongdoing and accept the penalty offered by the University." Such admonition, rather than the "objection," made, would have been so much more beneficial.

Chapter 87–Was James Henry Drew Drowned in the Tennessee River By UT Hospital Personnel?

On the morning of April 13, 1995, James Henry Drew fell and struck his head on a coffee table while watching TV. He was taken by ambulance to the UT Medical Center.

On the morning of the third day of his hospitalization Drew was discovered missing from his hospital room. UT Medical Center police conducted a search for Drew in the hospital and on the grounds but failed to locate him. On April 16, Drew's aunt, Ethelyne Avant, notified the Knoxville Police Department of Drew's disappearance and completed a missing person incident report.

A body was discovered in the Tennessee River, at the rear of 918 Cherokee Boulevard in Knoxville, on April 21, 1995. The body was removed from the river and taken to the UT Medical Center for autopsy. Drew's brother, Lloyd Fears, identified the remains as belonging to James Henry Drew.

A sad matter then took a bizarre turn–one leading to what was quite unlike any other I handled in my entire career.

THE STATE CLAIM

On August 31, 1995 a claim was filed against the state of Tennessee with the Tennessee Division of Claims Administration by the estate of James H. Drew, Jr. and a number of the estate heirs. Claims Commission No.50042501. The claimants sued for $11 million and alleged that Drew's death had resulted from medical malpractice and acts of negligence. Knoxville attorney George Underwood, a relative of the deceased, represented the claimants.

The claim transferred to the Claims Commission on December 1, 1995. The claim itself did not qualify as bizarre–what came next did. I learned from Underwood that it was his theory that Drew's death was intentional: UT police had presumably taken Drew to the river and thrown him in or had otherwise participated in a conspiracy with medical staff–and possibly administrators– to eliminate Drew. Discovery depositions focused, at times, on this completely incredible theory of causation. Motive for such action was not offered except, perhaps, via one off–the-wall question to the chief Medical Center administrator.

Sergeant Curtis Moore, a medical center security officer, was deposed at length regarding his familiarity with stairway exits from the Medical Center. The questioning appeared aimed at demonstrating Moore's ability to exit the hospital–perhaps accompanied by someone else or carrying a body–without being seen by staff at the nursing station.

More to my amazement, during the deposition of Medical Center Director, Dr.Charles Mercer, Underwood asked whether Mercer was familiar with "the Body Farm," a UT facility, operated by Dr. Bill Bass, which utilizes donated or unclaimed bodies for research purposes. The well-renowned site is located adjacent to the Medical Center.

To my surprise Mercer denied familiarity with the Body Farm. Even more to my surprise Underwood asked no follow-up questions. After all, if the Body Farm had no relationship to Drew's disappearance, why ask about it?

THE FEDERAL CLAIM

On December 5, 1995, Underwood filed a second lawsuit on behalf of the same claimants in the U.S. District Court for the Eastern District of Tennessee. The federal action named as defendants UT Medical Center, The University of Tennessee, Daniel S. Ely, M.D., David AreHart, M.D., Sergeant Curtis L. Moore, Judy Paulson, R.N. and Novella Brooks, R.N. Dr. AreHart was a fourth-year UT medical student practicing under the supervision of Dr. Ely.

Moore, Paulson and Brooks were specifically identified by plaintiffs as UT Medical Center employees. AreHart and Ely were not.

Plaintiffs demanded compensatory damages in the amount of $751,498 and punitive damages in the amount of $10, 248,000.

I provided legal representation to each of the named defendants and was assisted by UT Assistant General Counsel Rhonda Alexander. First challenge: obtain dismissal of the federal case on jurisdictional grounds.

Tennessee law provides that filing a claim under the Tennessee Claims Commission Act waives any right to proceed against a state employee, in a related action, in any other forum.

Less than two weeks after the filing of the federal complaint, a motion to dismiss was filed on behalf of the two state entities and defendants Moore, Paulson and Brooks. On March 15, 1996, U.S. District Judge Jimmy Jarvis, denied the defense motion.

Judge Jarvis found that plaintiffs had only filed a 13 page document entitled "Complaint Allegations" with the Division of Claims Administration and later wrote a letter requesting to withdraw their case (three days after the elapse of the 90 day period preceding transfer of the case to the Claims Commission). Estate of James Henry Drew, Jr., et al. v. UT Regional Medical Center Hospital, et al., No. 3:95-CIV-676, (U.S. District Court, E.D. Tenn. 1996). The District Court did grant the defense motion requesting dismissal of the Medical Center and University as defendants. Id.

Both plaintiffs and defendants appealed the District Court ruling to the U.S. Court of Appeals for the Sixth Circuit. In an August 5, 1997, 2-1 split decision, the Court of Appeals (Circuit Judges Alice Batchelder and Martha Craig Daughtrey; Circuit Judge Nathaniel Jones in dissent) reversed the District Court and granted the defense's motion to dismiss the case against the police officer and two nurses. The District Court dismissal of the suit against the University and Medical Center was affirmed. Estate of James Henry Drew, Jr., et al. v. UT Regional Medical Center Hospital, et. al., No. 96–5481 (6th Cir. 1997).

The Court of Appeals expressed sympathy with the plaintiffs' argument that they had not made a knowing, intelligent and voluntary waiver of their rights to bring action against officers and employees of the state. Id. p.6. However, the appellate court held that the Tennessee Division of Claims Administration had treated the filing as a claim, Id., and "although the courts have not specifically held that filing with the Division of Claims Administration constitutes filing for the purposes of the Claims Commission Act and thus waiving other claims, they have consistently appeared to treat Division of Claims Administration filings as such. [Citations omitted]" Id.p.8.

Further, the Appeals Court held, "While this result may seem harsh from the plaintiff's perspective, especially in view of the District Court's finding that the plaintiffs' waiver was not 'knowing and voluntary,' we have held that when a party was represented by competent counsel when she filed her action in the Court of Claims, then an adequate foundation for the finding of voluntariness is provided. [Citation omitted]" Id.pp.9-10. The Sixth Circuit concluded, "the State of Tennessee waives its Eleventh Amendment rights and allows filing of a claim against the state only upon such waiver by the plaintiffs, and counsel is presumed to know it. [Citation omitted]." Id. p.10.

The Court did note that under state law the waiver provision would be rendered "void if the commission determines that the act or omission was not within the scope of the officer's or employee's office or employment," and that "if the commission later determines that such is the case, the plaintiffs will be free to pursue their claims against the three state employees at that time, because the statute of limitations is tolled while the Claims Commission resolves the case." Id. pp. 10-11. The determination of whether an individual was acting within the scope of their office or employment was one which "must be made by the commission and not merely alleged by the plaintiffs in their federal complaint." Id. p. 11.

The highly favorable impact on the University of the Sixth Circuit's ruling was conveyed by General Counsel Brogan to President Johnson, Vice President Fly and the UT Medical Center administration, in a August 7, 1997 memorandum:

Great news!! Attached is an opinion from the United States Court of appeals for the Sixth Circuit reversing Judge Jarvis of the United States District Court in Knoxville, who had held that this action was not barred by an earlier claim filed with the Tennessee Division of Claims Administration. After Judge Jarvis's decision, we filed a motion to reconsider but it, too, was overruled. We then appealed to the Sixth Circuit Court of Appeals on behalf of the three UT Medical Center employees... .

The Court of Appeals reversed and dismissed the lawsuit holding that plaintiffs can only recover in the claims commission and that the filing of their claim waived any claim against the individual UT defendants. Because the District Court had earlier dismissed the UT medical Center and the University of Tennessee, this ends this action as far as the University is concerned.

You will note Judge Jones dissented. This was expected. I attended the argument in the Sixth Circuit Court of Appeals – Ron Leadbetter argued – and it was clear from the argument that Judge Jones would dissent. As you will notice from Judge Jones' dissent, he is of the opinion that a plaintiff can never waive federal rights on the basis of a state statute. He dissented in two earlier Sixth Circuit Court of Appeals decisions–one involving Ohio and the other involving the Tennessee claims commission act–which held that filing with the Claims Commission constitutes a waiver of the right to sue state officials in any form.

> We are delighted with this result, especially since plaintiffs sued for $11 Million. Ronald Leadbetter and Rhonda Alexander handled this case.

A motion for summary judgment was filed with the District Court in May 1998, this time on behalf of Drs. Ely and AreHart. Unlike the three individual defendants previously addressed, there was an issue as to whether the two qualified as UT (State) employees.

In a Memorandum Opinion of December 14, 1998 , Judge Jarvis concluded that the evidence revealed that Dr Ely was acting as a state employee for purposes of the claim. In reaching this conclusion Jarvis noted, inter alia, "It is undisputed that during the year 1995 Dr. Ely did not receive any income from treating patients privately apart from his salary received from the University of Tennessee. Further, the fact that a case presentation with residents and interns from the medical school was done with Mr. Drew on the day prior to his death is evidence that Dr. Ely was treating Mr. Drew in his teaching capacity as an employee of the University of Tennessee." Memorandum Opinion, p. 8.

The District Court also declined to exercise discretion to hear the remaining state law claim against Dr. AreHart since at the time of the incident AreHart was a fourth year student–not a physician–and the "remaining issue in this case is a complex one of state law; that is, what, if any, duty of care does a medical student owe to a patient at a teaching hospital when the student is a member of the patient's treatment team?" Memorandum Opinion, p. 12.

The District Court ordered Ely dismissed as a defendant. Plaintiff's action against AreHart was also dismissed but "without prejudice." Order of Dec. 14, 1998.

Once again, an appeal was filed with the U.S. Court of Appeals for the Sixth Circuit. This time plaintiffs contested the entry of summary judgment in favor of Drs. AreHart and Ely and the District Court's earlier dismissal, on sovereign immunity grounds, of claims brought against the University of Tennessee Medical Center.

By order of May 1, 2000 the Court of Appeals (Appellate Judges Nelson, Cole and Clay) unanimously affirmed the District Court rulings in every respect. The federal action against both the University entities and personally named defendants was concluded once and for all.

BACK TO THE STATE PROCEEDINGS

Trial was held before the Tennessee Claims Commission, Commissioner Vance W. Cheek, Jr. presiding, on May 2 and 3, 2002. All proceedings were held in a large conference room adjacent to the lower level, northeast entrance to UT's Thompson-Boling Arena–conveniently located a few yards from the entrance to the arena dining facility.

The facts of the case–from start to finish–were well described in the final judgment rendered by Commissioner Cheek four months later (officially filed September 12, 2002).

The general background of the claimant has been assembled from numerous sources in the record. James H. Drew, Jr. was a 50 year old man with a history of seizures. He was an honorably discharged Vietnam Veteran who developed an alcohol addiction following his tour of duty. In early 1990 after returning home from a detoxification program from a VA hospital, Mr. Drew was assaulted with a baseball bat to his head after an argument erupted while he was drinking with an acquaintance.

Mr. Drew was taken to the hospital and admitted to the critical care unit where he was semi-comatose. He remained there for several weeks. Apparently, Mr. Drew's injury was so severe that even after being home for several weeks he was still unable to recognize anyone including his wife, daughter, and brother.

Following Mr. Drew's head injury, chronic seizures began in conjunction with his intoxications. From then until his death, Mr. Drew suffered numerous seizures. From time to time, he would seek medical aid during and after seizures.

Turning to the events at issue in this claim, on the morning of April 13, 1995, Mr. Drew was watching television when he suffered a seizure and fell, injuring his head on a coffee table. He was taken to UT Medical Center by ambulance. From the emergency room, Mr. Drew was stabilized and admitted into UTMC, room1020 of Building 10 East… . The Physician's Orders of Dr. Daniel S Ely indicate that Mr. Drew was to be on guarded condition with routine vital signs ordered and neurological checks as well as blood labs. [pp 1-2].

***

At 7:30 a.m. on April 15, 1995, the third day of Mr. Drew's hospitalization, he refused meds and was noted as being agitated. [Citation omitted]. Dr. AreHart noted in the doctor's progress note of 4/15/95 at 9 a.m. that Mr. Drew refused to be examined stating he was doing okay and that the "patient was only interested in watching wrestling and refuses any exam." [p. 3].

***

When Dr. Ely arrived at Mr. Drew's room, he was not there. It was surmised quickly that Mr. Drew has left UTMC against medical advice ("AMA"). Dr. Ely notified the nurse, security, and the nursing supervisor. Also, Dr. Ely noted "RN called family – grandmother to inform them he was missing" [citation omitted]. Security was notified at approximately 9:40 a.m. asked to look out for Mr. Drew, as he appeared agitated, but added that Mr. Drew good leave the hospital if he so wanted. Dr. Arehart searched the tenth floor for Mr. Drew as well as numerous places on the first floor. Dr. Ely stated in his deposition "subsequently it turned out that one of the cleaning ladies had seen him leave the floor." [p. 4]

Cheek noted that although a search was conducted and a missing person report filed with the Knoxville Police Department, Drew was not seen again until his body was discovered in the Tennessee River the morning of April 21, 1995. [p.5]

Quite unlike the bizarre theories tossed out or alluded to by plaintiff's counsel in pretrial proceedings, the only issue addressed by the Claims Commission was whether, under state law, the State of Tennessee is liable to the Claimant for "medical malpractice committed by the UTMC nursing staff" or "for the damages he sustained while in the care, custody, and control of the State."[p.5].

In ordering judgment for the State "on all issues," [p.6], Commissioner Cheek made a number of dispositive findings.

> This commission cannot FIND the UTMC's conduct was a substantial factor in bringing about the drowning death of Mr. Drew. Additionally, UTMC had no legal authority upon which to rely to restrain Mr. Drew from voluntarily walking out of the hospital. The outcome of this case could change considerably if the Claimants had presented evidence to the Commission that Mr. Drew was adjudicated incompetent or if his doctors had ordered him to be restrained and confined in his room. None of this was the factual situation in the case at bar. The lack of legal or medical authority to restrain and confine Mr. Drew relieves UTMC from liability for his leaving the hospital against medical advice. [p.15].

Commissioner Cheek also found there was no breach of the professional standard of care which Drew was due. He found that expert nursing testimony introduced by claimants failed to outweigh the testimony of defense expert witnesses that no professional standard of care was breached. [p. 10}

Nor, was the State guilty of negligent care, custody and control of Drew since he was not a prisoner in the State penal system, not adjudged incompetent, and the State was not his appointed fiduciary. "There is not a scintilla of evidence in the record to show that the state had the ability to exert the legal doctrines of custody and/or control over Mr. Drew."[p.14]

Interestingly, while completely rejecting any basis for awarding compensatory damages, the Commissioner took an interesting poke at plaintiff's counsel on the subject of damages:

> **The COURT:** one thing that eludes me, and I may very well just be overlooking it, I am looking for damages. I'm looking for an assessment of damages. Help me out with that. Is that part of your closing or – as of right now, I don't see that there is anything in proof outside of just the obvious damages to the family area.
>
> **MR. UNDERWOOD:** that's a significant part of it. He was on food stamps, if you will. So really it's just the pain and suffering and mental anguish is a big part of it.

The Commission ordered that judgment be entered in favor of the State of Tennessee. On January 8, 2003 an order was entered by the Claims Commission denying the plaintiffs' request for an "en banc" hearing before all three Tennessee Claims Commissioners, Following that order no further appeal was taken by plaintiffs.

What started as a roar of bizarre claims, multi-million dollar demands, and attention–getting and jurisdictional challenges ended with barely a whimper. Any hint that UT hospital personnel drowned or otherwise caused harm to James Henry Drew was erased.

Chapter 88–Losing the Case You Expected to Win–Pinson vs. State

During my years of practice at the University I generally found that losing cases had far more emotional impact on me than winning. It was my general practice to litigate only those cases where I believed the University's position to be correct. For that reason victory was expected–although never taken for granted. There was satisfaction but no particular elation when victory was achieved.

Because victory was generally expected the occasional loss often distressed me greatly–where did I go wrong? But there were a number of exceptions to the general rule of rejoicing in victory and agonizing over defeat, and a range of responses. Cases described in the next few chapters cover the spectrum!

MICHAEL PINSON vs. STATE OF TENNESSEE

On August 25, 1984 Michael Pinson, a member of the UT Martin football team, suffered a blow to the head during football practice and was rendered unconscious for a period of 10 minutes. The UTM athletic trainer, James Richard Lyon, examined Pinson and summoned an ambulance. Pinson was transported to Volunteer General Hospital in Martin.

At the hospital, Pinson's head was X-rayed and found to be normal. However, a CT scan was not performed. The next day his physician advised him not to participate in football practice for a week and that, if any further trouble arose, he should return for further examination.

Although Pinson suffered headaches from the time he arrived at the hospital until August 30, the headaches became milder each day. On September 3 Dr. Ira Porter, the UT Martin team physician, found Pinson asymptomatic for concussion. He advised that Pinson could return to practice if there were no further problems.

Pinson returned to practice that day and subsequently traveled as a member of the UT Martin team and played in at least two games. What occurred next would later be described by the Tennessee Court of Appeals:

> Testimony from Pinson's mother, roommate and a girlfriend, indicated that Pinson suffered headaches and complained of dizziness, nausea and blurred vision throughout this three week period from September 3 to September 24. Lyon did not report any of these symptoms to Dr. Porter. On September 24, Pinson walked to the sideline during a practice, stated that he had been "kicked in the head" and collapsed unconscious.

Michael Ray Pinson v. State of Tennessee, Court of Appeals of Tennessee, Western section at Jackson, C.A. No. 02A01-9409–BC–00210 (1995).

Following the second incident, Pinson was taken to Jackson–Madison County General Hospital where he underwent brain surgery. He remained in a coma for several weeks and required intensive rehabilitative treatment. Pinson suffered severe and permanent neurological damage.

On August 26, 1985 Pinson filed a claim in accordance with the Tennessee Claims Commission Act, alleging that his injuries resulted from athletic trainer Lyon's failure to report the August headaches to his physicians. Around the same time Pinson filed suit in the Circuit Court of Weakley County for the negligent failure of healthcare providers to correctly identify Pinson's brain injury from the August 25, 1984 incident. Pinson was represented by Knoxville attorneys Sidney Gilreath and Richard Duncan as well as Lee Greer of Paris, Tennessee.

I took the position that the University was not liable for injuries resulting from the failure of physicians to properly examine Pinson following the first incident–and I secured expert testimony supporting that position. In addition I took the position that it was a second unrelated incident–during which Pinson was "kicked in the head"–which resulted in his severe injury. There was ample witness support for that position also.

The case was tried before the Tennessee Claims Commission on May 10–11, 1993. There was no surprise testimony at trial and I felt confident in the outcome of the proceedings. Misplaced confidence, unfortunately.

Commissioner Martha Brasfield entered judgment in favor of Pinson on June 27, 1994. She held that it was trainer Lyon's negligence that was the proximate cause of Pinson's injuries because he had failed to provide treating physicians with sufficient information to properly diagnose Pinson's first brain injury.

Commissioner Brasfield found that Pinson suffered damages in the amount of $1,500,000. Noting that others had been sued in the Circuit Court of Weakley County for their negligent treatment of Pinson, Brasfield found the State of

Tennessee liable for 30% of the damages suffered or $450,000. Because Tennessee's statutory cap on such awards was the $300,000, judgment in that amount was entered in Pinson's favor. Michael Ray Pinson v. State of Tennessee, Tennessee Claims Commission, No.60971.

Because I felt that Commissioner Brasfield had disregarded critical evidence I filed an appeal to the Tennessee Court of Appeals. The judgment of the appellate court (Appeals Judges Farmer, Crawford and Highers) was entered on December 12, 1995.

As noted by the appellate court, "Although all neurological checks were normal, hospital records show that Pinson complained of headaches to the hospital staff. Pinson complained that one of these headaches was so severe that it made him sick to his stomach." Michael Ray Pinson vs. state of Tennessee, C.A. No. 02A01–9409–BC–00210., p. 1.

Not only did Pinson advise the hospital staff of headaches, Pinson's mother, roommate and girlfriend each testified at trial that Pinson had complained of headaches and dizziness, nausea and blurred vision during a three-week period between September 3 and September 24. Id., p.2.

The appellate court recognized that Pinson, his mother and the hospital staff had failed to advise treating physicians of Pinson's headaches. Also noted by the Court was a sharp conflict in testimony of the witnesses as to whether Lyon's had actually informed Dr. Porter of Pinson's headaches. "Appellant further contends that Dr. Porter spoke with Lyons at a football practice on August 30. Dr. Porter denied that he ever had any such conversations with Lyons about Pinson. As such, there was a sharp conflict in the testimony of the witnesses as to whether Lyons had actually informed Dr. Porter of Pinson's headaches." Id. p.8

The Court of Appeals rejected the University's arguments and held that"Lyons' negligence in not reporting Pinson's headaches was a proximate cause of Pinson's permanent injuries." Id. p.11. In addition, the Court of Appeals affirmed the Commission 's finding that the second brain injury did not detract from Lyon's responsibility for the first:

> In the instant case, Dr. Joseph R. Roland, a neurosurgeon, testified that on September 24, 1984 he treated Pinson for a chronic subdural and an acute subdural hematoma. Dr. Roland testified that the chronic hematoma was of 3 to 4 weeks duration and that the acute subdural hematoma was of 1 to 5 hours duration. Dr. Roland testified that the acute clot was caused by direct trauma to the brain or by bleeding from the membrane of the chronic subdural hematoma.
>
> It is impossible and unnecessary to determine from the record whether Pinson's permanent neurological injuries stemmed from damage to his brain

from the acute or chronic subdural hematoma. The Claims Commissioner found that Pinson's first injury would have been properly diagnosed and treated if Lyon had reported the neurological symptoms exhibited by Pinson from August 26 to September 24.

Id. p.10. The judgment of the Claims Commission was affirmed.

This 1995 judgment constituted my largest monetary loss as University counsel. How did I feel? Horrible–it was a gut wrenching experience. Still, the next day was a new one. My approach was to tell myself to "suck it up and move on." Still, Pinson remains my most costly and unexpected litigation loss during my 35 year career.

Chapter 89–The Malaria Reversal–Elosiebo vs. State

Mechelle Elosiebo was a student at the University of Tennessee, Knoxville in 2000. Her family was originally from Nigeria. In August of 2000 she returned from a nineteen day trip there to visit family.

Several days after returning to Knoxville Elosiebo reported to the UT Student Health Clinic, complaining of a headache, back pain, fever and abdominal cramps. She was seen by Dr. Robert Rubright, a long time staff physician at the clinic.

Rubright worked full time at the clinic from 1970 to 1988 (and also served as team physician for UT men's athletics from 1988 to 1993). After 1988 he continued working for the clinic on a part-time basis (30–40 days annually) when the clinic was shorthanded.

The symptoms Elosiebo described to Rubright, were those consistent with influenza, viral infection and many other diseases–as well as malaria. Rubright was advised by Elosiebo that she had just returned from a 19 day trip to Nigeria but that she had taken and was continuing to take anti-malarial medication (and, in fact, needed to obtain a medication refill).

Although malaria was, in 2000, the leading cause of death in the world, instances of the disease in America were extremely rare. Rubright himself had long ago been infected with malaria while stationed abroad during military service. Although familiar with the symptoms, he had never encountered a single case of malaria during his years at the Student Health Clinic despite frequent treatment of students who had traveled abroad (I myself had taken antimalarial medication while traveling to Africa and had received medical assurance that it was highly effective).

Based on his experience and Elosiebo's representation that she was taking anti-malarial medication Rubright determined she did not have malaria and diagnosed her illness as "acute viremia." He prescribed fluids and told Elosiebo to return the next day for a follow-up. What Rubright did not know was that medication provided to her–by her father–was medication deemed ineffective in the treatment of malaria by healthcare professionals.

Elosiebo returned to the clinic the next morning and was given an IV and fluids by Rubright but, again, was not tested for malaria. The morning of the third day Elosiebo returned to the clinic, significantly worse. Rubright conducted a urinalysis on Elosiebo which indicated she was having kidney problems and required hospitalization.

Within roughly 48 hours of the time Rubright first examined Elosiebo, she was transported to the UT Medical Center and admitted. There, a pathologist diagnosed Elosiebo as having malaria–but even that diagnosis was incorrect.

When Elosiebo failed to improve with prescribed treatment she was re-examined. Hospital physicians determined that she had a more dangerous form of malaria–falciparum malaria. Her treatment was then altered but not before her physical condition declined dramatically. She lapsed into a coma for 10 or 11 days, developed pneumonia and suffered acute renal failure.

Hospital costs for Elosiebo's hospitalization exceeded $100,000. She spent two or three weeks in bed after being discharged and dropped out of UT for one semester, graduating later than her entering class.

On August 28, 2001, a claim was filed on behalf of Elosiebo with the Tennessee Division of Claims Administration. The claim alleged that Elosiebo's injuries resulted from the failure of Dr.Rubright to conduct a simple blood smear for malaria when Elosiebo first appeared at the clinic on August 23, 2000. Elosiebo asked for $300,000 in damages.

The case transferred to the Claims Commission, Eastern Division, on November 19, 2000. Claims Commissioner Vance Cheek presided over the litigation. Knoxville attorney Richard Duncan represented Elosiebo.

Much of the pretrial discovery, including depositions of medical experts for both parties, was focused on the issue of whether malaria was such a rarely encountered disease in the geographic area in which Dr. Rubright practiced that his failure to immediately test for or diagnose the disease did not fall beneath the "applicable standard of care."

I secured the services of Dr. William Schaffner, of Nashville whose credentials included a subspecialty of infectious diseases within the specialty of internal medicine. Shaffner worked with the Vanderbilt University student health clinic and had treated cases of malaria.

I presented Schaffner's testimony as evidence that even a physician specializing in the treatment of infectious diseases encountered malaria so rarely as to be excused from immediately recognizing and testing for the disease in a patient with generic symptoms such as those possessed by Elosiebo. That argument didn't work but an argument I never made yielded an odd but favorable ruling.

The case was tried on October 23, 2003. Commissioner Cheek's findings were issued immediately at the end of trial–"from the bench." From my perspective, the most palatable portion of the Commissioner's findings were his introductory remarks:

> THE COMMISSIONER: Gentlemen, you both tried a wonderful case today and I appreciate that. Someone said – – I had both claimants and generals in a trial recently that I had before and they said, oh, you always say that, and I said, no, I don't always. I do often because very often people do a great job in preparing cases and I don't throw that around lightly. And you both did a great job and you should be commended by each of your clients. I'm sorry that Dr. Rubricht had to leave but I would like for your clients to know your lawyers did a good job for you.

Mechelle E. Elosiebo vs. State of Tennessee, No. 202000293 (October 23, 2003),p.3.

While the compliments were much appreciated, I was dismayed with the Commission's finding on the issue of whether Rubright had acted in accordance with the applicable standard of care. Cheek addressed his remarks directly to Ms. Elosiebo who was seated at the conference table in the hearing room:

> I believe he [Rubright] rendered good service, but I'm also making a finding that he violated the standard of care.
>
> How can I do that? When you presented, Mechelle, to him you presented that you had just returned from 19 days in Nigeria. You had all of these – – these vague, for lack of a better term, symptoms, but they were consistent not only with the virus, not only with influenza, but also with malaria. You stated that you had been on anti-–malarial medicine and I believe there was one other – – and you came, of course, to refill your malaria pill prescription. Three huge red flags that screen test for malaria. I do not believe it is the standard of care in the State of Tennessee that every doctor has got to look at the patient and say, where have you been lately. I do not believe that is the standard of care and that is not this Commission's holding at all. Had you, Mechelle, shown up and just said, I don't feel well and it ended up being malaria, I would not find that he violated the standard of care because he watched you. He did his best to take care of you. But you presented with three firecrackers right there.... Does that hold him up to a higher standard? No, I don't believe it does. I think that you can still look and say that the majority of reasonable family practitioners in the state of Tennessee, when given those three bits of information, presented with a vivacious, healthy young woman with these types of symptoms is going to order the test.

The test is a blood strip test. It is not a difficult test.... So I am going to find that he breached the standard of care in that based on this specific presentation that you gave him, coupled with the fact that, of course, having malaria, having been a traveler himself, he was aware that Nigeria as well as New Guinea are fertile grounds for malaria. So I am going to make that finding.

Id. pp. 6-8.

Very disappointed I was in that ruling. However, Cheek was not finished:

But here's another finding I'm going to make. There are no – – there is no evidence before me today as to what the damages were for your two days..... And counsel for the claimant, Mr. Duncan, said it right in the very second thing I wrote down, he said, "We're talking about a forty – eight hour period of time here, Your Honor." And he is exactly right. It begins and ends then. You have got– –you were released from their care, the care of the University of Tennessee staff. You went to the medical center. I believe that they were an intervening circum stance. They misdiagnosed you. I believe they are the proximate cause for all of your injuries.

Now, there is– – there has got to be some quantification of your damages for those forty–eight hours. And I kept waiting for that and I kept waiting for that, and I kept waiting for it but it never came. I did not find it, I cannot find it. I even posed Mr. Duncan that question directly and I just cannot find a quantified set of damages for that breach of standard of care for that forty–eight–hour period. And that is a fatal flaw under the rules.

Id. pp. 9-10.

Judgment was then announced in favor of the defense and formally entered in favor of the State on December 2, 2003. My initial disappointment dissipated with a great sigh of relief. Ah, had only the litigation ended there!

Elosiebo appealed to the Tennessee Court of Appeals. The appellate court (Appellate Judges Herschel Franks, Michael Swiney and Gary Wade) enter judgment on November 29, 2004, affirming Commissioner Cheek's finding of breach of standard of care. Regrettably, the Court of Appeal reversed the Commission's ruling on damages.

The appellate court held that "the Commissioner's finding that the hospital's negligence in misdiagnosing the type of malaria was an intervening cause which cut off defendant's liability is an error, because the hospital's misdiagnosis was a normal and foreseeable consequence." Michelle E. Elosiebo v. State of Tennessee, No. E 2003– 0294 –COA–R3–CV, p.6. A most interesting ruling from my perspective!

While the State urges us to hold that the misdiagnosis by the hospital was an intervening and proximate cause of plaintiff's injuries, the State's attorney stated in his closing argument "we don't suggest that any physician who is treating her at the Medical Center did anything wrong." He went on to state:

To assess comparative fault would mean that the State would have to point a finger at one of the physicians and say you acted negligently or you acted out-side the appropriate standard of care. Our whole point is that malaria is a diffi-cult disease to diagnose, that's part of our defense.

Essentially, the State conceded that the hospital's misdiagnosis of the type of malaria was not extraordinary or unforeseeable. Dr. Rubright and the medical experts also conceded that the type of malaria could sometimes be misdiag-nosed. The evidence preponderates against the Commissioner's finding of an intervening cause.

Id. p. 6.

I wondered if the appellate ruling would have been the same had Rubright immediately sent Elosiebo to the hospital on the day she first appeared at the clinic–without testing her for malaria.

The Court of Appeals found that the claimant suffer damages "well in excess of the statutory limits" and awarded judgment in the amount of $300,000 in the claimant's favor one. Id. p.7.

This case stands as the biggest "reversal" I suffered while litigating on behalf of the University – going from a judgment in favor of my client to a $300,000 loss on appeal. Regrettable, but still a rare deviation from the University's record of litigation success.

And even in Elosiebo the news was not all bad. In January 2005 the case was settled for $240,000, saving the University $60,000.

Chapter 90–Who Won and Who Lost?
In Re: Adam Manookian and the Threat of Violence

Adam Manookian was a graduate student at the University of Tennessee, Knoxville where he maintained a 3.94 grade point average in the Master of Sci-ence Program for Rehabilitation Counselor Education. Manookian was a wheel-chair bound paraplegic. He was active in community affairs including organizations assisting people with spinal cord or brain injuries. Prior to the incident described here he had no history of disciplinary problems at the Uni-versity.

On October 20, 2003, Manookian attended a class taught by Dr. Amy Skinner. During the class Skinner returned graded mid–term examinations to students in her class including Manookian.

Manookian was extremely upset with the grade he received and, after class, verbalized to classmates his anger at Skinner for the grade she had given him.

A female student reported to UT authorities that Manookian had made remarks she construed as threatening physical harm to Skinner. She elaborated that Manookian had on a number of occasions, threatened to "F___ up" Skinner and "hire a hit man." She described his conduct as "physically violent and aggressive at the same time" –and she described his verbal threats as "life-threatening."

UT Police conducted an investigation, interviewing several student witnesses, and reported findings to UT Vice Chancellor for Student Affairs Tim Rogers. Rogers then met with UT General Counsel Catherine Mizell for advice as to how to proceed.

Following Rogers' meeting with Mizell Manookian was issued a letter charging him with violation of the UT Knoxville code of student conduct and immediately dismissed from the University. He was advised of his right to a hearing of the charges against him as well as his right to proceed in accordance with the Tennessee Administrative Procedures Act.

Knoxville attorney Greg Isaacs notified the University he would be representing Manookian. He requested a formal APA hearing for his client. In mid-November I received notice from Mizell that I would now be handling the Manookian matter.

On December 9, I met with Vice Chancellor Rogers–my first meeting with anyone involved in the disciplinary matter. I had previously reviewed incident police reports. The key witness whose report had led to the disciplinary charges and Manookian's dismissal, had not been personally interviewed by Rogers – or Mizell.

Contrary to my own standard operating procedure, in this case an interview of the key witness played no role in drafting the initial disciplinary letter or the decision to dismiss Manookian from the University. I had no opportunity to personally interview key witnesses before issuance of a formal charge letter.

On December 11, 2003, UT Chancellor Loren Crabtree issued a formal charge letter notifying Manookian that he was charged with "Conduct which threatens or endangers the health or safety of any person," "Possession, while on University–owned or–controlled property of any weapon" and "Commission of an act on University property that would be a violation of state law." It was specifically alleged that Manookian had engaged in the following conduct:

On or about October 20–21, 2003, Mr. Manookian uttered threats in the presence of one or more other University of Tennessee students to physically harm or accomplish the physical harm of UT faculty member Amy Skinner.

On or about October 27, 2003, Mr. Manookian had in his possession on UT property (the staff parking lot at Circle Park and Peyton Manning Pass) a survival type knife, which was concealed in his automobile, in violation of Tenn.

Code Ann 39-17-1309.

Manookian was also advised that administrative Judge Joanie Sompayrac would be in charge of the proceedings.

Ordinarily the law requires that a student be provided an opportunity for a hearing prior to being dismissed for disciplinary reasons. There is an exception when a student's continued presence on campus is deemed a significant threat of personal injury or property damage. In such exceptional cases, immediate dismissal is lawful provided the accused is promptly afforded an opportunity for hearing.

In the Manookian case, the exception applied. As legally required, I made every effort to schedule a prompt hearing–within 30 days of the issuance of the formal charge letter. My effort failed–miserably! At greater cost to the accused than the University as the proceedings would show.

On December 29 attorney Isaacs filed for and obtained from Knox County Chancellor John Weaver, a "temporary restraining order" preventing Manookian's suspension from the University prior to his receipt of a hearing. On January 7, 2004 I filed with the Chancery Court a motion to dissolve the TRO. In addition, I requested that the case be transferred to the Davidson County Chancery Court in Nashville–contending the Knox County Court lacked jurisdiction over the case.

The matter was argued on January 12 before Chancellor Weaver. At the close of the hearing the Chancellor granted the University's motion, dismissed the TRO and transferred the case to Davidson County Chancery Court. Knox Chancery No. 04-143 Part lll.

The next day's Knoxville News Sentinel headlined "Suspended student gets no aid from Knox judge" (Knoxville News-Sentinel, January 13, 2004, p.1). The article noted that Manookian would have to take up his case with the Chancery Court in Davidson County. (Id.) The article noted that Manookian had been suspended on October 27 by UT's Vice Chancellor for Student Affairs, Timothy Rogers. (Id.)

Even after the Chancery ruling efforts to schedule a prompt hearing were un-successful–largely as a result of "discovery requests" by Manookian's attorney and his scheduling conflicts. Months went by with little movement toward set-ting a hearing date. A date was not set until nearly a year after Manookian's dismissal from the University.

In the meantime, I met with all witnesses identified in police reports and a few others. I assessed the key witness in the case as "problematic." While her descriptions of statements made by Manookian were somewhat supported by other witnesses, her perception of danger to Skinner posed by Manookian was not.

The only undisputed fact was that UT police had found a knife on the floor of Manookian's automobile on University property, underneath a blanket and other items.

Being of the opinion that my key witness would do a poor job testifying live I elected to have her testify by deposition. Since she resided out of state that was a workable option. Her July 14, 2004 deposition served the purpose–the purpose of justice rather than simply winning

The hearing before administrative Judge Sompayrac was held on September 7, 2004. Lasting most of the day, the hearing was open to the public although few attended. The proceedings were uneventful and the outcome not particularly surprising. Each party was required to submit "proposed findings and conclusions" following adjournment of the proceedings.

Judge Sompayrac's "initial order" was issued on January 19, 2005. Her findings were well supported by the evidence.

Some of the more interesting findings:

Ms. Bomyea's sworn testimony repeatedly asserted that Mr. Manookian "ranted and raved" that he wanted to "hire a hitman" and "f___ up that bitch [Dr. Skinner]." Ms. Bomyea also indicated that Mr. Manookian mentioned having a gun and a clip, and that he was depressed and had been considering suicide. She later acknowledged that some of these admissions from Mr. Manookian had taken place during a role – playing exercise for class.
Initial Order p.13.

At the hearing, Vice Chancellor Rogers acknowledged that he had heard that the comment concerning Mr. Manookian's alleged possession of a handgun and clip was made within the context of a role – playing exercise in a counseling class.

Mr. Manookian's person, automobile, and apartment were searched by the UT Police Department with Mr. Manookian's consent. There was no evidence of a handgun or ammunition. (Transcript 21-22).
Initial Order p.12

The University witness, Tracy Silver, who was brought in to corroborate some of Ms. Bomyea's testimony was actually ended up questioning Ms. Bomyea's credibility. Ms. Silver acknowledged that Ms. Bomyea had a reputation among classmates as often placing herself in the role of victim and being someone who likes to get attention. Ms. Silver described Ms. Bomyea as someone who has consistently seen "express a very different view of an incident that has happened… [t]he perceptions that she expresses are so different from what I thought I saw or I thought what happened or what others have said to me or thought what happened."

... Quite frankly, this hearing officer had difficulty considering Ms. Bomyea's testimony as highly credible.

Initial Order p. 13-14.

Also of interest was Somayrac's finding that even though Manookian claimed his mother placed a knife in his car during a recent visit to their home in Nashville–and his mother was present at the hearing but not called to testify– there was a lack of any evidence he had "the intent to go armed" in violation of state law. Id. pp. 11, 17.

Sompayrac ordered that all charges against Manookian be dismissed and that he "be reinstated as a student in good standing at the University of Tennessee." Id. p.18. By letter of February 8, 2005, Chancellor Crabtree notified Manookian of his decision not to conduct a review of the initial order.

The following month, on March 7, the Davidson County Chancery Court dismissed Manookian's action against the University. Davidson Chancery No. 04-143 Part III.

At the conclusion of these proceedings I felt a bit dismayed–but not because of the adverse ruling by the administrative judge. I found her ruling supported by the evidence. It was for that reason did not request a review by Chancellor Crabtree.

My dismay resulted from the realization that a young man I took a personal liking to sustained significant damage to his academic career–losing more than a year of school–as a result of prolonged legal maneuverings. Not to mention his litigation expenses.

On the other hand, had Manookian refrained from abusive profanity and verbalized threats directed at his professor there would have been nothing for a classmate to misconstrue as threats of violence. Message served, lesson learned and justice done.

Which party won this case? Debatable. In the final analysis I was quite comfortable with the result.

Chapter 91–Losing Was Cheaper Than Settling– Bobby Moore vs. State

A legitimate purpose of settling litigation is avoiding the potential cost of losing. This is particularly true where fault of a defendant charged with causing injury is undisputed. Still, settlement is not always cheaper than losing.

On October 8, 1984, a University of Tennessee Center for the Health Sciences employee was driving east on Union Avenue in Memphis in a University vehicle. As he approached the intersection with Dunlap Street the driver decided to make a left-hand turn. There were three problems associated with that decision.

First, left hand turns from Union onto Dunlap are prohibited. Second, the University vehicle was traveling in the outside lane. Finally, in the process of crossing two or three eastbound lanes onto Dunlap the driver struck a motorcycle traveling west. Not that it mattered, from a liability perspective, but the motorcycle was operated by an on-duty Memphis police officer.

The police officer, Bobby E. Moore, filed a claim with the Tennessee Division of Claims Administration, which was transferred to the Tennessee Claims Commission on July 22, 1985, seeking recovery in the amount of $130,000 for injuries he suffered in the accident. Counsel for Moore was Memphis attorney Carlton Barnes.

Since liability was not at issue, following completion of depositions of Moore's treating physicians, I promptly contacted Barnes with an offer of settlement. My final offer was $70,000. Barnes' final offer was $95,000. We proceeded to trial on the issue of damages alone.

On April 28, 1986 the case was tried in Memphis before Tennessee Claims Commissioner Tom Anderson. Moore's injuries were undisputed: depressed fracture of the skull, protrusion of the right eye, fracture of the right clavicle and various lacerations and abrasions of the left hand and right thigh. He was hospitalized from October 8 to October 16, 1984 and remained off work until January 21, 1985. He was evaluated by his physician as having a 15% permanent partial disability rating to the body as a whole, including 10% attributed to his back and 5% to his head injuries.

On June 8, 1986, Commissioner Anderson entered a final decree awarding Moore the sum of $52,235.10. Bobby E. Moore v. State of Tennessee, No. 52267. At that point, the University ("the State") had saved more than $18,000 by having its settlement offer rejected.

Moore appealed the Claims Commission's ruling to the Tennessee Court of Appeals. The sole issue on appeal was the adequacy of the Claims Commission's award for Moore's injuries.

On December 29, 1986 the Court of Appeals of Tennessee, Western Section at Jackson (appellate judges Highers, Tomlin and Farmer), entered an order modifying and affirming the judgment of the Claims Commission. In so doing, the Court of Appeals increased the award of damages by $10,000–to $62,235.10. Bobby E. Moore vs. State of Tennessee, Shelby Claims Commission No. 2.

The University still saved almost $8,000 as the result of my final order being refused–and nearly $33,000 as a result of rejecting the claimant's final offer. Even considering the cost of litigation, losing was considerably cheaper.

Chapter 92–Winning Felt a Bit Like Losing– St. John's United Methodist Church

In early 1980 the University of Tennessee Center for Health Sciences learned that Memphian Arthur Porter, Jr. had died. The University learned from Porter's executor, Don Malmo, it had been named in Porter's will as a primary beneficiary.

At about the same time, the University learned that St. John's United Methodist Church in Memphis–where Porter was a longtime member–had for some time provided assistance to Porter in handling nursing home, healthcare and other bills. For that purpose, St. John's had been added by Porter as a party authorized to write checks from his checking account.

Immediately following Porter's death, a Church trustee (not Malmo) withdrew the balance of funds from Porter's bank checking account. Zero assets remain for fulfillment of Porter's bequest to the University.

After reviewing the facts I reluctantly concluded the only option was to file suit, seeking recovery of all funds removed from Porter's account following his death. A civil action was filed in the Shelby County Circuit Court on June 10, 1980 seeking recovery of $295,179.57 plus interest from St. John's United Methodist Church. The executor for Porter, represented by Memphis attorney Allen Wade, joined the University in its suit against St. John's. The case became Don Malmo and the University of Tennessee vs. St. John's United Methodist Church, 15th Judicial Circuit of Tennessee, No. 9203672.

A jury trial was held from March 21–23, 1983. On March 23 the jury rendered a partial verdict in favor of the University. Certain issues remain to be resolved by the court. UT Executive Vice President and the Vice president for Development Joe Johnson was quite pleased and said so in a letter to me of March 25, 1983. The letter was copied to UT Development officers.

Thank you for the excellent and encouraging report on the jury verdict in the case of Malmo and UT v. St. John's United Methodist Church. You certainly did a fine job on this one. The jury decision will mean $200,000 to $300,000 for the UTCHS to be used for scholarships for students in medicine.

Sometimes it pays to go to court against the church.

I was of course pleased to receive the compliment. The added observation–although obviously correct–caused me a bit of discomfort. I did not in any way enjoy suing a church.

Judgment in favor of the Porter estate was entered by the Court on November 25, 1983, addressing probate issues. The case was now in hands of the estate's attorney, Wade. On November 26, 1985, I received a call from Wade advising that he expected the case to be completed by the end of January 1986. He estimated that the University would receive approximately $500,000. The money was actually received in the spring of 1987

I received a memorandum on May 25 from Joe Johnson offering "Congratulations on the long-awaited resolution of the estate of the late Dr. Arthur R. Porter, Jr." The following day I received a congratulatory letter from UTCHS Chancellor Jim Hunt thanking me "for the outstanding contribution which you made in assuring the endowment at the National Bank of Commerce which was desired by the late Dr. Arthur R. Porter, Jr. " and notifying me that he had received notice "that the national Bank of commerce has received a check of more than $500,000 from Mr. Lewis Donelson's law firm as the major distribution of the estate."

I was extremely pleased with the final outcome for the University. At the same time I felt a countervailing discomfort knowing that I had removed substantial funds from the church. The correct legal result was reached–and the documented desires of Dr. Porter were carried out.

This was done notwithstanding my personal sympathies for St. John's.

Still, winning felt a little bit like losing.

Chapter 93–Losing that Felt a Lot Like Winning– Henry Grager

On rare occasions I felt as good–if not better–losing a controverted matter as I did following a win. A couple of cases come immediately to mind.

Employment cases involving nothing more than claims of poor work performance rarely were brought to my attention since "satisfactory work performance" involves supervisory judgment rather than facts to be proved or disproved by witnesses.

I remember well a UT Memphis hearing in the 1970s. A panel of five or six employees conducted the hearing. The disciplined employee was represented by legal counsel. Therefore, I was requested to represent the department. The charge: preparation of bad-tasting coffee for departmental functions.

I completed the hearing–and do not recall the results–but recall well that I successfully recommended that attorneys no longer be invited to participate in future "work performance" hearings and further opined that such hearings not even be held. Losing this area of responsibility felt great!

There was–for a time–an exception for cases proceeding on appeal to the UT Board of Trustees (a practice which was eventually eliminated by UT charter amendment). In those exceptional cases legal counsel would appear for the University even if the opposing side lacked legal representation. The case of Henry Grager was a prime example.

HENRY GRAGER–"ASLEEP ON THE JOHN"

Henry Grager was a custodial foreman at the UT Center for the Health Sciences. He was fired for "sleeping on the job" after his supervisor initially could not locate him but eventually discovered him "asleep on the john [toilet]"

Grager commenced a series of appeals. A UTCHS employee grievance committee affirmed Grager's dismissal. UTCHS Chancellor, Dr. Al Farmer, later affirmed the committee's decision. An appeal to UT President Ed Boling was denied. Grager then appealed for a hearing before the full UT Board of Trustees. A hearing of his appeal was scheduled for the October 15, 1976 fall Board meeting,

As was the custom, the Office of General Counsel was requested to present the University's position even in the absence of legal counsel for the opposing side. The responsibility for responding to Grager's appeal was mine. Handling the appeal to the Board was also my first involvement with the disciplinary proceedings – there had been no involvement of legal counsel to this point.

The Board of Trustees heard my explanation of the "facts of the case," recitation of the steps in the appeal process and rejection of Grager's appeal at every level – including the President. Grager then stood before the Board and denied he was really asleep on the job but his best argument followed that denial. He commenced to cry.

As he cried Grager pleaded "I just want my job." He repeated that plea two or three times. He had my sympathy–and that of others present.

The Knoxville News-Sentinel headlined a front-page article the following day, October 16, 1976, "UT Custodian Restored to Job by Board". A 12–4 vote by the Trustees to overturn the decision of President Boling and restore Grager to his position highlighted the article that followed.

I had felt compassion for Grager and was pleased with his victory. My smile surely equaled, if not exceeded, that which typically marked my face following a win.

THE EMPTY COKE BOTTLE CASE

Far less known than Grager was the case of another UTCHS custodian issued a dismissal letter for removing empty Coke bottles from an academic building across the parking lot from the administration building. As best I recall that case occurred in the late 70s (I'm not able to locate any record of the incident and must rely on memory).

The custodian in question was apprehended by a campus police officer with a box of empty soft drink bottles in his possession. While not arrested, the custodian was issued a dismissal letter for removing bottles from a UTCHS academic building and placing them in the trunk of his car despite a sign posted on the building's soft drink machine which warned against removal of empty bottles.

The custodian requested an informal hearing before an employee hearing panel. Because it was initially believed the custodian would be accompanied by legal counsel I was asked to be present also.

The proceeding was very informal and commenced with the custodian being asked by the panel chair to respond to the charge. Without hesitation the custodian – who appeared to have very limited education–denied he had removed any empty soft drink bottles from the academic building. He explained that during his lunch hour he had walked to a construction site a block away, collected empty bottles (to be turned in later for the deposit value), placed them in a box, then returned with the box to the academic building in which he was working and placed it near the doorway.

According to the custodian, when his wife arrived to pick him up after work he retrieved the box of bottles from the building and placed it in the trunk of her car. It was at that point the police officer apprehended him.

I asked the panel chair for a brief recess and met with the officer who had confronted the custodians with the bottles. When asked if he had actually seen the custodian remove bottles from the area adjacent to the soft drink machine the officer conceded he had not. He also admitted he had not asked the custodian where he obtained the empty bottles and merely assumed they had come from the soft drink machine.

I returned to the hearing and asked that the charge against the custodian be dismissed. The charge was dismissed and the custodian returned to work. Justice was done and I felt as satisfied with the results as if I had won a big case. Just another good day!

Chapter 94–Even a Loss Can Seem Like a Win–
The Mirabella Case

The University of Tennessee and the University of Florida have an intense, long-standing football rivalry. Fans of both universities are passionate about their team.

Saturday, September 19, 1992 was a rainy day. For Tennessee fans attending the UT v. Florida football game the poor weather conditions mattered little. UT won the game by a score of 31–14. Florida fans remaining in the stands of Neyland Stadium after the final whistle were noticeably disappointed with the outcome. At least one Florida fan allowed his passion and conduct to get well out of hand.

Sam Mirabella and wife Marie had traveled with their son Charles and his wife Joanne to Knoxville to attend the game. At the conclusion of the game the Mirabellas proceeded to exit the stadium. Charles Mirabella was unhappy – to say the least.

When Charles Mirabella encountered University of Tennessee police officer Keith Lambert he approached and initiated a dispute with the officer. During the dispute Mirabella shouted profanities at Officer Lambert. Because he detected an odor of alcoholic beverages and thought Mirabella's speech was slurred, Officer Lambert believed Mirabella to be intoxicated.

Lambert asked Mirabella to leave the stadium and the conflict between the two escalated. Officer Lambert proceeded to arrest Mirabella and the father moved to intervene. In the process, there was physical contact between Sam Mirabella and Lambert. In the process Sam Mirabella fell and broke his ankle.

Officer Lambert charged Charles Mirabella with public intoxication, disorderly conduct and resisting arrest. He also charged Sam Mirabella with assaulting an officer and resisting arrest. The Knox County grand jury subsequently returned a "not true bill" and the charges against both Charles and Sam Mirabella were dismissed.

On September 17, 1993 lawsuits were filed in three separate jurisdictions in Tennessee by the Mirabellas. One lawsuit was filed by the Mirabellas in Knox County Circuit Court. Named as defendants in that action were the University of Tennessee, the UT athletics department, UT Athletic Director Doug Dickey and UT police officials. The Circuit Court action was voluntarily dismissed by the plaintiffs by "notice of dismissal" two months later.

A second lawsuit by the Mirabellas was filed against the same University defendants in the U.S. District Court for the Eastern District of Tennessee in Knoxville. In that action the Mirabellas claimed that the defendants violated various constitutional rights afforded them by the United States Constitution. The federal court was also asked to exercise "pendent jurisdiction" and entertain claims under state law: assault and battery, malicious prosecution, false imprisonment, outrageous conduct, deprivation of liberty interest, unreasonable search and seizure, use of excessive force and arrest without probable cause were charged against the University defendants. Demand was made for recovery of compensatory damages in an unspecified amount.

The third suit was filed with the Tennessee Division of Claims Administration under the Tennessee Claims Commission Act. That action was brought against the State of Tennessee and the University of Tennessee claiming negligence, assault and improper arrest by state employees. Each of the four plaintiffs sued for damages in the amount of $250,000 for a total recovery of $1 million - the maximum recovery against the State permitted in a single case.

Charles and Joanne Mirabella were represented in each case by Knoxville attorney Steve Schope while Sam and Marie Mirabella were represented by Knoxville attorney Billy Stokes.

In November 1993 I filed a motion to dismiss the federal court action, contending that plaintiffs had waived their right to proceed in federal court by filing a claim "identical in all material respects" with the Tennessee Claims Commission. U.S. District Judge James Jarvis agreed. In a "reported" decision, citing precedent in other reported decisions involving the University of Tennessee, the District Court dismissed the Mirabellas' complaint on July 11, 1994. Mirabella v. University of Tennessee, 915 F. Supp. 925 (E. D. Tenn.1994). In so ruling, the District Court cautioned that the federal action could be reopened if the acts of University employees were found by the Claims Commission to be outside the scope of their employment. Id. p.928.

The Claims Commission litigation proceeded even while the federal suit was underway. Presiding over the proceedings, on special assignment by the Tennessee Secretary of State, was Administrative Judge Thomas Stovall with the Administrative Procedures Division.

A number of hotly contested issues of law and fact were raised by the parties over an 8 1/2 year period following the filing of the claim. Discovery depositions of parties and witnesses were held in Florida , North Carolina and Tennessee.

One of the contested issues was whether Officer Lambert had sufficient cause to arrest Charles Mirabella. Support for the University's position sometimes came from surprising sources.

Undisputed was the fact that immediately prior to the incident Officer Lambert was standing at his duty station in the stadium watching the crowd exit. Charles Mirabella passed in front of Lambert several bleachers below. While passing, Mirabella directed criticism and profanity at Officer Lambert. Lambert's initial response was to direct Mirabella to "keep moving." Rather than comply, Mirabella turned toward Lambert and continued to shout profanities at the officer.

Lambert advised Mirabella he would be arrested if he persisted in causing a disturbance and Mirabella responded "well then, why don't you arrest me, you a--hole?" The profanities continued and Lambert moved briskly down the bleachers to place Mirabella under arrest. At some point Sam Mirabella attempted to intervene, both verbally and physically. In the process he had physical contact with Officer Lambert, fell and broke his ankle.

Officer Lambert proceeded to arrest Charles Mirabella for public intoxication, disorderly conduct and resisting arrest and also charged Sam Mirabella with assaulting an officer and resisting arrest. The Knox County grand jury subsequently returned a "not true bill." That action played a role in the plaintiffs' "false arrest" claim against the defendants.

On January 20, 1994 I took depositions from the Mirabella family at the Tampa, Florida law office of my long time friend and former law school classmate, Dewey Hill (no charge to the University of Tennessee). During the course of these depositions Joanne Mirabella admitted that her husband had directed profanity at Officer Lambert during their encounter.

The following day I took the deposition of the plaintiffs' expert witness, Sheriff Charles Dean of Inverness, Florida. Sheriff Dean was a relative of the Mirabellas. He was designated an expert witness for the purpose of establishing proper training standards for police officers. His testimony offered unexpected support for the defense on the "unlawful arrest" argument.

Sheriff Dean's testimony, later introduced as proof at trial, was that in a situation where a person in a crowd comes "out of the line and comes over calling you an a_ _ hole, that kind of thing up in your face, leaving the line, leaving the crowd, yes, sir, that is provocative," and it might well justify an officer exercising his discretion to make an arrest. He further testified, "once someone comes up in a confrontation and puts his hands on our officer he is arrested. He puts his hand on my officer he is arrested right there. I don't care what the provocation was at that point."

Since the first opinion clearly applied to Charles Mirabella and the second to Sam Mirabella, I was quite pleased with the testimony of the opposing side's expert witness. As it turned out, the claims commission subsequently ruled that it had no jurisdiction to entertain an unlawful arrest claim. For that reason, it was never necessary to introduce the Sheriff's expert testimony.

A much more difficult issue was the cause of Sam Mirabella's ankle injury. Evidence on this issue offered a good lesson on the reliability of eyewitness testimony.

Eight witnesses offered testimony on the nature of contact between Officer Lambert and Sam Mirabella. One witness, Susie Lynn Jacobs, testified that she observed Sam Mirabella fall but that he had never had any contact at all with Lambert.

At the other end of the spectrum, Sam Mirabella testified that, in essence, he was thrown down by Officer Lambert. Lambert himself testified that he simply attempted to hold off Sam Mirabella as he was attempting to arrest his son. The remaining witnesses each had a different version of events. It seemed that no two witnesses saw the same encounter.

The case finally came to trial on September 7, 2000. On January 21, 2001 Administrative Judge Stovall issued his decision. Judgment was entered in favor of the State of Tennessee and University of Tennessee on all claims by Charles and Joanne Mirabella. In the Matter of Sam Mirabella, et. al. v. State of Tennessee, TCC No. 301901.

Stovall ruled that he lacked jurisdiction to entertain plaintiffs' false arrest claims but also noted that "[b]ased upon Charles Mirabella's behavior, Officer Lambert was clearly justified in placing him under arrest (even though the charges were ultimately dismissed)." (Record p.78). Stovall concluded that Charles Mirabella's had become embroiled in a heated discussion with Officer Lambert in which he persisted in shouting profanities at the officer. He also found that Officer Lambert justifiably believed that Mirabella was intoxicated (Record pp.75-76).

From his review of the varied testimonies of the manner of contact between Officer Lambert and Sam Mirabella, Commissioner Stovall concluded that as Officer Lambert made contact with Sam Mirabella in an attempt to reach Charles Mirabella, Sam Mirabella attempted to regain his balance by reaching out and grabbing the shoulders of Officer Lambert – while at the same time voicing opposition to his son's arrest. (Record p.77). Stovall found that it was Officer Lambert's "furious rush down the bleachers and hurriedly stepping in front of Sam Mirabella... [that] resulted in Sam Mirabella falling down the bleachers and breaking his ankle." (Record p.79.) He concluded that the injury to Sam Mirabella might have been avoided had Lambert simply walked rather than rushed to place Charles Mirabella under arrest. Id.

Stovall awarded Sam Mirabella medical expenses in the amount of $1,528 for the care of his broken ankle. (Record p.77) and $3,000 for "pain and suffering". (Record p.80) for a total of $4,528. Marie Mirabella was awarded $800 for lost wages–the result of her taking time off from her employment to assist her husband in dealing with his injury. Plaintiffs appealed the Claims Commission judgment. The State did not.

On appeal to the Tennessee Court of Appeals, the Mirabellas argued that the Claims Commission erred in ruling that it lacked jurisdiction to entertain a claim for false arrest. The Mirabellas further contested the Commission ruling that there was insufficient evidence to demonstrate that the University negligently failed to train officer Lambert in crowd control. The Commission's award of damages to Sam and Marie Mirabella was also challenged as inadequate.

On February 5, 2002 the Tennessee Court of Appeals (appellate judges Herschel Franks, Charles Susano and Houston Goddard) unanimously affirmed the Claims Commission's judgment in favor of the State of Tennessee as to plaintiffs Charles and Joanne Mirabella. Also affirmed were the Commission rulings on the false arrest and "failure to properly train" issues

Only with respect to Sam and Marie Mirabella's challenge to the Commission's award of damages was the Commission ruling modified. (The Mirabellas argued in their appellate brief that the amount awarded by the Commission did not even "cover the cost of obtaining the evidence in this case." Brief of Plaintiff's/Appellants p.19. An indisputable point.). The Court of Appeals increased the award to Sam Mirabella by $8,000 and the award to Marie Mirabella by $1,000. In the matter of Sam Mirabella, et al. v. State of Tennessee, No. E2001 –00960–COA–R3-CV.

The total judgment ($13,328) paid by the University of Tennessee at the conclusion of seven and a half years of litigation was far less than plaintiffs' cost of bringing the matter to trial–not counting plaintiffs' costs associated with litigating the previously dismissed federal and circuit court actions.

One more case where my smile at the conclusion of the proceedings was more suitable for a win than a loss. Given the circumstances it was understandable.

Chapter 95–University Health Systems Lease Agreement–Too Late to Correct a Thirty Year Error

In 1997 the Tennessee Legislature authorized creation of a nonprofit corporation for the purpose of operating the UT Memorial research Center and Hospital. The enabling legislation authorized transfer of all hospital assets to a nonprofit corporation.

At its June 1998 annual meeting the UT Board of Trustees adopted a resolution authorizing the administration to take necessary steps to create a nonprofit corporation and to develop agreements necessary to accomplish transfer of the hospital to the nonprofit corporation. A charter was subsequently filed with the Secretary of State creating University Health System, Inc.

Attorneys representing the University of Tennessee and UHS work on developing a lease agreement satisfactory to both entities. The attorney representing UT in developing the lease agreement was UT Deputy General Counsel Catherine Mizell while UHS was represented by attorney Kevin Outerson. The attorneys drafted the lease after receiving input from their respective administrators connected with either UT or UHS, respectively.

The final draft of the lease agreement was presented to the UT Board of Trustees for its approval at a special 7:30 a.m. meeting held before the Board's annual meeting on June 17, 1999. UT's next president, J. Wade Gilley attended the meeting. He was present during the Board's consideration of the lease agreement–as was I.

The lease payment provisions quickly became the topic of heated debate. As noted in the meeting minutes "Consideration for the proposed lease calls for UHS to defease the $100 million dollars plus indebtedness of the University of Tennessee on the buildings and equipment at the hospital, a front end payment of $25 million to the University, and payments of approximately $2.5 million a year for 20 years, or $50,000,000." Minutes of the Special Meeting, Board of Trustees, June 17, 1999, p.2.

Trustee Tom Kerney raised a concern: "There is a thirty year period in the lease agreement when the University is not receiving anything from the lease." While Acting President Joe Johnson noted that the hospital's debt would be paid off he conceded, "There will be no annual payments at the end of the first twenty-year period." Kerney then replied, "if UT has a 30 year period during which no compensation is being received, additional discussion should take place." p.3.

Another Trustee was even more direct:

> Charles Coffey asked why UT would agree to offer the use of the name and UT facilities to a lessor for zero lease payment for thirty years. He suggested the contract be made a 20 year contract and be re-examined at the end of twenty years. He said if there is to be a fifty year contract there should be fifty years of income. Mr. Coffey said in 2019 or 2020 the Trustees sitting around the Board table are going to wonder what was wrong with Trustees in 1999 who leased the hospital facility for thirty years without any income. Id. p.4.
>
> [Trustee and Vice Chairman William] Sansom said the same question was discussed the previous day with Mickey Bilbrey and Bill Rice. He said the lack of lease payments for the last thirty years of the lease is a major issue that has been raised by other Trustees. Mr. Sansom said the frustrating thing from his perspective is that Trustees are somewhat boxed in. The transfer agreement has been designed and the Board has been somewhat preempted about where it is. He expressed his regret with the situation facing the Board but said the issue needs to be addressed.

Mr. Sansom said his understanding is that the UT Board faces a problem because the bond agency sees a contract as it is written, as it has been prepared, which is unfortunate for the Board because it was written and the Board did not get to pass on it.

Id. pp. 4-5

President Johnson then "said what he suggests is for the board to find some way for the respective lawyers to put some language into the deal that would not necessarily commit anyone to do anything other than commit people twenty years from now to have a required conversation and negotiation about any future payments, dollar amount unspecified." Id. p.5.

Sansom recessed the meeting "to allow the attorneys an opportunity to come up with additional language for consideration by the Board before acting upon the proposed transfer." Id. p. 7. Following the regular board meeting the special meeting of the board was reconvened in the Board room, Andy Holt Tower at 11 a.m.

UT General Counsel Beauchamp Brogan was called upon by trustees to respond to questions, both about new proposed language and matters discussed earlier. Brogan replied that Catherine Mizell was the UT attorney who worked on the lease. Mizell was then called to respond to questions. Certainly appropriate since Mizell was the attorney representing UT in developing the lease.

But when Mizell was presented a question about the language of the lease - including proposed new language–she replied "that was something that Kevin Outterson handled". Outterson - the attorney for the party with which the University was contracting–then explained to the Board why the lease agreement said what it did and could not be changed:

> Mr. Kevin Outterson, counsel for UHS, said the proposed language was reviewed by the bonding advisors and bond counsel. The bond underwriters will not issue or underwrite the bonds for a twenty – year lease because the average maturity is past thirty years. He said if the language is changed to guarantee payment after twenty years or something stronger than the newly proposed language, the bonding agencies have indicated all the bond ratings will be downgraded significantly as a result of additional obligation that might be added. If the hospital happens to do very well over the next twenty years, additional lease payments can be added and an "A" bond rating can be maintained. Id. p.8.

Mizell said nothing in response to Outterson's comments–either in agreement or disagreement.

Sansom then noted that the new language presented by the attorneys said the "bonding agency 'must approve' and the proposed resolution that was read earlier in the day said review of the bond rating agencies would be limited. He said with the new language a concession was made and questioned why the change was made."

Mr. Outterson replied that "the bond counsel recommended removing the former clause because he did not think the bond insurers would accept it." Mizell offered no comment.

Outterson concluded the conversation with the statement, "they were asked not to include the word 'negotiate' in the language, but it would work as long as Board members understood the negotiated figure could be zero or one dollar." Id, p. 11. Two trustees brought the discussion to a close by expressing negative sentiment about the lease arrangement.

> Mr. Coffey said although it is personally a strain for him, he could support the language if 'negotiate' were included.
> Mr. Sansom said it is a strain for many of those involved. He said he felt as though Trustees were outrun, which bothers him, but the proposed language represents the best that can be done because of the restraints faced by Mr. Outterson and Ms. Mizell in working with the bond agencies.

The 50 year lease was subsequently approved by the Board.

Counsel for UHS performed well, gaining 30 years of free leasehold for his client. In 2019 or 2020 the answer to Coffey's question might be known. While UHS is contractually bound to "negotiate" - whether flush with cash or dead-broke - the University would be well served by securing legal representation from someone other than counsel for UHS.

Mizell did comment to the Board that "an effort was made to reflect the discussions from earlier in the meeting" but "called to the Board's specific attention that the proposed new language only says there would be a 'consideration' of an annual lease payment."

Was there a legally sound basis for the University to enter into a 50 year lease with only 20 years' lease payments? Perhaps. Had I been the attorney responsible for drafting the lease agreement I would have felt compelled to personally explain that basis to the Board of Trustees–not turn that responsibility over to the other party's attorney.

Had UT officials consciously discussed, negotiated and waived thirty years of lease payments I would have said so, identified the official who "cut the deal" and asked him to explain to the board why he believed a thirty year payment gap was good for the University. No one offered that explanation to the Board.

Under no circumstances would I have asked the attorney for UHS–the party benefiting from the 30 year payment gap–to respond to questions posed by the Board vice-chair and other members of the Board. Each party has its own legal counsel for a reason: to represent the legal interests of the party he or she represents.

Had I handled the UT-UHS lease in the manner described above, I would have to confess my approach was a "screw-up."

Chapter 96–Gilley's Nationwide Search for New UT General Counsel–Bogus From the Start

In late summer 1999 UT General Counsel Beauchamp Brogan advised UT President J. Wade Gilley that he would retire as UT General Counsel effective December 31, 1999 and as Secretary to the Board of Trustees effective June 30, 2000. In September the University issued a position announcement, advertising the upcoming vacancy.

Gilley had the title of the position changed to "Vice President, General Counsel and Secretary." He did so "because he wanted the new position to be an integral part of his staff, management staff." (Brogan deposition, p. 20).

The position announcement was mailed to all public institutions of higher education in the United States and was advertised in the Chronicle of Higher Education and elsewhere. (Brogan deposition, p. 37). All attorneys in the Office of General Counsel received a copy of the position announcement. While disappointed to learn of Brogan's retirement I was very interested in applying for his position.

When I read the one-page job advertisement for "Vice President, General Counsel, and Secretary" ("General Counsel") I immediately suspected something was amiss.

The introductory paragraph accurately described the UT employment setting:

POSITION ANNOUNCEMENT:
President J Wade Gilley of the University of Tennessee invites nominations and applications for Vice President, General Counsel, and Secretary of the University. The University is a large, multi-campus, public institution of higher education consisting of a comprehensive teaching, research/doctoral campus in Knoxville; regional teaching and research campuses in Chattanooga and Martin; a comprehensive health science center based in Memphis with statewide outreach; a high–technology graduate/research Institute in Tullahoma; and statewide programs of commitment to public service including cooperation with industry, agriculture, governmental agencies and other re-

gional institutions. The University maintains strong ties and extensive collaborative programs with the Oak Ridge National Laboratory. The University has more than 42,000 students, 14,000 faculty and staff, 235,000 alumni, and an annual operating budget in excess of $1.2 billion. The principal office of the University is in Knoxville, Tennessee.

The second paragraph of the position announcement was likewise accurate in describing duties of the position as it existed during the period of my employment in the Office of General Counsel:

GENERAL DESCRIPTION OF DUTIES:

The Vice President and General Counsel serves as the chief legal officer of the University, responsible for providing advice, counsel, and representation to the University administration and the Board of Trustees in all legal matters and for representing the University in all legal actions. The Vice President and General Counsel reports directly to the President, plays an integral role in the President's management team, and serves as a key advisor to the President. The Vice President and General Counsel has management, supervisory, and budgetary responsibility for a staff of 25 employees, including 12 attorneys. The position also serves as Secretary of the University, performing various duties related to the University's corporate status and the Board of Trustees.

The next section departed dramatically from the norm. The statement of **mandatory** qualifications struck me as odd or even bizarre. [Emphasis added].

QUALIFICATIONS:

The successful candidate must have the following minimum qualifications: (1) J.D. or L.L.B. from an accredited law school; (2) admission to, or immediate eligibility for, the Tennessee State Bar; (3) **a minimum of fifteen years of legal practice experience, at least ten of which must have been as full – time, in – house counsel for a multi-campus, public institution of higher education;** (4) experience in transactional matters and civil litigation; (5) Strong analytical skills; and (6) understanding of and commitment to affirmative action and to achieving the University's affirmative action objectives. [Emphasis added].

In addition to the minimum qualifications, the successful candidate will have at least one of the following preferred qualifications: (1) experience as the chief legal officer, **or first assistant to the chief legal officer,** for **a multi—campus, public institution of higher education;** (2) management and supervisory experience, including review of other attorneys work; and (3) experience working directly with the governing board of a **multi–campus, public** institution of higher education. [Emphasis added]

The requirement of 15 years of legal practice experience seemed excessive; the balance of the highlighted language, in my opinion, bordered on the absurd. Such language was guaranteed to eliminate highly qualified potential candidates–or virtually assure the selection of a preordained candidate.

The chief legal counsel for Harvard, Yale, Purdue and numerous other promi-

nent private institutions would not meet the mandatory minimum qualifications.
. An attorney with many years of experience heading a private law firm followed by years of experience–but less than ten–as General Counsel of a public, multi-campus institution of higher education also would not meet minimum requirements.

Beverly Ledbetter, General Counsel for Brown University and former president of the National Association of College and University Attorneys–a black female–was by reputation one of the top higher education attorneys in the nation. She clearly did not meet UT's published minimums. Even the Attorney General of the State of Tennessee–each and every one that ever served–would be unqualified to serve as UT General Counsel.

"First assistant?" Never in my years of handling employment matters for the University had I seen such a term used as a job qualification descriptor.

How about "multi–campus?" The relevance escaped me although I had such experience. Even if relevant, a **minimum** qualification? My suspicions were strong that the selection was a "done deal" and Gilley was merely "going through the motion" of appearing to conduct an open job search.

The job announcement requested that "nominations and applications" be sent to Roger Dickson c/o the Executive Vice President's office in Andy Holt Tower. Dickson was a Chattanooga attorney as well as a UT Trustee. He was designated to head the search–a one–man search committee!

Those reading the job announcement were advised: "Nominations and applications of women and minority candidates are strongly encouraged." Readers were notified that "the University of Tennessee is an Equal Employment Opportunity/Affirmative Action/Title VI/Title IX/Section 504/ADA/ADEA Employer."

While the inclusion of such language complied with well-established UT employment practice, the use of a one-man search committee did not. Without exception, administrative level candidate searches in the previous decade or more had utilized multi-member search committees with great effort being made to include females and minorities on each committee.

Neither the job description nor search procedure seemed to me a bona fide effort to secure the best qualified person for the position of Vice President, General Counsel and Secretary. On September 20, I called UT Trustee Susan Williams–a Trustee who I knew personally and for whom I had the utmost respect–to seek her input. I had heard rumors that President Gilley had already decided to select Deputy General Counsel Catherine Mizell to replace Brogan.

Williams said she would call Dickson and get back to me. A day or so later Williams called back. She informed me she had called Dickson and asked him if a decision had already been made by Gilley to hire Mizell.

Dickson's immediate response was, "What's the matter, you don't want a woman in the position?" According to Williams, Dickson then assured her a decision had not been made. Based on Williams' statement I took Dickson at his word–somewhat.

By letter of October 6, 1999, I presented to Dickson my application for the position of Vice President, General Counsel and Secretary.

Chapter 97–The Interview Process Confirmed Suspicion

The search process for high-level UT administrative personnel always involved multimember search committees, many hours of applicant interviews and contact with listed references. None of that proved true in the Vice President, General Counsel and Secretary ("General Counsel") search.

Listed on my resume as references were five prominent UT and community leaders: UT men's athletic director, Doug Dickey, UT women's athletic director, Joan Cronan, U.S. District Judge Leon Jordan, UT Vice President for the Institute for Public Service, Dr. Sammie Lynn Puett, and nationally prominent Knoxville attorney Robert Ritchie. Dickson contacted none of my references nor those for anyone else.

Numerous letters of recommendation were submitted on my behalf by persons well respected within the University and the State. A wide variety endorsed my candidacy.

UT Chief of Police, Ed Yovella, UTK Minority Engineering Program director, Jim Pippin, UT Chattanooga Chancellor Bill Stacy, UT Center for the Health Sciences Chancellor Bill Rice, former Vice President for the Institute of Agriculture, Pete Gossett, former UT Martin Chancellor Margaret Perry, chief pilot for UT, Steve Rogers and many others wrote letters of support.

UT Trustees Susan Williams and Charlie Coffey actively supported my candidacy, as did former Trustee Frank Kinser.

Congressman John J. "Jimmy" Duncan wrote an outstanding letter of endorsement concluding with:

> Obviously, I have a very high regard for Mr. Leadbetter. It has grown from the opportunity to know and observe him for many years. Seldom have I seen anyone approach a job with the skill and dedication that Ron has devoted to the University of Tennessee. That is why I wholeheartedly believe that he is the best choice for this position and would be a wonderful asset to the University system.

I was immensely grateful for my Congressman and long time friend's support. On October 7, I met with UT Board Vice Chair Bill Sansom and advised him of my interest in the position.

On November 17, 1999, I was interviewed by Dickson in the seventh floor conference room of the Office of General Counsel, Andy Holt Tower. The meeting lasted one hour and 15 minutes. Our discussion could best be described as "coffee chit chat" rather than a focused effort by Dickson to determine if I was qualified to assume the position of General Counsel.

Although I had submitted a three page letter reviewing my personal history and a five-page application detailing my qualifications position of General Counsel was not asked a single questions about the contents of either document. I found this very puzzling—and rather suspicious.

On the morning of November 30, I was called to a "pre–interview" by President Gilley. I arrived at his eighth floor office and he invited me in. "Have a seat." I took a seat in the lounge area in front of his desk and he did likewise. Gilley informed me I was a finalist for the position of General Counsel.

For five to ten minutes we discussed my interest in the General Counsel's position. Then the phone rang. Gilley got up, went to his desk and took the call.

For 15 or 20 minutes Gilley engaged in subdued chatter with someone on the other end of the line. Finally, placing one hand over the receiver, he turned toward me and said we would meet again and talk more. I took the cue and exited his office.

My official interview was held in Gilley's office on December 6. There was a general discussion of ideas I had for the Office of General Counsel. Gilley asked nothing whatever about my credentials. Not a single query concerning qualification listed in my resume or letter of application. This was not what I expected of someone making a bona fide effort to identify the very best candidate following a nationwide search.

On December 14, I was called by Gilley and notified he had decided to hire Catherine Mizell—the other finalist in the nationwide search for the position of Vice President, General Counsel and Secretary. I thanked him for considering me. My suspicions were confirmed—and were bolstered by future events.

On December 20, 1999 the Executive Committee of the UT Board of Trustees met at 9:30 a.m. by telephone conference call originating from the office of President Gilley.

The minutes of the Executive Committee note the recommendation made by President Gilley:

Recommendation by President J. Wade Gilley for Vice President, General Counsel and Secretary of the University. Dr. Gilley said Roger Dixon, at his request, conducted the search for candidates to be considered for the position. Mr. Dickson forwarded the credentials of three individuals to Dr. Gilley for review. Dr. Gilley said he interviewed two internal candidates twice. Based upon the interviews, careful consideration and the credentials forwarded to Trustees

(Exhibit 1), Dr. Gilley made the motion that Catherine S. Mizell be elected Vice President, General Counsel and Secretary of the University effective January 1, 2000 with the same total compensation as the current General Counsel and Secretary.

The motion was seconded by Mr. Amon Carter Evans and unanimously carried [six members plus Gilley].

Mr. Dickson said there were **two very strong internal candidates**. He said he intentionally talked with several external applicants, but Ms. Mizell had been on board for some time and provides the stability that is needed in the General Counsel position at the present time. [Emphasis added]

About the same time I received a letter from Gilley–as well as UT Knoxville Chancellor Bill Snyder and UT Athletic Director Dickey–inviting Therese and me to join the UT official party traveling to Tempe, Arizona for the upcoming Fiesta Bowl football game between #5 ranked UT and #3 ranked University of Nebraska. All expenses paid!

As recorded in my personal diary, on December 30, 1999, "Therese and I flew, as members of the UT official party, on a huge 777 in business class to Tempe, Arizona for the Fiesta Bowl. We checked in at The Butte Resort where the team and official party is headquartered. We joined Tom Cronan, Kristi [Tom and Joan Cronan's daughter], her fiancé, Betsy Roberts, her son Will and his wife for dinner in the café. Then a 2 hour soak in the outdoor whirlpool overlooking the Arizona desert."

The following day I also recorded, "We had breakfast in the coaches' hospitality room. Therese and I wound up the millennium at the New Year's Eve dinner and party in the Butte Ballroom (we actually celebrated the New Year at 12 midnight eastern time. Y2K was a nonfactor! Nothing happened.)"

Where were you as the world entered a new millennium? Thanks to President Gilley my wife and I were present and involved in a historic, unforgettable event! For that I was grateful to UT's new president.

The year 2000 certainly had an auspicious start. On January 1, "We celebrated New Year's day by leaving at 6:30 AM with Dick and Susan Williams and their daughter Halle to drive to the Grand Canyon. We made it as far as 10 miles south [of our destination before we] ran into a blizzard, left the interstate to check the weather reports, then turned around and drove back toward Phoenix. We paid a wonderful visit to Sonoma where we were awed by the desert scenery, toured the town and ate Tex–Mex food (including fried, sliced cactus w/salsa & guacamole sauce)."

On Sunday, January 2, "Therese & I attended chapel with the football team this a.m. Danny Buggs was the speaker. 'Tailgate lunch' at the Butte ballroom.

At 4:30 we left for the Fiesta Bowl stadium [Sun Devil Stadium]. Our seats are in the President's box (Box–2) with 10 others in three rows of seats high above the field. A fantastic evening (in our box was Will Carver–SGA president–Gealita Sylvester, VP, Beach, Mike & Judy DeVine, Katie & Reggie High. In the box next to us was Pres. Gilley, Gov. Sundquist, Cong. Duncan, Susan & Dick Williams, Eli & Kathy Fly and the Flys' daughter." Unfortunately, UT lost the game to Nebraska, 21–31.

My diary entry for the following day, January 3, well summarized my personal feelings about the Fiesta Bowl getaway. "Home to Knoxville on the incredible 777 with fantastic food and luxurious bus. class seating. In all, a FABULOUS trip for us!"

With this momentous beginning I had little doubt that 2000 could be a phenomenal year for me personally–despite not being selected as UT's next General Counsel. I was in an excellent position to benefit from my selection as a finalist for the position. All that was required was that I be a "team player." And, the "team player" concept was, in general, one I heartily endorsed.

2000 WAS IN MANY WAYS A GREAT YEAR!

The year 2000 was exceptional in many respects. Some benefits were directly related to my University position. Other benefits accrued only as a result of great scheduling latitude afforded me by my new boss, Mizell – as it had been afforded me in the past by Brogan. Examples of these benefits were numerous.

In March my wife and I spent four days in Dallas, Texas celebrating our first grandchild Daniel's first birthday. At the end of March I joined friends - former UT purchasing director Joe Fornes and Knoxville private investigator Barry Rice - for a week-long ski trip in Utah.

During May I spent four days in Fort Myers, Florida at the Sanibel resort for a National Association of College and University Attorneys Board of Directors retreat. From June 23 to June 29, I attended another meeting of the NACUA Board of Directors, followed by the annual meeting of NACUA in Washington, D.C.

10 days in July were spent with my wife in Hawaii as she attended a meeting of the UT Federal Credit Union (Therese was a member of the UTFCU Board of Directors).

One of the longest and most memorable getaway benefits came that fall– nearly one year after Mizell was selected as General Counsel. On September 22, 2000 Fornes, Rice, Phyllis Sheffer (the widow of Bill Sheffer, a great friend who had journeyed internationally with me in the past) and I departed for independent travel through Nepal, China (Tibet) and northern India. We returned to the U.S. on October 15 after an incredible three and half weeks spent with friends and families of friends in those three countries.

Even with phenomenal leisure time travel opportunities, the year remained packed with job-related responsibilities I enjoyed so much. My litigation schedule was full and other assignments plentiful.

20 major cases were litigated by me to conclusion in 2000. One case was tried in U.S. District Court in Chattanooga and another in U.S. District Court in Knoxville.

A Fair Labor Standards Act case appealed to the Tennessee Court of Appeals in Knoxville was argued and won. The vigorously contested Drew case (See Chapter 87) was successfully argued before the U.S. Court of Appeals for the Sixth Circuit.

Another hotly contested case (*Papachristou)* was finalized by the U.S. Supreme Court. The continued intensity of my workload was reflected in my diary entry for October 15, 2000, the day after I returned from Southeast Asia, "Back from Asia. Arrived at midnight," and my entry for the following day, "In to work at 5 a.m."

My record of litigation success remained largely intact. Fifteen wins counterbalanced three losses and two settlements. A costly defeat ($300,000) was sustained in a medical malpractice case but two other losses totaled less than $4,000 (on claims exceeding $300,000). While a settlement I considered foolish was imposed against my wishes (see Chapter 31. *Hernandez*), the year's litigation record was overall quite good.

I continued to represent the University statewide in various ways aside form in the courtroom. On August 30 I flew to Nashville on the UT plane with Gilley's newly appointed affirmative action director, Theotis Robinson, along with Sarah Phillips and several other UT administrators. We attended a Title VI meeting scheduled by the legislature. Phillips, Robinson and I each spoke and answered questions posed by state legislators in attendance.

I continued to represent the University in handling UT statewide rulemaking matters both in interactions with the Tennessee Secretary of State's office and the Legislature's Joint Government Operations Committee.

There was one development of note in 2000. During the year the office attorneys received an email from Mizell requesting that we not attend meetings of the Board of Trustees since Gilley thought there were "too many attorneys at the meetings." I found that odd since I was almost always the only attorney in attendance aside from the General Counsel.. Was there a problem with Board members having access to University legal counsel? Gilley might have had good reason to think so.

Even with administrative changes in the Office of General Counsel 2000 was a good year for me personally–a great year! It is unlikely I would have received criticism from anyone had I continued on the same track. No one other than me.

WAS THERE CAUSE TO CHALLENGE THE PRESIDENT'S HIRING DECISION?

During the General Counsel search process I learned that a number of NACUA colleagues from around the country, with whom I was well acquainted, had applied for the position. A number met all of the minimum requirements and were distinguished practitioners of higher education law. I knew those meeting the published criteria to be very well qualified; had any one of them been selected I would eagerly have continued serving the University under his or her direction.

Interestingly, the only candidate with higher education law experience, selected by Dickson for interview - outside the UT General Counsel's Office - was an attorney who failed to meet the minimum requirements.

Incredibly, each candidate selected by Dickson for interview, with a single exception, failed to meet the advertised minimum requirements for the position. One female candidate selected by Dickson withdrew her application before interview. She was employed in the State Attorney General's Office.

Candidate Richard Jackson, a black male, was selected by Dickson and interviewed. His name was not forwarded to Gilley for consideration because Dickson found him "not qualified." (Deposition of Dickson, p.57).

Bruce Anderson, whose wife Monique was employed by UT Knoxville, was a highly regarded Knoxville attorney in private practice. Dickson interviewed Anderson but declined to forward his name to Gilley because he too was "not qualified."(Id.).

Ted Ayers, Vice President and General Counsel of Wichita State University since 1996 – and General Counsel for the University of Colorado from 1984 to 1986 and General Counsel for the Kansas Board of Regents from 1986 to 1996 – was a superb candidate I knew well from NACUA. He met every published minimum qualification except one. His primary experience was with a single-campus university.

Ayers was interviewed by Dickson even though he was "not qualified" under the "multi – campus" requirement (Wichita State being a single -campus institution). He was included by Dickson in the pool of three finalists despite his undisputed failure to meet the minimum requirements for the position.

The fifth candidate selected for interview was Catherine Mizell. One requirement for the General Counsel position was "the successful candidate must have... (4) experience in transactional matters and civil litigation."

I had personal knowledge that Mizell did not have litigation experience. Years earlier she had requested to be relieved from handling litigation in Knox County Sessions Court and I had been asked by then-General Counsel Beach Brogan to relieve her of that responsibility. Mizell later declined my invitation to actively participate in the *Jain* trial in federal court. I was aware she had never questioned a witness on the witness stand or interrogated a witness under oath with opposing counsel present.

Oh yes, I met each and every published qualification for the position. Even a cursory review of my resume confirms that to be true.

Gilley never challenged Dickson's approach. He never asked why he presented him a final pool with only one candidate meeting the required qualifications for the position.

It was clear to me the entire search process blatantly violated established UT hiring policy and practice. I was further of the opinion that the sham process qualified as a "pretext for discrimination on the basis of sex." Gilley wanted a woman in the position. Someone he could control. It was my assessment that Gilley made employment decisions on the basis of illegal discriminatory preferences. That was the conclusion I reached after reviewing the facts of the General Counsel search–a conclusion soon to be bolstered by evidence in other employment actions taken by Gilley.

HIGH SCHOOL GRAD ROCKETS FROM TEMPORARY HOURLY PAID TO VICE PRESIDENT IN SIX MONTHS– THEOTIS ROBINSON AND THE RACE FACTOR

I was familiar with Theotis Robinson long before Gilley assumed the UT presidency. Robinson's community involvement and newspaper opinion columns were well-known. He was a former Knoxville City Councilman and Vice President of the 1982 World's Fair.

Robinson was also UT's first black student. I personally respected him. We had nothing but friendly encounters. I also knew Robinson had never graduated from UT or any other college or university.

At the time of Gilley's hire Robinson held a temporary, hourly paid position and had a small office on the eighth floor of Andy Holt Tower. He had no supervisory duties and no responsibilities in the area of affirmative action. UT policy excluded temporary positions from the standard policy requirement that position vacancies be advertised. For that reason the position filled by Robinson had never been advertised.

I was dumfounded to learn that in December 1999 Gilley moved Robinson from his temporary secretary-clerical, hourly-paid, position to the position of Equity and Diversity Administrator. Robinson received a salary increase from around $30,000 to $55,000. The position vacancy Robinson filled was not advertised as required by UT policy.

Six months later I was again stunned to learn that Gilley had just "reorganized" Robinson into the position of Vice President for Equity and Diversity – with a salary increase to $82,000. A top level University administrative position was now filled by a high school grad who had held a temporary secretarial-clerical position a few months earlier. A vice presidency filled by a person lacking any bona fide credentials for the position–a position filled without any search, let alone a bona search in accordance with University policy. Moreover, the vice presidency is one I would have applied for had a bone fide search been conducted. A classic discrimination lawsuit in the making!

On August 21, 2000 I met with the UT Knoxville affirmative-action officials Marva Rudolph–a black female–and Jenny Richter–a white female. Marva advised me she was considering going on a one-year education leave because of differences with Robinson. According to her "Theotis' philosophy (from Gilley) is if you need blacks and women just hire them." Marva feels this is racism–as does Jenny. Marva has seen the December or January announcement from Gilley announcing Theotis' appointment as Vice President (along with other appointments). Marva informed me that this decision was altered to "Director" or other title now held when Gilley was told that Theotis lacked a degree.

DISTRESS, PRAYER AND GOD'S MIRACULOUS ANSWER

As a litigator having extensive civil rights experience I was well aware of the challenges facing a civil rights plaintiff. I was also aware of the significantly greater challenge faced by a white male claiming discrimination on the basis of race and/or gender.

More daunting was the almost insurmountable "qualified immunity" hurdle faced by those bringing suit against public officials for alleged discriminatory acts involving acts of discretion–exercise of judgment. Absent clear and indisputable evidence of unlawful discriminatory "animus" or intent, the legal doctrine of "qualified immunity" would result in dismissal of any civil rights lawsuit brought against Gilley.

Added to the formidable barriers to litigation success was the presumed cost of failure–or even bringing suit. A number of "friends" would likely "disappear" –some out of fear of being associated with a "malcontent" and others out of belief that I was consumed by an attitude of "sour grapes."

More intimidating was the possibility my employment with the Office of General Counsel would be immediately terminated. I had not yet qualified for full retirement benefits and had no interest in retiring regardless. Even if my employment continued, the latitude and job assignments I enjoyed throughout my career would surely end.

Doing nothing had great appeal! But what about the countless seminars I had provided to UT employees and the advice I had given to many seeking counsel in equally or more challenging circumstances. "If you learn of illegal or unethical conduct step forward! Report it!"

Much of my litigation success was attributed to UT employees who followed my advice–employees who stepped forward, disclosed and even testified about inappropriate and illegal conduct of superiors and others.

My letter of application for the position of General Counsel included, as my final job qualification "bullet point," the following: "Last, but foremost, absolute commitment to integrity." If I failed to act, that "bullet point" would be false representation of who I was.

Specific to the search itself, I had year after year, in seminar after seminar, taught that employment discrimination on the basis of race and gender–with very narrow exceptions–was prohibited by law. Protection from discriminatory animus extended to whites as well as blacks and males as well as females.

Legitimate affirmative-action, aimed at eliminating "the vestiges of historic discrimination," required use of bona fide job descriptions, good faith candidate searches and employment decisions based on factors other than the race or sex.

If I failed to step forward and contest the process by which the General Counsel's position was filled–and the position by which Theotis Robinson became Vice President for Equity and Diversity–why would I expect anyone else to step forward under less egregious circumstances? I felt compelled to act.

No, I did not act precipitously. Both state and federal law requires that civil rights actions be commenced within one year of becoming aware of unlawful discriminatory employment action and I took full advantage of the time provided.

Securing competent and reputable legal counsel was an immediate necessity. One attorney came immediately to mind, opposing counsel in recent litigation, Blount County attorney David Duggan, had recently handled two civil rights cases against the University. The case of Dragan Stefanovic v. The University of Tennessee involved a claim that plaintiff was denied employment on the basis of sex (male), national origin (Slavic) and veteran status. Judgment was entered in the University's favor by the U.S. Court of Appeals for the Sixth Circuit in March 1999. (6th Cir., No. 97-5125)

A second case, Sarah Ledbetter v. The University of Tennessee, involved a claim of employment discrimination on the basis of disability brought in the U.S. District Court for the Eastern District of Tennessee. Judgment in that case was entered for the University in April 2000. (No.3:98-CV-694 Jordan/Phillips).

Although Duggan was my adversary I had great respect for him. Throughout our litigation Duggan came across as highly competent and–more important–

a person of high character.

In late June 2000 I phoned Duggan and asked if he might be interested in representing me in a civil rights action against Gilley. We met in his office in Maryville to discuss the details. Without hesitation Duggan agreed to take on the challenge.

On September 13, I again met with Duggan in his office and the paperwork for filing suit in federal court was completed. Nothing would be filed until the last minute. The opportunity to fold was still available.

As the clock ticked I continued to seek advice from close friends. My wife offered incredible support, well aware of the risks. And I prayed.

Quite memorable was my meeting with long time friend, Doug Dutton. A Knoxville lawyer, Doug was a schoolmate from law school. His family and ours attended church and vacationed together for many years. Our small "Promise Keepers" prayer group continues to meet.

On August 11, 2000, Doug and I met for coffee at Panera's on Cumberland Avenue adjacent to the UT Knoxville campus. Considerable time was spent discussing details of the General Counsel search and related legal issues.

My personal concerns were expressed. What would people think if I bought suit against Gilley? As we concluded Doug's memorable response was, "I think you should do it!" I agreed. My decision was final!

Still, I pondered what the future would bring. I prayed for God's guidance and courage. An answer was later provided–in a miraculous fashion! And, when I needed it most.

In mid September I signed formal charges for filing with the Tennessee Human Rights Commission and the Equal Employment Opportunity Commission at the latest date possible. That filing was timed so public notice of the filing would coincide with filing of a separate civil rights lawsuit in U.S. District Court.

Because Congressman Duncan had been a good friend over the years and had gone far beyond expectation in endorsing my candidacy for General Counsel I felt it incumbent on me, as a matter of courtesy, to notify him of my plans before suit was filed and he learned of the filing from another source.

On the morning of November 30, 2000 I made the short drive from Andy Holt Tower to Congressman Duncan's office. When I arrived I learned he was in Washington, D.C. carrying out his congressional duties. I met instead with Bob Griffiths, Duncan's chief assistant.

Bob is a good friend as well as a member of my Sunday school class. He listened attentively as I explained in detail the basis for my decision to bring suit against President Gilley. Bob was completely understanding and very supportive. He expressed confidence my friend Jimmy would feel likewise. I was most thankful for the expression of support! Still, it was not enough to head off a mounting sense of discouragement. As I left my Congressman's office a sense of despair consumed me. The worst feeling I've had in my life.

During the five-minute drive back to Andy Holt Tower I prayed "God, if there was just one other person to share this with me..." What I had in mind was some kind of co–plaintiff –someone to join with me as a partner in the litigation. Undeniably, my request was a bit far-fetched. A reasonable prayer might simply have asked for encouragement, leaving the details to God.

At 10 a.m. I entered the Andy Holt Tower parking garage. Almost immediately I spotted my friend, then-Vice Provost for Student Affairs, Tim Rogers, walking toward me. Rolling my window down I shouted, "Hey, Tim, how're you doing?"

"Not good," Rogers replied with fury in his voice. Surprised by his response I parked my car, got out and listened while he shared a stunning explanation for the fury.

Rogers explained that he and Interim Provost Cliff Woods had just left a meeting with President Gilley and Theotis Robinson. He and Woods had presented a recommendation that a current UT employee in the office of student affairs, Vinnie Carilli, be promoted to the position of Dean of Students.

According to Rogers, he had explained to Gilley–and Robinson–that a search committee, with female and minority representation, had conducted a lengthy search to fill the Dean of Students position. The committee had unanimously agreed on a final pool of three qualified candidates, a black male, a white female and Vinnie Carilli, a white male.

After interviewing all three candidates the committee unanimously agreed that the female candidate should be rejected even though she was well qualified "on paper" because she had poor interpersonal skills. The committee unanimously agreed that both Carilli and the black male were well-qualified but that a job offer should be extended to the latter. Theotis Robinson, personally extended a job offer to the black candidate after "wining and dining " the candidate in the Sky Box at Neyland Stadium.

For whatever reason, the preferred candidate declined the job offer and elected to remain with his current employer. Because the search committee was of the unanimous opinion that Carilli was highly qualified to assume the position the committee then unanimously recommended that Carilli be offered the deanship.

It was with this explanation that Rogers and Woods–Woods being black–recommended to Gilley that Carilli be hired. Both Gilley and Robinson immediately said "no!" Gilley asserted, "There's plenty of women and minorities out there–now go find one!"

Stunned by this disclosure, I knew Carilli would soon be receiving a call from a compassionate colleague! A prayer answered–and in a matter of minutes! Call it an amazing coincidence if you will. I did not and do not.

My feeling of despair was completely gone, never to return. That same afternoon I filed suit against J. Wade Gilley in federal court.

A front page article in the next day's Knoxville News Sentinel headlined "UT lawyer files suit claiming discrimination." (Knoxville News-Sentinel, December 1, 2000). The article explained:

A University of Tennessee lawyer charged in a federal lawsuit filed Thursday that he hasn't been promoted because he's white and male.

Ron Leadbetter, 53, the associate general counsel who investigated allegations of fraud in the UT athletic program a year ago, sued UT president J. Wade Gilley in U.S. District Court seeking at least $1.5 million in damages.

His filing claims Gilley denied him the equal protection of the law and discriminated against him in violation of his constitutional rights.

The Sentinel article further disclosed that it was the appointments of Mizell as Vice President and General Counsel, and Theotis Robinson, first as an administrator charged with "managing UT's diversity resources and educational services program," then as Vice President for Equity and Diversity, that led to my civil rights action.

The saga had just begun. Many surprising twists and turns would be encountered as the Gilley litigation proceeded. And the final results would not be as anyone imagined. Another prayer answered.

Chapter 98–Gilley Sued and the Evidence Grows

GILLEY SUED FOR SEX AND RACE DISCRIMINATION

At 1:38 PM on November 30, 2000 my federal lawsuit against the president of the University of Tennessee was filed. (Ronald C. Leadbetter v. J. Wade Gilley, No.3:00–CV–661, U.S. District Court, E.D. Tenn.). Although identified as president of the University of Tennessee, Gilley was sued in his individual capacity for both compensatory and punitive damages.

The Complaint presented federal constitutional ("equal protection") and State law employment discrimination claims. It was alleged that "in late December 1999 or early January 2000, the Plaintiff was denied promotion to the position of Vice President and General Counsel, on the basis of gender, the Defendant instead choosing for this position a woman less qualified than the Plaintiff on the basis of her gender."

Also alleged was that "in the winter of 2000 the Plaintiff was denied consideration for and selection for the administrative position having chief responsibility for managing the diversity resources and educational services program of the University of Tennessee, on the basis of his race, the Defendant instead choosing for this position an African–American, who was less qualified than the Plaintiff, on the basis of his race." Further, it was alleged that "on or about August 23, 2000, the Plaintiff was denied consideration for and selection to the position of Vice President for Equity and Diversity Affairs, the Defendant instead choosing for this position an African–American, who was less qualified than the Plaintiff, on the basis of his race."

Compensatory damages in the amount of $500,000, punitive damages in the amount of $1 million, back pay, front pay, employment benefits and interest, as well as attorney's fees were requested. The complaint concluded "THE PLAINTIFF DEMANDS A JURY TO TRY THIS CAUSE." Representing me was Blount County attorney David Duggan.

The Court's first formal action in the case was somewhat disappointing to me but entirely appropriate. On December 11, 2000, U.S. District Judge Leon Jordan filed a one-sentence order providing: "Pursuant to 28 U.S.C. section 455, it is hereby ORDERED that the undersigned disqualifies himself from further consideration of matters related to this civil action." It would of course have been completely inappropriate for one of my references for the position of General Counsel to be adjudicating the claim that I was unlawfully denied that position.

U.S. Magistrate Judge Thomas W. Phillips was appointed to replace Jordan. It was Phillips who would determine whether there was evidence of discriminatory intent sufficient to overcome Gilley's presumed "qualified immunity" under federal law. Absent such evidence the case would not proceed to trial. President Gilley would be exonerated (and presumably emboldened to continue his challenged employment practices).

OUTPOURING OF SUPPORT

Immediately following news reports of my lawsuit against Gilley, I began to receive a flood of expressions of support from co-workers, friends and others I had never met; phone calls, letters, office visits and words of encouragement from strangers on the street. All expressions were very much appreciated. A few I found especially memorable:

On December 4, I received a phone call from Congressman Jimmy Duncan expressing his support for me. Another call came from legendary Tennessee Vols Sports Information Director Haywood Harris.

UT Assistant General Counsel Lisa Atkins, a black female, called later the same day, expressing her full support for me. Another call came from Vinnie Carilli. He expressed his support and wanted to meet the next day to discuss Gilley's refusal to approve his selection as Dean of Students. We met the following day to discuss the prospect of what course of action he might take for being denied the position.

The morning of December 5 Assistant Vice President for Business and Finance, Charles Moss, came by my office and complimented me for "having the guts" to do what I was doing. He also revealed that he had learned from Mizell, before the search began, that Gilley wanted to hire her without a search.

Later that afternoon Lillian Mashburn, who had served as UT's Congressional liaison, congratulated me during a face-to-face encounter. She then stated she was furious that Gilley had selected Pam Reed to replace her as UT's representative to Congress. More about Reed later.

On December 6 Vice Provost Tim Rogers paid a personal visit to my office on the seventh floor–three doors down from Mizell's–and loudly announced his support for me as he arrived. A few days later I received a call from UT computer-security expert Slade Griffin. He was furious, supportive and offered technical help, should I need it.

Knoxville lawyer Billy Stokes called to say he had sent Gilley a letter of recommendation on my behalf and never received the courtesy of an acknowledgment. UT Associate Vice President Bob Levy greeted me in the seventh floor lobby one day with "Are people treating you as if you're contaminated? I'm not."

The calls of support continued, day after day. My concern that friends would disappear or think badly of me was largely unfounded.

DID I HAVE A CONFLICT OF INTEREST?
BOARD OF PROFESSIONAL
RESPONSIBILITY ASKED TO DECIDE

At 11 a.m. on December 4, 2000, shortly after my phone conversation with Congressman Duncan, I received a visit from UT Associate General Counsel Alan Parker. As he entered my office he announced, "I want to see what a million-dollar plaintiff looks like." Parker announced that Mizell wanted to see me in her office. I smiled (I hasten to add that I took no offense at Parker's involvement in the matter- he was just doing his job. We were and remain friends).

The meeting was conducted in Mizell's office behind closed doors. At the outset I was advised the meeting was for the purpose of discussing my having a possible conflict of interest –not my lawsuit. I was asked if I wanted to involve Duggan-a bit late to be asking–but I said no, as long as there was no discussion of the lawsuit.

Mizell advised that Parker would take the lead since she might be involved in the lawsuit. She later participated in the discussion anyway.

Parker and Mizell expressed their opinion that I could not ethically continue to represent the University as they thought that I had a conflict of interest. I did not agree.

Immediately following the meeting, at the urging of Parker and Mizell, I telephoned the Chief Counsel for the Board of Professional Responsibility, Lance Bracy. I requested his opinion as to whether I had a conflict of interest.

Bracy requested that I have Duggan provide him a copy of the complaint and a summary of the facts pertaining to the ethics issue. That same day Duggan wrote Bracy and provided the requested information.

The following day I received from Parker a letter marked confidential. The letter accurately reflected the discussion in our meeting the previous day–with the exception of a statement that I not only agreed I had a duty not to speak with any UT employees about my lawsuit but "would carry out that duty."

As a party to the litigation, not an attorney for a party, I was of the opinion I had no such duty; as a practical matter, and to remove any doubt, I refrained from any attempt to discuss the case with Gilley or any other UT official involved in the General Counsel search process.

By letter of December 7, 2000, Duggan wrote Parker and raised another ethics issue: "Initially I am compelled to raise with you my opinion that you and Ms. Mizell are in violation of DR [disciplinary rule] 7–104 pertaining to communication with one of adverse interest, by conducting your meeting with my client on December 4, 2000 without having had any communication with me. You know my client to be represented by an attorney, and you did not have my prior consent to conduct this meeting. " Duggan advised that he had reported his concerns to the Board of Professional Responsibility.

Duggan clearly said, "It is my client's position that he most certainly did not affirm and agree with your directive not to discuss with or to engage any University of Tennessee officials or employees in conversation regarding any of his claims or lawsuit, nor did he agree to carry out that duty." Then Duggan stated his "...opinion that such directive to my client constitutes an infringement of his First Amendment rights and purports to interfere with his ability to talk with witnesses in this case. If you persist in this type of action, your action will result in the assertion of additional constitutional deprivations against the University."

Knoxville attorney Edward G. "Ward" Phillips advised Duggan by letter of December 18, 2000, that he would be representing both Gilley in the U.S. District Court proceeding and the University of Tennessee in the companion EEOC charge. Just as was the case for Parker, I held no animosity toward Phillips for his representation of Gilley and the University in these proceedings. He was simply doing his job.

Additional communication was exchanged between legal counsel. A number of disputed issues of fact and law were raised. My employment with the University would terminate if the Board of Professional Responsibility ruled against me on these issues. I was in for a bit of surprise.

By letter of February 6, 2001, Bracy notified Duggan:

> The factual issues relating to the ethics inquiry concerning Leadbetter v. Gulley [sic], et. al. appear to be in dispute. We are unable to opine when factual issues are disputed. Please advise in the event you are able to submit an agreed or stipulated statement of facts and we will give the matter further consideration.

There was never a ruling on the issues presented to the BPR. Proceedings before the Board of Professional Responsibility were halted. Efforts to revisit the ethics issue were never resumed.

CARILLI WINS JOB!

According to Vice Provost Rogers, Gilley had made clear on November 30 that Carilli was no longer a viable candidate for the Dean of Students position. But only days after filing suit I received good news from Rogers: Gilley had rescinded his edict and Carilli's promotion could proceed.

By memorandum of December 15, 2000 to Cliff Woods, Gilley announced, "This is a follow up to my conversation with you and Vice Provost Tim Rogers regarding the dean of students position." He explained, "If this decision were mine to make I would extend the search in an effort to find a pool of at least three qualified candidates who are really interested in the job."

Gilley stated that "in the future" he would insist on a "final pool of at least two highly qualified external candidates who are truly interested in the position." But not this time. "Again, however, the decision on the dean of students is yours to make, and I will honor your decision." According to Rogers, rumor on the street was that my lawsuit led to the reversal.

Carilli got the job! I was pleased. Unfortunately for the University, in 2001 Carilli left the UT for a position at the University of Scranton; fortunately for the University, Carilli returned to UT to become Vice Chancellor for Student Affairs in January 2014 following Rogers' retirement from the position.

JOB DUTIES CHANGE DRAMATICALLY, BENEFITS REMAIN

Within a short time after commencement of the Gilley litigation my civil rights case assignments disappeared. My last civil rights cases concluded – each with judgements in favor of the University–in 2001.

My responsibility for reviewing affirmative action plans and UT compliance with civil rights law ended. I no longer was asked to attend meetings of UT affirmative action or human resources officers or provide seminars on the subject of civil rights or affirmative action.

During the latter part of 2001 and early 2002 my caseload shifted dramatically. A major shift involved the elimination of civil rights cases and addition of many tort cases–primarily claims of negligence causing bodily injury or property damage–to my caseload.

In 2003, for the first time ever, I was assigned responsibility for litigating workers compensation claims. I continued to handle a number of medical malpractice lawsuits although a smaller number due to the hiring of additional attorneys.

The responsibility for handling all aspects of UT compliance with the administrative procedures act remained mine. For example, I concluded three APA disciplinary proceedings in 2002–including one resulting in an adverse ruling by the Tennessee Supreme Court. I worked on five in 2003 (all successfully) and six in 2004 (all successfully).

My responsibility for handling UT rule changes remained unchanged. I continued to represent the University before the Joint Government Operations Committee of the State legislature in all rulemaking hearings.

Although the number of cases assigned to me remained roughly the same, the complexity of those cases declined. Over the next few years the actual work hours in my work-week plummeted. However, my salary was unaffected and I continued to receive customary pay increases and other University benefits. No complaints whatever on that score.

I was very pleased that Mizell did nothing to curtail my penchant for international travel and development of personal relationships abroad. My requests for leave of absence for travel purposes were handled fairly and favorably, much as they had been under Brogan's leadership as General Counsel.

In the final analysis, although certain responsibilities of my positions were altered – some significantly–my job remained exciting and rewarding while the Gilley litigation proceeded. I had no complaints from a purely personal perspective. My concerns were for the role of integrity and governmental efficiency as a dominant force at the University of Tennessee.

EVIDENCE OF RACIAL AND GENDER BIAS MOUNTED

Within a year from the date of Gilley's hire the number of blacks in administrative positions on Gilley's staff increased from zero to two while the number of females grew one to four. I certainly had no objection to that, if done lawfully.

Indeed, I had personally nominated a female, Kaye Koonce, my good friend from Charleston, South Carolina to the NACUA Board of Directors. Other females and blacks were nominated by me for positions on boards of charitable organizations. A major distinction was that my actions were focused on promoting and selecting persons on the basis of their qualifications–not their race or gender. Evidence strongly suggested that Gilley's selections were premised on race or sex rather than on qualifications.

DEREK ANDERSON FOLLOWS GILLEY TO KNOXVILLE

Derek Anderson, a black male in his mid-20s, worked as Gilley's special assistant when he was a student at Marshall University. In August 1999 Anderson was, at the urging of Gilley, hired by UT as research assistant in the office of Diversity Resources and Education Service at a salary of $25,000 a year. Gilley had urged UT Knoxville Chancellor Bill Snyder to assist in securing Anderson a two-year "limited term position" as he worked on his graduate degree.

I received several phone calls from Marva Rudolph, UT Knoxville affirmative-action officer, complaining that Anderson was able to "come and go" as he wished and engaged in improper conduct. Later I learned that Jimmy Naifeh, Speaker of the Tennessee House of Representatives, had demanded that Anderson, who had repeatedly traveled to Nashville with Gilley, cease representing himself as a legislative intern. Anderson had reportedly been permitted to serve in that capacity without going through the proper process.

According to a Chattanooga Times Free Press (electronic supplement) report on June 6, 2001:

The job [at UT] was advertised for 10 days, but Mr. Anderson was the only applicant, records show. Two months after Mr. Anderson was hired, Dr. Gilley appointed a "streamlining committee" to help reduce UT's administration through restructuring.

As a university employee, Mr. Anderson charged $403 in personal purchases to a university credit card, $346.49 in meals at the University club restaurant and accumulated $1,415.81 in unpaid housing fees, according to records obtained by the Times Free Press.

With those bills still unpaid, Mr. Anderson was fired on March 31, 2000, for falsifying his resume, records show. In an April 4, 2000, memo to Mr. Anderson from university officials, he was informed he was fired for falsifying his resume by claiming to have received a bachelor's degree in 1999 from Marshall, when he did not have that degree.

In later testimony Gilley conceded he had urged Anderson's employment but took no responsibility for urging the employment of an unqualified candidate. (Dep. of Gilley, p.283-86).

On November 14, 2001 the Knoxville News-Sentinel reported:

"UT lawyer files second suit, claims discrimination against white males." (p.B3). The Sentinel noted, "The second lawsuit by Ronald C Leadbetter, filed Tuesday, names only UT as a defendant and makes nearly identical claims as one he filed in November 1999 against former UT president J. Wade Gilley." (Id.)

"Tuesday's lawsuit states Leadbetter filed a charge of discrimination with the EEOC on November 15, 2000, and received a notice of right to sue on August 16, 2001." The News-Sentinel article also reported:

Tuesday's lawsuit claims UT, acting through Gilley and others, violated its long-standing published policy and practice of nondiscrimination based on race and gender preferences in taking the particular employment actions described in the complaint.

"Accordingly, (UT) has acted in derogation of the University's distinguished past practice of opening employment opportunities for females and minorities without discriminating against Caucasian males," the lawsuit states.

(Id.).

My second lawsuit was not in any way directed at the UT leadership in office at the time the suit was filed–only Gilley.

Chapter 99–Pamela Reed Enters the Picture– Gilley's Paramour

"In April 2000, Dr. Gilley authorized the creation of a new job title at the University of Tennessee at Memphis. Ms. [Pamela] Reed was hired for that job on May 1. She was the only applicant, records show." (Chattanooga Times Free Press (electronic supplement), June 6, 2001, p.1). Another gender-based employment action by the UT President?

SKIRTING UT POLICY FOR A WOMAN–PAMELA REED

The afternoon of February 27, 2001, I received my first tip from a reliable source–I swore not to disclose the tipster's identity–that Gilley had again skirted UT employment policy and procedures and was engaged in an affair with the beneficiary of his action, Pamela Reed.

My notes for the day:

Learned this afternoon that (1) Pam Reed has been promoted to Ass't Vice President (?) (2) Gilley visits her office (5th Floor) in casual attire w/ door shut (3) Many cell phone calls between the two (4) Pam stalked a stripper when Pam was a student- something involving Pam's husband! But the stripper was a student with a 4.0 who came and complained to Tim Rogers. (5) Pam is causing disruption in office staff of Sen. Thompson & Sen. Frist, etc. (6) May NOT have her law license.

I learned from another inside source that Gilley and Reed had traveled together to Washington, D.C. the week of March 12. Another member of Gilley's staff, Katie High, approached Gilley around the same time and advised him of negative aspects of Reed's record." Gilley reportedly "brushed her off."

On April 5, yet another source informed me of Reed's new position as Executive Director of a newly established UT Center of Excellence. The establishment of a Center of Excellence was always accompanied by a news release –except Reed's. A review panel conducted approval reviews for all Centers– other than Reed's.

On April 24, 2001 I received more incriminating evidence. I met Carla Parmele on my way to lunch. Parmele was, at the time, senior administrative services assistant to the Vice President for Agriculture, Dr. Jack Britt. She had previously served as Gilley's secretary.

During our conversation Parmele revealed that in the spring of 2000 Gilley asked her to schedule a meeting on a specified date. "That's Good Friday, Parmele responded." To which Gilley replied, "Go ahead and schedule it." According to Parmele, Gilley and Reed had their meeting in Andy Holt Tower– a locked building–on Good Friday, 2000.

It was during this same encounter that Parmele informed me that prior to UT's announcement of the nationwide search to fill the position of General Counsel she had heard Gilley express his intent to promote Mizell to the position.

At 6:00 a.m. the morning of May 15 Duggan and I met in his office to discuss litigation matters. One point of discussion was the absence of any media coverage of Gilley and Reed's interaction. We agreed that I should not be the one to initiate contact with the media. Duggan said he would call David Keim at Knoxville News-Sentinel later that morning.

There is a saying, "You can lie but you can't hide the truth." What transpired over the next few weeks offered evidence in support of that saying.

My personal notes for May 24 record more revelations concerning Gilley's presidency:

On 5/21 Gilley had meeting in his office w/Johnie Ammonette & others–day before Sentinel article on rumors of Gilley resigning. Phil Scheurer was rudely denied entrance

to Pres. office (to secure entrance for worker seeking access to a circuit breaker).
Ammonette obtained access.

$ is being poured into President's house. $1Million plus–incl. landscaping–according to John Parker [head of Facilities Management} Mid-July move in doubt. Tomorrow at 8:15 a.m. Pam Reed will be moved from A. H. Tower to Suite 211 Room F of the Conference Center. Two persons moved to get Pam a bigger office.

Pam brought in to help Gilley edit book.

Rumor: Has accused [verbally] a Dean in Memphis of sex. harass.

Earlier complaint filed vs. Delta Airlines for sex. harr.

The May 25, 2001 edition of the Knoxville News-Sentinel carried the front-page headline: "UT official under scrutiny." News-Sentinel staff writer David Keim provided the details:

A fast rising University of Tennessee administrator who has been working to implement President J. Wade Gilley's research initiatives is under review amid concerns that she embellished her resumes.

UT has created at least two new jobs and one special assignment for Pamela S. Reed since last May, a period during which Gilley has boasted of streamlining his administration.

Read, 44, was hired as an assistant director at UT's Health Science Center in Memphis in May 2000 after a nine-month stint with state government. During part of that time she worked as a state attorney without a license. To keep the job, according to a state personnel official, Reed would have to have had a law license.

Within a few months of being hired by UT–University officials are unsure exactly when–she went to work in Knoxville as a special assistant to Dwayne McCay, Vice President for Research and Information Technology.

Reed had business cards printed that listed her as an "assistant vice president," although she had to stop using them because the position was not authorized.

In March, she was named executive director of a Center for Law, Medicine and Technology at a salary of $75,000.

***

Gilley and his staff said they were unaware of possible falsehoods and embellishments on her resumes until the News Sentinel asked about them this week. "It's something somebody should have reviewed at some point," said Gilley.

Dean Henry G. Herod of UT's College of Medicine in Memphis, with Gilley's approval, supported creation of an assistant director of program development position.

Herod asked that the position be posted on April 24 and Reed was hired on May 1.

She was the only applicant.

***

By late summer, McCay said Reed was working in Knoxville.

He assigned office space to Reed on the fifth floor of the Andy Holt Tower, UT's main administration building.

"The president (Gilley) asked me if I could find space," McCay said. Information about who checked Reed's background prior to her assent into the UT administration remained unanswered Thursday.

"I didn't hire her," Gilley said with a shrug. "I didn't check her background."

***

My diary entry for May 25 reads:

Big article on Gilley in the Sentinel (the beginning of the end??) Maybe the public–and the Board of Trustees will catch on to Gilley's gross improprieties now. A little slow–but sure!

"Word is out today-Gilley has resigned!" reads my diary entry for June 1. By the following day the public began to learn the facts about Gilley's downfall.

"UT president resigns" headlined the June 2, 2001 issue of the Knoxville News–Sentinel. The front-page article reported the circumstances:

Despite denying four times in the past three weeks that he was planning to step down as president of the University of Tennessee, Dr. J. Wade Gilley resigned Friday afternoon effective immediately.

***

The executive committee of the UT board convened in the eighth–floor boardroom of the university's administrative tower to read Gilley's one–page resignation letter and to vote on whether to accept it.

Committee members James Haslam II, [Johnnie] Amonette, Susan Williams, Jerry Jackson and Clayton McWhorter voted without opposition to accept Gilley's decision.... The committee quickly voted–again without opposition –to appoint Eli Fly, executive vice president, as interim president.

On June 6, 2001 the Chattanooga Times Free Press headlined "Lawsuit charges hirings by Gilley questionable." The article described my November 2000 lawsuit alleging that Gilley had hired and promoted on the basis of race and gender without regard for qualifications. Specifically mentioned in the article were Theotis Robinson, Derek Anderson and Pamela Reed.

"UT looking into Gilley's relationship with official" headlined The Tennessean, from Nashville, in a front-page article on June 7, 2001.

University of Tennessee administrator Pamela Reed pressed UT President J. Wade Gilley hard to continue his mentorship of her and to approve the program for which she was named to a $75,000 executive director post, according to a series of e-mail communications released yesterday.

"What have I done that is so horrible that you will no longer "watch over me" until I can stand alone–I just needed a bit more time," Reed wrote in a December e-mail, responding to Gilley's statement that he would mentor her "on a more limited basis."

"I thank you for what you have done for me, it still sounds like you are signing off on me," Reed wrote in the December 15 email, "which you are telling me. You must realize my investments here are multi–financial, emotional and professional."

The Chattanooga Times Free Press reported the following day, June 8, 2001, "Gilley says he OK'd Reed job, not credentials." According to the article, " 'I never checked her resume, but I never checked people who were already there (at the University),' said Dr. Gilley, who resigned June 1, citing health and personal reasons."

Also, on June 8, 2001, the Knoxville News-Sentinel headlined, "Early exit breaks Gilley's contract." The article explained, "The trustee who signed Gilley's contract for UT, Knoxville businessman Bill Sansom, said he believes the contract was voided when Gilley resigned without notice and the board accepted his resignation."

On June 14, 2001 the Knoxville News-Sentinel reported "UT administrator Reed resigns." Reporter David Keim reviewed the contents of a report released by the University identifying resume embellishments and financial issues attributed to Reed.

Keim also reported, "UT continues to withhold emails that UT's General Counsel, Catherine Mizell, deems 'personal,' a half-inch stack of emails between Gilley and Reed documenting their 'working relationship'"–far outside the bounds of the UT personnel policies adopted early in my career and adhered to throughout the University prior to Gilley's arrival.

The July 20, 2001 issue of the Knoxville News -Sentinel disclosed the contents of the "personal" emails finally released by the University of Tennessee. "Gilley e–mail reveals sexual liaison with Reed," read the front-page headline. The details of a February19 e-mail from Gilley to Reed were provided.

"Gosh, I thought you were acting pretty frisky Friday and I was trying to please you, " Gilley said in one document, which shows that the message was sent from his private email account to hers the evening of Monday, February 19, "I am very sorry…

"I am sorry if I am not up to your expectations but at my age and health conditions

I don't know if I will ever be really sexually active again to any real degree."

What others and I discussed privately for some time was now publicly disclosed. Gilley's relationship with Reed was anything but an attempt to promote a uniquely qualified individual to a University position for which she was qualified.

"E-mail led to resignation," according to the front page article in the Chattanooga Times Free Press on July 31, 2001:

> A potentially embarrassing email message led University of Tennessee officials to demand the resignation of former university president J. Wade Gilley, sources have confirmed.
>
> Dr. Gilley, 62, was asked May 30 for his resignation and that of former administrator Pamela S. Reed by University trustee William B Sansom of Knoxville, who had seen an email message that suggested an attempted intimate encounter between Dr. Gilley and Ms. Reed.
>
> According to sources, Mr. Sansom called Dr. Gilley in Destin, Florida where he was attending a four-day meeting of Southeastern Conference university presidents. Mr. Sansom told Dr. Gilley to resign, or he would be terminated. Mr. Sansom also asked for Ms. Reed's resignation.
> Other trustees had designated Mr. Sansom to contact Dr. Gilley.

Now the public, as well as top-level UT officials, was aware that Gilley had lied about the reason for leaving the UT Presidency. The evidence was strong that Gilley parsed the facts to suit his needs. Would the District Court feel the same in determining whether my case against Gilley could proceed?

(Postscript: On January 14, 2002 I received a phone call at the office from a long time friend from UT days, Steve Bowers. Bowers was calling from the Chancellor's office at James Madison University. With him in the office was Ron Carrier, the retired president of James Madison U.

Bowers shared with me that Carrier had been listed by Gilley as one of his references when he applied for the UT presidency. He also shared with me that when a UT representative contacted Carrier to "check out the reference," Carrier responded that "he didn't think UT was a good fit for Gilley ."

Carrier was quite right.

PAMELA REED'S COURSE OF ACTION
AFTER DEPARTING UT

In June 2002 Pamela Reed filed a $14 million suit in U.S. District Court (E.D. Tenn.) against Catherine Mizell, Dwayne McKay, Katherine High and the University of Tennessee.

Reed claimed that Gilley had sexually harassed and made unwanted sexual advances in exchange for helping her career. She claimed the co-defendants had conspired to terminate her employment for pretextual reasons and had illegally accessed her personal records including her private email account.

The Chronicle of Higher Education, on July 5, 2002(p, A33), reported "Former Administrator Sues U. Of Tennessee at Knoxville Over E–mail Privacy. "

On November 8, 2002, the Knoxville News-Sentinel published a front-page article, "Audit says deceit, slipshod screening behind Reed's rise."

In February 2003 Reed's suit was amended to add Wade Gilley as a party defendant. Then in November 2003 Reed filed a defamation lawsuit against another Gilley successor–former UT president John Shumaker and other university and state officials.

I offer nothing further on the Reed litigation since I had little personal knowledge of the matters being litigated (aside from matters addressed elsewhere in the pages of this book). Except for revelations from one key party to the litigation - Pamela Reed herself!

A little past 11 a.m. the morning of December 20, 2001 I received a phone call from "Karen Lane." She spoke with me for 20 or 25 minutes about Gilley's termination of Pamela Reed and related matters. She would not tell me what UT department she was in.

On January 14, 2002 I received another call from "Ms. Lane." She provided me a wealth of information. Some I found very credible and some not so much. At the end of the conversation Ms. Lane provided me her phone number.

During February and March, 2002, I received calls from "Lane'" on a regular basis, Sometimes informative and always intriguing. During one call I was advised she had a handwritten "settlement agreement " with Gilley and that Gilley had recently called to threaten her if she disclosed anything about the agreement. No further comment on that.

My last recorded call from "Lane" –who by now I'm sure you realize was actually Pamela Reed–was received December 17, 2004.

So what was the most worthwhile subject we discussed during our last dozen or so telephone conversations–and we never met in person? Reed's spiritual well-being.

On a number of occasions I shared with Reed my Christian faith. She shared with me that she had been raised a Catholic. I emphasized the importance of faith in Christ over denominational affiliation. She expressed to me her interest in redirecting her life in a more spiritual direction. It has been a decade since we last communicated.

I am unaware of the final disposition of Reed's lawsuits. I am far more interested in knowing if Reed prevailed on the latter challenge.

Chapter 100–Evidence Against Gilley Mushrooms

Initial efforts by Duggan to secure documents from Gilley and schedule depositions of prospective witnesses were rebuffed. A motion was filed with the court seeking to compel compliance with plaintiff's discovery requests. A defense motion was filed on Gilley's behalf seeking "a protective order to provide him protection from the discovery sought by plaintiff which defendant deems inconsistent with the doctrine of qualified immunity." See: Ronald C. Leadbetter v. J. Wade Gilley, Memorandum and Order, No. 3:00-CV-661, August 31, 2001, p.1.

The District Court's August 31 ruling granted plaintiff's motion and denied the defense motion for a protective order. Discovery proceeded.

Between August 2001 and March 2002 numerous documents were exchanged between the parties and a number of depositions were taken. All but one deposition–my own–were initiated by Duggan.

As noted in my diary,

Duggan and I spent three hours in Ward Phillips' office reviewing and obtaining copies of records the afternoon of August 9, 2001. On Labor Day, September 3, I spent four hours that morning with Duggan in his office preparing for our first deposition – the deposition of J. Wade Gilley.

The Knoxville News-Sentinel's front-page article of September 5, 2001, announced that UT's former president would be in Knoxville for his deposition:

GILLEY TO TESTIFY ON HIRES
Details of ex-UT president's link with Reed may come to light
The University of Tennessee's ex-president will be required to answer
questions under oath, a federal magistrate has ruled.

> Dr. J.Wade Gilley is scheduled to give his deposition today in a $1.5 mil-
> lion civil suit filed against him last year by UT staff attorney Ron Leadbetter
> The suit alleges that in his 22 months as president, Gilley promoted
> women and minorities ahead of white men.
> Leadbetter, who is white, cited Reed as an example of discrimination
> against men.
>
>   ***
>
> Leadbetter's suit, filed last November, cited the promotion of
> Catherine Mizell to the postion of UT General Counsel and Theotis
> Robinson to a vice presidency of equity and diversity as evidence of
> discrimination by Gilley.

The article identified other Gilley hires where discriminatory bias may have been involved (including Carilli's initial rejection as Dean of Students). Gilley's denials of wrongdoing were also noted.

With respect to any salacious details of Gilley's relationship with Reed, Duggan quickly laid to rest any notion that such conduct would be a focus of discovery. As reported by the Sentinel: "Duggan said he doesn't plan to ask about Gilley's personal relationship with Reed. 'I'm primarily interested in just asking about why he made the decisions that he made with respect to certain employment matters,' Duggan said." (Id.)

The following day, the News-Sentinel headlined, "Deposition brings Gilley from Virginia Retirement." (Knoxville News-Sentinel, September 6, 2001,p. A-4).

A September 5 entry in my diary notes that Gilley's deposition in Phillips' office lasted from 9 a.m to 5:30 p.m. (excluding an hour or so for lunch). My deposition was set for September 7.

On the evening of September 6 Therese and I attended the funeral of long time friend and UT facilities manager, John Parker. "His Eye is on the Sparrow" was the last song played at Parker's funeral. I found encouragement in that instrumental even as I grieved the loss of a friend and prepared mentally for the next day's activity. Must have worked-the deposition lasted from 9 a.m. to 5:30 p.m. but seemed to breeze by. All went well.

A prospective witness, retired UT Vice President, Sammie Lynn Puett, was killed in an auto accident in Texas several weeks later. I attended her funeral on October 15.

Two weeks later Duggan deposed most of the witnesses deemed crucial to our case. Between October 29 and October 31 Duggan completed the depositions of eight key UT officials and employees. Two additional depositions were taken on March 22 of 2002.

Between the two sets of depositions a second lawsuit was filed in federal court, on November 31, 2001. (Ronald C. Leadbetter v. The University of Tennessee, U.S. District Court, No. 3:01-cv-534, E.D. Tenn.). That suit followed the Equal Employment Opportunity Commission's issuance of a "right to sue "notice following its failure to issue a finding as to whether the University had engaged in unlawful discriminatory employment action.

Some witnesses supported Gilley's employment decisions. Much testimony directly contradicted Gilley's testimony or undermined explanations he offered as to how and/or why he reached those decisions. Would the court accept Gilley's explanations as truthful? Or would the court find his explanations false – a pretext for unlawful discrimination on the basis of race or sex?

In order to proceed to trial by jury all that was needed was a finding by Magistrate Phillips that there existed sufficient evidence from which a jury could find that the latter scenario applied. It would then be for a jury to hear the testimony of witnesses, weigh the evidence and determine if a "preponderance," more than 50%, of the evidence indicated that Gilley discriminated unlawfully.

Chapter 101–
Sworn Testimony Placed Gilley's Truthfulness at Issue

The sworn testimony of Gilley and key University personnel was revealing on a number of key issues of fact relevant to my claims against Gilley. Excerpts of sufficient detail are provided in this chapter in order to allow readers to make their own "educated guess" as to how they would have ruled had this case been presented to them as jurors.

Did Gilley Announce Intent To Appoint Mizell Without a Search?

Duggan asked Gilley, at deposition on September 5, 2001, "Did you ever tell any member of your staff prior to commencement of the search that it was time to give Catherine a chance?" Gilley's answer: "I don't remember that – – doing that. I wouldn't have – –I wouldn't have done that." (Dep. of Gilley, p.168). Really?

Senior Associate Vice President for Business and Finance Charles Moss testified by deposition that prior to commencement of the General Council search process he was told by Vice President Eli Fly during a meeting in his office "something to the effect that Wade wants to put Catherine in the job without doing a search." (Id. p.9). As Moss left Fly's office he "walked out in the foyer they are in the lobby and Catherine was out there and I said something to the effect... I understand congratulations may be in order. And she kind of smiled and then we engaged in a very brief conversation and she said,' Wade wanted to put me in the job without doing a search, but I told him we had to do a search.' " (Id. pp.9-10).

There was an even earlier disclosure by Gilley of his intent to hire Mizell without a search. Just prior to public announcement of Brogan's plan to retire, Gilley revealed his intentions to his secretary, Carla Parmele.

    Q. All right. Did you ever have occasion during the time that you worked for Dr. Gilley to have any conversations with Dr. Gilley pertaining to Beach Brogan's retirement as General Counsel?

    A. One time.

    Q. Was that prior to the time that Mr. Brogan's retirement was announced?

    A. It was prior to the time his retirement was publicly announced.

    Q. Okay. What transpired during that discussion; what was said?

    A. I was at my desk and Dr. Gilley came in and said, "Have you heard that Beauchamp Brogan is retiring?" And I said, "Yes, I have heard that. We will miss him." And he said, "Well, I think it is time Catherine had a chance. Don't you?" (Dep. of Parmale, p. 5).

The evidence was strong that Gilley had voiced his intent to hire Mizell without a search. There was evidence he falsely denied doing so.

Did Gilley Participate in Preparation of the General Counsel Job Description?

According to Gilley it was General Counsel Brogan who drafted the General Counsel position announcement (Dep. of Gilley, p. 170). But, Gilley was admittedly involved in the process.

"Mr. Brogan did the first draft. He shared that draft with me. I made my comments. He made appropriate adjustments. He shared with Mr. Dickson and then they collaborated on the final draft." (Gilley, .pp. 176-77).

Did Gilley Choose a One-Member Search Committee As a Bona Fide Means of Conducting a UT Position Search?

In his September 5, 2001 deposition, President Gilley claimed a one – member search committee was justified because of the need to expedite the search following Brogan's mid-September announcement that he planned to retire by the end of the year. (Gilley, p.309). At the same time he "justified" his use of a multi-member search committee for head basketball head coach (and Gilley himself served on the basketball coach search committee). (Gilley, p.20):

> I didn't have to, but I think the–a lot more public interest in the basketball position. And, first, you want to share the responsibility during and after the decision. And so we–not unlike what has been done before, but we–and we had time. We knew well in advance. Basketball searches are conducted, once you start on the–or coaches–on a very fast track basis and you get exceptions from the Affirmative Action Office to do that.

In addition to evidence that "fast track" searches used multi member search committees, there was evidence the General Counsel search was never in fact considered in need of expedited handling. When asked if he recalled Gilley,

Brogan or anyone else ever talking to him about the need to expedite the search process, Dickson replied, "I don't." (Dep. of Dickson, p.48).

Gilley conceded he could not personally cite a single example of a one -member search committee conducting a nationwide search for an "administrative executive managerial" position. (Dep. of Gilley, p.189). He claimed that when he did so for the General Counsel search, "I relied on the recommendation of Brogan, the General Counsel, and Mr. Fly, the Executive Vice President. I was only on the job a month at that point in time." (Id.p.189).

In fact, Gilley was hired in mid- June (assuming the presidency on August 1). Gilley had three and a half months to conduct a search before Brogan retired. He offered no explanation of why a multi member committee would take longer than a single–member committee to do the job. In any event, why would an experienced university president think a search committee, composed of a single white male, had any ring of authenticity from an "affirmative action/ equal employment opportunity" perspective–unless of course the president presumed his selection of a female would avoid any charge of discriminatory practice?

Gilley credited Brogan with suggesting use of a one-member search committee ("at the University–wide administration, it had been done in the past and he [Brogan] gave me the specific example of the Vice President for Development"). (Dep. of Gilley, p.188). In fact, that search was conducted by a multi - member search committee. Even if there were an exceptional case in the past, was there a legitimate non-discriminatory reason for making an exception for the General Counsel search?

In my affidavit filed with the U.S. District Court I testified:
> It has long been the University practice that a multi–member search committee having minority and female members be appointed to identify and recommend a qualified candidate(s) for the position to be filled. To my knowledge there has not been a single upper level administrative position filled in the past 25 years utilizing a search committee composed of a single person. One major reason for utilizing multi-member search committees, discussed by me with affirmative action officials and personnel officials on a number of occasions, is to promote both the appearance and reality of a non-discriminatory employment decision being made.

(Affidavit of Leadbetter, p.7, par.18).

A jury might have concluded that Gilley's claim–that a one–member search committee was necessary due to the need to expedite the search–was false, concocted only as a "cover" for a scheme to assure the selection of the candidate for the position he pre-selected on the basis of her gender.

Were Minimum Requirements for the GC Position Intentionally

Ignored?

Dickson was asked why he interviewed applicants who did not meet minimum qualifications–all but one of those he selected to interview. He offered a succinct explanation:

> **Q.** If those persons were not qualified, why were they chosen
> for interview?
>
> **A.** Because I thought they may be a person that could do the job.
> (Dep. of Dickson, p.58).

A succinct explanation suspect on its face. Imagine the outcry had an unqualified male been selected over a female meeting all mandated qualifications. A key question was, did Gilley know that Dickson interviewed unqualified candidates? As noted below Gilley admitted he knew of the inclusion of an unqualified candidate in the final pool of three candidates, took no corrective action and expressed no concern.

Did Gilley Believe Mizell Lacked Litigation Experience?

Gilley took the position that both Mizell and I were qualified for the position of General Counsel. There was evidence he knew one of us did not meet all required qualifications for the job.

The entire responsibility of reviewing the candidates files was not left to Dickson–Gilley personally engaged in that review. "The two finalists I interviewed, I looked at their file." (Gilley, pp 143,152).

There was never a claim by Gilley that I failed to meet any published minimum requirement for the position. Gilley also admitted that Dickson offered no criticism of my qualifications:

> **Q.** Did Mr. Dickson make any critical comments of Mr. Leadbetter?
>
> **A.** No, he didn't.

Gilley swore under oath "I only had one question which I wanted the two candidates to respond to, and that was the question about the organization and management of the office. And they both, whether it was one interview or two interviews, gave me satisfactory responses to that question." (Dep. of Gilley, p.193). There was evidence that statement was false–that Gilley was concerned about Mizell's lack of litigation experience.

Yes, there was evidence from which a jury might conclude that Gilley knew Mizell lacked the required litigation experience. His claim that he left to the "search committee" any review of credentials, was arguably false.

> **Q.** Let's talk about civil litigation experience for a moment. What was Ms. Mizell's litigation experience that you were able to determine?
>
> **A.** I raised that question with Mr. Brogan and reviewed her resume. She had, according to Mr. Brogan, had had some experience as a litigator, but he didn't consider that – – having a litigator as being the manager

of the university's legal office was a critical factor.

Q. Well, and the reason you say that, apparently, it was not a key factor to them is because in fact, she had very scant litigation experience, isn't that true?

A. Compared to Mr. Leadbetter, she has limited litigation experience.

Q. But, nevertheless, it was a stated minimum qualification that there be litigation experience for this position?

A. Litigation and– –transactional and litigation experience. (Id. p. 212).

E-mails from Mizell to Gilley in late November and early December 1999 also evidenced deceptiveness in Gilley's claim he was unconcerned with Mizell's lack of litigation experience.

Q. [Referring to Exhibit 20, "the 11/30/99 email from Catherine Mizell to Dr. Gilley"] All right. She references a discussion about litigation skills and experience. Can you tell me what that was about?

A. I think she brought that up, because that was to – – but that wasn't the central to my question of her issue, the central issue, because I had already talked with Mr. Brogan and others about that. And that – – the level of litigation experience and skills was not a determining factor in the position. Some experience was required to understand, but not a determining.

Q. Do you know why she was concerned about that?

A. I don't know.... The University is a rumor mill. And maybe she had picked up or someone else had indicated to her that this was a concern or a factor, but it was not a factor and it wasn't something that I had any concerns about, other than the fact that the person meet the minimum standard, and which she was certified to me by Mr. Roger Dickson, who is, you know, a Trustee, an attorney, and a former judge. (Dep. of Gilley, pp. 240-41).

***

Q. So, you didn't have any questions in your mind about the strength of her litigation experience?

A. No.... That was not the factor that I was focusing on. (Id. pp.241-42).

***

Q. So, her comment to you in this email about litigation skills and experience, she wasn't responding to any type of inquiry you had made, she just did this on her own volition?

A. I think that she said in light of our discussion today, and, obviously, that was brought up. I don't remember this email, but that was brought up. And so, obviously, she wanted to follow up on that discussion. (Id. p.242).

***

Q. (Referring to "the 12/8/99 email from Catherine Mizell to Dr. Gilley, marked and filed as Exhibit 21) All right. On December 8, 1999, Ms. Mizell sent you another email , this time just a week before your memo to the Board of Trustees, saying that you had met on December 6 and that she had gathered information on fifteen University legal offices.

A. Uh–huh.

Q. Do you recall what that was about?

A. I think that was, again, her following up on our discussion regarding organization of the General Counsel's office at the University of Tennessee. And I don't know why she felt that she needed to follow up on that, but, apparently, she went out and followed up on that.

Q. Had you asked her to do that?

A. No, I hadn't. (Id. p.244).

Mizell's lack of litigation experience was confirmed by her boss, Brogan: "I don't recall Ms. Mizell ever trying a jury case or examining a witness in open court." (Dep. of Brogan, p. 57). Other than a single case he could not recall Mizell ever examining a witness under oath with adverse counsel present [as in a deposition]. (Id.p.62).

Brogan offered a reason for Mizell's lack of litigation experience. He noted there were two major areas of responsibility in the Office of General Counsel. "One, of course, was litigation. And the other was all the other work involving the University of Tennessee, which we call staff work or which a lot of lawyers would refer to as office work." (Dep. of Brogan, p.72).

Brogan explained "So, I wanted Catherine to be an office lawyer, a manager, to help me. I didn't want to bog her down in trial work, because being a trial lawyer, I know how much time it takes to take depositions and stuff like that. So, I didn't want to bog Catherine Mizell down. That is the only reason I didn't give her litigation." (Id.)

At an office meeting on April 17, 1996 Brogan made the following statement to the lawyers on his staff: "You make better all around lawyers if you do trial work." Brogan's statement helps explain the requirement that the successful candidate for General Counsel have litigation experience.

When Dickson was asked about his knowledge of Mizell's litigation experience he admitted he had none.

Q. Okay. Now, you told me that Ron would have more experience in the area of civil litigation. Did you formulate any opinions or do you have any knowledge of what Catherine Mizell's litigation experience was?

A. Less than Ron's.

Q. Okay. Do you know if she has ever examined a witness under oath?

A. I wouldn't know. I wouldn't care, but I wouldn't know. (Dep. of Dickson, p. 70).

A key issue for jury determination was whether Gilley knew, but didn't care that Mizell lacked litigation experience because she afforded him a chance to place a woman in the position of General Counsel.

ANALYTICAL SKILLS

Dickson said he thought Mizell had strong "analytical skills." He deemed this an important attribute of Mizell, with whom he had a personal friendship (Both were from Chattanooga). (Dep. of Dickson, pp.66-68). Yet, Dickson never asked questions aimed at determining whether my analytical skills were strong. "I know nothing of Ron's analytical skills." (Id.). Must not have been important. And Gilley apparently agreed.

TRANSACTIONAL MATTERS

Gilley acknowledged awareness of my experience in handling transactional matters. "Mr. Leadbetter had worked on the ESPN/ NCAA thing and I had been aware of that. I thought he did a very good job." (Gilley, p.143). He pointed to no criticism of my ability to handle transactional matters.

When asked about my experience handling compliance with the Tennessee Uniform Administrative Procedures act, Gilley agreed, "That is a transactional matter. I think that transactional matters were only one of many factors that were in the job description." (Dep. of Gilley, p.215-16).

IMPORTANCE OF QUALIFICATIONS

Gilley was asked, "How important are qualifications in the hiring process?" He responded, "Qualifications are the first criteria. A person has to be qualified. And that is – – Qualifications is a determining factor." (Dep. of Gilley, p.98).

ONLY DIFFERENCES BETWEEN FINALISTS DISCOVERED BY GILLEY'S INTERVIEW OF CANDIDATES
In his deposition, Gilley testified:

I wanted to ask Mr. Leadbetter and Ms. Mizell about streamlining, how many lawyers did we need, did we need twelve lawyers, when the University of Michigan has seven and the University of Virginia has five? Why did we need twelve? And that gave me some insight into them as a manager of the office. And that was the purpose of the interview. (Dep. of Gilley, pp. 144-45).

When asked if he was aware that Mizell believed the office of General Counsel needed more attorneys and Leadbetter believed the office needed fewer, Gilley responded: "Mr. Leadbetter was very forthcoming in his and he had a very distinct view that he needed – – that the office could do with fewer attorneys."(Dep. of Gilley, p.145)

Gilley described Mizell's response as "if certain conditions could be changed, the University could do with fewer employees and fewer attorneys in the General Counsel's office. But she had an understanding of the University has a unique position in regard to malpractice suits and residents that the University can't get out of easily and it has to defend residents." He also testified that Mizell told him she wanted to hire a "Deputy". (Id.)

Dickson was asked whether any questions were asked of the candidates regarding their management style or ideas for organizing the office. He said "No". (Dep. of Dickson, p. 72). When asked, "Did you formulate any opinions or conclusions about the merits of the two candidates, based upon asking those kinds of questions about how you would organize the office?" Dickson replied "No.". (Id.).

In my October 6, 1999 letter of application to Dickson, I stated that "I offer the following strengths in connection with this application." One of those was "Firm commitment to the practice of 'preventative' law through active participation of the General Counsel's office in providing to UT officials legal education, advice, and representation aimed at discouraging litigation and, where litigation is unavoidable, increasing the likelihood of success."

Dickson asked nothing about this "bullet point" in my letter of application. More significantly, Gilley asked me for no further explanation during my brief interview. A jury might conclude from that fact that Gilley was not truly interested in which of the final applicants could best do the job and was more focused on the gender of the preferred applicant.

Did Gilley Favor Mizell Because of Her Title or Position as Deputy General Counsel?

When asked if he believed the General Counsel position description was "designed to favor Ms. Mizell" Gilley responded:

A. I don't know. This is Mr. Brogan or Mr. Dickson in this. However, I do know that Mr. Leadbetter qualified under that and at one point he had been, before there was a Deputy, there were two Associate General Counsels and he was a Chief Assistant to the General Counsel of the University of Tennessee.

Q. Isn't it true that University officials, including yourself, were surprised to find out that he, Mr. Leadbetter, was able to meet that qualification?

A. I wasn't surprised. I didn't think about who would make the qualifications. (Dep. of Gilley, pp. 175-76).

Gilley testified that Mizell's title of "Deputy General Counsel" had no bearing on his decision.

Q. Do you believe that the higher title entitled Ms. Mizell to the promotion?

A. No, I don't." (Gilley, p.216). Any application of a concept of "natural progression" of an employee from one level to the next was clearly rejected by Gilley as a factor in this case.

Was Gilley's Stated Reason for Selecting Mizell False?

In his testimony Gilley essentially denied personal responsibility for selecting Mizell as General Counsel. When asked why he did not ask more questions during my interview, Gilley explained "Well, he [Leadbetter] had been one of the three finalists recommended by Mr. Dixon, and I was at that point relying on Mr. Dickson...." (Dep. of Gilley, p.142, 182).

Later Gilley testified, "absent other information, I was committed to taking the recommendation of the committee." (Id. pp.146-47).

Q. So, I take it from what you just said, that, absent receiving other information, you intended to take the search committee's recommendation?

A. Yes.

Q. But the only other information you sought in these interviews was their theory about how to organize the office; correct?

A. Yes.

Q. Did one candidate stand head and shoulders above the other in terms of how to organize the office?

A. I thought that both their answers were satisfactory. (Id. p.147).

Yet there is ample evidence Gilley did not simply take whatever recommendations were provided him without further inquiry.

Dickson recommended three candidates to Gilley, ranking Mizell first. He admitted that he did not know if a second candidate, Ayers, was unqualified because he was from a single campus public institution (Wichita State University). (Dep. of Dickson, p. 58). But, Gilley knew that Ayers was "from Wichita State, that is not a–Witchita State is not a multi-campus institution." (Dep. of Gilley, p. 206).

Because Ayres was unqualified Gilley made the decision not to interview him regardless of Dickson's recommendation. . Gilley made no complaint and made no request that the search continue. The absence of a black finalist seemingly merited no concern.

Gilley interviewed only two candidates–Mizell and me. (Dep. of Gilley, p. 192). Having only two qualified candidates–even assuming Mizell met the litigation requirement–caused him no concern.

Why even conduct interviews if relying on search committee recommendations?

> **Q.** All right. I want to be sure I understand. You have told me that you did not give Mr. Leadbetter the opportunity to talk about these alleged problems [in Memphis arising in the course of the Skoutakis case.] in his interview because you were relying upon Mr. Dickson?
>
> **A.** Right. (Gilley, p.142).

***

> **Q.** All right. So, you elected not to ask Mr. Leadbetter about these alleged problems at Memphis?
>
> **A.** Right.

***

> **Q.** Did those problems cause you concern; were they a negative factor, in other words, in terms of considering him?
>
> **A.** No, they were not a negative factor. (Gilley, p. 146)

Did Gilley's Handling of the Carilli Search Committee Recommendation Reveal His True Intent?

When asked "Why should Mr. Carilli, let's say, be penalized just because the other person [the black applicant] then decides I don't want the job?"

Gilley replied, "Well, I think that the standard ought to be at least three people who are fully qualified, able and willing to take the job." (Dep. of Gilley, p.110).

Gilley did not "depend " on the extensive search done by a multi-member search committee. He made the decision--at least initially.

The difference? A jury might find it depended on the race or gender of the applicant. They might have been influenced in that regard by the testimony of Vice Provost Tim Rogers following Gilley's initial rejection of the recommendation to hire Vinnie Carilli (See Chapter 97).

Was Reorganization a Ruse for Promoting Theotis Robinson Based on His Race?

With respect to the employment history of Theotis Robinson I made no claim of manufactured job description or bogus search. There was no job description, no advertised position and no candidate search whatever.

Under Gilley's direction a "temporary" employee with a high school diploma, holding a secretary–clerical position, was moved to an administrative position then a well-paid vice presidency–positions with job responsibilities completely outside the employee's prior experience. The move was accomplished under the guise of "reorganization."

As I testified in my affidavit:

16. Prior to defendant Wade Gilley becoming president it was University policy for more than two decades to permit promotions within the "chain of command" without any requirement that the position to be filled be advertised (with the exception of upper-level administrative positions specified in Geier). At the same time all positions not filled by "chain of command" promotions within a department were required to be filled in accordance with University employment policy and procedures requiring the position be advertised and selection of a successful candidate from a pool of qualified applicants. The University has never had, during this period, a policy or procedure creating an exception to this process for employees whose positions outside the "chain of command" are eliminated as a result of restructuring, reorganization or other purpose. During the period of my university employment the issue of such transfers has on a number of occasions been discussed by me with University personnel officers, and in no instance was a transfer or promotion to a position outside the "chain of command" approved except through utilization of standard University employment procedures, including job advertisement and selection of a candidate for hire or promotion from a pool of qualified applicants.

(Affidavit of Leadbetter, p. 6, par. 16)

In the following paragraph of my affidavit I described the reason for the policy described above:

17. The purpose of the University's long – standing requirement that job vacancies be filled only following preparation of a bona fide job description, conduct of a bona fide search and selection of a candidate for a position from a pool of qualified candidates, without regard to race or gender, is to meet the nondiscrimination and affirmative action requirements of University policies as well as federal and state law. This purpose has been discussed by me with University affirmative action officers, personnel officers and other officials on numerous occasions over the tenure of my employment in the Office of General Counsel.

(Affidavit of Leadbetter, p.6., par. 17).

From the above testimony a jury might have found that Gilley's testimony was false – a ruse to hide unlawful discriminatory motive.

Gilley justified his handling of Robinson's rise to a University Vice Presidency as follows:

> **Q.** No one but Theotis Robinson was considered for the positions of Administrator of Equity and Diversity and then Vice President?
> He was the only one considered for those positions; is that correct?
> **A.** He–in terms of reassigning duties to him at the initial phase, I was looking for somebody to do that. Among the positions that were being affected by the restructuring, and he was the most logical person to be reassigned those duties, just as Tom Ballard was the

most logical person to be reassigned to duties for State Governmental Relations.

Q. Well, of course, Theotis Robinson was, until he received these redesignations, he was a low ranking University of Tennessee employee, not a high-ranking administrator like these other persons. Isn't that a tremendous distinction between him and these other persons?

A. Well, several people moved from Assistant and Associate Vice President to Staff Vice President, which could be seen as an elevation, but I think the most important thing is, what are the duties and responsibilities that a person has and are conducting, far more–as you indicated earlier, *far more important than the title that they have.* (Dep. of Gilley, p. 259). [Emphasis added].

It was the testimony of Sarah Phillips, Executive Assistant to Gilley, that prior to Robinson being "reorganized" to the positions of administrator and vice president, he had no managerial responsibilities at the University nor did he have any affirmative-action responsibilities. (Dep. of Phillips, pp.61-62). Gilley claimed Robinson had other attributes justifying his rapid ascent up the job ladder.

Q. But it is true, nevertheless, is it not, that all of these other persons who were re-designated Vice Presidents or given new titles in the restructuring were administrators, not low level employees?

A. Well, he was an administrator, but I would hesitate to characterize him as a low-level employee. He is a prominent figure in the Knoxville community. He was a columnist for the newspaper. He was on a television show. He had been a Vice President of the World's Fair. He was a former member of the City Council. So, I would not characterize him as a low-level employee.

Q. Isn't it true that when you came to the University, Mr. Robinson was designated as a term or temporary employee, he was hourly, making $22,000 per year?

A. I don't know. I was told his salary was $30,000 a year, and he had been there for six or eight years.

Q. Isn't it true that his pay rate was at a secretarial, clerical, hourly level?

A. I don't know.

Q. Mr. Robinson has only a high school diploma; is that correct?

A. That is my understanding. (Gilley, p. 260).

Phillips was asked if, in her previous experience as an affirmative action officer for the University, a position announcement for "affirmative action or equity and diversity positions" would typically "have required at least a bachelors degree if not a masters degree?" She answered, "Typically." (Phillips, p.93.)

I testified that during the years of my University employment I was "very familiar with general qualifications of upper-level administrative officials at the University" and had reviewed qualifications of such university officials on numerous occasions. "I [was] unaware of a single instance during the period of my employment (except the promotion of Theotis Robinson) that a person without a college degree has been hired or promoted into such position." (Affidavit of Leadbetter, p. 14, par. 37).

Sara Phillips said she was well aware of my experience in training and working with affirmative-action officers, conducting civil rights legal updates for affirmative action and personnel officers and annual review of the affirmative action plans. (Dep. of Phillips, p.87). She agreed that my affirmative action job experience was superior to that of Robinson.

Phillips agreed that underutilization of minorities and women had been eliminated from all EEO (equal employment opportunity) job categories within the University- wide administration prior to Gilley becoming president. (Id. p.80). She further agreed that, at my recommendation, a footnote was placed in the 1999 UT Affirmative-Action plan announcing that "in prior years, university administration has eliminated underutilization in all applicable job groups." (Id. p.99).

Philips confirmed that another attorney in the UT Office of General Counsel, Karen Holt, had left her position as an attorney in the office of General Counsel to become an affirmative action officer for the University. (Id. pp. 89-90). Had I applied for an affirmative action position, had one been advertised, I would not have been the first lawyer in the office of General Counsel to do so. Since no openings were announced there was nothing to apply for.

I made clear in my affidavit testimony provided to the federal court that "I would have applied for the administrative position in which Robinson was placed had I had the opportunity to apply for the position." (Affidavit of Leadbetter, p. 12, par. 33).

"Likewise, I would have applied for the position of Vice President in which Robinson was subsequently promoted. Neither the Administrator position nor Vice President position was advertised nor was any search conducted, and I believe it would be futile to approach Dr. Gilley and request to be considered for either position because Robinson had already been selected. " (Affidavit of Leadbetter, pp. 12-13, par. 34).

From my testimony a jury could have concluded that I would have applied for either position had I only had the opportunity.

Did Gilley's Promotion of Pamela Reed's UT Employment Career Provide Further Evidence of Gilley's Discriminatory Intent in Employment Matters?

Gilley's deposition testimony justifying the manner in which he promoted Pamela Reed rapidly up the employment chain often contradicted his testimonial explanations for other employment actions.

When asked why Reed was hired into a position in Knoxville under Vice President McCay, Gilley explained "she was given additional assignments in Dr. McCay's office and at the university. She was working on a communications plan...." (Gilley. P. 292). "So, one of the responsibilities she had working with Dr. McCay and with the faculty in Memphis was developed a way in which faculty who have common interests could communicate and learn about the research initiatives of the University." (Gilley, p.293).

Gilley was then asked "Well, whether it was one time or not, she didn't have any communications experience prior to being given those duties, did she?" And Gilley responded "No, she didn't." He then provided examples of upper level administrators who had been assigned responsibilities they had not previously performed.[Id].

Gilley was asked about an "email that was reported in the News Sentinel, you told Ms. Reed concerning her title change: We'll have to be careful about the Affirmative Action/EEO stuff." What did you mean by that? He responded, "Well, there was a proposal to – that they were discussing about creating a title of assistant vice president for federal relations in Dr. McKay's office and that she would be–that might giving her that title and, basically, I told him and her that we could not create any new position. If we did at some time in the future create new positions, it would have to go through the affirmative action EEO exercise." (Gilley, p.295).

Gilley then testified that he opposed the title change for Reed because "1., we can't establish the position because we don't have positions to establish. 2., if we do, we will have affirmative action procedures to go through and that is very clear here at the University, but if you work for Dr. McKay and get experience in this area, then at some point if there is a position that, perhaps, you can be competitive for it." (Gilley, p. 296).

Gilley's interpretation of emails back and forth with Reed was quite revealing:

Q. In that same e- mail, you went on to say that the restrictions here are tighter than I have ever experienced. What restrictions were you referring to?

A. The affirmative action, EEO, and the Geier, all of that... . And routinely [at Marshall University], to expedite things, we would suspend part or all of the affirmative action rule, because that was permitted by our plan. That was not permitted here... .

Q. How did all of that relate to what you were discussing with Ms. Reed in this e-mail in terms of her future employment?

A. She was interested in federal relations. And, basically, I said that if in the future a position is created and if you gain some experience in the area, additional experience in the area working with Dr. McCay, you will be – – you may be a more viable – – it may help your chances of getting that position.

Q. But you didn't say in this e-mail that you were not eligible for this position right now, but you might be in the future; you didn't say that, did you?

A. No, I didn't. … .(Gilley, pp.296-97).

Q. What did you mean when you told Ms. Reed in this e-mail: "to be cautious"?

A. Not to push for things that were not achievable.

Q. You also say in this e-mail that: "how things in then how they seem at the beginning is more important." What did you mean by that?

A. I mean we couldn't do it. I had already said that we couldn't – – went to Dr. McCay, that we – – I didn't want to create this position and this title.

Q. So, "being careful" means we can't do it?

A. Right.

Q. Why didn't you just say we can't do it?

A. I probably should have. E-mails are such that, you know, it is – – (Gilley, p.301-2).

Q. Dr. Gilley, let me ask you this. One last question, I guess, pertaining to Ms. Reed. In general, what were her qualifications for the these various positions that she was being considered for?

A. Well, I don't know that she was being considered for any position, but she was given temporary duty assignments in Dr. McKay's office and also in connection with my office and Dean Hered's office. (Gilley, p.303).

Q. Whatever position or positions she held at the University while she was here, in your opinion, was she qualified to hold those positions?

A. Well, in terms of her original and permanent position with the College of medicine, they determined that she was qualified to do that.

Q. All right. Did you ever make any determinations about what her qualifi cations were or were not?

A. No, I did not. (Gilley, p. 304).

Were Race and Sex Employment Factors For Gilley?

The issue at the heart of my litigation with Gilley was whether he intention-ally selected Mizell as General Counsel on the basis of her gender and whether he intentionally selected Robinson as Administrator and Vice President on the basis of race. When asked, "So, race and gender never entered your mind in making these decisions?" Gilley replied, "It was never a determining factor." (Dep. of Gilley, p.55).

With respect to Robinson Gilley testified that race was considered "as a positive factor, but not a determining factor." (Id. p. 56).

It would be my challenge to disprove these "denials" by demonstrating that Gilley's explanations for his employment actions were false or lacking in credibility–nothing more than a pretext for discriminatory conduct. Determination of credibility of witnesses and truth of numerous contradictory allegations of fact were matters to be decided by a jury. Could a jury have determined that Gilley's answers were deceptive–aimed at covering up illicit behavior? The federal court said no. Reach your own conclusion.

Chapter 102–Gilley "Wins"–Did the Courts Get it Right?

District Court Rules Gilley Protected by Qualified Immunity

On February 1, 2002 Duggan filed a "Motion to Determine Whether Defendant is entitled to Qualified Immunity." With the motion was filed a 61 page brief with supporting affidavits and deposition testimony. An opposing defense motion for summary judgment was filed a short time later.

Magistrate Phillips issued his 52-page "Memorandum Opinion" on September 30, 2002. In accordance with that ruling an Order was entered by the District Court the same date. Plaintiff's motion was denied; defendant's was granted. "This case and plaintiff's claims of reverse discrimination in violation of 42 U.S.C. SS 1981 and 1983, and under the THRA, Tenn. Code Ann. S 4-21-01, et. seq., are DISMISSED."

Phillips elected to accept Gilley's explanation for his employment actions. The Memorandum Opinion concluded with:

Gilley is entitled to qualified immunity in this case because Leadbetter cannot establish facts from which a reasonable jury could conclude that Gilley intended to discriminate against Leadbetter because he is white or male in the three challenged decisions. Gilley is also entitled to qualified immunity on the reverse race discrimination claims because he reasonably believed he could use race as a positive factor in Robinson's assignments/ job titles without violating the equal protection rights of whites. (Id. p.51).

The Court reached its conclusion by accepting the arguments and evidence presented by the defense. Plaintiff's evidence and arguments were rejected. As the Court observed, "Gilley emphasizes he did not make the actual decision to promote Mizell, nor did he have the authority to do so." (Id. p. 12). With respect to Robinson, the Court again accepted Gilley's testimony as true. "Gilley asserts he understood from his staff that 'people could be reassigned to other offices, you could give them additional duties, [and] you could change their job title consistent with their additional duties' [Gilley Dep. at 255-256]." (Id. p.14)

The Court accepted as true Gilley's testimony that he did not discriminate: "Gilley testified that he did not consider Mizell's gender in his recommendation to the trustees" (Id. p. 29) –not "even as a positive factor." (Id. p.30). "Gilley admits he viewed Robinson's race as a positive factor–but not a determining factor... " in assigning Robinson administrative duties. (Id. p.17). Then the Court bought Gilley's explanation for Robinson being named Vice President:

In Gilley's view, the core responsibilities of the position [of Vice President] were already being performed by the incumbent, Robinson. Since there was no vacancy, Gilley did not consider anyone else for Robinson's new job title and responsibilities. Even if he had considered others, Gilley had no reason to believe Leadbetter would be interested." (Id. p. 20).

Magistrate Phillips noted that under U.S. Supreme Court precedent "at least five categories of evidence may provide evidence of discriminatory intent: (1) Discriminatory impact where a clear pattern, unexplainable on grounds other than race, emerges from the effect of the action; (2) Historical background particularly if it reveals a series of official actions taken for invidious reasons; ... (4) Substantive and procedural changes, for example, where there are departures from the governmental entity's normal procedural and substantive standards; ...In addition, pretext, whereby the reasons proffered by the governmental decision–maker are found to be not credible or false, is relevant to show discriminatory intent." (Id. p. 24).

Despite Duggan's extensive, detailed presentation of contradictory testimony and other evidence, Phillips elected to accept Gilley's version. Quite disturbing to me was the fact that a jury was denied the opportunity to decide the facts of the case. A notice of appeal to the U.S. Court of Appeals for the Sixth Circuit was filed on October 17, 2002.

A 53 page appellate brief was filed by Duggan on my behalf. The brief concluded with "Plaintiff would show unto this Court that he has produced evidence of numerous genuine issues of material fact that would fall into the categories recognized by the United States Supreme Court ...that would allow a jury to find intentional discrimination ... ."(Proof Brief of Appellant, p.46).

Oral argument before the Sixth Circuit was set for March 10, 2004. I joined Duggan for the drive to Cincinatti the night before.

Appellate judges Eric Clay and Boyce Martin entered as the Court was called to order. I knew both to be very liberal in their approach to civil rights matters.

Not a good sign.

The third member of the three- judge panel was U.S. District Judge Richard Mills from Illinois, sitting by designation. I was unfamiliar with Judge Mills but only two votes were needed to affirm the challenged ruling below.

Duggan did a phenomenal job arguing the appeal, in my estimation. Still, after Court recessed we agreed prospects for the case did not appear to bode well.

On September 29, 2004 our foreboding proved to be well founded. The Court of Appeals affirmed, in a 3-0 ruling, the judgment below. (Ronald C. Leadbetter v. J. Wade Gilley, No. 02-6360, U.S. Court of Appeals, 6th Cir.)(Electronic Citation: 2004 FED App. 0329P (6th Cir.).

The Court of Appeals held that I failed to establish a "prima facie case of discrimination" both as to the sex discrimination claim involving the position of General Counsel and the race discrimination claim involving the positions of Equity and Diversity Administrator and Vice President of Equity and Diversity.

There was no denial by the Court of Appeals that the position of Vice President, General Counsel and Secretary required that the "successful [General Counsel] candidate must have the following minimum qualifications:... (4) experience in transactional matters and civil litigation."(.Id. p.3)(Emphasis added). However, the Court rejected my claim there was evidence Mizell did not meet the litigation requirements:

"There is no dispute that Leadbetter sought and was qualified for the General Counsel position. However, the District Court found that Leadbetter failed to establish a prima facie case of discrimination because he did not show that Gilley was the unusual employer who discriminates against men and because he failed to show that Gilley treated differently employees who were similarly situated but were not members of the protected class." (Id. p.10)

"Leadbetter tried to show that Gilley's reasons for hiring Mizell had no basis in fact by arguing that Mizell had absolutely no litigation experience. In Leadbetter's view, Mizell had no litigation experience because she did not take depositions and did not make court appearances. Leadbetter has a self–serving and narrow view of the phrase 'litigation experience.' Mizell's management of the general staff, oversight of attorneys' work, and authorship of the University's only successful petition for certiorari to the United States Supreme Court are very significant litigation experience, even if the experience was not earned in court. Leadbetter claimed that Mizell's qualifications did not actually motivate Gilley's decision to hire her since Gilley made up his mind to hire Mizell as soon as he heard that Brogan was retiring. While it appears that Gilley was interested in immediately naming Mizell as Brogan's successor once he learned of Brogan's intended retirement, Gilley wanted to do this because Mizell was qualified, competent, and could hit the ground running. Thus, Gilley had a legitimate nondiscriminatory reasons for hiring Mizell." (Id. 13).

With respect to the positions filled by Theotis Robinson the Court correctly observed that "Leadbetter never applied to be Equity and Diversity Administrator or Vice President of Equity and Diversity. He tries to overcome this problem by arguing that his failure to apply should be excused because he had no opportunity to do so." (Id. p.14). The Court then held:

"While Gilley and Leadbetter dispute whether the University was required to advertise the positions Robinson secured and whether the positions were even vacancies, Leadbetter has clearly failed to show that he would have applied had he known of the position. At best, Leadbetter states that he might have been interested in becoming Equity and Diversity administrator if he could have been paid more than the $55,000 Robinson earned in that capacity. This is a statement of general interest, it is not evidence that Leadbetter would have applied for the position. Furthermore, Leadbetter offers no evidence to show that the University had a blacks only hiring requirement that would have made his failure to apply fruitless.

In addition to his failure to apply, Leadbetter fails to show that he and Robinson were similarly situated candidates for the position of Vice President of Equity and I Diversity. The bulk of the vice president's responsibilities were those that Robinson had performed during eight months as Equity and Diversity Administrator. As such, Robinson had actual experience performing the vice president's duties. Leadbetter lacked that experience. This critical difference is enough to show that Robinson and Leadbetter were not similarly situated." (Id. pp. 15-16)

Perhaps the most interesting finding of the Court of Appeals–at least to me– was the following:

"Leadbetter held a lower position than Mizell at the General Counsel's office, and he had no experience as chief legal officer or first assistant to the chief. He had no experience working with the governing board of a multi – campus public university, and his academic credentials did not meet Mizell's academic achievements. Furthermore, he had been removed from responsibility for the Memphis litigation following a series of mishaps that included inadequate preparation and the presentation of perjured testimony." (Id. p.12).

I wondered if the Court of Appeals paid any attention at all to Gilley's own testimony on the insignificance of title and his admission that I had served as a "first assistant to the chief."

Contrary to the Court's finding, I had extensive experience working with the UT Board of Trustees. The commentary on my being removed from Memphis litigation bordered on the absurd; while *Skoutakis* was a litigation disaster from my viewpoint I was never removed from Memphis litigation.

The appeals court was correct in stating that Mizell's academic achievements exceeded mine (I was never editor of the UT Law Review and I am certain her grade point average exceeded mine). Had we been competing for a position in 1972 that might have made a difference. In 1999 Wade Gilley had knowledge of candidate qualifications far more indicative of ability to effectively serve as General Counsel–including my litigation grade–94% of cases resulted in wins!

I'll not reargue my case in the pages of this autobiographical history. My lawsuit against Gilley is long over. I'll leave any further assessment of the facts to you, the reader. You have been provided the same evidentiary testimony provided to the District Court and the Court of Appeals. How would you have ruled?

THE GILLEY LITIGATION REACHES CLOSURE

In early March, 2004, following the adverse ruling of the Sixth Court, David Duggan was appointed Circuit Judge in Blount County and subsequently elected to the position. Very well deserved in my opinion!

With Gilley out of the picture and my "counsel of record" unable to represent me any longer my passion for pursuing litigation against the University was greatly diminished.

Efforts to obtain new counsel were unsuccessful and not vigorously pursued in any event. An offer of monetary settlement from the University was rejected – I would not agree to sign any agreement to refrain from discussing the litigation. My separate action against UT was eventually non-suited.

In spring 2005 the Gilley litigation was marked by closure. Surprisingly, my University career continued in a positive direction, at least for me personally, as it had all along.

Chapter 103–The Eli Fly Interlude–A Sliver of Orange

The UT Board of Trustees voted to accept J. Wade Gilley's resignation as president of the University of Tennessee on June 1, 2001. That same day the Board voted to appoint Eli Fly Acting President. I viewed Fly as a man of integrity and felt he would turn the University back in the right direction. One of his first administrative actions evidenced a commitment to utilizing known expertise and proved commitment to the University.

With Acting President Eli Fly's replacement of Gilley there was indeed an immediate uptick in integrity within the UT system administration–at least temporarily. The good news was reported by the Knoxville News-Sentinel on September 7, 2001: "UT to tighten hiring policies." The subheading of the front page article read "Acting president endorses panel recommendations." Details included in the article:

People who want jobs at the University of Tennessee will undergo more rigorous background checks–including reviews of their credit histories in some cases–under recommendations endorsed this week by Acting President Eli Fly.

The changes come in the wake of the June resignations of President Dr. J. Wade Gilley and fast-rising administrator Pamela S. Reed."

The Sentinel reported, "On June 21 Fly named a six-member task force to examine UT hiring procedures and had received the task force's report the previous day. Among task force recommendations: A standardized form should be used to assure that campuses statewide verify applicants references, educational qualifications, licenses and certifications." (Id.p.A7.)

By memorandum of July 23, 2001 to all UT student affairs officers and UT Martin Chancellor Dr. Katie High, Fly addressed the subject of Student Affairs Coordination:

Please be advised that I have asked Vice President for Operations Philip Scheurer to assume the role of coordinating the work of our Chief Student Affairs Officers system wide. These duties were formerly performed by Dr. Katie High before Dr. High assumed her current role at U.T. Martin [as Chancellor].

As you know, Mr. Scheurer has over 30 years experience in Student Affairs matters – 15 of those years were spent as the Chief Student Affairs Officer at U. T. Knoxville. Mr. Scheurer is assuming these new duties in addition to current responsibilities for operations on the Knoxville Campus and oversight of the Capital Outlay/Capital Maintenance and Real Estate Management functions for the University System.

I am sure you will be hearing from him soon and thanks in advance for your continuing support of the University in this time of change.

c: President's staff
Mr. Ron Leadbetter
Vice President Philip Scheurer

Fly's memorandum signified to me his intent to return university management to officials of known expertise and integrity. Student affairs officers David Belote, Odell Horton, Jr., Richard McDougall, Al Pujol and Tim Rogers each met that criteria in my estimation. Clearly, intentions were good but time was woefully short for accomplishing needed administrative changes. Taking precedence was the search for a new UT president.

The November 6, 2001 edition of the Knoxville News-Sentinel spelled out the parameters of the the presidential search pursued by the UT Board of Trustees and Tennessee Governor Don Sundquist:

List of UT presidential candidates revealed soon

By David Keim

NASHVILLE–The first slate of candidates to be considered for the presidency of the University of Tennessee will be made public within two weeks, but finalists aren't expected until January.

"I don't have any idea who they are," Gov. Don Sundquist said Monday after a meeting of the presidential search committee at the executive residence.

Sundquist, who chairs the committee and UT's board, told UT officials to get the University ready for its next leader by disposing of pending litigation and addressing other potential distractions.

He asked Acting President Eli Fly to take responsibility for an "immediate action list" that includes the "Gilley Legacy."

Dr. J. Wade Gilley resigned abruptly June 1 after just 22 months on the job. Revelations of romantic involvement with a controversial, fast-rising ex-administrator followed.

"The only thing I know to do there is to tell the truth," Fly said.

Fly also said that the only litigation involving the presidency is a lawsuit filed against Gilley by a staff attorney who contends Gilley promoted women and minorities ahead of white males. (Id., p. B1).

There was a clearly expressed desire to eradicate problems associated with the "Gilley legacy." A commitment to integrity was expressed. My involvement with Gilley was not harped on–I was not even mentioned by name. Hope springs eternal!

Chapter 104–The Shumaker Presidency– "Go for Two!"

After the Gilley debacle the UT Board of Trustees surely would take measures to assure that the next presidential search would be open and thorough, taking extra precautions to avoid another selection faux pas. Not so! A 2- inch thick stack of news articles and investigative reports tell the sad story.

How it all began was described by the Knoxville News-Sentinel in a front-page article on Sunday, August 3, 2003:" Shumaker's ex-wife claims search rigged."

"After Gilley's resignation, a two-pronged search process to replace him was initiated by [Governor] Sundquist. One prong, which was assisted by a 25 member advisory Council drawn from UT constituent groups, openly recruited candidates and produced [Marlene] Strathe, provost and vice president of academic affairs at the University of Northern Colorado, as a finalist.

The second prong was led by search consultant Bill Funk of Korn/ Ferry International, who was paid $90,000 to privately seek out active university presidents who might be suitable for UT. Shumaker, then president of the University of Louisville, was the only candidate to emerge from Funk's efforts.

The trustee panel picked Shumaker after grilling both candidates in a session that was broadcast live via the Internet. Critics of the process openly doubted whether the public arm of the search effort had ever been meant to generate viable candidates and pointed out that none of the candidates who emerged from the public pool had any experience as a college president." (Id. p.A21).

In late February 2002, I learned Shumaker had been selected by the UT Board of Trustees to serve as UT's next president. He would be making an introductory presentation at the University Center auditorium on the evening of March 6.

Several days before Shumaker's scheduled presentation, I made a phone call to Julie Hermann (former UT head volleyball coach, serving as senior associate athletic director for the University of Louisville at the time of my call). Our conversation proved to be enlightening – a week or two later after the call.

At the beginning of our conversation I queried Julie, "It looks like your president, John Shumaker, is going to be the next UT president… what can you tell me about him? Her response was encouraging. "Oh, he and his wife Lucy are great. Lucy and I are best friends – we go out running together every morning. Lucy is so excited to be going to Knoxville and the University of Tennessee."

Julie then added that there was a possibility she would be joining her friend and returning to Knoxville. I sensed genuine excitement in Julie's voice at that prospect

I attended the March 6 presentation by Shumaker in the University Center auditorium. Shumaker made a fine presentation. He certainly sounded like presidential material.

After the presentation Shumaker began greeting folks and shaking hands. I made my way down front to greet him. "Dr. Shumaker, I understand that we have a mutual friend–Louisville associate athletic director Julie Hermann."

Shumaker turned quickly toward his wife–who was standing 10 or 15 feet away–and shouted "Lucy, Lucy this gentleman knows Julie Hermann!" With that, Shumaker's wife walked over and engaged me in animated conversation about how much she thought of Julie Hermann and what great friends they were.

John Shumaker turned to greet other well-wishers as I completed my conversation with his wife and offered congratulations on coming to UT. She thanked me, appearing sincerely eager to move with her husband to Knoxville.

The UT Board of Trustees approved John Shoemaker's appointment as president on March 5, 2002. UT was getting not only an acclaimed educator as president but also an esteemed associate–his wife.

A few days later the bombshell dropped. Shumaker had filed for divorce. I sensed the University had been duped–once again. But, at least UT had a president–someone who would lead the University in its drive for excellence.

On August 24, 2002 the Knoxville News-Sentinel carried the front-page headline, "UT chief's pay 2nd in U.S." The article following disclosed that "University of Tennessee President John W. Shumaker is the second–highest-paid public university chief in the nation, according to a new report." His salary of $733,550 was second only to that of the $787,319 salary of the president of the University of Texas system. The third highest paid public university chief executive at the University of Michigan, earned only $677,500 (Id.). Shumaker earned $143,550 more than the next highest paid public university president in the Southeast conference. (Id.).

With this news came a saying that floated around the University community, "You get what you pay for." Assuming the truth of that statement, the University was on its way to excellence. UT paid the private search firm of Korn/Ferry International $90,000 for its work.

Chapter 105–Here We Go Again–
First Evidence of Shumaker Corruption

During the "Big Orange " era UT employees were fired for stealing toilet tissue, pilfering cash from cash registers and using UT motor pool vehicles for personal travel. UT officials went to prison for misappropriating UT property and paid UT punitive damages, as well as compensation, for their misdeeds. A coach was fired for lying. With a new era standards changed.

In 2002, UT pilot Steve Rogers was directed to fly an empty UT airplane to Birmingham, Alabama to pick up a female passenger he referred to as "President Shumaker's girlfriend, Carol Garrison." Garrison was a former official at the University of Louisville while Shumaker was president and was now president of the University of Alabama at Birmingham.

I later learned from Rogers that he had made a number of trips to Birmingham and Louisville for Shumaker -and sometimes Garrison. Rogers expressed his concern with the propriety of what was being done. I expressed my concurrence with his concern.

In the clear absence of any internal controls over Shumaker's access to UT aircraft, the use of the airplane in question continued for a period of time. Finally the news media caught on. Knoxville reporter Gene Paterson, with WATE 6, was one of the first to report on the growing scandal. State Senator Tim Burchett from Knox County was one of the first political leaders to become involved. Change was afoot by Spring 2003.

News reports on the Shumaker scandal mushroomed–yielding me a two- inch stack of copies of some of those reports. The following excerpt from "Wikipedia" provides a fair summary of Shumaker's misdeeds:

"The first allegations were made in June of that year [2003] when Knoxville, Tennessee news media reported that the University had paid for his personal travel on a university–owned airplane. Shumaker eventually reimbursed the University more than $30,000 (more than $5,000 in July, followed by more than $25,000 the following month) for his personal airplane use. In July 2003, additional questions arose regarding personal expenses that Shumaker had charged to a university credit card, a $300,000 consulting contract that the university had established with a Washington, D. C. attorney who was a long time friend and business partner of Shumaker's without going through a bidding process, and a revelation that Shumaker had failed to tell the University that he was serving as trustee of a college in Greece. In August, it was publicly revealed that in 1995 and 1996, shortly after serving as president of Central Connecticut State University, Shumaker had received $10,000 in personal payments from Hyundai, apparently related to a $110,000 contract he had signed with Hyundai to train students at the Connecticut school. He submitted his resignation on August 8, 2003, following public request for his resignation from at least one state senator and a member of the university's board of trustees, as well as a public statement by Tennessee Governor Phil Bredesen that the controversy was hurting the University.

After Shumaker's departure from the University of Tennessee, all three of the universities where he had been President undertook audits of his spending during his presidencies. The University of Tennessee found that Shumaker had incurred $165,000 in expenses for football–related entertainment and $73,000 in expenses for holiday receptions. He also ordered $493,000 in renovations and new furnishings for his official residence, which had been remodeled at a cost of $787,597 less than a year earlier. His unauthorized purchases for the home included $97,350 for a new sun room and closet, $77,270 to create two bedrooms for his sons, a new telecommunications system that cost $64,000, a $7,000 Persian rug, two $7,400 entertainment systems, and a $4,822 gas grill.

Officials in Connecticut deemed the Hyundai payments to be a violation of the state's ethics laws, but could not prosecute because of the statute of limitations.

Shumaker claimed severance pay under his employment contract with the University of Tennessee. Initially he asked for about $420,000 and at one time claimed that he was owed as much as $1.7 million, but eventually he received $175,000 after reaching a settlement with the University in January 2009." ("John Shumaker", Wikipedia, January 31, 2014 search result). (Citations omitted).

The second group of expenditures might be categorized as wasteful spending or simply poor work performance–by those looking to cut the President a little slack. Shumaker was just a wasteful spender was what his defenders wanted the public to believe.

However, the first group of expenditures contained activity falling clearly within the category of "misappropriation of state property"–"gross misconduct" under University of Tennessee personnel policies and procedures.

I'll not review further the sordid tale of a corrupt presidency except to the extent I had personal knowledge and involvement. I had no personal contact with Shumaker–aside from fleeting encounters at public events and passing in the hall–after our initial meeting at the University Center Auditorium.

However, I had plenty of contact with others. On February 18, 2003, I took a deposition in Nashville, then had lunch at Amerigo's with Lisa Atkins, a former attorney in the OGC. Next, I visited State Senator Tim Burchett in his office at Legislative Plaza. I shared with him a few concerns about illicit activities at the University.

The front page headline of the August 9, 2003 Knoxville News-Sentinel read "UT again leaderless." The sub headline read, "Controversy leads Shumaker to quit."

Almost four full pages of newsprint spelled out the details. I thought UT Trustee Lynn Johnson summarized it best:

"Trustee D. Lynn Johnson said the reputation of UT and the board of trustees has been damaged. 'We have to begin restoring both of those,' he said. 'I think the board has a lot of work to do in front of us, and it's not isolated to picking an interim president to restore the credibility of the university and the credibility of the board,' he said." (Id. p. A6).

As already indicated, Shumaker's extravagant spending and misappropriation of state property–and funds–was detailed in wide ranging news reports and is readily accessible to readers through a Web search. I focus attention only on a narrow sliver of reporting that drew little public attention and no corrective measures.

WHERE WAS UNIVERSITY LEGAL COUNSEL WHILE DISASTER WAS BREWING?

The *Courier–Journal*, a Louisville, Kentucky daily paper, carried an Associated Press release in its August 11, 2003 issue, "UT trustees: search on Shumaker lacked data." Details followed:

"Tennessee officials say that when they signed a $90,000 contract with search consultant Bill Funk to find a new president, they expected him to conduct thorough background checks.

But UT trustees say there is no mention in Funk's background check of the Kentucky marriage license that Shumaker applied for in 1995 to help a Chinese woman obtain a U. S. visa.

UT trustees also say they were not briefed about the controversy surrounding the University of Louisville foundation, a nonprofit entity established to accept private donations from individuals and businesses on behalf of the school.

The trustees say Funk and his search firm failed to mention that Shumaker and the foundation were involved in a legal battle with the Courier–Journal which sued to force it to open its records to the public.

'All of this information is something that any decent private investigator could've found out,' [Tennessee State Senator Tim] Burchett told the Knoxville News-Sentinel. 'I think the trustees acted on the best information they had, and clearly they wouldn't have made this decision if all this had been revealed to them.'

Trustee Andrea Loughry said she asked UT attorneys to review the background check performed by Funk's company, Korn/Ferry International."

The August 14, 2003 edition of the Knoxville News-Sentinel carried the following front-page headlines: "People will be mad," "Shumaker spending 'questionable'" and "Audit finds what Governor calls 'generalized failure of controls' at UT." Details of an audit report released by UT's internal auditing department "listed numerous violations of UT policy and identified $31,885.75 in 'questionable' expenditures." (Id.).

There was blame to go around but I'll focus on the area I was familiar with–the role of legal counsel.

"I think this audit's going to be the tip of the iceberg," [Senator Tim] Burchett said. "They need to get back to teaching Tennesseans and paying people a decent wage. Clearly, they are not in the mission of being a land grant institution, and any time we veer from that path we're are going to have trouble. The only solution to this is more disclosure on the part of higher education." (Id.)

He added: "The underlying fact is no one is advising them legally on what is right and what is wrong. Apparently, the only advice they're getting is telling them ways to get around the law." (Id. p.A13).

Where was UT's legal leadership during the developing disaster and what role did the General Counsel play? The August 15, 2003 audit hinted at the answer in reviewing a conflict of interest finding involving a man who served as one of three incorporators of a company doing business in China–John and Lucy Shumaker being the other two:

"Mr. Fishman's July 23[2002] letter was subsequently referred to Ms. Catherine Mizell, University General Counsel. Ms. Mizell stated since Mr. Fishman was an attorney she was under the impression that he would provide legal services associated with the development of the high school in Beijing and drafted an agreement with him accordingly. Ms. Mizell explained that her office did not have expertise in creating a corporation or other legal entity in China under Chinese law. If Mr. Fishman had not been required to perform these legal services, the University would have needed to hire additional legal counsel with expertise in foreign transactions. Ms. Mizell's draft indicates Mr. Fishman would provide all the legal services required for the project, including negotiating and drafting or reviewing any agreements or other legal documents required. Ms. Mizell stated her draft was forwarded to Dr. Shumaker and she did not see the final executed contract." (Id.p.21).

The UT audit disclosed serious concerns regarding a related contract between UT and a Chinese institution:

"On October 8, 2002, Dr. Shumaker signed an agreement between the University and Beijing Bohua Foreign Language School to establish a Sino–U.S. high school in Beijing and to examine offering graduate degree programs in China.

Because some of the discussion about this project involved an ownership interest, which according to the General Counsel's Office, the University was prohibited from holding, Dr. Shumaker decided to pursue the proposal through the University of Tennessee Foundation. University and foundation officials made a trip to China in January 2003 to discuss this matter.

Mr. Philip Scheurer, vice president for operations, was ultimately designated as the University's lead person for the project and took responsibility for developing a business plan for the school. Mr. Scheurer stated he did not feel comfortable that Mr. Fishman had performed adequate due diligence regarding the Chinese business partners. He said he had a difficult time obtaining financial data from Bohua and had little knowledge of the partners' backgrounds. He also stated Mr. Fishman was not completely familiar with applicable Chinese laws and additional legal expertise was needed. Therefore, Mr. Scheurer stated he asked Mr. Fishman to identify and retain a Chinese lawyer whose services were billed through Mr. Fishman's contract with the University." (Audit, p. 23).

Scheurer was, in my opinion–based on my long experience of working with him as a University administrator–highly capable and a person of integrity. He was not an attorney. In my estimation, University legal counsel should have been intricately involved in addressing legal issues surrounding the entire China project and was not. The audit made clear that sound legal review of the contract would have avoided serious and costly problems for the University:

CONCLUSIONS OF THE AUDIT

"The contract with Mr. Fishman was improperly classified as a legal services contract. Although Mr. Fishman provided legal services, including an understanding of various Chinese legal requirements and government regulations, it appears that most of the services provided related to a specific educational partnership proposal." (Audit, pp. 23-24).

Presumably, an attorney skilled in handling transactional matters–including contract review–would know that.

Shumaker's questionable use of UT aircraft was another matter warranting the attention of UT legal counsel. That matter also was addressed by the UT audit:

"Dr. Shumaker admitted that some of his air travel expenses incurred by the university were for personal reasons, generally trips to Louisville related to his divorce and trips to Birmingham to visit Dr. Carol Garrison, president of the University of Alabama at Birmingham (UAB), and other friends. Also, he said his personal travel usually was an extension of business travel. University travel policy states individuals combining business and personal travel will be reimbursed the lesser of actual expenses incurred or the amount that would have been incurred for the business portion only. ... No written or unwritten policy at the University allows personal use of the University airplane.

Past presidents Dr. Joseph Johnson and Mr. Emerson Fly stated they were not aware of any president using the airplane for personal reasons." (Audit, pp. 6-7).

The audit noted 14 trips on which "Dr. Shumaker combined personal and business travel in a manner that appeared to result in additional cost to the University." (Audit, p.8). Several trips were purely personal and contained no business-related component.

UT auditors concluded: "The analysis of air travel indicated that 18 trips by Dr. Shumaker were either personal or included personal segments that resulted in an estimated additional cost of $14,491.46 to the University. " (Audit, p.13).

Was UT counsel aware of Shumaker's questionable use of unity aircraft? If so, what action was taken by UT counsel to address the issue? Let's see what the record reveals.

Chapter 106–Add Lying to the Charges Against Shumaker

"More of Shumaker's spending comes under scrutiny; UT's top brass grilled" was the title of the report published by Knox News.com on August 22, 2003:

> UT's chief auditor, Mark Paganelli, told the Fiscal Review Committee [of the State legislature] that key information was apparently withheld from Shumaker's personal calendars that were turned over earlier this summer as part of an inquiry into his travels.
>
> "Shumaker was untruthful about sharing a motel room with Carol Garrison, president of the University of Alabama at Birmingham, during a trip to Texas last December," Paganelli said.
>
> During a five-hour hearing, several of UT's highest–ranking officials were apologetic and conceded they should have done something different to address Shumaker's activities. They testified that they were essentially helpless to stop Shumaker.
>
> "A separate set of calendars was found after Shumaker's Aug. 8 resignation when his office and Andy Holt Tower was being cleaned out," Paganelli said. "An auditor was standing by as the office was emptied of Shumaker's personal effects and the calendars were found on his desk."
>
> "They were not what was given to us," Paganelli said, adding that the calendars found on the desk contain information about trips to Birmingham, Ala., and Little Rock, Ark., that had previously been unavailable to auditors.

Several top UT officials took personal responsibility for the lack of oversight. The General Counsel was not among them.

According to the Knox News.com report :"[Chief of Staff Cathy] Cole, [Vice President for Business and Finance Sylvia]Davis, [Vice President and Treasurer Butch]Peccolo and [Vice President Phil] Scheurer each testified that they didn't contact UT trustees with their concerns because Shumaker had informed them at a staff meeting that they weren't supposed to have any private contact with trustees except through his office." Once again, there was no input from UT's General Counsel.

Rep. Donna Rowland, R- Murfreesboro, said Shumaker's behavior appeared to be "fraud or embezzlement" and wanted to know how UT could assure the public that future presidents won't abuse their position. "We've never had this problem before," she said. "That's a good question," Paganelli replied. (Id.)

The question of how to address fraud or embezzlement on the part of University officials was one previously addressed by the UT Office of General Counsel. Personally, I had no doubt as to the course of action to be taken in the present case. However, I was not asked.

On August 22, 2003, Tennessean.com, reported: "UT trustees give Shumaker

$422,956 severance package." Tennessean.com further reported that while the trustees voted unanimously to give Shumaker a severance package in that amount, "Some legislators said the severance was absurd in light of Shoemaker's spending practices." The article also said, "Tennessee Governor Phil Bredesen sided with the trustees–at least temporarily."

On September 4, 2003 Knox News reported that the "List of witnesses tentatively scheduled to appear today before the legislature's fiscal review committee" included "Catherine Mizell: UT vice president and the school's chief legal counsel. She had initially been scheduled to appear today but has instead provided a letter explaining Shumaker's severance package, officials said."

Nashville's "News 2", reporting the legislative Fiscal Review Committee's proceedings, included the following exchange:

"Questions were raised this summer about Shumaker's use of a state plane and making extravagant renovations to the UT president's home at a time of state budget cuts and higher tuition. The former president's chief of staff was grilled about who should have blown the whistle.

UT presidential chief-of-staff Dr. Cathy Cole said, 'Well, I said last time and I'll say it again today, I apologize. I think it was all of our responsibility.'" (Chris Bundgaard for News 2 , 9.4.03)

6 News Reporter Steve Gelbach , WATE. com also covered the proceedings in Nashville. With reference to Mizell's letter–since she did not appear in person–Gehlbach reported:

"UT's chief attorney Catherine Mizell said the Board of Trustees agreed to pay Shumaker's severance to avoid a lawsuit.

If Shumaker had sued over his contract, the University could have been tied up in court for more than a year and had to pay him $1.7 million. Instead, officials decided on a $423,000 settlement to cut ties with Shumaker for good."

(WATE.com Sept.4, 2003)

Amazing! The president lies, cheats and steals and the victim of the misdeeds, the University of Tennessee, is worried about a breach of contract! In my extensive experience handling such matters I took the position, consistent with settled law, that gross misconduct trumps any employment contract or buyout arrangement.

Fortunately, others also disagreed with the General Counsel's reasoning. On October 13, 2003 the Chronicle of Higher Education headlined "U. of Tennessee Rescinds Former President's $423,000 Severance Package." The article explained the reason:

"The University of Tennessee Board of Trustees voted unanimously Friday to rescind a $422,956 severance package that had been negotiated with the University's former president, John W. Shumaker, who resigned in August. The vote came a day after the state comptroller's office released a report stating that Mr. Shumaker had abused university credit cards and misled the university's internal auditors."

The 96 page report issued by the Tennessee Comptroller of the Treasury on October 9, 2003, did not–in my estimation–add a great deal to the report issued by UT auditors although additional evidence of Shumaker's dishonesty was documented. There was, in my opinion, sufficient evidence alluded to in the audit report to warrant immediate termination of Shumaker's UT employment for gross misconduct.

An introductory letter, addressed by Comptroller of the Treasury, John Morgan, to Governor Bredesen, the UT Board of Trustees, members of the General Assembly and UT President Joe Johnson, concluded with a criticism of UT's upper management:

"According to staff, since there was no one in the position of Vice President for Business, there was no one to see the "bigger picture." However, this should not be considered an excuse for upper management's failure to appropriately react to Dr. Shumaker's improper actions. In terms of operational realities, it does not appear that there was such a high degree of compartmentalization on the part of upper–level staff that they were really unable to see problems with Dr. Shumaker's actions. Rather, the situation was such that there was no one in the administrative staff who felt secure enough in his or her position to hold Dr. Shumaker accountable for violations of policy and unbridled spending and, perhaps more importantly, senior staff did not appear to realize the significance of the problems.

A fourth circumstance that contributed to the failure of university officials to promptly disclose inappropriate activity on the part of the president was lack of effective channels to communicate concerns to the Board of Trustees. Upper management indicated that Dr .Shumaker had instructed them that no one was to communicate with board members except through his office. Additional weaknesses were that the Board of Trustees lacked an audit committee and that the university's internal audit staff reported directly to the president. Combining these factors with a mind–set that difficulties should be resolved within the UT community rather than being publicized meant that Dr. Shumaker was not restricted in his activities and his improper acts were not disclosed and addressed at the time they occurred."

The special report detailed several matters that brought the role of the office of UT General Counsel under fire:

"For the year ended June 30, 2003, the University's General Counsel identified ten contracts for legal services, all of which had been obtained through a non-–competitive bidding process. The contract with Mr. Charles Fishman was one of the 10 identified.

State auditors contacted the Board of Professional Responsibility and determined that Mr. Fishman was not licensed to practice law in Tennessee. When asked about his lack of a license to practice law in the state of Tennessee, Ms. Catherine Mizell, UT General Counsel, stated that there was no conclusive answer as to whether Mr. Fishman could be considered to have practiced law in Tennessee. She stated that from her perspective, Mr. Fishman was a lawyer in Washington, D.C., and was handling transactions in China. However, Mr. Fishman was in Knoxville for nine days of his contract.

The contract with Mr. Fishman stands in sharp contrast to the other contracts the University had for legal services during the period in question. Thirdly, neither the finalized contract nor the amendments to the contract were reviewed by the University's legal counsel.

Mr. Fishman had already claimed to have provided services for two months before his July 23 letter to Dr. Shumaker outlining their agreement. In his letter, Mr. Fishman agreed to be available to consult with the University and with third parties on behalf of the University. After receiving this letter, Dr. Shumaker referred it to Ms. Sylvia Davis, Vice President of Budget and Finance, who apparently forwarded it to UT's legal staff. According to Ms. Mizell, once she received Mr. Fishman's July 23, 2002, letter, she drafted a proposed contract for legal services. Ms. Mizell's draft left no doubt that this was a contract for legal service. ... Ms. Mizell sent the draft contract to the president's office.

Regarding the contract with Mr. Fishman, [UT treasurer] Mr. Peccolo stated that it was anything but routine. The normal process for such contracts was for the General Counsel of the University to request the additional legal services and identify the vendor or to provide the services." (Special report, pp.7-8).

Based on these findings the Comptroller offered the following recommendation: "University officials need to remember that they cannot avoid responsibility by out- sourcing certain functions. For example, if the university seeks legal services, which obviously must involve the university's rights and obligations, the work obtained should be under the auspices of the university's internal legal staff and should be reviewed adequately by the university's legal staff." (Special Report, p. 12).

Many other instances of misconduct by Shumaker were described in the special report, as were related oversight failures by upper-level university administrators–including UT's General Counsel. One of the last matters addressed pertained to UT plane flights and falsification of University records relating to those flights:

"For purposes of illustration, the calendars discovered in Dr. Shumaker's office after he had resigned will be referred to as "Calendar A" because they reflect the original unaltered information. The calendars initially provided to the media and to the University's internal auditors will be referred to as "Calendar B," because they reflect deleted information. … .

Our comparison between Calendar A and Calendar B disclosed that Dr. Shumaker apparently substantially revised Calendar A by deleting almost all references to his travel to Birmingham and Louisville." (Special report, p. 46)

The Comptroller further found, regarding personal plane trips, "We determined that Dr. Shumaker evidently was less than truthful when he stated that all his trips were primarily business-related and that any of his personal travel would have been "embedded" with his overall business travel. The UT internal audit report and our review disclosed four occasions where his travel appeared to be wholly or primarily personal in nature." (Special Report, p. 49).

Toward the conclusion of the body of the special report, the Comptroller found: "Clearly several members of upper management knew about some of Dr. Shumaker's questionable activities but failed to take effective action, including notifying the board of their concerns. In light of the problems surrounding Dr. Shumaker's activities, it is imperative that the Board takes steps to create a system in which upper management, including internal audit, can more easily bring issues to the attention of the Board and that the Board members, collectively and individually, assume a more active oversight role in the activities of the university's upper management, particularly in the areas of honesty, integrity, and compliance with internal controls." (Special Report, p. 55).

Comptroller Morgan concluded his cover letter for the special report with notice that "The matters discussed in this report have been referred to the Office of the Attorney General, and where applicable, to the District Attorney General for the 6th judicial District (Knox County)." (Special report, p.5).

Neither the UT audit report nor the special report of the State Comptroller directly attacks the role of UT General Counsel. Yet that was the one position in the UT administration that was directly responsible to the Board of Trustees. Even Gilley "fully understood that this was a position that reported to the Board" (Dep. of Gilley, p 133).

Chapter 107–Role of the General Counsel in the Shumaker Travesty

What should the General Counsel have done in handling the Shumaker travesty? Years earlier I was provided the answer to that question by the General Counsel for the University of South Carolina.

In late July 1990, I flew to Columbia, South Carolina on UT business. I joined Gwen Fuller, a former law clerk in the UT Office of General Counsel for dinner at California Dreaming.

The next day I had lunch with my friend Paul Ward, General Counsel for the University of South Carolina, and Dr. Paul Hurray, a past member of the University of Tennessee faculty. Ward and I were friends from participating in various NACUA seminars and other activities (and Ward later served as president of NACUA during 1996–97).

After lunch Ward provided me a tour of the USC campus. As we visited, a sensitive topic came up. The highly paid and lavish spending president of USC, Dr. James Holderman, had just resigned amid charges of financial impropriety. How did Holderman's issues affect Ward?

Ward shared with me that he had learned of Holderman's improprieties and was faced with a choice: do nothing or report the president's misconduct to the Board of Trustees. He recognized that if he took the latter course his job would likely be in jeopardy.

Ward did the right thing–he fulfilled his duty as legal counsel to the Board of Trustees and reported the president's misconduct to the Board. The president was removed and Ward retained his position as General Counsel (leaving in 1991 to take the position of General Counsel at Arizona State University). I learned years later that Ward received a national award for promoting morality and institutional integrity in higher education. He certainly deserved it.

There is no question in my mind that UT's General Counsel should have promptly reported any knowledge of misconduct by Shumaker to the Board of Trustees. She was either unaware of what many others–including myself– knew or she simply failed to inform the Board of Trustees of information she had. Or perhaps the Board ignored what she disclosed. There may have been a combination of those three possibilities. To my knowledge the issue has ever been addressed by Mizell or anyone else.

On January 21, 2004, Tennessean.com headlined "Knox DA will not prosecute Shumaker." According to Tennessean.com:

"University of Tennessee trustees said yesterday it was time to move on after Knox County's District Attorney General decided not to prosecute former UT President John W. Shumaker.

Randy Nichols, the 6th Judicial Circuit's top prosecutor, wrote in a letter to state Comptroller John Morgan that his office had found no evidence of crimes by Shumaker. Shumaker resigned in August after about 14 months on the job, over questions about his spending of state money, including his use of the UT airplane, extravagant purchases for his official residence and expensive parties.

State auditors, who work in Morgan's office, reported in October that Shumaker might have broken four state laws by altering calendars he submitted to UT auditors to conceal personal trips; lying to auditors about a hotel stay in San Antonio, Texas, and taking personal trips on the UT plane or on commercial and charter flights paid for by the university."

Nichols acknowledged that Shumaker was 'less than forthcoming upon initial questioning, particularly relating to personal travel.' But, he continued, 'This conduct, although disappointing in a university president, does not fit the criteria for criminal conduct under the statutes mentioned above.'" (Tennessean.com Wednesday 1/21/04, by Michael Cass, Staff Writer)

The standard for successful prosecution of criminal charges is "proof beyond a reasonable doubt" - a very high standard. Successful prosecution of administrative charges of gross misconduct requires only that a disciplinary charges be proved by a "preponderance of the evidence"–more evidence supporting a charge than not.

Although the District Attorney General concluded there was a lack of sufficient evidence to meet the high standard for criminal prosecution of Shumaker, he and his staff spent more than four months reviewing the evidence and reaching that decision. There was ample evidence of wrongdoing–just not enough to justify criminal charges.

In fact, there was an abundance of evidence supporting administrative charges of gross misconduct against Shumaker. Misappropriation of University aircraft for personal use and falsification of university records alone would have supported a charge of gross misconduct and a penalty of job termination.

There is no doubt in my mind that an inexperienced lawyer fresh out of law school could have successfully prosecuted administrative charges against Shumaker. The evidence supporting administrative charges of gross misconduct was overwhelming! A "contested case" hearing in accordance with the administrative procedures act offered an excellent opportunity to bring the entire Shumaker debacle to closure – at no cost to the University (aside from minimal costs associated with the administrative process itself).

For some reason, incomprehensible to me, the University elected not to take the initiative and fire Shumaker for gross misconduct. Instead, it was Shumaker who took action, filing suit in August 2004 against the University for breach of his employment contract.

"Former UT president sues state for breach of contract

Former University of Tennessee President John Shumaker on Thursday filed a claim against the state asking for at least $425,000 for breach of his employment contract.

Shumaker, who resigned a year ago amid controversy over his financial dealings, may actually be entitled to $1.7 million or more, said Dan Warlick, his newly retained Nashville attorney.

Warlick cited a 2003 memo by Catherine Mizell, UT General Counsel, stating that amount would be required to buy out Shumaker's original contract."

(KnoxNews.com, by Tom Humphreys, August, 27, 2004)

Shumaker's suit was filed with the Tennessee Division of Claims Administration on August 26, 2004 and transferred to the Tennessee Claims Commission on November 24, 2004. Damages in the amount of $423,000 were demanded for alleged breach of contract, a contract Shumaker claimed was "negotiated and ratified in August 2003."(John W. Shumaker v. State of Tennessee, Claims Commission No. D20500301, Claims Commission of the State of Tennessee, Eastern Grand Division).

Vance Cheek was the presiding Commissioner. Assistant Attorneys General Kevin Steiling and Steven McCloud served as defense counsel for the State (the University of Tennessee).

Motions to dismiss and for summary judgment were filed on behalf of the State. On June 3, 2005, Commissioner Cheek issued an "Order Denying Defendant's Motion to Dismiss. " In his order, Cheek noted that the University of Tennessee and Shumaker had entered into a written contract of employment on May 9, 2002. (Order,p.2).

A little more than a year later, on August 7, 2003, Shumaker met with Governor Bredesen and UT Board Vice Chairman Clayton McWherter and tendered his resignation effective August 8, 2004. (Id.). In a special session held August 21, 2003 the UT Board met and adopted a resolution approving severance payment to Shumaker in the amount of $249,800. (Id.).

The State (UT) audit report was issued on October 9, 2003 and the Board voted on October 10 to rescind the August 21 approval of a severance payment. (Id. p.3)

Commissioner Cheek rejected the State's motion for summary judgment for lack of jurisdiction (Id. p.4), finding that Shumaker had sufficiently alleged the existence of documents incorporated into his employment contract. (Id. p.8). Then the Commissioner noted there were only six possible means by which Shumaker's employment could be terminated. (Id. p.9)

According to the Commission, "Subsection H is the only reference the Commission can find in the agreement regarding the mutual negotiation of Dr. Shumaker's termination. Subsection H states simply 'the Board and Dr. Shumaker may reach a mutual agreement for termination of this agreement at any time prior to the expiration of the term.'" (Id. p.10). It was Commissioner Cheek's conclusion that the "negotiated terms of the mutual termination agreement must be incorporated into the original agreement as if set forth verbatim therein."(Id.). In other words the Board's deal with Shumaker to pay him a "buyout" following his resignation became part of his employment contract.

Commissioner Cheek also noted that one of the other six bases for contract termination, set forth in "Subsection E," was "for cause" which "refers generally to "unsatisfactory performance, breach of the agreement, willful misconduct, gross misconduct, and/or criminal activity." (Id.p.10). Subsection E provided that in the event of termination "for cause" Shumaker "shall not be entitled to further salary, fringe benefits, perquisites, or any other form of compensation." (Id).

Incredibly, the UT General Counsel failed to invoke (or advise the Board to invoke) subsection E as soon as there was sound evidence of Shumaker's willful or gross misconduct—and that evidence dated back at least to June 2003, well before Mizell spoke of the advantages of a $423,000 buyout.

Shumaker's claim was ultimately settled for $175,000 in January 2009. That was a considerable saving over the $423,000 Mizell considered a good settlement offer in 2003. But it was a disastrous waste of time and money and a public relations nightmare which could have been avoided by terminating Shumaker for "gross misconduct" in 2003. It was the UT General Counsel who bore responsibility for failing to make that call.

Chapter 108–Redirection in the Office of General Counsel

With the January 2000 replacement of Beauchamp Brogan by Catherine Mizell, as General Counsel, came dramatic changes in the operation of the UT office of General Counsel.

As a general rule, Brogan had taken an "open door" approach to management, assuring accessibility to others, including staff. The actual door to his office was generally open. In contrast, Mizell habitually kept her door closed. It was understood within the office that meetings with her should be scheduled in advance. Neither co-workers nor "outsiders" dropped by "just to say hi." There were exceptions for the President, Trustees and others of sufficient standing.

When Brogan entered the office each morning his cheerful greeting was infectious; Mizell preferred a quiet entry utilizing a back hallway, avoiding the main entrance and rarely exchanging pleasantries of the day. Different personalities? For certain. And a harbinger of decline in office camaraderie that existed under Brogan.

Office staff meetings and occasional retreats offered invaluable opportunities for staff attorneys and the General Counsel to interact and discuss vital policy and legal matters in depth. A sound and successful management approach was utilized by Brogan! Mizell's was distinctly different.

In a May 22, 2000 e-mail Mizell notified OGC staff attorneys, "My schedule is subject to frequent and last–minute changes these days, so I am suspending weekly staff meetings for a while, perhaps until after the June Board meeting. If anyone needs to meet with me, please ask Joan to get you on my calendar. Thanks for your patience."

We never had weekly staff meetings - at most they were monthly. Monthly meetings went to none following Mizell's memorandum. The next office staff meeting was held on February 16, 2006–nearly six years after issuance of the May 22, 2000 memorandum!

Brogan celebrated his 70th birthday with a cookout at his home on July 24, 1999. All attorneys in the office were invited. Holiday celebrations and other special events for office staff were important to Brogan.

Social interaction between the General Counsel and office staff diminished with the change in leadership. Mizell rarely attended luncheons and dinners hosted by office staff at their homes. She never hosted such events herself.

With the change in leadership came staffing changes. In more than two decades under Brogan's leadership incoming staff attorneys rarely left. With Mizell's arrival a number of fine attorneys I had helped train in litigation exited.

Memphis attorney Sarah Hall left in July, 2000. Lisa Atkins left in October of the same year. Memphis attorney Odell Horton, Jr. left around the same time.

By memorandum of December 13, 2000, Mizell introduced to the Knoxville staff attorneys "New Staff in Memphis." Two attorneys, Tom McAlexander and Tanda Grisham, were hired on "full time, limited duration appointment, subject to continuation for a maximum of three years."

Two other attorneys were hired on a "part-time (20 hours per week), term appointment expected to last no more than one year." That limited term appointment approach did not strike me as a mechanism for developing teamwork within the office or promoting networking within the University community.

Alan Parker left UT for UT-Battelle in July 2001. A serious loss for the University in my judgment.

Tanda Grisham, one of Mizell's hires, left in the fall of 2003. A November 25, 2003, e-mail circulating among OGC attorneys and the State Board of Regents read: "Another UT attorney bites the dust."

A new deputy general counsel, Peter Foley, was hired in February 2002. An introductory memorandum (February 11, 2002) from Mizell explained that Foley had over 27 years of practice experience and most recently had served in the Peace Corps for a "two–year tour of duty in the Ukraine. His primary assignment was to serve as in-house counsel to the Yalta Sea Trade Port, and his responsibilities included negotiating international commercial contracts and supervising the resolution of international contract and port disputes."

Foley was billed as having "experience in a wide variety of civil litigation, including complex litigation in the fields of architectural/engineering malpractice, construction, anti-trust, trademark, and contract."

I was encouraged that Mizell had brought on board a skilled litigator and negotiator. It was also my hope that Foley would promote integrity, networking and teamwork.

Chapter 109–Networking Focus Removed

During the first years of Mizell's leadership I continued to serve as the lead University attorney working with UT human resource officers, as well as UT student affairs officers. For example, at the June 14–15, 2001 meeting of the chief human resources officers for each campus I addressed the subjects of "fingerprinting childcare workers" and recent federal legislation governing privacy of medical records.

At the August 2001 meeting of the chief student affairs officers I addressed topics such as the "contractual nature of campus catalogs" and appropriate language for inclusion in security brochures.

One major change came with staff attorneys being instructed that all matters must be processed through the General Counsel. No longer would someone outside the University having a need for legal assistance be directed by an office secretary to the attorney handling that area of legal practice. Instead, any request for assistance would be direct to Mizell. She would assign work at her discretion. "Walk-in" requests for assistance–often with instant resolution–became formalized requests for assistance that might take days or weeks to process.

Unlike Brogan, Mizell discouraged staff attorney interaction with UT Board members. This was an approach which started when Mizell advised OGC attorneys not to attend Board meetings because, "Dr. Gilley thinks there are too many lawyers at the Board meetings."

My leadership role with the National Association of College and University Attorneys was brought to an end by Mizell–along with the invaluable fount of information I had access to as a result of my membership and leadership in that organization.

One of the last topics I addressed as a speaker at NACUA's 40th annual conference in Washington D.C. in June 1999, was "Limiting and Litigating Your

Opponent's Attorneys Fees." In the early years of my practice I gained much valuable assistance on that and other topics from other NACUA attorneys. I recognized the value of the organization to the University of Tennessee.

In April 2002, I requested permission to attend the 2002 NACUA annual meeting. My request was denied. Perhaps cost was the issue? Excerpts from e-mails between Mizell and me on the subject offer what I would categorize as a "bureaucratic" response:

Date: 4/11/2002 10: 40 5 AM   Subject: Re: NACUA

Ron,

Please see my earlier emails of 8–14–01 and 3–15–02 notifying all attorneys that out–of–state travel for conferences will not be approved. I am not approving any out–of–state travel except for essential litigation purposes. All attorneys will have to obtain the required CLE credits through in – state courses. Plenty are available that are directly relevant to the work of this office.

Catherine

On 4/15/2002 at 7:35 AM I sent my e-mail response:

Would you be willing to approve my attending NACUA if I pay all expenses associated with out–of–state travel e. g. pay for the airline cost and waive any request for out–of–state per diem reimbursement? If UT will cover the conference fee and hotel I will cover all other expenses (and not request any per diem reimbursement).

Thanks for considering this request.

Ron

The "lock-step" response was received by email the same day at 11:22 AM:

"I am not approving any out –of –state travel except for essential litigation purposes. One–day CLE seminars are available in Knoxville, Nashville, or Chattanooga with significantly lower registration fees and no hotel expenses."

Of course, I had agreed to pay for the hotel.

The slightly lower registration fee was paid and I attended a local CLE conference that had little to do with higher education. Completely missed were the benefits of networking with other higher education attorneys.

A related opportunity to serve as the Southeast Conference representatives on a "presidential advisory board" for the National Collegiate Athletic Association was likewise nipped in the bud by Mizell (see Chapter 81). Once again the University lost a valuable networking opportunity–a vital source of information in many areas affecting higher education.

The networking focus which had worked so well to the University's benefit for more than a quarter of a century had been successfully eliminated.

Celebrating 25 years of employment in the UT Office of General Counsel. L to R: UT General Counsel Beach Brogan, Ron and Therese Leadbetter and UT President Joe Johnson (May, 1998).

Celebrating 35 years of employment in the UT Office of General Counsel. UT General Counsel Catherine Mizell, Ron Leadbetter and UT President John Peterson (December 14, 2007).

Big Orange, Black Storm Clouds and More   547

Chapter 110–Life Goes On Quite Well–For Me

With Gilley's departure from UT in June, 2001 there was a period of uncertainty in my life as University Counsel. I served first under the "acting presidency" of Eli Fly, with whom I had worked well for many years, then the presidency of John Shumaker. Considering my ongoing litigation with former President Gilley and parallel litigation against the University there was reason to doubt whether my personal and professional life would face bumps in the road.

I spent little time worrying about the bumps and any time spent worrying would have been wasted. Life actually went on quite well for me personally and professionally. Not so well for the University.

My litigation caseload remained what could be called, "predictably unpredictable." I was neither assigned an extraordinarily higher number of cases nor removed from handling significant litigation. In 2002 civil rights actions were removed from my area of responsibility while I saw an uptick in the number of tort claims assigned to me for handling.

In general, my litigation record remained the same. The year 2001 concluded with 13 wins and no losses. Three settlements–all tort claims–were finalized for a total of $66,953. Not a bad year.

The following year was significantly more challenging. Fourteen cases–all tort claims–concluded with favorable judgments for the University. However, four cases ended with judgments against the University. Judgments totaling $345,028 were assessed in favor of plaintiffs. Two additional tort claims were settled in 2002 for a total of $32,000.

Altogether the University paid out slightly more than $377,000 in judgments or settlements for the year – what would be my worst year ever as counsel for the University (excluding the Hartman contract case loss 2003, see Chapter 86). In a short time my worst year would take on a brighter hue compared to other monetary losses sustained by the University in the legal arena.

In 2003 the overall record improved to 12 wins, two losses and two settlements. The total payout dropped to $233,026 (of which $122,000 went toward settlements).

For the three-year "post –Gilley" period it is worth noting that the amounts paid out each year were a small fraction of the amounts sued for. Judgments requested were not always specified in dollars. The following totals are only for cases in which plaintiffs demanded specific dollar amounts.

2001 – $624,082 (Three demands exceeding $100,000)
2002 – $3,084,330 (Six demands exceeding $100,000)

2003 – $2,027,233 (Five demands exceeding $100,000)

(Excluding *Hartman*).

My litigation calendar was full. In July 2002 22,000 state employees were furloughed. Twenty or so employees in the Office of General Counsel were sent furlough notices. With upcoming trials and depositions, I was one of three given an exemption based on upcoming depositions and a trial. As OGC attorneys were advised by an office e-mail of June 28, 2002, "If there is a shutdown of state government, do not report to work on Monday morning unless Catherine has expressly authorized you to do so." I do not recall the duration of the government shutdown–I did not miss any days.

I continued to handle UT compliance with the Tennessee Administrative Procedures Act, including all rulemaking responsibilities –and represented the University before the Joint Government Operations Committee of the Tennessee State legislature. The majority of contested case hearings before UT administrative judges were handled by me.

I continued to travel statewide and work with all UT campuses. To cite a few examples from my diary:

6/28–29/01 Flew to Memphis this afternoon–after Locke hearing–then on to Jackson.

10/17/01 Met with Chancellor Bill Stacy and Dan Webb in Chattanooga.

12/6–7/01 Flew to Memphis, then on to Martin to meet with [Baseball] coach Bubba Cate

12/13/01 To Nashville for lunch with Martha Campbell, Attorney General's office.

1/28–29/02 Flew to Memphis, then to Union City, then Alamo (to meet with Claims Commissioner Randy Camp). Trial in Alamo (Campberry).

3/25/02 Chattanooga, APA hearing at UTC.

5/6/02 Nashville, Joint Government Ops meeting.

5/7–8/02 Memphis–Jackson–Memphis, depositions.

6/13/02 Chattanooga, search and seizure seminar for UTC police

6/18–20/02 Memphis and Jackson, depositions.

7/16–17/02 Memphis and Jackson, more depositions.

Mizell was most gracious in continuing to grant my requests for annual leave for family vacations and other personal purposes, with scheduling at my discretion. For me personally, the transition following Gilley's departure and during the Shumaker presidency which followed, was as satisfying and rewarding as ever. The same could not be said for the University of Tennessee.

Chapter 111–Joe Johnson, Interim President (2003-04) Another Sliver of Orange

My diary entry for August 8, 2003 reads: "President Shumaker resigns today! Good riddance to corruption, ego and sheer unmitigated greed. Maybe we can get an ethical person for our next president at UT."

LIFE GOES ON

In the meantime, my professional life continued at an exciting pace. On August 13, I flew to Albany, New York, and then drove to Stockbridge, Massachusetts for the deposition of Dr. Tony Segel in the Henry Harris case (See ,Chapter 43). I left Albany the following morning for the return flight home just hours before a massive blackout hit the Northeast and parts of Canada.

On the 18th, I traveled to Johnson City for the deposition of *Harris* expert witness Tony Katras. Then, the next day, according to my diary, "I flew to Winston-Salem for the evidentiary deposition of Dr. Howerton, claimant's expert in the Harris case. Back late this evening from the Wake Forest Medical Center in Winston-Salem."

Harris was tried in Johnson City on August 21–22. According to my diary entry for August 22, I "finished at 5 PM and a great 'burden' lifted (had two months to 'reconstruct' a case that another attorney had had two years to screw up. Worst case I've ever had to try). We'll see what the outcome is."

JOE JOHNSON BECOMES INTERIM PRESIDENT

Shortly after Shumaker's resignation the UT Board of Trustees appointed Dr. Joe Johnson as interim president of the University. Once again a sliver of the Big Orange glowed upon the University. And, once again I was motivated to step forward.

I knew beyond doubt that Johnson was a man of character and commitment to the University. The last two presidents had been abysmal failures from an integrity viewpoint and Johnson would be serving only briefly while a new president was selected. So why bother? I already had plenty to do with repeated trips to Clearwater, Florida to care for my aging parents.

In searching my files for documentary support for this book, I came across a writing I authored on Sunday, August 24, 2003. I had completely forgotten ever preparing the document and even now do not recall why I did. Regardless, the writing fully explains what happened the morning of August 24 and why I extended an offer of assistance to Interim President Joe Johnson.

ANSWERED PRAYER–August 24, 2003

At 6 AM this Sunday morning I was at the office doing odds and ends. I don't normally do devotions on Sunday morning, but whispered a brief prayer before heading for Panera's because of my deep ongoing concern for what role I should take in initiating an approach to "new" interim UT President Joe Johnson. It is my desire to contribute to resolving the mess created by the last two presidents (and the General Counsel's failure to do anything whatever to head off the crisis) but at the same time avoid jeopardizing my own employment.

My brief prayer: "Lord I'm willing to serve. Just show me what you want me to do." [Emphasis added].

As I arrived at Panera's at 7:00 the only other car in the lot was leaving. As I entered I saw only one other person in the bakery–a person I looked at briefly and, because of somewhat unkempt gray hair and black T-shirt, I took to be a street person. Carrying my order of cappuccino and pastry I took a seat on the opposite side of the fireplace from where I normally said, semi-consciously trying to avoid face-to-face contact with the street person who was seated right next to where I would normally sit.

The headline article in the Sunday paper was yet another story in the series on the Shumaker scandal. This article commented on the previous week's selection by the UT Board of Trustees of Joe Johnson to lead the University during the interim between Shumaker's resignation and the selection of a new president. As I read I contemplated what contact, if any, I should attempt with President Johnson, the easiest and safest course being one of inaction.

As I turned to and commenced to read the second page of the paper I heard a voice from behind comment on the article I was reading. I turned to look at the gentleman who spoke and was surprised to see he was not a street person but instead was a minister with a black "vestment" type T-shirt and a large gold cross. The article on which he commented on the headline "God in government."

Soon my new friend, Bill Willis, a retired Methodist minister from Georgetown, Georgia, and I were engaged in a spirited discussion of the role of God in our lives. Rev. Bill observed that our society seems to be one in which God speaks but we're not listening. He receives our attention on Sunday and then we exclude him the rest of the week. Our primary concern is to "go along to get along."

These comments by the Reverend could not have been more clearly directed to me from the Lord. I needed to go make contact with Joe and not concern myself with what negative response I might receive. And, if there was any doubt in my mind what God was saying He soon made the message even clearer.

A little after 7:00 a second Methodist minister added his presence to the sparse crowd at Panera's. The Rev. Bob Tripp, former candidate for Tennessee governor, entered by himself and a few minutes later I walked up to him, introduced myself, reminded him we had previously met (at a West Knox Republican meeting). Minutes later Bob walked over to me and, much to my amazement, informed me [that] God had placed me in his path this morning. He proceeded to relate to me the experience by which God had called him in a vision to run for governor–not to get elected, just to run–and now he had called him to seek the presidency of UT (by vision of a "power T").

Most significant to me [was] it is not for us to worry about assuring the results. Nor are we to be concerned with whether the actions God directs meets with popular approval. Bob's assertion was that when God calls we must respond.

Ironically, both Tripp and Willis made the same statements to me that God had directly spoken to them but that most people would not understand. How amazing to hear them confirm the very miracle I was in the process of receiving!

I introduced the two ministers and we agreed to meet again – Bob later sent me an email documenting our God–inspired encounter and reiterating that God had placed me in his path (while in truth it was God who placed him in my path).

God was not finished.

I knew it was God's will for me to approach Joe with an offer to help UT through its troubles. I wanted additional confirmation. It was on the way.

A bit before 9:00 I picked up [graduate student] Jorge Ureta [from Panama at Laurel apartments [near the UT campus] for church [as I did each Sunday]. Minutes later we arrived at Central Baptist in Bearden, just as we completed a discussion of the situation at UT. In response to Jorge's query of what would happen next I enigmatically responded that the route to be taken would "likely be determined Monday," an oblique reference to my God–led decision to contact Joe Johnson the following day with an offer to help.

No more than 2–3 minutes later Jorge and I arrived at the front door of the church where deacon Steve Jones greeted me with "It's good to know the University is now in the hands of you and Joe Johnson." What an affirmation!

And, following an emotion–tinged record number of baptisms at the start of the service Rev. Larry Fields followed with a sermon reiterating the very same theme presented twice previously at Panera's. Larry reiterated God's desire that we not follow the ways of the world just to get along. So certain was I on the direction of the sermon I even wrote down on the bulletin the word "Episcopal," knowing In ADVANCE that Larry would mention that church is an ex-

ample of how even churches get caught up in trying to please men rather than God–and, yes, Larry mentioned the Episcopal church by name 4-5 minutes after I wrote the name on the bulletin and I do not ever recall Larry mentioning the Episcopal church previously.

The invitational hymn was "I Surrender All."

Yes, I went to Joe Johnson's office at 8 AM Monday morning and delivered a note offering my support and assistance. He responded with a hand-written note of thanks the next day.

As a sort of postscript, I have prayed that one of the trustees would contact me with a request for input. Although I am not certain what the implications are, one of the trustees I have known for quite a few years and had a good relationship with, Barbara Castleman of Martin, did the next best thing. The Sunday following my message from the Lord, I was again approaching the sanctuary doors [at Central Baptist Bearden]–greeted again by Steve Jones– when I was shocked to meet Barbara Castleman waiting to enter. She was visiting with her daughter and her fiancé, a UT law student. The encounter afforded me an opportunity to encourage Barbara to ask tough questions such as "How did we get in this mess?"

Time will tell what the results of my contacts will be. In the meantime I am assured that the RESULTS are in God's hands and not mine!

Ron Leadbetter

As indicated in my "devotional" I went to Johnson's office the next morning. He was not in. I left a hand-written note: "Joe, welcome back! You're the man to restore the university's image of honor and integrity. I stand ready to serve the effort–please call on me if I can help.   Ron"

Later the same day I received Joe's hand-written response at the top of my note: "Ron–Thanks a lot. I appreciate your support. Joe". Moving in the right direction–at least short-term.

Chapter 112–During the Orange Sliver Life Went On

During the period of Joe Johnson's interim presidency life went on for me as before–quite well. Challenging, always something new and never dull. A few examples taken from my diary:

10/22/03–Met with Dr. William Schaffner, UT's expert in Elosiebo in Nashville.

10/23/03–"Elosiebo trial today. In a rare treat Commissioner Lance entered judgment from the bench (in favor of the state). A nice win! " [Unfortunately, not a permanent one].

11/9–10/03–Depositions at Duke Medical Center (Raleigh – Durham, NC) in the Nichols case.

11/14/03–My volleyball team, "The Misshits", won the UT faculty-staff league championship this afternoon.

11/16/03–Several friends met with me at my home to discuss plans for "independent" travel on Russia's "Trans-Siberian Railway." Present at the planning meeting were Joe Fornes, Steve Hillis, Barry Rice and Tom Cronan.

11/28–12/3/03 In Clearwater, Florida with family.

12/10/03–I Presented a legal seminar, "Liability Prevention," to UT surgery residents at the UT Medical Center in Knoxville.

12/16/03–"Our office was invited to a fantastic dinner prepared by Karen [Sprouse] at the Sprouses. Most of GC Office came–of course GC Mizell did not (and never has)."

1/12/04–Argued defense motion for TRO, in Manookian, before the Knox County Chancery Court.

1/19/04–Met with Duggan in his law office in Maryville to prepare for oral argument of appeal in Gilley to the U.S. Court of Appeals for the Sixth Circuit.

1/23/04–Met with an expert witness in Nashville this morning in the Patsy Smith case.

1/27/04–Retirement reception this afternoon at the University club for UT Assistant Vice President for Human Resources Sara Phillips.

1/28–29/04–Patsy Smith trial in Johnson City.

2/4/04–"State Claims Commissioner Vance Cheek issued his findings in favor of the State (UT Medical Center) in a 45-50 minute telephone conference ruling following last week's two-day trial in Johnson City of a case that arose in 1993 –11 years ago! Great victory!"

2/18–22/04–In Clearwater, Florida with family.

2/24/04–"Today in particular I am awestruck by how much God has blessed me–last week my parents were better than they've been in a long time. Yesterday I received a visit from an "ancient history" co-worker, Cliff Koen, a UT Memphis personnel official from the early 1980s–nice visit with Cliff (plus gracious gift of cake from New Orleans). Today: great surgery relief on my left foot by Dr. Ivan Cooper this a.m. ... . This afternoon: 2-day trial conflict with my Sixth Circuit hearing (Leadbetter v. Gilley) canceled out–so I'm on my way to Cincinnati with Dave Duggan on March 10."

3/8/04–"A UT Admin. intern, Zack Lewis, joined me for a trip to Nashville today. Lunch with [former OGC colleague] Lisa Atkins and a three-minute appearance before the Gov't Operations Comm. (Legislature).

3/9/04–Off to Cincinnati with David Duggan.

3/19/04–Attended reception at the UT ""TREC" [UT recreation center] for director Harold Denton, celebrating his retirement after 33 years at UT.

3/22/04–"Dropped by UT Medical Center to see how Tom Cronan's surgery went (Doc thought it went very well–malignant tumor on pancreas removed)." [Much to my dismay, Cronan was diagnosed with pancreatic cancer; he would not be joining me for the journey on the trans-Siberian railway].

3/30/04–Breakfast event at "Club LeConte" to hear UT football coach Phil Fulmer speak.

4/1/04–"Five racquetball games with UT football coach Phil Fulmer at lunch (TREC Center). I won all 5 but it was fun to play w/ Phil–He's a competitor!"

4/15/04–Drove to Nashville today for depositions in the Guereux case.

4/16/04–Bridge this evening at Roy and Linda Painter's [Linda was Associate Provost for UT Knoxville; Roy was–and remains–co-director of my Sunday School department at church].

4/22–26/04–In Clearwater, Florida with family.

When I returned from Florida on the 26th, I got word that the next president of the University of Tennessee would be John Peterson, Provost and Executive Vice President for Academic Affairs at the University of Connecticut. Another chapter in the life of the University of Tennessee–and my own–would soon begin.

Chapter 113–Checking Out The Next UT President– John Peterson

Once again the search for a new UT president encountered controversy. "An anonymous letter and an outdated resume have cast a cloud over the search for a new president at the University of Tennessee, where Utah State University President Kermit Hall was a finalist last month," reported the Desiree Morning News on May 18, 2004.

"Hall and American Council on Education lawyer Sheldon Steinback characterize the search, which ended with John D. Peterson being named UT president on April 21, as "tainted" and "flawed," the article continued. The concern: "Negative information about "several" of the final six candidates, including Hall, was submitted anonymously to key people involved in the search. Hall didn't find out about a secret letter about him until after Peterson was chosen." (Id.)

Given the disastrous results of the past two presidential hires by the University I thought it might be wise to do my own background check on the incoming president. I would leave to others any investigation of a search process screw-up.

One of my good friends from the National Association of College and University attorneys was Paul Shapiro, the recently retired General Counsel of the University of Connecticut. I left a message with his former office, asking him to contact me. Shapiro responded by email on the morning of April 29:

Hey, Ron, it's great to hear from you! I'd be happy to speak with you.

Retirement is wonderful. [Excluded is a paragraph outlining the benefits and advantages he experienced in retirement]. I do miss that, and the friendships. In my mind, there is no organization, of lawyers or anyone else, that matches the professionalism and collegiality that NACUA provided. And I sure miss talking women's hoops with you each year!

So, call by all means–[telephone number omitted].

Paul M Shapiro

[address in Storrs, Connecticut, telephone number and email address omitted]

The benefits of networking–particularly my involvement with NACUA–are evidenced by Shapiro's email.

Later that same day I spoke by telephone with Shapiro for one hour and 15 minutes. The only issue even remotely bearing on ethics concerned a house Peterson built on University-owned property. But, it was paid for with his own money. He made arrangements whereby U Conn. could buy out the house. Did not strike me as a matter of concern.

According to my notes,

Paul says he has a "fine" relationship, but not a "strong" relationship with John. Not a close personal relationship. Said to one new Dean: "you don't want to spend too much time with this guy."

Not impulsive (can be confused as being indecisive–but he likes to get ALL information before acting. But he did close the geology department. Nice person, not in it for the $. Swedish. Doesn't like conflict! E.G. Deans bickering John/Carol are devoted couple! Devoted to Carol's aging parents in Calif. (LA area)

Shapiro let me know he had sent Peterson an email saying, "You need to call on a good friend of mine, Ron Leadbetter." I thanked him for doing that. And I thanked him for his friendship and input.

Concluding that Peterson lacked the character flaws dominating the previous two presidents I felt good. I was concerned by Shapiro's strongly stated assessment that Peterson "doesn't like conflict," being well aware that one responsibility of a university president was to confront and resolve conflict–in a diplomatic manner whenever possible.

My first taste of Peterson's penchant for conflict-avoidance was soon to come.

Peterson officially took office as UT president on July 1, 2004. Thanks to Shapiro's email Peterson invited me to his office for a meeting shortly after his arrival.

We met on July 9. According to my diary, "I met with UT President John Petersen in his office for the first time today. A very candid meeting. We'll see where it takes us–God knows!" The emphasis of my presentation was that the current General Counsel, Mizell, was skilled in certain areas of legal practice but not leadership. The University would be better served with new leadership –and not necessarily me.

Peterson and I met again on October 13. According to my diary, "I met with UT President John Petersen this a.m. from 10 to 10:45–a good meeting with discussion of several items of easily understood screw-ups by Mizell included. We'll see what he does with it."

As any employee, I recognized I was taking a chance in criticizing my boss's performance. Still, I knew if I did not voice my concerns it was unlikely anyone else would.

More than a month later, on November 22, I received Peterson's reaction to my input. His letter of November 19 made for one thing clear–if I could not support my boss I should go for employment elsewhere. It was clear to me that Peterson had no interest in pursuing the matter further and was comfortable with the leadership in the Office of General Counsel. I was ready to move on –in my existing job, not elsewhere.

Chapter 114–The Russia Connection–Easier to Arrange Than Intra-Office Communication

2004 was a year of interesting challenges. The difficulty of each challenge was not always what one might expect.

One challenge began with a March 4, 2004 memorandum to General Counsel Mizell from me:

> I would like to request authorization to take annual leave from August 2–August 27, 2004. Several friends and I have been invited to visit the former "Secret Nuclear City" of Zheleznogorsk in Siberia and this would be a good opportunity to utilize some of my "over–accumulated" annual leave while developing some good international relationships at the same time.
>
> Thanks.

I received no immediate response. Instead, on July 13 I received an unrelated memorandum from Mizell:

"It is my understanding that you were absent from June 9 until June 28 due to a scheduled medical procedure. You did not request my permission or notify me of your absence. You reported only two days of sick leave, June 9 and 10. Do you have an explanation?"

When I read the memorandum I was somewhat amused. In 2004 my office was in the UT Communications and Student Services Building while Mizell's was in Andy Holt Tower. The buildings are connected. Our offices are no more than a 10 minute walk apart.

I thought it odd that more than a month had passed without a visit to my office, or at least a phone call to my secretary, to find out where I was. The question was easily addressed. My memorandum of July 14 began with, "Yes, I have an explanation."

First, I noted that "going back to 1972 I have never used an entire day of sick leave–only two half days–for my own illness or injury. Only in the past couple of years have I used any sick leave at all and that leave was utilized in connection with severe health care needs of my aging parents."

I then explained that I had undergone "out-patient" surgery on June 9 to address non-–resolving problems resulting from a broken bone in my foot. "I was placed on medication and advised to stay home, with my foot elevated, with driving and placing any form of pressure on my foot for more than five minutes each hour being proscribed." That was the explanation for taking two days sick leave. But what about the balance of the period between July 10 and June 28.

"Given Dr. Cooper's medical advice, it would certainly have been appropriate for me to have taken sick leave for several weeks in order to permit my foot to heal properly. For good or bad, I let my work ethic and commitment to my University responsibilities take precedence over my doctor's good advice.

Even on June 9, the date of my surgery, I called the office and advised Tish of my surgery results and my physician's directives but that I would be available if anyone needed me. Due to pain medication taken following surgery, I refrained from doing any UT work on June 9 or 10. However, I stopped taking pain medication the morning of June 10 and determined to resume my normal responsibilities the following day. On June 11, I transformed my dining room into my 'office away from the office.' All necessary litigation files were brought to my temporary work quarters." (Id.)

The balance of the memorandum was consumed in delineating the various trials and depositions I had prepared for at my home office. But, "I was in fact in the office frequently during the June 11–28 period, often in the early morning or late afternoon or evening and on at least two Sundays, largely due to the fact that I had to rely on others to transport me to and from the office."

I explained that I made regular use of wheelchairs and on June 18 "spent almost the entire day in depositions in the Nichols case at the UT Medical Center, thanks to Nursing Administration's arrangement for wheelchair transport for me."

As the net result of my work efforts during the period June 11 through June 28, I maintained a full work schedule and fully attended to each and every one of my job responsibilities. My litigation and other assignments are, as always, current and fully attended to.

Toward the end of the July 14 memorandum I requested permission to take leave the following week to provide assistance to my parents in Clearwater. I concluded with an observation that, "My work is completely up to date and I will be available by cell phone to address any issues that arise during that period."

The next day I received another memorandum:

SUBJECT: Request for Annual Leave and Reporting Use of Leave

I certainly understand and appreciate the need to take care of aging parents and therefore approve your request to take annual leave July 19 through July 23.

After your return, I will address further the matter of proper reporting of leave [which, in fact, I heard nothing more about].

In March you sent a memorandum to me requesting to take annual leave from August 2 through August 27 to travel to Siberia. Neither you nor I could possibly know five months in advance that your work responsibilities will allow you to be out of the country for four consecutive weeks. Are you still requesting this extended leave?

Thank you.

Later that same day, July 15, I responded:

Thanks for approving my request for annual leave July 19 through July 23, 2004.

Yes, I am still requesting the extended leave mentioned in the March memorandum. Indeed, I have done everything to ensure that the extended leave does not in any way affect my work responsibilities. For example, I have had all depositions, hearings, and other litigation matters set after August 27 (or the week prior to August 2).

Again, thanks.

Five days later I received a letter from Mizell advising that she was "pleased to inform" me that I had been approved for a 3% salary increase. Five days after that, on July 27, I received another welcome message from Mizell:

I approve your request to take annual leave August 2 through August 28. Please let me know how you can be reached if necessary, and if possible, please call the office periodically to see if any urgent matter has arisen.

I hope you have a good trip.

I thanked Mizell for her approval and explained that a "telephone contact from Siberia and Mongolia (particularly on the railway) may not be possible, you may reach me by e-mail to a friend, Elena Snejkina [e-mail address omitted] and I will respond ASAP."

The trip went well. I stayed in touch with the office by telephone and e-mail. No problems arose which were not handled expeditiously (the term "expeditiously" being a favorite of mine that I have traditionally used for "voicemail" messages when I am unavailable). Ah, if only communication within our office could have been handled as simply and expeditiously.

Chapter 115–Russian Connection With UT Blossoms

After returning from a successful month-long journey across nine time zones in Russia with former UT employees Steve Hillis and Joe Fornes, I returned to Knoxville. I authored an article about the trip for the Knoxville News-Sentinel. "Tennessee travelers take 'independent' approach to trans-Siberian railway" was published in the October 24, 2004 edition of the Sentinel (page F1). An editorial note advised readers that "Veteran traveler Ron Leadbetter is employed as Associate General Counsel at the University of Tennessee."

One of my group's many stops along the Trans-Siberian route was in the city of Penza, 450 miles south of Moscow. Penza was home to Elena Snejkina. Snejkina introduced us to another resident, Olga Meshcheryakova.

Meshcheryakova, at age 26, founded the "Lingua Center," a non-profit aimed at teaching children, young people and adults English and several other languages. Thousands had been served by the Center. When asked by Hillis if the Center had any particular needs, Meshcheryakova replied, "Books in English."

Hillis spearheaded a drive to collect a shipping container load of a wide variety of books in the English language from Blount County and Knoxville area. $4,000 in shipping costs were covered by area donors (including the Hillises, Therese and me).

Plans were made for the opening of the American Library at Penza State University, where Meshcheryakova served on the English faculty and as director of international education (and Dr. Meshcheryakova currently serves as the Head of the International Office of Penza State University).

Hillis and I returned to Penza for the opening of the American Library in December 2005. The grand opening ceremony was held at Penza State University on December 8.

Attending and presenting opening remarks, in addition to PSU officials, were the Deputy Governor of the Penza region, Elena Stolyarova, and the Vice Mayor of the city of Penza, Yuri Alpotov. The event was well covered by the news media.

Both Hillis and I spoke at the ceremony. I read congratulatory letters from Congressman Jimmy Duncan and UT Knoxville Chancellor Loren Crabtree to those gathered.

An article about the grand opening of the American Library at Penza State University appeared in the "Maryville Times" on December 25, 2005.

The American flag flies in the library. A framed photo of Meshcheryakova with UT Women's Head basketball coach Holly Warlick and Assistant coach

Dean Lockwood, taken during a trip by Meshcheryakova to UT in 2006, greets library visitors.

The Knoxville area and UT received a visit from Olga Meshcheryakova and Snejkina in September 2006. Meshcheryakova, who arrived first, joined a group from church for a whitewater rafting trip I led down the Ocoee River.

The following day Meshcheryakova joined Therese and me for the UT v California football game. She joined us for Knoxville's Boomsday (Labor Day fireworks) celebration the day after.

On the afternoon of September 7 Chancellor Crabtree, as well as members of his staff (Jan Simek and Mary Papke) met with our Russian friends in his office for more than an hour. Crabtree and his staff expressed their sentiment that a formal relationship between UT and PSU would seem to fit well within UT's "Ready for the World " program–a program promoting better international understanding–initiated under Crabtree's leadership.

Crabtree's interest in promoting a formal relationship between UT and Penza State University deepened as time went on. Before leaving for another trip to Penza in the fall of 2007 I stopped by Crabtree's office to see if there was any additional information he would like me to obtain while in Penza.

"See if you can find any faculty who would be interested in teaching UT students in English," Crabtree requested. "Quite a challenge," I thought. I told Crabtree I would see what I could come up with.

Soon after I arrived in Penza, I met with the Rector (President) of PSU, Vladimir Volchikhin. At the end of our meeting I explained Crabtree's request. Volchikhin nodded but said nothing more. As I left his office I hoped my request had not been offensive or presumptuous.

Late that afternoon I received a phone call from someone in the Rector's office. Someone responding to the Chancellor's requests would meet with me at noon the next day at the American Library.

The following day was a busy one and I barely made it to the Library by noon. As I approached the facility I saw no one else entering. My assumption was that the faculty member–or perhaps two or three–who had expressed interest was already inside.

As I entered the library I was stunned. An open seating area in the library was packed with 45 or 50 Penza State faculty members. Vice Rector Meshcheryakov–Olga Meshcheryakova's father-in-law–was present as were several of his staff.

After introductory remarks by the Vice Rector I added a few explanatory remarks of my own. The next hour and a half was spent shooting video of one faculty member after another. Included were faculty from law, business, political science, engineering and other disciplines.

Each faculty member extended greetings to Chancellor Crabtree and–each in his or her own way–described the discipline taught and stated how happy he or she would be to teach students from the University of Tennessee. The English spoken by the vast majority of those videoed was easily understood.

After returning to Knoxville I had a follow-up meeting with Crabtree. After I completed a video showing of the Penza State faculty, I shared with him that I was amazed at the turnout for the video. "Not as amazed as me, " replied Crabtree. It seemed as if plans for an international center for US–Russian co-operation was well under way. Only one snag developed.

On January 4, 2008 breaking news on local media revealed that Chancellor Crabtree had resigned from the University. As reported by Channel 8–WV LT on the morning of January 4, 2008:

> There's been a change in leadership at UT–Knoxville campus. Chancellor Loren Crabtree has resigned effective immediately.
>
> Volunteer TVs Liz Tedone has more on what was a shocking announcement to many.
>
> It's been no secret that Chancellor Crabtree and University President John Petersen have disagreed on governing the flagship campus.
>
> Chancellor Loren Crabtree's resignation comes as a shock to many university faculty members.

I always made it my habit to stay out of administrative disputes and stick to the practice of law. Still, I quickly recalled the "inside information" I received that President Peterson did not like "conflict."

Just as quickly I reminisced that presidents during the "Big Orange" era also had conflicts with chancellors from time to time. Back then diplomacy and a spirit of teamwork routinely trumped conflict.

Crabtree's last meeting with Stephen occurred shortly after his resignation was announced. It was reported to me by one of his staff that, at that meeting, Crabtree announced his regret he would not be able to carry through on the UT –Penza State project. Crabtree described that project as the best tangible result of the "Ready for the World" effort.

Therese and I attended a going away event for Crabtree in the University Center on the afternoon of January 17, 2008. From there we proceeded to a fundraiser in Maryville: "David Duggan for Circuit Judge." UT lost a good Chancellor; Blount County later gained a fine judge.

Dr. Jimmy Cheek became Chancellor of UT Knoxville on February 1, 2009. I made several efforts to schedule a meeting with him to discuss the possibility of establishing a cooperative venture between UT and Penza State U. No response of any kind was provided.

I followed up my proposal with an offer to raise funds for the project. Still no reply from the Chancellor–not even an "I'm not interested."

In spring 2011 I led a small group with UT ties, including the head of the UT Russian Department, Dr. Stephen Blackwell, to Penza State University. Shortly after I returned to Knoxville I authored an article for the Knoxville News-Sentinel, "UT group explores prospects with Russian University." The July 17, 2011 article identified various Russian education leaders the group met with and describe their "deep commitment to developing cooperative educational relationships [with the University of Tennessee]."

Even without active support–or even acknowledgement–by Cheek–efforts to develop a cooperative relationship between UT and PSU and our communities have continued. As recently as December 1, 2013, I e-mailed a proposal to UT Knoxville Chancellor Jimmy Cheek at the urging of a top UT development officer:

> Subject: Ron Leadbetter proposal for establishment of cooperative educational relationship between UT and Penza State University (Penza, Russia).
>
> Dear Chancellor Cheek:
>
> First, and foremost, I hope you and your family had a wonderful Thanksgiving!
>
> The rest of this email is offered as the result of a UT staff member's suggestion that I make contact with you in the light of your expressed interest in making the University of Tennessee a "Top – 25" institution of higher education.
>
> Specifically, I have a vision of creating a high – profile partnership between UT and Penza State University in Penza, Russia aimed at promoting establishment of an international center for Russian – American cooperation in higher education. As with the University itself, focus would be on teaching, research and public service.

The Chancellor was provided additional history of the project, including efforts both in Penza and within the UT community. My proposal concluded with:

> There is much more I would be pleased to share with you by way of explaining relationships already established and ideas for the future (e. g. Dr. Meshcheryakova proposes organizing a Russian – American symposium/workshop aimed at discussing/developing a joint plan for combating terrorism in the world). My question to you is, are you interested in pursuing further the concept I have presented. If so, I'll be more than happy to meet with you and discuss in more detail.

The Chancellor was invited to contact me by e-mail or by telephone. I confirmed with the Chancellor's secretary that he received my e-mail. I never received a response. The effort continues. In fall semester 2013 the first UT student enrolled for a semester of study at Penza State University. A UT graduate accepted an assistantship at PSU for fall 2014.

In March 2014 UT Knoxville's Center for International Studies hosted Meshcheryakova for a "one–week university networking and professional visit" in conjunction a 3-month Fulbright Russian International Education Administrators Fellowship she received.

As Meshcheryakova explained by e-mail to Dr. Mark Bryant, Director of the UT International House, in requesting UT sponsorship, "The focus of [the Fulbright] program is to enhance and hone the professional skill sets of university administrators who work with and develop programs for incoming international students from around the world and especially those from the U.S. It is also designed to provide fellows with an opportunity to build on current partnerships with U.S. universities or investigate programs of interest." [January 9, 2014 e-mail to Bryant]

Meshcheryakova added a more personal reason for requesting UT sponsorship:

There is also another reason of my desire to choose UT for my networking week. This is professional relations and even friendship with some of the people who work for your university [a number being listed by name and position]. Some of them have already been to Penza, others encouraged their students to do so. Anyway, this time I hope will have time and opportunity to come with more ideas for international cooperation to the benefit of our two universities.

Hopefully, the University will eventually take advantage of a golden opportunity to promote educational cooperation and friendship with a world power often perceived as an adversary. Both Russia and the U.S. could benefit from the effort. And my former boss, Mizell, can take partial credit for such networking achievement by having authorized my extended leave of absence for travel to Russia back in 2004.

Chapter 116–During the Peterson Presidency All Again Went Well–For Me

Disregarding the leadership encounter at the beginning of Peterson's presidency, the University's third president in four years and I got along without any further confrontations. In fact, at the end of my UT career Peterson made clear that even our initial disagreement had been fully resolved.

Unlike the Gilley and Shumaker presidencies, whenever I encountered Peterson we exchanged greetings and perhaps a few other pleasantries; unlike the Boling, Alexander and Johnson presidencies I had no direct working relationship with Peterson. The General Counsel saw to that.

While I certainly would have enjoyed a personal working relationship with Peterson, my career and life continued along a marvelous pathway during his presidency. As in the past, I had no complaints of personal or professional mistreatment. Quite the contrary.

As time went on my workload actually decreased. During the last few years of my employment in the office General Counsel my secretary, Tish, and I often joked that I had a 15 hour work week. Not really a joke–absolutely true!

From a taxpayer's viewpoint, "Sad, but true." But from a purely personal viewpoint life during my last three or four years in the office of General Counsel was equivalent to a part-time job with full-time pay.

I continued to arrive at the office at 5:15 each morning. Morning devotion - Bible reading and prayer–started the day. In the past, the next two or three hours were spent reading and dictating legal documents and correspondence - tasks benefiting from the early morning quiet of an office uninhabited by other employees. That habit was replaced, more often than not, by early departure for a nearby establishment–on or off campus–for coffee and breakfast, catching up on the news and networking and socializing with other early-morning risers. Back in the office around eight I habitually spent the first 15 minutes or so greeting staff and exchanging family and personal updates. The balance of the morning was generally spent interviewing witnesses, attending depositions, or engaging in a wide variety of litigation and other work-related activities.

Unless in court (or out of town) I took my standard 2 1/2 hour lunch break. The afternoon was typically spent on people–oriented legal activities. At 4 o'-clock I left the office–most days.

Even during what I would call my "work hours," I often found I had no pending work-related responsibilities. On those occasions I worked on personal projects–planning my next independent travel trip abroad, studying Russian or taking care of personal business. Of course, these personal projects never took place when there was UT work to be done.

The substantial reduction in work hours was very easily explained. With the addition of more attorneys in the Office of General Counsel I received fewer case assignments–although I continued to receive challenging and complex case assignments. However, what I would term as "walk-in business" –University officials and others seeking legal advice by telephone or dropping by the office–virtually disappeared. Mizell required that all such requests for legal assistance be directed initially to her. My phone logs reflect a dramatic drop in contacts with others for UT legal purposes.

Fewer requests for seminar presentations and complete elimination of civil rights/affirmative action responsibilities in 2002 further reduced my work hours.

As a result, my independent travel abroad each year was even less likely to pose a conflict with my work assignments.

Oddly, even with three or four UT attorneys in the Memphis office, I continued to handle cases in West Tennessee. One interesting example involved an Administrative Procedures Act hearing at UT Martin in August 2006.

A newly trained administrative judge from UT Knoxville, Angi Smith, joined me for a flight to Memphis the morning of August 27. The following morning we departed the Memphis airport Radisson for the 2 1/2 hour drive to Martin.

The "Abner Smith" case was heard by Angi Smith in Martin later that morning–August 28. The hearing concluded later that same day. Smith and I drove back to Memphis for the return flight to Knoxville later that evening.

Knoxville attorneys (including me) were assigned medical malpractice cases in Memphis and Memphis attorneys were assigned medical malpractice cases in Knoxville. I found that interesting.

Coincident with reduction in work responsibilities, I spent fewer late nights, weekends and other times in what I would term "outside normal work hours," traveling on UT business. That translated into more free time for me–which I was not seeking but took advantage of. Not good for the University. Wasted resources. Happily, the General Counsel was satisfied with my work performance.

MY FIRST PERFORMANCE EVALUATION EVER IN 2007

In June 2007, I received my first formal performance evaluation ever. For whatever reason Mizell (and Baugh and Brogan before her) had elected not to conduct formal job performance evaluations for office attorneys.

I received from Mizell the highest rating possible– "exceptional" – in the categories of "efficiency and timeliness," "planning and organization of work" and "relationship with support staff." Scores of "commendable" were given in the categories of "presentation skills," "productivity," "working cases to disposition (litigators)," "initiative and industry/growth and development," and "relationship with clients."

Scores of "satisfactory" are given in 14 remaining categories. I received no "fair" or "unsatisfactory" ratings. Given the fact that Mizell had made clear that there was an absolute limit as to the number of "exceptional" and "commendable" ratings that could be given, I was extremely pleased and a bit surprised.

Each staff member was afforded an opportunity to respond to the performance evaluation and I responded to mind. I expressed disagreement with my evaluation in the category of "efficiency and productivity." I rated myself "unsatisfactory" in that category. I also suggested steps that might be taken to correct that deficiency: assign me more cases.

Mizell addressed my responses in a positive fashion:

SUPERVISOR'S ADDITIONAL COMMENTS

Ron brings the valuable assets of discipline and efficiency to his work. He is also an extremely positive individual who, I believe, genuinely expects to prevail in virtually every matter he handles. This positive spirit is admirable and may sometimes actually affect outcomes. At the same time, a balanced assessment of the strengths and weaknesses of the University's position and appropriate balancing of policy and other considerations are critical to determining legal strategy.

Ron has indicated an ability and willingness to handle a greater volume of work. We will consider additional assignments that might be made to take advantage of his efficiency and productivity.

Catherine S. Mizell]
Vice President and General Counsel

The kind comments were much appreciated. Good intentions were clear. Over the next few weeks I received several additional major case assignments. In late August, the hiring of a new full time attorney-the first ever for the UT Chattanooga campus–was announced. On September 19, 2005 I drove to Chattanooga–a one and a half hour drive from Knoxville–to handle five student loan default cases in Hamilton County Sessions Court. I was back in Knoxville by lunch time.

I traveled again to Chattanooga on March 26, 2007 to handle six more student loan cases in the Hamilton County Sessions Court. The entire proceeding took 15 minutes.

Then, on September 24, 2007–after the employment of the full-time attorney at UTC–I drove to Chattanooga and handled 12 more collection cases before returning to Knoxville early that afternoon. (Post note: none of the student loan collection cases are included in my litigation records–the extreme simplicity and routine nature of the cases did not warrant their inclusion).

It was clear to me that Mizell had good intentions in her approach to managing the Office of General Counsel. Equally clear to me was the fact that my philosophy for handling legal matters for the University was quite different.

Despite the differences, all went well–for me. Perhaps not so well for the Office of General Counsel and the University.

Chapter 117–Too Many Chiefs

Change can be good. In the legal field change from "what's not working" to "what works best" will predictably produce client benefits. But change just for the sake of change can be wasteful or even counterproductive–something to be avoided. I consciously crafted my own practices in accordance with those principles throughout my career. And those same principles were almost uniformly adhered to by the University and the Office of General Counsel during the "Big Orange" period. Not so much during the Gilley presidency and that of his successors.

For the first nearly three decades of my career a single attorney was routinely assigned responsibility for defined areas of legal practice affecting the University. Aside from training purposes only one attorney was typically involved in trying any particular lawsuit. That approach worked well as evidenced by the results–documented evidence of litigation success!

With the introduction of what I call the "black storm clouds" of the Gilley presidency, the OGC moved in the direction of what I characterize as "too many chiefs." OGC had multiple layers of responsibility and shifting responsibilities. The new approach was less effective. As also evidenced by the documented results.

Almost from the day she became General Counsel Mizell became actively involved in questioning litigation strategy and requesting information on specific cases – far beyond what Brogan had ever done. A two level case management approach. Then Peter Foley was hired in February 2002 as Deputy General Counsel. Mizell assigned Foley supervisory responsibility for cases and legal matters in which I (as well as other attorneys) was well experienced. A third level of management.

The new management approach was best described by Mizell in a January 3, 2007 memorandum "To all staff" announcing the "Delegation of Litigation Matters to Deputy General Counsel:

"With the encouragement and approval of President Peterson, I am delegating to Peter Foley responsibilities related to day–to–day management and supervision of litigation with the accompanying title of Deputy General Counsel. This delegation will relieve my workload and allow me to devote more time to other responsibilities of my position, including my significantly increased responsibilities to the Board of Trustees. Peter's assumption of these additional responsibilities will also allow for greater oversight of litigation activities on a regular basis.

Peter and I have worked closely on litigation matters over the past several years, and I have developed confidence in his skills and judgment. It is this confidence that allows me to delegate the day–to–day supervision of litigation matters to Peter with assurance that he will carry out my expectations in this important area.

Effective immediately, all litigation matters (administrative, state court, federal court, and Tennessee Claims Commission) will be staffed to me through Peter. Peter will be the attorney's immediate supervisor with respect to litigation matters, with full authority to assign work and direct action. Your communications concerning litigation matters will be addressed directly to Peter, and as a general rule, there will be no need initially to include me in those communications. Peter and I will continue to confer regularly about litigation matters, and he will bring to my attention what I need to know. I will continue to review motions to dismiss and motions for summary judgment filed in state or federal court, except those raising only the standard defenses of employee immunity under [section] 9–8–307 (h) and waiver under [section] 9–8–307 (b) I will also review dispositive motions in some Claims Commission Cases."

Clear? Three levels of supervision in an office with 15 attorneys–less than half of whom were actively involved in litigation. Would this approach improve on the 94% win record and the low dollar judgment/settlement payout record I accumulated prior to the management change? The cases and statistics speak for themselves.

THE MANOOKIAN SNAFU

By the time I received the Manookian case I had a virtually unblemished record of handling more than 100 formal hearings. One secret to success: meet and speak with key witnesses before initiating charges.

In *Manookian* the General Counsel advised the Vice Chancellor for Student Affairs to proceed with immediate suspension of the subject of disciplinary action without first interviewing a key witness who was readily available. By the time I received the case Manookian had already been dismissed from the University for allegedly threatening to kill his professor. The case could have been prosecuted as a lesser offense and possibly settled had a serious snafu not occurred at the outset.

Brogan's approach was to avoid direct involvement in litigation and leave all details to the attorney experienced in handling such cases. His was the better approach as the Manookian snafu demonstrates.

THE HARTMAN DISASTER

The Scott Hartman case provides perhaps the best example of the what I call, "too many chiefs" approach–and the failure of that approach. (See Chapter 90). With absolute certainty, the introduction of additional levels of management did nothing to improve the outcome. Perhaps an adverse judgment in excess of $1 million would have been saved had no change been implemented. We'll never know.

The UT CHATTANOOGA "RAPE" EMBARRASSMENT

In fall 2005, six UT Chattanooga football players were arrested and charged with rape of a female first-year UTC student by local law enforcement authorities. The UTC Office of Student Affairs consulted the UT General Counsel's office as to how to proceed.

Initial handling of the case was by Deputy General Counsel Peter Foley. On his advice all six football players were dismissed from the University. Each of the accused was advised of his right to a hearing and each elected to receive a hearing in accordance with the administrative procedures act. At that point I was asked to become involved and handle the APA proceedings.

Once again, the die was cast by the time I became involved. As in *Manookian* the key witness–the female student whom the rape charges concerned–was readily available for interview before any administrative charges were filed. She was enrolled as a student at UTC. I was the first university official to speak with her. My practice would have led me to speak with the accuser–my key witness–before disciplinary charges were issued and the students were dismissed.

A brief e-mail from Mizell, dated November 15, 2005, reveals the unnecessary complexity of a process I handled successfully many times in the past.

Ron:
At least three of the UTC students accused of rape have already indicated through counsel that they will elect an APA hearing to contest student conduct charges, and you will need to be prepared to handle the hearings. Please consult with Peter on all pre--hearing issues, including selection of an ALJ, FERPA issues, joinder of hearings, deferral of hearings pending the outcome of the criminal matter, etc. Peter will be receiving a draft of the initial notification of charge letters from Mary Lynn on Wednesday, and he will send them to you for review.
Thanks,
Catherine

Not a single issue was one I had not handled successfully in the past. Just not with a committee of three.

An Associated Press report published in the November 20, 2005 edition of Knox News.com, headlined "Chattanooga embarrassed by rape case." The article continued:

"Rape charges against six football players at the University of Tennessee at Chattanooga have embarrassed this city, which prides itself on a family–friendly reputation.

A female student who was drunk says she was raped by the group of players at a campus apartment, while an attorney for the players contends she consented to the sex with multiple men.

A police report shows the woman told investigators she got drunk at a lambda Chi out of a fraternity party. When the party broke up around 2:30 AM, she said she was taken to an apartment where 7–10 men began taking turns having sex with her.

University Chancellor Roger Brown has said the accused players were suspended from classes and are no longer enrolled pending a student conduct code hearing. He also said the university reported the fraternity to its national headquarters.

The accused players, all free on bond, were suspended from the team by [head football coach Rodney] Allison before they were charged. The six players, Muhammad Ahmad Abdus-Salaam, Lironne Davis, DeJuan Payne, Cori Stukes,

Terrence Thomas and Larry White, have a preliminary hearing set Dec. 12."

After a three-way discussion–Mizell, Foley and me–Joanie Sompayrac was appointed administrative judge by UTC Chancellor Brown. Following a good deal more three-way e-mail discussions, formal administrative charge letters were issued to each of the six accused students.

Getting to that point was a bit of a struggle. There was debate as to whether FERPA (Federal Education Rights and Privacy Act) privacy protection afforded student records precluded conducting all six hearings at the same time. Fortunately, I was able to secure acceptance of my view that FERPA did not apply and it would be completely unreasonable to request the young lady to go through six hearings.

The hearing was set for January 12, 2006. The accuser had dropped out of school and I faced a new challenge: locating the young lady and persuading her to meet with me for interview prior to the hearing. Initially she did not want to be further involved in the proceeding. A developing problem was detected.

On January 11, one day before the hearing was set to commence, I was finally able to arrange a meeting with my key witness. Definitely not the way I ever proceeded in the past.

I met with J. A. in a conference room at the UT Chattanooga student affairs office. Like pulling teeth. Although I cannot disclose the contents of our conversation suffice to say I expected a tough hearing the next day. I was not disappointed.

Just prior to the start of the hearing J. A. advised me she was not willing to testify. Each of the accused, six attorneys, and the administrative judge were in the hearing room and ready to proceed. I was in the hallway outside seeking to persuade the accuser to testify and explain how she could do so without looking at anyone.

After 10 or 15 minutes of intense words, alternating between begging and mild threatening, my witness agreed to testify. We entered the hearing room to the awaiting assembly

Sompayrac called the hearing to order and set out procedural rules governing the hearing. . Chattanooga attorneys Myrlene Marsa, Hank Hill, Mike Little, Dave Barrow, Jerry Summers and Jeff Schaarschmidt were present and each identified the football player he or she represented as the hearing got underway.

I called J.A. as my first witness and she took the witness stand. With eyes focused on the floor in front of her she testified fully and forthrightly, as best I could tell. What she had to say was not anything to be proud of but certainly implicated the accused.

Cross examination killed any thought I had of proving a "rape" charge. J. A. conceded she had published remarks "bragging about …taking on the football team." She admitted being an active participant at the party and knowingly departing in the wee hours of the morning for another destination.

The accuser's claim that she was intoxicated at the time she engaged in sexual acts with the accused faced strong contradictory evidence introduced by defense attorneys. At the same time evidence that each of the accused had sex with the accuser was iron–clad and never at issue.

The hearing lasted two days. On the second day, following final arguments, Sompayrac took the case under advisement. At 2:30 in the afternoon I left UTC for the return drive to Knoxville.

Four months later, on May 16, 2006, Sompayrac issued an "initial order" finding each of the six accused innocent of rape. She also found each of the accused guilty of "physical abuse" and "lewd, indecent or obscene conduct". The penalty of "indefinite suspension" was imposed on each defendant.

One of the accused, Terrence Thomas, filed a petition for judicial review with the Hamilton County Chancery Court (Docket No. 06–0568) on July 14, 2006. I filed a motion to dismiss on August 6. That motion was granted by Chancellor Howell Peoples' Order of Dismissal entered August 15, 2006.

The Hamilton County criminal charges against the six defendants were ultimately dismissed for lack of evidence.

From my perspective the correct result was reached as to each of the six accused football players. There was little doubt in my mind that a negotiated resolution could have been easily been reached with each defense attorney at the outset had a "rape" charge not been included. Had the accuser been interviewed by University counsel immediately following the incident there is little doubt a charge of "rape" would not have been included.

"Too many chiefs" consumed time debating procedural details when prompt assessment of the validity of the accuser's charge would have better served the

University. I saw only increased expenditure of time and cost resulting from the change in practice I had routinely followed in the past.

Chapter 118–2007 Was a Great Year!

In 2007 I marked 35 years of employment in the University of Tennessee office of General Counsel. Was my 35th year as exciting as the first? Absolutely!

Judge David Duggan, his wife Kerry and other friends came to our home for dinner the evening of January 5. Wonderful visit and we talked a bit about UT history.

Early Saturday morning January 20, I picked up Bahodoor Kosimov, a UT–based Fulbright scholar in journalism from Tajikistan, for breakfast. I had recently been introduced to Kosimov by Dr. Peter Gross, head of the UT Department of Journalism and Electronic Media.

The first OGC staff meeting in seven years was scheduled by Peter Foley. On January 24 Foley, Steve Sprouse, Rhonda Alexander and I met in a conference room and hooked up by conference call with OGC Memphis attorneys. We discussed various legal developments of mutual interest. A welcome return to a practice that worked well in years past.

Following the morning staff meeting I flew to Memphis then drove to Jackson for the evening. The next morning I tried the case of Barry Clark v. State of Tennessee before the Tennessee Claims Commission–Commissioner Miller–Herron presiding–in Camden.

I enjoyed traveling about the State of Tennessee –at one time or another I had visited every one of Tennessee's 95 counties at some point in my career.

After completing the Clark trial, according to my diary entry for January 25, I then drove to Martin for afternoon meeting with witnesses in Peggy Jackson v. State. This evening I attended the UT Martin men's and women's basketball games with Phil and Debbie Dane (UTM Athletic Director) and had courtside dinner (very nice meal sitting at tables at the end of the court during the women's game!). Super evening.

The next morning I attended depositions in the Chancellors conference room at UT Martin. I drove back to Memphis for the flight home later that day.

A March 27, 2007 memo from Mizell announced that the Steve and Karen Sprouse planned to retire effective June 30. Steve was the longest-serving attorney in the office of General Counsel, aside from me.

Mid-May featured a 10 day trip to Ireland with friends Sandra and Steve Foster. Sandra was employed in the UT Knoxville personnel office in the '70s.

My diary entry for August 17 documents the legal services I continued to provide the UT Medical Center at the opposite end of the state.

Flew to Memphis for the day. Won the Copeland case (argued State's S. J. Motion & won) Karen Williams, J [Circuit Judge]. This makes three S. J. wins in a row in Memphis in three big dollar cases–with all other defendants in each case remaining in the case (Roberson, Connor and Copeland). A good record!

Another trip abroad was taken in the fall. On August 24, I departed for Russia and Central Asia with a UT "affiliated" group. I was joined on the trip by Barry Rice (a UT graduate whose son Brian is an announcer for UT athletics), Helen Hewitt, (whose grandfather, Brown Ayers, was a former UT president and has one of the University's most famous buildings, Ayers Hall, named for him) and Olga Meshcheryakova, who met the rest of us in Moscow's Domodedovo Airport for travel onward to Central Asian.

In Tajikistan we met up with former UT Fulbright scholar Bahodoor Kosimov and a future UT Fulbright scholar in journalism, Muhayo Orifova.

Following our September 16 return to the U.S. I authored a full-page article about the exotic independent travel adventure for the Knoxville News-Sentinel. Titled "Road less traveled provides a memorable journey," the article tells the story of our group's travel through "the Stans" including a seldom traversed "highway" route through the desolate but fascinating Pamir mountains. (Knoxville News-Sentinel, November 4, 2007, p. F4).

The entire staff of the Office of General Counsel enjoyed Christmas lunch during the week before Christmas holiday at the Italian Market and Grill. Many years had gone by without such office holiday camaraderie. The time together was enjoyable–another welcome return to a good past practice.

The annual UT Service Awards Luncheon was held in the University Center on December 14. I was recognized for 35 years service in the office of General Counsel. A photograph was taken of me with President Peterson and General Counsel Mizell.

Yes, 2007 was a great year for me! It also seemed to be a better year for the Office of General Counsel–except for the departure of Steve and Karen Sprouse, both of whom had given years of valuable service to the University.

Chapter 119–My Litigation Record in 2007– Check the Stats

My litigation experience in 2007 was the mix I enjoyed so much throughout my career. The stats tell much of the story (and several case reviews follow).

A total of 30 cases were brought to finality by me in 2007. There were 24 wins, five losses and one settlement.

WORKER'S COMPENSATION CLAIMS

Workers compensation cases, being a "horse of a different color" are dealt with separately for statistical purposes. In 2007 four WC cases were concluded with compensation claims being rejected by the Tennessee Claims Commission. In each case the Commission concluded that the injury for which compensation was sought was not work-related. Of course there is really no way to assess the dollar value of rejected claims. But there would certainly have been cost to the University had the claims been granted.

In two cases the Commission ruled in favor of the Workers Comp claimant. $16,102 was awarded in one case and an unspecified amount in another (with the amount to be determined based on future treatment). A third WC case was settled for $15,000. The estimated total value of all claims paid or affirmed was $40,000.

CONTESTED CASE PROCEEDINGS

Five University of Tennessee contested case administrative proceedings were concluded in 2007. Four were conducted in accordance with the Tennessee Administrative Procedures Act and one in accordance with informal procedures set out in the UT Knoxville student handbook ("Hill topics"). All five concluded with University action being upheld.

TORT CLAIMS

A total of 15 tort claims were litigated to completion in 2007. Tort litigation involved both claims of bodily injury and property damage. Claims involved automobile accidents allegedly caused by UT drivers, bodily injury resulting from "slip and falls" due to claimed or actual defects on University property, an amputated finger resulting from a faculty member's claimed negligence in operating a dangerous piece of equipment and other acts of negligence attributed to UT employees.

Judgments in favor of the University were entered in 13 of the 15 tort cases. Claims in those cases totaled $530,471. A couple of the winners were quite interesting. Two other cases resulted in judgments against the State (University of Tennessee).

Total tort claims against the University in 2007 amounted to $880,882.56. Judgments in the two losses totaled $56,250.

MEDICAL MALPRACTICE CLAIMS

In 2007 final judgments were entered in three medical malpractice cases. Two cases with total claims in the amount of $900,000 resulted in judgments in the University's favor.

One suit for $1 million resulted in a judgment against the University in the amount of $250,000. I found all three cases challenging and quite interesting.

The loser got most of my attention.

CIVIL RIGHTS AND CONSTITUTIONAL AL LAW

There were no cases in my areas of specialty, civil rights and constitutional law, concluded in 2007 as none had been assigned me since 2002. Since the vast majority of those cases were litigated in federal court my federal practice likewise concluded in 2002. On a practical note, my 95% win record in those case categories remained intact.

TOTAL EXPOSURE AND PAYMENT FOR 2007

A total of $2,780,882 in claims–excluding workers compensation–filed against the University or State of Tennessee for alleged acts of negligence of University of Tennessee employees, were brought to conclusion in 2007.

Roughly $40,000 was awarded on worker's compensation claims and $306,250 on all other claims falling under my responsibility.

Aside from failure to appeal the $250,000 judgment in *Chumley*, 2007 was a very good year litigation–wise! (See Chapter 123). My last full year of litigation for the University was a winner!

Post script:

So how did other attorneys perform by comparison? I have refrained from commenting on how other OGC attorneys performed–in part because I handled by far the largest caseload of anyone in the office. It would also be imprudent to comment on cases about which I lacked sufficient information. One limited exception involves tort claim dating back to 2002.

The March 18, 2006 Knoxville News-Sentinel's front page headline announced, "UT ordered to pay student $300,000 for injuries from campus assault." Tennessee Claims Commissioner Vance Cheek "found that UT failed to provide adequate lighting near the Lake Avenue parking garage, providing an inviting atmosphere for the Nov. 13, 2002, assault. The $300,000 is the maximum amount allowed by state law." (Id.)

I had one case in my career that hit the maximum for non-contract actions brought under the APA (*Pinson*). From what I knew of the facts of the present case the results were quite surprising.

As the Sentinel reported:

"Smith had parked her bright orange Volkswagen in the Lake Avenue garage after working at a clothing store in West Town Mall. She spoke to her boyfriend in Chattanooga by cell phone as she crossed Terrace Avenue and ascended steps leading to the Presidential Complex and her dormitory.

She told her boyfriend she had a creepy feeling of being followed. That's when Christopher J. Gann, then 25, implemented his plan to steal Smith's car.

Gannon smashed Smith in the head with a brick, but the athletic woman fought back. She shoved Dan down the steps and ran before falling to one knee from the blow to her head.

Gann later told police he got mad because Smith pushed him. He retrieved his brick and chased after the woman, hurling the brick at her. The brick struck Smith's back, allowing Gann to catch her.

Gann dragged Smith off the steps and repeatedly smashed her head with a brick. He stopped striking her with the brick, he told police, only because Smith wouldn't stop screaming.

Cheek initially awarded Smith $1.5 million in damages but reduce that amount to $1.25 million, [Smith's attorney] said. Cheek told the attorneys that he found Smith had some comparative fault because she was not paying attention to her surroundings while walking to her dorm.

She declared that Smith was 25% at fault and UT had the remainder. But with a limit of $300,000 on claims against the state, Cheek awarded Smith the maximum amount." (Id. p. A9).

I was quite puzzled by the findings and thought back to one interesting incident I heard about near the conclusion of the four-day hearing was proceeding on the UT campus. One key witness for the University exited the hearing, saw me in the area and described an incident had just been privy to.

According to my source, immediately after Commissioner Cheek announced a recess, he blistered attorneys on both sides for the manner in which they had conducted themselves during the hearing. Both sides repeatedly raised objections and those objections were repeatedly overruled. Cheek concluded his tongue lashing with, "If Ron Leadbetter had been handling this matter the hearing would have been over in two days!"

Only a year or two earlier I had asked Commissioner Cheek the number of cases being tried by University attorneys in his division. I was stunned to learn that no other University attorney had pursued litigation to trial. The Smith ruling may have encouraged that pattern to continue.

On March 19, 2008 Knoxville News-Sentinel readers learned that "UT loses appeal in attack case." (Knoxville News-Sentinel, March 19, 2008, B1). The Sentinel reported that the Tennessee Court of Appeals had rejected the University's appeal from Commissioner Cheek's ruling. (Id.)

In the same issue the editor of the Sentinel offered an editorial contending "UT should make its peace in Jessica Smith case." After reviewing the horrendous facts of the matter the editor opined, "UT presumably can appeal the case to the state Supreme Court. However, at this point, the school runs the risk of losing more in credibility and goodwill–if it hasn't lost these already–than it can in legal approval. Two hearings ago was a good time for UT to settle this case and move on. It is past time now." (Id. p. B4).

I remain of the opinion the University could have achieved a better result in

Smith–and not necessarily by settling the claim at the outset. Promoting an effective working relationship with the adjudicating body is often helpful.

Chapter 120–The Two 2007 Tort Losses

The case of Robert Baker Eadie v. State of Tennessee was a *tort claim I expected to win–but lost.

Eadie, a student in the College of Veterinary Medicine, was palpating a cow at the large animal clinic with his right hand. Palpating is a medical term that has been described to me as the process when a healthcare worker feels a person or animal for the purpose of determining how the body's tissues or muscles feel in such categories as shape, size, swelling, firmness, or location of the fetus in a pregnant female. While palpating the animal, Baker placed his left hand on a hydraulic lift operated by a Vet school intern–and UT employee–Dr. Moira Roberts. The middle finger on Eadie's left-hand was partially amputated–crushed–by the hydraulic lift.

Eadie filed suit in the Claims Commission in June 2004 for $300,000 in damages, claiming that his injury resulted from Dr. Robert's negligence. The University's position was that it was Eadie's negligence in placing his hand on the hydraulic lift, despite a posted warning, that caused his injury. Eadie was represented by my good friend, Knoxville attorney, Robert Stacey.

The case was tried on November 29, 2006. Commissioner Stephanie Reevers ruled in Eadie's favor on August 20, 2007, allocating 25% of the fault to the claimant.

The Commissioner found that Eadie had suffered damages in the amount of $55,000, therefore he was awarded a judgment in the amount of $41,250. (Claims Commission No. 20401057). Stacey did a fine job presenting his client's case and deserved the win. No appeal was recommended.

A second tort claim judgment against the University in 2007 involved an automobile accident on Magnolia Avenue in Benton County (Camden, TN). UT Martin driver, Jane "Rene" Bard, was admittedly at fault in the accident but the University disputed the amount of damages claimed by the claimant, Barry Clark. (Barry L. Clark v. State of Tennessee, Claims Comm. No. 20050817).

Clark, filed suit in March, 2005 seeking recovery for injuries and property damage he suffered while riding a bicycle and struck by a UT vehicle operated by Bard. He demanded compensatory damages in the amount of $50,411.71. Due to the minor nature of the claimant's injuries the figure was disputed.

The case was tried in Camden on January 25, 2007. Commissioner Nancy

Miller–Herron presided.

Two days later, on January 29, 2007, Commissioner Miller-Herron awarded Clark judgment in the amount of $15,000. On my case card I entered a note: "This amount is GOOD for UT." A "loss" on my litigation record but a "good" loss for the University."

As I have mentioned in other chapters, a tort is a legal term for when one person suffers a loss due to the negligence of another in civil terms, not criminal.

Chapter 121–Two Memorable 2007 Tort Wins– An Injured Horse and the Errant Golf Ball

THE HORSE CASE-CRIDER v. STATE

The case of Charles Crider v. State of Tennessee (Claims Comm. No. 20060213) was filed in September 2005. Crider was the owner of a horse named "Indian Sage," an Appaloosa mare. Indian's specialty was barrel racing.

Indian underwent surgery on her throat at the College of Veterinary Medicine for breathing problems. Following surgery, the Vet tech said that Indian unexpectedly "threw a fit," as her anesthesia wore off, and injured her leg – dislocating it at the knee. As a result, she could no longer barrel race.

Crider sued for $53,000, which included the claimed $50,000 value of Indian, cost of surgical procedures and aftercare. The case went to trial on October 10, 2006. Judgment was entered in the State's favor by Claims Commissioner William Shults on October 31, 2007. Commissioner Shultz identified the evidentiary basis for his conclusion:

In his fourteen (14) years at the University of Tennessee, Dr. [Thomas] Doherty has never seen an occurrence like this during recovery from a laryngotomy. Under examination by Mr. Leadbetter, Dr. Doherty also stated that the horse at no time thrashed about with its legs or struck an object. He also testified it was common for a horse to get up after two attempts, and that he had never seen an animal get up in the fashion in which Indian Sage did and break its leg. (Final Judgment, p.7).

What happened to Indian Sage is obviously regrettable. However, there is simply no testimony taken from an expert before this Commissioner which would indicate that the usual and customary standard of care for bringing a horse out from under anesthesia, without injury, was breached in this case. Dr. Holder, the surgeon, deferred to the opinion of Dr. Doherty, the attending anesthesiologist here, who testified that it was not foreseeable that Indian Sage would break a forelimb after such a routine surgery. In fact, he testified he had never seen this occur and that the usual and customary practices for this type of surgery were followed in the case of this animal.

The owner himself admitted that he did not know what the standard of care was in similar situations. Further, Mr. Crider was not present in the recovery room and thus, there is absolutely no other evidence before me contradicting Dr. Doherty's testimony that all proper measures were taken in connection with the recovery of the horse.

(Final Judgment, p.13). There was no appeal from the Commission's judgment.

Far more challenging than Crider was the case of Audrey Connor.

THE GOLF BALL CASE—CONNER v. STATE

Conner was a negligence case arising out of a golf event at the Stone Bridge Golf Club in Memphis on September 17, 2003. The UT Academy of Students of Pharmacy annually sponsored the event.

Dr. Stephanie Phelps, a faculty member of the UT Center for the Health Sciences College of Pharmacy, served as a faculty advisor for the Academy and made contractual arrangements with Stonebridge for use of the club facilities for the tournament.

Audrey Conner, a student in the College of Pharmacy, had volunteered to work the event and "drive around the course [in a golf cart] to check on the different player groups to make sure things were going smoothly. It is undisputed that plaintiff had never been on a golf course before and knew very little about how the game was played." (Circuit Court's Memorandum Opinion, p.3).

A foursome consisting of Dr. Phelps and students Leigh Price, Steve Phillips and Paula Carter were out on the course as the tournament progressed. At one point, Conner and golf cart companion Kelli Hall stopped by to engage in conversation with Dr. Phelps and another member of the foursome at what he said was "hole number six" while waiting for another foursome to clear the area in front of them so they could proceed.

As the second foursome cleared the area Phelps' foursome returned to the fairway to resume play as Connor and Hall drove off in their golf cart. Members of the Phelps foursome, one after another, drove his or her ball out into the fairway.

No one in the foursome observed that the golf cart had driven into the area adjacent to the fairway. Unfortunately, Leigh Price's long drive at hole number six exited the fairway, descended toward the cart path and struck Connor in the head. Connor sustained a severe brain injury from the blow.

Connor filed suit against the State of Tennessee in the Division of Claims

Administration in September 2004. She alleged her brain injury resulted from negligent supervision by Dr. Phelps and requested damages in the amount of $300,000.

The claim against the State was subsequently joined for further proceedings with a suit filed by Conner against Stonebridge Golf Club and Leigh Price in the Shelby County Circuit Court. (Audrey Conner vs. Leigh Price, Linkscorp LLC d/b/a Stonebridge Golf Club, and The State of Tennessee, No. CT–005257–04 Div. II and Audrey Conner vs. the State of Tennessee, No. CT–002707–06 Div. II).

Following completion of discovery–deposition of witnesses–all three defendants filed motions for summary judgment, contending that the undisputed facts show there was no negligence on the part of the defendants. The motions were argued before Circuit Judge James Russell, on April 27, 2007.

On June 7, 2007 the Circuit Court entered its "Memorandum Opinion and Order Granting in Part and Denying in Part Motions for Summary Judgment." Two defendants prevailed on their motion and one did not.

The State's motion to have the case dismissed was denied. Judge Russell found that "although [in the claims commission action] the plaintiff's theory of recovery is predicated upon allegations of negligence as to Dr. Stephanie Phelps acting in her capacity as faculty advisor for the Academy of Students of Pharmacy [in the Circuit Court action] Dr. Phelps is sued in her individual capacity as a player (as opposed to any official capacity in her role as faculty advisor). (Id. p.11).

The Court ruled, "with regard to Dr. Phelps' alleged negligence with regard to the actions of the ASP students in putting on the golf tournament, the State's motion to dismiss is hereby denied." Although Judge Russell ruled the State was not entitled to judgment as a matter of law he ruled that the deposition evidence showed the State was titled to summary judgment based on undisputed facts:

"For purposes of this motion only, there may well be a disputed issue of material fact as to whether Dr. Phelps had a duty to instruct tournament players, such as Leigh Price, on rules of golf etiquette and safety and it may also be a disputed issue of material fact as to whether Dr. Phelps had a similar duty to spectators and non— participants such as plaintiff. However, even if such a duty existed–which the state denies–it is clear that any breach of these duties had no causal connection to the injuries suffered by plaintiff." (Id. pp.12-13).

For example, the Court found that Connor already knew the relevant rules of golf etiquette:

"…but Kelly told me that if the ball is in play that you would wait … If a ball was in play, we waited, and then after people had finished their turns, we would go on.

… if they were in the middle of hitting golf balls, we didn't go. But yes, we would stop and if they were hitting golf balls, yes, I saw golf balls going through the air." (Id. p.13).

The Court also focused on the plaintiff's response to my question as to what she would have done differently had Dr. Phelps sat down with her and explained golf rules of etiquette–which Connor responded "I wouldn't have done anything differently." (Id.p.14).

Finally, the Court noted that Connor was not even present before the tournament commenced: "Moreover, had Dr. Phelps given such instructions and warnings to the non-playing participants, by the time plaintiff arrived the tournament had already commenced and Dr. Phelps was out playing golf." (Id. p.14).

For the foregoing reasons, summary judgment was granted in favor of the State. Connor took no appeal from that ruling.

Summary judgment was also granted in favor of the Golf Club. The student defendant, Leigh Price, had her motion denied and remained a defendant. I have no information how the case ended for the Price. For the State the case concluded with the Court's ruling that UT employee Dr. Stephanie Phelps had no liability even if she had acted negligently.

Chapter 122–The Late Arriving Surgeon and the Missing Skull Fragment

Two major medical malpractice cases involving medical faculty at UT Memphis were concluded in 2007. The road was challenging.

ROBERSON v. STATE OF TENNESSEE
THE MISSING PHYSICIAN

Timothy Roberson was scheduled for surgery at Methodist Hospital on August 16, 2000. The surgery was to be performed under the supervision of Dr. Kevin Foley. UT surgery residents would begin the surgery and Foley would complete the more challenging aspects of the surgery.

Roberson was placed under anesthesia before 8 a.m. and surgery began at 9 a.m. Foley did not come to the operating room until 3 p.m.–almost 7 hours after Roberson was put to sleep. Foley's procedure took five and a half hours–placing Roberson under anesthesia for a total of nearly 11 hours. Somewhere in the process Roberson suffered nerve damage to his upper extremities.

Timothy and wife Gwendolyn Roberson, filed suit with the Division of Claims Administration on August 1, 2001. The claimants requested damages in the amount of $600,000. (Claims Commission No. 20200260 W.D.)

The Robersons' action against the state alleged professional negligence of UT surgery residents, Dr. Christie Mina and Dr. L. Madison Michael. Claimants were represented by Memphis attorney Duncan Ragsdale.

At about the same time, claimants (a/k/a plaintiffs) filed suit in the Shelby County Circuit Court (No. CT-007255-04 Div. 8) against a number of private defendants, including Semmes–Murphy Clinic, Methodist Hospital Central, The Medical Anesthesia Group, Dr. Kevin Foley, and several other privately employed healthcare workers.

The evidence showed that surgery residents Mina and Madison were in the operating room performing surgical procedures on Roberson long before Foley's arrival. But the Robersons' contended that while the surgery residents acted in a timely manner they did nothing to address what they termed "the abandonment" of Tim Roberson by Dr. Foley.

It was also the Robersons' claim that the padding and positioning of Tim Roberson were inadequate and contributed to his injuries.

The Roberson case was originally assigned to OGC Memphis attorney Tanda Gresham. It was reassigned to me in December 2003 when Gresham resigned her position at UT for employment elsewhere.

In October 2004 the Claims Commission case was ordered transferred to the Shelby County Circuit Court. The case was officially filed in that court on December 29, 2004. (In the Circuit Court of Tennessee for the 30th Judicial District at Memphis, No. CT–007255–04 Div. VIII).

It took a number of depositions of witnesses beyond those deposed by Grisham. Included was the deposition of plaintiffs' expert, Dr. John Leonard, a physician in Greenville, North Carolina. Another expert, Dr. John Ogden, was deposed in Atlanta. The defendants deposed both the injured patient, Timothy Roberson, and his wife Gwendolyn.

After deposing the claimants and their expert I filed a motion for summary judgment along with a detailed "Statement of Undisputed Material Facts" - one of the key facts being that Dr. Foley was called as soon as decompression was completed by Dr. Mina. It was our argument that there was no negligent delay.

Other defendants filed motions for summary judgment and oral arguments were presented to Shelby County Circuit Judge D'Army Bailey on December 14, 2006. Judge Bailey issued an oral ruling from the bench and granted the State's motion. Interestingly, the motions filed by the remaining defendants were denied.

On January 5, 2007 the Circuit Court entered an "Order on Defendant State of Tennessee's Motion for Summary Judgment." Plaintiffs immediately filed an application for an "extraordinary appeal pursuant to Rule 10, Tennessee

Rules of Appellate Procedure." On January 11, 2007 the Tennessee Court of Appeals entered an order denying plaintiffs' application. A difficult, high dollar case, was over – at least for the University (and, as was my customary practice, I made no effort to determine the outcome of the remaining claims and have no knowledge of their outcome).

Postscript: No effort was made to settle the case early on because my early review of the case file– and the preliminary work done by Gresham –persuaded me that UT medical residents had done nothing wrong. Even in a high dollar case I believed it was ill-advised to settle a claim where the evidence weighed substantially in favor of the party I represented.

THE MISSING SKULL FRAGMENT
COPELAND v. STATE

William Copeland, an adult resident of Senatobia, Mississippi, was injured in an automobile accident on April 20, 2003 when he was ejected from the vehicle by the force of the collision. Copeland was taken from the scene of the accident to the Regional Medical Center at Memphis located in Memphis, Shelby County, Tennessee.

When examined with x-rays and a CT scan at "the Med", Copeland was found to be suffering from a "frontal subdural hematoma"–a brain injury–among numerous other injuries. UT surgery resident Mark D. Smith, M.D. and his UT faculty supervisor, surgeon Morris Ray, M.D., performed a "frontotemporoparietal craniectomy" and several other procedures on Copeland. Lifesaving procedures!

A portion of Copeland's skull was removed in order to treat and repair his brain injury. The skull fragment or "bone flap" removed by Drs. Ray and Smith was provided to staff members of "the Med" for storage and safe keeping until reduced swelling of the brain permitted additional surgery to replace the bone flap in Copeland's skull.

On June 30, 2003 Copeland was scheduled for surgery to replace the bone flap in his skull. When Copeland arrived at the hospital he was informed by Dr. Scrantz, the physician scheduled to conduct the surgery, that the surgery had been canceled because Copeland's flap could not be located; it was lost.

Surgery was rescheduled. On July 25, 2003 a metallic mesh was inserted in place of the missing bone flap. Copeland's treatment was complete. But Copeland was not satisfied.

On April 20, 2004 Copeland filed suit in the Circuit Court for the Thirtieth Judicial District at Memphis (Shelby County Circuit Court) against doctors Ray and Smith, as well as the Shelby County Healthcare Corporation, for $5 million in damages. The same day Copeland filed suit against the State of Tennessee, seeking the $300,000 maximum recovery against the State permitted by law for a single claimant). Memphis attorneys Dee Shawn Peoples and R. Lindley Richter, Jr. represented the claimant/plaintiff.

In March 2005 Copeland took a "voluntary nonsuit" in the Circuit Court action as to defendant Mark Smith. By filing suit with the Tennessee Claims Commission, Copeland had waived his right to proceed against Mark Smith, a UT employee.

By Order of April 13, 2005 the Claims Commission proceeding (No. 20401644, W. D.) was transferred to the Shelby County Circuit Court. (No. CT-002874–05, Div. III) to be joined for trial with the existing circuit court proceeding (Docket No. CT–002255–04, Div. III). The presiding judge was Karen Williams, Circuit Judge.

The 49 page complaint bore the following introductory listing of the grounds under which relief was requested:

"COMPLAINT FOR THE FOLLOWING:

I. BAILMENT

II. NEGLIGENT STORAGE, MAINTENANCE, AND PROTECTION OF HUMAN BODY PARTS

III. RES IPSA LOQUITUR

IV. VIOLATION OF OBLIGATIONS OF A WAREHOUSEMAN

V. CONVERSION

VI. MEDICAL MALPRACTICE

VII. BREACH OF WARRANTY

VIII. NEGLIGENCE OF PHYSICIANS

IX. REPLEVIN

X. DETINUE

XI. NEGLIGENT ENTRUSTMENT

XII. NEGLIGENT ENTRUSTMENT [Sic]

XIII. SPECIAL ASSUMPSIT

There were numerous allegations in the complaint, many repetitive, some incomprehensible and a few downright absurd. To cite a few of the hundreds of interesting allegations contained in the complaint:

"24. That as a direct and proximate result of the breach of the duties, obligations, and responsibilities of the defendants, Regional Medical Center at Memphis, Morris W. Ray, M.D., and Mark D. Smith, M.D. the plaintiff has suffered severe and serious personal injuries that were readily foreseeable, to-wit: the plaintiff has been permanently disfigured, and suffers, and will continue to suffer, from tinnitus, dizziness, neurological deficits, headaches, blurred vision, loss of balance and vertigo; the plaintiff suffers from anxiety, loss of self-esteem, and nervousness; the plaintiff has lost large sums of money that he otherwise would have earned and will lose large amounts of money in the future that he otherwise would have earned; that said conditions are permanent and progressive; the plaintiff has significant limitations on his daily activities; said injuries, pathological fear of further injury, disfigurement, anxiety, nervousness, tinnitus, neurological deficits, headaches, blurred vision and dizziness result in severe and serious pain and suffering, and are permanent and progressive; the plaintiff has been compelled to spend large sums of money for medical, hospital, plastic surgery and pharmaceutical care in an attempt to cure and alleviate said condition, and will continue so to do in the future; the plaintiff has been denied and prevented from receiving the optimum medical care and treatment for the aforesaid medical conditions; the plaintiff has lost the opportunity to have the removed portion of his skull reattached rather than being replaced by a prosthetic device; the implantation of the titanium mesh prosthetic device exposes the plaintiff to a known carcinogenic appliance; the plaintiff has been prevented from engaging in his normal applications, amusements and hobbies; and, the plaintiff is unable to engage in his normal social activities.

WHEREFORE PLAINTIFF, William Copeland, prays for judgment against the defendants, Regional Medical Center at Memphis, Morris W. Ray, M. D. and Mark D. Smith, M. D., Jointly and severally, in a sum in excess of Five Million Dollars ($5,000,000.00) and his costs of suit." (Complaint, pp. 5-6).

Count II of the complaint contained the following explanation of how the defendants were guilty of "negligent storage, maintenance, and protection of human body parts":

"17. That defendants, Morris W. Ray, M.D. and Mark D. Smith, M.D. as agents and servants of defendant, Regional Medical Center at Memphis, and individually as physicians for the plaintiff, retained possession of that portion of the skull of the plaintiff for its storage, maintenance, and protection, until such time as the condition of the plaintiff would permit its permanent replacement; however, said defendants lost, mislaid, or otherwise disposed of said portion of the skull of the plaintiff, all in violation of the rules and procedures of their principal and master, defendant, Regional Medical Center at Memphis, and in violation of their duties, obligations and responsibilities to provide for the safe, adequate and proper storage of human body parts.

18. That defendants… by removing, retaining possession, and accepting said portion of the skull of the plaintiff as a depository of human body parts and as licensed physicians, were under a continuing duty at all times relevant hereto, to know the whereabouts of said portion of the skull of the plaintiff;…" (Complaint, p.8).

Similar allegations relating to the missing skull fragment, i.e. bone flap, the titanium metal substitute and the horrific impact of the substitution on

Copeland's physical, mental and financial well-being consumed nearly 50 pages of print.

The deposition of William Copeland was held on February 17, 2006 in Memphis. When I entered the conference room where the deposition was to be held I saw the plaintiff for the first time. He had arrived earlier, along with his attorneys.

I had expected to see someone whose head was grossly distorted in some fashion. Instead, I encountered a young black male who appeared normal in every respect.

I took a seat at the conference table several feet from Copeland. As discreetly as possible I examined Copeland's head at every opportunity. During the deposition I asked Copeland to point to the exact location where the titanium mesh had been surgically implanted as replacement for the missing bone flap.

Copeland did as requested, but I saw nothing. His hair had grown back at the surgical site and not even a surgical scar was noticeable. There was no bulging, no indentation... nothing.

I requested and received photographs of the injury site. Of course, even had the bone flap not been lost scarring at the surgical site would have been expected – both from the initial surgery and the surgery needed to return the flap to its original location.

In September 2006, I filed a motion for summary judgment on behalf of the State contending that the State's employee–Dr. Smith had engaged in no negligent act and had caused no injury to the plaintiff.

10 more depositions were taken during the first half of 2007. A particularly valuable deposition was taken of Kevin Scott with the Midsouth Tissue Bank. It was his testimony that titanium mesh implants were common substitutes in skull injury cases such as Copeland's.

The State's motion for summary judgment was argued before Judge Williams on August 17. She issued an oral ruling from the bench: Motion granted

A formal order granting the State's motion for summary judgment was entered by the Court on August 21, 2007. No appeal was taken from the Circuit Court's order.

The "high dollar" case could likely have been settled for a "reasonable sum" early in the proceedings. No settlement offer was ever made.

Again, the University of Tennessee benefited financially by not "caving in" in the face of "risk." As important, the University stood behind a young physician who, in my view of the evidence, had done nothing wrong.

Chapter 123–The Sure Loser: An Appeal Not Taken– Chumley vs. State

One thing is certain in the legal world: the judge is always right, at least for legal purposes, unless reversed on appeal. The only appeal which cannot be won is the one not filed. The following case provides an example of a horrendous judicial ruling against the State which should have been appealed, but was not.

KRISTEN CHUMLEY, ET. AL. V. STATE OF TENNESSEE

A single medical malpractice case was responsible for over 70% of litigation judgment/settlement costs to the University for cases I concluded in 2007. That case dated back to a November 12, 1998 office visit to a private (non-UT affiliated) clinical facility in Knoxville by 11-year-old Kristin Chumley.

Kristen's mother, Misty Chumley, sought treatment for her daughter's lingering fever. Dr. Fred Grello, a UT employee working at the clinic as part of his faculty assignment, examined Kristen and recommended she be given an injection of Vistaril.

Because Kristen asked that the shot did not be given in her buttock, Grello prescribed the shot be given in her deltoid muscle. The injection itself was given by a medical assistant, Clay Madison, who was employed by the clinic–not the State.

Even as the injection was given, Kristen screamed in pain. Her pain continued after she left the clinic. Later medical examination confirmed she had suffered nerve injury while being injected.

On November 10, 1999 a claim alleging medical malpractice and negligent supervision was filed against the State by Kristen's parents, Jerry and Misty Chumley, on her behalf and theirs. The claim's major allegations were that Dr Grello had prescribed an excessive dose of Vistaril, failed to properly advise Misty Chumley of the potential for nerve damage from administering the injection in Kristen's arm, and that, as result of the injection in her arm, Kristen suffered severe nerve damage.

An award of damages in the total amount of $1 million was requested by the Chumleys. The case was tried in Nashville on December 1, 2006 before Claims Commissioner Nancy Miller-Herron.

On January 26, 2007 judgment was entered in the claimants' favor. Claimants were awarded the sum of $250,000. (Kristen Chumley et. al. v. State of Tennessee, Claims Commission No. 20000808). I was flabbergasted. In my estimation the commissioner's findings were completely at odds with the evidence –and the testimony of claimant's own expert witnesses.

By memorandum of February 2, 2007 I recommended to Deputy General Counsel Peter Foley that the case be appealed.

Peter,

We have a problem with a "plaintiff's lawyer" –who is now a Claims Commissioner –who has "run amok" and seemingly deems it her duty to ensure that claimants are not burdened with the responsibility of proving their case with credible evidence (of a breached standard of care, in this case). Also, money is clearly no object to this commissioner; the $250,000 award for a "peripheral nerve" injury to a young lady who was playing organized basketball a short time after the incident in this case makes the McDonald's "hot coffee spill" verdict look downright reasonable and even stingy! Compare the Chumley award to another commissioner's recent, very reasonable $15,000 award in the Barry Clark case where the State was unquestionably at fault, the claimant had pain–sometimes intense–following a bike accident with a UT vehicle, accrued $3,155 in med bills, five weeks of rehab and continuing minor problems with his lower back.

I recommend an appeal of the judgment, on the ground the judgment is contrary to a clear preponderance of the evidence and the damages awarded are grossly excessive and a remittitur should be granted even if the proof supported the Commission's findings as to breached duty and causation.

I prepared a 22-page memorandum outlining proof supporting an appeal and presented that to Foley on February 9. Four days later Foley announced his decision: no appeal. Case over. Good for me–less work. Bad for the University– a quarter million dollars paid that might have been saved. Below are excerpts from the Commissioner's rulings and evidence from the record–primarily testimony from claimants' expert witnesses–suggesting an appeal was in order.

THE COMMISSION'S FINDINGS

Commission Miller-Herron premised her quarter–million-dollar judgment in favor of the claimants on a two-part finding that Dr. Grello breached the acceptable recognized standard of professional practice. First, the Commissioner found that "Dr. [Fred] Grello breached the recognized standard of acceptable professional practice in the medical profession and the specialty of pediatrics by allowing Clay Madison to give claimant an injection of Vistaril in [Kristin Chumley's] deltoid muscle." (Judgment, p. 31).

Second, the Commissioner found that "Dr. Grello's failure to discuss the risks of giving the injection in the deltoid muscle with Kristin Chumley's mother was a breach of the standard of care." (Judgment, p. 32). The Commission surmised that "claimant's harm could have been reasonably foreseen by Dr. Grello." (Judgment, pp. 33–34), and that if Dr. Grello had discussed with claimant's mother the potential of nerve injury" a reasonable person in claimant's mother's position who had been advised of potential nerve injury would not have consented to have this injection in the deltoid muscle of an 11-year-old." (Judgment, p. 31).

With respect to causation, the Commission found that "Dr. Grello's decision to allow Clay Madison to give the injection of Vistaril in Kristin Chumley's arm was the cause in fact of her injuries." (Judgment, p. 32). Commissioner Miller-Herron rested her conclusion on the testimony of claimants' expert, Dr. Weinstein, that within a reasonable degree of medical certainty, Kristen's injury was "secondary to the injection of Vistaril." (Judgment, p. 29).

Testimony of Chumleys' Expert Witnesses Contradicting the Commission's Findings

I urged an appeal because the Commissioner's findings were completely contrary to the testimony of claimants' expert witnesses and other undisputed evidence. To begin with, claimants' expert, Dr. Weinstein, testifid he could not state whether Kristin's injury resulted from the Vistaril or from the needle in which the Vistaril was contained (Deposition of Weinstein, p.26-27).

It was undisputed that Grello prescribed Vistaril–but it was a non-state employee, Clay Madison, who administered the injection. As conceded by claimants' second expert, Dr. Swan, it was Madison who was solely responsible for administering the shot in the correct location and in the proper manner. (Dep. of Swan, p. 23).

Grello examined Kristen's arm shortly after the incident and noted that "[the] injection site was–it was on the triceps muscle, about halfway down the arm, maybe a third of the way down the arm... It was lower than the deltoid muscle." (Dep. of Grello, p.30).

The Vistaril package insert specifically warned that the injection in the deltoid "should not be made into the lower and mid third of the upper arm."(Dep. of Swan, Exbt. 5). No contrary evidence was introduced that Madison gave the injection in the authorized location–the deltoid muscle. (See Dep. of Swan, Exbt. 5).

It was Mrs. Chumley's testimony:

Q. Now, at the time that Mr. Madison started to give the shot, did you say anything to him?

A. I just said, do you have to give it in her arm? That looks like a really big needle.

Q. What did he say?

A. That's where it's supposed to go.

Q. Had he already inserted the needle at the time you made the statement?

A. It happened very quickly, but I said that before the needle went in and as the needle was in.

Q. So as the needle went in, what happened?

A. She started crying.

Q. Immediately?

A. Yes. (Trial Transcript, "TR," p. 68).

Mrs. Chumley testified during her discovery deposition: "I asked him [Clay Madison] why is she screaming? What's going on," as Kristen cried out "Mommy, make him get it out, make him get it out," and that Madison said: "I'm sorry," but that he wouldn't take it out, and at one point it looked like he moved the needle. It actually wiggled and she screamed worse." (Tr. 69-70)

Dr. Swan specifically testified she herself was not qualified to testify to the standard of care of a medical assistant [Clay Madison]. (Dep. of Swan, pp. 29–33). In fact, Dr. Swan testified that she relied entirely on nurses to give injections and did not give injections herself. (Id. pp.34, 38-39). She also testified that nurses typically do not consult her before administering injections:

The most common scenario is they go in to give a shot at the recommended site and the child says I don't want it. Our nursing staff is well-versed in that and usually can actually talk to the family and explain why they get it there. If the family still does not want to get it, then I will go in and talk to the family. (Dep. of Swan, p.34).

When asked whether she "as the physician has the discussion with the patient about the importance of giving the shot in one location versus another," Dr. Swan replied "Either myself or our R.N. does."(Dep. of Swan, p.34). Swan also offered clarification in response to my question of whether "the physician must manipulate the arm and determine how big the muscle is":

Physicians are not the ones that primarily give injections. It's typically nurses, other trained professionals that give it. They are trained to when you give an injection in the arm to feel the muscle and inject it into it. That's a procedure that they do. Physicians are not involved with. (Tr. 119-20).

Therefore it was claimant's expert, Dr. Swan, who made clear in her testimony that Dr. Grello was not the one responsible for administering the injection of Vistaril. Swan's testimony directly contradicted the Commissioner's finding that Grello was responsibility for the administration of the injection.

With respect to the dosage issue, the Commissioner did not conclude that Grello had prescribed improper dosage. In any event, the undisputed evidence showed that Kristen's pain was instantaneous, occurring within one or two seconds–three seconds at most–of the beginning of the injection. (Tr. 37–38), and injection took only 20–25 seconds to complete. (Tr. 21). In any event, the administered dose,75 mg., was only 13% more than the recommended dose of

66.5 mg.

Dr. Swan identified the "side effect from giving too much Vistaril....Sedation is the big one. Drowsiness, tremors." Swan admitted there was no reference at all in the "Physicians Desk Reference" to nerve damage being a side effect of administering too much Vistaril. (Tr. 20-21). Nerve injury was not identified as a possible side effect by any witness.

There was also an issue as to whether Kristen had a well-developed deltoid muscle. Dr. Swann claimed that Dr. Grello breached the applicable standard of care by authorizing the injection of Vistaril in Kristen's deltoid muscle.

However, under cross examination, Swan admitted that many injections are given to children in the deltoid.

Q. Well, okay, let me see if I can break it down a bit. Nurses give shots, not physicians?

A. That is correct.

Q. And you understand that shots are given, injections are given in the deltoid in the arm?

A. That is correct.

Q. And they are given to children?

A. Correct.

Q. And we're talking about Vistaril in this case, but for just a moment let's talk about other shots. There are a whole host of injections that are given to children in this deltoid?

A. That is correct.

Q. And that could be to a 10-year-old, 11-year-old, 12-year-old, any age child, correct?

A. Correct.   (Tr. 119-20)

Dr. Weinstein, claimants' other expert, who treated only pediatric patients – children – confirmed that a variety of injections are given in the deltoid muscles of children. (Tr. 7, 27). There was no exception for the administration of Vistaril.

Q. But you understand you can, in appropriate circumstances, administer an injection of Vistaril in the deltoid muscle?

A. In certain cases.

Q. What are those certain cases?

A. Again, I reference the PDR. It's in a well developed deltoid muscle in certain adults and older children.

Q. Older children. Is there any literature that you're aware of that deals with the administration of this drill that defines what an older child is?

A. Not that I'm aware. (Dep. of Swan, p.14)

Dr. Swan offered her opinion that "An 11-year-old's deltoid is not well-developed enough." (Tr. p.22). When asked to assume that Kristen had a well-developed deltoid muscle, Dr. Swan replied, "It's hard for me to assume that an 11-year-old would have that."(Tr. 17). But Swan admitted she had never personally examined Kristen. (Tr.96). She was unaware of any evidence as to whether or not Kristen had a well-developed deltoid muscle. (Dep. of Swan, p.16).

Dr. Swan conceded that "if a doctor gave a patient who had a well-developed deltoid an injection of Vistaril, that would be considered within the standard of care." (Tr. p.18). She admitted she had never seen any literature specifying when the muscle mass in the arm of a child of a specific age reaches a particular level.

A. It varies by age. It also varies by child, so it's much harder in children to make those assessments, because every child is different depending on what their growth philosophy is, how large they are, their frame size, it's not nearly as easy to make those assessments.

Q. And you have not done any studies yourself as far as when a child reaches a certain stage in muscular development where you can say, well, at this age, I have found that 80% of 12-year-olds have a fully developed deltoid muscle?

A. No. That's why we always have to rely on examining the muscles.
(Tr. 134-35).

When claimants' other expert–Dr. Weinstein–a pediatrician who actually examined Kristen, was asked if she had a well-developed deltoid he responded in the affirmative.

Q. Doctor, you conducted a physical examination of Ms. Chumley during the first–her first visit to you August 25, 1999?

A. Yes.

Q. And you–I take it you examined her arm, the one she complained of having pain in?

A. Yes, sir.

Q. Would it be fair to say she had pretty well-developed deltoid muscles?
Mr. Pryor: object. Object to form.
The Witness: Yes, I think she had fairly well-developed muscles in her arm.
(Tr. p.23).

Dr. Grello also was of the opinion that Kristen had a well-developed deltoid: "She was a tall, athletic, well developed adolescent, nearly 12 years old, approximately 130 pounds… (Dep. of Grello, p.25). Grello further described Kristen:

Well, she was average size approximately for an 18-year-old, so my purposes in both determining dose and the injection site I considered her to be an adult.

Q. As far as having a well-developed deltoid muscle?

A. I would say that she qualified–I'd say all her muscles were well- developed. She was, in terms of her maturity, also, her tanner stage, she was developing and was essentially–she essentially look like a high school senior in terms of size. She was a swimmer, and I recall that she was athletic. She was muscular, she's a sturdy young lady. I would just have to say that I considered her to be the size of an adult. (Tr. 26).

Last, but not least, was the issue of the magnitude of the injury that Kristen suffered. Claimants' expert made it clear that whatever nerve injury Kristen suffered was minor.

Q. Was it your understanding that Ms. Chumley continued to participate actively in sports, including basketball, during the time you were seeing her, that is, after your first visit with her?

A. It's my understanding that she did.

Q. All right. Did she ever tell you she had to stop because of pain in her arm?

A. I don't believe that it kept her from participating in sports.

Q. All right, and was it your understanding that she did receive relief from whatever pain she had in her arm by taking Keppra?

A. Yes.

Q. And you have not seen her since March 17, 2003?

Q. Excuse me. Back in 1999.

A. Yeah.

Q. Okay. Did you have the feeling that she did not perhaps appreciate how much she had improved since you first saw her?

A. That's pretty typical, that people forget how much pain they used to have.

Q. Okay. The last time–the last time you saw Kristen, is it fair to say that her –the continuing effects of her injury were very minor in nature?

A. They were mild in nature.

I advised Foley that it "borders on the absurd to think the State should fork over $250,000 for a mild injury that does not in any significant way prevent Kristin from enjoying life.

FAILURE TO APPEAL
A SURE LOSER

The real tragedy, from my viewpoint, was not that the Commissioner entered a quarter million dollar judgment against the State; the tragedy was that a decision was made by the Office of General Counsel not to appeal the Commissioner's ruling.

An appeal would have risked little and opened the possibility of saving $250,000 for the University. The failure to appeal served as affirmation of the Commission's ruling and removed all doubt. A sure loser!

Chapter 124–Political Challenge Leads to Retirement

At the commencement of 2008 there were issues in administration of the office of General Counsel. The University of Tennessee was also dealing with yet another administrative meltdown at the presidential level.

For me personally, though, life was good! Both personally and professionally I could not have asked for more. So I had no interest in retirement. What was best for me was not the issue.

2008 was an election year. Almost since the day I arrived in the state of Tennessee I was involved in the local political process in one way or another. I had not run for office myself but had assisted others in seeking elective office.

The 18th district seat in the state House of Representatives was held by two-term incumbent Stacey Campfield who was running for a third term. While Campfield and I shared many political views we disagreed vigorously over the best way to implement those views.

Campfield had developed a local, statewide and even national reputation for expressing conservative viewpoints in a way that portrayed him as an extremist.

He was known for his inability to work with opponents across the aisle–and even fellow House members in the Republican Party. As a result, while he introduced many bills he rarely got one passed.

While I had no interest in running against someone who was serving the public well in the state legislature, I saw a problem that needed to be addressed. The Republican Party and the voters of the 18th district needed a representative who effectively represent them in the State legislature. I had a solid background in the workings of state government, including the legislative branch, and believed I could help. Just as important, I was more than willing to make the necessary commitment to serve.

I was under no illusion–Campfield was a highly effective campaigner. He had defeated opponents in two previous House races by tirelessly campaigning door-to-door. He flooded the district with his red and white campaign signs. However, he was not an effective fundraiser.

I was ready for the challenge and prepared to vigorously campaign door-to-door. But I had a job. Legally I could campaign while still employed by the University but I was not willing to take that route. That presented a major problem.

Ideally, I would have commenced campaigning for the District 18 House seat the previous autumn. But I had a number of pending cases and other University responsibilities I was not willing to abandon.

The Republican primary was set for August 7 and would likely determine of the next seat holder in a heavily Republican district. Time was of the essence. On the other hand I was committed to avoiding any charge that I had abandoned unfinished business to campaign. Or that I had any conflict of interest between my UT position and campaigning for a legislative seat.

I first announced my intentions to General Counsel Mizell by e-mail of February 18, 2008:

Catherine,

I want to give you a "heads up" on my likely pursuit of the District 18 House seat in the Tennessee General Assembly. I've taken out and completed the necessary petition to run but will not make a final decision (and will not file my petition) until the end of the month. If I proceed with the House race I will also plan on retiring from the University effective March 31–I don't want even a hint of conflict of interest–and will provide you a formal "notice of retirement" letter at the same time. Of course I will work with my successor to make sure all pending cases are smoothly transferred (and all cases are currently up to date in any event). I'll keep you advised.

Ron

That same day the Knoxville News-Sentinel issued a similar announcement: "Leadbetter may seek House seat" (Knoxville News-Sentinel, February 18, 2008, p. B1):

"Ron Leadbetter, associate general counsel at the University of Tennessee, has picked up a petition to run against fellow Republican Rep. Stacey Campfield for the state House's 18th District seat in the Aug. 7 state primary.

"I'm thinking strongly in that direction. I will be making a decision by the end of the month. I want to make sure this is public-service oriented and not just something I'm doing," Leadbetter said.

He will retire from his UT position if he runs, he said. "Anybody who's been around here would be a fool to run and have a state position. Even if I campaigned in the evening, someone would be pointing it out as a potential conflict of interest," he said.

Leadbetter, 60, has been at UT for 35 years. In 2000, he filed two lawsuits against UT and then-President J. Wade Gilley alleging that Gilley discriminated against white men by hiring and promoting less-qualified women and minorities. Leadbetter lost one lawsuit against Gilley and withdrew one against the University."

On February 29, 2008 I provided Mizell my official retirement letter:

Dear Catherine:

At the beginning of last week I indicated to you that I was giving serious consideration to running for a House seat in the Tennessee General Assembly and that, if I decided to do so, I would be retiring from the University of Tennessee. Since that time I have made a decision to seek the House seat.

Although I might legally continue employment with the University until such time as I am elected to the House seat–assuming, of course, my election effort is successful –I believe the better course of action is to retire in the near future in order to avoid even the appearance of a conflict of interest. Further, I prefer to campaign full time, rather than only on weekends and evenings. Accordingly, I will retire effective March 31, 2008.

Needless to say, I will continue to diligently pursue pending cases and will work with whichever attorney (s) is assigned to succeed me in order to ensure that nothing "falls through the cracks." To the extent possible I will be glad to assist anyone handling these cases after my retirement date.

I absolutely and unequivocally have enjoyed my years of employment in the Office of General Counsel and have frequently wondered whether I ought to be paying tuition for the incredible opportunities and experiences provided rather than receiving a salary for doing what I enjoy so much. Despite the great pleasure I have received from serving the University and those associated with it for more than 35 years, it is now time to move in a different direction and pursue another aspect of public service.

I extend to you and the rest of my colleagues in the office my very best wishes for a bright and successful future. I will surely miss participating in that future even while exulting in the challenges and rewards of my "second career."

Sincerely,
Ronald C. Leadbetter
Associate General Counsel

Even in moving to campaign mode, the University connection did not end. My campaign treasurer was famed UT Sports Information Director Haywood Harris. Both he and his long time UT sports broadcasting partner, Gus Manning were actively involved in my campaign.

My campaign manager was a UT graduate, Gary Casteel. One of my first campaign contributors was world-renowned Body Farm founder, Dr. Bill Bass.

Former UT Trustee Susan Williams was an active advisor and contributor.

Many current and former UT employees supported my campaign in one way or another.

My last day of work was March 31, 2008. Retirement day was celebrated with an office lunch at Regas restaurant downtown.

The event was attended by everyone in the office–and joined by Therese. We had dessert back at Andy Holt Tower and I received a symbolic retirement gift from General Counsel Mizell–a sturdy, lovely wooden rocking chair! Everyone present got a good laugh, knowing I would not likely use it soon. That was correct.

One month before I retired–at the end of February–my last major litigation concluded. The case symbolized in many ways the exciting aspects of the job I held for more than 35 years. It was the input of opposing counsel, however, that affirmed what I treasured most about my service as legal counsel for the University of Tennessee.

Chapter 125–My UT Career's Grand Finale– "The Death of Cupid"

Dr. Roseanne Barker, M.D. is a prominent urologist who practices in Knoxville, Tennessee. In addition, Dr. Barker is an accomplished equestrian. In 2004 she not only owned five horses but had ridden in various jumping competitions. Barker boarded her horses at Kimberden Farms in Knox County. Both she and her daughter rode and took lessons there several times each week.

One of the horses Barker owned was a seven-year-old "Dutch Warm Blood" gelding named "Cupid." Barker purchased Cupid in August 2004 from Peter Vanderkallen in the Netherlands. Vanderkallen had trained Cupid and ridden him in competition.

Barker left Knoxville following the 2004 Christmas holiday to spend New Year's with family in Indiana. Cupid and Barker's other horses were left in the care of trainers at Kimberden Farms.

On December 31 Cupid was run through vigorous jumping exercise by Caley Thomas, one of the trainers. The next morning morning, January 1, 2005, Cupid seemed fine. However, around 4 p.m. Thomas noticed that Cupid had not eaten any hay all day. Recognizing that something was wrong, Thomas called a local veterinarian, Dr. Lillard, who prescribed a dose of banamine–a pain medication.

An hour and a half after the injection of banamine Cupid's heart rate was a bit elevated at 70 and his temperature was low at 99.7°. The trainer called Dr.

Lillard a second time and arrangements were made to have Cupid transported to the UT Veterinary Teaching Hospital for treatment.

Cupid arrived at UT around 10 p.m. Dr. Sarah Wiggins a veterinary intern in the College was assigned Cupid's care. Because Wiggins was not yet licensed to practice veterinary medicine in Tennessee, she practiced under the supervision of Dr. Carla Sommardahl, a faculty member in the UT College of Veterinary Medicine. However, Sommardahl was not physically present at the clinic when Cupid arrived.

At the time Cupid arrived at the University he was bright and alert. Thomas thought the ride to UT in a horse trailer might have dislodged gas in his bowel, bringing about relief. Cupid appeared to behave well at the clinic. He did not claw while being examined and was described by his trainer as being "happy and bright."

Dr. Wiggins performed a complete physical on Cupid and found his heart rate and pulse rates were high. Wiggins conducted rectal and ultrasound examinations, both of which showed normal results. However, a blood test returned a white blood cell count that was abnormally low.

Wiggins elected not to conduct an abdominocentis or "belly tap" since she was concerned about the risk of lacerating the horse's small and large intestines, Cupid did not exhibit any signs of pain and all other signs, except for elevated heart rate, were normal.

From the time of Cupid's presentation at the animal hospital at 10 p.m. until 3 a.m. the morning of January 2 there were no overt signs of abdominal pain. With Cupid's condition appearing to improve trainer Thomas left the University sometime before midnight on the 1st.

Once Cupid was settled in, fourth year veterinary students monitored his condition and Wiggins left the hospital around midnight. Around 3 a.m. on January 2 Wiggins received a call from one of the students alerting her to the fact that Cupid was acting "colicky" and pawing and trying to roll in his stall–evidence he was in pain.

Wiggins immediately returned to the hospital and determine that Cupid was extremely ill–in serious pain. She contacted Dr. Sommardahl who arrived at the hospital around 3:30 a.m. Barker also was called and told of Cupid's grave condition. She arrived at the hospital later that afternoon.

Cupid died around 8:30 that evening. An autopsy two days later revealed that at the time of death Cupid had a 180° torsion or twisting of his large colon and "endotoxemia"–presence of bacterial toxins.

On May 19, 2006 Barker filed a claim with the Tennessee Division of Claims Administration seeking recovery of damages in an amount between $250,000 and $300,000. The case was assigned to Claims Commissioner William O.

Schults. (Rosanne Barker, M.D. vs. State of Tennessee, Claims Commission of the State of Tennessee, Eastern Grand Division, Claim No. T-20060928). Barker was represented by Thomas Miller, senior partner in the Lexington, Kentucky law firm of Miller, Griffin and Marks. Miller was experienced in handling equine cases.

Barker's claim alleged that Cupid died as the result of the professional negligence of Dr. Sara Wiggins. More specifically, Barker alleged that the applicable professional standard of care required that Wiggins conduct a "belly tap" on Cupid at the time of his admission to the UT Veterinary Teaching Hospital; Wiggins violated that standard by failing to conduct the procedure.

According to the claim, had Wiggins conducted a belly tap, she would have discovered the presence of colon torsion. The torsion caused endotoxemia and led to Cupid's death. With early detection of torsion, according to the claim, Cupid's life could have been saved with corrective surgery.

The State's answer was filed on May 26–one week after the filing of the claim. On July 10 a motion to dismiss was filed on behalf of the State. The State's motion was denied by order of the Claims Commission entered September 22, 2006. It quickly became clear that critical facts were in dispute and this case would not be resolved by summary judgment.

It was my opinion from the outset that the weight of evidence disproved negligence on the part of Dr. Wiggins. Therefore, no settlement offer was made. I urged that the case proceed to trial. My recommendation was accepted both by Mizell and Foley.

The discovery process was intense. Many phone calls and preparatory meetings preceded each deposition as well as the review of Cupid's medical record. . Trial preparation proved to be challenging and quite interesting. I spent two days in Canandaigua, New York (near Rochester) preparing for, then participating in, the discovery deposition of Dr. Wiggins. Her deposition had been scheduled at the request of Claimant's attorney.

On February 1, Miller deposed UT Veterinary faculty members Dr. James Blackford and Dr. Carla Sommardahl, as well as three of the students. I provided the deponents a full day of preparation the day before their depositions.

In April, by agreement, Miller took the depositions of trainer Caley Thomas and the owner of Kimberden Farms, Kim Burnette-Mitchell, by telephone. Both resided in Florida. Although my general practice was to be personally present at depositions–to get to know the witness and observe body language, in the present case I did not believe a trip to Florida would be productive. All went well and there were no surprises.

The deposition of Claimant's expert, Dr. Martin Crabo, of Tucson, Arizona, was a different matter. I elected to fly to Arizona for the deposition of the Doctor of Veterinary Medicine. Miller elected to attend by conference call.

I arrived at Crabo's horse ranch in the desert outside Tucson well before the deposition was scheduled to begin. The time was spent with Crabo and his family–getting to know a bit about Crabo's involvement with horses over a cup of coffee. Very interesting and extremely informative! The court reporter arrived in time to set up and Miller called in on time. The deposition went very well.

I had an opportunity to join a long time friend and UT grad, Dr. Jerry Lemler, and his wife, for dinner in Tuscon before catching my return flight to Knoxville.

I took the discovery deposition of Dr. Barker at her office in Knoxville on July 16, then returned to Canandaigua on August 20 to take the evidentiary deposition of Dr. Wiggins. Wiggins' deposition was later introduced at trial as evidence rather than calling her to testify personally–which she had agreed to do if asked. I felt the better option was to go the deposition route.

On July 30 the parties deposed Peter Vanderkallen, by long distance conference call to the Netherlands. A personal appearance would have been nice but not justified under the circumstances.

Peter Vanderkallen, of the Netherlands, testified that he actively engaged in buying horses in Europe and selling them in the United States. 99% of his experience with selling horses in America involved Dutch and German Warmbloods. Vanderkallen also rode horses at the Grand Prix level. He had trained horses since he was 13. The silver medal winner of an event at the 1996 Atlanta Olympics was one of the horses he trained.

Vanderkallen had ridden Cupid in competition and testified that he was comparable to some of the top horses he sold during his career. He rode Cupid in November 2004 and detected no problems or defects. Cupid was compared by Vanderkallen to three horses which all had the same sire, or father, as Cupid. One of those horses had a similar bloodline on its mother's side and was ridden in the 1996 Olympics. The owners turned down an offer of $1.2 million for the horse.

On June 6, 2006, Vanderkallen prepared an appraisal of Cupid and opined that on January 2, 2005, he was worth between $250,000 and $275,000. ! (Dep. of Vanderkallen). I had no evidence to the contrary. The case would be determined on the basis of fault rather than amount of damages. Cupid was clearly a valuable horse.

The State's expert was Dr. Keith Chaffin, Doctor of Veterinary Medicine. Chaffin was a twenty-year member of the faculty of the Texas A&M College of Veterinary Medicine. He served as a full-time professor of Equine Internal Medicine and had been Board Certified in large animal medicine in 1991.

I mailed Cupid's medical record to Chaffin and spent hours on the telephone with him in advance of his scheduled deposition. On September 25, I flew to

Houston, Texas and spent additional hours reviewing the case file with him.

Later that afternoon we conducted the discovery deposition–by telephone–requested by Miller. After the Miller's deposition was concluded we took a short break. Following the break I took Chaffin's deposition for proof–for introduction at trial.

Trial was held before Commissioner Shults on October 25 and 26, 2007 in a conference room at the UT Thompson Boling Arena. There was evidence on both sides and Miller was a skilled adversary. He presented well the evidence supporting his client's position. Following the conclusion of trial Shults took the case what he termed as "under advisement" and announced he would let us know his decision when one was reached.

MILLER'S POST-TRIAL LETTER TO
UT PRESIDENT PETERSON

My most treasured yield from the vigorously contested Barker proceedings came a few days after trial concluded. I received in the mail a copy of a letter from attorney Tom Miller dated October 30, 2000. The letter was addressed to UT President John Peterson.

Dear Dr. Peterson:

My purpose in writing is to compliment Ron Leadbetter, your chief legal counsel at the University of Tennessee.

Because the focus of my practice is litigation, I come across many attorneys with whom I am an adversary all over the United States. In the 34 years I have been licensed to practice, my experience with those attorneys has been widely diverse. Particularly, in more recent years, our profession has become increasingly contentious, in a bad way. Therefore, it is somewhat novel to come across an adversary who is both highly competent while maintaining a professional demeanor and a pleasant personality. Ron fits into that category.

Periodically I deal with the attorneys at the University of Kentucky, and, on occasion, I have represented one of its subdivisions. Therefore, I do have a sense of what is involved in representing the University and its employees.

Ron is an excellent attorney who aggressively defends his clients while playing by the rules and shows every reasonable courtesy toward his opposing counsel, the adversarial parties and witnesses. He is also a very hard worker and, as in the case I have with them, is willing to go to great personal sacrifice to travel to difficult–to–reach locations for depositions.

You are lucky to have Ron in your employee.

Sincerely,

Thomas W. Miller

In one short letter an adversary stated succinctly the principles that drove my professional career. I was deeply honored by Miller's comments. That the letter was written before the Commission entered judgment in the case was most humbling. The outcome of the case had no bearing on the letter.

I came across Peterson at lunch a few days after I received a copy of Miller's letter. Peterson offered congratulations and seemed quite sincere in doing so.

THE FINAL JUDGEMENT

Commissioner Schultz issued his Final Judgment on February 15, 2008 (and the Judgment was filed officially on 26, 2008). Shults' seventy-one page ruling detailed the findings on which the judgment was based. In those findings he carefully reviewed the testimony of each of the witnesses. Shults took note of the conflicting evidence as to whether Dr. Wiggins violated the applicable standard of professional care my failing to perform a "belly tap" on Cupid. He also weighed conflicting evidence as to whether Cupid had colon torsion when he was brought to the Veterinary Hospital or developed that torsion shortly before his death. Shults also noted the conflict in evidence as to the actual cause of Cupid's death.

A summary of the findings supporting Shults' judgment are found in the last few pages of that document:

> Regardless of whether the [colitis] predated the colon torsion, or not, the critical inquiry in this case is whether UT was negligent in timely diagnosing the torsion by conducting a diagnostic abdominocentesis:
>
> A conclusion that the University and its employees were not negligent in this case is suggested by some of Dr. Crabo's was own testimony. For example, he confirmed that in a horse presenting as did Cupid, toxic colitis, in fact, would have been higher on his list of diagnoses than colonic torsion which would still be a reasonable possi bility.
>
> Additionally, all testifying veterinarians, including Dr. Crabo, opined that a horse with colonic torsion usually will have severe unrelenting pain and there was no his tory of such a level of pain in Cupid until 3 a.m. on January 2, 2005. In fact, trainer Caley Thomas testified that in a severe case of colic horses will typically roll about, curl their lip, perhaps straighten their necks, and appear to desire to get on the ground. With Cupid, she testified that his stall did not have the appearance of a place in which a horse had been rolling around and that during the course of the day he had passed seven bowel movements. The fact that the horse defecated seven times on January 1 at Kimberden Farms and an additional four times at UT, along with the observation of Dr. Sommardahl that she felt partly digested fecal matter when she performed a rectal examination around 4 a.m., seems to support the conclusion that a painful colon torsion had not eventuated by the time Cupid was brought to the hospital.

(Final Judgment, pp. 64-65)

It is clear from the record that Cupid did not seem particularly ill when he arrived at the University. Admittedly, his heart and respiration rates were elevated indicating some form of illness may have been occurring. However, he did not present as a se verely ill animal. Dr. Wiggins performed a thorough pre–admission examination of the horse according to not only her testimony but also that of Ms. Thomas, the trainer. Colic, rather than a colonic torsion severely obstructing the bowel to the extent that it was dying, seemed at that time, according to the proof, more probable.... . Further, Drs. Wiggins, Sommardahl, and Blackford performed four separate rectal exams be tween 10 p.m. on January 1 and 3 p.m. on January 2 and felt neither the torsion nor the effects of a torsion one would expect had it been present. Further, Dr. Chaffin, an eminently qualified and Board Certified veterinarian testified that the abdominocentesis the claimant so vigorously argued should have been done between 10 and 11 p.m. on January 1, is really more diagnostic of small intestine disorders than the conditions seen in Cupid. Dr. Blackford, the only practicing surgeon testifying, stated that at the time of autopsy he visualized the area not only of the torsion but also other areas of the horse's intestines which would have been affected and which he and Drs. Sommardahl and Wiggins had actually touched on January 1 and 2, 2005. He testified unequivocally that what he saw at that time did not indicate tissue which had been dead, as a result of torsion, since midmorning on January 1st. He did not observe a phenomenon known as "rarification" which he opined would have occurred within thirty (30) minutes after intestinal tissue died.

(Final judgment, pp. 65-66)

The Claimant's primary contention is that an abdominocentesis (belly tap) should have been done immediately upon presentation of the horse at the University. How ever, three board-certified experts, Drs. Sommardahl, Blackford, and Chaffin did not agree with this proposition. ... .

Dr. Crabo is neither Board-Certified nor a practicing surgeon. Although he has been in active veterinary practice since 1991, he testified he has not performed surgery in four to five years. In fact, he does not even assist in surgery at this time although he maintains his practice is solely with horses.

The evidence in this case is clear that the care Cupid received at the University of Tennessee far exceeded that of a "day nurse" as opined by Dr. Crabo. Dr. Wiggins thoroughly evaluated Cupid upon his arrival at UT, including obtaining a negative sonogram and negative results on rectal examination. She left the hospital around 12:30 on January 2, 2005, but immediately returned when notified that Cupid's condition had declined precipitously between 3:00 and 3:30. She then attempted a belly tap which was unsuccessful with a 1,275 pound animal which was moving about. Attempting this procedure was clearly a risk to both her and Cupid.

Prior to attempting the belly tap, Dr. Wiggins contacted Dr. Sommardahl who immediately came from her home to the hospital around 4 a.m. Dr. Sommardahl competently evaluated the horse and when surgery then became the consideration, summoned her colleague, Dr. Blackford, who likewise not only examined the horse but actually was able to get Cupid to stand on January 2, 2005.

This is not a picture of negligent or incompetent care.

(Final Judgment, pp.69-70)

Commissioner Shults then concluded that "based upon all the evidence presented to this Commission at the trial of the matter, this Commissioner cannot find that the defendant was negligent in the care of Dr. Barker's horse, Cupid. Therefore, this claim against the state must be respectfully, DISMISSED."
(Id. p. 70).

No appeal was taken by Barker from the Claims Commission judgment. My litigation career at the University of Tennessee concluded as it had begun–with a judgment favorable to the University–this one documented by a 71-page ruling.

More important to me, the principles and values to which I strived to adhere during my University career were documented in a gracious letter from opposing counsel.

Chapter 126–Post-Retirement UT Activity

My race for State Representative ended with the August 7, 2008 primary election. It was a close race and I came in second (close of enough to motivate me to run again against Campfield two years later for the State Senate, again finishing second, in a three way Republican primary, obtaining 36% of the vote to Campfield's 40% and third candidate Steve Hill's 22%). On to other interests!

My passion for international travel and networking in the former Soviet Union, the Middle East and elsewhere surged. I took on more and more responsibilities for international mission work abroad as a representative of my church. Soon I learned the meaning of the phrase heard often from friends who had retired before me, "I'm so busy I don't know how I ever had time to work!"

My involvement at UT continued. Regular attendance at sporting events, activity as an alumnus and retiree and interest as a concerned citizen are some of the ways I remained tied to the University. There were also ways more tied to my legal roots at the University.

UT President John Petersen, under pressure from the UT Board of Trustees, resigned the UT presidency on February 18, 2009, effective June 30. In a Knoxnews.com post dated February 19 my long-time friend State Senator Tim Burchett criticized the manner in which the past few UT presidents were chosen: "I hope the University will try to look within the system, or find someone locally." Burchett said. "We've gone through three presidents in a relatively short period of time. These national search firms haven't done well by us, in my opinion."

Quite true, in my opinion too. Yet, the source of the problem was not entirely with the national search firms. Some of the responsibility lay within the University.

Several months after Peterson's resignation from the UT presidency he paid a visit to Panera's Bakery on N. Peters Rd. in Knoxville, where I was meeting-with my early morning coffee group. I introduced Peterson to the group. After introductions I asked Peterson, "How are you doing?" His reply: "Not as well as in the past and your former boss is a big part of the reason why." No further explanation was requested or received. Peterson went on his way–departing Tennessee for a new residence in the Carolinas.

Even though retired, I was available for consultation–at no charge. On rare occasions I was called for assistance by the Office of General Counsel. I received no direct calls from General Counsel Mizell–only those who reported to her.One case of note involved a traveling minister, Reverend John McGlone.

I received a call from McGlone sometime during the latter part of 2008. He had heard that I was the UT attorney who had handled the past issues involving"preaching on campus." According to McGlone, University police and other UT officials were restricting or prohibiting him from speaking on campus.

I emphasized to McGlone the University's right to regulate the "time, place and manner" in which speech was uttered in locations open to the public. Beyond that, I opined, restrictions based on speech content, such as expression of religious views, were prohibited by the First Amendment to the United States Constitution.

Sometime later I received a call from Matthew Scoggins, a fine young attorney in the OGC who began his career, as I did, serving as a law clerk in the office. Scoggins mentioned McGlone's activities on campus. He asked that I review with him the advice I had given University officials in the past when addressing the issue of itinerant preachers preaching on campus. I gladly did so and reviewed a bit of University history on that issue.

I received no further request for input although I later heard that UT had successfully defended a U.S. District Court action brought by McGlone. The story did not end there.

The August 3, 2013 issue of the Knoxville-Sentinel healined "Preacher wins appeal courtg of UT ban." (p.4A) Details followed:

A federal appeals court on Friday issued an injunction barring
the University of Tennessee from blocking a traveling evangelist from
spreading the gospel on campus.

In an opinion authored by 6th circuit U.S. Court of Appeals Judge
Boyce Martin Jr., John McGlones' lawsuit against UT-tossed out by a district judge has been resurrected and a temporary injuctiion approved.)

The article further noted that McGlone had been "told by UT attorney Matthew Scoggins that he needed to be invited by "students, faculty or staff," but had earlier been told by Maxine Davis, UT's dean of students, "that he could no longer proselytize on campus without sponsorship from a UT organization." (Id.).

The appellate court ruled–according to the article–that "as a result of the inconsistency between the two policies, it is unclear to the ordinary person who has authority to grant sponsorship" and that "makes UT's policies unconstitutionally vague and opens the door for arbitrary and discriminatory application of the policies." (Id.). The cost to the University was around $75,000 in attorney's fees and an embarrassing religious liberty indictment by the liberal wing of the Sixth circuit.

This was a case i would have settled quickly--handling McGlone as visiting ministers were handled in the past. I suspect it was not Scoggins who made the final call in pursuing this matter to court.

There was another matter that followed my retirement involving issues with which I had much experience. I was not consulted but would have been glad to help. The results were extremely costly for the University in more ways than one.

Chapter 127–The Bruce Pearl Tragedy–
Who Dropped the Ball?

The University of Tennessee fired Bruce Pearl as its head basketball coach on March 21, 2011. Pearl and three assistant coaches were later found guilty by the NCAA of recruiting violations and providing false and misleading information concerning those violations. The NCAA assessed a three-year "show cause" penalty against Pearl and a one year "show cause" penalty against the assistant coaches, barring the coaches from coaching at any NCAA institution during the term of the penalty.

A brief discussion of what led to the end of Pearl's UT coaching career is found in the July 24, 2001 issue of the Knoxville News Sentinel, p. 1D, "Lies dunked basketball staff." Excerpts from the article provide the necessary framework for understanding what went wrong.

Joyce Thompson, one of the NCAA's head investigators for the probe into Tennessee's athletic department, clutched a photograph as she sat across from Bruce Pearl during a June 2010 interview. Also present was Mike Glazier, the University's lead attorney.

Neither Pearl nor Glazier were caught off guard. Six days earlier, the NCAA's en forcement staff had informed Glazier that the infamous photograph of Pearl and prized prospect Aaron Craft taken inside Pearl's home would be part of the interrogation.

"Have you, and I apologize, this is a grainy photo that we received in our office, and I received this through E–mail just to let you know," Thompson said, looking at Pearl. "But, um, we received this picture and it purports to be you with Aaron Craft.

"Do you have any recollection of that incident or maybe where this picture was maybe taken from and…?"

"That's Aaron, that's me," Pearl said. "I don't really know where that's taken."

"OK," Thompson said. "Any place on campus but you don't know?"

Glazier interjected. "Do you recognize the woman that's in the picture?" He asked, referring to a shot of Jana Shay, the wife of Pearl's assistant coach Jason Shay, positioned with her head down in the background.

"No," Pearl said. "I really don't."

"Coach," Glazier said, "is that in your home anyplace?

"No," Pearl said.

"OK," Thompson said.

And with that, the end had officially begun.

(Id.).

But further analysis of the impending tragedy is warranted. The best approach is to answer the question, "How were such matters handled in the past?"

USE IN-HOUSE COUNSEL WITH RELEVANT EXPERIENCE

"Puzzled" best describes my reaction when I learned that outside counsel–the law firm of Bond, Schoeneck and King of Overland Park, Kansas–had been retained to handle NCAA issues for the University of Tennessee. For three decades the University had very successfully handled such matters in-house.

In reviewing the "Notice of Allegations" issued by the NCAA on February 21, 2011, I found nothing extraordinary, certainly nothing requiring special investigative expertise. Given the University's intense involvement with athletics surely one of the staff attorneys in the Office of General Counsel had been trained to take my place in handling NCAA matters (and I could have been contacted and requested for assistance - as I was on a number of other matters following my retirement). In my opinion, if there was no in-house counsel trained in handling NCAA infractions claims there should have been!

Being personally acquainted with UT personnel–particularly in athletics–proved highly beneficial to me in conducting in-house investigations. Having firsthand knowledge of the inner workings of the University likewise proved very helpful. Through no fault of their own, outside counsel–particularly from another state–would understandably lack those investigative advantages.

The use of outside counsel proved costly–in more ways than one. According to The Knoxville News-Sentinel, August 18, 2011,p. 1C, ("Legal fees for NCAA surpass $300,000"): "UT has paid $317,178.06 to the firm Bond, Schoeneck and King, according to an invoice figure provided by UT on Wednesday to the News Sentinel. That's an increase of more than $115,000 since the beginning of February."

The article noted that the firm had first been hired to handle NCAA matters in November 2009. I retired in March 2008. Seemingly the General Counsel had sufficient time to train or hire in-house counsel to handle NCAA issues.

AN INSTITUTION'S INVESTIGATION SHOULD PRECEDE– NOT FOLLOW–THE NCAA'S

My first order of business was always to investigate the facts before proceeding to trial or hearing of any sort–or any meeting with NCAA investigators. It was important to learn the correct answers to questions likely to be asked of a party I represented or had ties to, prior to the commencement of any adversarial proceeding including those before NCAA investigators.

Although I cannot be certain, I am confident the University received the photograph which led to Pearl's downfall well before providing that photo to outside counsel. For certain outside counsel received that photo six days prior to Pearl's meeting with NCAA investigators. But Pearl never saw the photo until shortly before his meeting with NCAA investigators.

The firm hired to represent the University at the NCAA investigative hearing on June 14, 2010, had six days to meet with Pearl and his assistant coaches and thoroughly investigate their knowledge of the photograph presented by the NCAA. Unfortunately, the key witnesses having knowledge about the photo were not questioned until approximately one hour before the NCAA investigators commenced their own investigative interviews.

Outside counsel Mike Glazier and Kyle Skillman met with Pearl and his three assistant coaches together–my personal practice was to interview potential witnesses separately in order to avoid intentional or unintentional "synchronization" of testimony–with little emphasis placed on identifying when and where the mystery photograph was taken.

When the coaches stated they didn't recognize where the photograph was taken, the matter was dropped. There was no further effort to identify the location (although a couple of weeks later it would become clear that further questioning would most assuredly have produced that information).

"Coach, the NCAA did not send us this photograph with the hope we would return it to the rightful owner. Take your time, take a close look and let's see if we can identify where this photograph was taken," is the question I would have asked–"interrogation" akin to the approach followed in determining the facts from key parties in the NCAA "tutoring scandal."

PROMOTE TRUTHFULNESS/
WARN OF PENALTIES FOR LYING

My approach to dealing with potential witnesses and valued members of the University community was to first and foremost emphasize the importance of truthfulness and the consequences of testifying falsely. While outside counsel advised the coaches to be forthright and "tell the truth", there was reportedly no discussion of penalties for lying. No reminder was given the coaches that lying constitutes a "primary infraction" under NCAA rules and may result in job loss for the offender and severe penalties being imposed on the University.

Somewhat counterproductively, Pearl and his assistants were advised to be truthful, but to answer the questions asked and "don't elaborate." My own standard advice to potential witnesses was to answer "yes" or "no" when possible but to provide an explanation when necessary in order to provide an accurate response. The example I used on numerous occasions with prospective witnesses is one familiar to attorneys: "Have you stopped beating your wife?" A "yes" or "no" answer will not suffice. "Elaboration" is highly recommended. "No, because I never started beating her to begin with," would be a much better response.

LAST MINUTE, INCOMPLETE PREPARATION OF
WITNESSES IS ILL-ADVISED

It has been my personal experience in litigating cases that even persons of the highest moral caliber often come unglued when placed in an adversarial setting, such as a deposition, trial or proceeding before NCAA investigators. Given adequate preparation and adequate time to think about it, persons of integrity perform well. Without adequate preparation and sufficient time to replace instinctive responses with those which are carefully considered and true, even those of the highest integrity may succumb to an instinctive urge to testify falsely. I am 99.9% certain that is what happened in Bruce Pearl's case.

Without question, Pearl and assistant coaches erred by falsely telling NCAA investigators they did not know the location depicted in the photograph shown them by NCAA investigators on June 14. It is equally certain the temptation to lie could have easily been nipped in the bud. Evidence supporting this conclusion is ironclad, in my view. Here is a summary of the supporting facts:

THE CIRCUMSTANCES GIVING RISE TO
PEARL'S CAREER ENDING LIE

Transcripts of NCAA interviews and related sources confirm the following:

1. Pearl and his three assistant coaches were called to meet collectively with University attorneys in the first floor conference room of the UT Office of General Counsel on June 14, 2010. The only attorneys present were "outside coun-

sel"–no attorney on the OGC staff was present.

2. The coaches were advised by outside University counsel that NCAA investigators would be interviewing them regarding reports of impermissible recruiting–related phone calls being made.

3. Glazier displayed a photograph, reportedly "pulled out of his personal belongings," and asked each coach if he could identify where the photograph was taken. Each coach replied that he could not say where the photograph was taken. Little, if any, follow-up questioning was undertaken. Most significantly, Pearl was not made aware of or shown this photo until less than an hour before the NCAA investigators entered the conference room.

4. Counsel advised the coaches to tell the truth but made no mention of penalties for failing to do so. Although advised to answer questions by the investigators the coaches were also advised "don't elaborate." The coaches were not asked by outside counsel if they had any questions.

5. The preparatory meeting lasted less than one hour. All coaches left the conference room and NCAA investigators arrived soon thereafter.

6. Each coach was called separately for interview by the NCAA investigators. Present at the meeting were Mike Glazier and Kyle Skillman, "outside counsel for NCAA compliance and infractions matters," Joyce Thompson, NCAA associate director of enforcement and Kristen Matha, NCAA assistant director of enforcement/Basketball Focus Group.

7. Each investigative interview was conducted under the direction of Thompson. She commenced each meeting by asking those present to identify themselves. Then, Thompson asked each coach the following questions:

(1) "[it's my understanding that you have read the NCAA interview notice form, is that correct?"

(2) "And do you understand that form as you've read it?

(3) " …do you understand that you have an obligation to be truthful and forthcoming as far as the information you provide me today?"

(4) "And do you also understand that should you provide any false or misleading information that that could have a negative or adverse effect on any employment opportunities that you may have at the University of Tennessee or at any other NCAA institution in the future?"

(5) "And I'm also obligated to tell you that you have a right to be represented by personal legal counsel and do you understand that right?"

(6) "And do you understand that neither Kyle or Mike are representing you as your personal legal counsel for the purpose of this interview?"

(7) "And do you waive your right to personal legal counsel for the purposes of this interview?"

Each coach interviewed answered each of the questions in the affirmative.

UT COUNSEL NOT YOUR PERSONAL ATTORNEYS

After obtaining their answers to the above questions Thompson explained the purpose of the interview:

> I'm also obligated to tell you the purpose of this interview, and the purpose of this interview is to... determine whether or not you have any knowledge and/or have been involved in any NCAA violations while you've been employed at the University of Tennessee, and do you understand the purpose of this interview?

At this point each coach might understandably have experienced a sense of isolation or abandonment. The coaches had been called a short time earlier to meet with University counsel in the conference room of the UT Office of General Counsel, for the express purpose of preparing for investigative interviews by the NCAA. Each received advice from UT outside counsel on how to respond to NCAA investigators.

I never prepared a single person for trial if I did not represent that person. It was the NCAA investigator–Thompson–who reminded Pearl and the other coaches that the UT attorneys who had called them to meet and prepare for the NCAA investigation were not their attorneys. I found the NCAA notice disturbing. During my career I often represented University employees in legal proceedings. So long as those employees were acting in good faith to carry out their job responsibilities the University never hung employees "out to dry"– left to their own resources.

If an employee engaged in criminal activity, willful misconduct or conduct for personal financial gain he or she was on his own. Otherwise the employee could count on me for support and assistance. I represented UT police officers, medical personnel, faculty–and coaches–sued for job related acts of negligence resulting in personal injury or property damage to others. The University paid any monetary judgments awarded. From the perspective of those UT employees I was certainly considered their "personal legal counsel."

It was not surprising for me to learn that none of the coaches asked for adjournment of the hearing in order to obtain personal legal counsel. Career criminals may routinely demand an attorney but law-abiding citizens often do not –even when they should.

A request for adjournment to secure legal counsel might be construed as an admission of wrongdoing. After all the announced purpose of the NCAA investigative hearing was to investigate whether excessive phone calls had been made–not whether a recruit was impermissibly in a coach's home!

In my opinion Pearl's answer to Thompson's question as to whether he could identify the location where a photo was taken in which he and Aaron Craft appeared (and whether he knew the identity of a woman in the picture) was solicited under unacceptable conditions.

It soon became clear that Pearl answered falsely–and did so instinctively and reflexively out of a sense of fear. Only an hour or two earlier he had told University counsel he could not identify the photo location or the lady in the photo. Pearl knew all along that the photo was taken in his home and the woman in the photograph was Jana Shay, wife of assistant coach Jason Shay.

Pearl's false testimony to NCAA investigators constituted a primary infraction of NCAA rules. I am confident that a serious, "primary" infraction could easily have been avoided had a different process been followed by University counsel. How can I be certain of that? The best evidence was provided by Pearl himself.

A couple of weeks after providing false information to the NCAA, Pearl came forth on his own initiative, conceding he had not been completely truthful with NCAA investigators and needed to meet with them again in order to "come clean." See: Knoxville News Sentinel, July 23, 2011, p. 1A.

As reported in the July 24, 2011 issue of the Sentinel, "'I panicked,' Pearl said, 'I wanted it to go away. It goes against a lot of things that I've worked for that I sorta stand for.'" Id. p. 5D.

Immediately following the events of June 12 Pearl met with his coaches and initiated a repair attempt:

HAVING SECOND THOUGHTS
Second thoughts raced through Pearl's head immediately after his initial interview with the NCAA.

He called a meeting with his assistance later that day, something the NCAA also considered to be a compromise of the investigation's integrity. His questions focused solely on the photograph.

"... he, Coach Pearl, came back and said that he recognized that it was his house," [assistant coach] Shay said in his follow-up interview with the NCAA.

"OK," Thompson said, "and what was your, what was your reaction to that?"

"I mean I–if he said it was then I agreed with him."

Shea said he, Jones and Forbes each notified Pearl that they didn't recognize the photographs setting.

It was then, Shea said, that Pearl decided he would contact the NCAA to say that "we've got additional information."

(Knoxville News-Sentinel, July 24, 2011,p. 5D.)

A description of events leading to the panic was also reported by the Sentinel:

Attorney Michael Glazier, who represented UT in its case with the NCAA, had knowledge of the photo six days prior to the coaches being interviewed, but did not share that information with the staff.

Pearl has since said that he and his staff were under the impression the

NCAA was coming to interview them about secondary violations involving impermissible phone calls, and had he known the possibility of a major violation existed, he would have retained his own legal counsel.

(The Knoxville News-Sentinel, September 29, 2011, p.1C.)

On August 5, 2010, Pearl again met with NCAA investigators. OGC attorney Matthew Scoggins was present for the second interview, along with outside counsel and the NCAA's Joyce Thompson. This time Pearl testified truthfully. The photo with Aaron Craft was taken at his home. Included in the photograph was Jana Shay, the wife of Jason Shay. Pearl admitted he knew all of this during the first interview and did not tell the truth.

Pearl's confession was good for the soul, but not for his job. The damage was done from the NCAA's perspective. UT, as well as the coaches, would suffer severe consequences as the result of the coaches' false denials of knowledge of a minor or secondary infraction of NCAA rules.

On September 9, 2010 Director of Men's Athletics, Mike Hamilton, wrote Pearl a four-page letter captioned "Notice of Termination of Employment Agreement." The first three pages of the letter delineated a number of infractions and claimed infractions of NCAA rules attributed to Pearl. Included was a detailed description of events at the June 14 meeting at which Pearl "knowingly furnished the NCAA enforcement staff and the University's outside counsel with false and misleading information concerning the photograph. Although not necessary to a finding of gross misconduct, our conclusion is that your false and misleading statements to the NCAA on June 14 were deliberate and premeditated...."

Following the review of underlying facts, the disciplinary charge was announced. "Based on the facts described above, Chancellor Cheek and I have determined that you engaged in gross misconduct, including dishonesty and other acts involving intolerable behavior." Hamilton then explained that, "As a result, the University is terminating your employment agreement for adequate cause under article XVII.F.1(vii).

The balance of the letter left me dumbstruck.

The effective date of the termination of your employment agreement is October 8, 2010 ("Effective Date"). On the Effective Date, you will become an employee at will with no definite term of employment and will remain an employee at will until the university enters into a new employment agreement with you.

The concluding paragraphs of the letter notified Pearl that he could request a hearing if he wished to contest the contract termination. Also, he was placed on notice that "if the University develops a good faith belief "that he engaged in additional NCAA violations not currently known to the University" he would be subject to additional disciplinary action. The assistant coaches also received similar letters charging them with failure to be forthcoming in their NCAA interviews.

Unbelievable! During the entire period of my employment I never encountered an employment case in which an employee charged with gross misconduct –let alone conduct characterized as "dishonesty and other acts involving intolerable behavior"–did not have there employment terminated or at least suspended. Although I hasten to add that, in my personal view, had UT attorneys done their job Pearl would not have been in this situation to begin with.

Another observation: almost every non-faculty employee at the University is an "at will" employee (as I was for nearly 36 years). Thousands of University employees have retired from the University after serving as employees-at-will for decades. I suspect not one of them thought of "at will" employment as disciplinary action. Oh, yes, it is true Pearl's salary was reduced by 25%. Given his top tier salary level, that hardly reflects a penalty appropriate for the charge described in Hamilton's letter.

I do not in any way attribute the absurdity of Mike Hamilton's letter to Hamilton–a gentleman I hold in high esteem on a personal level. An attorney crafted the letter.

The tragedy continued. As I earlier noted, the NCAA issued a "Notice of Allegations" on February 21, 2011. The 26 page document alleged a number of infractions primarily involving excessive phone calls and impermissible contacts with recruits and family members by UT football Head Coach Lane Kiffin, assistant football coaches and basketball coaches. Virtually all of these infractions fell into the secondary category. Twelve did not and fell into the primary category.

Allegations against Pearl relating to the Aaron Craft photograph fell into the primary category. Those allegations related entirely to Pearl's conduct on June 14 - during and shortly after the meeting. Aside from the photo–related allegations, Pearl was charged with nothing constituting a primary infraction. Nor were any of his assistant coaches.

UT fired Pearl and the assistant coaches on March 21, 2011. The action against Pearl was taken on the premise that an additional, so called "bump" with a prospect had occurred after issuance of the September 9 disciplinary letter.

Even if that conduct (when added to the "gross misconduct" described in the September letter) constituted a terminable offense, immediate dismissal and immediate cessation of pay would logically result. Instead Pearl received a payout in the amount of $948,728.

Assuming, for the sake of argument, that Pearl truly bore responsibility for the infractions leading to his dismissal–the photo incident followed by what typically would have been an inconsequential secondary "bump" infraction–a million-dollar payout was a totally inappropriate expenditure of University funds.

On June 11 the NCAA held a hearing in Indianapolis. "The ["bump"] violation was appealed by UT and Pearl and found not to have merit by the NCAA committee on infractions at the June hearing, but the damage had already been done. Pearl and his staff had been fired months earlier." Knoxville News-Sentinel, September 29, 2011,p. 3C.

On August 24, 2011 the NCAA announced a three-year show -cause penalty for Pearl based on recruiting violations and "the provision of false and misleading information about them, and the inducement of others to do the same." The assistant coaches received one year show-cause sanctions. Knoxville News-Sentinel, July 14, 2013, p. 1D.

In this final stanza of the Bruce Pearl tragedy it once again became clear to me what might've been had a sound approach been taken by University counsel prior to Pearl's initial meeting with NCAA's investigators. Of course it was not my problem. I was retired.

Still, if only I had been called upon for input. It would have been gladly provided. Likely with a far better outcome for my Alma Mater and former employer, The University of Tennessee.

Post note #1: I met with Bruce Pearl for coffee at Panera's on N. Peters Rd. in Knoxville for more than an hour the afternoon of February 5, 2014. We discussed the NCAA issues affecting Pearl's career and the contents of this chapter. My analysis of the events leading to Pearl's termination was affirmed in every respect–from admission of guilt to confirmation of being poorly informed and ill-prepared for the NCAA interview.

Post note #2: Auburn University hired Pearl as its Head Basketball Coach on March 17, 2014. One Auburn official playing a key role in attracting Pearl to Auburn was former NCAA rules compliance head David Didion. At the time Pearl was sanctioned by the NCAA Didion was NCAA's Director of Enforcement. UT's loss was Auburn's gain, some might say.

Chapter 128–Conclusion

This publication has taken more than two years to craft. Meticulous review of voluminous records I accumulated over many years and many hours spent organizing those records explain the duration of the effort.

It is my hope and prayer that you, the reader, have found this historical treatise informative and entertaining. I trust I have added to your understanding of the wide and often bizarre variety of legal matters addressed by an institution of higher education–in this case, the University of Tennessee.

Perhaps you'll agree that my autobiographical account describes a unique and incredibly entertaining career. More important, l hope you have found the revelations of history from within the administrative sanctum of the University of Tennessee enlightening. I would be quite disappointed to learn that you already knew most of what I've written. And shocked!

Also, I hope you have found food for thought in the many principles engrained in and lessons learned by others and me during the course of my professional career as legal counsel for UT–principles and lessons documented in these pages. A few of my favorites:

Higher education is about more than just teaching, research and public service. It is about people.

Formation of friendships in the workplace and community adds joy to a mere job.

Networking offers a valuable means of achieving professional success–and genuine friendships.

Do the right thing, not what's easy (otherwise the "KISS" principle–"keep it simple stupid"–is the one I embraced).

Money is important but people are more valuable.

Change for the sake of change is ill-advised; beneficial change should be embraced.

Check the stats, then proceed accordingly. If you've never failed or lost you've never tried (a case or anything else).

Document, document, document.

Fear of failure is destructive. Lessons learned from failure breed success.

Failure is human. Forgiveness is divine.

Integrity is a centerpiece of success.

And then a personal principal: When all seems hopeless remember: God never fails.

Times change and the influence of the above principles and lessons at the University came and went. From my unique position within UT Office of General Counsel I watched the "Big Orange" achieve a long term radiant glow–then fade as the black storm clouds of the Gilley-Shumaker era moved in–then brighten somewhat as an era of uncertainty moved in. As a Vol fan it is my ultimate hope that full radiance of the "Big Orange" will eventually return.

Postlude

As we come to the end of what was a long project in the making for many years, I must say a very special thanks to the many hands that came together to help me realize my dream of putting my years of notes and recordkeeping into the form of a book. As the saying goes, "It takes a village."

First, as I wrote in my dedication, all my love and appreciation goes to my family beginning with Therese-my sweetheart. She has been a wonderful wife and mother and, as you have read, shared with me in many of the events and activities described in this book. We called upon her excellent secretarial skills, too, as she came through and typed some of the most detailed and confusing sections contained herein. My children, Cara and Lee, are the two greatest children a father could have ever had and I love them to the depths of my being. Their encouragement and support for my efforts on this book were a huge help, too. They have blessed us with their marriages and seven grandchildren.

It was my great fortune to employ three other women who worked long hours on this project and deserve a mention here.

Once again, my adage of, "I cannot do everything, but I can hire someone who can," came to light. I feel blessed that these fine women came into my life just when I needed them. Together we have been able to cross the line and score. After all, we live in the great State of Tennessee, the University of Tennessee is our Alma Mater, and our blood runs deep orange.

Ron Leadbetter 2015

Photo Album

Wedding Day for Theresa and Ron: June 28, 1969

Republican
National
Committee.

February 13, 1973

Mr. Ronald C. Leadbetter
203 Administration Building
University of Tennessee
Knoxville, Tennessee

Dear Ron:

    What a fantastic job you did on the dinner! Thanks,
thanks, thanks -- for making it such a terrific evening.

Yours very truly,

George Bush
Chairman

Leadbetter served as chairman of the 1973 Lincoln Day Dinner sponsored by the Knox County Young Republicans. Mayor Kyle Testerman and Ron met the guest speaker for the event at the airport. George Bush, who was later to become U.S. President #42, was the president of the Republican National Committee in 1973.

Tim McGee,
University of Tennessee wide receiver and All-American (1982-86).

Many thanks to Jim Stanton and the University of Tennessee for permission to use football photos. Thanks, too, to our good pal, Tom Mattingly, for helping to arrange it.

Reggie White-UT defensive lineman (1980-83). All-American in 1983.

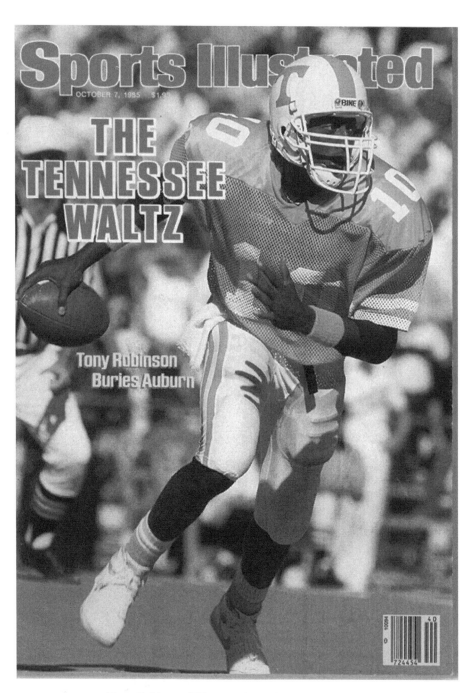

Tony Robinson-UT quarterback (1982-85).
A candidate for the Heisman trophy in 1985.

Heath Shular-UT quarterback (1991-1993) Heisman Trophy runner-up in 1993.

LADY V🏀LS

THE UNIVERSITY OF TENNESSEE WOMEN'S INTERCOLLEGIATE ATHLETICS ● BASKETBALL
Pat Head Summitt, Head Coach   Mickie DeMoss, Assistant Coach   Holly Warlick, Assistant Coach

January 29, 1987

Ron and Therese Leadbetter
6316 Creekhead Road
Knoxville, Tennessee 37919

Dear Ron and Therese:

    I wanted you to know how much I appreciate your participation as guest coaches for the North Carolina game. Mickie, Holly and I hope you enjoyed the experience in the locker room as well as behind the bench, and that you will be back to watch the Lady Vols play throughout the season.

    Please know your interest in Women's Athletics and willingness to support our program is very important to the entire Department and I hope we can count on your friendship for years to come.

    Thank you again for joining us and congratulations on your victory!

Sincerely,

Pat Summitt

PS/Mk

JOHN J. DUNCAN, JR.
2ND DISTRICT, TENNESSEE

2267 RAYBURN HOUSE OFFICE BUILDING
WASHINGTON, DC 20515-4202
PHONE: (202) 225-5435
FAX: (202) 225-6440

800 MARKET STREET, SUITE 110
KNOXVILLE, TN 37902
PHONE: (865) 523-3772
FAX: (865) 544-0728

252 EAST BROADWAY
MARYVILLE, TN 37804-5782
PHONE: (865) 984-5464
FAX: (865) 984-0521

6 EAST MADISON AVENUE COURTHOUSE
ATHENS, TN 37303-4297
PHONE: (423) 745-4671
FAX: (423) 745-6025

Congress of the United States
House of Representatives
Washington, DC 20515-4202

November 7, 2005

COMMITTEES:
TRANSPORTATION AND INFRASTRUCTURE
SUBCOMMITTEES:
WATER RESOURCES AND ENVIRONMENT—CHAIRMAN
AVIATION
HIGHWAYS, TRANSIT, AND PIPELINES

RESOURCES
SUBCOMMITTEES:
NATIONAL PARKS, RECREATION, AND PUBLIC LANDS
FORESTS AND FOREST HEALTH

GOVERNMENT REFORM
SUBCOMMITTEES:
NATIONAL SECURITY, EMERGING THREATS, AND
INTERNATIONAL RELATIONS
GOVERNMENT MANAGEMENT, FINANCE,
AND ACCOUNTABILITY

Rector Volchihkin Vladimir Ivanovich
Rector
Penza State University
40 Krasnaya Street
Penza, Russia 440026

Dear Rector Volchihkin:

I want to offer my sincere congratulations to you and your
colleagues on the occasion of the opening of the Lingua Center
at the Penza State University.

My long-time friend Mr. Ronald Leadbetter, an attorney at the
University of Tennessee's Office for General Counsel, has shared
many of the details of this project with me. I am grateful to
Mr. Leadbetter, as well as, to Mr. Stephen Hillis for their
numerous efforts in assisting you and the Lingua Center
Director, Professor Olga Meshcheryakova in making this opening
possible.

The Lingua Center is an excellent example of educational
collaboration between our two nations, and I am confident this
Center will prove to be a tremendous resource to your
University.

Congratulations again, and I wish you the very best in your
future endeavors.

With kindest regards, I am

Yours truly,

JOHN J. DUNCAN, JR.
Member of Congress

JJD:dr

Tennessee delegation at American Library in Penza, Russia in 2011.
Ron Leadbetter shown in middle front row.

Vadim Supikov, a leader in the Penza, Russia regional "Duma" or Legislature, wears a
UT Vols hat in front of his Penza home. (Fall 2007).

A reunion of old political friends from university days at the Leadbetter's home in Knoxville before a UT football game. Left to right: Jim Hager, Cong. Jimmy Duncan, Ron Leadbetter, Allen Gottlieb (September 3, 2011).

Helen Ashe, Martha Rose Woodward, Ellen Turner, (January 2012)
Helen and Ellen are owners of the Love Kitchen.

At the American Library at Penza State University in Penza, Russia: Ron Leadbetter,Olga Meshcheryakova and Chuck Pate (May 2014). Prominently displayed is a framed photo of Congressman Jimmy Duncan and Mescheryakova taken in Duncan's Knoxville office.

Ron (left) Vadim Supikov, Leader of Penza, Russia Duma or Legislature (middle) Steve Hillis (right) in 2007.

Theresa and Ron celebrate UT retirement with a trip on the
Volunteer Princess as they cruise down the Tennessee River within sight of
the University of Tennessee.

It's great to be a Tennessee Vol!

Index by Chapters

(References are by **chapter numbers)**

Aberdeen, Stu, 19 (**Look in Chapter 19, not page 19)**
Adkisson, Grady, 16
Aldmon, Howard 3, 21, 56, 57
Alexander, Lamar, 11, 13, 19, 52,53, 70
Alexander, Rhonda, 31, 87, 118
Alissandratos, D.J., 38, 45
Anderson, Derek, 98
Anderson, Tom, 91
Andrews, Jim, 31
AreHart, David, 87
Ashe, Helen, 41
Ashley, Ray 24
Asp, Carl, 74, 79, 80
Atkins, Lisa, 105, 108
Ault, Lawrence, 63
Aydelott, Zed, 46
Ayers, Ted, 97
Bailey, D'Army, 122
Baker, Howard, 22, 56
Baker, W.R., 83
Baldridge, O.S. ('Syl"), 30, 84
Barber, Kaddie, 19, 52
Baretz, Mark, 67
Barker, Ron, 79
Barker, Roseanne, 29, 125
Barnes, Carlton, 91
Barrett, Lida, 24
Bass, William ("Bill"), 10–12, 59,124
Bates, Bill, 71
Battle, Bill, 36
Batts, Lonnie and Perry, 55
Baugh, John, 3, 5, 8, 9, 11, 12, 14, 23, 53
Baynes, Brodie, 12
Baxter, Jimmy, 3, 52
Bearman, Leo, 70
Beaty, Scarlett 58
Becker, Gerald, 56
Bell, Sheila Trice, 15
Bennett, Edward, 19, 56, 58, 59
Bensel-Meyers, Linda, 79, 80
Benson, Kirsten, 75
Benson, King and Katsy, 1
Berke, Andy, 62
Bernard, Pam, 15, 81
Berrien, Roberta, 14

Berry, Al, 14
Berst, David, 73
Bevins, E.S., 23
Bishop, Clifford 40
Black (vs. UT and McKinney), 64
Blackford, James, 125
Blackwell, Robert, 67
Blackwell, Steve, 115
Blake, Cleland, 42
Blanton, Ray, 13
Bobbitt, Denise, 67
Boling, Edward J., 3, 7, 9, 21, 23, 25, 52, 53, 57, 68, 70, 71
Bond, Schoeneck and King, 127
Bootle, W.A., 64
Boring, Richard, 75
Bowen, Earle 52
Bowers, Stephen, 99
Bowie, Brooke, 76
Bozeman, Sam, 52, 67, 68
Bracey, Lance, 98
Bradberry, Homer 61
Brake, Al, 3
Brasfield, Martha, 41, 88
Brewer, James Allen, 66
Brightman, Tamala, 11, 18
Brock, Karen, 19, 67
Brogan, Beauchamp E. ("Beach"), 11, 12, 17, 25, 30-35, 41, 52, 53, 55, 57, 58, 64, 69-73, 84, 95, 96, 101, 108
Brookshire, Mike, 52, 63
Brown, Clarence (OFCCP), 52
Brown, Doug, 83
Brown, Ed, 12
Brown, Mark, 31
Brown, Roger, 117
Bruwiler, Sallee, 56
Bryant, Felice (Boudleaux), 36
Buck, In re:, 27
Burchett, Charles, 6
Burchett, Tim, 105, 126
Burks-Jelks, Patricia, 52
Burnside (Nursery), 64
Burkett, Steve, 64
Burson, Charles, 37, 46, 60, 70
Butler, John, 67
Burton, Larrimore, 64
Bush, George, 22
Buuck, David, 80, 86
Calage, Cleo, 21, 56

Campfield, Stacey, 124, 126
Capps, Bryan, 80
Carbajal de Garcia, Isis, 15
Cardwell, Susan, 19
Carilli, Vinnie, 86, 97, 98
Carman, Howard, 40
Carruth, Harvey, 82
Carter, S. Daniel, 63
Cate, H. David 38, 63
Casteel, Gary, 124
Castleman, Barbara, 111
Cavallo, Jimmy, 40
Central Baptist Church Bearden,11, 18
Chaffin, Keith, 125
Chapman, E.J., 64
Chapman, E. Winslow, 39
Chauke, Amon Ben (Linah, et. al.), 48
Cheek, Jimmy, 115, 127
Cheek, Vance, 29, 42, 43, 87, 89,119
Chesney, Dave, 22
Children's Center, 9
Chumley, Kristen, 123
Clapp, Andrea, 58
Clark, Barry, 118, 120
Clark, Raymond, 40
Clements, Cecil, 69
Cody, Mike, 53, 70
Coffey, Charles, 95, 97
Coffey, Don, 66
Cohen, Neal, 37
Cohen, Steve, 38
Coker, Bryan, 86
Cole, Cathy, 105
Cole, Elsa, 81
Colson, 61, 64
Combs, Lewis, 23
Combs, Michael, 20
Connell, Mary Ann, 15
Conner, Audrey, 11
Contessa the Python, 30
Cooper, B.B., 66
Copeland, William, 122
Copeland, William B., 44
Cox, Ben, 43, 58, 59
Crabtree, Loren, 53, 90, 115
Creekmore, Betsey, 7, 52
Crider, Charles, 121
Crisp, Kyle, 16
Crocker, Diane, 31, 56

Index by chapters

Cronan, Joan, 11, 18, 19, 22, 25, 38, 56
Cronan, Tom, 11, 18, 19, 22
Croushorn, James, 55
Crowe, Kyle, 69
Cutting, Joann, 41, 61, 70
Dane, Phil, 118
Darsie, John, 23
Davidson, Paul, 83
Davis, Herman (Darnell), 41
Davis, John Clarence, 84
Davis, Robert, 60
Davis, Ron, 75
Davis, Sylvia, 105
Dean, Charles, 94
Dee, Paul, 66
Denson, Fred, 59
Demaree, Rebecca, 62
Derrington, Bill, 67
Dessart, Don, 24
Devoe, Don, 18
Dickey, Doug, 11, 18, 19, 37, 58, 71-79, 83
Dicks, John, 64
Dickson, Roger, 96, 97, 101
Didion, David, 127
Dodge, Lola, 56, 82
Donati, Don, 31, 40, 56, 58, 61, 68, 70
Doran, Wil, 67
Douglas, Ben, 5
Drew, James Henry, 87
Drinnon, Jim, 5, 8, 11, 13, 20, 53
Dry, Larry, 22
Duggan, David, 56, 58, 97-102, 115, 118
Dunagan, Nick, 25, 28
Duncan,Jr., John J. ("Jimmy"), 1, 5,9, 22, 97, 115
Duncan, John J., 1, 56
Duncan, Lynn, 22
Duncan, Richard, 88, 89
Dunn, Winfield, 6
Dutton, Doug, 22, 97
Eadie, Robert Baker, 120
Earl, A.D., 25
Ebersole, Luke, 20, 52, 56
Echols, Marsha, 13
Edge, Murray, 41, 83
Eisenberg, Marcia, 41
Elam, Tom, 5, 57
Eldridge, John, 28
Ellington, Buford, 7, 53

Elosiebo, Mechelle, 89
Ely, Daniel, 87
Emert, Stan, 85
English, Burton, 79
Evans, Richard, 70
Farmer, Al, 28, 52
Fendley, Susan, 11
Ferraris, Gary, 56
Fisher, Homer, 13, 38
Fisher, Wayne, 5
Fleetwood One Hour Photo, 64
Fleming, Scott, 63
Flory, Joseph, 56
Fly, Emerson ("Eli"), 30, 35-37, 52,53, 57, 103
Foley, Kevin, 122
Foley, Peter, 43, 83,108,117, 118,123
Ford, Deborah, 68
Fornes, Joe, 82, 115
Fox, Bill and Debbie, 29
Fox, Andy, 29
Fraker, Stephen, 63
Francisco, Jerry, 45
Francisco, Linda, 82
Franz, Linda, 82
Friedman, Robert, 26
Frost, Sheila, 18
Fuller, Gwen, 11, 107
Fulmer, Phillip,11,25,37,75,86
Furrow, Ann and Sam, 25, 57
Gabel, Cynthia, 75, 77
Gaston, Finus, 36
Gault, Willie, 72
Gehlar, James A., 56
Geier, Rita Sanders, 52, 53
Gibbons, Julia, 31,40,58,61,68
Gigou, Henry, 64
Gilbert, Bob, 57
Gilbert, Bud, 37
Gilbert, James, 67
Gilles, Jim 60
Gilley, J. Wade, 11,13, 33,52, 55,79, 95-102, 109
Gilreath, Sid, 80, 88
Glazier, Mike, 127
Glazier, Ralph, 58
Glenn, Robert, 28
Gosa, Alan, 56
Gossett, Pete, 53
Grager, Henry, 93
Granger, Ben, 55
Gray, Frank 53
Gray, Victoria, 79, 80
Gregory, Donald, 40

Grello, Fred 123
Griffey, Leticia ("Tish"),11,12
Griffin, Hugh, 40
Griffiths, Bob, 97
Grisham, Tanda, 108, 122
Gross, Charles, 64
Gross, Francis, 28, 66
Gross, Peter, 118
Gurley, Laverne, 56
Hager, Jim, 2, 3
Haile, Henry, 14, 24
Hall, Sara, 108
Haltom, Bill, 47
Halworth, Eugene, 84
Hancock, John Mark, 37
Hamilton, Mike, 127
Hamilton, Ray, 82
Hammonds, Benny, 73
Harlan, Charles, 59
Harris, Fred, 58
Harris, Haywood, 98, 124
Harris, Henry (Virginia),43,111
Harrison, Jimmy, 13
Hartman, Scott (Kay, Cleon), 13,29, 83, 117
Harvey, Robert, 20
Hatcher, Paul, 41
Hatton, Sue, 56
Haynes, Bobby (Kenny), 4
Hazeur, Camille, 56
Hedrick, Russ, 80
Hemmeter, John, 14, 52
Herbstritt, Mike, 82
Hermann, Julie,11,18,56,104
Hernandez, Felipe, 31
Herndon, Walter, 24
Herring. Leslie, 55
Hewitt, Helen, 118
Heyder, Stephen, 58
Higdon, Bill, 73
High, Katie, 13, 14, 99
Hill, Dewey, 94
Hill, Norm, 56
Hilliard, Richard, 73
Hillis, Steve, 115
Hineline, Ginger, 56
Hitchcox, Mike, 21
Holland, Carolyn, 56
Holmes, Peter, 57
Holt, Andrew D., 3, 5, 11, 25
Holt, Donna, 47
Holt, Charles, 67
Holt, Karen, 37, 53, 62
Holtzcaw, Craig, 28
Hooban, Roger, 14, 25

Index by Chapters

Hooban, Roger, 14,25
Horak, Jan Williams, 12, 22
Horton, Charles, 19
Horton, Odell, 70, 108
Hosty, Thomas, 79
Houser, Wayne, 40
Huddleston, Charles, 6
Hudson, Margaret, 11
Hudson, Marilyn, 28, 31
Hull, Thomas, 58
Hunt, James C. ("Jim"), 11, 26, 30,31, 40, 41, 52, 53, 55, 56, 58, 61,62, 64, 67, 68, 70, 92
Hunt, Tripp, 37
Huntsman, Stan, 83
Ingram, Reggie, 75
Isaacs, Greg, 90
Itson, James, 55
Ivester, Jack, 40
Jacobs, Katie, 13
Jain, M.K., 58
Jarvis, Jimmy, 56, 58, 63, 87, 94
Jenkins, Roger, 74
Johnson, Bill (Trustee), 57,64
Johnson, Joe, 19
Johnson, Joseph E. ("Joe"), 5, 7,13, 14, 19, 20, 25, 27, 33, 36-38,52, 53, 56, 57, 59, 65,66, 71, 73, 74, 82, 92, 95, 111
Jones, Janet Kite, 9
Jones, Julie Lisa, 43
Jones, Mark, 74
Jones, Robert, 71, 72
Jones, Tom, 73
Josberger, Marie, 56
Jordan, Leon, 58, 60, 85, 98
Jordan, Ray, 38
Kami, Peter, 1, 3
Keele, Roxanne, 28
Keith, David, 18
Kerin, Tim, 66, 83
Kerney, Tom, 95
Kersavage, Joseph, 85
Kilcrease, Irving, 28, 62
Killifer, Fred, 83
Kinser, Paul, 23
Kneier, Kimberly, 12
Knox County Young Republican, 7
Koksal, Ron, 43
Koonce, Kaye, 15, 98

Kosmalski, Len, 8
Kozar, Andrew ("Andy"), 9, 11, 14,18, 19, 35, 52, 57, 63
Kramer, Roy, 73
Krelstein, Ron, 64
Kressin, Geoffrey, 64
Kyle, James, 37
Laird, Timothy, 84
Lambert, Keith, 40, 94
Lambert, Walter, 37
Lance, Harrison, 58
LaRosa, Tino (and Carmen) 18
Larry, O.D. (Fnny), 11
Laszlo, Andy, 19
Laughlin, Harry, 63
Leadbetter (Jones), Cara, 9, 11,12, 15, 18, 19
Leadbetter, Lee, 9,11,18,19
Leadbetter, Therese, 5,9,12, 13,16, 18, 19, 22, 52, 82
Ledbetter, Beverly, 73
Ledbetter, Sarah, 58
Lemler, Jerry, 58
Levy, Bob, 98, 101
Lewis, George, 26
Littlejohn, Dennie, 13
Locke, Eric (Richard), 86
Lockridge, John, 20, 58
Lockwood, Charlie, 21
Logan, Judd, 83
Logan, Twyla, 40
London, Jim 31
Lyle, Helen Hobbs, 28
Lyon, James Richard, 88
Maddox, Robert, 58
Madison, Michael L., 122
Mahood, Chester, 64
Majors, Johnny, 58, 71, 73
Malmo, Don, 92
Mancuso, Captain, 3
Mann, John, 22
Manning, Gus, 124
Manning, Peyton, 31, 36, 37
Manookian, Adam, 90, 117
Marius, Richard, 2
Marron, Bill, 71
Martin, David, 22, 52
Martin, Tony, 25
Martinez, Jesse, 76
Mashburn, Lillian, 98
Mashburm, Pauline, 55
Matthews, Doug, 19
May, Scarlett, 56
Mays, Hardy, 59
McAlexander, Tom, 80, 108

McCalla, Jon Phipps, 40
McCartney, Ron 11
McCleskey, JJ, 76
McConkey, Cindy, 71
McDaniel, Rudolph, 55
McDonald, Fred, 40, 56
McDowell, Bob, 23
McGee, Tim, 72
McGlone, John, 60, 126
McInnis, Malcolm, 27, 31, 37, 38, 40, 63, 71-73, 76, 79
McLean, Hite, 56
McRae, Robert, 14, 21, 28, 35, 55, 56, 58, 70
McReynolds, Dana, 40
McWherter, Boyd, 71
Mears, Ray, 16, 18, 19, 71, 73
Mercer, Charles, 87
Merryman, Clyde, 66
Meshcheryakova, Olga, 115, 118
Miller-Herron, Nancy, 69, 120, 123
Miller, Tom, 29, 125, 118
Miller, William, 5
Mina, Christie, 122
Mingey, Tim, 73
Mirabella, Charles, et. al., 40, 94
Mizell, Catherine, 13, 31, 34, 43, 53, 80, 81, 83, 90, 95-98, 105-110, 114-118, 124, 127
Moeller, Gene, 73
Moncier, Herb, 40
Moody, Todd, 58
Moon, Pam, 13
Moore, Bobby E., 91
Moore, Curtis L., 87
Moore, Gloria, 40
Moriarty, Thomas, 85
Morgan, Charles Van, 40
Morgan, John, 105
Morris, Ken, 69
Morse, Henry, 21, 64
Morton, L. Clure, 55
Moss, Charles, 98, 101
Muirhead, Eric, 45
Mullowney, William, 15
Murray, Barbara, 19
National Association of College and University Attorneys, 15
Neese, Bill, 58
Nelson, David, 56
Nelson, Rodney Q., 59
Nettles, Mario, 40
Newcomb, Vester, 38
Newkirk, William, 5
Nicely, Hazel, 11, 12, 84
Nichols, Trent, 41

Index by Chapters

Nolley, Robert, 55
Norris, Bob, 56
North, William, 13
Norton, Frederick, 52
Nwauwa, Wilfred, 31
Obear, Fred, 53
O'Brien, Theresa Elizabeth
Cecelia,1
O'Neill, Kevin, 75
Outterson, Kevin, 95
Overholt, Robert, 71
Owen, Jim, 30
Paganalli, Mark, 106
Papachristou, Mark, 28
Parker, Alan, 21, 38, 68, 98, 108
Parker, John, 58, 82, 100
Parmele, Carla, 99, 101
Patterson, Richard, 26
Patriotic Observance Committee,1
Pearl, Bruce, 127
Peccolo, Butch, 19
Peltz, Roger, 18
Peoples, Carlton, 71
Peoples, Dee Shawn, 44, 122
Perry, Margaret, 53
Peters, John, 79
Peterson, John, 29, 112-116, 118, 125. 126
Phelps, Stephanie, 121
Phillips, Edward G. ("Ward"), 97, 100
Phillips, Sara, 36, 52, 97, 101
Phillips, Thomas, 40, 58, 60, 100, 102
Pinson, Michael, 88
Pippin, James, 11
Porteous, David, 9
Postel, Joy, 26
Postlethwaite, Arnold, 61
Porter, Arthur, 92
Porter, Ira, 88
Prados, John, 53
Presley, Elvis, 45
Priest, Tim, 66
Professional Food Services
Management, 64
Puchett, Bettie, 12
Puett, Sammie Lynn, 84, 100
Quinn, John, 58, 73
Ragsdale, Duncan, 122
Ratliff, Leslie, 77Raulston,
Leonard, 5
Ray, Morris, 44, 122
Ray, Gloria, 57, 71
Reed, Pamela, 99
Reed, William, 27

Reese, Jack, 11, 24, 25, 40,53, 63,66
Reevers, Stephanie, 120
Reno, David, 40
Reveiz, Fuad, 71
Rhea, Daniel F.B., 8, 12, 14, 20
Rice, Barry, 11
Rice, Bill, 53
Rich, John, 11, 52
Richey, Trent, 71
Richter, Jennifer, 27, 38, 86, 97
Richter, R. Lindley, 44, 122
Ridley, Reggie, 80
Riley, Spencer, 80
Ritchie, Robert ("Bob"), 28, 66
Roach, Bill, 16, 19
Roads, Steve (Kimberly Roads
Schlapman), 12, 18
Roberson, Deborah, 56
Roberson, Timothy (Gwen-
dolyn),122
Roberts, S.H. ("Bo"), 11
Robinson, Bill, 11, 13, 19, 66
Robinson, Milton, 30, 55
Robinson, Theotis, 52, 97
Robinson, Tony, 66, 71
Rogers, Steve, 19, 105
Rogers, Timothy ("Tim"),11,28, 38,40,55,60,63,75,86,90,97,98
Rollo, Mike, 78, 127
Rothchild, Nate, 84
Rowan, Robert, 58
Rubright, Bob, 89
Rucker, Richard, 83
Rudolph, Marva, 97
Russell, James, 121
Ryan, Michael, 70
Sanderson, Michael, 25, 28
Sansom, William ("Bill"), 25, 95, 97
Saum, Bill, 19, 73, 76
Savage, Pat, 10
Salky. Irvin14, 31, 64
Scarbrough, Jerry, 58
Scheurer, Phil, 11, 56, 71, 72, 75
Schmidt, Bill, 11
Schmid, Al, 20
Schwarz, Ilsa, 28
Scoggins, Matthew, 60,126, 127
Scott, David, 15
Schaffner, William, 89
Scroggins, Troy Gene, 47
Seelbinder, Oscar, 27
Sells, Jack, 19, 27, 73

Selvidge, Barry, 28
Sexton, Jimmy, 76
Shadko, Warren, 40
Shapiro, Paul, 113
Shelby, Clinton, 53
Sherrer, John, 40
Shope, Steve, 94
Shuler, Heath (Joe, Benji),74
Shults, William, 121, 125
Shumaker, John (Lucy), 104, 106,107
Simons, Gray, 8, 11
Skillman, Kyle, 127
Skinner, Bill, 83
Skoutakis, Vasilios ("Bill"),11, 70
Slagle, William, 26
Sly and the Family Stone, 64
Small, Neal, 56
Smith, Angi, 116
Smith, Charles, 14, 21, 23, 56, 71
Smith, Hilton, 55
Smith, Loren, 85
Smith, Patsy (Shawn), 42
Smrt, Charles, 75
Snejkina, Elena ("Helen"), 114, 115
Snodgrass, William R., 70
Snyder, William ("Bill"), 25, 28, 38,
56, 58, 60, 74, 82, 97
Sobieski, John, 40
Sommardahl, Carla, 125
Sompayrac, Joanie, 28, 90, 117
Soni, Raj P., 24
Speight, Harry Max, 61
Sprouse, Steve, 69, 118
St. Johns United Methodist
Church,92
Stacey, Robert, 120
Stacy, Bill, 62
Stafford, D.T., 56
Stair, Billy, 37, 79
Stair, Caesar, 24, 56
Stanley, Larry, 52
Steele, Connie, 11
Stefanovic, Dragan, 56
Stevens, James, 61
Stewart, Marcus, 5
Stockdale, Jim, 52, 55, 63
Stokes, Billy, 29, 94, 98
Stokes, Raymond, 61
Stovall, James, 40, 94
Stovall, Tom, 94

Index by Chapters

Story, Julie, 41
Stowers, Arthur B.("Art"),8,12
Strickland, R. David, 69
Stuart, Ford, 1
Sullivan, David, 40
Summitt, Pat Head,11,18, 56
Summitt, Robert, 56, 61
Sundquist, Don, 22
Susano, Charles, 5, 24, 56
Taliaferro, Ron, 64
Taylor, Robert, 5, 14, 20, 24, 25,56, 64
Teaford, Hugh, 40
Tegano, Carmen, 74
Temple, Charles, 11, 19
Testerman, Kyle, 22
Thacker, Jack, 4, 25
Tharpe, James, 64
Thompson, Charles, 6
Thompson, Joyce, 127
Todd, James, 58
Trembley, John, 11
Tripp, Bob, 111
Tucker, Fred, 59
Turley, Tim, 28
Turner, Jerome, 55, 56
Underwood, George, 87
University Physicians Foundation,64
"UTC 6" (Rape case), 117
Ureta, Jorge, 11, 48, 111
Van de Vate, Nancy, 12, 20
Vaughn, Troy, 40
Veterans Against the War, 6
Victor the Dancing Bear, 18
Volchikhim, Vladimir, 115
Von Beulow, Peter, 85
Vora, Chandan, 58
Wade, Allen, 92
Wade, Jerry, 64
Wadley, Fredia, 59
Walkup, Knox, 4
Walker, Cas, 1
Walker, Clark, 16
Walker, Robert, 40
Wall, Pat, 66
Wallace, George, 21
Walters, Herbert, ("Hub"), 5
Waters, William L. ("Bill"), 29
Watts, George, 83
Ward, Paul, 15, 107

Watkins, Phil, 13, 19
Watson, Michael Jerome, 55
Weaver, Charles, 1, 2, 64
Webb, Bill (UTCHS), 46
Webb, Bill (Track and Field), 83
Weaver, John, 90
Weekly, Karen (Ralph), 38, 62
Weisberg, Mike, 76
Welford, Harry, 58
Wells, Jack, 28
Wesson, Tina, 11, 18
West, Mike, 58
West Knoxville Sertoma Club, 9,11
White, Barry, 36
White, Reggie, 71, 72
Whited, Jamie, 31, 78
Whitehead, Tom, 25
Whittle, Chris, 1
Widgery, William, 27
Wiggins, Sarah, 125
Williams, Alan, 73
Williams Horack, Jan, 22, 35, 70
Williams, Karen, 122
Williams, Rita, 47
Williams, Susan, 96, 97, 124
Willis, Bill, 111
Wilson, Frank, 62
Wilson, Richard, 38, 62
Winchester, Lee, 46
Wirtz, Richard, 28
Wiseman, Thomas, 53
Witt, Al 29
Witt, Bob, 29
Witt, Maureen, 64, 67
Witten, Jason, 86
Woodruff, Bob, 25
Woods, Cliff, 86, 97, 98
Woods, Melvin, 55
Woodside, Marianne, 58
Woodson, Roland, 52
Woody, Alice, 53
Woolf, Lou, 12, 20
Woolsey, Telena, 61
Workman, Dale, 41
Wormsley, Neal, 19
Wright, Robin, 79, 80
Wu, Shaojun (LeFan), 48
Wyant, Gary, 37
Wynn, Trina, 40
York, Clyde, 5
Young Americans for Freedom,1,6
Yovella, Ed, 3, 11, 40, 60
Zenner, Kim, 18, 56
Ziegler, Dhyana, 82